D0096992

Wales

David Atkinson
Neil Wilson

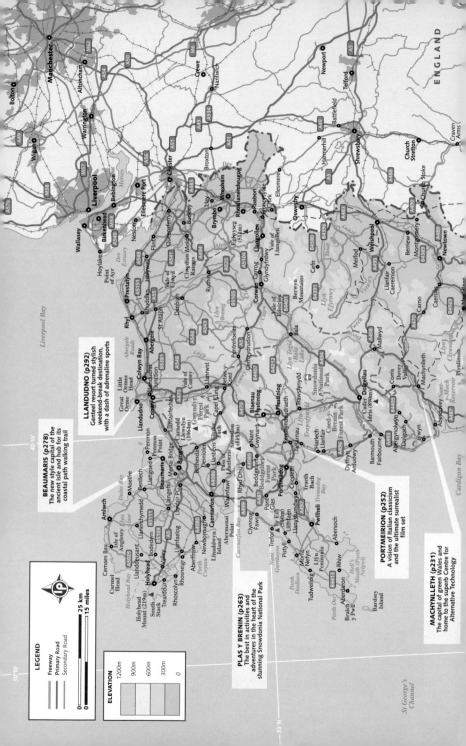

LEGEND

Freeway
Primary Road
Secondary Road

0 ———— 25 km
0 ———— 15 miles

ELEVATION

1200m
900m
600m
300m
0

BEAUMARIS (p278)
The new style capital of the ancient isle and hub for its coastal path walking trail

LLANDUDNO (p292)
Genteel resort turned stylish weekend-break destination, with a dash of adrenaline sports

PLAS Y BRENIN (p263)
The best in activities and adventures in the heart of the stunning Snowdonia National Park

PORTMEIRION (p252)
A vision of Italian classicism and the ultimate surrealist film set

MACHYNLLETH (p231)
The capital of green Wales and home to the superb Centre for Alternative Technology

ENGLAND

Liverpool Bay

Cardigan Bay

St George's Channel

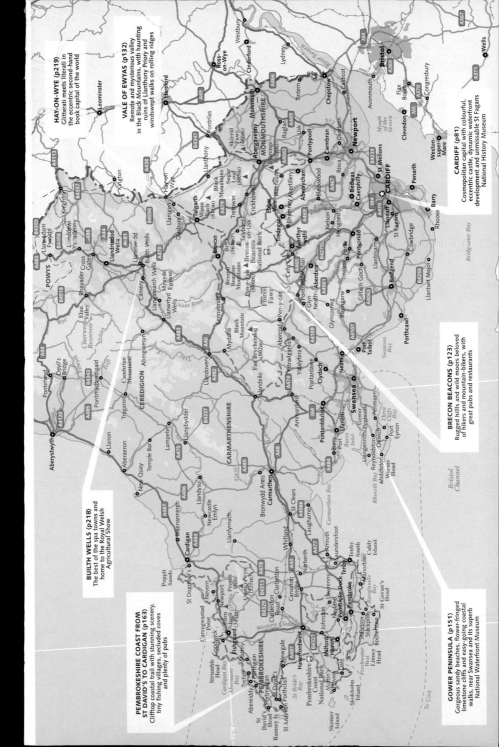

HAY-ON-WYE (p219)
Glitterati meets literati in the eccentric second-hand book capital of the world

VALE OF EWYAS (p132)
Remote and mysterious valley in the Black Mountains, with haunting ruins of Llanthony Priory and windswept walks on rolling ridges

CARDIFF (p81)
Cosmopolitan capital with colourful, eccentric castle, dynamic waterfront development and unmissable St Fagans National History Museum

BUILTH WELLS (p218)
The best of the spa towns and home to the Royal Welsh Agricultural Show

BRECON BEACONS (p123)
Rugged hills and wild moors beloved of hikers and mountain-bikers, with great pubs and restaurants

PEMBROKESHIRE COAST FROM ST DAVID'S TO CARDIGAN (p163)
Clifftop coastal trail with stunning scenery, tiny fishing villages, secluded coves and plenty of pubs

GOWER PENINSULA (p151)
Gorgeous sandy beaches, flower-fringed limestone cliffs and easy-going coastal walks, near Swansea and its superb National Waterfront Museum

Destination Wales

The Welsh spirit is the country's defining feature. Indeed, for its entire history Wales has struggled against waves of invaders who have sought to subjugate its people; but, as the invaders found out, it's a country that just won't lie down.

Today the spirit of Wales is stronger than ever. Welsh arts, film and, above all, rock music have taken the world stage by storm and killed off the hackneyed old stereotypes of desolate pit villages, lovespoons (spoons with an elaborate handle that are a traditional artisan craft) and teashops.

The new Wales is a vibrant place where history is alive and Welsh culture finds new forms of expression. The mix of defiant tradition and New-World sophistication is one of Wales' greatest assets today. The male voice choirs may still keep a welcome in the valleys, but an alternative culture flourishes in urban hubs, a healthy dose of hedonism oozes from gourmet kitchens and hip hotels, and a strong motif of environmental awareness underpins the country's forward-looking perspective.

Wales remains a superb outdoors location: grab your hiking boots or a mountain bike and lose yourself in timeless rural scenery laced with waterfalls, lakes and jagged peaks, winding roads and sandy beaches. You can tour villages with tongue-twisting names before settling down in a cosy pub with a pint of local ale, or join the adrenaline junkies in a quest for the ultimate adventure – Welsh style.

Wales is a place that becomes an obsession, beckoning back its visitors year after year with its friendly locals, fine food, remarkable landscapes, white-knuckle adventures and admirably green credentials. These are the marks of a country looking firmly towards a rosy future.

MARK DAFFEY

Cardiff

Take a tour, or go and see a rugby match at the imposing Millennium Stadium (p88) in Cardiff

Watch yachts race in Cardiff Bay (p88)

Revel in flamboyant Gothic fantasy at Cardiff Castle (p85), restored by the Bute family with delightful eccentricity

Southeast Wales & Brecon Beacons

JON DAVISON

Be inspired by Tintern Abbey's haunting ruins (p115)

Climb to the summit of Pen-y-Fan (p124), the highest peak in South Wales

CHERYL FORBES

Swansea, the Gower & Carmarthenshire

NIC CLEAVE PHOTOGRAPHY / ALAMY

Enjoy the spectacular views of the
Carmarthenshire countryside from
Carreg Cennen Castle (p158)

NEIL SETCHFIELD

Visit Dylan Thomas' grave at Laugharne (p161)

Learn about Welsh history at the impressive National Waterfront Museum (p143) in Swansea

JEFF MORGAN / ALAMY

Pembrokeshire

Watch the puffins around Skomer and Skokholm Islands (p183), one of many unique species present

ANDREW PARKINSON

MANFRED GOTTSCHALK

Ride the waves in Whitesands Bay (p189), one of Wales' best beaches for surfing and water sports

Visit St David's Cathedral (p184), which has been standing for almost a thousand years

DAVID TIPLING

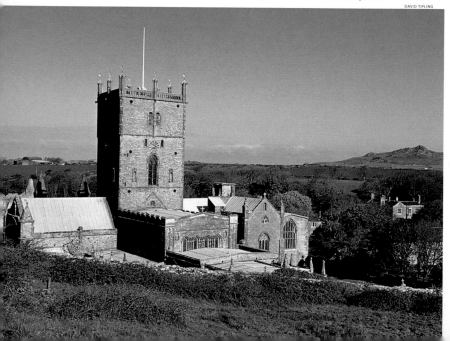

Mid-Wales

WORLD PICTURES / ALAMY

Take a ride on the narrow-gauge Vale of Rheidol Railway (p213), which runs from Aberystwyth

GREG GAWLOWSKI

Soak up history at the superb Powis Castle (p228) in Welshpool

Be bemused by the World Bog Snorkelling championships (p217) held in August at Llanwrtyd Wells

PAUL GLENDELL / ALAMY

Snowdonia & the Llŷn

Walk in Edmund Hilary's footsteps in the glorious Snowdonia National Park (p237)

GARETH MCCORMACK

EOIN CLARKE

Visit one of the world's greatest medieval castles, World Heritage Site–listed Caernarfon Castle (p255)

Stay in Italianate Portmeirion (p252), an embodiment of the 'strange necessity' of beauty

NAGELESTOCK.COM / ALAMY

Anglesey & the North Coast

PATRICK HORTON

Take a canal-boat ride on Thomas Telford's masterpiece, Pontcysyllte Aqueduct (p299), over the River Dee

Overleaf:
Fall in love with nature in the Snowdonia National Park (p237), with its pristine mountain streams and oak woodlands

GARETH McCORMACK

ANDERS BLOMQVIST

Stroll through windswept Beaumaris Castle (p278)

Promenade along genteel Llandudno beach (p292), before getting active with some adventure sports

DAVID POOLE / ALAMY

Contents

Regional Map Contents

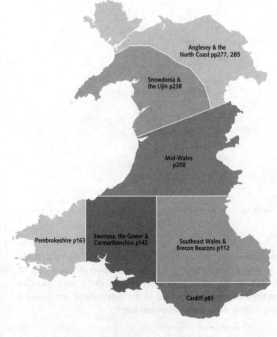

The Authors

DAVID ATKINSON
Introductory Chapters; Mid-Wales; Snowdonia & the Llŷn; Anglesey & the North Coast

Working on the Wales book is something of a prodigal return for David Atkinson. Born just across the border in North Wales, and a veteran of family holidays from Snowdonia to Anglesey, David has since carved a career as a travel writer with guidebook assignments taking him from Japan to South America. Summer 2006 saw him back in Wales and marvelling at how the country has moved forward since those halcyon days of building sand castles on the beach at Beaumaris aged seven. What's more, he took a fresh pair of eyes with him to survey the landscape, accompanied by his baby daughter.

My Favourite Trip

My favourite trip? Tricky. For activities, it's glorious summer day-walking in the Clwydian Ranges (p302), or learning a new skill at the Plas y Brenin National Mountain Centre near Capel Curig (p263). For deserted beaches and some great Welsh ozone, it's hard to beat hugging the coast of the Isle of Anglesey by car or on foot (p280), followed by some hearty local fare and a pint of bitter from a local microbrewery (p251). But, most of all, my two personal favourites are Machynlleth for its Centre for Alternative Technology (p234) and Portmeirion (p252) for its fairy-tale village and a chance to spend the night in a castle.

NEIL WILSON
Cardiff; Southeast Wales & Brecon Beacons;
Swansea, the Gower & Carmarthenshire; Pembrokeshire;
Pembrokeshire Coastal Path; Directory; Transport

Neil's first trip to Wales was as a geology student more than 20 years ago, breaking rocks in Anglesey and trying to pronounce Llanfairpwllgwynwotsitsname. He has been back to explore the Welsh landscape many times, whether rock-climbing in the Llanberis Pass, trying to surf (and failing miserably) in the Gower Peninsula, or cruising the coast from Caernarfon to Pembrokeshire in a traditional wooden sailboat. On this trip he added Pen-y-Fan and Cribyn to his list of Welsh summits gained, explored the more remote reaches of the Pembrokeshire Coast Path, and developed a taste for cockles and laver bread.

My Favourite Trip

As a fan of good food as well as the great outdoors, I really enjoyed travelling through the Brecon Beacons National Park, which offers the chance to combine the two. From the foodie capital of Abergavenny (p125) I headed north into the magical Vale of Ewyas (p132), with its haunting ruined priory and wild, windswept hills, before returning to civilisation and a giant scoff at the Bear in Crickhowell (p130). Then I donned my hiking boots for an ascent of Pen-y-Fan (p124) above Brecon, followed by a slap-up meal in Brecon's Felin Fach Griffin (p137). Finally, a meander southwest to see the caves of Dan-yr-Ogof (p138) and Carreg Cennen Castle (p158) was topped off with dinner at the King's Head in Llandovery (p159).

Getting Started

Dust off your rucksack, fish out your hiking boots and you're ready to go. The only difficult thing about planning a trip to Wales is deciding where to visit first. Do you go for the all-action hiking-cycling-surfing-rafting route, play the history buff and soak up the sights, or wallow in cosy pubs after windswept walks? Luckily nothing is too far away in Wales and it's easy to squeeze in a bit of everything – even on a short trip. Public transport is reasonable, there's accommodation to suit all budgets and, above all, the locals are very friendly.

See Climate Charts (p309) for more information.

WHEN TO GO

Wales is beautiful at any time of year, but the soggy Welsh weather means that summer (June to August) remains the busiest time for visitors. Most of the rain is concentrated in autumn and early winter, with the worst of the downpours generally between October and January. Winter days are startlingly short, and although you may get a picturesque blanket of snow, many smaller attractions, tourist offices and B&Bs close for the entire low season (October to Easter).

After January the rain slackens off and as temperatures pick up and days lengthen it's a good time to get out walking. Spectator sports, too, hit their peak, with both the rugby and football calendars coming to a close.

July and August is high season for Wales, coinciding with the major school-holiday period across Britain (see p313), hence attractions, accommodation and roads can get choked with visitors, prices are often inflated and even the kindest of locals can get annoyed with the crush. However, this is prime time for a long, lingering night at one of Wales' countless festivals or a concerted assault on its highest mountains.

To beat the crowds, May and September are great times to visit, combining the best of the weather with the colours of the countryside, but without the clogged roads and accommodation rush of midsummer.

HOW MUCH?

Ticket to national rugby game £15

B&B en-suite double room £50

Local newspaper 50p

Average single bus journey £1.20

A coffee and two slices of *bara brith* (spicy fruit loaf) £2.50

Three-course dinner £15

One hour's car parking £0.40

See also Lonely Planet Index on inside front cover.

COSTS

Prices in Wales will seem expensive to many overseas visitors; the cost of accommodation and restaurants tends to be slightly higher than in many other parts of the UK. Prices are noticeably higher around Cardiff and Snowdonia, and more expensive generally in high season (June to August), while prices everywhere tend to drop in the low season (October to Easter).

Backpackers using public transport, staying at hostels and eating a combination of supermarket food and modest restaurant meals could scrape by on about £30 per day. If you plan to hire a car, stay in B&Bs, eat out at midrange

---

DON'T LEAVE HOME WITHOUT...

Some swear by packing light, and you'll be very glad you did if you're lugging your backpack down a one-track road followed by a herd of rogue sheep; others pack for contingencies and feel safest with an outfit and accessory for every occasion. Just remember, everything you could ever need will be readily available in Wales.

Do pack your rain gear, however, as a downpour is a distinct possibility. Take some cool-weather gear as well, as cold snaps are also common, even in summer. Hostellers will be glad if they carry a padlock, while die-hard campers shouldn't leave home without good boots and a torch (flashlight), and the seriously active will need a compass and first-aid kit.

Lastly, don't forget a copy of your travel-insurance documents (see p313 for more details).

places and see some sights you'll need to budget about £80 per day. Those opting for top-end hotels and facilities should plan on about £150 per day.

For travellers with families it's worth looking into family passes for transport (p330) and sights and asking hotels for special family deals. All national

---

TOP TENS

Must-See Films

For a quick-fix taste of Wales before you leave home, nestle down on the sofa and nurture those daydreams with these flicks. Most of these films are reviewed on p45.

- *How Green Was My Valley* (1941)
  Director: John Ford

- *Twin Town* (1997)
  Director: Paul Turner

- *The Englishman Who Went Up a Hill…* (1995) Director: Chris Monger

- *Solomon and Gaenor* (Solomon a Gaenor; 1998) Director: Paul Morrison

- *The Citadel* (1938)
  Director: King Vidor

- *Above Us the Earth* (1977)
  Director: Karl Francis

- *Hedd Wynn* (1994)
  Director: Kevin Allen

- *Tiger Bay* (1959)
  Director: J Lee Thompson

- *Eldra* (2002)
  Director: Tim Lyn

- *Human Traffic* (1999)
  Director: Justin Kerrigan

Top 10 Novels

Wash away the old stereotypes and get a grasp of Cool Cymru with these top page-turners. Some of these books are reviewed on p42.

- *Work, Sex and Rugby* (1993)
  Lewis Davies

- *Rape of the Country Fair* (1998)
  Alexander Cordell

- *Aberystwyth Mon Amour* (2001)
  Malcolm Pryce

- *Sugar and Slate* (1992)
  Charlotte Williams

- *The Green Bridge* (1992)
  John Davies (Ed)

- *My People* (1915)
  Caradog Evans

- *Entertainment* (2000)
  Richard John Evans

- *How Green Was My Valley* (1939)
  Richard Llewellyn

- *Flesh and Blood* (1974)
  Emyr Humphreys

- *One Moonlit Night* (1995)
  Caradog Pritchard

Our Favourite Festivals & Events

Party with the best of them on Wales' packed festival circuit. From the divine to the dangerous there's almost always something of interest going on around the country.

- Six Nations Rugby Championship
  (Cardiff) February/March

- Urdd Eisteddfod
  (changing venues) May/June

- Hay Festival
  (Hay-on-Wye) May/June

- Man vs Horse Marathon
  (Llanwrtyd Wells) June

- International Musical Eisteddfod
  (Llangollen) July

- Sesiwn Fawr Festival
  (Dolgellau) July

- Cardiff Festival
  (Cardiff) July/August

- Brecon Jazz Festival
  (Brecon) August

- Victorian Festival
  (Llandrindod Wells) August

- Abergavenny Food Festival
  (Abergavenny) September

museums and galleries are free and most other attractions don't charge for children under five.

TRAVEL LITERATURE

Welsh travelogues range from the old and not so politically correct to the rosy-eyed and romantic. Some of the following titles are now out of print but can be found via online bookstores or in secondhand bookshops.

For a good overview of Welsh people and culture, Dannie Abse's stimulating *Journals from the Antheap* (1988) is a compilation of humorous accounts of his trips through Wales, musing with droll satire on the state of the nation.

Anthony Bailey's *A Walk Through Wales* (1992) is an engaging account of a three-week cross-country ramble that attempts to make sense of the legend-rich land through his encounters with farmers and poets, nationalists and clerics.

A more romanticised version of Wales is proposed in Jan Morris' *Wales: Epic Views of a Small Country* (1984), as she recounts her search across the valleys and mountains for the very origins of Welsh character, folklore and culture.

Muse over the passage of time and the shaping of a nation in *I Know Another Way* (2002), a compilation of stories by six of Wales' leading writers, which reflect on their journeys along an ancient pilgrimage route from Tintern to St David's.

Three astounding 18th-century guides to Wales are combined in *A Tour in Wales* (1773) by Thomas Pennant. The original works were largely responsible for the popularity of Wales with the Romantic Movement.

George Borrow's *Wild Wales: Its People, Language and Scenery* (1862) is an evocative and entertaining account of an 1854 walking tour of Wales, with the author's illuminating, if condescending, observations on Welsh people and places.

Hugh Oliff's *On Borrow's Trail: Wild Wales Then and Now* (2003) is a modern interpretation of Borrow's book as the author retraces his steps, recording changes in the landscape and people in a rich commentary accompanied by evocative photographs and illustrations.

INTERNET RESOURCES

Activity Wales (www.activitywales.com) The one-stop shop for everything from golf to abseiling.

Data Wales (www.data-wales.co.uk) A marvellous miscellany of cultural titbits.

ICWales (www.icwales.co.uk) Comprehensive and detailed news, plus features on all aspects of Welsh life.

Lonely Planet (www.lonelyplanet.com/destinations/europe/wales) Extensive information and links and tips from travellers.

V Wales (www.vwales.co.uk) A bottomless pit of information on Wales.

VisitWales (www.visitwales.com) A comprehensive website from the official Welsh tourism authority.

Itineraries

CLASSIC ROUTES

SOUTH WALES & THE PEMBROKESHIRE COAST   10 Days

If you're short on time and want to see a good cross-section of Wales, the southern end of the country is probably the most accessible.

Start off with the sights and sounds of **Cardiff** (p81), including its fantasy **castle** (p85), sparkling **Cardiff Bay** (p88) and the incredible **National Museum** (p86). When you've finished, take a side trip to whimsical **Castell Coch** (p105) and **Caerphilly Castle** (p105) before getting a real insight into Wales' past at the **St Fagans National History Museum** (p104) and **Rhondda Heritage Park** (p119).

When you've had your fill of history, head for the **Brecon Beacons National Park** (p123) for a breath of fresh mountain air and some excellent walking. From here head south and breeze through **Swansea** (p141) and on to Wales' first declared Area of Outstanding Natural Beauty (AONB), the **Gower Peninsula** (p151), a hot spot for adrenaline junkies. Head further west to Pembrokeshire, where some good spots to visit include **Tenby** (p165), **Manorbier** (p169), **Carew Castle** (p181) and **Tidal Mill** (p181), and the puffin colony on **Skomer Island** (p183). It's also well worth walking part of the clifftop **Pembrokeshire Coast Path** (p197), perhaps from Dale to Martin's Haven, before finishing up with a bracing walk along the fine sandy beaches of **St Bride's Bay** (p182).

See the best of South Wales and the Pembrokeshire Coast on this leisurely 190-mile trip around heritage sites, moody mountains and surf-swept shores.

THE WELSH LOOP   Three Weeks

One of the most popular routes is a wide loop taking in all the Welsh highlights: castles and mountains, a good dose of spectacular countryside and the buzzing capital.

Begin in **Cardiff** (p81) for a taste of modern Welsh life before heading north for your first glimpse of Wales' spectacular scenery at the **Brecon Beacons National Park** (p123). From here head west to **St David's** (p184) with its cathedral and gateway to the **Pembrokeshire Coast National Park** (p163). A good pit stop north of here is the university town of **Aberystwyth** (p211), only a short hop from the **Vale of Rheidol Railway** (p213) and incredible **Devil's Bridge** (p215). North again are cosmopolitan **Machynlleth** (p231) and the superb **Centre for Alternative Technology** (p234). Fans of kitsch shouldn't miss the Italianate village of **Portmeirion** (p252) before the essential trip to **Snowdonia National Park** (p237). **Betws-y-Coed** (p260) makes the best base with a slew of hiking and biking trails within easy reach of town. More World Heritage Sites await in the imposing castles of **Caernarfon** (p254) and **Conwy** (p288), then it's time to relax at the elegant seaside resort of **Llandudno** (p292), which is today reinventing itself as a stylish weekend break with a dash of adrenaline-sport chic.

The 480-mile Welsh Loop takes in all the classic pit stops from cosmopolitan Cardiff to the stunning scenery of the national parks, the mighty grandeur of Wales' best castles and the scarred slopes of the southern coal valleys.

ICONS OF WELSH CULTURE   **One Week**

This route celebrates the very essence of being Welsh, taking in the birthplaces of national icons and visiting towns most closely associated with the Welsh identity.

Start in **Portmeirion** (p252) near the home of visionary architect Sir Clough Williams-Ellis, before heading west to the Llŷn Peninsula and following the backroads around the peninsula to Nant Gwrtheyrn and its **Welsh Language and Heritage Centre** (p274) to learn about the renaissance of the Welsh language. The journey back to Porthmadog takes in the whitewashed village of **Aberdaron** (p271), the home base of firebrand preacher turned poet RS Thomas, with views offshore to the mystical **Bardsey Island** (p272), the alleged resting place of some 2000 saints. Also, just outside Pwllheli lies the village of **Llanystumdwy** (p268), the final resting place of David Lloyd George, the late great Welsh political leader.

Head south with the Cambrian Coast line to **Aberystwyth** (p211) where the National Library of Wales, a prestigious seat of learning, celebrates its centenary in 2007. Follow the Pembrokeshire Coastal Path south from here to **St David's** (p184), the cathedral town named after Wales' very own patron saint and the epitome of saintly virtue. Finally, skirt the bottom of the country with a dash across Carmarthenshire to **Swansea** (p141), the town most closely associated with that great icon of Welsh culture, Dylan Thomas.

Take a trip through the places associated with Welsh cultural icons to get under the skin of the national identity on this 300-mile trip.

ROADS LESS TRAVELLED

THE VALLEYS   Three Days
The Welsh valleys boomed with Britain's Industrial Revolution and were devastated by its demise. Today they are scarred and suffering but the tightly packed pit villages and rusting relics give a telling insight into the history and the plight of rural South Wales.

Start off at the **Rhondda Heritage Park** (p119) near Cardiff, a fascinating introduction to the industrial life of the valleys. From here head north to **Aberfan** (p121) for a poignant reminder of the risks of industrialisation. Further north you'll hit Merthyr Tydfil, a former iron and steel centre, where you can visit **Cyfarthfa Castle** (p120) and the **old ironworks furnaces** (p120), and take a trip on the **Brecon Mountain Railway** (p120). Continue east to **Blaenavon** (p121) to visit its Unesco World Heritage Sites highlighting the best and worst of the Industrial Revolution.

East of the iron and coal valleys, you'll find the meandering Wye Valley where you can explore Britain's last medieval castle in **Raglan** (p115) and the famous fortified bridge at **Monmouth** (p111). The drive south from here rolls through a lush stretch of waterway. The jewel in this valley, though, is **Tintern Abbey** (p115), one of the most hauntingly beautiful ruins in Wales. From here you can wander **Offa's Dyke Path** (p124) or the **Wye Valley Walk** (p111) before finishing in **Chepstow** (p116) to ramble around the Norman castle or spend a day at the races.

Go underground in mining towns and at heritage sites on the Valleys tour, and trace the course and consequence of Wales' headlong industrialisation before gently meandering down the glorious Wye Valley. This quick trip covers 70 miles.

TO THE ENDS OF THE EARTH   Three Days

One of the least explored and least spoilt regions for tourism is the Llŷn Peninsula, an expanse of verdant countryside and coastal walks that personifies Wales' rural idyll.

Start in **Criccieth** (p267) with its fairy-tale castle. Head southwest to **Pwllheli** (p268) to stock up on brochures at the only official tourist office on the peninsula. Then point the car south and head out to join the waxheads and beach bums at **Abersoch** (p270), the peninsula's main centre for water sports. Continue on to **Aberdaron** (p271) where boats depart for **Bardsey Island** (p272), a mystical place linked to the legend of King Arthur. Head northeast along the west coast of the peninsula to **Morfa Nefyn** (p273), a small village with stunning views from the headland and a glorious beach to wander along en route to the **Ty Coch Inn** (p273), a historic pub that has also been used as an atmospheric film set. The ultimate destination, however, is the village of **Llithfaen** (p274), home to **Nant Gwrtheyrn** (p274) and the Welsh Language and Heritage Centre. This centre for residential Welsh language courses feels like the end of the earth and, indeed, is the ultimate location to lose yourself in the Welsh culture.

This alternative route travels 100 miles along the backroads and country lanes of one of the least-known but most scenic areas of Wales.

TAILORED TRIPS

GREEN WALES

Get in touch with the green Wales movement by blazing a trail to save the planet.

Start things off at Swansea and hook up with **Dryad Bushcraft** (p73), a cooking school with a difference: teaching students how to live off the land not exploit it. Then head west to **St David's** (p184), the spiritual home of Wales' patron saint and original father of the green movement who lived off and cared for the land. Tipi West, Wales' original alternative community with

the ultimate in green-friendly accommodation, is further north overlooking **Cardigan Bay**. Head east to the spa towns of Mid-Wales, which are littered with options for sleeping and eating that adhere to a strict environmental policy. Of these, the workaday town of **Builth Wells** (p218) is a great spot for organic produce.

Northwest of here is the country's green capital at **Machynlleth** (p231), home to the **Centre for Alternative Technology** (p234) and the nation's green conscience. Finally, hightail up north to the genteel seaside resort of **Llandudno** (p292). Not only is the north coast of Wales home to a growing army of wind farms, but several of the hotels here have won a Green Dragon Award under the Welsh environmental scheme.

WALES FOR ADRENALINE JUNKIES

Wales is a great place to get your heart-racing kicks.

Start off in the **Brecon Beacons National Park** (p123) for some excellent walking, caving and biking. From there head to the **Gower Peninsula** (p151), the

home of Welsh surfing and great climbing. West of here is the **Pembrokeshire Coast National Park** (p163), famous for kayaking, coasteering and as a place to climb sea cliffs. Surf, windsurf and kite surf at **Dale** and **Newgale** beaches (p183); or go diving at the dive sites around **Skomer** (p183) and **Ramsey** (p188).

Head north to **Machynlleth** (p231) for some excellent mountain biking or further north to climb the crags at **Tremadog** (p252). Roll on to **Snowdonia National Park** (p237) and indulge in some thrilling climbs, white-water rafting and excellent mountain biking. Inland, water rats should also take a trip to **Bala** (p245). In North Wales hop over to **Prestatyn** (p276) to begin the walk along **Offa's Dyke Path** (p124) back to where you started.

WALES FOR KIDS

From beaches and barnyards to castles and caves, Wales has plenty to keep both you and the little darlings on the back seat happy.

Start off in Cardiff at the **National Museum Wales** (p86), a fantastic place with great displays on dinosaurs and volcanoes, as well as some massive marine life. Then head for **Techniquest** (p90) to blow square bubbles and find out why bogeys are green. Just south of Cardiff are the reconstructed houses of the **St Fagans National History Museum** (p104) or head north and descend into the depths at **Big Pit** (p122) in Blaenavon. Then head west to the Pembrokeshire coast to search for seals near **St David's** (p184), or build empires in the sands of **St Bride's Bay** (p182). Head north to take in the **Welsh Wildlife Centre** (p210) before turning inland to pan for gold at **Dolaucothi Gold Mine** (p159). Discover giant insects as you crawl through the mole hole at the **Centre for Alternative Technology** (p234) in Machynlleth. Further north is **Anglesey Sea Zoo** (p282), with wave tanks and sea pools teeming with marine life, and the family-friendly resort of **Llandudno** (p292).

ON THE TRAIL OF KING ARTHUR

The legend of King Arthur is deeply engrained in Welsh folklore and recalled in many place names. This journey leads through beautiful countryside and takes in ancient monuments – a true quest for the Holy Grail.

Start off in **Monmouth** (p111), where the 12th-century Benedictine monk, Geoffrey of Monmouth, first popularised the Arthurian legend in *Historia Regum Britanniae*. Then head for **Carmarthen** (p156), which is alleged to be the birthplace of Merlin the magician. According to local legend, the hill outside the town is his final resting place. From here follow the trail north to **Blaenau Ffestiniog** (p259) close to where Arthur is said to have fought his final battle, the Battle of Camlan. Marchlyn Mawr near **Llanberis** (p263) is said to be the site of buried Arthurian treasure, while **Ruthin** is associated with another battle, in which Arthur took revenge on his enemy Huail; the site is now marked by a boulder in the town's Peter's Square. The quest for the Holy Grail terminates at **Llangollen** (p297) – legend says this most treasured Christian relic is contained within the walls of Castell Dinâs Bran.

Snapshot

From Llandudno to Llandaff, the topics under discussion in pubs, classrooms and community centres across the country all return to one subject: what does it mean to be Welsh in the early 21st century? Overall there is a positive sense that being Welsh is about looking to the future.

Wales has been battered in recent decades by industrial decline, rural poverty and a loss of its traditional identity. These spectres still make their presence felt occasionally, but Wales today is more hopeful, buoyed by a renewed sense of Welsh culture and pride, and spurred on by initiatives to embrace new industries and new cultural forms of expression. As such, it's high time to assign the hackneyed stereotypes to the dustbin of history and move on.

First and foremost Wales is growing: the population of Wales is just a whisker away from reaching the three-million mark, with the country predicted to reach the landmark figure by 2008. Since the expansion of the European Union (EU), when 10 new states joined in 2004, an influx of Eastern European workers has significantly boosted the figures.

FAST FACTS

Population: 2.9 million

Sheep population: 10.2 million

Inflation: 2.4%

Unemployment rate: 4.5%

GDP per capita: £12,000

Size: 20,000 sq km

Rate of house price inflation: 10.5%

The issue of political devolution has dominated Welsh politics in recent years. While many people felt removed from the political process and voter turnout has been low in regional elections, the new National (Welsh) Assembly is now established as the voice of the country. Furthermore, Wales took a step towards a full parliament during the summer of 2006 when the Queen signed into law the Government of Wales Act 2006.

Under the new Act, the Assembly Government will be able, from May 2007, to draw up its own laws for the first time – provided Westminster agrees first. The current Welsh Secretary, Peter Hain MP, said the new Act was more momentous than the 1998 legislation that set up the National Assembly. The move also boosts the position of Rhodri Morgan, who has long styled himself as the first minister of the Welsh Assembly Government.

On the financial front, the Welsh economy is improving and the National Assembly is portraying the country as an ideal location for foreign investment. But Wales still qualifies for EU aid and traditional industry is all but dead. While the Bay area and Mermaid Quay in Cardiff may seem to have experienced a renaissance, the closure of a major semiconductor plant by South Korean TV and electronics firm LG, near Newport, is a reminder that the recovery is fragile and Asian investment not a catch-all solution.

How to compete economically as well as solve the social and environmental problems of the 21st century were the primary concerns of the inaugural Innovation Wales Conference in 2006, with hi-tech companies, venture capitalists and public and private bodies considering how Wales can capitalise on its vast innovative potential.

At a more personal level, green and health issues are moving on apace, with the National Assembly Government announcing in 2006 that it would ban smoking in all enclosed public places in Wales from 2 April 2007.

Finally, the hot topic for all concerned with the Welsh identity was the popular TV series *Big Brother*'s 2006 final. Welsh finalist Glyn Wise, an 18-year-old student from Blaenau Ffestiniog, came in second place behind Tourette's sufferer Pete Bennett. Interviewed on the show, Wise draped a Welsh flag around his shoulders and professed his desire to see the Welsh language and culture continue to flourish.

How ironic that it fell to a reality TV–show contestant to convince the world that Wales is truly moving with the times.

History

Wherever you go in Wales, history is in evidence: the landscape rises and falls with the outlines of Stone Age tombs, Celtic earthworks, countless castles, disfigured hills and rusting machinery; towns display their medieval walls, dour chapels and evocative graveyards; and people talk – about their saints, their princes and their national heroes. Travel through Wales with its history in mind and you'll find it easier to understand Welsh anger and pride.

PREHISTORY & THE CELTS

Little is known about Wales' early history, but rare discoveries, including a human tooth in a cave near Denbigh, date the earliest human habitation back to 250,000 BC. The country is, however, littered with stone monuments and burial chambers dating back to Neolithic times, such as the massive Pentre Ifan dolmen in Pembrokeshire (p195).

It was much later, around 600 BC, that the first wave of Celtic warriors arrived on Wales' shores from central Europe and with them the poets and druid-priests who would change the course of Welsh history forever. The Celts had a defining role in Wales, making enormous technical and artistic advances and introducing a new language, social hierarchy and belief system. Their all-knowing druids were the driving force behind the changes and acted as godlike go-betweens with the pantheon of gods they worshipped. Revered as much for their knowledge as their divine power, the druids were integral to the start of an oral tradition of storytelling and song writing – one that is celebrated to this day.

THE ROMANS

By the time Julius Caesar landed in Britain in 55 BC, the Celts had occupied Wales for almost five centuries; when the Romans invaded in mid-1st century AD they put up staunch resistance. Mona (Anglesey) was the centre of druidic power and the site of a raging battle in AD 60. Although the Romans took control of Wales they never really conquered it. The interior held little attraction for them, few roads were built and the Celts managed to live alongside the Romans, adopting and adapting to the new cultural force.

The best surviving remains from this time are at Segontium (p256) and at the incredible Isca Silurium (p108), where a stunning amphitheatre and baths are open to the public.

BIRTH OF WALES

Wales' isolated position meant that it missed out on the heaving battles that spread across Europe in the wake of the Roman departure, and this comparative lull gave rise to a number of separate kingdoms. Around this time a British leader, possibly by the name of Arthur, emerged and proved victorious against Saxon invaders. Whether this was the legendary King Arthur or not is largely immaterial; the seed of a story, now embellished by years of romanticism, had been planted.

Along with Irish invaders came faithful missionaries, spreading Christianity and founding basic churches. The most important of these was St David (see

Go to www.bbc.co.uk /wales/history /davies for the accessible web version of leading historian John Davies' acclaimed work *A History of Wales*, an authoritative, wide-ranging and detailed guide from the earliest times to the 20th century.

The superb *When Was Wales*, by Gwyn Williams, uses myth, legend, poetry and the stories of ordinary Welsh people to explore Welsh national identity since the time of the Celts.

To survey the history, culture and traditions of Wales try the easily navigated www.britannia .com/celtic/wales.

250,000 BC	600 BC
Earliest evidence of human habitation in Wales	Celtic people begin to settle in Wales

the boxed text, below), who performed miracles, wooed the crowds and established his eponymous town as a centre of religion and learning (see p184).

The written word gradually moved from biblical purposes to literature, and the poems of Taliesin and Aneirin, from the late 6th and early 7th centuries, are the earliest surviving examples of Welsh literature. By then a distinct Welsh language had emerged and *Cymry,* a word describing the land and its people, had been established.

Isolated and compressed, the once disparate people were becoming something new, distinct and solid: Welsh. Their stories became legends and their beliefs religion. An intense, highly durable culture was born.

The Taliesin Tradition,
by Emyr Humphreys,
brilliantly traces the
identity of Wales and the
Welsh over a millennium
and a half, exploring the
influence of literature,
history, religion and
politics on the Wales
of today.

EARLY WELSH RULERS

Despite cultural assimilations, territorial scuffles continued throughout the country. One present-day reminder of this unstable time is Offa's Dyke (p63), a 178-mile fortification built in the 8th century to mark the boundary between two kingdoms: the Welsh on one side and the English (the Saxons in the form of the Kingdom of Mercia under King Offa) on the other.

During the 9th and 10th centuries savage coastal attacks in the south by Danish and Norse pirates forced the small kingdoms of Wales to cooperate. Rhodri Mawr (Rhodri the Great, d 878), a charismatic leader, managed to unite most of the kingdoms, only to see them split among his sons. His grandson, Hywel Dda (Hywel the Good, d 950), reunified the country and then went on to consolidate its laws, decreeing communal agricultural

---

WHO WAS ST DAVID? *Nona Rees*

St David, or Dewi Sant, is the only truly native patron saint of his country in the British Isles. His biography was compiled in the 1080s by Rhygyfarch ap Sulien, using earlier material. His parents, Sant and Non, were of noble descent and David's life spanned most of the 6th century.

His birth probably took place on a cliff top near present-day St David's (p184). His mother, Non, was protected from the murderous intent of a local chieftain by a mighty storm and by standing stones that moved to protect her. A spring of water miraculously burst forth, which today is a holy well. David was hence known as the Waterman and drank only water. He subdued the appetites of the flesh by standing up to his neck in cold water and reciting the psalms. He was attended by an angelic presence and worked miracles of healing.

Like many young men of good birth, David was educated by monks. He went on to found churches across South and East Wales. In company with Saints Teilo and Padarn he made a pilgrimage to the Holy Land, eventually returning to West Wales.

David established his monastery beside the River Alun where the cathedral now stands. His claim to the site was disputed by Boia, a local chieftain, whose scheming wife made her maidens dance naked in the river to tempt the monks. Predictably it did not work: she went mad and disappeared and a passing pirate murdered Boia.

David's healthy, if spartan, way of life required a diet of bread, herbs and water, early rising, manual labour, care for the poor, reading, writing and prayer. Fellow churchmen acclaimed his spiritual stature when he preached at the Synod of Brefi (Ceredigion). The ground rose under him and a dove, representing the Holy Spirit, landed on his shoulder.

David died on Tuesday, 1 March, in either 589 or 601. In 1123, Pope Callistus II recognised his sainthood and he became a focus for Welsh identity. His emblem is the leek.

Nona Rees is the author of St David of Dewisland.

AD 410	1066
Rome severs ties with Britannia, and a number of Welsh kingdoms emerge	The Normans invade Wales and a prolonged period of Welsh resistance begins

practices and affording women and children greater rights than other legal systems of the time.

Ironically, as Wales was becoming a recognisable entity, it was forced to acknowledge the authority of the Anglo-Saxon king of England in return for an alliance against the marauding Vikings.

WALES UNDER THE NORMANS

By the time the Normans arrived in England in 1066, the Welsh had returned to their warring, independent ways. To secure his new kingdom, William the Conqueror set up powerful, feudal barons – called marcher lords – along the Welsh border. From here the barons repeatedly raided Wales, taking as much territory as possible under their control.

Curiously enough, Welsh literature flourished during this time of strife. Under the patronage of the warring kings, court poets honed their craft and fantastic tales were soon transcribed. You can see the oldest surviving Welsh-language manuscript, the 12th-century Black Book of Carmarthen, in the National Library of Wales at Aberystwyth (p213).

Bards and musicians were also greatly valued in the royal courts and it was one of Wales' great leaders, Rhys ap Gruffydd (Lord Rhys), who convened the first bardic competition – Wales' original *eisteddfod* (see p47) – for a seat of honour in his house.

Meanwhile, conflict continued, with the Welsh being pushed back further and further until only Powys and Gwynedd remained independent. Successive Welsh monarchs regained territory through more bloody battles, but it was not until Llywelyn ap Gruffydd (Llewellyn the Last) that a true leader emerged. Having gained control of most of Wales, he adopted the title 'Prince of Wales' and by 1267 had forced England's Henry III to recognise him as such.

Llywelyn's triumph was short-lived, however, and by 1277 he had lost much of what he had achieved. Edward I campaigned hard to control the Welsh upstart and eventually killed both Llywelyn and his brother Dafydd. He then set up his 'Iron Ring' of imposing castles to prevent further Welsh revolt. Four of these (Conwy, p289; Caernarfon, p255; Harlech, p248; and Beaumaris, p278) stand as testimony to the bravado of Edward's plans. Caernarfon, perhaps the most famous of all, is the ultimate expression of military and royal authority, and it was here that Edward fulfilled his promise to give the Welsh a prince who didn't speak English. His infant son, Edward II, was born here and crowned Prince of Wales, a title bestowed, to this day, on the eldest son of the reigning monarch.

OWAIN GLYNDŴR

By 1400 resentment against the English was rife throughout Wales and years of famine, plague and greedy lords boiled over into rebellion. Owain ap Gruffydd (better known as Owain Glyndŵr, or Owen Glendower to the English), a descendant of the royal house of Powys, became the uprising's unlikely leader, declaring himself Prince of Wales and attacking neighbouring marcher lords.

Henry IV reacted harshly and passed a series of penal laws imposing severe restrictions on the Welsh. This only increased support for the rebellion and by 1404 Glyndŵr controlled most of Wales, capturing Harlech and Aberystwyth and summoning a parliament at Machynlleth. Crowned Prince of Wales at

10th-century Welsh law allowed women to divorce their husbands on the grounds of impotence, leprosy or bad breath.

Wales has more castles per square mile than any other country in Western Europe. For all you'll ever need to know about the castles and strongholds of Wales visit www .castlewales.com.

1400	1536 & 1543
Welsh hero Owain Glyndŵr leads the Welsh in rebellion	The Tudor Acts of Union unite Wales and England, and grant equal rights and parliamentary representation to the Welsh

---

THE LANDSKER LINE

The so-called Landsker Line, which runs roughly along the present-day A40 through Pembrokeshire, is considered something of a cultural divide between the 'Welshry' and coastal 'little England'. The line was originally created by a series of castles and strongholds built by the Normans after their invasion of West Wales in the 11th century. The *landsker*, the Norse word for frontier, marked the edge of their conquered lands and protected them from the Welsh in the north. The south of what is now Pembrokeshire became anglicised, leaving the north a bastion of Welsh language and culture – a feature still evident today.

---

the meeting of parliament, he began forming alliances with Scotland and France, whose enmity with England made them natural allies.

Glyndŵr met his match in Prince Henry, son of Henry IV and hero of the Battle of Agincourt. After a series of defeats, his allies deserted him and in 1406 Glyndŵr was forced to retreat north. Gradually the English regained control and Glyndŵr simply disappeared.

A Machynlleth Triad, by Jan Morris and Twm Morys, is an insightful and often funny account of Machynlleth at the time of Glyndŵr, as it was in the mid-1990s and on into an unknown future.

To follow Glyndŵr's attempts to unite the country, visit the Owain Glyndŵr Centre (p233) or tackle some of Glyndŵr's Way (p63), a long-distance path passing many sights connected with the rebellion.

THE TUDORS & THE ACTS OF UNION

The remainder of the 15th century saw the Welsh and English learning to coexist in many ways, though old tensions remained.

As the English fought the civil Wars of the Roses, the Welsh waited for a prophesied ruler who would restore their fortunes and lead them to victory over their age-old enemy. Most agreed that Henry Tudor best fit the role. A descendant of the Tudor family of Penmynydd in Anglesey, who managed at best a shaky claim to the throne, Henry was the most prominent Lancastrian (red rose) in opposition to Richard III (white rose). After years of exile in Brittany, Henry defeated Richard in the Battle of Bosworth Field in 1485 and ascended the throne. This began the Tudor dynasty, which would reign until the death of Elizabeth I in 1603.

Welsh hopes were high but apart from a removal of restrictions imposed by the penal laws things didn't improve much. Little attention was paid to Wales until the reign of Henry VIII, when the Tudor Acts of Union in 1536 and 1543 finally established English sovereignty over the country. The lawless Marches (the border area between Wales and England) were reorganised and Welsh counties were established. Although the Welsh became equal citizens and were granted parliamentary representation, Welsh law was abolished and English was declared the official language of law and administration. The gentry – already mostly bilingual – leapt at the chance to enhance their status and cooperated fully with the Tudors, turning their backs on the Welsh language.

THE WELSH CHURCH & WELSH LANGUAGE

Throughout these volatile years the Cistercian abbeys at Valle Crucis (p297) and Strata Florida (p216) had become centres of Welsh culture and learning. Their glory years came to an end, however, when Henry VIII converted to Protestantism and then dissolved the abbeys in 1536.

1588	1759–82
Translation of the complete Bible into Welsh, which established Protestantism and propped up the Welsh language	Dowlais and Merthyr Tydfil ironworks started and Bethesda's slate quarry opened

William Morgan, vicar of Llanrhaeadr-ym-Mochnant, produced the first complete Bible in Welsh in 1588, solidifying Protestantism as the national religion and propping up the Welsh language. As a spoken tongue, its position was unassailable, and it would remain the language of the majority until well into the 19th century. It was the production of grammars and dictionaries during this period, however, that helped preserve Welsh as a literary language.

EDUCATION & NONCONFORMISM

The late 17th and early 18th centuries witnessed the first attempts to educate the masses in Wales. The first printing presses were established and a huge increase in the number of books printed in Welsh followed. Most of these were religious works, aimed at instilling knowledge of the Gospel.

A similar religious motivation fuelled the educational initiatives of the period, including the system of circulating schools founded by Griffith Jones in the 1730s. Jones decided to use Welsh as the medium of instruction, as 70% of the rural population spoke no English. By the time he died in 1761 more than 200,000 men, women and children had learned to read the Bible.

Welsh national feeling was high and the evangelical services of the Methodists became popular. The powerful preaching and uplifting hymns spread Methodism throughout the country by the end of the 18th century. Other Nonconformist (non-Anglican) groups, such as the Independents and the Baptists, experienced an increase in religious fervour. By the 19th century most Christian worshippers in Wales no longer chose the Established Church.

The equal sign in maths was invented by a Welshman, Robert Recorde of Tenby, in the 16th century.

ROMANTIC WALES

Towards the end of the 18th century the influence of the Romantic Revival made the wild landscapes of Wales fashionable with genteel travellers. The works of landscape painters such as Richard Wilson did much to popularise the rugged mountains and ruined castles, and the rediscovery of Celtic and druidic traditions fuelled a growing cultural revival and sense of Welsh identity.

Scholars were increasingly concerned about the need to preserve the culture and heritage of their country and efforts were made to collect and publish literature. Edward Williams (Iolo Morganwg to use his bardic name) went on to revive ancient bardic competitions and held the first 'modern' *eisteddfod* in Carmarthen in 1819.

A Welsh colony was founded in Patagonia in 1865 and you can still visit a Welsh teahouse there in the village of Gaiman.

TWM SIÔN CATTI

The legendary Thomas Jones was born in 1530, the bastard son of a Tregaron landowner. It is said that Jones – who was living with his mother in near-poverty – turned outlaw at the age of 18 to save the two of them from starvation.

His banditry developed into a Robin Hood–style crusade to redistribute regional wealth. A master of disguise with a sense of humour, he relied on trickery rather than violence, retreating when necessary to a secret hideout near the River Tywi. His speciality was sheep and cattle rustling. He was never caught and in later life bought himself a royal pardon and went straight, writing poetry (winning a prize at the Llandaff *eisteddfod*) and stories (many about his own exploits), marrying the daughter of the high sheriff of Carmarthenshire and even serving as mayor of Brecon.

Welsh kids still grow up with stories about Twm Siôn Catti, most of them unfettered by genuine historical fact.

1819	1916
First modern *eisteddfod* is held as part of a Welsh cultural revival	David Lloyd George becomes Prime Minister of the UK

At this time Augusta Hall (Lady Llanover) invented the Welsh national costume: she considered the out-of-date fashions worn in Wales to be quaint, and generations of schoolgirls have been condemned to wear her designs on St David's Day ever since.

INDUSTRIALISATION

Eighteen signatories on the American Declaration of Independence were of Welsh descent.

The Welsh economy had long been based on agriculture, with few exports other than the herds of animals driven to market in England. When parliament restricted grazing rights on common land, smallholders were forced to migrate to the towns, fuelling a major development in Welsh history.

The iron industry had been growing in Wales since the mid-18th century. Ironworks proliferated around Merthyr Tydfil (p119) and workers arrived in droves. Roads, canals and tramways were constructed and English industrialists took control. The valleys were changed forever. Pioneering engineering developments from this period litter modern Wales, including Thomas Telford's spectacular Pontcysyllte Aqueduct (p299) and his graceful suspension bridges over the Menai Straits (p277) and at Conwy (p290).

The Industrial Revolution ploughed on, but its workers were getting fed up with the appalling working conditions and low rates of pay. Trade unions emerged and the first half of the 19th century was characterised by protests and calls for a universal right to vote. In 1839 the Chartist Riots broke out in towns such as Newport when a petition of more than one million signatures was rejected by Westminster. Between 1839 and 1843 the Rebecca Riots ravaged the rural southwest. The name 'Rebecca' refers to a biblical verse in Genesis: 'And they blessed Rebecca, and said unto her, Thou art our sister, be thou the mother of thousands of millions, and let thy seed possess the gate of those which hate them'. The 'Daughters of Rebecca' (men dressed in women's clothes) would act out a pantomime and tear down the turnpike tollgates on the order of 'Mother Rebecca'.

Wales was the first nation in the world to employ more people in industry than in agriculture.

In 1847 the Commission on Education published a damning report, known as *The Treason of the Blue Books,* on the state of education in Wales. It questioned Welsh morality and blamed the influences of Nonconformity and the Welsh language for allegedly lax morals. The introduction of the 'Welsh Not', a ban on speaking Welsh in schools, created a tide of anger and drove an ever-widening rift between the Welsh Nonconformists and the English Anglicans.

POLITICS & DEPRESSION

By the second half of the 19th century industry had grown, coal had superseded iron and the sheer number of migrants from England threatened to weaken the fabric of Welsh society. Nonconformists began to politicise their teachings and liberalism gained a firm hold in Wales.

John Ford's Oscar-winning film *How Green Was My Valley* is an evocative Hollywood interpretation of the hardship and suffering of the industrial valleys.

Finally in 1867 industrial workers and small tenant farmers were given the right to vote and elections in 1868 were a turning point for Wales. Henry Richard was elected as Liberal MP for Merthyr Tydfil, and brought ideas of land reform and native language to parliament for the first time.

The Secret Ballot Act of 1872 and the Reform Act of 1884 spread suffrage even further and gave a voice to the rising tide of resentment over the hardships of the valleys and the compulsion to pay tithes to the church. Liberal Nonconformity held sway over much of Wales during the late 19th and early

1925	1964
Plaid (Cenedlaethol) Cymru, the Welsh Nationalist Party, is formed	Jim Griffiths, first Secretary of State for Wales, is elected

20th centuries, even producing a prime minister, David Lloyd George (see p36). In 1900 Merthyr Tydfil returned Keir Hardie as Wales' first Labour MP.

National sentiment grew and education improved substantially. During WWI Wales boomed and living standards rose as Welsh coal and agriculture fed the economy. A quarter of a million people were employed in Wales' coal industry in the 1920s; the results of this industrialisation can be seen at the former mining town of Blaenavon (p121), a Unesco World Heritage site.

Between the world wars the country suffered the results of economic depression and thousands were driven to emigrate in search of employment. The Labour Party weathered the storm and, as the 20th century progressed, became the political force of the nation, as rugby (see p40) had become its sport.

In 1925 six young champions of Welsh nationalism founded Plaid Cenedlaethol Cymru (the Welsh Nationalist Party; later shortened to Plaid Cymru) and began the slow but assured campaign for self-government.

Lawrence of Arabia, TE Lawrence, was born in Tremadog, North Wales, in 1888.

POSTWAR WALES

The coal industry boomed during WWII, but afterwards went into decline; inefficient mines were closed and a bitter struggle ensued as unemployment levels rose to twice the UK average. The Welsh language was suffering and the people felt powerless.

In 1957 the village of Capel Celyn, near Bala, and the surrounding valley were flooded to provide water for the city of Liverpool, despite campaigning. There were too few Welsh MPs in the House of Commons to oppose the project and resentment still lingers over the issue, intensified in dry summers by the appearance of the chapel, school and farms above the waters of Llyn Celyn.

The 1960s became a decade of protest in Wales, and Plaid Cymru gained ground. In 1962 Cymdeithas yr Iaith Gymraeg (the Welsh Language Society) was founded, which campaigned for legal status for the language and for Welsh-speaking radio and TV. At the same time Welsh pop began to flourish and Welsh publishing houses and record labels were set up. Cardiff was declared the Welsh capital in 1955, and in 1959 Wales finally got an official flag.

In Wales' worst mining disaster 439 men and boys were killed at the Universal Colliery, Senghenydd, about 4 miles northwest of Caerphilly, in 1913.

In 1964 the position of Secretary of State for Wales was created and two years later Gwynfor Evans became the first Plaid MP. Support for Plaid Cymru soared in the wake of his victory and further electoral successes by the party in the 1970s started people thinking about a measure of Welsh self-government.

With only a shaky parliamentary majority the Labour Party was doing all it could to maintain Welsh support. In 1976 the Welsh Development Agency

MADOG

As part of Wales' Romantic renaissance, the story of Madog (Madog ab Owain Gwynedd, son of a prince of North Wales), who is said to have set off and discovered America in 1170, was also revived. Used during Elizabeth I's reign to justify the colonisation of America, it was now deployed to give the Welsh a sense of pride in their past. Madog and his followers had supposedly intermarried with native Americans, and early settlers to America had reputedly come across Welsh-speaking natives. In 1796 John Evans, the leader of a party that helped map the River Missouri, sought to find these Welsh-speaking Indians, but failed to find them. Given that many small American tribes disappeared soon after colonisation, due to the effect of European diseases and through loss of their lands and food sources, Evans' conclusion has not satisfied those who believe in the Madog story.

1970s	1980s
Wales is the most feared opponent on the rugby field	Margaret Thatcher's Conservative government makes drastic cuts to Wales' coal and steel industries; unemployment soars

THE RISE OF LLOYD GEORGE (1863–1945)

A genuine political radical, David Lloyd George began his career as the champion of Welsh populist democracy and a critic of society and its institutions. He came from a family of staunch Nonconformists, preached at Temperance Society meetings and earned a reputation early as a fiery solicitor willing to defend the people against the authorities.

A talented and witty orator, he won his first seat as Liberal MP for Caernarfon Boroughs and at 27 became the youngest member of the House of Commons. As Chancellor of the Exchequer he launched a broad but controversial programme of social reform, including the introduction of old-age pensions, a 1909 budget that taxed the wealthy to fund services for the poor, and the 1911 National Insurance Act to provide health and unemployment insurance.

Elected Prime Minister in 1916 after a divisive alliance with the Conservatives, Lloyd George went on to become an energetic war leader; he excelled at a time when strong leadership was needed, dismissing red tape and forcing his opinion when necessary.

At the Paris Peace Conference in 1919, Lloyd George was credited with negotiating a middle ground between the harsh demands of Georges Clemenceau and the idealistic proposals of Woodrow Wilson. The treaty was well received in Britain and in August 1919 he was conferred with the Order of Merit by the king.

Domestic problems, however, continued to trouble him. Postwar industrial unrest and economic reconstruction dogged the country, while civil war raged in Ireland. Lloyd George eventually agreed to Irish independence, a solution the Conservative alliance never forgave.

Meanwhile, continuing accusations of corruption, extreme financial greed and the selling of honours began to ruin his reputation. Radicals, Welsh nationalists and campaigners for women's rights all felt betrayed. Whatever convictions he had begun with seemed to have been lost in a quest for power and fame. In 1922 the Conservatives staged a party revolt and broke up the shaky coalition. Lloyd George resigned immediately.

His popularity had faded, the Liberal Party was in disarray, political allies had abandoned him and both the Welsh and the British working class felt thoroughly deceived. Lloyd George's political career had reached a sad anticlimax. He died in 1945 at Llanystumdwy, where there is now a small museum devoted to his life (p268).

(WDA) was established to help Wales make the awkward transition to new sources of employment. Political responsibility began to devolve to Cardiff and on St David's Day in 1979 a referendum on limited devolution was put before the Welsh people. A resounding 'no' vote was returned.

The Labour Government collapsed soon after and Margaret Thatcher's Conservative Party swept to power. In the 1980s the most drastic cuts to the now-nationalised but increasingly inefficient coal industry began. The Thatcher years of privatisation also led to severe cuts in the manufacturing and steel industry. Agriculture, too, was in a state of disarray and unemployment began to soar. Welsh living standards lagged far behind the rest of Britain, and with the collapse of the Miners' Strike of 1984–85 Welsh morale hit an all-time low. Extreme action on behalf of Welsh nationalism by activist group Meibion Glyndŵr (Sons of Glyndŵr) brought widespread condemnation as English holiday homes in North Wales were fire-bombed and the populace moved ever further from separatist ideals.

In 1982 the pressure on the Welsh language abated after a hunger strike by Gwynfor Evans forced the Conservatives to come good on election promises and establish S4C (Sianel Pedwar Cymru), the Welsh-language TV channel (see

1982	1999
S4C, the Welsh-medium TV channel, begins broadcasting	First National Assembly elected

p45). Support and enthusiasm for the Welsh language increased, night courses popped up all over the country, Welsh-speaking nurseries and schools opened, university courses were established and the number of Welsh speakers started to stabilise at around 20% of the population. At the same time Plaid Cymru began to broaden its base and develop serious policies, embracing all things European as well as arguing for a Welsh authority to oversee public expenditure.

DEVOLUTION

In 1997 a general election brought 'New Labour' to power and the devolution process got off the ground once again. In September of that year a referendum on the establishment of the National Assembly scraped through by the narrowest of margins.

The Assembly got off to a shaky start. Alun Michael, First Secretary in the new Assembly, was quickly ousted by a vote of no confidence and was replaced by the widely popular and populist MP Rhodri Morgan. Lacking the powers granted to the Scottish Parliament, the Assembly was always going to have a hard time convincing the world – and the Welsh – of its merit. Inane political debate, a lot of bad press and a farcical series of events over its new building didn't help the cause. Outside the political arena, though, Welsh pride flew high; Wales played host to the world's rugby elite in its sparkling Millennium Stadium, Welsh rock bands were making headlines with a slew of high-profile releases and the concept of 'Cool Cymru' swept through Britain.

The Assembly has now settled down (some say too comfortably) in a quest for a new national identity.

The Welsh Extremist, a nonfiction work by Ned Thomas, explores the issues of oppression and freedom that spurred the anti-English bombings in the 1970s.

WALES TODAY

At the turn of the millennium, Wales and its capital city Cardiff both underwent major transformation. On 26 November 2004 the £106 million Millennium Centre opened belatedly as a new permanent home for, among others, the Welsh National Opera. The move marked the culmination of Cardiff's regeneration, which can be traced back to the mid-1980s when the Cardiff Bay Development Corporation was set up to oversee the transformation of the waterfront area. Over the years a total public and private urban renaissance project costing £1.8 billion has been put into effect with the aim of redeveloping 4.2 sq miles of deprived docklands in the bay formed by the estuary of the Rivers Taff and Ely.

The unveiling of the new National Assembly building and the ratification of the Government of Wales Bill (due to take effect from May 2007) have helped to assuage initial concerns about the validity of the new seat of government and allowed it, under Rhodri Morgan, to become part of the fabric of daily Welsh life. Furthermore, the renewed sense of confidence continues to filter down to all levels of society: Wales strides the sporting field like a colossus, Welsh-language culture is blossoming, and new industries are spreading like a hi-tech plague across the country, many flashing their green credentials alongside their desire to boost the local economy.

Age-old problems remain (rural poverty, manufacturing decline and depopulation) while the three biggest factors that will shape Wales' future (demographics, globalisation and climate change) are major concerns. But overall there's a sense that Wales today is not just moving forward but finally holding its head high once more.

London's Big Ben was most likely named after a bulky Welshman – the industrialist and Commissioner of Works, Benjamin Hall.

2005	2006
Cardiff celebrates its centenary as a city and its 50th year as Wales' capital with a year-long festival of cultural events. And Wales wins the Rugby Grand Slam.	The Government of Wales Bill proposes the biggest transfer of power from Westminster to Wales since the Welsh National Assembly was set up in 1999

The Culture

In the past Wales has battled with the world's perception of it as an un-sophisticated place, an uncool appendage to England. Much has changed in recent years and Welsh pride and international standing have been buoyed by the success of pop and rock stars, authors and film makers, and the establishment of the National (Welsh) Assembly. Never before has the sense of national identity and pride risen so high.

For a multitude of links about Wales try www .walesonline.com.

THE WELSH IDENTITY

A complex blend of historical association, ingrained defiance and Celtic spirit defines the notion of 'Welshness'. In recent years, though, Wales has evolved in many ways and the old stereotypes of the Welsh as pious but unsophisticated country folk have largely given way to a more cosmopolitan consciousness.

For the convivial Welsh the most prominent feature of their culture is the language: a wonderful, sing-song lilt littered with an incomprehensible mix of double 'l's and consecutive consonants. For centuries the Welsh have had to fight for its very survival and this has done much to underpin anti-English sentiment, especially in the heavily Welsh-speaking northwest, as well as strengthen their identity as a separate nation. In 2001 a political storm ensued when census forms did not include a box to tick for Welsh nationality.

Expertly written and photographed, *Wales in Our Own Image*, by Gwenda Williams, will replace your romantic notions of Wales with a far more compelling account of this small nation.

Identification as a nation is one of the essential prerequisites for political power and the attitude to devolution has also changed in recent years, from firm opposition to cynical acceptance. Although the National Assembly's lack of power and limited authority dominate most criticism, few would consider a return to Westminster control. In the hope of gaining political clout the Welsh have also begun side-stepping Britain and aligning themselves with other small EU nations.

While urban Wales embraces international values and the young migrate to the cities, the ageing population of rural Wales clings to vanishing small-farm traditions. The decline in farming and subsequent losses to rural communities is a major concern. Since the foot-and-mouth epidemic of 2001, the Welsh rural landscape has become a higher priority for most, and a collective new voice championing the cause of sustainability has emerged.

Sheep outnumber people in Wales by almost four to one.

LIFESTYLE

Welsh lifestyles can differ vastly from one part of the country to another. Urban residents live in a culture of hard work and long hours much like the rest of Britain, while in rural areas the pace of life tends to be slower and more traditional. Small family farms are still the cornerstone of rural society, but the farmers' way of life is under threat as incomes fall, the farming population ages and young people make for the bright lights of the city.

WHAT'S IN A NAME?

Probably the greatest insult you can give the Welsh is to refer to their country as 'England'. It may seem an obvious point but it's important to get it right.

England dominates the UK to such an extent that not only the English but most of the world tends to say 'England' when they mean the UK. When you cross the border into Wales, it pays to remember you're in another country. England, Scotland and Wales make up Great Britain; add in Northern Ireland and you've got the UK: the United Kingdom of Great Britain and Northern Ireland.

There has been a general loss of vitality in many rural communities; schools have closed and the deterioration of public transport in these areas has caused further isolation. Meanwhile, urban areas are expanding and developing, catering for these patterns of migration and resulting in a new-found affluence in the cities.

After the fallout from the collapse of industrial mining and steel manufacturing, Wales recovered by switching to light manufacturing. Women increasingly became the new breadwinners and there was a gradual change in thinking within the traditionally patriarchal society; however, many of the jobs created were low-skilled positions. The standard of living in Wales is among the worst in the UK and much of the country still qualifies for European Union (EU) funding, allocated to the most disadvantaged areas in Western Europe. Low-income employees earn about £11,000 per annum, while the average salary is roughly £20,000; top earners average about twice that figure. Both wages and disposable income fall well below the UK average, and unemployment levels, although declining, are higher than most of Britain.

The fabric of family life is also changing: children leave home rather than work the land; the birth rate is now the lowest on record; and as church-going figures fall, the pub has taken its place as the focal point for community life. Rugby is still the lifeblood of the nation though and the country's passion for sport has to be experienced to be believed.

> Wales is not represented on the British flag.

Alternative Lifestyles

Attracted by the serene countryside, relative isolation and cheaper living, a steady stream of migrants have crossed the border into West and Mid-Wales in search of an alternative lifestyle. The process began in earnest in the 1960s, and by 1974 the Centre for Alternative Technology (p234) had been established to showcase the cravings for something new and wholesome. A few years later a controversial tepee camp was established as a permanent settlement in Carmarthenshire.

> Few houses in Wales have house numbers; most people prefer to name their homes.

The 1980s saw a new wave of alternative lifestylers head west, and now you can bump your head on dream catchers, eat lentils, and source books

---

SPA & YOGA RETREATS

If you're more of an overworked urbanite than adrenaline junkie and need some time away from it all, then just breathe deep, relax and let someone else massage your weary soul. Wales has a number of excellent spa and yoga retreats; choose from luxury countryside sanctuaries specialising in yoga, alternative therapies and meditation to hotel-based spas where five-star opulence will woo you into deep relaxation.

- **Celtic Manor** (www.celtic-manor.com) Exclusive five-star spa in the city of Newport that has every luxury on offer.

- **Gaia Cooperative** (www.gaiacooperative.org) A wide range of courses in healthy living and environmental awareness near Hay-on-Wye on the Welsh borders.

- **Heartspring** (www.heartspring.co.uk) Individual retreats in Llansteffan (south of Carmarthen) with a combination of tailor-made complementary therapy and teaching sessions.

- **Hurst House** (www.hurst-house.co.uk) Luxurious treatments and pampering at this country-house hotel.

- **Mary Madhavi Yoga** (www.marysyoga.co.uk) Holistic weekends featuring a full programme of yoga, relaxation and experiential classes.

- **St David's Hotel and Spa** (www.thestdavidshotel.com) Pop in for a quick fix or stay for a city break at Cardiff's top-notch hotel and spa.

on how to run a Native American–style sweat lodge in most small towns to be found across West and Mid-Wales.

POPULATION

For a look at what people have said about the Welsh and what they've said about themselves, see *A Most Peculiar People: Quotations about Wales and the Welsh*, edited by Meic Stephens.

With only 2.9 million people Wales is sparsely populated compared to the rest of Britain and even this figure is misleading, as large urban centres in South Wales account for a good chunk of the population, while Mid-Wales is serenely quiet. In many places sheep far outnumber people.

The indigenous Welsh are mostly of Celtic stock and about 20% of the population speaks Welsh. Anglesey and the Llŷn are bastions of the language and culture, with smaller strongholds in the Swansea Valley and eastern Carmarthenshire. The heavily populated, urbanised south has far fewer Welsh speakers. Migration trends are focused primarily on the move from rural to urban areas and the influx of English people; a huge chunk of the population – 22% – was born in England. That means there are now more English people in Wales than there are Welsh speakers – a worrying figure for Welsh-language activists.

SPORT

The Welsh are passionate about sport, in particular the Holy Grail of rugby and football. Roughly speaking, rugby is the national game, although followed with a particular passion in the south, while North Wallans reserve their most fervent support for football. For competition purposes Wales is a country in its own right and all home matches of the national rugby and football teams are played in the Welsh pride and joy: Cardiff's sparkling Millennium Stadium (p88). Arguably the UK's finest international sports arena, it has hosted football's FA Cup Final and the Rugby World Cup for several years now while the much-delayed Wembley Stadium project in London has been mired in problems.

Lawn tennis was invented in Wales.

Rugby

Rugby in Wales is more than just a passion – it has been turned into a national sport. Fans verge on the fanatical and the sterling performance of the home team, winning the Grand Slam in 2005, has served to fuel the fanaticism. Rugby Union, the 15-player form of the game, is by far the most popular, while Rugby League, the 13-player version, tends to languish in relative obscurity, although the newly formed Celtic Crusaders are doing their best to buck that trend.

The four Welsh regional clubs playing in the Celtic League are Newport-Gwent Dragons (playing at Rodney Parade, Newport); Llanelli Scarlets (Stradey Park, Llanelli); Neath-Swansea Ospreys (The Knoll, Neath); Cardiff Blues (Cardiff Arms Park). You can catch club matches between September and Easter.

For information and news, see www.wru.co.uk.

Football

Dip into *The Wisdom of Wales*, Paul Barrett's collection of proverbs and superb photography, for some nuggets of wisdom from the land of the leek.

Football (soccer) has been second fiddle to rugby in recent years, with the Welsh rugby team winning the Grand Slam in 2005. Nevertheless, Wales' national soccer squad have also shown promise. Wales narrowly missed out on qualifying for Euro 2004 under former player-turned-manager Mark Hughes and now, under new manager John Toshack, the aim is to rebuild the squad plus source new young talent to line up with established Premiership stars, such as Ryan Giggs (Manchester United) and Craig Bellamy (Liverpool).

The Welsh Premier League is a semiprofessional league and home to teams such as NEWI Cefn Druids and the New Saints. As Wales' national league, high-performing teams at this level qualify for European competition.

WELSH LANGUAGE WOES

Although support for the Welsh language has strengthened in recent years and other minority cultures look to Wales as a shining example, in reality the threat to the Welsh language is acute.

Economic hardship in rural areas, particularly Welsh-speaking communities, has led to migration to urban centres. Meanwhile, large numbers of non-Welsh speakers have been moving in, changing the cultural dynamic of rural Wales in a very short time. Few of these migrants learn the Welsh language or become involved in local traditions, and their presence inflates house prices and forces local people out.

During the rise of nationalism from the 1960s to 1980s, opposition to the English 'invaders' rose steadily and anti-English slogans and graffiti were common. Slogans such as *'Dal dy dir'* (Hold your ground) and *'Ildiwch'* (Surrender) still adorn the mountain sides and rural walls. A radical underground organisation, the Sons of Glyndŵr, went even further, firebombing English-owned holiday homes and, in doing so, causing much harm to the nationalists' cause.

Today, peaceful 'No Colonisation' campaigns attack estate agents in England who are selling Welsh properties to outsiders, and pressure group Cymuned has brought the case for state regulation of the housing market to both the National Assembly and the UN. Several local authorities have now proposed controversial moves to limit the capacity of nonlocals to buy or build property – the favoured approach to redress the balance.

For more information visit www.wales4sale.com and www.bbc.co.uk/wales/history/sites/language/pages/timeline.shtml.

Cardiff City (Championship), Wrexham (League Two) and Swansea City (League One) play in the otherwise English Football League, though the high-flying Bluebirds have aspirations to play Premiership football.

Major English football events have been held at the Millennium Stadium until the new Wembley Stadium is finished, but you won't hear too many fans complaining. Cardiff City is the only club ever to take the FA Cup out of England, beating Arsenal in 1927, but for now at least, fans will have to contend with seeing English teams rule the roost, albeit on their home turf.

For more information, visit www.icwales.co.uk/soccernation.

Take a crash course in the Welsh language at www.nantgwrtheyrn.org.

MULTICULTURALISM

Wales has a small ethnic minority, only about 2% of the population, most of whom are based in Cardiff, followed by Newport (where there's a large mosque) and Swansea. Most of these communities are well integrated and Butetown (formerly known as Tiger Bay) in Cardiff is one of Britain's oldest and most successful multiracial communities.

For comprehensive coverage of arts, politics and current affairs in Wales visit www.planetmagazine.org.uk.

The largest minority group in Wales is Asian people from India, Pakistan and Bangladesh, and other groups are so limited in size and location that they do not fit in with the government policy of placing asylum seekers in communities where they will be easily assimilated and supported. Consequently Wales has received relatively few asylum seekers and has largely avoided the raging debates on asylum that have dogged the rest of the UK in recent years.

In northern Wales, however, young nationalists have recently been targeting non-Welsh speakers and the tiny minority population of Blacks and Asians. Although you shouldn't encounter any problems as a tourist, be aware that ill feeling can exist.

MEDIA

Welsh media has strengthened in recent years, though newspapers are generally populist titles taking a lightweight view of Welsh affairs and doing little to provoke thought or debate; significantly, the three major papers are controlled by one company (Trinity Mirror). Alternative voices are heard through

A Welshman cofounded the *New York Times*.

an increasing number of top-quality Welsh magazines. Due to launch in 2007 is *Y Byd* (The World), the first-ever Welsh-language newspaper. For more details, check the website www.ybyd.com.

TV and radio in Wales are far ahead in terms of innovative programming and quality broadcasting, churning out many award-winning TV programmes and, at the best of times, working as a catalyst for change. BBC Radio Wales and BBC Radio Cymru transmit English- and Welsh-language news and features, while a host of commercial stations turn up the music for listeners. BBC Wales and local Welsh-language broadcaster S4C (Sianel Pedwar Cymru; see the boxed text, p45) successfully produce a variety of excellent TV viewing.

RELIGION

St Patrick was a Welshman.

Although the Welsh once had a strong image as a god-fearing, church-going nation, this stereotype no longer holds true. Religion in Wales has a remarkable history but little contemporary support. About 72% of the population is Christian but church-going figures are thought to be as low as just 7%.

Since the 18th century, Nonconformist Protestant denominations have held most sway over the people of Wales, bringing a puritanical strain to Welsh life. Today, Methodists, based mainly in rural areas, are the largest group, followed by the Congregationalists, who are strong in South Wales, and smaller groups of Wesleyans and Baptists. Of non-Christian religions, Islam has the largest following.

Mon Mam Cymru: The Guide to Anglesey, by Philip Steels & Robert Williams, is an excellent guide to the island home of the druids.

The growth of alternative spirituality and paganism in Mid-Wales is largely undocumented, but many 'New Agers' subscribe to the concepts of ancient beliefs in some form or another. Celtic druidism (see the boxed text, p276), pagan shamanism and many traditional Eastern religions are now the focus of workshops and gatherings attended by increasing numbers of people.

ARTS

The Welsh arts scene, which has a history of showcasing fine works, is thriving at the moment thanks to some excellent creative talent and an injection of funds from the National Assembly. Launched in 2001, Cymru'n Creu (Wales Creates) is a consortium of public agencies aimed at encouraging a culturally diverse, creatively rich and entrepreneurial arts industry. The programme appears to be providing momentum and focus for emerging talent.

The National Museum of Wales in Cardiff and the National Library of Wales in Aberystwyth celebrate their centenary in 2007.

Literature

Check out the latest books, reviews and publications at www .gwales.com.

Wales has an incredibly rich literary history, with storytelling firmly embedded in the national psyche. From 2000-year-old bardic poetry to the Welsh-inspired 'sprung-rhythm' of English poet Gerard Manley Hopkins, latter-day Welsh writers have had a store of impressive works to refer to.

However, it is primarily 20th-century writing that has brought Welsh literature to a worldwide audience. A milestone was the 1915 publication of the controversial *My People,* by Caradoc Evans (1883–1945), in which he exposed the dark side of Welsh life with stories of 'little villages hidden in valleys and reeking with malice'. Up until then, writers had pursued established nostalgic themes.

In an international sense it was the 'roaring boy' of Welsh literature, Dylan Thomas (1914–53), who was Wales' most notable export, his reputation for outrageous living almost equalling that of his literary works. He is acclaimed for writing half a dozen of the greatest poems in the English language, including such timeless works as *Fern Hill* and *A Refusal to Mourn the Death, by*

Fire, of a Child in London. Thomas, however, is probably most famous for his hugely comic radio play, *Under Milk Wood,* describing a day in the life of an insular Welsh community.

Although Thomas rarely touched on it, a recurrent theme across Welsh literature was the pain and politics of coalminers and quarry workers in the Depression years. Richard Llewellyn (1906–83) brought these hardships and the suffering to a world audience with his romantic roller coaster of a novel, *How Green Was My Valley,* a popular but dubious gathering of all the myths, stereotypes and truths of the industrial valleys.

Welsh literature matured in the work of home-grown heroes taking on the clichés of valley life and developing more realistic, socially rooted works. Poet and painter David Jones (1895–1974) began the trend with his epic of war, *In Parenthesis,* published in 1937. His testament to WWI was based on his experiences in the trenches and the language produced is an enduring literary achievement.

Remembered best for her short stories and novels, Kate Roberts (1891–1985) explored the experiences of working men and women in rural Wales, often evoking qualities of a time since past. One of Wales' most outstanding 20th-century writers, her novel *Feet in Chains* explores the struggles of a North Wales slate-quarrying family over almost 40 years, and her novel *Tea in Heather* is an insightful observation of the struggles of a little girl growing up in Gwynedd in the early 20th century.

Finely observed and incredibly dark and witty, Rhys Davies' stories in *A Human Condition* examine small-town life and rural mentality. The elegant *On the Black Hill,* by Bruce Chatwin (1940–89), also evokes the joys and hardships of small-town life, exploring Welsh spirit and cross-border antipathy through the lives of torpid twin-brother farmers.

Poetry has been strongly represented in recent years with fine work tumbling out of Wales from a number of authors. Names to look out for include Robert Minhinnick (editor of *Poetry Wales*), Gillian Clarke, T Harri Jones and John Barnie.

For a compelling overview of Wales and the Welsh, take a look at the *Land of the Living* sequence of seven novels by Emyr Humphreys. The first novel, *Flesh and Blood,* is a triumph of character and a beautiful observation of the ways in which people are shaped by their environment.

Discover Welsh legends and folktales through the eyes of a child in the beautiful quirky memoir *A Welsh Childhood* by Alice Thomas Ellis.

Lime, Lemon and Sarsaparilla is Colin Hughes' wonderful evocation of Italian life in South Wales when the café was central to many small communities' social life.

POET, PRIEST & PATRIOT

One of Wales' most passionate and most reclusive modern writers, the priest-poet RS Thomas (1913–2000), was an outspoken critic of Welsh 'cultural suicide' and a staunch supporter of unpopular causes. Nominated for the Nobel Prize for literature, his uncompromising work has a pure, sparse style, which he used to explore his profound spirituality and the natural world.

RS Thomas was also more politically controversial than any other Welsh writer, becoming the Welsh conscience and campaigning fervently on behalf of indigenous language and culture. His unflinching support of Welsh issues did not always extend to his compatriots, however, with him proclaiming at one point that they were 'an impotent people/sick with inbreeding/worrying the carcass of an old song'. In the late 1980s and early 1990s he was at the centre of a highly public row when he publicly praised the arsonists who firebombed English-owned holiday homes in Wales. He claimed that English speakers were destroying the country and asked 'What is one death against the death of the whole Welsh nation?' His inflammatory views were picked up by the rock band Manic Street Preachers (see p47), who used a line of his for their hit album *This is My Truth, Tell Me Yours.*

Despite his fierce passions, English is the language of his poetry, although he wrote some prose, including his enigmatic autobiography *'Neb'* (Nobody), in Welsh.

Another excellent introduction to Wales and an insight into its changing values is *The Green Bridge*, edited by John Davies, a compendium of short stories by Wales' leading authors, exploring love, politics, sport, satire, industry and the countryside.

Except for Leonora Brito's *Dat's Love*, a heady tale of life and love, mundanity and surrealism in Cardiff's cultural melting pot, the literary voices of Blacks and Asians in Wales are rarely heard. Charlotte Williams, however, also broke the mould with her exploration of Welsh-Guyana roots in her autobiography *Sugar and Slate*, an examination of belonging and geographical, cultural and racial dislocation.

James Hawes' *White Powder, Green Light* is a scathing yet hilarious look at the Welsh media industry, Welsh-language die-hards and Soho bigwigs.

The most recent contemporary novels from Wales are an irreverent look at youth culture and its strange mix of sketchy tradition and drug-infused haze. Lewis Davies' critically acclaimed debut novel, *Work, Sex and Rugby*, is a hideously funny weekend odyssey of nights on the pull and days on the dole in the South Wales valleys. Other authors, such as Richard John Evans in his darkly comic novel *Entertainment*, have explored a much darker side of the postindustrial, drug-dissipated valleys.

For a bizarre look at modern Wales, the Chandler-esque crime caper *Aberystwyth Mon Amour*, by Malcolm Pryce, is as ridiculous as it is sublime. Its deadpan delivery of the most absurd events is clever comedy at its best.

For more information on literature in Wales, visit www.seren-books.com or www.gwales.com.

WALES' LITERARY MOVEMENT   *Iwan Llwyd*

The loss of the referendum for devolution in March 1979 was a catharsis for modern Welsh literature in Wales. Like the investiture of Prince Charles as the Prince of Wales in July 1969, it heralded a flood of political and engaged writing and poetry, most notably the left-wing historian Gwyn Alf Williams' re-evaluation of Welsh history in his masterpiece *When Was Wales?*

Also important were the poets T James Jones and the Welsh-American Jon Dressel's *Janus* poems, submitted for the Crown at the National Eisteddfod in Caernarfon, also in 1979. Judged the winning entry by the adjudicators, the poems, comparing the debacle of the devolution referendum in 1979 with the death of Llywelyn ap Gruffydd, the last native Prince of Wales in 1282, were declared invalid by the Eisteddfod establishment because they were the work of more than one poet.

This apparent capitulation to the inevitability of the death of Welsh Wales sparked a renaissance among a younger generation of Welsh poets and novelists. Poets such as Steve Eaves, Menna Elfyn, Gerwyn Williams, Myrddin ap Dafydd, Ifor ap Glyn, Elin ap Hywel and Iwan Llwyd decided that poetry had to be taken out of the chapel, study and lecture room and performed in pubs, clubs and cloisters. This led to a series of poetry tours such as *Syched am Sycharth* (celebrating the Welsh rebel Owain Glyndŵr) and *Taith y Saith Sant* (a celebration of the Celtic saints of the dark ages), making Welsh-language poetry once again a popular medium of protest and performance.

At the same time Welsh-language novelists such as Wiliam Owen Roberts, whose seminal work *Y Pla* (Pestilence) has been translated into several European languages, Mihangel Morgan, Bethan Gwanas, Eurig Wyn, and Caryl Lewis have recharged the Welsh imagination with a combination of humour, satire and magic realism.

Boosted by the establishment of S4C and BBC Radio Cymru, the Welsh-language TV and radio stations, during the 1980s (see opposite), a generation of professional Welsh-language writers have for the first time enabled Welsh poetry, drama and prose to have a life outside the traditional amateur and academic enclaves.

Recent years have also seen an increasing crossover between Welsh and English poetry and literature, as well as poets and musicians such as Twm Morys and Gwyneth Glyn establishing new audiences with their blend of words and music.

Iwan Llwyd is a poet and author based in Porthmadog.

Cinema & Television

Welsh TV and film-making have been leading the cultural revival in Wales and although English media still dominates the moving image, Wales has recently been packing a punch disproportionate to its size.

The stereotypes of Welsh life as depicted in early classics (such as *The Citadel*, the story of an idealistic doctor in a Welsh mining town, and *How Green Was My Valley*, a film that probably annoys the Welsh more than any other) held fast for many years despite the fact that they featured non-Welsh actors, English or American directors and few if any Welsh locations. The first genuinely Welsh film was Karl Francis' *Above Us the Earth* in 1977. Based on the true story of a colliery closure, it featured an all-amateur cast in real valley locations.

In recent years the beginnings of a new film industry have emerged. Film workshops have been established, as well as a Welsh media agency, BAFTA awards and an international film festival. Meanwhile, S4C (see below) has been instrumental in supporting emerging talent and promoting Welsh culture to the outside world.

This renewed confidence and greater independence has strengthened the Welsh film identity once forged only by Hollywood greats Sir Richard Burton, Sir Anthony Hopkins and, more recently, Catherine Zeta-Jones. Rising Welsh star Rhys Ifans, previously lead singer in the band Super Furry Animals (see p47), has also made it big in tinsel town with appearances in *Notting Hill*, *51st State* and *The Shipping News*, and at home with the funny but clichéd revenge comedy *Twin Town*.

Two of S4C's greatest success stories have been Welsh-language docudrama *Hedd Wyn*, nominated for an Oscar for Best Foreign Language Film in 1994, and *Solomon a Gaenor*, nominated in the same category in 1999. Another S4C production *Eldra*, a coming-of-age tale about a young

Hedd Wyn, directed by Paul Turner, is a film of the life of a farmer's son, who was conscripted into WWI and killed without knowing he had won the highest honour for a Welsh poet.

Solomon and Gaenor, directed by Paul Morrison, is a tale of forbidden love set against the backdrop of the South Wales coalfields at the turn of the 20th century.

BRINGING WALES TO THE WORLD

It took a hunger strike by Welsh nationalist Gwynfor Evans and heavy campaigning by Cymdeithas yr Iaith Gymraeg (the Welsh Language Society) to prevent the government from reneging on the promise of a Welsh-language TV station. Yet today, the broadcasting baby is credited with rejuvenating a threatened language, strengthening Welsh national identity and bringing Wales to the world.

Although heavily subsidised, Sianel Pedwar Cymru (S4C; Channel 4 Wales) has been an enormous success since it began broadcasting in 1982. The channel has been instrumental in the renaissance of the Welsh language and encouraging people to learn Welsh. Long-running soap opera *Pobol y Cwm* (People of the Valley) is even transmitted with subtitles to the rest of Britain. The establishment of a Welsh channel has also created jobs and attracted young people to places such as Bangor and Caernarfon, previously unknown to young media graduates, and is helping to reverse the brain-drain to Cardiff and London.

The station has also helped to establish a stronger sense of cultural identity for Wales both within the country and internationally. Oscar-nominated films, such as *Solomon a Gaenor* and *Hedd Wyn* (see above), have helped raise the profile of Wales and Welsh film-making, and acclaimed documentaries such as *The Celts* and *Space Tourists* have been sold worldwide, further strengthening the Welsh presence in the international arena.

However, it is the channel's assault on the world of animation which has won it the most international respect. In 1982 its cuddly yellow bear, *Super Ted*, became the first-ever British animation series to be broadcast by Disney. Success continued worldwide with *Fireman Sam*; Oscar nominations for *Famous Fred* and *The Canterbury Tales*; a worldwide cult following for the dysfunctional Stone Age family *The Gogs*; cutting-edge film-length animation in *Other World*; and a slew of South Korean and Israeli children following the adventures of *Sali Mali*, a forgetful little old lady with a heart of gold.

The Englishman Who Went Up a Hill but Came Down a Mountain is a light-hearted film about a village changing its image – and doing whatever it takes.

Romany girl growing up in a slate-quarrying community in North Wales, won the 2003 'Spirit of Moondance' award at the Sundance Film Festival in Colorado. Other films to look out for include the edgy *Human Traffic,* which immortalised Cardiff's club scene, and for novelty value Charlotte Church's cinematic flop *I'll Be There,* a tale of a rebellious teen pursuing her dreams of becoming a singer.

S4C and BBC Wales have also been a springboard for small-screen success, challenging preconceptions and fuelling independent production. Between the religious and farming programming, soap operas and game shows are some Welsh gems. One recent BAFTA award winner was the hard-hitting documentary *Ar y Stry* (Streetlife), which follows the lives of homeless heroin addicts. The film did much to dispel the myth that the issue remained an imported problem by including middle-class Welsh speakers.

Ivor the Engine, a wannabe choir-singing locomotive, entertained children for 30 years on British TV.

More recently the revival of BBC TV series *Doctor Who,* set in Cardiff, and its spin-off series, *Torchwood,* have introduced sci-fi fans to Cardiff as the centre of alien activity.

Wales' oldest claim to cinematic fame, however, is as a location. Popular with directors since the 1920s, the country now hosts major productions on a regular basis. The stunning landscape of Snowdonia is by far the leader of the pack with modern movies such as *First Knight* and *Tomb Raider 2* being shot here. TV classics were also filmed in Wales, with Portmeirion used as the backdrop for cult classic *The Prisoner.*

See the boxed text, p303, for more.

Music

1960s hero Bob Dylan changed his surname in homage to the Welsh poet Dylan Thomas – he was previously known as Bob Zimmerman.

Music has always been important in Wales and could never be stamped out despite years of both political and religious suppression. However, the ancient traditions of competitive performance and the sweet sounds of country folk hardly grabbed the world and made it listen.

ROCK & POP

Sixties sex bomb Tom Jones injected some much-needed life into the otherwise predictable music flow, and the brazen allure of Shirley Bassey singing *Goldfinger* brought James Bond fans to their knees. The 1970s saw the emergence of great rock bands such as Man and Budgie, but their fine quality did not translate into fame. It took a roar from the red dragon in the late 1990s to hit the international big time with the heady sounds of

TOP 10 MUST-HAVE ALBUMS

- Manic Street Preachers *Everything Must Go* (Epic)
- Catatonia *Way Beyond Blue* (Blanco Y Negro)
- Super Furry Animals *Mwng* (Placid Casual)
- Gorky's Zygotic Mynci *Bwyd Time* (Ankst)
- Man *Endangered Species* (Evangeline)
- Budgie *Squawk* (Notworthy)
- The Alarm *Strength* (IRS)
- Y Cyrff *Atalnod Llawn 1983–1992* (Rasal)
- Ffa Coffi *Pawb Am Byth* (Placid Casual)
- Llwbr Llaethog *Hip-Dub Reggae-Hop* (Ankst)

As compiled by Spillers Records of Cardiff, see p101.

a host of mega-groups, including Manic Street Preachers, Catatonia and Stereophonics. Their innovative sounds, clever lyrics, rabble-rousing rock and poignant ballads have escaped across the borders and have changed the staid image of Wales as a nation of melodious harpists and male voice choirs forever.

The Manics paved the way with a series of successful albums after *Generation Terrorists* (1992) established it as a key 1990s band. The three-piece Stereophonics followed with a string of infectious singles, and Cardiff-based Catatonia shot to stardom after *International Velvet* (1998) and its now-classic anthem, 'Every day when I wake up I thank the Lord I'm Welsh'.

Meanwhile, bilingual cult band Super Furry Animals churned out a blend of infectious alternative sounds, proving its stellar talents to the world with *Mwng*, the biggest selling Welsh-language album of all time. Other big players worth looking out for are Feeder and Lostprophets.

Today, the Welsh music scene may not be as overhyped by the media as it once was, but its true substance has come to the fore. An important new network of artists, labels and agencies has been established. Young pop scamps the Automatic are blazing a trail for Wales, while from the dark heart of the Rhondda Valley come soon-to-be-stadium-sized rock giants Funeral For a Friend and Bullet For My Valentine, heading a fertile metal scene. And there's an eclectic array of rising stars waiting in the wings for their main chance, from the expansive rap of Akira the Don and blissed-out Welsh-language folktronica pioneer Jakokoyak, to the decadent pop of the Hot Puppies and wired guitar rock of the Poppies.

The 1995 disappearance and presumed suicide of Manic Street Preachers guitarist Richey Edwards was a turning point for the band. Their 1996 album, *Everything Must Go*, made them famous worldwide.

THE EISTEDDFOD

You could put the *eisteddfod* (ey-*steth*-vot; plural *eisteddfodau*, ey-*steth*-vuh-dye; literally a gathering or session) down as nothing more than a hick country folk festival, but miss it and you'll overlook one of Europe's strongest cultural traditions.

A truly Welsh celebration, the eisteddfod is the descendant of ancient tournaments in which poets and musicians competed for a seat of honour in the households of noblemen. The first genuinely regional tournament seems to have been held in 1176 at Rhys ap Gruffydd's castle in Cardigan, though references exist to earlier gatherings. *Eisteddfodau* grew less frequent and less lively following the Tudor Acts of Union, a process accelerated in the 17th and 18th centuries as dour Nonconformism took hold. But in the late 18th century Edward Williams (better known by his bardic name, Iolo Morganwg) reinvented the *eisteddfod* as a modern festival and an early, informal one took place in Carmarthen in 1819.

The first **Royal National Eisteddfod** (www.eisteddfod.org.uk) was held in 1861 and has since become Europe's largest cultural shindig. Poetry, theatre, choral singing, rock music, dance, pageantry and tradition collide in this quintessentially Welsh event, which attracts over 150,000 visitors. Over the years it has become a barometer of Welsh culture with aspiring bands and emerging artists making their debut here. The whole event takes place in Welsh but larger events are simultaneously translated and there's loads of help on hand for non-Welsh speakers. The festival is held during the first week of August, alternately in North and South Wales.

Another massive session takes place every July in Llangollen, where the **International Musical Eisteddfod** (www.international-eisteddfod.co.uk) kicks off for a week of unrivalled action. As many as 50,000 music disciples pour in from over 40 countries to get their fix of folk tunes, choral harmony, rock, dance and recitals. Competitions take place daily and famous names take to the stage for gala concerts every night.

The third national event is the roving **Urdd National Eisteddfod** (www.urdd.org), a festival of performing and visual arts for children. This is Europe's largest youth festival, and brings together roughly 15,000 performers chosen from all over Wales. Most self-respecting young adults, however, head for the fringe activities of the Royal National Eisteddfod.

FOLK

If you'd like to see some traditional folk music the best place is at the annual *eisteddfodau* (see p47), but you can also stop in at a session at pubs, folk clubs or smaller festivals. Robin Huw Bowen is Wales' leading harpist. Elinor Bennett, Delyth Evans and singer-harpist Sian James are hot on his heels. Bands such as Hin-Deg, Calenning and Mabsant blend traditional and contemporary Welsh sounds with international influences and are all worth looking out for. Also worth catching are Twm Morys, for his upbeat Celtic rock, and Dafydd Iwan, a captivating performer with a political bent to his songwriting.

> The triple harp is the predominant instrument in Welsh folk music.

CLASSICAL

Classical music also enjoys a high profile in Wales and it's well worth attending performances by the BBC **National Orchestra of Wales** (NOW; www.bbc.co.uk/wales/now) and the **Welsh National Opera** (WNO; www.wno.org.uk). The WNO has fostered the careers of many young opera singers but by far its biggest name these days is Bryn Terfel, plucked from a North Wales sheep farm to become the nation's hero.

Architecture

Wales is a great place to delve into the past for architectural gems. The industrial age left some fine testimonies in the country. Blaenavon's (p122) great ironworks, quarries and workers' houses are now a source of national pride, as are the superb engineering works by Thomas Telford: Pontcysyllte Aqueduct (p299) and his suspension bridges over the Menai Strait (p277) and the River Conwy (p290).

> Wales is home to about 600 castles and has the dubious distinction of being one of the most densely fortified countries in Europe.

Ecclesiastical attractions include secretive St David's Cathedral (p184) and also the magnificent ruined abbeys of Tintern (p115), Strata Florida (p216) and Valle Crucis (p297). On the secular side, there are several fine country houses, including Tredegar House (p108) and Plas Newydd (p281).

It is probably castles that are the country's most famous architectural attraction and Wales is covered in them – 'The magnificent badge of our

---

STAYING IN HISTORIC BUILDINGS IN WALES   *Dr Greg Stevenson*

Historic buildings make enjoyable day trips, but staying in them is an entirely more satisfying experience. Those travellers who are looking for accommodation with a difference should investigate the following:

- **Elan Valley Trust** (www.elanvalley.org.uk) has the best-preserved long house in Wales (Llannerch y Cawr) as well as the wonderfully isolated farmhouse of Tynllidiart, a mile down its own track.

- **Landmark Trust** (www.landmarktrust.org.uk) lets a tower in Caernarfon castle, a Victorian fort in Pembrokeshire and what is probably Britain's fanciest chicken shed at Leighton.

- **National Trust Cottages** (www.nationaltrustcottages.co.uk) lets Abermydyr, a Georgian estate cottage designed by no less than the architect John Nash, as well as the Old Rectory at Rhossili, which is the only building above what is possibly Wales' finest beach.

- **Portmeirion** (www.portmeirion-village.com) provides the opportunity to stay in Clough's architectural masterpiece in either self-catering cottages, the waterfront hotel or the newly converted Castell Deudraeth.

- **Under the Thatch** (www.underthethatch.co.uk) specialises in traditional thatched cottages but also lets a converted Edwardian railway carriage by the sea at Aberporth and a couple of traditional Romany caravans.

Dr Greg Stevenson is a Honorary Research Fellow at University of Wales, Lampeter

subjection', as the writer Thomas Pennant put it. The finest are those built by Edward I in North Wales: Caernarfon (p255), Harlech (p248), Conwy (p289) and Beaumaris (p278), collectively listed as a Unesco World Heritage Site. Meanwhile, Cardiff boasts two rather different castles – Cardiff Castle (p85) and Castell Coch (p105) – designed by William Burges, a Victorian specialist in love-it-or-hate-it repro-Gothic.

The equivalent of the National Trust in Wales is **Cadw** (www.cadw.wales.org .uk), the division within the National (Welsh) Assembly with a responsibility for protecting, conserving and promoting an appreciation of the historic environment.

Magnum photographer David Hurn's beautiful book Wales: Land of My Father looks at the dramatic cultural changes that took place in the last two decades of the 20th century.

Visual Arts

Wales has a long tradition of visual arts and currently has more energy, inspiration and experimentation in this area than at any time in its history. In a brave attempt to stake Wales' claim to international recognition, the landmark Artes Mundi (Arts of the World) award, the world's largest art award ever at £40,000, has been established. Elija-Liisa Ahtila, a visual artist and film-maker from Finland won the 2006 prize for her video installations; the 2004 prize was won by Xu Bing, a printmaker and installation artist born in China, but now based in New York.

Wales was first recognised by the arts world as a fashionable place for landscape painters, particularly at the end of the 18th century, when the French Revolution effectively closed Europe to British artists. The rugged mountains and rolling valleys around Dolgellau (p241) made it a popular retreat, while rolling hills and romantic ruins were popular with artists such

For Welsh arts information online visit www .artswales.org.uk or the National Galleries of Wales site at www .nmgw.ac.uk.

ICONIC WELSH BUILDINGS   *Dr Greg Stevenson*

Welsh architecture has far more to offer than just castles and cottages, but it is these that seem to catch the imagination of most visitors. You are never very far from a castle in Wales and the pick of the South must include **Pembroke** (p171), **Carreg Cennen** (p158) and **Caerphilly** (p105) with its famous sinking tower that even out-leans that of Pisa. For pure fantasy indulge yourself in the fairy-tale castles of **Cardiff** (p85) and **Castell Coch** (p105), which were refurbished to the Victorian tastes of the world's wealthiest man.

To talk about Welsh architecture as opposed to that which is British, you must look to the rich vernacular traditions of the principality. Isolated from the fickle fashions of urban England, much of rural Wales developed regionally distinctive building forms that used locally available materials to create buildings that answered local needs. These are best exhibited in the rural cottages and farms that vary from county to county (and in some cases from village to village). Look out for locally distinctive traditions such as slate roofs grouted with cement washes in Pembrokeshire, ancient oak-framed buildings in Montgomeryshire, and humble earth-walled thatched cottages in Ceredigion and Carmarthenshire. Selections of the best traditional buildings have been re-sited at the **St Fagans National History Museum** (p104), and the **St David's peninsula** (p184) will reward with untouched farmsteads and simple rustic cottages. For towns and villages made picturesque by their traditional buildings, visit **Dolgellau** (p241).

Although it is probably Wales' historic buildings that draw in most of its visitors, its more recent architecture deserves some attention. Portmeirion, designed by the eccentric **Sir Clough Williams-Ellis** (p252), brings a touch of Italy to Penrhyndeudraeth; the **Millennium Stadium** in Cardiff (1999; p88) brings the capital to life on match day; and Norman Foster's Great Glasshouse (2000) at the **National Botanical Garden of Wales** (p157) embodies a simple beauty. Among the mostly unadventurous apartment blocks of Cardiff Bay, the **Wales Millennium Centre** (2004; p90) stands out alongside the **Senedd** (home to the **National (Welsh) Assembly**, p88) completed in 2005 by the Richard Rogers Partnership.

Dr Greg Stevenson is a Honorary Research Fellow at University of Wales, Lampeter

as Richard Wilson and later Turner, who painted both the Wye Valley (p111) and Valle Crucis (p297).

Introduced to the world at the 1913 Armory Show in New York, Augustus John (1878–1961) created the 'Bohemian' figure in painting and rivalled Dylan Thomas for his outrageous private life. He was, however, an incredible draughtsman and created big, bold canvases often showing the influences of postimpressionism from Europe.

For artists and artworks, old and new, take a look at www.welshartsarchive.org.uk.

Frank Brangwyn (1867–1956), poet-painter David Jones (1895–1974; see p43) and Ceri Richards (1903–71) make up Wales' 20th-century hall of fame. Richards, influenced particularly by Matisse, is probably the most notable figure and his work can be seen on permanent view at the Glynn Vivian Gallery in Swansea (p143).

Industrial Wales, particularly the parts found in the coal valleys, was the subject of a number of fine artists in the second half of the century and was also the subject matter of the 'Rhondda Group' – Ernest Zobole (1927–99), Charles Burton (1929–) and Glyn Jones (1936–). The thickly layered oils on canvas of Sir Kyffin Williams showed a return to the Welsh landscape for inspiration, while the younger Welsh artists such as Kevin Sinnott and Peter Prendergast have brought a new vigour to the sights and figures of South and North Wales respectively.

In recent years radical art at the cutting edge of political engagement has brought Iwan Bala, Ivor Davies and David Garner fame. Other names to look out for include Brendan Stuart Burns and Mary Lloyd Jones, and sculptors David Nash and Robert Harding.

It's well worth dropping into local galleries and exhibitions to check out what's on show. For big names try the National Museum and Gallery of Wales (p86), while you'll generally find more contemporary work at Wales' two leading arts centres: the Aberystwyth Arts Centre (www.aberystwythartscentre.co.uk; p215) and Cardiff's dynamic Chapter Arts Centre (www.chapter.org; p99).

Theatre & Dance

Wales is awash in theatre, from amateur Welsh-language shows in rural hired halls to top English-language productions with world-class stars in Cardiff. There are some 20 major theatre companies and a host of smaller community and educational groups. Many Hollywood stars, including Charlie Chaplin, Sir Anthony Hopkins and Catherine Zeta-Jones, first trod the boards at these regional theatres.

For more information on Welsh companies and performances visit www.theatre-wales.co.uk.

Cardiff, Bangor, Mold and Milford Haven all have their own well-regarded theatre companies, but attempts to establish a Welsh national theatre have failed due to bickering between regional factions.

MALE VOICE CHOIRS

Born out of the Temperance Movement in the mid-19th century, the male voice choir *(cor meibion)* was one solution to the grave problem of drink. The Methodists in particular encouraged this wholesome activity and breathed life into what became an institution in the coal-mining towns of the southern valleys.

With the collapse of the old coal-mining communities, choirs have struggled to keep numbers up and some have even allowed women to join their ranks. You'll still find choirs hanging on tenaciously in all the main towns, practising religiously and many competing internationally. Most choirs are happy to have visitors sit in on rehearsals. One of the best can be found each Monday at the Greyhound Hotel in Builth Wells (p218).

Wales' leading English-language professional company is **Theatr Clwyd** (www.clwyd-theatr-cymru.co.uk) at Mold, attracting top names such as Sir Anthony Hopkins and Janet Suzman. One of its main aims is to put new Welsh writing on an international stage.

Cardiff's acclaimed theatrical organisation the **Sherman Theatre Company** (www.shermantheatre.co.uk) produces a wide range of productions each year, including theatre for young people, inventive adaptations of classic dramas and new writing projects.

The highly acclaimed Music Theatre Wales, a pioneering force in contemporary opera, has a growing international reputation and tours annually across Europe. Its innovative productions vary from contemporary classics to newly commissioned works, and win rave reviews wherever they go.

The Welsh National Opera is one of the world's leading opera companies.

Two big names on the Welsh-language stage include **Theatr Gwynedd** (www .theatrgwynedd.co.uk) in Bangor (see pp288), and **Dalier Sylw** (☎ 01222-236650), at the Chapter Arts Centre in Cardiff (see p99). Experimental theatre companies include the **Fiction Factory** (www.fictionfactoryfilms.com), geared to original work with a Welsh voice, and **Green Ginger** (www.greenginger.net), a bizarre Tenby-based group that produces street and fringe shows as absurd as they are memorable.

Dance lovers should look out for **Earthfall** (www.earthfall.org.uk), Wales' leading dance-theatre company and one of the most sought-after companies across Europe. Its pioneering dance theatre combines political and social agendas with live music and strong visual imagery.

A good place to catch a variety of performances from modern and classical drama to solo recitals is the Bute Theatre in Cardiff. The university theatre has six separate performing areas and is often free for daytime events.

Environment

For a small place, Wales packs an incredible punch. You can lurch from craggy peak to rugged coast across a patchwork of rolling fields littered with sheep and still have only touched on it. The landscape has astounding diversity and is incredibly important to the Welsh people, for historic, cultural and economic reasons. The National (Welsh) Assembly has recognised this, making Wales one of only three countries in the world with a commitment to sustainable development built into its constitution. An elusive concept at the best of times, it remains to be seen whether the Assembly can turn theory into firm policy.

THE LAND

Wales can claim one of the richest and most diverse geological heritages in the world; and it is geology, more than anything else, that has helped shape the destiny of Wales in modern times. Its mountainous terrain helped protect the Welsh from rampaging invaders who rarely made it across the peaks to the coast, and the Welsh language flourished in these protected western locations, strongholds of the culture to this day.

As early as the 17th century, geologists were drawn to the mysteries of Wales' rippled rocks, ice-scooped valleys and puzzling fossils. Some of the oldest exposed rocks in the world are around St David's Head (p189), while the rest of the country is an evolutionary baby at only 200 million years old. The jagged peaks and u-shaped valleys of Snowdonia, darlings of the climbing set, were created when an ancient ocean dissecting Britain was obliterated by a dramatic continental collision. Marine life was entombed as fossils on the summit of Snowdon and it took the persistent power of an Ice Age to carve out the steep slopes of the valleys. The only remnants of these long-lost glacial monsters are the dark dramatic waters of lakes such as Llyn Idwal near Capel Curig.

In South Wales, extremes of temperature split and shattered the rock, and the mountains eroded into the red-sandstone moorland and grassy, flat tops of the Brecon Beacons. The porous limestone cliffs then became perforated with waterfalls, creating massive cave systems such as Dan-yr-Ogof (p138).

The ultimate inspiration for Welsh daydreams, *Eternal Wales* looks at places of significance in Welsh history and consciousness through the vivid accounts of Gwynfor Evans and the stunning photography of Marian Delyth.

The dune system near Porthcawl on the Glamorgan coast is the largest in Europe, rising to over 61m.

Britain's deepest cave is in Ogof Ffynnon Ddu near Abercraf. It has a depth of 308m below the surface and is 30 miles long.

TRAVEL WIDELY, TREAD LIGHTLY, GIVE SUSTAINABLY – THE LONELY PLANET FOUNDATION

The Lonely Planet Foundation proudly supports nimble nonprofit institutions working for change in the world. Each year the foundation donates 5% of Lonely Planet company profits to projects selected by staff and authors. Our partners range from Kabissa, which provides small nonprofits across Africa with access to technology, to the Foundation for Developing Cambodian Orphans, which supports girls at risk of falling victim to sex traffickers.

Our nonprofit partners are linked by a grass-roots approach to the areas of health, education or sustainable tourism. Many – such as Louis Sarno who works with BaAka (Pygmy) children in the forested areas of Central African Republic – choose to focus on women and children as one of the most effective ways to support the whole community. Louis is determined to give options to children who are discriminated against by the majority Bantu population.

Sometimes foundation assistance is as simple as restoring a local ruin like the Minaret of Jam in Afghanistan; this incredible monument now draws intrepid tourists to the area and its restoration has greatly improved options for local people.

Just as travel is often about learning to see with new eyes, so many of the groups we work with aim to change the way people see themselves and the future for their children and communities.

The geological history of both these areas changed the face of Wales and its history of settlement forever. Rich deposits of coal south of the Brecon Beacons and the slate mountains of Snowdonia fuelled the Industrial Revolution, and the hoards of workers who came to make their fortune settled in the rows of terraced houses lining the scarred slopes of the valleys today.

WILDLIFE

The wildlife of Wales may not be your first reason to visit, but certain parts of the country offer opportunities for unexpected encounters, from seal pups to dolphins and raucous sea birds to rogue sheep.

For government information on national wildlife conservation and environmental protection visit www.ccw.gov.uk.

Animals

Ice ages and human intervention killed off big game long ago, and today any scurrying in the bushes is likely to be something small and furry rather than wild and dangerous. In the mountains you'll occasionally see herds of wild ponies, while pine martens and polecats can be found almost everywhere.

Coastal wildlife is still some of Wales' most fascinating. The main attraction is the Atlantic grey seals that give birth to almost one thousand pups on the Pembrokeshire shore in late September and early October. Other marine attractions include bottlenose dolphins in Cardigan Bay (see Endangered Species, below), the occasional passing porpoise and the cockle harvest at low tide in the Burry Inlet on the Gower Peninsula.

Offshore islands are internationally renowned habitats for sea-bird colonies, and even if you're not an avid twitcher the sheer numbers and raucous noise are quite something. Grassholm Island (p183) harbours one of the world's largest gannet colonies (30,000 pairs), while the rock faces of Skomer and Skokholm Islands (p183) are crowded with colonies of guillemots, razorbills, storm petrels, kittiwakes and puffins. Thirty per cent of the world's population of Manx shearwaters – that's 150,000 pairs – call this and Ramsey Island their northern home. Ramsey and Bardsey Islands are also host to a few pairs of rare choughs. The best time to visit sea-bird colonies is between April and mid-August.

Step carefully in Tregaron Bog; it's the British black adder's only habitat.

Inland, the Dee estuary has Europe's largest concentration of pintails, while an exceptional number of red kites (see the boxed text, p54) nest in the southern Cambrian Mountains of Mid-Wales. Otters are re-establishing themselves along the River Teifi and in the border area of northern Powys, but salmon, sea trout and brown trout are diminishing. Most unusual of all, however, is the elusive gwyniad, a unique ice-age relic of a fish found only in Llyn Tegid (Bala Lake; p245).

ENDANGERED SPECIES

Almost 200 species in Wales have been identified as in need of conservation. Intensive farming, loss of habitat and acidification are all serious threats to diversity, but financial resources to reverse these trends are severely lacking.

Your best chance of catching up on endangered species may also be one of the most dramatic. A major group of bottlenose dolphins can be seen in Cardigan Bay (p211) year-round and further out to sea you can spot Risso's dolphins, common dolphins and minke whales.

Wales is the only place in the UK where you'll find horseshoe bats. You can see them between March and October at their recently restored home, St Cadoc's Church in Llangattock Lingoed, near Abergavenny. Barbastelle bats can be seen at Pengelli Forest National Nature Reserve in north Pembrokeshire or along wooded valleys across the country, during the summer months just before dark.

Check out activities, events and natural wonders in the Pembrokeshire Coast National Park at www.pembroke shirecoast.org.

KITE COUNTRY

Doggedly fighting its way back from the verge of extinction, the majestic red kite *(Milvus milvus)* is now a common sight in Mid-Wales. This aerobatic bird with its 2m-long wingspan was once common across the UK and was even afforded royal protection in the Middle Ages. However, in the 16th century it was declared vermin and mercilessly hunted until only a few pairs remained.

This fragile breeding population in the Tywi and Cothi valleys of Mid-Wales was saved by a group of committed campaigners who launched an unofficial protection programme that was to last 100 years, the longest-running protection scheme for any bird in the world. Despite persistent threats from egg-hunters and poisoned baits (meant for crows or foxes), there are now more than 300 pairs throughout Wales. An ecotourism initiative, the Kite Country Project, was launched in 1994 to encourage visitors to see the red kite in action without disturbing or endangering the species. It runs six Kite Country Centres (see p226) where visitors can watch kites being fed at close range.

For more information contact **Kite Country** (www.kitecountry.co.uk) or the **Welsh Kite Trust** (www.welshkitetrust.org).

Plants

Agriculture, shipbuilding, charcoal burning and mining cleared Wales of its indigenous oak forests, and woodland now covers only 12% of the country. Most of this is non-native sitka spruce, a fast-growing timber crop disliked by most wildlife. To get an idea of how the Welsh landscape once looked, visit Pengelli Forest in Pembrokeshire or one of the areas managed by Forest Enterprise Wales, such as the Coed y Brenin Visitor Centre near Dolgellau (p245).

David Williams' *Landscape Wales/Tirlun Cymru* captures the moods and seasons of the Welsh landscape through powerful images, and makes suggestions for activities with maps and practical details.

Cultivation and overgrazing have led to erosion in many parts of Wales, which in turn has damaged habitats and prevents rooting or reseeding of native species. Native ash, recognisable by its finely toothed leaves, however, is common everywhere, especially along rivers and in woods in the Gower Peninsula and Brecon Beacons. In its shade you'll find common dog violets, a delicate purple flower blooming from March to May, and several species of orchid with small deep purple, or sometimes white, flowers on a tall stem.

In mountainous areas such as Snowdonia and the Brecon Beacons, fragile alpine-Arctic plants breed away from grazing sheep and goats. Between the rocks you'll see purple saxifrage, a cushiony plant with tiny bowl-shaped flowers and overlapping leaves, and moss campion, a low plant with dense foliage covered in pink flowers. These plants live a precarious life on the higher slopes, so take care if you're hiking or climbing; you can do irreparable damage by disturbing them.

The Making of Wales, by John Davies, traces how the landscape of Wales has evolved and been shaped by humans from prehistory to contemporary society.

Myrtle, a strongly scented bush with dark green leaves and bright orange flowers, and crowberry, a small shrub with needlelike leaves and black berries, thrive in the inland bogs and soggy peatlands. Also look out for the rare, slender cotton grass, with its distinctive tuft of white cotton in midsummer, and bog pimpernel, a delicate pink funnel-shaped flower. Cwm Cadlan, near Penderyn, is a wet grassland boasting butterwort, one of Britain's few insectivorous plants. It has small blue or purple flowers on tall slender stems and large sticky leaves at ground level for trapping its prey.

On the coast, amid the sand dunes, you may find evening primrose, a tall plant with bright yellow flowers; sea bindweed, easily spotted by its pink-and-white striped flowers; and marram grass, the hardy windswept grass growing on the seaward side of dunes. The Gower Peninsula is a good place for thrift, a small pink flower on a tallish stem, and samphire, a strong-smelling small herb bush with long spiky leaves.

ENDANGERED SPECIES

One of Wales' most endangered plants is the Snowdon lily. A remnant of the last Ice Age, it has survived on the slopes of Mt Snowdon for 10,000 years. The lily has thin leaves and looks a little like a grass plant until its white flowers emerge between late May and mid-June. Warming climates and overgrazing have shrunk its habitat and reduced plant numbers to worrying figures. Only six tiny patches of the plant now survive on Snowdon and there are no higher slopes where the plant can migrate for cooler conditions.

Another species on the critically endangered list is Ley's whitebeam, a distinctive large deciduous shrub that flowers in late May and early June and is only seen in the limestone outcrops north of Merthyr Tydfil (p119). Of more interest to most is the delicate green-flowered fen orchid (one of Europe's rarest plants), which is being closely protected in the Kenfig National Nature Reserve near Port Talbot.

Snowdonia: The Official Park Guide, by Merfyn Williams and Jeremy Moore, celebrates the beauty and diversity of Snowdonia through evocative and authoritative text and some spectacular photography.

NATIONAL PARKS

Almost a quarter of Wales is protected by its three national parks and five Areas of Outstanding Natural Beauty (AONBs).

On top of this, Wales has one marine nature reserve, more than 60 national nature reserves and over 1000 Sites of Specific Scientific Interest (SSI); all of which combine to make the highest density of nature conservation sites anywhere in Europe. There are at least six other categories of protected land as well.

These environmental assets have brought the local people economic benefits from tourism that outweigh any restrictions imposed by the parks' protected stature. For many years the parks of Wales have drawn crowds and as the Rev John Parker noted in 1831, 'There is no place more public than the higher ground of Eryri (Snowdonia) in the summer'.

The popularity of Snowdonia has ensured its future in a very real way. When a huge chunk of Mt Snowdon came up for sale in 1998, the National Trust (NT) began an urgent campaign to prevent it falling into the hands of commercial developers; £4m was needed in 100 days. Welsh-born actor Sir Anthony Hopkins donated £1m, and within four months, more than £5m had been secured and Snowdonia was saved. Hopkins basked in Welsh glory until he took out American citizenship two years later, to the disgust of his compatriots.

Brecon and Snowdonia include majestic mountain regions, while Pembrokeshire offers a protected coastline and wildlife islands. Snowdonia is the second largest national park in Britain at 845 sq miles, Brecon covers an area of 519 sq miles and Pembrokeshire is the smallest national park with 225 sq miles consisting mainly of the coastline of the County of Pembrokeshire.

Visit www.eryri-npa .co.uk for the low-down on recreation, conservation, weather and places to visit in Snowdonia National Park.

Full of information on history, flora and fauna, Roger Thomas' vibrant *Brecon Beacons: The Official Park Guide* is essential for any trip to the hills. For information on activities, events, news and weather in the Brecon Beacons visit www.breconbeacons.org.

NATIONAL PARKS IN WALES

National Park	Features	Activities	Best Time to Visit	Page Reference
Brecon Beacons	High plateau and rolling hills; ponies, grouse, pine martens	Walking, cycling, canoeing, caving	Apr–Oct	p123
Pembrokeshire Coast	Rugged cliffs and sandy beaches; gannets, grey seals, dolphins	Walking, kayaking, surfing, coasteering	Apr–Oct	p163
Snowdonia	Dramatic mountains and ridges; polecats, buzzards, goats	Mountaineering, walking, rafting, windsurfing	May–Sep	p237

For information on envir-
onmental issues contact
Environment Agency
Wales (www.environ
ment-agency.wales.gov
.uk), Friends of the Earth
(www.foe.co.uk), or the
Wildlife Trusts (www
.wildlifetrusts.org).

AREAS OF OUTSTANDING NATURAL BEAUTY (AONBS)

The five AONBs are: the Anglesey coast (p275), which has rocky coves, towering sea stacks and limestone cliffs and is popular for climbing and water sports; the Llŷn coast (p267), which features cliffs, coves and beaches and is a magnet for surfers and windsurfers; the Clwydian Ranges, a landscape of rolling green hills and upland moors, which is hiking heaven; the Gower Peninsula (p151), which has beautiful beaches and undulating farmland and is popular with surfers, kayakers and walkers; and the Wye Valley (p111), a majestic riverside glen, which plays host to walkers and canoeists.

ENVIRONMENTAL ISSUES

There is deep concern in Wales about the environment, on which many jobs and the success of the tourist industry depend. Much work has been done to clean up the worst industrial scars; the air is cleaner than it has been for centuries and the government has committed itself, and the country, to a sustainable future; however, serious threats to the welfare of the countryside remain.

Many issues are inextricably linked with agricultural practice. Wales has the highest density of sheep in the EU and overgrazing and soil erosion are serious problems. Runoff from pesticides, slurry and silage is destroying the water, and the dwindling numbers of full-time farmers means that the essence of Welsh rural life is threatened. The foot-and-mouth epidemic in 2001 was only one of a long string of crises to hit the rural economy.

Out of the burning pyres, however, came a greater understanding of the land. People saw for the first time that agriculture wasn't necessarily the biggest money-spinner in rural areas and that saving the brand image of Wales as a clean, green, rural idyll was just as important as the coveted EU farm aid.

For a look at green
issues in Wales visit the
Campaign for Rural Wales
at www.cprw.org.uk.

The introduction of Tir Gofal, an agri-environment scheme that rewards farmers for what they do with their land as much as for what they produce, has created enormous demand since its establishment in 1999. Combined with expected Common Agricultural Policy (CAP) reform to steer money away from unnecessary production and into alternative rural activities, it should mean a visible improvement in countryside protection and enhancement. The scheme pays farmers to farm in an environmentally sensitive way: managing wildlife habitats, increasing public access, reducing grazing levels and pesticide use and creating buffer zones along rivers to prevent leaching of fertilisers. It is a commendable start for sustainable development, with over 15% of the area of Wales now being managed under the scheme. Landscape changes are noticeable where the scheme is active, particularly where hedgerow management has been undertaken. In addition, access opportunities created by the scheme can be found alongside new access to the countryside on the Countryside Council for Wales website (www.ccw.gov.uk).

Other environmental issues affecting Wales include the continuing debate on waste management, landfill and incineration; increased road congestion and public transport issues; and biodiversity challenges and the monoculture ethic in forestry.

For some of the best
countryside activities visit
Festival of the Country-
side at www.foc.org.uk,
which promotes sustain-
able, environmentally
sensitive tourism in
Wales.

Industrial pollution continues to dog the countryside, and discharge from metal mines, abandoned coal pits and the increasing numbers of open-cut mines in South Wales are also a major concern. Tourism, too, is taking its toll. The growing tourist traffic in the national parks has led to serious footpath erosion, especially in the Brecon Beacons and Snowdonia (see the boxed text, p264).

Most campaigners agree that environmental issues need to be seen in a wider political context. There is a need for interdepartmental consultancy

ALTERNATIVE SOURCES OF ENERGY

Innocuous though they may seem, land-based wind turbines have become one of the most contentious and divisive issues in rural Wales.

Wales has been moving towards increased use of renewable energy for some years, but opposition to insensitively sited wind farms has been steadily mounting. Nobody disputes the need for sustainable energy and few object to community-based schemes that bring much-needed income to small towns and villages. However, the huge visual impact of commercial schemes on the landscape and their irregular output has brought both locals and campaigners out in droves. It's an emotive issue, though, pitting one environmental campaign group against another and raising serious questions about the planning process involved.

When a massive scheme in Cefn Croes, Ceredigion, was given approval by the Secretary of State in 2001, people were outraged: 1300 objections and a call for a public inquiry had been disregarded. The planning system came under fire and the National Assembly's very role was questioned. Meanwhile, the Assembly has set a target of achieving 20% of Welsh energy demands from renewable resources by 2010, and many say this is overambitious. Campaigners argue that the provision of renewable energy goes far beyond the theories of green policy and they fear the government's narrow political agenda in pushing their targets.

The focus has also turned to offshore wind farms and tidal power as viable alternatives. The battle continues with every new planning application, though, and many who never saw themselves as activists are now finding a voice and leading campaigns across the country.

The most recent controversy, meanwhile, surrounds plans to grow the fuel of the future in hydrogen farms in Wales. The Carmarthenshire Energy Agency is embarking on a joint project with Ireland to produce hydrogen from trees in a series of farms in West Wales. The Wales and Ireland Rural Hydrogen Energy Project aims to release hydrogen contained in fast-growing willow trees. Hydrogen promises limitless energy with no pollution, drinkable water being the only emission from its use. But the barrier to a hydrogen economy is production because an electrical charge is necessary to release hydrogen from water and most electricity is produced by fossil fuels.

Dr Richard Dinsdale, of the University of Glamorgan, who is involved in the project, said: 'The hydrogen farm concept was identified as part of the Objective One–funded "Hydrogen Wales" project and it provides an ideal route for the development of research performed in Wales into technologies which can provide social and economic benefit to rural areas.'

The hydrogen would power cars and other vehicles through the use of fuel cells. There are hydrogen fuel-cell motors already in operation in Canada, the USA and other countries, including, notably, England on London's RV1 bus route. These fuel cells are nothing new, however. They were first invented in 1839 by a Swansea lawyer, Sir William Robert Grove, who called his original device a 'gas battery'.

Could Wales be at the forefront of the hydrogen revolution? Only time will tell.

so that economic, social and environmental issues are addressed in a holistic manner providing true protection for one of Wales' greatest assets.

At the same time, progress is constantly being made. The Welsh Assembly's drive to reduce the amount of rubbish sent to landfill sites is proving successful with nearly a quarter of all Welsh municipal waste now recycled or composted. Across Wales the figure for the amount of waste recycled or composted has increased to 23%, up from 20% in 2005. In 1999 only 7% of rubbish was being recycled or composted.

It's a sign that Wales is taking seriously the commitment to sustainable development built into its constitution and looking to the future.

Outdoor Activities

Whether you're someone who wanders into outdoor shops to stroke shiny ka-rabiners while muttering about needing to get into it all, or a weather-beaten veteran of craggy peaks and bitter winds, Wales has something to offer. From a host of multiactivity centres, where you can get a taste of adventure, to some of Britain's best walking (p62), climbing (opposite) and caving (opposite), as well as the world's best mountain biking (p61), Wales packs a lot into a small space. The landscape is stunning, access is easy and there's always a cosy pub with a warm fire nearby when you need to dry out.

For hard-core climbers and wannabe adventurers, Paul Williams' *Rock Climbing in Snowdonia* offers plenty to aspire to.

This chapter will give you an overview of what's on offer; local trails, activity centres and facilities are identified in the regional chapters. Whatever you're planning to do, take a look at www.adventure.visitwales.com and order a free copy of the *Adventure Wales* brochure from the Welsh Tourist Bureau (WTB). It's packed with information from adventure junkies, and includes tips on how to get started, the best places to go and a directory of operators.

BEACHES

For a wide-ranging site covering all major adventure sports and tailor-made packages for activity holidays, check out www.activity.visitwales.co.uk.

The 2006 *Good Beach Guide* commended beaches across Wales for their excellent water quality. The annual survey, published by the Marine Conservation Society (MCS), the UK charity dedicated to the protection of seas, shores and wildlife, found that the UK's beaches are now the cleanest since the guide was launched in 1987, with more than 500 of the 800 beaches tested across the UK recommended for bathing in the 2006 survey. The award is the UK's highest commendation for water quality standards. Of 120 MCS-recommended beaches across Wales, 19 were found on the Isle of Anglesey alone, with many accorded Blue Flag status, an international award for well-managed beaches with EC Guideline standard water quality.

According to the MCS, this year's increase in the number of recommended beaches is due to dry weather conditions in recent years, which have served to substantially reduce the amount of storm pollution entering the sea, hence improving bathing water quality; more information is available from www.good beachguide.co.uk.

One of the recommended beaches, Rhosneigr Beach on the Isle of Anglesey, is a mix of shingle and soft sand set in a sheltered bay and edged by sand dunes. The beach is particularly popular with sports enthusiasts; scuba diving, surfing, sea canoeing and windsurfing are among the most popular activities. Surfboards are available for hire at the beach, and there is zoning for water sports with a boat lane marked out.

Llandudno West Shore Beach (see p292), meanwhile, presents a quieter side to Llandudno than the popular North Shore Beach. The large expanse of shallow water makes it ideal for kite surfing, while the extensive sand revealed at low tide creates ideal conditions for kite buggying. For walkers, a coastal path leads along the nearby Great Orme headland.

In 2006 the Gower Peninsula celebrated its 50th anniversary as the first Area of Outstanding Natural Beauty (AONB) to be designated in England and Wales. To mark the occasion, the National Trust (NT), which owns and manages three-quarters of the Gower Peninsula coastline, inaugurated five new walks along the coastal path: Penmaen Burrows (2.5 miles), Pennard Cliffs (3.5 miles), Bishopston Valley (3.5 miles), Whiteford Burrows (4 miles) and Rhossili Bay (5 miles).

For more information check the National Trust website at www.national trust.org.uk/wales.

CAVING

If you fancy crawling through crevices, slithering down slopes and scrambling up rocks, Wales is riddled with magnificent cavernous limestone valleys. There are more than 1000 caves to explore, 300 of which were naturally formed.

The largest cave area is in a band stretching across South Wales from Crickhowell (p130) to Carreg Cennen Castle (p158), and other caves can be found on the Gower Peninsula, in Pembrokeshire and across North Wales. Top sites include Ogof Draenen, north of Blaenavon, which has more than 40 miles of passageways, and the UK's deepest cave, Ogof Ffynnon Ddu (p139). For beginners Porth-yr-Ogof (p138) in the Brecon Beacons National Park and Paviland Cave (p153) on the Gower Peninsula are also good spots to start.

There are several caving clubs across Wales; check out the **British Caving Association** (www.british-caving.org.uk), or www.caving.uk.com for listings. A full day's caving will cost about £65 per person for a group of six.

Martyn Farr's *Darkworld* is a lavishly illustrated account of the success and frustration of determined exploration in some of the most spectacular and colourful caves in the world under Llangattock Mountain in Crickhowell, Powys.

CLIMBING

The peaks of Snowdonia and sea cliffs of the Welsh coast are some of Britain's best climbing locations and have nurtured the talent of some of the world's finest mountaineers. With an abundance of climbing options in the area, both well-versed rock fanatics and complete beginners can satisfy their cravings to climb.

During the summer it can be hard to find a cliff without brightly clad climbers making an ascent, but spring and autumn are less crowded, and ice-climbing in Snowdonia is a popular pursuit in winter. Don't underestimate the power of the weather – check the forecast with the local tourist office or the **Met Office** (www.metoffice.com), and make sure you're fully equipped for emergencies.

You shouldn't attempt your first climb without some expert advice; there are centres all over Wales offering those crucial initial climbing lessons. Many centres offer climbing as part of a multiactivity course, or you can take specific lessons. Expect to pay around £200 for a two-day course to learn the basics. One of the best places to take a course is **Plas y Brenin** (National Mountain Centre; www.pyb.co.uk) in Capel Curig (p263).

Remember that climbing is a serious undertaking and always seek expert advice at the planning stage. Climbers should also check with the local tourist office, local climbing shops, climbers' cafés such as Pete's Eats (see p264) in Llanberis, and specialist climbing guidebooks.

For more information on climbing in Wales contact Plas y Brenin or the **British Mountaineering Council** (☎ 0870 0104878; www.thebmc.co.uk); for indoor climbing, check the website www.indoorclimbingwalls.co.uk.

Sir Edmund Hillary and his team trained in Snowdonia before their successful assault on Everest.

Terry Marsh's comprehensive guide *The Mountains of Wales* is an essential book for avid walkers who are intent on scaling any of Wales' 600m-high peaks.

CYCLING

Wales is a great place to get out on a bike; official cycle trails, bicycle-only routes and quiet back roads provide a wonderful perspective on the Welsh landscape, while some more serious off-roading can be had on a bevy of world-class mountain-bike trails. You can hire bikes all over the place (see the regional chapters for details) and make up your own day trips, or you can bring your own pride and joy and ride across the country.

Bicycles can be ridden on any track identified as a bridleway on Ordnance Survey (OS) maps, but you generally can't cycle on public footpaths. The best roads for cyclists are the calm, unnumbered country roads and lanes between villages, which are quietest outside the traffic-choked months of July and August.

Information

Lonely Planet's *Cycling Britain* has details of the best bike routes, information on places to stay and eat, and a useful section on bicycle maintenance.

VisitWales publishes *Cycling Wales,* a free introduction to Wales' long-distance and regional routes (which cater for road rides, bicycle-only trails and mountain biking), with listings of tour organisers, cycle-hire outlets and useful regional publications. The WTB also produces a map pack that gives details of local routes that can be done over a short break (between three and seven days) at one of nine specially chosen cycle destinations. More information can be found at www.cycling.visitwales.com, or check the website www.cyclesmart.org.

The **Cyclists' Touring Club** (CTC; ☎ 0870 8730060; www.ctc.org.uk) offers comprehensive information (free to members) about cycling in the UK and overseas – including suggested routes, local contacts, organised cycling holidays, a bike-hire directory, and mail-order OS maps and books. Annual membership costs £34 per adult and £55 for a family. Some cycling organisations outside the UK have reciprocal membership arrangements with the CTC.

Cycling Without Traffic: Wales, by John Price, details 30 easy and safe cycle routes. You'll find tips on what to see and where to go, as well as practical information on terrain, distance, public-transport access and parking.

Cycling Routes

There are two main long-distance cycle routes in Wales, both part of the National Cycle Network (NCN). Their end points are on the rail network, so you can go out by bike and back by train, or vice versa. Sustrans (see below) publishes an array of maps and guides (prices from £5.99 per map) with information on services and accommodation for each route. See the shop section at www.sustrans.org.uk.

LÔN LAS CYMRU

The most difficult of the NCN challenge routes, **Lôn Las Cymru** (Greenways of Wales; the Welsh National Route; NCN Rtes 8 and 42) stretches about 254 miles through the heart of Wales. Starting from the Anglesey port of Holyhead it passes through the mainly Welsh-speaking northwest and mountainous Snowdonia before hitting the green hills and mountains of rural Mid-Wales, and then on into the former industrial Welsh Valleys and finally to Cardiff. From Brecon to Cardiff the route coincides with the Taff Trail, a combined walking and cycling route (see p124). An alternative braid of the route (NCN route 42) runs through Abergavenny to Chepstow.

According to Sustrans, the traffic-free North Wales Coastal Route is thought to be the best on the whole of the UK National Cycle Network (NCN).

LÔN GELTAIDD

A more leisurely route, **Lôn Geltaidd** (Celtic Trail; NCN Rtes 4 and 47) covers 220 miles from near Chepstow, via Newport and Swansea, to Fishguard on the north Pembrokeshire coast. Billed as a 'Journey of Discovery', the trail

---

SUSTRANS & THE NATIONAL CYCLE NETWORK

Sustrans is a sustainable transport charity encouraging people to walk, cycle and use public transport in order to reduce motor traffic and its adverse effects. Its brainchild, the National Cycle Network, now comprises 10,000 miles of track and is currently coordinated by more than 2000 volunteer rangers who donate their time to maintain routes in their communities.

When Sustrans announced its plans in 1978 it was barely taken seriously, but the growth in popularity of bicycles, coupled with near-terminal road congestion in the UK, has focused much attention on the idea of cycle paths. The incredible project now has the support of more than 450 local authorities and other organisations. The network now carries more than 230 million journeys each year.

For more information on cycling in Wales and the rest of the UK, interactive mapping and more than 400 maps and guides, visit www.sustrans.org.uk or call ☎ 0845 113 0065.

picks up the varied landscape, history and culture of South Wales. The route includes 13 miles of superb car-free cycling through the magnificent new Millennium Coastal Park, and a separate high-level mountain-bike section between Pontypridd and Neath.

The NCN also includes a number of high-quality routes without traffic that are ideal for cyclists of all abilities. The seaside promenade from Colwyn Bay to Prestatyn is thought to be the best of these in the whole of the UK. It's part of a longer route, the North Wales Coastal Route (NCN Rte 5).

For information on any cycling route, contact Sustrans (opposite).

Mountain Biking

Wales has become something of a mountain-biking mecca in recent years, offering some of the best purpose-built mountain-biking facilities in the world. A stunning all-weather single-track radiates from seven excellent mountain-biking centres, five of which have world-class ratings.

For more information, VisitWales produce the brochure *Mountain Bike Wales,* which has details of six mountain-biking routes across Wales; also check the website www.mbwales.com, a comprehensive site listing everything you need to know about trails, centres and conditions. See the regional chapters for details of local operators.

OS maps and specific mountain-bike guides are available for most areas but remember that many trails cross fragile upland environments and you should always keep an eye on your map and respect marked routes.

In North Wales head for some of the country's best purpose-built tracks at Coed y Brenin Forest Park (p245) and epic rides at Gwydir Forest Park (p238) near Betws-y-Coed. Explore the wilds of Mid-Wales on some excellent networks by basing yourself at Machynlleth (p231) or Llanwrtyd Wells (p216), just two towns where mountain biking has almost become a way of life. Other good facilities in this area include wild Nant-y-Arian near Aberystwyth and the Hafren Forest near Llanidloes.

In South Wales, Afan Forest Park, east of Swansea, is also in the world-class rankings. Other good tracks can be found in the Brechfa Forest, northwest of Llandeilo, in Carmarthenshire, and there's a superb new specialist downhill course at Cwmcarn, northeast of Caerphilly (p105).

FISHING

There are some 240 rivers and streams in Wales for anglers to choose from. Catches include brown trout in spring (on the Rivers Usk and Teifi, as well as the Wye, Dee, Seiont and Taff); Wales' own shy sewin (sea trout) in spring and summer (on the Towy, Teifi, Rheidol, Dyfi, Mawddach and Conwy); salmon in autumn (on the Usk, Teifi and Conwy); and grayling in autumn and winter (on the Wye, Dee and upper Severn). You can also angle for sea fish, either from the rocks or from a chartered boat, in many spots along the coast.

Fishing is fairly tightly regulated in the UK and many prime stretches of river are privately owned, so fishing in Wales can be amazingly expensive. For practical information on getting a licence, and the best time of year to catch different kinds of fish, try the **Environment Agency** (www.environment-agency.gov.uk/fish).

For further information, VisitWales produces the brochure *Fishing Wales,* which has details of fishing clubs, tackle shops and places to fish; see also the website www.fishing.visitwales.com.

GOLF

In 2003 the International Association of Golfing Tour Operators awarded Wales its prized Undiscovered Golf Destination of the Year award. Wales hasn't looked back since. With more than 200 courses ranging from world-class

Wales' mountain-bike trails have been officially dubbed the best in the world by the International Mountain Bicycling Association (IMBA).

Tackle the best mountain biking in Wales with the help of Pete Bursnall's pocket-sized *North Wales Mountain Bike Guide.*

championships links to hilly nine-hole courses, the country is now gearing up to take the golfing world's spotlight when it hosts the Ryder Cup, scheduled to be staged at the Celtic Manor Resort in September 2010.

For more information, VisitWales produces the brochure *Wales: Golf as It Should Be;* see also the website www.golfasitshouldbe.com for details of Welsh golf operators, course profiles and an index of courses.

Some of the best courses include Royal Porthcawl and Royal St David's, both of which appeal to the professional player. For a more laid-back round of 18 holes, try clifftop Cardigan, leafy Cradoc in the heart of the Brecon Beacons, or the windswept Nefyn and District course.

HORSE RIDING & PONY TREKKING

A good website for horse riders is www.equestrian wales.org.uk.

Wales is an ideal place to get out on a horse and enjoy the long sandy beaches, glorious rolling hills and lush forest. You don't need any riding experience, as riding schools cater to all levels of proficiency and they're littered all over the country. Some of the most beautiful riding is in the national parks, and Mid-Wales is also an excellent spot to see the world from horseback.

Rides generally cost about £15 per hour and if you're an experienced rider there are numerous equestrian centres with horses for hire. Some are mentioned in the regional chapters, and tourist offices have details of others.

WALKING

For hiking information, check out www.ramblers .org.uk/wales.

Wales' incredibly lush and varied landscape, replete with thousands of miles of walking trails, makes it a walker's paradise. Walks can be as relaxing or as vigorous as you wish, taking in canalside lanes, national-park scrambles or brisk sea-cliff strolls.

The most challenging walks are in the national parks of Snowdonia (p237) and the Brecon Beacons (p123). Snowdonia is Wales' biggest national park and is home to its highest mountain, along with a host of other impressive peaks and dramatic glaciated valleys. Base yourself at Betws-y-Coed (p260) and meander through the woodland or plan a full-on mountain adventure. In the Brecon Beacons you can scale craggy escarpments from the market town of Brecon (p133) or head for the western end of the park and walk for days without meeting another soul.

Outside of the national parks, secluded trails and long-distance paths crisscross the country (see opposite) and cover a range of territories. Any time of year is good for walking, though expect crowds in July and August, a good soaking of rain at any time and restrictively short days in winter.

On Foot in Snowdonia, by Bob Allen, is an indispens- able guide to the best 100 walks in Snowdonia. There are excellent instructions, good maps, route ratings and some stunning photography.

The walks described in this chapter are more suited for long-distance walking; for details of shorter walks, see the destination chapters.

Rights of Access

Welsh weather is fickle and even on short walks you should arm yourself with good rain gear, warm clothing and proper footwear. For more serious hikes, check the weather forecast with the tourist office, take a map, compass, first-aid kit, food and water and make sure someone knows where you've gone and what time or day you'll be back.

Today there are 24,855 miles of public footpaths, bridleways and byways in Wales, many of them marked with yellow arrows or waymarks. From May 2005 the public's rights of access to countryside has included most open country, common land, public forests and other dedicated land across Wales. These areas cover 1737 sq miles – about one fifth of Wales, or five times the area of accessible land previously available. The new access was granted under the Countryside and Rights of Way Act 2000. For more information, and details of how to adhere to the new Countryside Code (launched in 2004), contact the **Countryside Council for Wales** (☎ 0845 1306229; www.ccw.gov.uk).

Be aware that some of the rights of way cross private land owned by the Ministry of Defence (MoD); look out for red flags warning that access is denied because manoeuvres or firing are underway.

National parks and other protected areas are *not* open to unlimited access. The parks have been established to protect the country's finest landscapes, and their popularity with walkers means it's easy to damage the surrounding environment. Don't stray off the trails and always get permission from a landowner before pitching a tent.

Information

Lonely Planet's detailed guide *Walking in Britain* includes the three national trails in Wales, a dozen other long-distance paths and a wide selection of shorter walks and day-hikes.

The **Ordnance Survey** (OS; www.ordnancesurvey.co.uk) publishes several series of excellent, widely available maps covering all of Wales, and official guides for most trails are available from tourist offices, newsagents, bookshops and outdoor-equipment shops.

The free WTB publication *Walking Wales* has an introduction to the best long and short walks, and tourist offices have publications on local walks. For more information, check out www.walking.visitwales.com, which also lists private companies offering organised walking tours in Wales.

Trails

Serious walkers and anyone with a desire to see rural Wales should consider a multiday walk or two. Civilisation is never far away so it's easy to assemble a walk of your choice of duration that connects with public transport and that is punctuated by villages and hostels or bunkhouses. You can choose from 18 regional routes and three National Trails (see below).

For more information on the trails, check the website www.walking .adventurewales.com, or try www.ramblers.org.uk/wales, www.ldwa.org.uk or www.nationaltrail.co.uk. Many of the trails have their own websites.

NATIONAL TRAILS

The three national trails are open to walkers, cyclists and horse riders, and are waymarked with an acorn symbol.

Glyndŵr's Way (132 miles; www.nationaltrail.co.uk/glyndwrsway) This undulating route, zigzagging from Knighton to Machynlleth and back to Welshpool, passes many sites connected with the rebellion led by Owain Glyndŵr in the early 15th century. The birdlife found along this trail is another highlight. Accommodation is scarce in some sections and the hilly terrain means the going can be slow. Machynlleth has the best transport connections and gives easy access to mine-scarred valleys. The trail between Dyfnant Forest to Vyrnwy Lake is recommended for shorter walks. See p207.

Offa's Dyke Path (177 miles; www.offas-dyke.co.uk) Following an 8th-century grand earthwork project this trail skirts the Wales–England border through an astonishing range of scenery and vegetation. The best-preserved sections of original dyke are near Montgomery, and the Clwydian Ranges are stunning. This strenuous trail is best done south to north. Shorter walks include Chepstow to Monmouth, and through the Black Mountains to Hay-on-Wye. See p124.

Pembrokeshire Coast Path (186 miles; www.pembrokeshirecoast.org.uk, www.visitpembroke shire.com/walking) Hugging the sea cliffs of the Pembrokeshire Coast National Park, this is one of the UK's most beautiful walking routes. It passes incredible coastal scenery, tiny fishing villages and secluded coves. South to north is the preferred direction, but continual steep ascents and descents make this walk more challenging than the mileage suggests. If you're short on time, stick to the northern half, from Sandy Haven or Marloes to Cardigan (particularly the section between Dale and Martin's Haven). See p197.

For action and adventure in Snowdonia, check out www.snowdonia-active .com. It contains news, information and a directory of operators.

For the lowdown on the best pitches for your tent, Jonathan Knight's *Cool Camping: Wales* is the definitive guide.

For a sense of the trail's rich heritage, David Hunter's *Walking Offa's Dyke Path – A Journey Through the Border Country of England and Wales* is an essential companion for long-distance walkers.

SAFETY GUIDELINES FOR WALKING

Before embarking on a walking trip, consider the following points to ensure a safe and enjoyable experience:

- Pay any fees and obtain any permits required by local authorities.
- Be sure you are healthy and feel comfortable walking for a sustained period.
- Obtain reliable information from park authorities about physical and environmental conditions along your intended route.
- Be aware of local laws, regulations and etiquette about wildlife and the environment.
- Walk only in regions and on trails within your realm of experience.
- Be aware that weather conditions and terrain vary significantly from one region, or even from one trail, to another. Seasonal changes can significantly alter any trail. These differences influence the way walkers dress and the equipment they carry.
- Before you set out, ask about the environmental characteristics that can affect your walk and how local, experienced walkers deal with these considerations.

RESPONSIBLE TREKKING

To help preserve the ecology and beauty of Wales, consider the following tips when trekking.

Rubbish

- Carry out all your rubbish. Don't overlook easily forgotten items, such as silver paper, orange peel, cigarette butts and plastic wrappers. Empty packaging should be stored in a rubbish bag. Make an effort to carry out rubbish left by others.
- Never bury your rubbish. Digging disturbs soil and ground cover and encourages erosion. Buried rubbish will likely be dug up by animals, who may be injured or poisoned by it. It may also take years to decompose.
- Reduce waste by taking minimal packaging and no more food than you will need. Take re-usable containers or stuff sacks.
- Sanitary napkins, tampons, condoms and toilet paper should be carried out despite the inconvenience. They burn and decompose poorly.

Human Waste Disposal

- Contamination of water sources by human faeces can lead to the transmission of all sorts of nasties. Where there is a toilet, please use it. Where there is none, bury your waste. Dig a small hole 15cm deep and at least 100m from any watercourse. Cover the waste with soil and a rock. In snow, dig down to the soil.
- Ensure that these guidelines are applied to a portable toilet tent if one is being used by a large trekking party. Encourage all party members, including porters, to use the site.

Washing

- Don't use detergents or toothpaste in or near watercourses, even if they are biodegradable.
- For personal washing, use biodegradable soap and a water container (or even a lightweight, portable basin) at least 50m away from the watercourse. Disperse the waste water widely to allow the soil to filter it fully.

■ Wash cooking utensils 50m from watercourses using a scourer, sand or snow instead of detergent.

Fires & Low-Impact Cooking

■ Don't depend on open fires for cooking. The cutting of wood for fires in popular trekking areas can cause rapid deforestation. Cook on a lightweight kerosene, alcohol or Shellite (white gas) stove and avoid those powered by disposable butane gas canisters.

■ If you are trekking with a guide and porters, supply stoves for the whole team. In alpine areas, ensure that all members are outfitted with enough clothing so that fires are not a necessity for warmth.

■ If you patronise local accommodation, select those places that do not use wood fires to heat water or cook food.

■ Fires may be acceptable below the tree line in areas that get very few visitors. If you light a fire, use an existing fireplace. Don't surround fires with rocks. Use only dead, fallen wood. Remember the adage 'the bigger the fool, the bigger the fire'. Use minimal wood, just what you need for cooking. In huts, leave wood for the next person.

■ Ensure that you fully extinguish a fire after use. Spread the embers and flood them with water.

Erosion

■ Hillsides and mountain slopes, especially at high altitudes, are prone to erosion. Stick to existing trails and avoid short cuts.

■ If a well-used trail passes through a mud patch, walk through the mud so as not to increase the size of the patch.

■ Avoid removing the plant life that keeps topsoils in place.

Wildlife Conservation

■ Do not engage in or encourage hunting. It is illegal in all parks and reserves.

■ Don't buy items made from endangered species.

■ Don't attempt to exterminate animals in huts. In wild places, they are likely to be protected native animals.

■ Discourage the presence of wildlife by not leaving food scraps behind you. Place gear out of reach and tie packs to rafters or trees.

■ Do not feed the wildlife as this can lead to animals becoming dependent on hand-outs, to unbalanced populations and to diseases.

Camping & Walking on Private Property

■ Always seek permission to camp from landowners.

■ Public access to private property without permission is acceptable where public land is otherwise inaccessible, so long as safety and conservation regulations are observed.

ENVIRONMENTAL ORGANISATIONS

For further information, contact the **Forestry Commission Wales** (☎ 0845 604 0845; www.forestry .gov.uk/wales), or check the website www.snowdonia-society.org.uk.

LIFE ON THE EDGE

If you fancy some rock climbing with the sea snapping at your heels, head for the Pembrokeshire coast, where the high-adrenaline sport of coasteering was born. Equipped with wetsuit, flotation jacket and helmet, you make your way along the wave-thrashed coastal cliffs by a combination of climbing, traversing, scrambling, cliff jumping and swimming.

Routes are graded so you can choose the level of difficulty, but you must be reasonably fit and a confident swimmer. By any standard it's a demanding and fairly risky activity, so don't just head out there on your own; join a group with a qualified leader who has a good knowledge of the coastline, water and weather conditions, and then you will see why the sport has taken the world by storm.

Two reliable centres offering coasteering adventures either as single activities or as part of residential, multiactivity programmes are **Twr-y-Felin** (TYF; ☎ 01437-721611; www.tyf.com) at St David's and **Preseli Venture** (☎ 01348-837709; www.preseliventure.com), which is near the Pembrokeshire Coast National Park and also near Fishguard.

REGIONAL ROUTES

There are 18 regional routes, the pick of which are as follows.

Cambrian Way (274 miles; www.cambrianway.co.uk) From Conwy to Cardiff through much of Wales' highest, wildest and most gorgeous countryside, the Cambrian Way is the longest, least used and most rugged of the regional routes. Remote and isolated in places, and covering demanding terrain, this trail is only for the experienced, dedicated walker. Several hotels and walking outfits along the route have banded together to offer accommodation and walking holidays on sections of the route. See p207.

> Tackle Wales' toughest long-distance path with the help of AJ Drake's *Cambrian Way: A Mountain Connoisseur's Walk.*

Dyfi Valley Way (108 miles) From Aberdovey to Llyn Tegid (Bala Lake) and back along the other side of the valley to Borth, north of Aberystwyth. See p235.

Taff Trail (55 miles; www.tafftrail.org.uk) From Cardiff up the Taff Valley and across the Brecon Beacons National Park to Brecon. There's an easy canal walk around Brecon. Highlights include the ascent of Taipalan and the viaduct at Cefn Coed. See p124.

Usk Valley Walk (50 miles) From Newport and the Severn Estuary up the Usk Valley to Abergavenny and Brecon. For a shorter walk, try Abergavenny to Brecon. See p110.

Wye Valley Walk (136 miles; www.wyevalleywalk.co.uk) From Chepstow up the valley of the River Wye via Builth Wells to the Mid-Wales market town of Rhayader. See p111.

COASTAL PATHS

> Wales has 750 miles of coast, 605 of them walkable on long-distance trails.

The coastal paths of Wales are growing, and join together to form 605 miles of coastal walking.

Carmarthen Bay Coastal & Estuaries Way (55 miles) Armoth to Gower.

Ceredigion Coastal Path (70 miles) Ynyslas to Cardigan.

Edge of Wales Walk (47 miles) Caernarfon to Bardsey Island.

Glamorgan Heritage Coast Path (14 miles) Newton Burrows to Gileston.

Isle of Anglesey Coastal Path (125 miles) Isle of Anglesey circular route.

Llŷn Coastal Path (95 miles) Caernarfon to Porthmadog.

North Wales Path (60 miles) Prestatyn to Bangor.

Pembrokeshire Coastal Path National Trail (186 miles) Poppit Sands to Amroth.

> The Pembrokeshire Coastal Path, a Practical Guide for Walkers, by Dennis Kelsall, is an essential handbook containing practical details for long-distance routes and day trails as well as pointing out interesting features along the way.

Walking Festivals

Newport Bay Spring Walking Festival (☎ 01239-820627) 29 April to 1 May

Llanelli Festival of Walks (☎ 01554-776606) 26 May to 29 May

Conwy Walking Week (☎ 01492-575290) 19 July to 26 July

Barmouth Walking Festival (☎ 01341-280787) September

Llandrindod Wells Weekend Walking Festival (☎ 01579-822600) 8 September to 10 September

Cardigan Festival of Walking (☎ 01239-615554) 6 October to 8 October

WATER SPORTS

Whether you want to tour along glassy inland lakes and rivers, surf or paddle on sheltered bays, or take a thrilling ride down a white-water river, you'll find somewhere in Wales just waiting to be discovered. For information on Wales' beaches, see p58.

Most paddle sports are easy to pick up, and centres across the country have lessons for beginners and improvers alike, many of which can be combined with weekend breaks. For more information about water sports, check the website www.adventure.visitwales.com.

Some bigger activity centres for various water sports:

Plas Menai (National Water Sports Centre; ☎ 01248-670964; www.plasmenai.co.uk)
Plas y Brenin (National Mountain Centre; ☎ 01690-720214; www.pyb.co.uk)
Preseli Venture (☎ 01348-837709; www.preseliventure.com)
Tyr-y-Felin (TYF; ☎ 01437-721611; www.tyf.com)
West Wales Wind, Surf & Sailing (☎ 01646-636642; www.surfdale.co.uk)

> Coasteering originated in Pembrokeshire in the 1980s.

Canoeing & Sea Kayaking

For flat-water enthusiasts looking to explore hidden coves, discover sea caves and paddle around towering cliffs, the coasts of Pembrokeshire, the Llŷn and Anglesey have stunning scenery as well as internationally renowned sea-bird colonies near the islands of Ramsey (p188), Skomer (p183) and Bardsey (p272).

Inland waterways worth exploring include Llyn Tegid (Bala Lake; p245) and Llyn Gwynant in North Wales; Llangorse Lake (p137) in the Brecon Beacons; the Brecon Canal (p128); slow-moving rivers such as the Teifi near Cardigan (p209); the Wye in East Wales and the Dee in North Wales.

For the more adventurous, the Pembrokeshire coast is one of the UK's finest sea-kayaking areas and is Britain's only coastal national park; powerful tidal currents create huge standing waves between the coast and offshore islands. Freshwater West and Newgale are the best places to head for. Other popular spots around Wales include Rhossili (p154) and Llangennith (p154) in the Gower; Caswell Bay near the Mumbles (p146); Hell's Mouth (p270) on the Llŷn; and Rhosneigr, Holy Island (p282) and the Menai Straits in Anglesey (p285). A half-day introductory course costs about £40.

Most Welsh inland waterways are privately owned, but the **Welsh Canoeing Association** (WCA; www.welsh-canoeing.org.uk) has negotiated agreements to allow use by canoeists on designated sections of certain rivers at certain times of the year and under certain flow conditions. Check the website for regulations, and never assume that permission to launch on one section of a river entitles you to pass through downstream sections.

Diving

Steep underwater cliffs, stunning submarine scenery and a surprising array of sea life make Wales an excellent place for some subaquatic action. Indeed, people have been diving in Wales since the 1970s, but in the last few years it has become more accessible as a sport. Pembrokeshire probably has the best diving in the country and its offshore reefs, such as the Smalls, where grey seals spend summer, offer fantastic deep diving. Closer to shore, Ramsey Sound, Skokholm Island (p183) and Skomer Island Marine Nature Reserve are well worth checking out. In North Wales head for Bardsey Island (p272), the Skerries just north of Holyhead, or the Menai Straits.

> Skomer Island Marine Nature Reserve is one of only three marine nature reserves in the UK.

Be aware that many of Wales' best dive sites have raging tidal currents that can be dangerous to dive. Current-swept sites should be dived in areas of water without current, and even experienced divers should seek local advice before taking the plunge.

KITE SURFING & LAND YACHTING

Been there, done that? Looking for a new high? Kite surfing and land yachting are some of the fastest-growing sports in Wales and should be on every adrenaline junkie's must-do list.

Kite surfing takes the best of board sports and combines it with incredible airborne action. Aficionados of surfing, skateboarding and snowboarding will recognise the moves, but you'd be advised to take some lessons before hitting the water. Rhosneigr in Anglesey is the best place to try it but Pembrokeshire and the Gower Peninsula are also popular.

For further information contact the **British Kite Surfing Association** (www.kitesurfing.org), or check out recommended operators at www.adventure.visitwales.com. A two-day course typically costs about £175.

With speeds of up to 75mph, land yachting is incredibly exhilarating and also really easy to pick up. The giant sandy beach at Cefn Sidan, Pembrey Country Park, which has an 8-mile stretch of sand that is more than 3-miles wide, is an ideal spot to try out these wheeled demons. Other good spots include Pendine Sands in Carmarthenshire, Newgale in Pembrokeshire, Criccieth (p267) on the Llŷn and Rhosneigr in Anglesey. For more information, contact the **British Federation of Sand and Land Yacht Clubs** (www.bfslyc.org.uk), or try www.britishlandsailing.co.uk.

In the 1920s Sir Malcolm Campbell broke all land-speed records when he drove *Bluebird*, a turbo-powered car, on Pendine's vast beach at more than 170mph.

There are plenty of dive shops and schools in Pembrokeshire and Anglesey; check out www.adventure.visitwales.com for a list of schools and operators. At PADI centres, a Try-dive course will cost about £55 and a one-day diver course to learn the basics will cost about £150.

Surfing

Surrounded by sea on three sides, Wales is an ideal location for those wanting to learn to surf, and for more experienced wave riders there's plenty of more earnest action. The tidal range is immense – 4.5m to more than 7m – so you can find completely different sets of breaks at low and high tides.

September to April is peak wave-riding time and although some of the most popular beaches do get crowded, with a bit of effort there should be no problem finding your own space. Thanks to the North Atlantic Drift, sea temperatures are often warmer than they seem, but you'll need a wetsuit in any season (and possibly boots, hood and gloves in winter).

WHERE TO GO

Two excellent sources of surfing information are www.coldswell.com and www.a1surf.com. Both feature weather reports, beach guides, reviews and links to other sites.

The real home of Welsh surfing is the Gower Peninsula. There's a wide choice of breaks in a small area and plenty of *après*-surf activity. Caswell Bay, the Mumbles (p145), Langland Bay, Oxwich Bay and Llangennith (p154) are all good choices.

In Pembrokeshire the best breaks are at Tenby South Beach, Manorbier (p169), Freshwater West and West Dale Bay. Along St Bride's Bay (p182) try Broad Haven South and Newgale – a beautiful long beach that's rarely crowded. St David's immense Whitesands Bay (p189) is good for beginners, but very popular and often disappointingly busy. Along Cardigan Bay, Harbour Trap in Aberystwyth is worth a dip.

The best the Llŷn has to offer is the popular 4-mile stretch of bay at Porth Neigwl (Hell's Mouth) near Abersoch (p270); other possibilities are at Aberdaron (p271) and Porthor (Whistling Sands; p271). On Anglesey's southwest coast you may find modest breaks at Cable Bay and Rhosneigr.

COURSES

The best possible introduction to surfing is to take a few lessons; within a few days you'll be catching waves and getting a decent ride. Most surf beaches have surf schools; some good spots for learners include Llangennith, Whitesands and Hell's Mouth.

For more information on surf schools and gear hire, see the regional chapters or try www.adventure.visitwales.com for a list of WTB-approved operators. The **Welsh Surfing Federation Surf School** (www.wsfsurfschool.co.uk) is another good bet.

White-Water Rafting

Despite Wales' substantial rainfall and mountainous terrain, the opportunities for white-water rafting are somewhat limited. Swallow and Conwy Falls near Betws-y-Coed (p260) are popular spots, as is the River Conwy, which caters to all levels and glides through the spectacular scenery of Snowdonia. The River Dee between Corwen and Llangollen and the River Usk have some Grade 2 to 4 rapids (Grade 1 is gently flowing water and Grade 6 is unrunnable). The dam-released River Treweryn near Bala (p246), one of the few Welsh rivers with big and fairly predictable summertime white water, has Grade 3 to 4 rapids.

For more information, contact the **National White-Water Centre** (www.welsh -canoeing.org.uk) or check the websites www.adventure.visitwales.com or www.uk rafting.co.uk.

Windsurfing

There's great potential for windsurfing all around Wales' coast and on many inland lakes, too. Most of the beaches listed under Surfing (opposite) are also suitable for windsurfing and have gear hire and lessons available. New board designs are more stable than in the past, making it much easier to learn; after a couple of hours you should have no problem staying upright and getting a feel for the wind.

The Gower Peninsula around Port Eynon (p153) and Llangennith (p154) are great spots with a variety of conditions and various wind directions, while Oxwich Bay has flatter water for learners. In Pembrokeshire, Freshwater West and Newgale are the hot spots; while in North Wales, Rhosneigr in Anglesey, and Hell's Mouth on the Llŷn (p270) are good places to head. Inland lakes, such as Llyn Tegid (p245) in Snowdonia, are also worth checking out.

The majority of windsurfing centres are open from April to October, but avoid midsummer to beat the hordes; a two-day course to get up and running generally costs around £130. For more information, contact the **UK Windsurfing Association** (www.ukwindsurfing.com), or check out the website www.forces-of-nature.co.uk.

Delight in the thrills of North Wales with Terry Storry's guide to the area's best water-sports places: *Snowdonia White Water Sea and Surf.*

Food & Drink

Traditionally, Welsh food was based on what could be grown locally and cheaply. This meant that oats, root vegetables, dairy products, honey and meat featured highly in most recipes. Food was functional and needed to satisfy the needs of manual labourers – hearty and wholesome but not quite *haute cuisine*.

These days, something of a minirevolution is happening in Welsh dining, and restaurateurs, hotel managers and even farmers have discovered the value of promoting quality Welsh food. Organic cheeses, succulent meats, vegetables pulled fresh from the ground and fantastic fish are all making their way onto menus across the country.

The Very Best Flavours of Wales is a celebration of the best of Welsh cooking with cordon bleu chef Gilli Davies.

This isn't to say that everywhere you go in Wales you can expect gastronomic delights, but with a little effort you can find the gems and get a taste of Wales at its very best. Look out for the dragon and daffodil logos of the True Taste scheme, which encourages excellence in food production.

STAPLES & SPECIALITIES

Traditional Welsh dishes include the hearty *cawl*, a classic one-pot meal of bacon, lamb, cabbage, swede and potato. It's one of those warm, cosy dishes that you long for when you're walking in the hills. Another traditional favourite is Welsh rarebit, a kind of sophisticated cheese on toast generously drizzled with a secret ingredient tasting suspiciously like beer.

Check out the website www.walesthetruetaste.com for a taste of Welsh cuisine.

The most famous of Welsh specialities is laver bread, which is not bread at all but boiled seaweed mixed with oatmeal and served with bacon and toast for breakfast.

Succulent upland lamb and beef are known well beyond Wales. Lamb in particular is a national speciality, although the traditional meat – bacon – remains a firm favourite.

THE RISE OF WELSH HAUTE CUISINE *Colin Pressdee*

Great progress has been made in all areas of the food industry in Wales. In the last decade there has been a huge increase in the number of local farmers markets and food festivals. These have made the public aware that good produce has to be paid for, and while it is more expensive than supermarkets, the quality is far higher. Examples of outstanding farm shops and farmers markets are the Rhug Organic Estate, Corwen; Haverfordwest Farmers Market and Cardiff Riverside Market. Outstanding produce shops include Edwards of Conwy, Langfords of Welshpool and Blas ar Fwyd of Llanwrst.

At the same time there has been a huge increase in the number of restaurants in Wales that make a point of sourcing and using food from local suppliers. There are now many seriously good country-house hotels with fine-dining experiences – examples include Fairyhill in the Gower Peninsula, Plas Bodegroes in Pwllheli, Ye Olde Bulls Head Inn in Beaumaris, and Ynyshir Hall in Eglwysfach, near Machynlleth.

The biggest improvement has been the rise of the gastropub, both in towns and rural locations. The White Horse at Hendrewydd, the Wynnstay in Machynlleth, the Fox Hunter in Nant y Derry, the Welcome to Town in Gower and the Hardwich Abergavenny, are some of the many who now take pride in the Welsh food experience.

Chefs in Wales have embraced country produce, taking traditional food and showing how it can be presented in modern gastronomy. Foods such as Welsh lamb, Welsh Black beef, sewin (wild sea trout), Penclawdd cockles, Conwy mussels, laver bread and farmhouse cheeses have their place in every kitchen of the increasing number of good eating places in Wales.

Colin Pressdee is the author of Food Wales.

Seafood is a speciality around the coast: herring and mackerel are the traditional catch, although salmon or sewin (wild sea trout) are also popular. Oysters are harvested in the Gower as a cash crop rather than a food source, so it is cockles that usually make it to the kitchen table.

Welsh cheese is also a speciality, the best known variety being Caerphilly, a crumbly, salty cheese once popular with miners. There's little cheese being made in Caerphilly these days, but cheese-making in general is undergoing a revival. Cheese-freaks should comb the delis for Caws Cenarth, Celtic Blue, Llanboidy, Nantybwla, Pantysgawn or Teifi.

The sweet-toothed should look out for Welsh cakes: fruity little griddle scones or *bara brith*, a spicy fruit loaf made with tea and marmalade. Moist fruit cakes such as *teisen lap* are also delicious, even more so with an infusion of spicy goodness as is the case in *teisen carawe* (caraway cake) and *teisen sinamon* (cinnamon cake).

> For a comprehensive look at Welsh food, from recipes and producers to awards and food fairs, try www.foodwales.com.

> The leek and daffodil are the symbols of Wales.

DRINKS

The pub in Wales is part of the social fabric of the country and most pubs serve an impressive range of beers: ales, lagers, stouts and porters. Beers are usually served at room temperature, which can be a shock if you've been raised on ice-cold lager, but it does bring out the subtle flavours of beer hand-pumped from the cask.

Beers are usually served in pints (570mL) and half-pints (285mL). In southern Wales order a pint of Brains, which is brewed in Cardiff and claimed by locals to be one of the best drops in the UK. Also worth quaffing is Double Dragon Premium, a fragrant Felinfoel bitter. Look out for local ales at brewpubs, which usually stock the best offerings from the regional microbreweries. The **Great Welsh Beer and Cider Festival** (www.gwbcf.org.uk), held in Cardiff in November, is also a great place to taste the best home-grown brews.

Wales has also begun to produce its own whisky again (see the boxed text, below), plus there's wine from Pembrokeshire vineyards and gin and vodka from the Brecon Beacons.

> The Campaign for Real Ale (Camra) champions the cause of traditional ales. Visit www.camra.org.uk.

WHERE TO EAT & DRINK

There's never been a better time to eat out in Wales, but it's still possible to drive into any town and stumble upon nothing more wholesome than the local greasy spoon. Put in a little effort, though, and you'll find those elusive hideouts of good food.

Pub grub is convenient and affordable, but not always impressive. Much pub food has improved in recent years, though, and you can get a perfectly

---

THE NATIONAL SPIRIT

Whisky was once produced throughout Wales, but the temperance movement killed off production of the devil's drink and the last distillery closed in the 1890s.

A hundred years later the process of putting Welsh whisky back on the map got off to a bad start when a dodgy distillery was revealed as nothing more than a blending and bottling plant. The Scotch Whisky Association was none too pleased and had it shut down.

In September 2000 a new distillery in the picturesque village of Penderyn, 10 miles west of Merthyr Tydfil, made history when it distilled the first Welsh whisky in over a century. On 1 March 2004, the first release of the delicate Penderyn Single Malt Whisky took place. Main stores have been left to age and develop more complex flavours but connoisseurs are queuing up to sample the limited edition.

For more information visit www.welsh-whisky.co.uk.

WALES' TOP EATERIES

Armless Dragon, Cardiff Seriously fresh international fare with an innovative Welsh twist; see p96.
Bear Hotel, Crickhowell Award-winning flavours at every price level at this old-time coaching inn; see p130.
Carlton House, Llanwrtyd Wells Dine in theatrical surroundings with personal attention from the Michelin-star chef; see p217.
Drawing Room, Builth Wells Excellent foodie retreat somewhat spoiled by the frosty welcome; see p219.
Felin Fach Griffin, Brecon Big flavours and stylish presentation at this gorgeous gastropub; see p137.
Foxhunter, near Abergavenny Bold and brilliant modern classics in contemporary country surroundings; see p130.
Plas Bodegroes, Pwllheli Romantic Michelin-star retreat in the wilds of Wales serving exquisite modern classics; see p270.

---

reasonable lunch or dinner at a surprisingly good price. Most pubs serve food between noon and 2pm, and 5pm and 9pm.

An increasing number of places are championing local produce and bringing the concept of the gastropub to Wales. The trend for talented chefs to abandon their urban stomping grounds, wind down a peg or two and get closer to their ingredients is making waves in rural Wales, and could turn your quick pit-stop lunch into a long, lingering affair.

TV chef Ena Thomas is something of a legend in Wales and has published a range of Welsh cookbooks. Try *Four Seasons with Ena* for some seasonally inspired dishes.

In larger towns and cities you'll find switched-on bistros and restaurants serving up anything from decent to inspired food. An extension of the restaurant business is the restaurant-with-rooms idea, where fine dining and a cosy bed are generally only a staircase apart. Most of these places combine gourmet food with a small number of lovingly decorated rooms – so you can linger as long as you like over that final brandy.

For most restaurants you'll need to book ahead, particularly at the weekend, and a 10% to 15% tip is expected on top of the bill. In smaller towns, the only food available on Sunday may be the popular, pricey roast served at pubs and hotel restaurants.

Café society is blooming all over Wales, though its standards vary from twee tea-and-bun fests to hip hang-outs for the young and underemployed. Most serve up cheap breakfast fry-ups and a varied menu of snacks and sandwiches, though more enlightened establishments will stretch to something more imaginative. Wholefood cafés have sprouted all over Mid-Wales and West Wales, where alternative lifestylers have ordered in the tofu and set up shop.

Vegetarians should head straight for the famous Glamorgan sausage, made from a heady mixture of cheese, breadcrumbs, herbs and chopped leek.

When it comes to drinking in Wales, the local pub is about the only place to go. You can buy alcohol at most supermarkets and at off-licences (liquor stores), but you'll miss out on a great part of Welsh culture if you never make it through the swinging doors and onto the sticky carpet of the local. Welsh pubs vary enormously, from cosy watering holes with big fires and an inviting atmosphere to tough inner-city bars where solo women travellers may feel decidedly ill at ease. Chain bars, with little character, have spread into Welsh towns; it's well worth seeking out the older and more atmospheric places to get a real sense of local culture. Evidence so far suggests that the relaxation of the drinking laws has not significantly increased Welsh consumption of alcohol.

VEGETARIANS & VEGANS

Happily, vegetarianism has taken off in a big way in Wales; practically every eating place, including pubs, has at least one token vegetarian dish, though don't expect it to always be inspired. Things are decidedly easier in larger towns as well as in Mid-Wales and West Wales, where alternative lifestyles have blossomed. Many cafés in these areas are strictly vegetarian and even vegans should be able to find a decent meal. In addition to the listings throughout this book, check out www.happycow.net for some more suggestions.

EATING WITH KIDS

If you're travelling with children, eating out and satisfying all those cravings for crisps and sweets can start to cost the earth after a few days. Picnic lunches can help keep costs down and every town has a supermarket or open-air market to stock up on supplies.

Pub food is generally the cheapest bet for a hot lunch or dinner and most pubs are licensed and willing to have children on the premises until about 7pm. Practically all pubs serving food have a children's menu and many also have beer gardens with climbing frames to keep the little ones entertained. Most restaurants are also child-friendly and have highchairs and half portions available; generally the more expensive and exclusive the restaurant, the more intolerant the staff can be, so ask when you make a booking.

For more information on travelling with children, see p332.

The Welsh Table by Christine Smeeth is a delightful combination of simple traditional Welsh dishes, kitchen anecdotes and words of wisdom.

COOKING COURSES

Try your hand at making your own Welsh supper at the following venues:

Abergavenny Food Festival (www.abergavennyfoodfestival.co.uk) Lessons from master chefs at this September festival of food; see p128.

Elan Valley Hotel (www.fungiforays.co.uk) Two-day breaks for fungi freaks on a quest for mushroom heaven; see p226.

Drovers Rest (www.food-food-food.co.uk/courses.htm) Private and group classes in the UK's smallest town; see p217.

Dryad Bushcraft (www.dryadbushcraft.co.uk) Outdoor survival and bushcraft cookery for the more adventurous; navigate to the wilderness gourmet course through 'courses' on the website.

Porth Farm Cookery School; Caersws, Montgomeryshire (☎ 01686-688171; www.mont-hols.co.uk/members/18/) Top tips from a cordon bleu chef in a specially designed demonstration kitchen at the heart of a 15th-century country house.

EAT YOUR WORDS
Out to Eat

Table for ... please.
  Bwrdd i ... os gwelwch yn dda.   boordh ee ... os *gwe*·lookh uhn dhah
Can I see the menu, please?
  Ga i weld y fwydlen, os gwelwch yn dda?   gah ee weld uh *voo*·eed·len, os *gwe*·lookh uhn dhah
The bill, please.
  Y bil, os gwelwch yn dda.   uh bil, os *gwe*·lookh uhn dhah

First Catch your Peacock, by Bobby Freeman, is the classic guide to Welsh food and an entertaining read, combining authentic and proven recipes with cultural and social history.

In the Pub
I'd like a (half) pint of ...
Ga i (hanner o) beint o ...   gah ee (*han*·er oh) baynt oh ...

bitter	*chwerw*	*khwe*·roo
cider	*seidr*	*say*·duhr
lager	*lager*	*lah*·guhr
orange juice	*sudd oren*	seedh *o*·ren
water	*dŵr*	door

Cheers!
  Iechyd Da!   *ye*·khid dah

Traditional Dishes

bara brith	*ba*·ra breeth	A rich, fruit tea-loaf.
bara lawr	*ba*·ra lowr	Laver seaweed boiled and mixed with oatmeal and traditionally served with bacon for breakfast.
cawl	kowl	A broth of meat and vegetables.

caws caerffili	kows kair·*fi*·li	Caerphilly cheese, a crumbly salty cheese that used to be popular with miners.
ffagots a phys	*fa*·gots a fees	Seasoned balls of chopped pork and liver in gravy served with peas.
lobsgows	*lobs*·gows	A Northwalian version of cawl.
pice ar y maen	*pi*·ke ahr uh main	(lit: cakes on the griddle stone) Small, fruited sconelike griddle cakes, also known as Welsh cakes.

Myths & Legends

Wales is littered with the stuff of legend: the grand peaks and wild passes; the caves, cairns and *cromlechs* (burial chambers); the *menhirs* (standing stones), ruined fortresses and ancient abbeys. The mysterious power of these landmarks couldn't help but be intensified in a nation of small, close-knit communities, dependent on the skills of generations of storytellers, musicians and poets to enrich their lives. Even today these centuries-old traditions are a source of pride and enthusiasm in *eisteddfodau* (gatherings; see the boxed text, p47) – the modern-day celebration of Welsh literature and culture.

It's not just the landscape, however, that makes people tell tales; Wales' rich and dramatic history has itself inspired stories of giants, saints and fairies, King Arthur and the devil, mythological beasts and supernatural events. From the time of the Celts and their druid priests, through Roman occupation and Saxon struggles to the arrival of Christianity during the 5th and 6th centuries, there was always ample fodder for a god-fearing, death-fearing audience that had been invaded, suppressed and occasionally treated to moments of glorious victory.

Professional storytellers held a lofty but precarious position and were responsible for boosting the morale and massaging the self-esteem of their noble patrons. Choosing the right theme for the master's mood was always an issue, but the favourite tales recounted battles against evil, adventures of heroic leaders and tales of magic, mystery and enchantment – all of them full of fairies and ghosts. By the 9th century, a collection of tales featuring everything from mysterious lakes and stones to the heroic King Arthur had appeared in *Historia Brittonum* written by Nennius, thought to have been a monk from Bangor.

Few of these stories, however, were ever written down by the Welsh in their own language, so most have either been dressed up almost unrecognisably in the clothes of other cultures or have been lost. Only a handful of fantastic tales derived from myths of the Celtic gods have survived, in two remarkable 14th-century compendia called *The White Book of Rhydderch* and *The Red Book of Hergest*. By the 15th century, with the addition of specifically Welsh heroes to the cast of characters (Llewelyn the Great, his grandson Llywelyn ap Gruffydd, Owain Glyndŵr and others – all seen as leading the resistance against the English conqueror), the source material was richer than ever.

The stories were later translated into English as the *Mabinogion* (Tales of a Hero's Youth) and today they provide us with the best insight into Welsh mythology and the magical, sometimes terrifying, pagan Celtic world.

STONES, LAKES & HOLY WELLS

Some of the most enchanting Welsh myths step straight from the world of fairy tales, featuring locations that seem strange and mysterious even today.

Llyn y Fan Fach, a small alpine lake of dark waters in the Black Mountain area of eastern Carmarthenshire, is the setting for the best known of Wales' many Lady-of-the-Lake stories. The tale is of a farmer's son who falls in love with a fairy-woman from the lake, and is permitted to marry her on the condition that he does not strike her three times in anger. For more on this legend, see the boxed text, p159.

These mythical maidens that appeared from lakes are only one of the strange mysteries associated with water in Wales. Another association is with many of Wales' prehistoric *menhirs*. These megaliths – said to have been thrown into their positions by giants, saints, King Arthur or Merlin – often have the added mystery of allegedly wandering off for a drink at certain times.

Read about the history of Welsh gods and goddesses and their fantastic tales at www.realmagick.com /articles/33/2033.html.

The town of Beddgelert (the Grave of Gelert) is said by some to be named after a legendary dog that saved Prince Llywelyn's baby from a wolf.

The *Mabinogion*, by Gwyn Jones and Thomas Jones, is a contemporary translation of Wales' Celtic tales and ancient myths. Visit www.gouk.about .com/cs/mythslegend1/ for useful links.

Samson's Stone (near Kenfig, South Wales) goes down to the River Sker on Christmas morning; the immense Fish Stone (near Crickhowell in southern Powys) pops into the River Usk for a Midsummer Eve's swim; and the four standing stones at Old Radnor (east of Llandrindod Wells in southern Powys) sip from Hindwell Pool when the village church bells ring at night.

The Welsh Gwyllgi (Dog of Darkness) is a terrifying apparition of a huge hound that's said to wander lonely roads by night.

Strange markings on many of these stones, and on equally ancient burial chambers, are taken to be fingermarks of the devil or King Arthur when they threw the stones. Perhaps the burial chamber with the spookiest association is at St Lythan's (5 miles to the southwest of Cardiff), set in the so-called Accursed Field (where nothing will grow) and whose capstone is said to spin around three times each Midsummer's Eve.

The many ancient burial mounds scattered throughout Wales have their own legends: some as the graves of giants, or of Roman soldiers, as with the Twyn Tudor mound on Mynydd Islwyn in South Wales; and some that have been deposited by the devil. Treasure seekers and others with the nerve to poke around on these mounds have often met with misfortune or disaster (see the boxed text, p79). There is even a nugget of truth in some of the stories. For years the so-called Mound of the Goblins (Tomen yr Ellyllon, near Mold in North Wales) was said to be haunted by a horseman in gold armour. When it was excavated in 1833 a man's skeleton was found, wrapped in a gold cape some 3500 years old.

The Coblynau were good-humoured mine spirits who helped the miners by knocking in places with rich mineral or metal lodes.

A good many other Welsh legends – notably those about floods and submerged cities – are probably based on fact. The most famous of these concerns Cardigan Bay, said to have once been dry land, a fertile region called Cantref Gwaelod (The Lowland Hundred). The legend recounts how Seithenyn, keeper of the dikes that held the sea at bay, got drunk one night and forgot to shut the sluice gates, and the land, together with 16 cities, was inundated. You can supposedly still hear the tolling of sunken church bells in the area today. A similar legend, complete with church bells, is also told about Llangorse Lake (p137), near Brecon.

The arrival of Christianity in Wales gave a new slant to many ancient stories: markings on stones previously attributed to a giant or Arthur's horse became the footprints of saints, and mysterious mounds miraculously rose from the ground to form pulpits for preachers. Most commonly, wells once worshipped in pagan rites, and supposedly guarded by dragons or huge eels, acquired associations with Christian saints and amazing curative powers.

The best known is St Winifred's Well, around which the town of Holywell in North Wales has flourished. In the 7th century, Winifred, niece of St Beuno, rejected a wily young chieftain called Caradoc, who promptly expressed his displeasure by decapitating her. A spring – with healing powers, of course –

THE RED DRAGON

One of the first mythical beasts in British heraldry, the red dragon is a powerful symbol in ancient legends. Nobody really knows when it first appeared in Britain, but it was apparently used on the banners of British soldiers on their way to Rome in the 4th century, and was then adopted by Welsh kings in the 5th century to demonstrate their authority after the Roman withdrawal.

At any rate the Anglo-Saxon king, Harold, and Cadwaladr, 7th-century king of Gwynedd, liked it so much they made it their standard in battle, forever associating the symbol with Wales. In the 14th century Welsh archers had the red dragon as their emblem and Owain Glyndŵr used it as a standard in his revolt against the English Crown. A century later, quarter-Welsh Henry Tudor (later King Henry VII) made the dragon part of the Welsh flag, though it was only in 1959 that Queen Elizabeth II commanded that the red dragon, on a green and white field, be recognised as the official flag of Wales.

MAPPING THE FAIRIES

When geographer Brian John decided a few years ago that he would map the distribution of fairies (well, fairy tales, actually) in Pembrokeshire, he was not sure what to expect. This was in the context of the Pembrokeshire Folk-Tale Project, which in 1991–96 led to the collection of over 500 folk tales from the county, and the publication of four volumes giving the tales and their sources. The tales were grouped as follows: tales of the saints; heroic deeds; strange happenings; fairy tales; witchcraft and magic; signs, omens and portents; ghostly tales; and folk heroes. He noticed that certain types of tales were concentrated in certain areas. When he came to map the fairy tales he observed that they were far more frequent in the northeast of the county than in other districts; and this might well be expected, for according to tradition Gwlad y Tylwyth Teg (Fairyland) is located out in Cardigan Bay, beneath the waves and on invisible green islands. Contrary to the Victorian stereotype, the fairies are not particularly small, and neither do they have gossamer wings, but they are more virtuous than human beings, and have a preference for red and green clothing. If you deal honestly with them, or do them some special service, you may be invited to pay them a visit in order to sample the delights of their peaceful and comfortable kingdom.

For details of the folk-tale collection, see www.books-wales.co.uk.

Brian John is the author of the Angel Mountain Saga (www.angel-mountain.info).

---

appeared where her head hit the ground. Meanwhile, Caradoc's descendants were cursed by St Beuno to bark like dogs unless they humbly immersed themselves in the spring's waters. Luckily for Winifred, St Beuno managed to join her head back to her body with a prayer, and she later became an abbess.

One of the favourite folk stories, and one that still resounds around the hills and farmlands of North Wales even today, revolves around the legend of Teggie, Wales' answer to the Loch Ness monster. For more on this legend see the boxed text, p246).

ARTH FAWR THE BEAR

King Arthur has inspired more legends, folk tales and curiosities, and given his name to more features of the landscape in Wales, than any other historical figure. His story is so interwoven with myth and mystery, folklore and fiction that his true identity remains unknown. Was he a giant of superhuman strength or a dwarf king who rode a goat instead of a horse? Was he a Celtic god associated with the constellation Ursa Major, the Great Bear (Arth Fawr in Welsh)? Or, as most historians suspect, was he a 5th- or 6th-century cavalry leader who led the early Britons against the Saxon invaders, his story increasingly romanticised as time went on?

One of the earliest, most tantalising descriptions about such a hero appears in the *Historia Brittonum*. By the 9th century Arthur's fame as a fighter against the Saxons had reached every corner of the British Isles. Legends cropped up from Cornwall to Scotland, associating him with local caves, ancient megaliths (named Arthur's Chair, Arthur's Table and Arthur's Quoit), mountains (battle scenes and treasure-troves) and lakes (the magical source of his great sword).

Prose romances and epic poems soon transformed Arthur into a heroic king of marvels and magic deeds, at the head of a phalanx of other famous heroes and aided by the wise magician Myrddin (Merlin; see p78). Arthur is also present in the 12th-century *Llyfr Du Caerfyrddin* (The Black Book of Carmarthen), the oldest surviving Welsh manuscript.

In the centuries that followed, other writers – most recently and perhaps most famously the Victorian poet Alfred Lord Tennyson – climbed on the bandwagon, weaving in love stories, Christian symbolism and medieval pageantry to create the romance that surrounds Arthur today.

Maen Chwyfan, an early medieval stone cross in Flintshire, protected the treasure supposedly buried beneath it by zapping any gold diggers with lightning.

The Adventures of King Arthur in Snowdonia and Anglesey, by John Morris and Gareth Roberts, brings the legends of King Arthur to life through a host of real-life characters and their unique Welsh perspectives.

Tintagel in Cornwall has the strongest claim to being Arthur's birthplace, Cadbury Castle in Somerset contends it's the site of Camelot (his court), and Glastonbury Abbey his burial place; however, the Welsh – especially those living in southern Wales – make many fervent claims of their own. The 12th-century historian-novelist Geoffrey of Monmouth asserted that a grassy mound at Caerleon (p108), near Newport in Gwent, was the site of Arthur's first court, describing it as populated with hundreds of scholars, astrologers and philosophers as well as many fine knights and ladies. And why not? Caerleon had already been favoured by the Romans, serving as headquarters of the elite, 6000-strong Second Augustan Legion. The remains of its fine amphitheatre are still visible today (doing double duty in the mind's eye as Arthur's great Round Table).

Camlan, the site of Arthur's final battle (curiously well pinpointed at around AD 542), may have been in Cornwall, Somerset or Cumberland, but Wales has at least two candidates: Camlan Hill in Cwm Cerist in North Wales and Maes Camlan in Mid-Wales. As for Avalon (Avallach in Welsh) – the blessed 'island of apples' where the dying Arthur was taken by Merlin – could it not be Wales' saintly Bardsey Island, which is just off the tip of the Llŷn Peninsula?

Many other places in Wales have used natural features or curiosities to suit the Arthurian legends, notably the Preseli Hills of northern Pembrokeshire – the source of the bluestone megaliths that form the inner circle of Stonehenge in England and the site of many Neolithic monuments bearing Arthur's name. The Gower Peninsula's scattered megaliths have been drafted in, notably a massive burial chamber on Cefn Bryn near Reynoldston (p155), whose 25-tonne capstone is well known as Arthur's Stone. Castell Dinas Brân at Llangollen (p299) is said to hide the Holy Grail – the vessel used by Christ at the Last Supper and imbued with supernatural qualities – which Arthur and his knights sought obsessively in later stories.

More intriguingly, some places have directly inspired Welsh versions of the hero's exploits. The Pembrokeshire coast is where, according to the 10th-century story *Culhwch and Olwen,* Arthur and his knights started the hunt for a ferocious magic boar. On Mt Snowdon, Arthur slew Rita Gawr, a giant notorious for killing kings and making coats of their beards. Snowdon also provides an alternative version of the king's death and burial, following a fierce battle at Bwlch-y-Saethau (Pass of the Arrows), after which his knights took refuge in a nearby cave called Ogof Lanciau Eryri (Cave of the Lads of Eryri). Of course, other Welsh caves, including Craig-y-Ddinas in South Wales, also lay claim to this role.

Ultimately, in most stories, Arthur and his followers end up in a cave – not dead, perish the thought, but in a kind of mythical cold storage – asleep until the Once and Future King is again called upon to defend Britain.

MERLIN THE MAGICIAN

The story of this great Welsh wizard is probably modelled on a 6th-century holy man named Myrddin Emrys (or Ambrosius). Carmarthen (whose Welsh name, Caerfyrddin, means Merlin's City) lays claim to his birth, thought to have been during the time of Vortigern, a legendary leader of the Roman British against the Saxons.

It's said that Myrddin's mother was a strict Christian and his father an evil man of magical powers. Myrddin inherited the wizardry minus the wickedness and became famous for his prophecies. By the 10th century these prophecies were common currency across Western Europe and gave hope to many Welsh princes in their struggles with the Anglo-Normans. One of the most potent of these early rallying prophecies concerns two dragons, one red and one white, revealed by Myrddin to be lurking in a cave on Dinas

---

Trace the true location of Arthur's kingdom right into the heart of Wales with the help of *The Keys to Avalon,* by Scott Blake and Scott Lloyd.

For a tailored tour of Pembrokeshire, taking in legendary Stone Age and Celtic sites, visit www .celticwestwales.com.

Emrys, Snowdonia, a place where Vortigern had tried unsuccessfully to build a tower. The dragons started fighting, Myrddin explaining to the king that the struggle symbolised the fight between Britons (or the Welsh) and Saxons. Naturally the red dragon, symbolising Wales, won (and Myrddin kept Dinas Emrys as the site for his own fortress).

In his book, Geoffrey of Monmouth changed Myrddin's name to Merlin and presented him as the wise wizard and advisor to Arthur's father, King Uther Pendragon. One of his seminal acts was to disguise Uther one night as Duke Gorlois, to enable Uther to spend the night with the duke's wife, Ygerna, who duly conceived Arthur. It was Merlin, too, who planted the prediction that Uther Pendragon's true heir would draw a sword from a stone, and who advised Uther to establish a fellowship of knights (and who actually made the Round Table at which those knights would eventually sit). These stories would become essential ingredients in the highly romanticised Arthurian legend that developed in the following centuries, most notably in the hands of the French poet Chrétien de Troyes in the 12th century, and in the English-language *Morte d'Arthur*, written by Sir Thomas Malory in the 15th century.

As Arthur's own counsellor, Merlin continued to be the pivot around which all revolved. It was through Merlin, of course, that Arthur obtained his miraculous sword, Excalibur, from a Lady of the Lake (one of many lakes to claim this role is the lily pond at Bosherston, in south Pembrokeshire). It was Merlin who predicted Arthur's demise, and it was thanks to Merlin that his remaining knights afterwards found safety on the Scilly Isles.

Merlin himself appears to have come to an ignominious end, trapped by that same Lady of the Lake in a cave on Bryn Myrddin (Merlin's Hill) just east of Carmarthen, where groans and the clanking of iron chains are still part of local lore. Other versions sustain the hopes of believers by insisting that Merlin is not dead but held in a trance in Brittany (where many Britons found refuge from the Saxons in the 5th century) or in a glass house on Bardsey Island, where he guards the Thirteen Treasures of Britain

Read more about Welsh myths and legends, from women of Arthurian mythology to Merlin, the red dragon and where to find the Holy Grail in Wales at www.welsh dragon.net/resources /myths/index.shtml.

Find out about contemporary Welsh fairy witchcraft at www.tylwythteg .com/welsh1.html.

DEATH & DISASTER

Scoff if you like, but don't say we didn't warn you. Here are a few myths to ignore at your peril.

Cader Idris, Snowdonia
Inhabited by a mythical giant, the 893m summit of this peak in southern Snowdonia is known as the Chair of Idris. Spend a night here and you'll wake up either blind, mad or a poet.

Llyn Irddyn, North Wales
Keep a blade of grass in your pocket as you walk around this lake or the malicious fairies will come and get you.

Maen Du'r-arddu, Snowdonia
A couple who sleep by this boulder in Snowdonia will find by morning that one has become a poet and the other has gone mad.

Tinkinswood, near St Nicholas, Cardiff
Dance around this Neolithic burial chamber on a Sunday and you'll end up like the group of women who once did: they were turned into the stones that now surround the chamber.

Twmbarlwm Hill, near Risca, Gwent
Don't meddle with this mound (said to have been the site of a druid court of justice) or you'll be attacked by a swarm of bees (which is what happened in 1984 to a group of workmen trying to restore the mound).

Twyn Tudor, Mynydd Islwyn, South Wales
If you dig into this mysterious mound for treasure you'll provoke a terrific thunderstorm.

GEOFFREY OF MONMOUTH

Geoffrey of Monmouth, the Benedictine monk whose colourful *Historia Regum Britanniae* (The History of the Kings of Britain) became a 12th-century bestseller, changed Myrddin's name to Merlin (supposedly to spare his Norman French readers from any indelicate association between 'Myrddin' and *merde*), and shamelessly embellished the old stories.

(including a magical cloak, a cauldron, a robe, a ring and a chessboard with pieces that play by themselves).

Tales like this still have a grip on the Welsh imagination. The stump of a 17th-century oak tree, nicknamed 'Merlin's Tree', once stood inconveniently in Carmarthen's Priory St. One of Merlin's well-documented prophecies was that 'When Myrddin's tree shall tumble down/Then shall fall Carmarthen town'.

The tree died of old age and was removed in 1978, but Carmarthen is still there, although some years after the tree died, the River Tywi burst its banks and flooded the town. Pieces of the tree are still kept under glass at Carmarthen's civic centre.

Get the lowdown on Welsh deities at www .timelessmyths.com /celtic/welsh.html.

Cardiff

The roar that went up from Cardiff's Millennium Stadium when Wales clinched victory in the 2005 Six Nations rugby championship – their first grand slam since 1978 – seems to still echo around the city today. The Welsh team's return to form gave a massive boost to national confidence, a feeling reflected in the optimistic buzz that makes Cardiff such an appealing place to visit.

Cardiff was shaped in the 19th century by the world's richest man – John Patrick Crichton-Stuart, third marquess of Bute – whose architectural legacy ranges from the colourful kitsch of Cardiff Castle to the neoclassical elegance of the Civic Centre. But the 21st century is making its presence felt as the sprawling docks that generated the Bute fortune continue their transformation into the glitzy waterfront development of Cardiff Bay, centred on the futuristic flourishes of the Wales Millennium Centre and the Welsh Assembly Building.

There's plenty to explore in the city itself, but one of Cardiff's great attractions is the ease with which you can escape the urban clamour: vast acres of parkland stretch north from the castle's doorstep to the bucolic setting of Llandaff Cathedral, and the Taff Trail cycle route follows a leafy river bank to the fairy-tale setting of Castell Coch.

A short day trip by bus or train will take you to the old-fashioned seaside suburb of Penarth, the gritty industrial heritage of a rapidly regenerating Newport, or the magnificent medieval fortress and cheese capital of Caerphilly.

HIGHLIGHTS

- Gawping open-mouthed at the high-camp Victorian kitsch of **Cardiff Castle** (p85)
- Taking a tour or, better still, seeing a rugby match at the **Millennium Stadium** (p88)
- Enjoying great art at the **National Museum Wales** (p86)
- Watching the yacht-racing, cold beer in hand, at a table overlooking **Cardiff Bay** (p88)
- Strolling through 500 years of history at the open-air **St Fagans National History Museum** (p104)

National Museum Wales ★

St Fagans National History Museum ★

★ Cardiff Castle

Millennium Stadium ★ ★ Cardiff Bay

■ TELEPHONE CODE: 029   ■ POPULATION: 321,000

CARDIFF (CAERDYDD)

HISTORY

The Romans were first here in AD 75 and built the fort where Cardiff Castle now stands; the name Cardiff probably derives from the Welsh Caer Tâf (Fort on the River Taff).

After the Romans left Britain the site remained unoccupied until the Norman Conquest. In 1093 a Norman knight named Robert Fitzhamon (later earl of Gloucester) built himself a castle here – the remains stand within the grounds of Cardiff Castle – and a small town grew up around it. Both were damaged in a Welsh revolt in 1183 and the town was sacked in 1404 by Owain Glyndŵr during his ill-fated rebellion against English domination.

The first of the Tudor Acts of Union in 1536 put the English stamp on Cardiff and brought some stability. One of the few city-centre reminders of medieval Cardiff is St John's Church. But despite its importance as a port, market town and bishopric, only 1000 people were living here in 1801.

The city owes its stature to iron and coal mining in the valleys to the north. Coal was first exported from Cardiff on a small scale as early as 1600. In 1794 the Bute family (see the boxed text, below) – who owned much of the land from which Welsh coal was mined – built the Glamorganshire Canal for the shipment of iron from Merthyr Tydfil down to Cardiff. In 1840 this was supplanted by the new Taff Vale Railway. A year earlier the second mar-

quess of Bute had completed the first docks at Butetown, just south of Cardiff, getting the jump on other South Wales ports. By the time it dawned on everyone what immense reserves of coal there were in the valleys – setting off a kind of gold-rush fever – the Butes were in a position to insist that it be shipped from Butetown. Cardiff was off and running.

The docklands expanded rapidly, the Butes grew staggeringly rich and the city boomed, its population mushrooming to 170,000 by the end of the 19th century and to 227,000 by 1931. A vast, multiracial workers' community known as Tiger Bay grew up in the harbourside area of Butetown. In 1905 Cardiff was officially designated a city, and a year later its elegant Civic Centre was inaugurated. The city's wealth and its hold on the coal trade persuaded Captain Robert Scott to launch his ill-fated expedition to the South Pole from here in 1910. In 1913 Cardiff became the world's top coal port, exporting some 13 million tonnes of the stuff.

But the post-WWI slump in the coal trade and the Great Depression of the 1930s slowed this expansion. The city was badly damaged by WWII bombing, which claimed over 350 lives.

Cardiff's designation in 1955 as Wales' capital – making it Europe's youngest capital city – gave it a new lease of life. It was chosen via a ballot of the members of the Welsh authorities. Cardiff received 36 votes to Caernarfon's 11 and Aberystwyth's four. Other cities who vied for the position included Swansea and

---

THE BUTE FAMILY

The Butes, an aristocratic Scottish family related to the Stuart monarchy, arrived in Cardiff in 1766 in the shape of John, Lord Mountstuart, who had served briefly as prime minister under King George I. He married a local heiress, Charlotte Jane Windsor, acquiring vast estates and mineral rights in South Wales in the process.

Their grandson, the second marquess of Bute, grew fabulously wealthy from coal mining, then in 1839 gambled his fortune to create the first docks at Cardiff. The gamble paid off. The coal-export business boomed, and his son, John Patrick Crichton-Stuart, the third marquess of Bute, became one of the richest people on the planet. He was not your conventional Victorian aristocrat; an intense, scholarly man with a passion for history, architecture, ritual and religion, he neither hunted nor fished but instead supported the antivivisection movement and campaigned for women's right to a university education.

The Butes had interests all over Britain and never spent more than about six weeks at a time in Cardiff. By the end of WWII they had sold or given away all their Cardiff assets, the fifth marquess gifting Cardiff Castle to the city in 1947. The present marquess, the seventh, lives in the family seat at Mount Stuart House on the Isle of Bute in Scotland's Firth of Clyde; another maverick, he's better known as Johnny Dumfries, the Formula One racing driver.

Machynlleth. Today, with the continuing regeneration of Cardiff Bay, the opening of the Welsh Assembly Building, and booming media and service sectors, Cardiff is on the up again.

ORIENTATION

Cardiff city centre is a compact area on the east bank of the River Taff, stretching south from Cardiff Castle for 500m to Cardiff Central train station and bus station, and from the vast Millennium Stadium east to Cardiff Queen Street station. The tourist office is bang in the centre on the Hayes.

Bute Park stretches north from the castle. To its east lie the government and university buildings of Civic Centre and the student

suburb of Cathays. To its west, along Cathedral Rd, are the leafy upmarket suburbs of Pontcanna and Canton, filled with good-value guesthouses and B&Bs.

The redeveloped dockland area of Cardiff Bay lies a mile south of the city centre, clustered around the Wales Millennium Centre – not to be confused with the Millennium Stadium!

INFORMATION
Bookshops

Troutmark Books (Map p86; ☎ 2038 2814; 41-43 Castle Arcade) Biggest secondhand bookshop in the city.
Waterstone's (Map p86; ☎ 2066 7549; 2a The Hayes; ⏱ 9am–6pm Mon–Sat, till 8pm Thu, 11am–5pm Sun) Lots of Welsh-interest books, maps and guides.

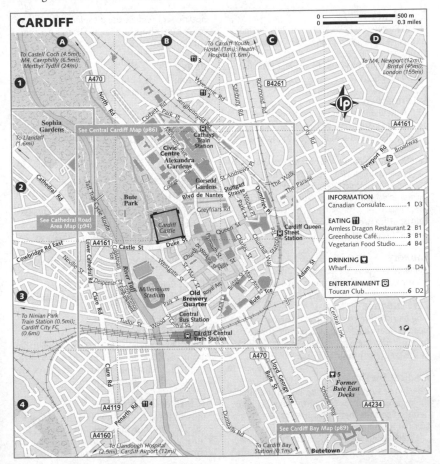

CARDIFF

INFORMATION	
Canadian Consulate	1 D3

EATING 🍴	
Armless Dragon Restaurant	2 B1
Greenhouse Café	3 B1
Vegetarian Food Studio	4 B4

DRINKING 🍷	
Wharf	5 D4

ENTERTAINMENT 🎭	
Toucan Club	6 D2

CARDIFF

CARDIFF IN...

One Day
In the morning take a look around the **National Museum Wales** (p86), then stroll through the Victorian **shopping arcades** (p101) before stopping for lunch at **Café Minuet** (p96). After a post-prandial walk in **Bute Park** (opposite), enjoy a guided tour of the spectacular Victorian Gothic interiors at **Cardiff Castle** (opposite), then take the Waterbus down the river to **Cardiff Bay** (p88) for dinner by the waterfront at **Bosphorus** (p97) or **Ba Orient** (p97). If you're up for a late night, take the bus back to town for some live music at **Clwb Ifor Bach** (p100).

Two Days
Follow the one-day itinerary, and kick off day two with a tour of the **Millennium Stadium** (p88), or a walk or bike ride out to **Llandaff Cathedral** (p91). After lunch, take a bus to **Castell Coch** (p105) or the **St Fagans National History Museum** (p104). Return to the city for dinner and in the evening try to catch a performance at the **Wales Millennium Centre** (p90).

Emergency
Heath Hospital (☎ 2074 7747; Heath Park) Two miles north of the Civic Centre, with an accident and emergency department.
Police Headquarters (Map p86; ☎ 2022 2111; King Edward VII Ave)

Internet Access
BT Internet booths These coin-operated booths are dotted around the city centre; they cost 10p per minute, 50p minimum. They also act as wi-fi hot spots for anyone with a BT OpenZone account.
Cardiff Central Library (Map p86; ☎ 2038 2116; John St; ☷ 9am-6pm Mon-Wed & Fri, 9am-7pm Thu, 9am-5.30pm Sat) Free internet access; housed in this temporary building until the new library opens on the Hayes at the end of 2008.
Tourist office (see Tourist Information below) Internet access for £1 per 30 minutes.

Laundry
Laundrette (Map p94; 87 Pontcanna St) This laundrette is convenient to the Cathedral Rd area.

Left Luggage
The **tourist office** (see Tourist Information opposite) offers a left-luggage service for £3 per item per day; there are no left-luggage facilities at the train station or airport.

Medical Services
Pharmacies rotate late opening hours; check the regional newspaper, *South Wales Echo*, for details. **Boots the Chemist** (Map p86; ☎ 2023 1291; 36 Queen St) is open till 8pm on Thursdays.
   Cardiff Shopmobility (Map p86; ☎ 2039 9355; Bridge St) is a charity that provides wheelchairs and electric scooters for the disabled to get around the central shopping area. There's no charge but donations are welcome.

Money
All major UK banks (with ATMs and currency desks) are represented along Queen St and High St.

Post
Main post office (Map p86; 45-46 Queens Arcade, Queen St; ☷ 9am-5.30pm Mon-Sat)
Post office Cathedral Road area (Map p94; 91 Pontcanna St); Cardiff Bay (Map p89; Bute St)

Tourist Information
Cardiff Bay Visitor Centre (Map p89; ☎ 2046 3833; The Tube, Harbour Drive; ☷ 9.30am-6pm)
Tourist office (Map p86; ☎ 0870 121 1258; www .visitcardiff.com; Old Library, The Hayes; ☷ 9.30am-6pm Mon-Sat, 10am-4pm Sun, till 7pm Mon-Sat Jul & Aug)

Travel Agencies
STA Travel (Map p86; ☎ 2038 2350; Duke St Arcade, 11 Duke St)

Universities
Cardiff University (☎ 2087 4000; www.cardiff.ac.uk) About 15,000 students study here, most living in the neighbourhoods of Cathays and Roath, north of the city centre.

SIGHTS & ACTIVITIES
Many of Cardiff's main sights, including the castle, Millennium Stadium and National Museum Wales, are clustered around the city centre. A mile to the southeast, Cardiff Bay –

once the old docks, now the city's fastest-developing district – has plenty more to see.

Central Cardiff
CARDIFF CASTLE
The Bute family, who transformed Cardiff from a small town into the world's biggest coal port, also transformed **Cardiff Castle** (Map p86; ☎ 2087 8100; www.cardiffcastle.com; Castle St; adult/child incl guided tour £6.95/4.30, grounds only £3.50/2.20; ⏰ 9.30am-6pm Mar-Oct, 9.30am-5pm Nov-Feb) from a medieval ruin into the landscaped grounds and kitsch Gothic fantasy you see today.

The castle complex is hidden behind high walls that follow the outline of the original Roman camp and was a secret world cut off from the outside until the Butes donated it to the city in 1947. It's a collection of buildings arranged around a grassy, peacock-inhabited courtyard, the oldest of which are the 12th-century motte-and-bailey **Norman keep** and the 13th-century **Black Tower** beside the castle entrance.

The castle's site was first occupied by the Romans in the 1st century AD. Part of the **Roman walls** remain in the southeast corner, dating from the 3rd century AD and measuring 3m across at the base. It faces a scene-stealing sculpted frieze (created by Frank Abraham in 1983) that gives a muscular impression of life under Roman occupation.

A house was built here in the 1420s by the earl of Warwick and was extended in the 17th century by the Herbert family (the earls of Pembroke), but by the time the Butes acquired it a century later it had fallen into disrepair. The first marquess of Bute hired architect Henry Holland and Holland's father-in-law, the famous landscape-architect Lancelot 'Capability' Brown, to get the house and grounds into shape.

The most recent part of the castle is the array of 19th-century towers and turrets on the west side, dominated by the colourful 40m **clock tower**. This mock-Gothic extravaganza was dreamed up by the mind-bendingly rich third marquess of Bute and his architect William Burges, a passionate eccentric who used to dress in medieval costume and was often seen with a parrot on his shoulder. Both were obsessed with Gothic architecture, religious symbolism and astrology, influences that were often combined in many of the features Burges designed, both here and at the Butes' second home at Castell Coch (p105).

The 50-minute guided tour takes you through the highlights of this flamboyant fantasy world, from the **winter smoking room**, with décor reflecting the seasons of the year (and a fright for anyone who dares listen at the door – look up as you pass through the doorway!), through the elaborate Moorish decoration of the **Arab room** (marble, sandalwood, parrots and acres of gold leaf), to the mahogany-and-mirrors narcissism of **Lord Bute's bedroom**, with a gilded statue of St John the Evangelist (the marquess' name saint) and 189 bevelled mirrors on the ceiling, which reflect the name 'John' in Greek.

The **banqueting hall** boasts a fantastically over-the-top fireplace depicting the legend of Robert the Consul and is overlooked by that medieval must-have, a minstrels' gallery. The **nursery** – perhaps the most sympathetic room in the castle – is decorated with fairy-tale characters and the **small dining room** has an ingenious table, designed so that a living vine could be slotted through it, allowing diners to pluck fresh grapes as they ate. The **roof garden** seems to underline how much of a fantasy all this really was – designed with southern Italy in mind, rather than Wales.

Housed in the Black Tower is the **Welch Regiment Museum** (Map p86; ☎ 2022 9367; www.rrw.org.uk; admission included in entry to castle grounds; ⏰ 10am-5.30pm Wed-Mon Mar-Oct, 10am-4.30pm Wed-Mon Nov-Feb), which records the military achievements of South Wales' infantry regiment.

The southeastern corner of the castle complex was being redeveloped at the time of writing and is scheduled to open in late 2007 as an interpretation centre, tearoom and new home for the Regimental Museum of 1st The Queen's Dragoon Guards.

BUTE PARK
To the west of the castle flows the River Taff, which is flanked to either side by lovely parklands that extend northwest for 1.5 miles to Llandaff. Bute Park, landscaped in the 1870s by Scots landscape architect Andrew Pettigrew and donated to the city along with the castle in 1947, Sophia Gardens, Pontcanna Fields and Llandaff Fields were all part of the Bute holdings that once extended to Castell Coch.

The southern edge of Bute Park, running west from the castle along Castle St, is a low wall topped with stone figures of lions, seals, bears and other creatures. The **Animal Wall** was designed by castle architect William Burges but only completed in 1892 after his death;

CARDIFF

it was extended and more animals added in the 1920s. A newspaper cartoon strip in the '30s brought the animals to life and many Cardiff kids grew up thinking the animals came alive at night.

In Cooper's Field, the part of the park just west of the castle, is a stone circle – not Neolithic but *fin de siècle* – erected in 1899 when Cardiff hosted the Royal National Eisteddfod (see p47). Such so-called **gorsedd stones** are found all over Wales where *eisteddfodau* (gatherings or sessions) have been held.

Nearby are the foundations of the 13thcentury **Blackfriars Priory**, which was destroyed in 1404 when Owain Glyndŵr attacked Cardiff, and later rebuilt, only to be finally vacated in 1538 when the monasteries were dissolved.

NATIONAL MUSEUM WALES

Northeast of Cardiff Castle is the Civic Centre, an early 20th-century complex of neo-Baroque buildings in gleaming white Portland stone, set around the green lawns and colourful flowerbeds of Alexandra Gardens. It houses the City Hall, police headquarters, law courts, crown offices and Cardiff University.

In the southeast corner is the splendid **National Museum Wales** (Map p86; ☎ 2039 7951; www.museumwales.ac.uk; Gorsedd Gardens Rd; admission free; ☒ 10am-5pm Tue-Sun), one of Britain's best museums, covering natural history and geology, art and archaeology. At the time of research the museum was undergoing a major refurbishment, scheduled for completion in late 2007; during this time some of the galleries may be closed.

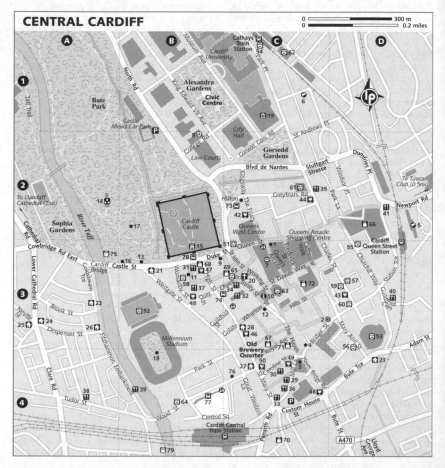

CENTRAL CARDIFF

The Evolution of Wales exhibit takes you through 4600 million years of geological history, with a rollicking multimedia display that places Wales into a global context. Spectacular films of volcanic eruptions and aerial footage of the country's stunning landscape explain how its scenery was formed, while model dinosaurs and woolly mammoths help keep the kids interested.

The natural-history displays range from cunningly camouflaged insects to the awesome 9m-long skeleton of a humpback whale that washed up near Aberthaw in 1982. The world's largest turtle (2.88m by 2.74m), which was found on Harlech beach, is now stuck here, suspended on wires from the ceiling.

The art gallery houses an incredible collection – many Impressionist and postimpressionist pieces were bequeathed to the museum in 1952 (with more in 1963) by the Davies sisters, Gwendoline and Margaret, granddaughters of 19th-century coal and shipping magnate David Davies (see p231). Treasures include luminous works by Monet and Pissaro, Sisley's *The Cliff at Penarth* (the artist was married in Cardiff) and portraits by Renoir, including the shimmering, soft and extraordinarily attractive *La Parisienne*. The sisters' favourite was Cézanne, but there are works by Matisse, too, and the anguished *Rain: Auvers* by Van Gogh, who killed himself just a few days after finishing the painting. The Pre-Raphaelites are well represented, as is Rodin, with a cast of *The Kiss*. Older works include those by El Greco, Poussin and Botticelli.

Welsh artists such as Richard Wilson, Thomas Jones, David Jones and Ceri Richards are all here, as well as Gwen and Augustus John – a highlight is John's beguilingly angelic portrayal of Dylan Thomas. Modern works include pieces by Francis Bacon, David Hockney and Rachel Whiteread.

The museum's Glanely Gallery is an interactive area where you can peer at items from the collection through microscopes and use interpretive computers. There are numerous changing exhibitions, recitals and a holiday programme of children's events.

You'll need at least three hours to see the museum properly – and it could easily take up a whole day. There are half-hour tours focusing on various aspects of the gallery every Saturday at 2pm, and regular classical and jazz concerts – call or check the website for information.

MILLENNIUM STADIUM

The giant **Millennium Stadium** (Map p86; ☎ 2082 2228; www.cardiff-stadium.co.uk; Westgate St; tours adult/child £5.50/3; ☼ 10am-6pm Mon-Sat, 10am-5pm Sun) squats like a stranded spaceship on the River Taff's east bank. Attendance at international rugby and football matches has increased dramatically since this 72,500-seat, three-tiered stadium with sliding roof was completed in time to host the 1999 Rugby World Cup.

Not everyone is happy with it: one critic called it 'an absurdly overexcited structure… that rears over the surrounding streets like a sumo wrestler'. The stadium cost £110 million to build – money that some feel could have been better spent elsewhere in the city – and big matches paralyse the city centre. But when the crowd begins to sing, the whole city resonates and all is forgiven.

The stadium has seven restaurants and 22 public bars (drinking is allowed during rugby matches but not football matches). The grass turf is actually grown on thousands of palettes (at RAF St Athan in the Vale of Glamorgan), which can be taken up for big concerts.

It's well worth taking a tour – you get to walk through the players' tunnel and sit in the VIP box. The entrance for guided tours is at Gate 3 on Westgate St. For details of matches, see p101.

ST JOHN'S CHURCH

Jutting above the city-centre shopping street is the graceful Gothic lantern tower belonging to the 15th-century parish church of St John the Baptist, with its delicate stonework that's almost like filigree. A church has stood on this site since at least 1180. Inside are simple, elegant arches: a calm retreat from the street. Regular lunchtime organ concerts are held here.

Cardiff Bay

In the 1880s Cardiff grew from one of the smallest towns in Wales to the largest, thriving on the money made by the rapidly expanding coal-export industry. In 1913 more than 13 million tonnes were exported from Cardiff docks, but after WWII demand slumped. The docklands deteriorated into a wasteland of empty basins, cut off from the city by the railway embankment. The bay outside the docks – which has one of the highest tidal ranges in the world (more than 12m between high and low water) – was ringed for up to 14 hours a day by smelly, sewage-stained mudflats. The nearby residential area of Butetown became a neglected slum.

Since 1987 the area has been completely redeveloped as Cardiff Bay, a massive commercial centre filled with gleaming new shopping centres, hotels, restaurants and government buildings. A state-of-the-art tidal barrage has turned the stinking mudflats into a vast freshwater lake, alive with yacht races on summer weekends.

On Sundays from mid-June to September there are street performers and various shows around the bay. The Cardiff Harbour Festival takes place on the August Bank Holiday weekend, with watery action in the bay itself as well as live music and fireworks.

Cardiff Bay Visitor Centre (Map p89; ☎ 2046 3833; Harbour Drive; ☼ 9.30am-6pm), housed in an oval tubular structure on the eastern side of the harbour known as the Tube, has an immense model of Cardiff Bay and stocks maps and booklets on the area and its history.

NATIONAL ASSEMBLY BUILDING

The **Pierhead Building** is one of the area's few Victorian survivors, a red-brick French-Gothic Renaissance confection built with Bute family money for the Cardiff Municipal Railway Co to impress the maritime traffic; the architect was a pupil of William Burges (who designed Cardiff Castle and Castell Coch). It now houses the **National Assembly Visitor Centre** (☎ 2089 8200; www.wales.gov.uk; admission free; ☼ 10.30am-6pm Easter-Sep, 10.30am-4.30pm Oct-Easter), a glitzy PR exercise explaining who's who and what's what at the Assembly using state-of-the-art exhibits and interactive computer displays.

Looming over it like a giant manta ray is Wales' most controversial architectural project, the **National Assembly Building** (Map p89; ☎ 2089 8477; www.wales.gov.uk; admission free; ☼ 8am-6pm Mon & Fri, 8am-8pm Tue-Thu year-round, 10.30am-6pm Sat & Sun Easter-Sep, 10.30am-4.30pm Sat & Sun Oct-Easter) – Y Senedd in Welsh – a striking structure of concrete, slate, glass and steel with a dramatic canopy roof. The underside of the roof is lined with red cedar and undulates in waves, mimicking the waves in the bay. It houses the debating chamber of the Welsh National Assembly, committee rooms and a public gallery where you can observe the debating chamber.

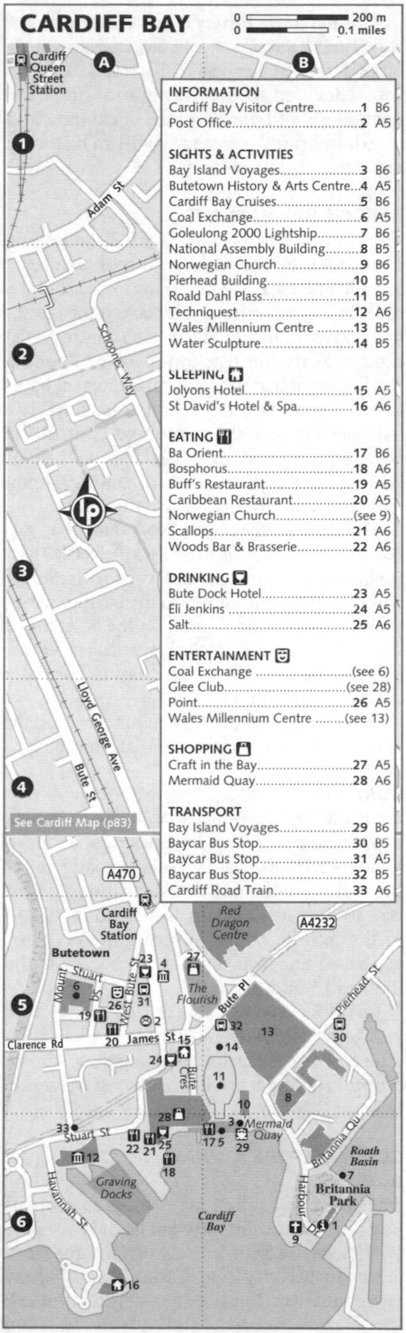
CARDIFF BAY
0 200 m
0 0.1 miles
INFORMATION
Cardiff Bay Visitor Centre 1 B6
Post Office 2 A5
SIGHTS & ACTIVITIES
Bay Island Voyages 3 B6
Butetown History & Arts Centre 4 A5
Cardiff Bay Cruises 5 B6
Coal Exchange 6 A5
Goleulong 2000 Lightship 7 B6
National Assembly Building 8 B5
Norwegian Church 9 B6
Pierhead Building 10 B5
Roald Dahl Plass 11 B5
Techniquest 12 A6
Wales Millennium Centre 13 B5
Water Sculpture 14 B5
SLEEPING
Jolyons Hotel 15 A5
St David's Hotel & Spa 16 A6
EATING
Ba Orient 17 B6
Bosphorus 18 A6
Buff's Restaurant 19 A5
Caribbean Restaurant 20 A5
Norwegian Church (see 9)
Scallops 21 A6
Woods Bar & Brasserie 22 A6
DRINKING
Bute Dock Hotel 23 A5
Eli Jenkins 24 A5
Salt 25 A6
ENTERTAINMENT
Coal Exchange (see 6)
Glee Club (see 28)
Point 26 A5
Wales Millennium Centre (see 13)
SHOPPING
Craft in the Bay 27 A5
Mermaid Quay 28 A6
TRANSPORT
Bay Island Voyages 29 B6
Baycar Bus Stop 30 B5
Baycar Bus Stop 31 A5
Baycar Bus Stop 32 B5
Cardiff Road Train 33 A6
Cardiff Queen Street Station
Adam St
Schooner Way
Lloyd George Ave
Bute St
See Cardiff Map (p83)
A470
A4232
Cardiff Bay Station
Butetown
Red Dragon Centre
The Flourish
Mount Stuart Sq
West Bute St
Bute Pl
Pierhead St
Clarence Rd
James St
Bute Cres
Mermaid Quay
Stuart St
Britannia Quay
Roath Basin
Britannia Park
Harbour Dr
Havannah St
Graving Docks
Cardiff Bay

The building has won awards for its environmentally friendly design, which includes a huge rotating cowl on the roof for power-free ventilation and a gutter system that collects rainwater for flushing the toilets. The lobby and surrounding area is littered with public artworks, including the 'meeting place', a curved bench made of 3-tonne slate blocks from Blaenau Ffestiniog, thoughtfully provided as a place for protesters to rest their legs.

The Assembly usually meets in a plenary session from 2pm on Tuesday and Wednesday, and seats in the public gallery are on a first-come, first-served basis. Guided tours of the building are available, taking in the debating chamber, committee rooms and the visitor centre. It's advisable to book a tour, but you can drop in at the Pierhead visitor centre and ask; if there's space available, they will usually let you tag along with a larger group.

HARBOURSIDE

The main commercial centre at Cardiff Bay is called **Mermaid Quay**, stacked with bars, restaurants and high-street shops, rising above the Waterbus jetty. To its east is **Roald Dahl Plass**, a vast public space (it used to be a dock basin) named after the Cardiff-born writer that serves as an open-air performance area, overseen by a soaring, stainless-steel **water sculpture**.

On the east side of the harbour, looking like it's popped out of the pages of a storybook, is the **Norwegian Church** (Map p89; ☎ 2045 4899; Harbour Dr; admission free; 🕒 9am-5pm), a white-slatted wooden building with a black witch's-hat spire. Built in 1869 beside the long-gone Bute West Dock, it was a seamen's mission, modelled on the lines of a traditional Norwegian village church. It fell into disrepair, but remained a place of worship until 1974; Roald Dahl was christened here, and served as president of the preservation trust that restored and renovated the church. It has now been reincarnated as an arts centre with an excellent café, interesting exhibitions, concerts and arts courses.

Nearby is the bright-red **Goleulong 2000 Lightship** (Map p89; ☎ 2048 7609; www.lightship2000.org.uk; admission free; 🕒 10am-5pm Mon-Sat, 2-5pm Sun), which used to be stationed off Rhossili, warning sailors away from the Helwick Swatch, a treacherous sandbank. It now houses a Christian centre with bookshop, café and exhibitions; you can also check out the neat little cabins and climb to the top of the light tower for the view.

CARDIFF

WALES MILLENNIUM CENTRE

The centrepiece and symbol of Cardiff Bay's regeneration is the outstanding **Wales Millennium Centre** (Map p89; ☎ 0870 040 2000; www.wmc .org.uk; Bute Place; admission free), an architectural masterpiece of stacked Welsh slate in shades of purple, green and grey topped with an overarching bronzed steel shell.

The roof above the main entrance is pierced by 2m-high, letter-shaped, stained-glass windows that spell out the words '*Creu Gwir fel Gwydr o Ffwrnais Awen*' (Creating truth like glass from inspiration's furnace), and 'In these stones horizons sing', composed by Gwyneth Lewis, Wales' National Poet 2005–06.

The centre is home to several major cultural organisations, including the Welsh National Opera, Academi (Welsh National Literature Promotion Agency), HiJinx Theatre, Ty Cerdd (Music Centre of Wales) and the dance company Diversions. You can wander through the public areas at will, or go on an official **guided tour** (adult/child £5/4; ☯ 9am-5pm) that will take you behind the giant letters, onto the main stage and into the dressing rooms.

TECHNIQUEST

The biggest and best science and technology discovery centre in Britain, **Techniquest** (Map p89; ☎ 2047 5475; www.tquest.org.uk; Stuart St; adult/child £6.90/4.80; ☯ 9.30am-4.30pm Mon-Fri, 10.30am-5pm Sat & Sun) has more than 160 engrossing, fun, hands-on exhibits with absorbing explanations. You can explore whirlwinds, race bubbles, play a harp with no strings and more – equally enjoyable for under-fives, stoned students and inquisitive adults. The shop has lots of quirky stuff and is reasonably priced. There's also a planetarium, which stages night-sky demonstrations and science shows.

BUTETOWN

Mount Stuart Sq, 300m northwest of the waterfront, is the heart of Victorian Butetown, once the residential district that housed the dock workers. The old **Coal Exchange** (Map p89; ☎ 2049 4917; www.coalexchange.co.uk; Mount Stuart Sq) was once the nerve centre of the Welsh coal trade, and for a time the place where international coal prices were set – it was here in March 1908 that a coal merchant wrote the world's first-ever £1 million cheque. The Exchange now houses a vibrant arts and performance venue.

The **Butetown History & Arts Centre** (Map p89; ☎ 2025 6757; www.bhac.org; 4-5 Dock Chambers, Bute St; admission free; ☯ 10am-5pm Tue-Fri, 11am-4.30pm Sat & Sun) is devoted to preserving oral histories, documents and images of the docklands, and its exhibits put the area into both an historical and present-day context.

CARDIFF BAY BARRAGE

The Cardiff Bay Barrage is a 0.75-mile-long dam enclosing the harbour. It took five years to build and created a new waterfront around 8 miles in length – a freshwater lake at the mouth of the Rivers Taff and Ely. It was a controversial project, as its construction involved flooding mudflats that had provided an important habitat for migrating and breeding waterfowl. The barrage includes sluice gates to control the water flow, three lock gates to allow passage for boats, and a fish pass that lets migrating salmon and sea trout enter and leave the rivers.

The toy-town **Cardiff Road Train** (Map p89; ☎ 2052 2729; adult/child return £4/2; ☯ hourly 11am-5pm), with live commentary, runs from Stuart St (opposite Techniquest) to the barrage along a landscaped embankment on the east side of Cardiff Bay (and is the only way to travel this route – the east side of the bay is normally closed to the public).

You can also get there by bus or car (head for Penarth Marina) or take the Waterbus ferry.

BOAT TRIPS

Bay Island Voyages (Map p89; ☎ 01446-420692; www .bayisland.co.uk) offers a range of cruises aboard high-speed RIBs (rigid inflatable boats), ranging from a half-hour thrash around Cardiff Bay to a two-hour trip to Flatholm Island in the middle of the Severn Estuary. They are based at a trailer kiosk parked near the Pierhead Building.

Cardiff Bay Cruises (Map p89; ☎ 2047 2004; www .cardiffbaycruises.com) operates three-hour evening cruises (£43 per person including three-course dinner) leaving from the marina at Mermaid Quay at 7.30pm.

GETTING THERE & AWAY
Boat

The most appealing way to reach Cardiff Bay is on the **Cardiff Waterbus** (Map p86; ☎ 07940 142409; www.cardiffwaterbus.com), which runs from jetties in the city centre to Mermaid Quay along the River Taff (£2 one way, 25 minutes); there are departures hourly, from 11.30am to 5.30pm, from Taff Meade Embankment near the train station, and twice daily, at 12.30pm and 4.30pm, from Cardiff Bridge near the castle. There are also Waterbus services from Mermaid Quay to the Cardiff Bay Barrage at Penarth (£2 one way, 20 minutes), with departures hourly from 10am to 5pm daily, and also from 6.30pm to 10.30pm on Saturdays.

Bus

The Baycar shuttle bus 6 runs to Cardiff Bay from the city centre (£1, 10 minutes, every 10 to 15 minutes), with stops outside the Hilton Hotel (on North Rd, east of the castle), St Mary St and Penarth Rd (just south of Cardiff Central train station).

Train

Shuttle trains run from Cardiff Queen St station to Cardiff Bay station (£1, four minutes, four hourly Monday to Saturday, seven daily on Sunday), from where the harbour is a quartermile walk. From Cathays or Central stations you have to change at Queen St.

Llandaff

Llandaff is a peaceful suburb 2 miles north of the centre, a village clustered around a green that has been swallowed up by the expanding city. Set in a hollow on the west bank of the River Taff is the imposingly beautiful **Llandaff Cathedral** (Map p89; ☎ 2056 4554; www.llandaffcathedral .org.uk; Cathedral Rd; admission free; ⏰ 7.30am-6pm Mon-Tue, Thu & Sat, 7.30am 7.30pm Wed, 7.30am-6.30pm Sun), built on the site of a 6th-century monastery founded by St Teilo.

The present cathedral dates from 1130 – it crumbled throughout the Middle Ages, and during the Reformation and Civil War it was used as an alehouse and then an animal shelter. Derelict by the 18th century, it was largely rebuilt in the 19th century and extensively restored after being damaged by a German bomb in 1941. The towers at the western end epitomise the cathedral's fragmented history – one was built in the 15th century, the other in the 19th. Inside, plain glass windows provide a striking clarity of light. A giant arch carries the organ and the huge, aluminium sculpture *Majestas* – its modern style a bold shock in contrast to Sir Jacob Epstein's gracious, vaulted space. Pre-Raphaelite groupies will like the Burne-Jones reredos (screens) in St Dyfrig's chapel

and the stained glass by Rossetti and William Morris' company.

Buses 24, 25, 33, 33A and 62 (15 minutes, every 10 to 15 minutes) run along Cathedral Rd to Llandaff.

WALKING TOUR

This tour consists of two parts. The first is a meander around the city centre, taking in the major sights. The second part strikes out through Bute Park to reach the cathedral at Llandaff.

For the first part of this walk, start from **Cardiff Bridge (1)** on Castle St, head east towards Cardiff Castle on the north side of the street, and take a look at the creatures perched on top of the **Animal Wall** (2; p85). Originally by the castle's south gate, the animals were moved here after WWI. Turn right on Womanby St, which is lined with warehouses. 'Womanby' has Viking roots and possibly means 'the strangers' quarter' or 'quarter of the keeper of the hounds'. On your right you'll see the **Millennium Stadium** (3; p88) looming over you.

Take a left on Quay St, then right on High St and left again to enter the **Central Market (4)** – this cast-iron market hall has been selling fresh produce and hardware since 1891. There's an old market office and clock tower in the centre. Exit on the far side on Trinity St; across the street to your right is the **Old Library (5)**, which houses the tourist office. The south façade features figures representing calligraphy, literature, printing, rhetoric and study. The motto *'Ny bydd ddoeth ny ddarlleno'* means 'he will not be wise who will not read'.

Go left around the Old Library and then north on Working St towards the castle, past **St John's Church** (6; p88). When you reach the junction with Queen St go right, then left into the Friary. Continue across the Blvd de Nantes (named after one of Cardiff's twin towns) to leafy **Gorsedd Gardens (7)**. Looming over the gardens are the splendid **City Hall (8)**, the **National Museum Wales (9**; p86) and the **Law Courts (10)**. Turn left, and cross busy North Rd to enter **Bute Park (11**; p85).

For the second part of the walk, follow the path into the park past the ruins of **Blackfriars Priory (12**; p86) on the right, then turn right and follow the east bank of the river northwards along a tree-shaded path for a mile until you reach a weir. Cross the footbridge

CARDIFF

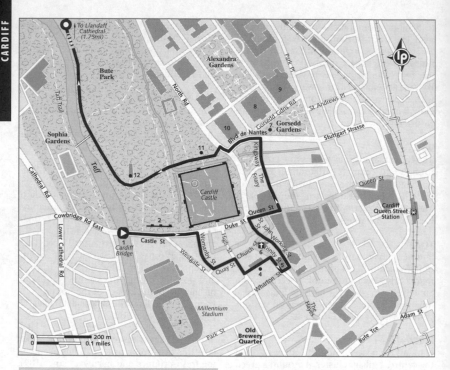

WALKING TOUR

Part One 1 mile, 30 minutes
Part Two 2 miles, one hour

above the weir and take the footpath that bears slightly left across the playing fields (signposted Pontcanna).

When you come to a sealed, tree-lined path turn right and follow it for another half-mile to the busy road of Western Avenue. Turn left, cross the road via the footbridge and continue past Llandaff Rugby Club, then turn right on a footpath that passes between rugby pitches on the left and a cemetery on the right. You will emerge at the foot of Cathedral Close with **Llandaff Cathedral** (p91) rising beyond.

CARDIFF FOR CHILDREN

A friendly, manageable city, Cardiff is a great place for kids and has a particularly good range of child-friendly sights. Possibly best of all is **Techniquest** (p90) at Cardiff Bay, but the **National Museum Wales** (p86) is also well geared towards younger visitors. Children will enjoy

the **Cardiff Road Train** (p90) at Cardiff Bay and **boat trips** (p90) to visit the barrage. If the sun's shining, there are the wide expanses of **Bute Park** (p85) to explore. Just outside Cardiff is the splendid **St Fagans National History Museum** (p104), with lots of activities during the summer, and the great castles of **Caerphilly** (p105) and **Castell Coch** (p105).

TOURS

City Sightseeing (☎ 2038 4291; www.guidefriday.com; ☑ daily Apr-Oct, Sat & Sun only Nov-Dec & Mar) runs open-top bus tours of the city, departing every 30 to 60 minutes from outside Cardiff Castle and taking in the Civic Centre, Cardiff Bay and the Millennium Stadium. Tickets (adult £7.50, child £3) are valid for 24 hours, and you can hop on and off at any of the stops. A nonstop circuit takes an hour.

There's a one-hour, wheelchair-friendly **Creepy Cardiff Ghost Tour** (☎ 07980 975135; www .creepycardiff.com; adult/child £5/4) that starts outside the National Museum Wales at 7.30pm most nights; book in advance.

See also p90 for details of boat trips from Cardiff Bay.

FESTIVALS & EVENTS

The biggest event on Cardiff's calendar is the five-week **Cardiff Festival** (☎ 2087 2087; www.cardiff -festival.com), running from late June to early August. Events in the festival include the Welsh Proms (10 days of concerts at St David's Hall); as well as jazz, roots and world music at a variety of venues; an international food and drink festival; funfairs, music and street theatre; open-air theatre at the St Fagans National History Museum; and a carnival at Mermaid Quay with samba bands and dance troupes. The fun culminates with the UK's largest free outdoor festival, the Big Weekend (first weekend in August), with the Lord Mayor's Parade, a funfair and live bands at the Civic Centre.

Cardiff's gay pride festival, **Mardi Gras** (☎ 2046 1564; www.cardiffmardigras.co.uk), is held in late August or early September at Cooper's Field, behind the castle. It gets bigger every year and local clubs hold special postcarnival events.

Gŵyl Ifan (☎ 2056 3989; www.gwylifan.org) is a Welsh folk-dancing festival held over three days in late June. It includes a grand procession through the city centre, a fair on the lawns outside City Hall, mass dancing at Cardiff Bay and workshops at the Thistle Hotel.

The 11-day **International Film Festival of Wales** (☎ 2031 1082; www.iffw.co.uk) is held in November, with sessions promoting new Welsh talent, glitzy premiere screenings, debates and guest appearances. There's also the opportunity to vote in the Audience Award for the best Welsh feature film.

SLEEPING

It can be almost impossible to find a bed in the city centre on big sporting weekends, especially rugby internationals, so keep an eye on the fixtures and choose another date or book well in advance. The tourist office can book a room for you for a fee of £2.

A Space in the City (☎ 0845 260 7050; www.aspace inthecity.co.uk) is an agency that lets out luxury, short-stay apartments in the city centre and at Cardiff Bay; rates begin at around £90 a night for a one-bedroom flat and there's a minimum two-night stay.

The best area for midrange accommodation is tree-lined Cathedral Rd, a 15- to 20-minute walk from the centre, or a £3 to £4 taxi ride from the train or bus station.

City Centre

BUDGET

NosDa @ Cardiff Backpackers (Map p86; ☎ 2034 5577; www.cardiffbackpacker.com; 98 Neville St; dm s/d £18/28/43) This is a well-run, popular independent hostel just over half a mile from the train and bus stations. There are singles, doubles and dorms, and a funky, late-opening bar to match the cheery brightness of the rest of the place.

NosDa @ The Riverbank (Map p86; ☎ 2037 8866; www .nosda.co.uk; 53-59 Despenser St; dm/s/d £19/36/52; P ⌨) You won't find a budget bed any closer to the city centre than this stylishly refurbished hostel right across the river from the Millennium Stadium. It's family-friendly, and there's an attractive in-house bar and restaurant.

Millers Tavern (Map p86; ☎ 2023 7605; janet@the millerstavern.com; 3-5 Brook St; s/d from £25/40) If you don't mind staying upstairs from a lively real-ale pub, this no-frills B&B is another decent city-centre choice, with a guest kitchen where you can rustle up your own grub.

Austin's Guest House (Map p86; ☎ 2037 7148; www .hotelcardiff.com; 11 Coldstream Tce; s/d from £35/45) The location is the main attraction here, just five minutes' walk from the castle. The bedrooms are pretty basic (there are cheaper ones with shared toilets) and the owner is friendly and helpful.

MIDRANGE

Sandringham Hotel (Map p86; ☎ 2023 2161; www .sandringham-hotel.com; 21 St Mary St; s/d from £40/55) They don't come much more central than the Sandringham. It may be nothing special in the décor department, but it's friendly and welcoming, and right in the thick of things – a good place to stay if you're here for the nightlife. There's a 24-hour reception, and no questions asked if you stagger in at 3am. Ask for a top-floor room at the back if you want to avoid street noise.

Big Sleep (Map p86; ☎ 2063 6363; www.thebigsleep hotel.com; Bute Tce; d £58-120; P ⌨) Billed as a 'designer hotel on a budget' and housed in a mirrored tower block, this place feels stark and functional despite the self-consciously cool colour schemes, Ikea furniture and (mostly) spacious rooms. Not bad value – especially on Sunday nights, when prices plunge – given the location and comfort level.

TOP END

Angel Hotel (Map p86; ☎ 2064 9200; www.paramount -hotels.co.uk/angel; Castle St; s/d from £95/105; P ⌨)

CARDIFF

Across the street from the castle, this lavishly refurbished Victorian confection was founded in 1883 by the third marquess of Bute. The rooms are richly furnished – many have castle views – and the lavish décor just manages to stay on the right side of chintzy.

Royal Hotel (Map p86; ☎ 2055 0750; www.theroyal hotelcardiff.com; 10 St Mary St; d £119-169; 🖳) Egyptian cotton sheets, goose-down pillows and fluffy bath robes contribute to a high pamper factor at this central boutique hotel, with sharp styling in shades of chocolate and cream with splashes of red. Just across the street from the train station.

Cathays Area
Cardiff Youth Hostel (YHA; Map p86; ☎ 0870 770 5750; 2 Wedal Rd, Roath Park; dm £18; 🅿 🖳) A spacious, modern red-brick hostel 2 miles north of the city centre, this place has a large, well-equipped kitchen and also has secure cycle storage. Take buses 28, 29 or 29B from the bus station.

Cardiff University (Map p86; ☎ 2087 4702; www .cardiff.ac.uk/resid; Southgate House, Bevan Pl; s from £22)

Single rooms with en suite in the Talybont Halls of Residence, 1.5 miles north of the city centre, are available from June to September on a B&B or self-catering basis.

Cathedral Road Area
Long, leafy Cathedral Rd is lined with loads of midrange accommodation, nearly all of it in restored Victorian town houses – wander along and take your pick.

BUDGET
Cardiff Caravan Park (Map p94; ☎ 2039 8362; Pontcanna Fields, off Cathedral Rd; sites per person £4.25, per car £2.70) This is an excellent camp site – a peaceful spot surrounded by wooded parkland but only a short walk from the city centre. Bicycle hire available on-site.

Welsh Institute for Sport (Map p94; ☎ 2030 0500; www.welsh-institute-sport.co.uk; Sophia Gardens; s/d from £27/54) Just off Cathedral Rd, this institute offers plain but functional rooms, some of them equipped for wheelchair users; guests can use the pool and fitness room for free. It gets booked out for big weekend sports events, so call ahead.

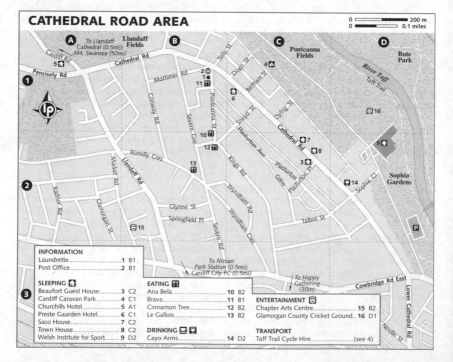

CATHEDRAL ROAD AREA

0   200 m
0   0.1 miles

INFORMATION		
Laundrette	1	B1
Post Office	2	B1

SLEEPING 🛏		
Beaufort Guest House	3	C2
Cardiff Caravan Park	4	C1
Churchills Hotel	5	A1
Preste Gaarden Hotel	6	C1
Saco House	7	C2
Town House	8	C2
Welsh Institute for Sport	9	D2

EATING 🍴		
Ana Bela	10	B2
Brava	11	B1
Cinnamon Tree	12	B2
Le Gallois	13	B2

DRINKING 🍺 🍷		
Cayo Arms	14	D2

ENTERTAINMENT 🎭		
Chapter Arts Centre	15	B2
Glamorgan County Cricket Ground	16	D1

TRANSPORT		
Taff Trail Cycle Hire	(see 4)	

MIDRANGE

Preste Gaarden Hotel (Map p94; ☎ 2022 8607; www .cosycardiffhotel.co.uk; 181 Cathedral Rd; s/d £35/55) Expect a friendly welcome at this Victorian B&B, which offers good value despite some rooms (especially the bathrooms) being a bit cramped. There are cheaper rooms with shared bathrooms.

Town House (Map p94; ☎ 2023 9399; www.thetown housecardiff.co.uk; 70 Cathedral Rd; s/d from £45/63; (P)) Yet another elegant Victorian town house with a welcoming owner, the Town House retains lots of period features, including mosaic-tiled hallway, original fireplaces and stained glass, though the décor in the bedrooms is a bit on the flowery side.

Beaufort Guest House (Map p94; ☎ 2023 7003; www .beauforthousecardiff.co.uk; 65 Cathedral Rd; s/d from £49/65; (P)) The Beaufort has a plush, upmarket feel, and despite having had a thorough refurbishment it retains a Victorian atmosphere with period-style furniture, gilt mirrors, heavy drapes and even the odd portrait of Queen Vic herself.

Churchills Hotel (Map p94; ☎ 2040 1300; www .churchillshotel.co.uk; Cardiff Rd; s/d from £65/75; (P)) A stylish town-house hotel on the edge of Llandaff Fields, the Churchill offers bright, modern bedrooms in the main building plus attractive suites with separate lounges in the adjoining mews cottages.

Saco House (Map p94; ☎ 0845 122 0405; www.saco apartments.co.uk; 74-76 Cathedral Rd; 1-/2-bedroom apt £123/153; (P)) This Victorian town house has been given a stylish contemporary makeover and converted into serviced apartments, complete with comfortable lounges and fitted kitchens. The two-bedroom apartments are good value for families with kids and there's an extra sofa bed in the lounge.

Cardiff Bay

There's not much in the way of budget accommodation in Cardiff's shiny new waterfront development.

Jolyons Hotel (Map p89; ☎ 2048 8775; www.jolyons .co.uk; 5 Bute Cres; d £85-195) A touch of Georgian elegance in the heart of Cardiff Bay, Jolyons is a small boutique hotel with six individually designed rooms combining antique furniture with contemporary colours and chic lighting. There are slate tiles in the stylish bathrooms (one with a whirlpool bath), crisp cotton sheets on the luxurious beds and a snug lounge bar with leather sofas and log-burning stove.

St David's Hotel & Spa (Map p89; ☎ 2045 4045; www .thestdavidshotel.com; Havannah St; d £260, ste £290-550; (P) (□)) A glittering, glassy tower topped with a sail-like flourish, St David's has become Cardiff Bay's signature skyline, a Sydney Opera House on the Taff. Expect five-star luxury – every room has a private balcony with harbour view – smart, understated style, and attentive service. The hotel's marine spa offers a range of therapies, as well as a pool, sauna and fitness rooms.

EATING

The Cardiff restaurant scene is booming, whether you'd like a bacon butty (bacon sandwich) or a bed of rocket.

If all you're after is some inexpensive fast food, look no further than the burger triangle of Mill Lane, Caroline St and St Mary St, the main refuelling centre for Saturday night clubbers, or City Rd in the student quarter northeast of the city centre, a mile-long strip of kebab and curry heaven.

City Centre

BUDGET

Cornish Bakehouse (Map p86; ☎ 2066 5041; 11 Church St; snacks £1.50-4; ☾ 9am-6pm Mon-Sat, 10.30am-5pm Sun) This bakery conjures up every imaginable variety of Cornish pasty, from traditional steak, potato and onion, to cheese and bacon or lamb and mint, as well as muffins and coffee, which you can eat standing up or take away.

New York Deli (Map p86; ☎ 2038 8388; 20 High St Arcade; mains £2-4; ☾ 9am-5pm Mon-Sat) This tiny wood-panelled café serves up giant, US-style sandwiches – one between two is enough for most mortals – stacked bagels and big mugs of coffee. There's a good breakfast menu too, but get in early as there are only a couple of tables.

Vegetarian Food Studio (Map p83; ☎ 2023 8222; 109 Penarth Rd; mains £3-5; ☾ 10am-9.30pm Tue & Wed, 10am-10pm Thu-Sun) This is an unassuming café and takeaway south of the city centre, which has earned a reputation for serving the tastiest and most authentic Gujarati vegetarian cuisine in the city.

Madame Fromage (Map p86; ☎ 2064 4888; 18 Castle Arcade, High St; mains £3-6; ☾ 9am-5pm Mon-Sat) One of Cardiff's finest delicatessens, with a wide range of charcuterie and French and Welsh cheeses, Madame also has a café with tables in the arcade, serving tasty platters of cheese with bread and salad, all kinds of sandwiches, and excellent coffee.

Café Minuet (Map p86; ☎ 2034 1794; 42 Castle Arcade, High St; mains £4-6; 🕑 10am-5pm Mon-Sat) Don't be fooled by the bare floorboards, folding chairs and paper tablecloths – this unassuming café produces some of the best Italian food in town. The menu includes several good vegetarian dishes, such as *stracciatella alla Romana* (a light soup of vegetable stock with pasta, beaten egg and parmesan, served with garlic bread) and deep-fried mushrooms stuffed with spinach and cheese.

Cardiff Central Market (Map p86; ☎ 2087 1214; St Mary St; 🕑 8am-5.30pm Mon-Sat) The city's handsome Victorian covered market is the place to stock up with picnic goodies such as fresh bread, cheese, cold meats, barbecued chicken, cakes and pastries.

MIDRANGE

Ask (Map p86; ☎ 2034 4665; 24-32 Wyndham Arcade, Mill Lane; mains £6-8) We don't normally bother recommending chain restaurants, but this Italian pizza and pasta joint really stands out as a good-value, family-friendly place with really tasty food, where the kids are made just as welcome as the adults.

Bali (Map p86; ☎ 2037 4700; 30-32 Caroline St; mains £6-9) Smiling waiters, low lighting and crisp linen napkins make for a warm and inviting atmosphere at this Southeast Asian restaurant. The menu gets your mouth watering with a list of Malay, Singapore and Indonesian classics such as satay, laksa, sambal, rendang and nasi goreng, and the kitchen does not disappoint, turning out authentically fragrant and spicy dishes.

Riverside Cantonese (Map p86; ☎ 2037 2163; 44 Tudor St; mains £7-10; 🕑 noon-11.30pm Mon-Sat, noon-10.30pm Sun) A stylish Chinese restaurant that eschews the traditional red and gold décor and paper lanterns for a more modern blonde-wood, apricot and green colour scheme, the Riverside is well known for its authentic Cantonese cuisine, including classic dishes such as salt-and-pepper prawns. There's also a dim-sum menu (served noon to 5pm).

Thai House Restaurant (Map p86; ☎ 2038 7404; 3-5 Guildford Cres; mains £8-12; 🕑 closed Sun) Wales' oldest Thai restaurant has been around for more than 20 years and is still winning awards. Warm yellow walls, polished wood and candle light make for an intimate atmosphere, and the Thai chefs certainly know their stuff, using fresh ingredients flown in from Bangkok every week.

Juboraj II (Map p86; ☎ 2037 7668; 10 Mill Lane; mains £8-12; 🕑 closed Mon) No flock wallpaper or Bollywood soundtrack here – Juboraj sports a stylish, modern brasserie look and serves a selection of classic north Indian and Bangladeshi dishes; try the tandoori trout, crisp outside, spicy and succulent within, or the duck karahi, cooked with peppers, onions, tomatoes and spices.

Champers (Map p86; ☎ 2037 2164; 61-62 St Mary St; tapas £3-4, mains £10-16; 🕑 noon-2.30pm & 7pm-midnight Mon-Sat, 7pm-midnight Sun) This relaxed Spanish wine bar has Andalucian-style wooden furniture set on a sawdust-scattered floor, lots of basket-work lampshades and low ceiling beams. Order a bottle of Rioja, then choose fish or meat from the counter to be cooked as you like, a plate of Serrano ham sliced from the bone or a selection from the tapas menu.

Zushi (Map p86; ☎ 2066 9911; The Aspect, 140 Queen St; sushi portions £1.50-3.50; 🕑 noon-10pm Mon-Sat, noon-5pm Sun) Popularised by local celebs (it's a favourite of Welsh rugby international Gavin Henson and girlfriend Charlotte Church), this is a desperately trendy sushi bar complete with colour-coded dishes on conveyor belts. OK, it ain't exactly Nobu, but the sushi is fresh and prettily prepared, and won't break the bank.

TOP END

Da Venditto (Map p86; ☎ 2023 0781; 7-8 Park Pl; mains £11-20; 🕑 closed Sun) Polished-wood floors, white linen tablecloths and blue napkins help create a formal, elegant setting for a menu of modern Italian cuisine, with offerings such as platters of smoked fish with lemon vinaigrette, crab and laver-bread risotto, linguini with lobster, and fillet steak with a white wine, cream and parmesan sauce.

Cathays

Armless Dragon Restaurant (Map p86; ☎ 2038 2357; 97 Wyeverne Rd, Cathays; mains £11-18; 🕑 closed Sat lunch, Sun & Mon) One of Cardiff's first foodie restaurants and still one of the best, the Dragon pretty much created what is now called 'modern Welsh cuisine' – that is, taking the finest Welsh produce and traditional Welsh recipes and giving them a contemporary gourmet twist.

Greenhouse Café (Map p83; ☎ 2023 5731; 38 Woodville Rd; 1-/2-/3-course menu £10/15/18; 🕑 closed Sun & Mon) A quirky little place with bare floorboards and mauve walls, this restaurant cooks up imaginative and adventurous vegetarian and vegan dishes accompanied by an excellent wine list.

AUTHOR'S CHOICE

Le Gallois (Map p94; ☎ 2034 1264; 6-10 Romilly Cres, Canton; mains £17-26; ☺ closed Sun) The name says it all – Le Gallois is French for 'the Welshman', and the Welsh owner-chef Padrig Jones has made his name by giving a Continental twist to the best of Welsh produce. An unfussy dining room of pale cream walls, polished-walnut tables and starched-linen napkins makes sure the focus is on the food – the menu of half-a-dozen starters and half-a-dozen main courses changes with the seasons, but signature dishes include confit of rabbit with roast langoustine, tomato and basil risotto, and roast monkfish and crispy noodles with claret sauce and Asian pesto. This is the place for a very special dinner or, if you want to sample some very special cooking without breaking the bank, an extremely good-value set lunch.

Cathedral Road Area

Happy Gathering (Map p94; ☎ 2039 7531; 233 Corbridge Rd E; mains £6-12; ☺ noon-10.45pm Mon-Thu, noon-11.45pm Fri & Sat, noon-9pm Sun) It's always a sign of a good Chinese restaurant when you see the local Chinese community eating there, and you'll see them in force at this popular, long-established place (it's been around for more than 30 years). Noisy, good-natured atmosphere, good service, and kids are made welcome.

Brava (Map p94; ☎ 2037 1929; 71 Pontcanna St; mains £8-12; ☺ 9am-3.45pm Mon, 9am-9pm Tue-Sat, 10am-3.45pm Sun) A cool café decorated with modern prints by local artists, with tables spilling onto the pavement in summer, Brava not only serves great coffee and wine, but also has a menu of bistro favourites, from risotto or steak sandwiches to stir-fried noodles.

Cinnamon Tree (Map p94; ☎ 2037 4433; 173 Kings Rd; mains £7-13) A cut above your usual curry house, the Cinnamon Tree has stylish, modern décor and a menu of specialities that includes unusual dishes such as *tharav sofyani* (duck seasoned with chilli, coriander and fenugreek in a thick, spicy sauce) and *hiran champan* (venison cooked with roast garlic cloves, onion and coriander seeds).

Ana Bela (Map p94; ☎ 2023 9393; 5 Pontcanna St; mains £15-21; ☺ noon-1.45pm & 7-9pm) This is a good place for a romantic dinner – chic but laid-back, with low light and candles, art on the walls and cool tunes – provided you don't mind putting your hand in your pocket. Prices are steep, but the food is superb. Try seared salmon fillet with puy lentils and bacon in a red-wine jus, roast loin of lamb with roasted red-pepper chutney. There's excellent house wine at just £12 a bottle.

Cardiff Bay

Norwegian Church (Map p89; ☎ 2045 4899; Harbour Dr; mains £3-6) Housed in a whitewashed wooden church that now houses an arts centre, this is a homely little café with a view of the harbour, serving excellent cakes, waffles, sandwiches and light lunches.

Buff's Restaurant (Map p89; ☎ 2046 4628; www .buffsrestaurant.co.uk; 8 Mount Stuart Sq; mains £4.75-13; ☺ noon-11pm) Hidden away from the crowds on the waterfront, this is a snug wine bar and restaurant that's popular with local business people, serving straightforward but well-prepared dishes such as crab cakes, fillet steak and roast lamb.

Caribbean Restaurant (Map p89; ☎ 2025 2102; 14 West Bute St; mains £7-9) Decorated in sunny Caribbean colours, this is a small, no-frills, family-run restaurant that dishes up hearty Caribbean home cooking. Service can be slow, but that's all part of the charm – you can natter away over a couple of cans of Red Stripe before tucking into a plate of jerk chicken or saltfish with a bowl of rice-and-peas.

Ba Orient (Map p89; ☎ 2046 3939; 27 Mermaid Quay; set lunch £9, mains £8-11; ☺ food served noon-3pm & 6-11pm Mon-Fri, 1-10pm Sat & Sun) One of the hottest spots at Cardiff Bay, this sophisticated cocktail and dim-sum bar cultivates an oriental atmosphere with low tables, carved wooden benches and Japanese tatami mats. The dim sum is both delicious and beautifully presented, and there are larger dishes such as aromatic crispy duck, plus an accomplished cocktail menu to explore.

Bosphorus (Map p89; ☎ 2048 7477; Mermaid Quay; mains £10-14) Sitting out over the water on its own private pier, this Turkish restaurant enjoys good views all round; the best of all are from the outdoor tables at the far end of the jetty. The food is as far removed from the humble kebab as Cardiff is from Istanbul, based on imperial Ottoman cuisine – succulent *piliç güveç* (chicken casserole), charcoal-grilled lamb, and crisp scallop and bacon shashlik.

Scallops (Map p89; ☎ 2049 7495; 2 Mermaid Quay; mains £11-17; ☯ noon-3pm & 7-10.30pm) No surprise that pride of place on the menu here goes to fresh seafood – from seared scallops with pea and mint purée to full-on lobster thermidor. The brightly decorated dining room is complemented by an attractive al fresco terrace with a view of the bay.

Woods Bar & Brasserie (Map p89; ☎ 2049 2400; Stuart St; mains £11-17; ☯ closed Sun dinner) Housed in the historic Pilotage Building, but given a minimalist, modern makeover inside, Woods is frequented by politicians from the nearby Welsh Assembly. The cuisine is modern European, light and flavoursome, with dishes such as roast fillet of red snapper with tomato and basil sauce, and vegetarian lasagne with hazelnut pesto.

DRINKING

Cardiff is a legendary boozing town, and right up there with Dublin and Prague when it comes to hen and stag parties – most Friday and Saturday nights see the city centre invaded by hordes of beered-up lads dressed in ladies' underwear, and sparkly stetsoned, stilettoed ladettes tottering from club to karaoke bar to kebab shop. Wednesdays are student nights, with cheap drink promos prompting a wave of midweek overindulgence.

The main pub-crawl area is the triangle formed by Mill Lane, Caroline St and St Mary St (tacky is a word that comes in handy here – it covers the décor, the music and the feel of the floors underfoot) but away from here Cardiff offers plenty of appealing places to drink, from traditional Edwardian pubs to stylish designer bars.

Don't forget to try the local Brains SA (meaning Special Ale, Same Again or Skull Attack depending on how many you've had), brewed by the same family concern since 1713.

City Centre

Goat Major (Map p86; ☎ 2033 7161; 33 High St) Solidly traditional, with armchairs, a fireplace, and lip-smacking Brains Dark real ale on tap, the Goat Major (ask the bar staff about the name) is an oasis of old-fashioned calm amid the noise and bustle of trendy city-centre bars.

Cantaloop (Map p86; ☎ 2037 7014; 23 Greyfriars Rd) Set in a lovely old red-brick building, Cantaloop is a terminally hip designer lounge bar, with lots of polished wood and leather sofas, an extensive cocktail menu and a Havana

cigar bar. There's also a nice outdoor terrace for summer-evening drinks.

Yard (Map p86; ☎ 2022 7577; 42-43 St Mary St) Occupying the site of an 18th-century brewery, Yard sports an industrial-chic décor of stainless steel, polished copper pipes and zinc ducting, with a trad-looking bar in front and clubby sofas in back. Outdoor tables, good food and a child-friendly policy pulls in families at lunchtime, while cocktails and DJs attract a young party crowd at night.

Bar Cuba (Map p86; ☎ 2039 7967; The Friary) A colourful Cuban-themed bar, where you can lounge on the big sofas and sip a San Miguel or Cuba libre (happy hour from 7pm Friday) before heading to the dance floor to show off your red-hot Latin moves (if they're not so hot, there are salsa classes at 8.30pm on Tuesday).

Tafarn @ NosDa (Map p86; ☎ 2037 8866; 53-59 Despenser St) A cool little bar attached to an upmarket backpacker hostel (see p93), Tafarn has outdoor tables on a riverside terrace, a big screen for watching all the rugby action and an all-day menu of tasty Welsh snacks.

Cottage (Map p86; ☎ 2023 8228; 25 St Mary St) A long, narrow pub with a traditional atmosphere – wooden floor, brass drip trays, polished mahogany bar – the Cottage attracts a mix of characters, from weary shoppers to local office workers, and offers guest real ales as an alternative to the ubiquitous Brains.

City Arms (Map p86; ☎ 2022 5258; Quay St) A friendly, unpretentious, old-fashioned pub with a classics-crammed jukebox, the City Arms is predictably packed out on rugby weekends (the Millennium Stadium is right across the road), but offers a pleasant place for a quiet pint on weekday afternoons.

Cathedral Road Area

Cayo Arms (Map p94; ☎ 2039 1910; 36 Cathedral Rd) This is a real-ale pub with warm atmosphere and a loyal band of regulars. It serves a fine range of Tomos Watkins real ales, plus guest beers such as Old Speckled Hen, and is filled to bursting on match days.

Cardiff Bay

Salt (Map p89; ☎ 2049 4375; Mermaid Quay) A huge, modern, nautical-themed bar (ocean-liner décor, blue-and-white drapes, bits of driftwood, pictures of the Welsh coast) with plenty of sofas and armchairs for lounging around and, best of all, a 1st-floor open-air terrace with a view of the yachts out in the bay.

Eli Jenkins (Map p89; ☎ 2044 0921; 7-8 Bute Cres) Named after the vicar in Dylan Thomas' *Under Milk Wood*, this is a trad-style pub set in a Victorian terrace, with wood-panelling, bookcases and a big screen for the rugby. It's a popular spot for an after-show drink for performers at the Wales Millennium Centre across the square.

Bute Dock Hotel (Map p89; ☎ 2065 1426; W Bute St) Originally a Victorian coaching inn, the Bute Dock is a proper local pub, a welcome antidote to the trendy bars of Mermaid Quay. Open-mic sessions on Friday nights keep the pub-singer tradition alive, with amateurs belting out renditions of Tom Jones classic hits.

Wharf (Map p83; ☎ 2040 5092; 121 Schooner Way) A huge glass-and-brick building with a Victorian-industrial look, the Wharf is a big family-friendly pub with a children's area and picnic tables overlooking the water. There's regular entertainment, with live music Monday and Saturday, and stand-up comedy on Thursday.

ENTERTAINMENT

Cardiff's club scene is hardly going to set the night on fire, but there's plenty to explore, especially if you're into the alternative side of things, and there's no shortage of decent live-music venues. The sporting calendar is a busy one, offering everything from county cricket to international rugby, while culture vultures can choose between the Welsh National Opera at the Millennium Centre, or the Welsh Proms at St David's Hall. *Buzz* is a free monthly magazine with up-to-date entertainment listings in the city, available from the tourist office and entertainment venues.

Cinemas

Chapter Arts Centre (Map p94; ☎ 2030 4400; www .chapter.org; Market Rd, Canton) The city's main arts centre has a full and varied programme of arthouse cinema.

Vue (Map p86; ☎ 08712 240 240; www.myvue .com; Millennium Plaza, Wood St) Huge 14-screen multiplex.

GAY & LESBIAN CARDIFF

Cardiff has a relaxed and thriving gay and lesbian scene, with most clubs and bars centred around Charles St – for listings and general information check www.gaywales.co.uk.

The big event is the annual **Mardi Gras festival**, held in late August or early September (see p93) – the local clubs run special nights over this weekend too.

Pubs, Clubs & Saunas

Bar Icon (Map p86; ☎ 2034 4300; 60 Charles St) A newcomer on the scene, Icon is an ultrastylish cocktail bar decked out in designer shades of olive green and chocolate brown, with comfy sofas and laid-back tunes; it pulls in a mixed crowd of gay and straight, male and female, young and old.

Golden Cross (Map p86; ☎ 2039 4556; www.thegolden.co.uk; 283 Hayes Bridge Rd) One of the oldest pubs in the city and a long-standing gay venue, this Victorian bar retains its handsome stained glass, polished wood and ceramic tiles. A daytime atmosphere of relaxed local drinking den escalates into full-on party mode in the evenings, with a crowded programme of drag, cabaret, quiz and karaoke nights.

Kings Cross (Map p86; ☎ 2064 9890; www.kxcardiff.co.uk; 25 Caroline St) Prominently positioned at one end of Cardiff's café quarter, the recently tarted-up KX (as its known) is a stalwart of the gay scene, with cabaret on Wednesday, DJs on Friday and Saturday, and karaoke on Sunday.

Club X (Map p86; ☎ 2025 8838; www.club-x-cardiff.co.uk; 35 Charles St; admission £5; ⏰ 10pm-3am Wed, 9pm-4am Fri, 9pm-6am Sat) Cardiff's biggest gay club has two dance floors, with a great chill-out bar and covered beer garden upstairs. Wednesday night is student night, with cheap drinks, but Saturday is the big one, with chart hits out front and dirty house in the back room. It's also open on the last Sunday of the month (11.30pm to 4am).

Exit Bar (Map p86; ☎ 2064 0102; www.exitcardiff.com; 48 Charles St) A friendly, attitude-free bar with DJs filling the two dance floors and retro disco hits and dance music every night of the week till 2am or 3am. The Exit is another popular, long-standing gay venue.

Locker Room (Map p86; ☎ 2022 0388; www.lockerroomcardiff.co.uk; 50 Charles St; admission £11; ⏰ noon-11pm Mon-Fri, nonstop noon Sat-10pm Sun) Gay men's health club and sauna.

Cineworld (Map p86; ☎ 0871 200 2000; www.ugc cinemas.co.uk; Mary Ann St) An even huger 15-screen multiplex.

Clubs

Clwb Ifor Bach (Map p86; ☎ 2023 2199; www.clwb.net; 11 Womanby St) Also known as 'the Welsh club' (or just Y Clwb in Welsh), this is Cardiff's longest-standing and most eclectic nightspot, with three dance floors promoting a range of club nights, from the hard rock, metal and goth of Tuesday's Planet Rock to Saturday night's Clwb Cariad, dedicated to classic Welsh-language rock and pop.

Chilli's (Map p86; ☎ 2064 1010; 3 Churchill Way) Formerly the University of Wales student union, Chilli's is a stylish chill-out bar and terrace with two dance floors. It's popular with students on weeknights, but pulls in a mixed crowd at weekends when they have Lamerica (www.lamericapromotions.com), a brilliant soulful/funky house night.

Coal Exchange (Map p89; ☎ 2049 4917; www.coalexchange.co.uk; Mount Stuart Sq, Butetown) Butetown's historic exchange building is a regular venue for Cool House (www.cool-house.co.uk), Cardiff's most famous house-music night, with top UK and international DJs attracting clubbers from as far afield as London and Manchester.

Toucan Club (Map p83; ☎ 2049 1061; www.toucanclub.co.uk; 95 Newport Rd) This funky little space, all bold colours and swirly mosaics, is the centre of Cardiff's independent club scene, promoting funk, world music and cutting-edge hip hop, as well as exploring new beats and staging live dance acts, acoustic acts and performance poets. Well worth a look.

Wish Club (Map p86; ☎ 2022 6600; www.wishclub.co.uk; 5-9 Church St) Wish is the place where all those hen nights are headed – cool dance floor, glamorous dress code, massive sound system, and a string of top-name touring DJs (think Goldie, Axwell, Tidy Boys, Seb Fontaine, X-press2, Layo and Bushwacker).

Classical Music, Opera & Ballet

Occasional classical music concerts are held in Cardiff Castle, Llandaff Cathedral and St John's Church.

St David's Hall (Map p86; ☎ 2087 8444; www.stdavidshallcardiff.co.uk; The Hayes) The National Concert Hall of Wales, this is the main venue for performances by the BBC National Orchestra of Wales, and home of the Welsh Proms (www.welsh

proms.co.uk), a 10-day series of concerts held in July.

Wales Millennium Centre (Map p89; ☎ 2040 2000; www.wmc.org.uk; Bute Pl, Cardiff Bay) Cardiff's biggest venue provides a permanent home for the Welsh National Opera, as well as several dance and drama companies.

Live Rock, Pop & Jazz

Major musicals and pop concerts are staged at the **Cardiff International Arena** (Map p86; ☎ 2022 4488; www.cclive.co.uk/cia; Mary Ann St) or, if they're really huge, at the **Millennium Stadium** (see p88).

Clwb Ifor Bach (Map p86; ☎ 2023 2199; www.clwb.net; 11 Womanby St) Founded in the early 1980s, this is Cardiff's most famous live-music venue, and the best place to catch gigs by up-and-coming new bands.

Barfly (Map p86; ☎ 0870 907 0999; www.barflyclub.com; Kingsway) Part of a UK-wide chain of music clubs, the Cardiff Barfly is a major live-music venue with gigs six nights a week, providing a stage for local talent as well as major bands on tour.

Cardiff University Students' Union (Map p86; ☎ 2078 1458; www.cardiffstudents.com; Park Pl, Cathays) The students' union hosts regular live gigs by big-name bands, from Newport rappers Goldie Lookin Chain and chart-toppers the Magic Numbers to ageing heavy-metal rockers Motörhead. The box office is on the second floor of the union building and is open noon till midnight.

Point (Map p89; ☎ 2046 0873; www.thepointcardiffbay.com; Mount Stuart Sq, Butetown) Set in a beautifully converted Victorian church, the Point has hosted gigs by a wide range of bands since opening in 2003, including the Stereophonics, Super Furry Animals and the Darkness. It's now one of the city's best live-rock and metal venues, with gigs several nights a week.

Café Jazz (Map p86; ☎ 2038 7026; www.cafejazzcardiff.com; Sandringham Hotel, 21 St Mary St) It's not exactly your traditional smoky jazz basement, but this appealing hotel café-bar is the city's main jazz venue, with live jazz kicking off at 9pm Monday to Thursday, and blues from 10pm Friday (on Saturday nights it's a piano bar). Monday-night jam sessions give new talent a chance to sit in with the house band.

Theatre

Chapter Arts Centre (Map p94; ☎ 2030 4400; www.chapter.org; Market Rd, Canton) Probably the city's most interesting arts venue, the Chapter has a varied programme of contemporary drama, as well as art exhibitions, workshops, alternative theatre and dance performances; it's also an appealing, arty place to hang out and there's a good café-bar with Cardiff's biggest range of beers.

Sherman Theatre (Map p86; ☎ 2064 6900; www .shermantheatre.co.uk; Senghennydd Rd, Cathays) The Sherman is home to South Wales' leading theatre company and stages a wide range of material from classics and children's theatre to works by new playwrights.

New Theatre (Map p86; ☎ 2087 8889; www.newtheatre cardiff.co.uk; Park Pl) This restored Edwardian playhouse – Anna Pavlova and Sarah Bernhardt are among those who have trod the boards here – hosts various touring productions, including big West End and Broadway shows, musicals and pantomime.

Comedy

Jongleurs (Map p86; ☎ 0870 787 0707; www.jongleurs .com; Millennium Plaza, Wood St) This well-established comedy chain stages regular stand-up shows on Friday and Saturday nights, with a trademark mix of well-known names, regulars and raw newcomers.

Glee Club (Map p89; ☎ 0870 241 5093; www.glee.co.uk; Mermaid Quay, Cardiff Bay) The Glee Club is another comedy chain providing a similar mix of acts.

Sport

If you stand in Bute Park on certain Saturday afternoons you can hear the crowds roaring at three different sports grounds.

Millennium Stadium (Map p86; ☎ 2023 1495; www .millenniumstadium.com; Westgate St) All national and international rugby and football matches take place at this stadium. Tickets for international fixtures are difficult for mere mortals to get hold of; national matches are easier. Football matches here are family affairs, with no drinking allowed inside during the match.

Cardiff Arms Park (Map p86; ☎ 0870 013 5213; www .cardiffrfc.com; Westgate St) Just north of the Millennium Stadium, this is the home ground of the Cardiff Rugby Football Club, founded in 1876. Rugby union is this city's favourite sport, and the Cardiff Blues are Wales' richest, most star-studded club, having fed over 200 players into the national team.

Ninian Park (☎ 0845 345 1400; www.cardiffcityfc.co .uk; Sloper Rd) A mile west of the centre is the home of Cardiff City Football Club. Fans still hark back to 1927 when the Bluebirds took the English FA Cup out of England for the first (and only) time – Welsh football's

equivalent of Owain Glyndŵr's rebellion. Take Cardiff bus 1 from the central bus station, or a Pontypridd-bound train to Ninian Park train station.

Glamorgan County Cricket Ground (Map p94; ☎ 2040 9380; www.glamorgancricket.com; Sophia Gardens) This is the home to Glamorgan County Cricket Club, the only Welsh club belonging to the England and Wales Cricket Board. At the time of writing it was undergoing redevelopment.

The city's newest sports team – founded in 1986 – is the premier-league ice-hockey club, the **Cardiff Devils** (☎ 0845 434 9055; www.thecardiff devils.com). At the time of writing, the club was homeless following the closure of the Welsh National Ice Rink.

SHOPPING

Cardiff is a major shopping city and has all the usual high-street names ranged along Queen St, the main commercial drag, and in the big city-centre malls. The Capitol Shopping Centre is at the east end of Queen St (housing the Virgin Megastore, Fat Face, Karen Millen) and the St David's Centre is between Queen St and Hill St (Debenhams, Marks & Spencer, Topshop). The shopping mall at Cardiff Bay, Mermaid Quay, at present has more bars and restaurants than shops.

Note that most of Cardiff's city centre, from Queen St south to Bute Tce, is slated for a major redevelopment that will create the biggest shopping centre in the UK – St David's 2 – scheduled to open in 2009.

Cardiff's most distinctive shopping feature is the High St Arcades, a series of glass-roofed Victorian and Edwardian arcades running off High St and St Mary St, lined with quirky fashion boutiques, speciality shops and cafés.

High St Arcade (Map p86; High St & St John St) This arcade abounds with fashion boutiques, shoe shops, nail salons and gift shops – check out cool shoes and bags at Buzz & Co, funky women's fashion and sparkly accessories at Pussy Galore, and smart, streetwise clothes at Road. Hobo's is great for secondhand 1960s and '70s clothing

Spillers Records (Map p86; ☎ 2022 4905; www.spillers records.co.uk; 36 The Hayes) The world's oldest record shop, founded in 1894 (when it sold wax phonograph cylinders) and still occupying its original premises, Spiller's is a national treasure. It stocks a huge range of CDs and vinyl, prides itself on catering to the nonmainstream end of the music market (it's especially good on punk), and promotes local talent through regular in-store gigs.

Cardiff Antiques Centre (Map p86; ☎ 2039 8891; 10-12 Royal Arcade, St Mary St & The Hayes; ⏰ 10am-5.30pm Mon-Sat) Spread over three floors of an Edwardian arcade, this centre has more than a dozen little stores selling Welsh porcelain and china, antique jewellery and silver, stamps, coins and collectables.

Castle Welsh Crafts (Map p86; ☎ 2034 3038; 1 Castle St) If you're after stuffed dragons, lovespoons, Cardiff T-shirts or a suit of armour (£2000 and wearable, if you're interested), this is the city's biggest souvenir shop, conveniently located across the street from the castle.

Craft in the Bay (Map p89; ☎ 2048 4611; 57 Bute St, Cardiff Bay; ⏰ 10.30am-5.30pm daily) This retail gallery showcases work created by contemporary Welsh artists and craftspeople, with a wide range of ceramics, textiles, woodwork, jewellery, glassware, paper, baskets, bookbinding and ironwork.

Jacob's Market (Map p86; ☎ 2039 0939; W Canal Wharf; ⏰ 9am-5.30pm daily) A four-floor red-brick building housing more than 50 stalls, Jacob's sells secondhand and antique furniture, vintage clothes, books, military memorabilia and bric-a-brac.

Markets

For a spot of old-fashioned shopping, head for **Cardiff Central Market** (Map p86; entrances on St Mary St & Trinity St; ⏰ 8am-5.30pm Mon-Sat), which is packed with stalls selling everything from fresh fish to mobile phones, or go across the Taff to the **Riverside Real Food Market** (Map p86; Fitzhamon Embankment; ⏰ 10am-2pm Sun) for fresh local produce and organic food.

GETTING THERE & AWAY
Air

Cardiff airport (☎ 01446-711111; www.cwlfly.com) is 12 miles southwest of the centre, near the suburb of Barry. On most days there are direct flights to Cardiff from destinations around the UK and continental Europe; see p320.

Bus

All local and regional bus and coach companies use Cardiff Central bus station on Wood St, right next to Cardiff Central train station. For information on local and national bus timetables and fares, contact **Traveline** (☎ 0870 608 2 608; www.traveline-cymru.org.uk).

The main intercity bus operators out of Cardiff are:

First Cymru (www.firstgroup.com) Swansea shuttle.

National Express (www.nationalexpress.com) Swansea, Newport, Chepstow, Bristol, London Heathrow, London Gatwick.

Stagecoach (www.stagecoachbus.com) South Wales Valleys, Merthyr Tydfil, Abergavenny.

Direct bus services from Cardiff (showing approximate one-way fares) are shown in the table below. The Beacons Bus connects Cardiff with various destinations in the Brecon Beacons National Park.

For details of buses to Cardiff from London and the rest of the UK, see p323.

Car & Motorcycle

The fastest access to Cardiff city centre from the M4 is via the A48 (Eastern Ave) from junction 29 or 30 or, from Swansea, the A470 (Northern Ave) from junction 32. The A4232 (Grangetown and Butetown Link) from junction 33 provides direct access to Cardiff Bay.

Try to avoid arriving in Cardiff, or even driving along the M4 nearby, during rush hours (7.30am to 9.30am and 4.30pm to 6.30pm Monday to Friday).

Train

The main train station in the city is Cardiff Central, on the southern edge of the city cen-

DIRECT BUS SERVICES FROM CARDIFF

Destination	Bus	Fare	Duration	Frequency
Abergavenny	X3	£4	1½hr	hourly
Aberystwyth	X40	£14	4¼hr	hourly
Brecon	X43	£4	1½hr	5 daily
Chepstow	201	£4.50	1hr	2hr
Swansea	100	£4	1hr	45min

tre. It is served by direct trains from major UK cities such as London (Paddington), Manchester, Bristol, Birmingham and Nottingham; see p323 for details. Call the **National Rail Enquiry Service** (☎ 08457 48 49 50; www.nationalrail.co.uk) for timetable information.

Arriva Trains Wales (www.arrivatrainswales.co.uk) operate all train services in Wales. For direct services from Cardiff (with one-way fares), see the table below.

Destination	Fare	Duration	Frequency
Abergavenny	£8	40min	hourly
Chepstow	£6	40min	hourly
Haverfordwest	£16	2½hr	2hr
Llandovery	£12	1½hr	1 daily
Merthyr Tydfil	£4	1hr	hourly
Shrewsbury	£27	2¼hr	hourly
Swansea	£4	1hr	45min

To get from Cardiff to North Wales by train, you will have to change at Shrewsbury.

GETTING AROUND
To/From the Airport
The X91 Airbus Express service (£3.70, 30 minutes, at least hourly) runs from the airport to the central bus station (stand E1).

A free shuttle bus links the airport terminal to nearby Rhoose-Cardiff Airport train station, which has regular trains into the city (£2.80, 35 minutes, hourly).

A taxi from the airport to the city centre takes 20 to 30 minutes, depending on traffic, and costs about £22.

Bicycle
Cyclists rejoice: Cardiff is one of Britain's flattest cities. The Taff Trail starts here and offers a pleasant route to Castell Coch and other sights. At **Taff Trail Cycle Hire** (Map p94; ☎ 2039 8362; off Cathedral Rd), in Cardiff Caravan Park, bike rental costs £7.25 per three hours and £10.10 per day. It has some bikes adapted for disabled cyclists.

Bus
City and suburban bus routes are operated by **Cardiff Bus** (Map p86; ☎ 2066 6444; www.cardiffbus .com; St David's House, Wood St); for timetable enquiries call **Traveline** (☎ 0870 608 2 608). Fares range from 90p to £1.80 depending on distance; buy your ticket from the driver, and have the exact fare ready (no change given).

A free transport map showing bus routes is available from the Cardiff Bus office and the tourist office.

There is a range of travel passes that work out cheaper than a single ticket to some of the destinations they cover. A **Day To Go** ticket (adult £3, child £2) is valid until midnight on the day of purchase, on all buses run by Cardiff Bus in the Cardiff, Penarth and Barry area.

A **Network Day Rider** (adult/child £6/£4) covers destinations as far-flung as Merthyr Tydfil, Blaenavon, Newport, Abergavenny, Monmouth and Chepstow on buses operated by Cardiff Bus, Stagecoach and several other local companies.

Both of the above tickets can be bought from the driver. For full details see the Cardiff Bus website.

Car & Motorcycle
Parking in the city centre can be a problem. There are convenient car parks at Castle Mews (on North Rd, just north of the castle) and Sophia Gardens (off Cathedral Rd, west of the city centre); charges are around £3 for up to two hours, £6 for up to six hours. There is free, unrestricted, on-street parking further out on Cathedral Rd, about 20 minutes walk from the city centre.

CAR RENTAL
For car rental try:
Avis (☎ 2034 2111; www.avis.co.uk)
Budget (☎ 2072 7499; www.budget.co.uk)
Europcar (☎ 2049 8978; www.europcar.co.uk)
Hertz (☎ 2022 4548; www.hertz.co.uk)
National (☎ 2049 6256; www.nationalcar.co.uk)

Taxi
Official black cabs can be hailed in the street, ordered by phone, or picked up at taxi ranks outside the train station, in Duke St opposite the castle, and at the corner of Greyfriars Rd and Park Pl.

Reliable taxi companies include **Capital Cars** (☎ 2077 7777) and **Dragon Taxis** (☎ 2033 3333).

AROUND CARDIFF

One of the great things about Cardiff is the variety of attractions around its outskirts. You can go down to the seaside at Penarth, explore the hulking moat-encircled castle at Caerphilly, or the high-camp, fairy-tale Castell Coch,

CARDIFF

wander around the amazing St Fagans National History Museum, or explore the remains of a major Roman army base at Caerleon.

ST FAGANS NATIONAL HISTORY MUSEUM

From the oldest surviving farmhouse in Wales to a row of miners' cottages from Merthyr Tydfil, historic buildings from all over the country have been dismantled and re-erected in a beautiful rural setting at the **St Fagans National History Museum** (☎ 2057 3500; www.museumwales .ac.uk/en/stfagans; St Fagans; admission free; ☼ 10am-5pm). More than 40 buildings are on show, including farmhouses of timber and stone, barns, a watermill, a school and an 18th-century Unitarian chapel, with native breeds of livestock grazing in the surrounding fields.

Highlights of the open-air museum include a farmhouse dating from 1508, redolent with the smells of old timber, beeswax and wood smoke, and a row of six miners' cottages from Merthyr Tydfil, each one restored and furnished to represent different periods in the town's history, from the austere minimalism of 1805 to all the mod cons of 1985.

You can see craftspeople at work in many of the buildings, showing how blankets, clogs, barrels, tools and cider were once made, and the woollen mill sells its own handmade blankets. It's a great place for kids, with a number of special events in the summer.

You'll need at least half a day to do justice to the museum, which also includes indoor exhibitions dedicated to traditional costume, farming implements and daily life. There's a café-restaurant in the visitors' centre, and summer-only tearooms at two other points.

Getting There & Away

St Fagans is 4 miles west of Cardiff. Take Cardiff buses 32 or 320 (20 minutes, hourly) to a small gate at St Fagans Castle, 500m from the visitors centre.

By car, take the A4232 south from junction 33 on the M4. From the city centre, head out on Cathedral Rd and continue straight along Pencisely Rd (B4488) and St Fagans Rd. There's a £2.50 charge for parking.

PENARTH

☎ 029 / pop 24,300

Penarth is a quaint, old-fashioned seaside resort, stuck somewhere between the 19th and 20th centuries, with a bright-blue spindly Victorian pier staggering out to sea, a trim seafront lined with attractive Victorian terraces, and a mature population wielding Thermos flasks. It's a good place to come for a brisk seaside walk, a world away from the bustle of the city, and makes a good half-day excursion.

From Penarth train station or the bus stop at Windsor Arcade in the centre, it's a five-minute walk through Alexandra Gardens down to the esplanade. There's a **tourist office** (☎ 2070 8849; Penarth Pier; ☼ 10am-5.30pm Apr-Sep) at the entrance to the pier.

A block east of the train station, the **Turner House Gallery** (☎ 2070 8870; www.ffotogallery.org;

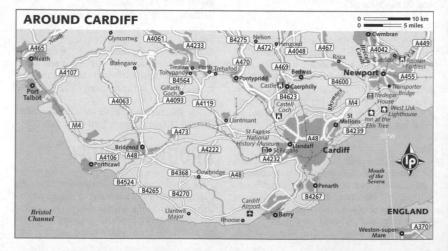

Plymouth Rd; admission free; 🕙 11am-5pm Wed-Sun), housed in a red-brick building, has changing art exhibitions, and runs summer workshops where kids can do stuff like print-making and pinhole photography.

At the north end of the town, next to Penarth Marina, is the **Cardiff Bay Barrage** (p90).

From May to October, **Waverley Excursions** (☎ 0845 130 4647; www.waverleyexcursions.co.uk) runs cruises on either the *Waverley*, the world's last seagoing paddle steamer, or its sister ship the *Balmoral*, departing from Penarth pier three or four times weekly for a trip across the Bristol Channel to Holm Island or to Ilfracombe in Devon. You can book by phone, online or at the tourist office; tickets can also be bought on board, or at the Cardiff Bus office in Cardiff.

Getting There & Away
Penarth is almost a suburb of Cardiff, lying on the south shore of Cardiff Bay. Cardiff buses 89 and 89A (20 minutes, half-hourly Monday to Saturday, hourly Sunday) run to Penarth, and there are frequent trains from Cardiff Central (10 minutes, every 20 minutes).

There's also a Waterbus ferry from Mermaid Quay in Cardiff Bay to the barrage (20 minutes), with departures hourly from 10am to 5pm daily, and also from 6.30pm to 10.30pm on Saturdays.

CASTELL COCH
Perched atop a thickly wooded crag on the northern fringes of the city is Cardiff Castle's little sister. The fanciful, fairy-tale **Castell Coch** (Cadw; ☎ 2081 0101; Tongwynlais; adult/child £3.50/3; 🕙 9.30am-6pm Jun-Sep, 9.30am-5pm Apr, May & Oct, 9.30am-4pm Mon-Sat & 11am-4pm Sun Nov-Mar) was the summer retreat of the third marquess of Bute and, like Cardiff Castle, was designed by William Burges in gaudy Victorian Gothic style, complete with working drawbridge and portcullis.

Raised on the ruins of the first Castell Coch (Red Castle) built by Norman Gilbert de Clare in the 13th century, the Butes' Disneyesque holiday home is a monument to high camp. Lady Bute's huge, circular bedroom is pure fantasy – her bed, with crystal globes on the bedposts, sits in the middle beneath an extravagantly decorated and mirrored cupola, with 28 painted panels around the walls depicting monkeys (fashionable at the time, apparently; just plain weird, now). The corbels are carved with images of birds nesting or feeding their

young, and the washbasin is framed between two castle towers.

Lord Bute's bedroom is small and plain in comparison – the WC isn't even en suite – but the octagonal Drawing Room is another hallucinogenic tour de force, the walls painted with scenes from Aesop's fables, the domed ceiling a flurry of birds and stars, and the fireplace topped with figures depicting the three ages of man.

Getting There & Away
Cardiff bus 26 (30 minutes, half-hourly Monday to Saturday, hourly Sunday) to Tredegar stops at Tongwynlais, from where it's a 10-minute walk to the castle. The same bus continues to Caerphilly Castle, and the two can be combined in a day trip. Bus 26A (four daily Monday to Friday) stops right at the castle gates.

It's also an easy cycle from Cardiff to Castell Coch along the Taff Trail.

CAERPHILLY (CAERFFILI)
☎ 029 / pop 31,000
The town of Caerphilly – now almost a suburb of Cardiff – guards the entrance to the Rhymney valley to the north of the capital. Its name is synonymous with a popular variety of hard, slightly crumbly white cheese (similar to cheddar, but saltier) that originated in the surrounding area. It has long been famous for its magnificent castle, and more recently for the quirky Big Cheese festival (see the boxed text, p107).

The **tourist office** (☎ 2088 0011; Twyn Sq; 🕙 10am-6pm Apr-Sep, 10am-5pm Oct-Mar) is just east of the castle, itself clearly visible 500m north of Caerphilly train station (along Cardiff Rd).

Caerphilly Castle
You could be forgiven for thinking that **Caerphilly Castle** (Cadw; ☎ 2088 3143; adult/child £3.50/3; 🕙 9.30am-6pm Jun-Sep, 9.30am-5pm Apr-May & Oct, 9.30am-4pm Mon-Sat & 11am-4pm Sun Nov-Mar) – with its profusion of towers and crenellations reflected in a duck-filled lake – was a film set rather than an ancient monument. Indeed, it often *is* used as a film set and makes a spectacular backdrop for the annual Big Cheese festival. But it is also one of Britain's finest examples of a 13th-century fortress with water defences.

Unusually, Caerphilly was never a royal castle. Most of the construction was completed between 1268 and 1271 by the powerful English baron Gilbert de Clare (1243–95), Lord Marcher of Glamorgan, in response to the threat of Prince Llywelyn ap Gruffydd, prince of Gwynedd (and the last Welsh Prince of Wales). In the 13th century Caerphilly was state-of-the-art, being one of the earliest castles to use lakes, bridges and a series of concentric fortifications for defence; to reach the inner court you had to overcome no fewer than three drawbridges, six portcullises and five sets of double gates.

Edward I's subsequent campaign against the Welsh princes put an end to Llywelyn's ambitions and Caerphilly's short-lived spell on the front line came to an end without ever tasting battle; the famous leaning tower at the southeast corner is a result of subsidence rather than sabotage. In the early 14th century it was remodelled as a grand residence and the magnificent Great Hall was adapted for entertaining, but from the mid-14th century onward the castle began to fall into ruin.

Much of what you see results from restoration from 1928 to 1939 by the fourth marquess of Bute; work continued after the state bought the castle in 1950. The Great Hall was given a magnificent wooden ceiling in the 19th century and the Gothic windows were restored in the 1960s; it is now used to host special events. On the south dam platform you can see reconstructions of medieval siege weapons; they are working models and lob stone projectiles into the lake during battle re-enactments.

Eating & Drinking

Glanmor's Tearoom (☎ 2088 8355; 22 Castle Ct; snacks from £2) Just north of the tourist office and opposite the castle, this is a cheerful old-fashioned tearoom with good homemade meals, fresh pastries and home-baked scones.

Courthouse (☎ 2088 8120; Cardiff Rd; mains £4-7) Parts of this atmospheric old pub date from the 14th century. It enjoys a great setting, with a beer garden overlooking the castle, serving basic pub grub and an all-day breakfast.

Getting There & Away

The easiest way to reach Caerphilly from Cardiff is by train on the Rhymney or Bargoed service (single/return £2.80/4.50, 20 minutes, four per hour Monday to Saturday, every two hours Sunday).

Stagecoach bus 26 (45 minutes, hourly Monday to Saturday, five daily Sunday) goes from Cardiff bus station to Castle St near the tourist office; this is the same bus that goes to Castell Coch, and the two castles make a good day trip.

NEWPORT (CASNEWYDD)

☎ 01633 / pop 140,000

Hello. My name is Newport, and I'm a bit of a dump. Ah well – they say the first step on the road to recovery is admitting you have a problem, and poor old Newport has been saddled for too long with a reputation for grim urban squalor and an alcoholic, binge-fuelled nightlife. But with the turn of the millennium it has pulled itself together and is determined to clean up its act.

Newly crowned with the title of 'city' in 2002, Newport is shrugging off the air of decline that settled over it in the late 20th century, and has set out on an ambitious programme of regeneration aimed at transforming the city centre from 1970s ugly to 21st-century hi-tech. The face of the city is changing almost daily – the latest additions include the stylish Riverfront Theatre & Art Centre (opened in 2004) and the striking Usk Footbridge (opened in 2006) – as the city gears up to host the Ryder Cup international golf tournament in 2010.

In the meantime, the city centre is still pretty grungy, its streets spotted with chewing gum and spattered with spilt booze and kebab sauce. Nevertheless, Newport offers some intriguing visitor attractions, from spectacular industrial heritage (the elegant Transporter Bridge) to indie music mecca (the legendary TJ's).

History

The town takes its name from the fact that it was built after the 'old port' at Caerleon, further upstream, following the construction of Newport Castle in Norman times. Like many harbour towns in South Wales, it grew rich on the back of the iron and coal industries in the 19th and early-20th centuries.

In the second half of the 20th century, Newport's shipbuilding industry disappeared, and the docks declined in importance as coal exports shifted to Barry and iron-ore imports to Port Talbot. In 2001 the huge Llanwern steelworks closed down. Today, the city is busy reinventing itself as a centre for the service sector and technology industries.

But the most famous event in Newport's history – perhaps fittingly, considering its present-day nightlife – was a street riot. Chartism, a parliamentary reform movement that arose during the early years of Queen Victoria's reign, was particularly strong in Wales. On 4 November 1839 some 5000 men from the Usk, Ebbw and Rhymney Valleys con-

THE BIG CHEESE

Any festival that includes a Cheese Olympics and a Tommy Cooper Tent has got to be worth a look. Each year, at the end of July, Caerphilly welcomes more than 70,000 people to the Big Cheese (admission free), a weekend of family-oriented fun and games that offers everything from fireworks to falconry, comedy acts to cheese-tasting, along with medieval battle re-enactments, food and craft stalls, archery demonstrations, live music and a traditional funfair.

The Cheese Olympics are held Friday evening, and include cheese-throwing, -rolling and -stacking events. The Tommy Cooper Tent – named after the much-loved British comedian, who was born in Caerphilly and died in 1984 – stages comedy acts, including a Tommy Cooper tribute act.

For more details, see www.caerphilly.gov.uk/bigcheese.

verged on Newport, intent on taking control of the town and sparking off a national uprising. They tried to storm the Westgate Hotel, where several Chartists were being held; police and infantrymen inside fired into the crowd, killing at least 20 people. Five men were subsequently imprisoned and three – including John Frost, who was a major organiser – were deported to Australia.

The event is celebrated in several plaques and monuments around town, notably the Westgate Hotel on Commercial St, where the entrance pillars are still bullet-scarred. Outside, among the hurrying shoppers, is an ensemble of angry bronze figures memorialising the Chartist riot.

Orientation & Information

The city centre lies on the west bank of the River Usk, stretching south from the train station along pedestrianised High St and Commercial St to the 1970s shopping plaza of John Frost Square. The entrance to the bus station is at the northern end of this square; the **tourist office** (☎ 842962; John Frost Sq; ☼ 9.30am-6pm Mon-Thu, 9am-6pm Fri, 9.30am-5pm Sat) is at the south end.

Sights

Not much remains of Newport's pre-industrial past, apart from the ruins of **Newport Castle** (admission free; ☼ 24hr) close to the train station – the three towers, now squeezed between traffic-clogged Kingsway and the river, were largely rebuilt after being trashed by Owain Glyndŵr in 1402 – and **St Woolos Cathedral**, a 10-minute walk west of the city centre, parts of which date from pre-Norman times.

There's more to see at the impressive and interesting **Newport Museum & Art Gallery** (☎ 656656; John Frost Sq; admission free; ☼ 9.30am-5pm Mon-Thu, 9am-4.30pm Fri, 9.30am-4pm Sat), in the same building as the tourist office, which covers the

town's history from the Romans at Caerleon to the rise of the coal and iron industries.

Nearby is the **Riverfront Theatre & Art Centre** (☎ 656757; www.newport.gov.uk/riverfront; Bristol Packet Wharf), the city's swish new cultural centre that stages theatre, opera, classical music and dance, as well as cinema, comedy and pantomime.

The town centre is an open-air museum of quirky modern sculpture. Northeast of the bus station, by the river, is the huge red circle of *Steel Wave* (1990) by Peter Fink, now almost a civic trademark. In John Frost Square, *In the Nick of Time* is a hilarious clock tower that falls to pieces on the hour. *Stand and Stare*, a ghostly shrouded figure on Commercial St, is dedicated to local writer WH Davies, author of *The Autobiography of a Super-Tramp*. There are several others, described in a leaflet available from the tourist office.

About a mile south of the city centre along Commercial St and Commercial Rd (A4042) rise the elegant spidery towers of the **Transporter Bridge** (cars & light vehicles 50p, pedestrians free; ☼ 8am-6pm Sat, 1-5pm Sun), which celebrated its 100th birthday in 2006. A remarkable piece of

THE LEGENDARY TJ'S

No account of Newport would be complete without a mention of **TJ's Disco** (☎ 216608; www.tjs-newport.demon.co.uk; 16-18 Clarence Pl). This notorious dive has been nurturing local talent since the 1970s, and still boasts a packed programme of live indie and alternative music from both local and international bands. The sticky floors and poster-plastered walls have heard it all, from the Buzzcocks and Echo & the Bunnymen to Oasis, Catatonia and Green Day, and legend claims that it was here that Kurt Cobain proposed to Courtney Love.

Edwardian engineering, it was built to carry traffic across the river while allowing high-masted ships to pass beneath. It is still part of Newport's road network, carrying up to six cars in a gondola suspended beneath the high-level track, but traffic has declined since the opening of a new road bridge in 2005. The neighbouring **visitors centre** (☎ 250322; Usk Way; ☺ 10am-5pm Sat & Sun) provides details of the bridge's history.

Getting There & Around

The fastest and easiest connection with Cardiff is by mainline train (£3.60, 13 minutes, six per hour). Buses are much slower (45 minutes) and less frequent. Local bus routes and timetables are available online at www.new porttransport.co.uk.

For one week in early June and for five weeks from late July to late August **City Sightseeing** (☎ 263600; www.city-sightseeing.com/newport) operates hop-on-hop-off, open-top bus tours (£6, four a day) that link the bus station to all the main sights, including Caerleon, the Transporter Bridge, Tredegar House and St Woolos Cathedral.

AROUND NEWPORT
Tredegar House

The seat of the Morgan family for more than 500 years, **Tredegar House** (☎ 01633-815880; park admission free, house adult/child £5.40/3.95; ☺ park 9am-dusk year-round, house 11.30am-4pm Wed-Sun Easter-

Sep, visitor centre 10.30am-5.30pm Wed-Sun Easter-Sep) is a stone garland–bedecked, red-brick 17th-century country house set amid gorgeous gardens and is one of the finest examples of a Restoration mansion in Britain. The Morgans, once one of the richest families in Wales, were an interesting lot – Godfrey, second Lord Tredegar, survived the Charge of the Light Brigade; Viscount Evan kept a boxing kangaroo; and Sir Henry was a 17th-century pirate (Captain Morgan's Rum is named after him) – and the house (guided tours hourly) is a monument to their wealth and taste.

Tredegar House is 2 miles west of Newport city centre. Take bus 15A or 30 from Newport bus station (15 minutes, four an hour).

Caerleon Roman Fortress

After the Romans invaded Britain in AD 43, they controlled their new territory through a network of forts and military garrisons. The top tier of military organisation was the legionary fort, of which there were only three in Britain – at Eboracum (York), Deva (Chester) and Isca (Caerleon).

Caerleon (Welsh for 'City of the Legion') was the headquarters of the elite 2nd Augustan Legion (they fought against the Picts in Scotland and helped build Hadrian's Wall) for more than 200 years, from AD 75 until the end of the 3rd century. It wasn't just a military camp but a purpose-built township some 9 miles in circumference, complete with a 6000-seat amphitheatre and a state-of-the-art Roman baths complex. Today it is one of the largest and most important Roman settlements in Britain. The Cadw guidebook *Caerleon Roman Fortress* (£2.95) is worth buying for its maps, sketches and aerial views, which help to visualise the settlement among the distractions of the modern town.

Begin with a visit to the excellent **National Roman Legion Museum** (☎ 01633-423134; admission free; ☺ 10am-5pm Mon-Sat, 2-5pm Sun), which displays a host of intriguing Roman artefacts, from jewellery to armour, teeth to tombstones, and shows what life was like for Roman soldiers in one of the remotest corners of Empire.

Head next for the **Roman Baths** (Cadw; ☎ 01633-422518; High St; adult/child £2.90/2.50; ☺ 9.30am-5pm Apr-Oct, 9.30am-5pm Mon-Sat, 11am-4pm Sun Nov-Mar) a block to the southeast. Caerleon's baths were once as huge and splendid as the one in Cluny

---

THE NEWPORT SHIP

In 2002 construction work for the new Riverfront Art Centre uncovered the remains of the most complete medieval ship ever found. Buried in the mud on the west bank of the River Usk, the 25m-long Newport Ship dates from around 1465 and was probably built in France (archaeologists discovered a French silver coin that had been placed in one of the ship's timbers by the boat builder). Some 1700 individual timbers have been recovered, and are currently undergoing conservation so that the ship's remains can be reassembled and put on display in a purpose-built facility beneath the new arts centre. In the meantime, some of the artefacts discovered in the ship are on display in Newport Museum. For more details, see www.thenewportship.com.

AUTHOR'S CHOICE

West Usk Lighthouse (☎ 01633-810126; www.westusklighthouse.co.uk; St Brides Wentloog, near Newport; d £95-110; **P**) Quirky doesn't even begin to describe this place – from the autographed Dalek in the lobby to the flotation tank in the summerhouse, this restored 19th-century lighthouse is one of Wales' more unusual B&Bs. Occupying a lonely spot where the River Usk flows into the Severn estuary, the building is short and squat rather than tall and thin, with four guest bedrooms ranged around a central spiral staircase like the slices of a cake. Our favourites are the two on the south side, both of which have four-poster beds and sea views. The décor is homely, a little worn at the edges but filled with endearingly eccentric details – an upside-down model ship steaming across the ceiling, an old fishing rod used as a curtain rail, a traditional red telephone box recycled as a shower cubicle. The lighthouse is at the end of a private road off the B4239, 2 miles south of Junction 28 on the M4 just west of Newport.

Evening meals are not available, but a few miles along the road you'll find the **Inn at the Elm Tree** (☎ 01633-680225; www.the-elm-tree.co.uk; St Brides Wentloog; mains £15-18), a contemporary country inn with log fires, leather armchairs and an intimate, candle-lit restaurant offering a modern European menu. It also has single/double rooms available from £80/90.

---

in France, and remained standing until the 12th century. Parts of the outdoor swimming pool, apodyterium (changing room) and frigidarium (cold room) are on show under a protective roof, and give some idea of the scale of the place.

Broadway, the side street opposite the museum, leads to a park on the left where you'll find the turf-covered terraces of the **Roman Amphitheatre** (admission free; ⏰ 24hr). The oval structure is the only fully excavated Roman amphitheatre in Britain; it lay just outside the old Roman city walls.

Caerleon is 4 miles northeast of Newport. Buses 2 and 7 (15 minutes, four per hour Monday to Friday, hourly Saturday and Sunday) run from Newport bus station to Caerleon High St.

Southeast Wales & Brecon Beacons

The southeast corner of Wales, where the River Wye meanders along the border with England, is the birthplace of British tourism. For more than 200 years people have come to explore this tranquil waterway and its winding, wooded vale where the majestic ruins of Tintern Abbey have inspired generations of poets and artists. But today there is more to the region than the pleasant market towns and rural by-ways of the Lower Wye.

To the west stretch the serried vales of the South Wales valleys, once the country's industrial heartland, where names such as Rhondda, Rhymney and Ebbw Vale speak of close-knit communities forged in the hard graft of coal mines and iron works. The mines may be closed and the iron works gone, but the communities survive and are carving out a new role for these scarred postindustrial landscapes with attractions such as the Rhondda Heritage Park, the Big Pit National Coal Museum and the Unesco World Heritage Site at Blaenavon.

Move north and the landscape changes yet again to the majestic upland scenery of the Brecon Beacons National Park, a magnet for hikers, hill walkers and mountain-bikers. Beneath the hills runs the River Usk, flowing through the lively towns of Brecon, Crickhowell and Abergavenny, whose lush surrounding farmland produces some of the finest food in Wales, and where you can enjoy one of the highest concentrations of quality restaurants in the country.

HIGHLIGHTS

- Strolling among the romantic ruins of **Tintern Abbey** (p115)
- Enjoying the tranquillity of the magical **Vale of Ewyas** (p132)
- Descending into a real coal mine at **Big Pit National Coal Museum** (p122)
- Reaching the summit of **Pen-y-Fan** (p124), the highest peak in South Wales
- Exploring the underground delights of the **Dan-yr-Ogof Showcaves** (p138)

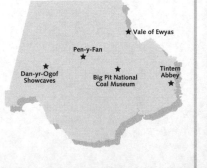

GETTING THERE & AROUND

Stagecoach is the southeast's main long-distance bus operator; call **Traveline** (☎ 0870 608 2 608; www.traveline-cymru.org.uk) for information.

If you'll be using buses frequently, you may save money by getting a travel pass. The Network Rider pass (£6/20 for a day/week) can be used on all buses operated by Stagecoach South Wales, Chepstow Classic Buses, Welcome Travel, Glyn Williams Travel and H&H Coaches; it is not valid on the X43 Cardiff–Merthyr Tydfil–Brecon–Abergavenny service operated by Sixty-Sixty Coaches.

LOWER WYE VALLEY

The River Wye flows 154 miles from the mountains of Mid-Wales to the River Severn at Chepstow, much of it designated an Area of Outstanding Natural Beauty (www.wyevalley aonb.org.uk) famous for its limestone gorges and dense broadleaved woodland. The most beautiful stretch lies between Monmouth and Chepstow, along the border between Monmouthshire and England. For a long time the county of Monmouthshire was considered to be in England, but it was finally recognised as part of Wales in 1974.

The **Wye Valley Walk** (www.wyevalleywalk.org) is a 136-mile waymarked riverside trail running from Chepstow to the river's source on the slopes of Plynlimon Fawr. From Monmouth downstream the trail runs mainly along the river's western side, past the splendid ruins of Tintern Abbey. The tourist offices in Chepstow and Monmouth have maps and information on walking short sections of the trail.

MONMOUTH (TREFYNWY)

☎ 01600 / pop 10,000

Against a background of pastel-painted Georgian prosperity, the compact market town of Monmouth bustles and thrives. It sits at the confluence of the Rivers Wye and Monnow, and has hopped in and out of Wales over the centuries as the border shifted back and forth. Today, it feels more English than Welsh.

The town is famous as the birthplace of King Henry V, victor at the Battle of Agincourt in 1415, and immortalised by Shakespeare. Other locals who have passed into history include Geoffrey of Monmouth (p78), the 12th-century historian, and Charles Stewart Rolls, co-founder of Rolls-Royce.

In modern times Monmouth's main claim to fame is the nearby Rockfield recording studio, a few miles to the northwest. Established in the 1960s, the studio has produced a string of hit albums including Queen's *Bohemian Rhapsody*, Iggy Pop's *Soldiers* and *(What's the Story) Morning Glory?* by Oasis, and has been used by bands from Mott the Hoople to Coldplay. It's not unknown for rock stars to be spotted in Monmouth's pubs and restaurants.

Orientation

The centre of town is Agincourt Sq, with the Shire Hall on its east side and Monnow St, the main shopping street, running southwest from here to the pedestrianised Monnow Bridge. Regional buses stop just off Monnow St near the Somerfield supermarket.

Information

IT Centre (☎ 714344; 2-4 Monnow St; ✆ 9am-5.30pm Mon-Sat; per 30 min £1)
Monmouth Hospital (☎ 713522; Hereford Rd) For emergency services go to Abergavenny.
Monmouth Library (☎ 775215; Whitecross St; ✆ 9.30am-5.30pm Mon, Tue & Fri, 9.30am-8pm Thu, 9.30am-4pm Sat) Free internet access.
Police Station (☎ 712321; Chippenham Gate St)
Post Office (27 Monnow St; ✆ 8.30am-5.30pm Mon-Fri, 8.30am-4pm Sat)
Rub-a-dub-dub (Cinderhill St; ✆ 7.30am-7.30pm Mon-Fri, 8am-8.30pm Sat) Self-service laundrette.
Stephen's Bookshop (3 Church St) A warren of floor-to-ceiling secondhand books.
Tourist Office (☎ 713899; Shire Hall, Agincourt Sq; ✆ 9am-5.30pm Jul & Aug, 10am-5pm Sep-Jun)

Sights

Agincourt Sq is dominated by the arcade of the 1724 **Shire Hall**, and a statue of former Monmouth resident Charles Stewart Rolls (1877–1910), one half of the team that founded Rolls-Royce. Not only a pioneering motorist and aviator, he was the first British citizen to die in an air accident (his statue is clutching a model of the Wright biplane in which he died). The square hosts a market on Friday and Saturday.

Nearby on Castle Hill are the meagre remains of **Monmouth Castle**, where Henry V was born in 1397. Except for the great tower, it was dismantled in the 17th century and the stone used to build **Great Castle House** next door, now headquarters of the Royal Monmouthshire Regiment. Inside is the volunteer-run **Regimental Museum** (admission free; ✆ 2-5pm daily

SOUTHEAST WALES & BRECON BEACONS

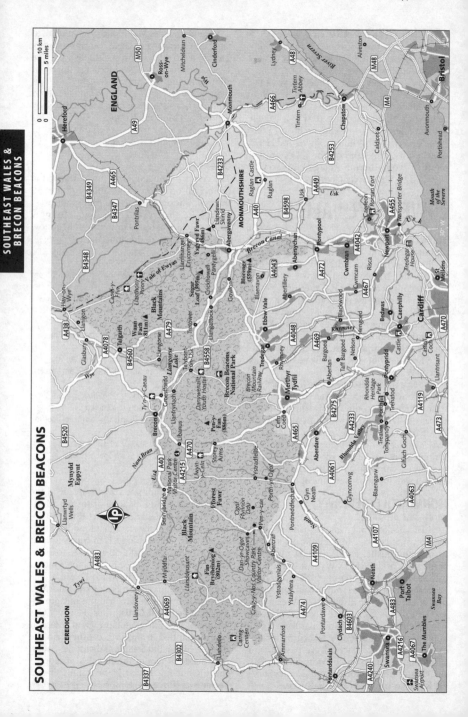

THE WYE TOUR

The Wye Valley has a valid claim to be the birthplace of British tourism. Boat trips along the River Wye began commercially in 1760, but a best-selling book – in fact, one of the first ever travel guidebooks – called *Observations on the River Wye and Several Parts of South Wales,* by William Gilpin, published in 1771, inspired hundreds of people to take the boat trip down the river from Ross-on-Wye (in England) to Chepstow, visiting the various beauty spots and historical sites en route. Early tourists included many famous figures, from poets William Wordsworth and Samuel Taylor Coleridge and painter JMW Turner, to celebrities such as Admiral Lord Nelson, who made the tour in 1802. Doing the Wye Tour soon became *de rigueur* among English high society.

Local people made good money providing crewed rowing boats for hire, which were equipped with canopies and comfortable chairs and tables where their clients could paint or write, while inns and taverns cashed in on the trade by providing food, drink and accommodation. It was normally a two-day trip, with an overnight stay in Monmouth and stops at Symonds Yat (a gorge on the English–Welsh border), Tintern Abbey and Chepstow Castle, among others. In the second half of the 19th century, with the arrival of the railways, the hundreds increased to thousands, and the tour became so commercialised that it was no longer fashionable.

You can still do the Wye Tour today, but these days it's a DIY affair. You can hire a two-person Canadian canoe from various places along the river, camping or staying overnight in B&Bs, but you'll need a guide to navigate the tidal section of the river downstream from Bigsweir Bridge, near Tintern. Beginners can opt for a half-day trip through the gorge at Symonds Yat, or an evening's leisurely paddle from Monmouth down to Redbrook.

For more information, contact **Monmouth Canoe & Activity Centre** (below) or **Mountain & Water** (☎ 01873-831825; www.mountainandwater.co.uk).

Apr-Oct, 2-4pm Sat & Sun Nov-Mar), a labour of love squeezed into a cupboard-sized space, tracing the regiment's history from the 11th century to the Gulf War.

Admiral Horatio Nelson visited Monmouth twice in 1802, officially en route to inspect Pembrokeshire forests for timber for his ships (though it may have had more to do with his affair with local heiress, Lady Emma Hamilton). Despite this tenuous connection Lady Llangattock, local aristocrat and mother of Charles Stewart Rolls, became an obsessive collector of 'Nelsoniana', and the results of her obsession can be seen in the **Nelson Museum & Local History Centre** (☎ 710630; Priory St; admission free; 🕒 10am-1pm & 2-5pm Mon-Sat, 2-5pm Sun). It's fascinating to see how complete Nelson worship was in 19th-century Britain, with forged relics such as locks of his hair, alongside copies of his first attempt to write with his left hand. Children can make Nelson hats and so on. There's also some general Monmouth history, illustrated by old photographs.

Monnow Bridge, at the southwest end of Monnow St, is the UK's only complete example of a late-13th-century fortified bridge. Much of what you see now was restored in 1705. On the far side of the bridge is the partly Norman **St Thomas's Church**.

Activities

Monmouth Canoe & Activity Centre (☎ 713461; www.monmouthcanoehire.20m.com; Castle Yard, Old Dixton Rd) offers half-day/full-day/week-long trips on the Wye in two-seater Canadian canoes (£25/30/180) or single kayaks (£18/20/120). Canoe transport and guides/instructors cost extra.

Sleeping

Monnow Bridge Caravan & Camping (☎ 714004; Drybridge St; sites per person £5) Just across the Monnow Bridge from the town centre, this tiny site has a quiet riverside location.

Casita Alta (☎ 713023; www.monmouthbedandbreakfast.co.uk; 15 Toynbee Close, Osbaston; s/d from £33/42) This B&B, in a quiet suburb 10 minutes' walk north of the town centre, enjoys beautiful views over the Monnow valley and is decorated with paintings by the owner, a trained artist. There are two rooms, one en suite and the other with a private bathroom across the hall.

Church Farm Guest House (☎ 712176; www.churchfarmmitcheltroy.co.uk; Mitchel Troy; s £30-45, d £52; **P**) Found in a tiny village 2 miles southwest of Monmouth, this sprawling 16th-century farmhouse retains its dark oak beams and stone fireplaces, and is peaceful, warm and welcoming. There are family rooms sleeping three or four, and vegetarian breakfasts.

Queen's Head Inn (☎ 712767; www.queensheadmonmouth.co.uk; St James St; s/d/tr £35/45/60) Recently refurbished, the Queen's Head is an appealing 16th-century pub with half a dozen brightly decorated bedrooms, all en suite.

Punch House Hotel (☎ 713855; punchouse@sabrain .com; 4 Agincourt Sq; s/d from £44/54) An old coaching inn bang in the centre of town, the Punch House offers comfortable rooms with a traditional feel, upstairs from a popular pub. Ask for the four-poster room (£64) if you fancy something special.

Eating

Wedges Coffee House (☎ 713513; 94 Monnow St; mains £2-4; ☙ 9am-5pm Mon-Sat) This is a cosy family coffee house, serving excellent home-cooked soups, curries and vegetarian dishes. In summer, the tables spill out into a sunny garden at the back.

Thyme Out (☎ 719339; 31-33 Monnow St; mains £3-6; ☙ 9am-5pm Mon-Sat) Located upstairs in the Salt & Pepper kitchenware shop, this stylish little café serves the best coffee in town, and also does breakfast (croissants, eggs or a fry up, 9am to 11am) and lunch (soup, quiche, baked potatoes, noon to 2.30pm).

Courtyard Café (☎ 719720; 2 Beaufort Arms Ct; mains £5-9) Grab an outdoor table in the cobbled courtyard here, among pot plants and flowers, and order succulent crab salad or bubbling Welsh rarebit, washed down with a glass of wine.

Misbah Tandoori (☎ 714940; 9 Priory St; mains £5-10; ☙ noon-2pm & 6-11pm) One of the best curry houses

SOUTHEAST WALES & BRECON BEACONS

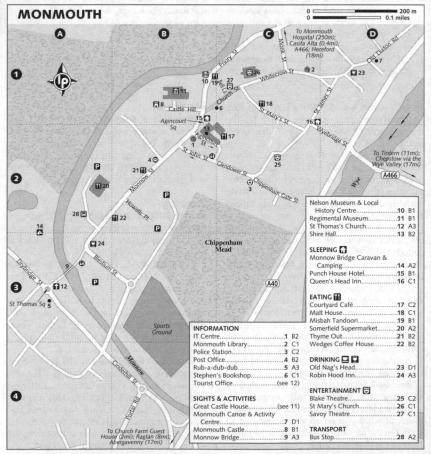

MONMOUTH

Information	
IT Centre	1 B2
Monmouth Library	2 C1
Police Station	3 C2
Post Office	4 B2
Rub-a-dub-dub	5 A3
Stephen's Bookshop	6 C1
Tourist Office	(see 12)

Sights & Activities	
Great Castle House	(see 11)
Monmouth Canoe & Activity Centre	7 D1
Monmouth Castle	8 B1
Monnow Bridge	9 A3
Nelson Museum & Local History Centre	10 B1
Regimental Museum	11 B1
St Thomas's Church	12 A3
Shire Hall	13 B2

Sleeping	
Monnow Bridge Caravan & Camping	14 A2
Punch House Hotel	15 B1
Queen's Head Inn	16 C1

Eating	
Courtyard Café	17 C2
Malt House	18 C1
Misbah Tandoori	19 B1
Somerfield Supermarket	20 A2
Thyme Out	21 B2
Wedges Coffee House	22 B2

Drinking	
Old Nag's Head	23 D1
Robin Hood Inn	24 A3

Entertainment	
Blake Theatre	25 C2
St Mary's Church	26 C1
Savoy Theatre	27 C1

Transport	
Bus Stop	28 A2

not only in Wales, but the whole of Britain, the Misbah is an authentic Bangladeshi family restaurant with a large and loyal following.

Malt House (☎ 772052; 10-12 St Mary's St; tapas £3-4, mains £7-11; ☷ 8am-10.30pm Mon-Sat, 5-11pm Sun) In this town of tearooms and cafés, the Malt House stands out with its chic designer décor and Spanish menu – choose from traditional tapas such as chorizo in wine, tortilla or calamari, and main dishes such as fish casserole or chicken brochettes with rosemary and lemon. There are also all-day breakfasts and a lunch menu of panini, pizza, pasta and tapas.

Self-caterers can stock up at the **Somerfield** (10 Oldway Centre, Monnow St; ☷ 8am-8pm Mon-Sat, 10am-4pm Sun) supermarket.

Drinking & Entertainment

Robin Hood Inn (☎ 719591; 126 Monnow St) The most family-friendly pub in town, the Robin Hood has a warm atmosphere, good food, and a big beer garden with children's play area.

Old Nag's Head (☎ 713782; Granville St) The Old Nag's Head is an old-fashioned, no-frills neighbourhood pub with friendly staff and a selection of real ales on tap. There's live Irish music on Thursday nights, and karaoke on Saturdays.

Savoy Theatre (☎ 772467; www.savoytrust.org.uk; Church St) This gorgeously decorated auditorium, built in 1928 on the oldest theatre site in Wales (its predecessor, the Bell Inn, opened in 1794), hosts modern drama, music gigs, live comedy and cinema.

Blake Theatre (☎ 719401; www.theblaketheatre.org; Almshouse St) The local theatre stages a varied programme of drama, music and children's shows.

St Mary's Church (☎ 740336; www.monmouthchoral .org.uk; Whitecross St) This church is the venue for regular performances by the Monmouth Choral Society.

Getting There & Away

Bus 69 runs along the Wye Valley between Monmouth and Chepstow (£4, 50 minutes, eight daily Monday to Saturday, four daily Sunday), calling at Tintern. Bus 83 runs from Abergavenny (£4, 40 minutes, six daily Monday to Saturday, four daily Sunday) to Monmouth via Raglan.

National Express coach service 536 goes from Cardiff to Monmouth (£9, one hour, one daily) and continues to Birmingham and Edinburgh.

AROUND MONMOUTH
Raglan Castle

Magnificent **Raglan Castle** (Cadw; ☎ 01291-690228; adult/child £2.90/2.50; ☷ 9.30am-6pm Jun-Sep, 9.30am-5pm Apr, May & Oct, 9.30am-4pm Mon-Sat & 11am-4pm Sun Nov-Mar) was the last great medieval castle to be built in Wales. Designed more as a swaggering statement of wealth and power than a defensive fortress, it was built in the 15th and 16th centuries by Sir William ap Thomas and his son, the earl of Pembroke.

A sprawling complex built of dusky pink sandstone, its centrepiece is the lavish **Great Tower**, a hexagonal keep ringed by a moat. It bears a savage wound from the Civil Wars of the 1640s, when it was besieged by Cromwell's soldiers – the tower was bombarded and undermined, until eventually two of the six walls collapsed.

The impressive courtyards beyond the Great Tower display the transition from fortress to grandiose palace, with ornate windows and fireplaces, gargoyle-studded crenellations and heraldic carvings.

Raglan village is 8 miles southwest of Monmouth and 9 miles southeast of Abergavenny. Bus 83 from Monmouth to Abergavenny stops at the Beaufort Arms in the centre of Raglan (25 minutes, six daily Monday to Saturday, four Sunday), a five-minute walk from the castle.

TINTERN
☎ 01291 / pop 750

The A466 road follows the snaking, steep-sided valley of the River Wye from Monmouth to Chepstow, passing through the straggling village of Tintern with its famous abbey. A mile or so upstream from the abbey is **Tintern Old Station** (☎ 689566; admission free, parking per 3/5 hr 50p/£1; ☷ 10am-6pm Easter-Oct), a Victorian train station with old railway coaches that house a tourist information desk, an exhibition about the long-gone Wye Valley railway, and a café. There's a large grassy play area for kids, and easy riverside walks.

Sights & Activities

The spectral ruins of **Tintern Abbey** (Cadw; ☎ 689251; adult/child £3.50/3; ☷ 9.30am-6pm Jun-Sep, 9.30am-5pm Apr, May & Oct, 9.30am-4pm Mon-Sat & 11am-4pm Sun Nov-Mar) sit by the River Wye, the worn stone scabbed with lichen and mottled grey, purple, pink and gold. Founded in 1131 by the Cistercian order, this sprawling monastic complex is one of the most intact medieval

SOUTHEAST WALES & BRECON BEACONS

abbeys in Britain, its soaring Gothic arches and ornate tracery a testament to Cistercian wealth and power.

The haunting ruins and their riverside setting have inspired poets and artists through the centuries, including William Wordsworth, who penned *Lines Composed a Few Miles Above Tintern Abbey* during a visit in 1798, and JMW Turner, who made many paintings and drawings of the abbey.

The huge abbey church was built between 1269 and 1301, and remains almost complete except for its roof; the finest feature is the magnificent west window. Spreading to the north are the remains of the cloisters, the infirmary, the chapter house, the refectory, the latrines and a complex system of drains and sewers. The site needs two hours at least to do it justice, and is best visited towards the end of the day after the coach-tour crowds have dispersed.

There are plenty of possibilities for riverside **walks** around Tintern. One of the best begins at the old railway bridge just upstream from the abbey, and leads up to the **Devil's Pulpit**, a limestone crag on the east side of the river with a spectacular view over the abbey (2.5 miles round trip).

Sleeping & Eating

Parva Farmhouse (☎ 689411; www.hoteltintern.co.uk; s/d from £55/74, 4-course dinner £23) This cosy 17th-century farmhouse has low oak-beamed ceilings, leather Chesterfield sofas and a wood-burning stove in the lounge, and a garden with beautiful views across the valley. The bedrooms are chintzy and appealingly old-fashioned (two have four-posters; £85 per double), and the atmospheric Inglenook Restaurant serves fresh local produce and locally made wines.

Old Station Campsite (☎ 689566; Tintern Old Station; sites per person £2; ☉ Easter-Oct) This basic, no-cars campsite is a handy overnight stop on the Wye Valley Walk or Offa's Dyke Path.

Getting There & Away

Bus 69 runs every 1½ to two hours from Chepstow (£2.20, 20 minutes) and from Monmouth (£2.70, 30 minutes), Monday to Saturday, stopping right in front of the abbey.

CHEPSTOW (CAS-GWENT)

☎ 01291 / pop 11,000

Chepstow is an attractive market town nestled in a great S-bend in the River Wye, with a splendid Norman castle perched dramatically on a cliff above the river. The town is also home to one of Britain's best known racecourses.

Chepstow was first developed as a base for the Norman conquest of southeast Wales, later prospering as a port for the timber and wine trades. As river-borne commerce gave way to the railways, Chepstow's importance diminished to reflect its name, which means 'market place' in Old English.

Orientation

Chepstow sits on the west bank of the River Wye, at the north end of the old Severn Rd Bridge. The train station is 250m southeast of the compact town centre (follow Station Rd); the bus station is 250m west. There are convenient car parks off Welsh St and next to the castle.

Information

Chepstow Bookshop (13 St Mary St; ☉ 9am-5.30pm Mon-Sat, noon-4pm Sun) The best of the local bookshops.

Chepstow Library (☎ 635730; ☉ 9.30am-5.30pm Mon & Fri, 10am-5.30pm Tue, 9.30am-4pm Wed & Sat, 9.30am-8pm Thu) Free internet access.

Tourist Office (☎ 623772; chepstow.tic@monmouthshire.gov.uk; Castle Car Park, Bridge St; ☉ 10am-5.30pm Apr-Oct, 10am-3.30pm Nov-Mar)

Sights

Magnificent **Chepstow Castle** (Cadw; ☎ 624065; Bridge St; adult/child £3.50/3; ☉ 9.30am-6pm Jun-Sep, 9.30am-5pm Apr, May & Oct, 9.30am-4pm Mon-Sat & 11am-4pm Sun Nov-Mar) perches atop a limestone cliff overhanging the river, guarding the main river crossing from England into South Wales (the best view is from the far bank – cross the 1816 Old Wye Bridge and turn left). It is one of the oldest castles in Britain – building began in 1067, less than a year after William the Conqueror invaded England – and the impressive Great Tower retains its original Norman architecture.

The castle's history is explained in an exhibition in the Lower Bailey, where you can see the oldest surviving castle door in Europe, a massive wooden barrier dated to before 1190. Nearby, beside the stairs down to the wine cellar, take a peek into the latrine and imagine baring your backside over this draughty stone box with a giddy drop straight down to the river. Kids will enjoy the castle grounds – lots of green space and plenty of staircases, battlements and wall-walks to explore.

A cave in the cliff below the castle is one of many places where legend says King Arthur and his knights are napping until the day they're needed to save Britain.

Just across the road from the castle is **Chepstow Museum** (☎ 625981; Bridge St; admission free; ⏰ 10.30am-5.30pm Mon-Sat & 2-5.30pm Sun), housed in an 18th-century town house. Good displays cover Chepstow's industrial and social history and a lot of effort is made to make it child friendly; upstairs are depictions of Chepstow Castle as well as some intriguing hair-styling devices, including a perm machine that looks like a 1950s sci-fi brain fryer.

The 13th-century **Port Wall**, the old town fortification, runs along the west side of the town centre. You can see it from the Welsh St car park and near the train station. Chepstow's main street, High St, passes through the **Gate House**, the original city gate, which was restored in the 16th century.

Chepstow Racecourse (☎ 622260; www.chepstow-racecourse.co.uk), set in rolling parkland alongside the River Wye found just north of the town centre, is one of Britain's most famous horse-racing venues and is home to Wales'

most prestigious race meeting, the Welsh National on 27 December.

Activities

The classic **Tintern and Return** walk begins at the tourist office and heads upriver along the Wye Valley path to Tintern Abbey, returning via the Offa's Dyke Path on the eastern bank. The total distance is around 13 miles; allow a full day, with lunch at Tintern. The tourist office sells a leaflet to accompany the walk (£1.25), but you'll also need Ordnance Survey (OS) Landranger map No 162 (also available from the tourist office). You can cut the walk short at Tintern and return to Chepstow (or continue to Monmouth) by bus.

Festivals & Events

The month-long **Chepstow Festival** (www.chepstowfestival.co.uk) takes place every second year in July (even-numbered years), with medieval pageantry, drama and music, outdoor art exhibits, comedy, street entertainment and Shakespeare in the castle.

The second weekend in July sees the annual **Two Rivers Folk Festival** (www.tworiversfolkfestival.com),

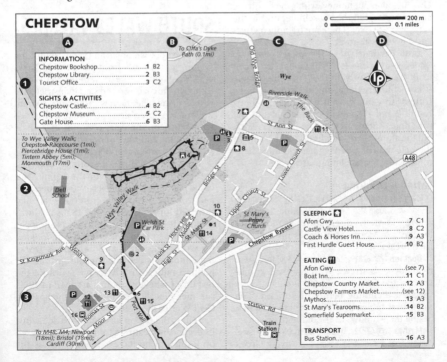

CHEPSTOW

0 — 200 m
0 — 0.1 miles

INFORMATION
Chepstow Bookshop.....................1 B2
Chepstow Library...........................2 B3
Tourist Office..................................3 C2

SIGHTS & ACTIVITIES
Chepstow Castle............................4 B2
Chepstow Museum........................5 C2
Gate House.....................................6 B3

To Wye Valley Walk;
Chepstow Racecourse (1mi);
Piercebridge House (1mi);
Tintern Abbey (5mi);
Monmouth (17mi)

To Offa's Dyke
Path (0.1mi)

Old Wye Bridge

Wye

Riverside Walk

The Back

St Ann St

St Mary's Priory Church

Welsh St Car Park

Hocker Hill St

Middle St

St Mary St

Bank St

High St

Upper Church St

Lower Church St

Bridge St

Chepstow Bypass

A48

Dell School

Wye Valley Walk

St Kingsmark Ave

Welsh St

Thomas St

Moor St

Port Wall

Station Rd

Train Station

To M48, M4; Newport
(18mi); Bristol (18mi);
Cardiff (30mi)

SLEEPING 🛏
Afon Gwy.......................................7 C1
Castle View Hotel..........................8 C2
Coach & Horses Inn......................9 A3
First Hurdle Guest House............10 B2

EATING 🍽
Afon Gwy...................................(see 7)
Boat Inn.......................................11 C1
Chepstow Country Market.........12 A3
Chepstow Farmers Market.....(see 12)
Mythos...13 A3
St Mary's Tearooms....................14 B2
Somerfield Supermarket...........15 B3

TRANSPORT
Bus Station..................................16 A3

three days of traditional music, morris dancers and concerts in the castle, which happily coincides with a beer and cider festival at the Coach & Horses Inn.

On the last Sunday of each month, weather permitting, the **Chepstow Garrison** (www.chepstowe .co.uk) living history group performs some fancy footwork at the castle, dressed in 17th-century costume.

Sleeping

First Hurdle Guest House (☎ 622189; www.firsthurdle guesthouse.co.uk; 9-10 Upper Church St; s/d £35/50) This elegant Georgian-style house has a top location right in the middle of town, and nine smallish, unfussy rooms with period furniture and en suites.

Coach & Horses Inn (☎ 622626; www.thecoachand horsesinn.co.uk; Welsh St; s/d £35/50; P) The owners of this welcoming pub-cum-B&B are from South Africa, a connection reflected in the décor of the bright but basic bedrooms (pics of antelopes, lions and giraffes everywhere). There's a family room that can sleep up to five.

Afon Gwy (☎ 620158; www.afongwy.co.uk; 28 Bridge St; s/d/tr £45/65/80) The four bedrooms at the Afon Gwy are plain but homey, with pine furniture and en suites, but the big selling point is the view over the river. There are friendly owners and a good restaurant.

Castle View Hotel (☎ 620349; www.hotelchepstow.co .uk; 16 Bridge St; s/d/ste £55/77/85) Converted from a 300-year-old private residence, the Castle View is filled with delightful historic details, from 18th-century wall paintings (in bedrooms 2 and 4) to hand-painted glass in the back door. Rooms are small and floors creaky, but the atmosphere is authentic. The 'suite' in the neighbouring cottage has a double bedroom with separate lounge area.

Eating & Drinking

St Mary's Tearooms (☎ 621711; 5 St Mary's St; mains £2-4; ☾ 9am-5.30pm Mon-Sat) A traditional tearoom serving home baking, sandwiches and hot lunches, St Mary's also dishes up a decent fried breakfast.

Boat Inn (☎ 628192; The Back; mains £9-14) A great riverside pub strewn with nautical knick-knacks, the Boat has a good menu of daily specials, including plenty of seafood. The three best tables in the house are upstairs, beside the windows overlooking the river.

Mythos (☎ 627222; Welsh St; mains £9-15; ☾ noon-2am Mon-Sat, 5pm-midnight Sun) This lively Greek bar and restaurant serves authentic Mediterranean mezes, from tzatziki and *spanakopita* (spinach-filled pastries) to souvlaki and *stifado* (rabbit and red wine casserole).

Afon Gwy Inn (☎ 620158; www.afongwy.co.uk; 28 Bridge St; 2-/3-course dinner £14/16, mains £11-14) This riverside restaurant is a local favourite, especially in summer when you can dine outdoors in the garden overlooking the river. The food is no-nonsense home cooking, with dishes such as roast Welsh lamb with redcurrant and rosemary gravy.

Self-caterers can stock up at **Somerfield supermarket** (Thomas St; ☾ 8am-8pm Mon-Sat, 10am-4pm Sun), or check out the local produce at **Chepstow Country Market** (Cormeilles Sq; ☾ 8am-noon Fri) or **Chepstow Farmers' Market** (Cormeilles Sq; 2nd & 4th Sat of month).

Getting There & Away

First buses X10 and X14 run to Chepstow from Bristol (£4, 50 minutes, hourly); bus X14 continues to Newport (50 minutes). Bus 69 links Chepstow with Monmouth via Tintern (see p115).

There are daily direct train services to Chepstow from Cardiff (£6, 40 minutes, hourly) via Newport.

SOUTH WALES VALLEYS

The valleys of Glamorgan and Monmouthshire, fanning northwards from Cardiff and Newport, were once the heart of industrial Wales. Although the coal, iron and steel industries have withered, the valley names – Rhondda, Cynon, Rhymney, Ebbw Vale – still evoke a world of tight-knit working-class communities, male voice choirs, and rows of neat terraced houses set amid a scarred, coal-blackened landscape.

The valleys' industrial economy emerged in the 18th century, based on the exploitation of the region's rich deposits of coal, limestone and iron ore. At first the iron trade dictated the need for coal, but by the 1830s coal was finding its own worldwide markets and people poured in from the countryside looking for work. The harsh and dangerous working conditions provided fertile ground for political radicalism – Merthyr Tydfil elected Britain's first ever Labour Party MP in 1900, and many locals went to fight in the Spanish Civil War in the 1930s.

Today, the region has fought back against its decline by creating a tourist industry based on industrial heritage – places such as the

Rhondda Heritage Park, Big Pit National Coal Museum and Blaenafon Ironworks are among Wales' most impressive tourist attractions.

RHONDDA VALLEY

Northwest of Cardiff, the Rhondda valley – the most famous of the South Wales valleys – was once synonymous with coal mining. The closure of the last pit in 1990 left the valley bereft, but since then Rhondda has succeeded in converting its abandoned colliery into a stunning exploration of the region's industrial heritage.

Rhondda Heritage Park (☎ 01443-682036; www .rhonddaheritagepark.com; Lewis Merthyr Colliery, Trehafod, Rhondda Cynon Taff; adult/child £5.75/4.45; ☑ 10am-6pm Apr-Sep, 10am 6pm Tue-Sun Nov-Mar) brings new life to the old colliery buildings of the Lewis Merthyr coal mine (which closed in 1983). The highlight is the Underground Tour, where you don a miner's helmet and lamp and, accompanied by a guide (all are ex-miners), experience a simulated descent to the coalface. The compelling commentary vividly re-creates the experience of mine workers in the 1950s, and hammers home the social impact of the coal industry.

Back at the surface, the Black Gold multimedia show explores the history of coal mining in South Wales, including what life was like for women and children. There's also an adventure playground for kids. Allow at least two hours for your visit.

The park is 12 miles northwest of Cardiff, just off the A470 between Pontypridd and Porth. There are frequent trains from Cardiff Central station to Trehafod (£3, 35 minutes, every half hour). Alternatively, take Stagecoach bus 132 (£2, one hour, half-hourly Monday to Saturday, hourly Sunday).

MERTHYR TYDFIL

☎ 01685 / pop 55,000

Merthyr Tydfil (*mur*-thir *tid*-vil) occupies a spectacular site, sprawled across a bowl at the head of the Taff Valley, ringed and pocked with quarries and spoil heaps. It was even more spectacular 200 years ago when the town was at the heart of the Industrial Revolution, and this bowl was a crucible filled with the fire and smoke of the world's biggest ironworks.

Today, all the industry has gone. Unemployment (6.6% in 2006) runs at around 20% more than the national average, and shopfronts such as Employment Matters, Tydfil Training and Army Careers Office are prominent in the town centre. But the town is turning itself

around, redeveloping former industrial sites, attracting new businesses, and turning its past into a tourist attraction. There are museums to visit at Cyfarthfa Castle and Joseph Parry's Cottage, and wild landscapes to explore in the nearby Brecon Beacons National Park, whose border lies just north of Merthyr.

Perhaps unusually for such an industrial town, Merthyr Tydfil has produced two internationally famous fashion designers – Laura Ashley (famed for her flowery, feminine designs in the 1970s) and Julien Macdonald (he of the shimmery, figure-hugging dresses favoured by Kylie and Britney).

History

Merthyr Tydfil means 'the place of Tydfil's martyrdom' according to legend, the town was named in honour of a Welsh princess who was murdered for her Christian beliefs in the 5th century. St Tydfil's Church is said to mark the spot where she died.

Merthyr remained a minor village until the late 18th century, when its proximity to iron ore, limestone, water and wood led it to become a centre of iron production. The subsequent discovery of rich coal reserves upped the ante, and by 1801 a string of settlements, each growing around its own ironworks – Cyfarthfa, Penydarren, Dowlais, Pentrebach and others – had merged together to become the biggest town in Wales (population 10,000, eight times the size of Cardiff at that time). Immigrants flooded in from all over Europe, and the town's population peaked at 81,000 in the mid-19th century.

By 1803, Cyfarthfa was the world's biggest ironworks. Ever more efficient ways to make iron were pioneered, on the backs of overworked labourers (including, until 1842, women and children as young as six) who lived in appalling, disease-ridden conditions. By the 19th century Merthyr was a centre of political radicalism. The Merthyr Rising of 1831 was the most violent uprising in Britain's history – 10,000 ironworkers, angry over pay-cuts and lack of representation, faced off against a handful of armed soldiers, and rioting continued for a month.

As demand for iron and steel dwindled in the early 20th century, one by one the ironworks closed down. Unemployment soared, reaching as high as 60% in 1935. In 1939 a Royal Commission even suggested that the whole town should be abandoned. But community ties were strong and people stayed on, despite the lack of work, and today the town is slowly getting back on its feet.

Orientation & Information

Merthyr sprawls across the head of the Taff Valley, and you'll need to do a bit of walking or cycling to see all the sights. The train and bus stations are close together at the south end of town; Cyfarthfa Castle is a mile to the north.

The **tourist office** (☎ 379884; tic@merthyr.co.uk; 14 Glebeland St; ☼ 9.30am-5.30pm Mon-Sat Apr-Oct, 9.30am-4.30pm Mon-Sat Nov-Mar) is in a shop beside the bus station.

Sights

For a measure of the wealth that accumulated at the top of the industrial pile, check out **Cyfarthfa Castle** (☎ 723112; Brecon Rd; admission free; ☼ 10am-5.30pm Apr-Sep, 10am-4pm Tue-Fri, noon-4pm Sat & Sun Oct-Mar), built in 1824 by Cyfarthfa's owner, William Crawshay II, overlooking his ironworks (now gone). The basement now houses an excellent exhibition on Merthyr's gritty history, including a section on the Cornish engineer Richard Trevithick, who in 1804 built the world's first steam locomotive to haul a load on rails. Set into the hillside across the river from the castle are the **Cyfarthfa Blast Furnaces**, all that remains of the ironworks that made the Crawshays rich; there are plans to convert the site into a tourist attraction.

A half-mile to the south of the castle, a row of pint-sized 19th-century ironworkers' houses, built by the Crawshays, stands in bald contrast to Cyfarthfa Castle. At No 4 is **Joseph Parry's Cottage** (☎ 723112; 4 Chapel Row; admission free; ☼ 2-5pm Thu-Sun Apr-Sep) furnished in 1840s style. It was the birthplace of Welsh composer and songwriter Joseph Parry.

Across the river from the bus station is **Ynysfach Engine House**, which once housed the huge beam engines that created the blast of hot air for the iron furnaces. If all goes according to plan, the engine house should be open to the public from 2007.

Trainspotters will relish **Trevithick's Tunnel**, site of the first test of Trevithick's steam-powered locomotive in 1804 – it hauled 10 tonnes of iron for 9.5 miles, at a speed of 4mph. It's off the A470 in Pentrebach, 1.25 miles south of Merthyr.

The narrow-gauge **Brecon Mountain Railway** (☎ 722988; www.breconmountainrailway.co.uk; return £8.50; ☼ 9.30am-6pm Easter-Oct), which operated between 1859 and 1964, once hauled coal and passengers between Merthyr and Brecon. A 5.5-mile section of track, between Pant Station and Torpantau at the head of Pontsticill Reservoir, has been restored and operates steam locomotive trips. There are five or six departures a day (the first at 11am) and the trip takes 65 minutes, with a 20-minute stop at Pontsticill (you can stay longer if you like and return on a later train). Pant Station is 3.5 miles north of Merthyr bus station; take bus 35 (20 minutes, four per hour Monday to Saturday only) to the Pant Cemetery stop, from where it's a five-minute walk. The Beacons Bus B6 service (p125) stops at Pant Station.

Activities

The **Taff Trail** runs along the river on the western edge of town, crossing the handsome railway viaducts of Cefn Coed (the third biggest in Wales) and Pontsarn, both completed in 1866, as it heads up to Pontsticill Reservoir (5 miles from the bus station to the Brecon Mountain Railway). The tourist office can provide details on half-day walks around town.

Fit walkers can hike across the Brecon Beacons from Merthyr to Brecon via the Taff Trail and the Gap Rd (18 miles), or you can cycle there following the Taff Trail all the way (25 miles).

The Forestry Commission's Garwnant Visitor Centre, at the head of Llwyn Onn Reservoir (5 miles north of Merthyr on the A470) is the starting point for a couple of easy forest walks, and also has an adventure play area and rope-swing 'assault course' for kids.

At Taff Bargoed, near Trelewis, 8 miles south of Merthyr, is the huge **Welsh International Climbing Centre** (☎ 01443-710749; www.indoorclimbingwalls .co.uk; Trelewis, Treharris; admission £5-7.70; ☼ 9am-10pm), one of Europe's biggest indoor climbing facilities, offering instruction in rock climbing, caving and abseiling.

Sleeping & Eating

Penylan Guest House (☎ 723179; 12 Courtland Terrace; s/d £20/40) A tidy terraced house off Union St, just 200m east of the train station, the Penylan is as central as you'll get. Rooms are good value, but nothing special.

Llwyn Onn Guest House (☎ 384384; www.llwynonn .co.uk; Llwyn Onn, Cwm Taff; s/d £40/70; P) A 200-year-old farmhouse set in a quiet village 4 miles north of Merthyr on the A470, this guesthouse has spacious and stylish rooms and a beautiful garden with views across Llwyn Onn reservoir.

Tregenna Hotel (☎ 723627; www.tregennahotel.co.uk; Park Tce; s/d £50/68; P) The Tregenna is 500m north of the train station, and has comfortable, if rather chintzy and old-fashioned, rooms.

Bessemer Hotel (☎ 350780; www.bessemerhotel.co.uk; Hermon Close, Dowlais; s/d from £60/65; P) Named after a steel-making process, the Bessemer has forged a reputation as the best place to stay, and to eat, in Merthyr. Still shiny and new with lots of polished wood, the rooms are spacious, the service professional, and the carvery roast lunches very good indeed. Meals are available for £6 to £12.

Wellington Boot Brasserie (☎ 370665; 1 Bethesda St; mains £8-12; ☼ 7-9.30pm Tue-Sat, 12.30-2.30pm Sun) Merthyr is not exactly a gourmet's delight, but this inviting pizzeria–wine bar down by the river serves excellent Italian food, and also does traditional Sunday lunches.

Coffee Grandee (Beacons Place Shopping Centre, John St) a Starbucks-style coffee shop with comfy sofas and armchairs, this is the only place in town for decent espresso and cappuccino.

The nearest budget accommodation is the bunkhouse at the **Welsh International Climbing Centre** (☎ 01443-710749; www.indoorclimbingwalls.co.uk; dm £12), 8 miles south, or at **HoBo Backpackers** (☎ 01495-718422; www.hobo-backpackers.com; Morgan St, Tredegar; dm £12) in Tredegar, 7 miles east of Merthyr.

The nearest campsite is at Llwyn Onn, 4 miles north on the A470.

Getting There & Away

From Monday to Saturday, Stagecoach bus X4 runs from Cardiff (£4, one hour, every 15 minutes) to Merthyr, and from Merthyr to Abergavenny (£5, 1½ hours, hourly). There is no Sunday service. Sixty-Sixty bus X43 (Cardiff to Abergavenny service) runs from Merthyr to Brecon (£3, 35 minutes, every two hours Monday to Saturday, twice on Sunday) and on to Crickhowell and Abergavenny. Bus services are limited or nonexistent on Sunday, with the exception in summer of the Beacons Bus (p125).

Merthyr is also linked to Cardiff by train (£4, one hour, hourly Monday to Saturday, every two hours on Sunday).

BLAENAVON (BLAENAFON)
☎ 01495 / pop 6000

The coal and iron town of Blaenavon (blye-*nahv*-on) is home to the best-preserved 18th-century ironworks in the world. The bleak industrial landscape around the town, with its abandoned coal and iron ore mines, limestone quarries and primitive railway system, became a Unesco World Heritage Site in 2000, as testament to South Wales' global importance as a producer of iron and coal in the 19th century.

In addition to its status as an industrial heritage site, Blaenavon has attempted to muscle in on Hay-on-Wye's territory by re-inventing itself as a 'book town' (see www .booktownblaenafon.com). In 2006 the plan faltered amid infighting and lack of funding, and the future of the project is uncertain. At the time of research, Broad St was in the process of being refurbished and prettified, and still had four secondhand bookshops who

---

THE ABERFAN DISASTER

On 21 October 2006 a low-key memorial service marked the 40th anniversary of one of the worst disasters ever to strike Wales. On that day in 1966, heavy rain loosened an already dangerously unstable spoil heap above Aberfan, 4 miles south of Merthyr Tydfil, and sent a half-million-tonne mudslide of liquefied coal slurry down onto the village. It wiped out a row of terraced houses and ploughed into Pantglas primary school, killing 144 people, most of them children.

To cap tragedy with scandal, the state-owned National Coal Board refused to accept responsibility for the mudslide and the Labour government of the day raided the disaster relief fund of £150,000 to pay for the removal of the remaining spoil heaps. In 1997, a newly elected Labour government repaid the money. But despite the fact that the 1966 amount would have been worth £1.5 million in 1997, they repaid only £150,000; many people feel this was a shabby gesture, and call for the government to repay the full amount to help maintain Aberfan cemetery and memorial.

Today, the A470 Cardiff to Merthyr Tydfil road cuts right through the spot where the spoil heap once stood. The site of the school has been turned into a memorial garden, while the village cemetery contains a long, double row of matching headstones, a mute and moving memorial to those who died.

were determined to make a go of things, plus a smattering of antique shops and cafés.

There's nowhere to stay overnight in Blaenavon; the nearest accommodation is in Abergavenny.

Orientation & Information

Blaenavon sits at the head of the Llwyd Valley, 16 miles north of Newport. Most buses stop in High St, in the centre of town. Broad St, with its bookshops, is a block to the east. Blaenavon Ironworks is 400m west of High St: walk up-hill to the top of High St, turn left on Upper Waun St, then left again on North St. Big Pit National Coal Museum is another mile west of the ironworks.

The **tourist office** (☎ 792615; www.blaenavontic.com; North St; ♥ 9.30am-4.30pm Mon-Fri, 10am-5pm Sat, 10am-4.30pm Sun Apr-Oct) is at the entrance to Blaenavon Ironworks.

Sights

When it was completed in 1788, **Blaenavon Ironworks** (Cadw; ☎ 792615; North St; adult/child £2.50/2; ♥ 9.30am-4.30pm Mon-Fri, 10am-5pm Sat & 10am-4.30pm Sun Apr-Oct) was one of the most advanced in the world. Its three huge coal-fired blast furnaces were provided with air powered by a steam engine, making them much more powerful than older, smaller furnaces fired with charcoal and blasted with air from a waterwheel-powered bellows. Within a few years it was the world's second-biggest ironworks, after Cyfarthfa at Merthyr Tydfil. Innovation and development continued here until 1904, when the last furnace was finally shut down.

Today the site is one of the best-preserved of all the Industrial Revolution ironworks. You can follow the whole process of production, from the charging of the furnaces to the casting of molten iron in the casting sheds. Also on display are the ironworkers' tiny terraced cottages. The surrounding hillsides are pitted with old tramlines, mines, tunnels and 'scouring' sites, where water was released from holding ponds to wash away topsoil and expose ore seams.

The atmospheric **Big Pit National Coal Museum** (☎ 790311; www.museumwales.ac.uk; admission free; ♥ 9.30am-5pm Feb-Nov, 10am-4.30pm Dec & Jan, guided tours 10am-3.30pm) provides an opportunity to explore a real coal mine and feel what life was like for the miners who extracted coal here for 200 years. Visitors descend 90m into a genuine coal mine and explore the tunnels and coalface in the company of an ex-miner

guide. It's sobering to experience something of the dark, dank working conditions, particularly considering the children who once worked here by candlelight.

Above ground, you can see the pithead baths, blacksmith's workshop and other colliery buildings, filled with displays on the industry and the evocative reminiscences of ex-miners.

You'll be decked out in hard hat, power pack and other safety gear weighing some 5kg, and won't be allowed to take matches or anything electrical (including photo equipment and watches) down with you. It's cold underground, so take extra layers, and wear sturdy shoes. Children must be at least 1m tall. Disabled visitors can arrange tours in advance.

The **Pontypool & Blaenavon Railway** (☎ 792263; www.pontypool-and-blaenavon.co.uk; return adult/child £2.40/1.20; ♥ departures half-hourly 11.30am-4.30pm Sat, Sun & bank holidays Apr-Sep) was built from Pontypool to Brynmawr to haul coal and passengers up and down the valley. Passenger traffic ceased in 1941, and coal haulage stopped when the Big Pit was closed in 1980.

Since then a 0.8-mile section, running northwest from Furnace Sidings near Big Pit, has been restored and maintained by local volunteers. Whistle Halt, at the north end, is the highest train station in England and Wales at 396m. The Whistle Inn Pub, beside the station, has a huge collection of miners' lamps. In 2006 approval was obtained to extend the line 1.25 miles south to Blaenavon, but it will be a few years before it opens.

Eating & Drinking

Old Lipton's Coffee Shop (☎ 792828; 76 Broad St; snacks £2-5) Housed in a converted grocery, this is a friendly traditional café serving tea, coffee, sandwiches, homemade soup and greasy-spoon standards such as sausage, egg and chips.

Pottery (☎ 790395; Llanover Rd; mains £6-12; ♥ Wed-Sun) This welcoming pub has an array of real ales and a beer garden with views over the hills, and dishes up excellent bar meals, including a great Sunday lunch. It's uphill from the roundabout on the A4043 on the southern edge of town.

Getting There & Away

Stagecoach bus X24 goes direct from Newport to Blaenavon (£3, 40 minutes, every 15 minutes Monday to Saturday); bus 23 serves the same route hourly on Sunday. Bus 30 from Newport to Blaenavon (hourly) continues to

Brynmawr; four per day (check times in advance) stop at Big Pit on the way.

At Brynmawr you can change to bus X4 (every 30 minutes) for Abergavenny, Merthyr Tydfil or Cardiff.

BRECON BEACONS

BRECON BEACONS NATIONAL PARK

Founded in 1957, the Brecon Beacons National Park (Parc Cenedlaethol Bannau Brycheiniog) stretches from Llandeilo and Llandovery in the west to Hay-on-Wye and Abergavenny in the east, encompassing some of the finest scenery in South Wales. High mountain plateaus of grass and heather, their northern rims scalloped with glacier scoured hollows, rise above wooded, waterfall-splashed valleys and green, rural landscapes.

There are four distinct regions within the park, neatly bounded by main roads: the wild, lonely **Black Mountain** (Mynydd Du) in the west, with its high moors and glacial lakes; **Fforest Fawr** (Great Forest), which lies between the A4067 and A470, whose rushing streams and spectacular waterfalls form the headwaters of the Rivers Tawe and Neath; the **Brecon Beacons** (Bannau Brycheiniog) proper, a group of very distinctive, flat-topped hills that includes Pen-y-Fan (886m), the park's (and southern Britain's) highest point; and, from the A40 northeast to the English border, the rolling heathland ridges of the **Black Mountains** (Y Mynyddoedd Duon) – don't confuse them with the Black Mountain (singular) in the west.

In 2005 the western half of the national park was given geopark recognition by Unesco. The **Fforest Fawr Geopark** stretches from Black Mountain in the west to Pen-y-Fan in the east, and it takes in important landscape features such as the ice-sculpted northern faces of the Brecon Beacons, the gorges and waterfalls around Ystradfellte, and the caves and limestone pavements of the southern Black Mountain.

Information

The **National Park Visitor Centre** (☎ 01874-623366; www.breconbeacons.org; Libanus; admission free; ☒ 9.30am-5pm Mar-Jun, Sep & Oct, 9.30am-6pm Jul & Aug, 9.30am-4.30pm Nov-Feb; meals around £4), set high on a ridge with fine views of Pen-y-Fan and Corn Du, is the park's main information point with full details of walks, hiking and biking trails, outdoor activities, wildlife and geology. It has easy disabled access, and there's a book and gift shop, tearoom, and picnic tables. During school holidays there are kids' activities, organised farm visits, guided walks and themed minibus tours.

The centre is off the A470 road 5 miles southwest of Brecon and 15 miles north of Merthyr Tydfil. The Beacons Bus B6 stops at the centre. Otherwise, Sixty-Sixty bus X43 (Cardiff–Merthyr Tydfil–Brecon–Abergavenny) stops in Libanus village, a 1.25-mile walk from the centre.

The **Craig-y-Nos Country Park Visitor Centre** (☎ 01639-730395; Brecon Rd, Pen-y-Cae; admission free; ☒ 10am-6pm Mon-Fri & 10am-7pm Sat & Sun May-Aug, 10am-5pm Mon-Fri & 10am-6pm Sat & Sun Mar, Apr, Sep & Oct, 10am-4pm Mon-Fri & 10am-4.30pm Sat & Sun Nov-Feb) is in the western part of the park near Dan-yr-Ogof caves. As well as park information, there are easy forest walks and picnic areas.

There are tourist offices at Abergavenny, Crickhowell, Brecon, Merthyr Tydfil, Llandeilo and Llandovery.

Out & About, the national park's free visitor newspaper, is available at tourist offices, and is full of useful information. OS Landranger maps 160 and 161 cover most of the park, and have all the walking and cycling trails marked.

Activities
WALKING

There are hundreds of walking routes in the park, ranging from gentle strolls to strenuous climbs. The park's staff organise guided walks and other active events throughout the summer – details are listed in *Out & About.* They also supply a booklet, *Walks in the Brecon Area* (£1.50), which details many hikes including the standard route up Pen-y-Fan and walks along the Monmouthshire and Brecon Canal.

Three long-distance walking trails pass through the park:

Beacons Way

The Beacons Way (www.breconbeaconspark society.org) is a 100-mile trail that wends its way across the park from Abergavenny to Llangadog (on the A40 between Llandovery and Llandeilo), taking in all the highest summits in the Black Mountains, the Brecon Beacons, Fforest Fawr and Black Mountain; the recommended time for the entire route is eight days. An illustrated route guide, *The Beacons Way* by John Sansom and Arwel Michael (£12), is available from bookshops and information centres.

Taff Trail

The Taff Trail (p66) walking and cycling route from Cardiff to Brecon cuts right across the middle of the park. The main route follows minor roads north from Merthyr Tydfil past the Pontsticill Reservoir to Talybont-on-Usk and the Monmouthshire and Brecon Canal. An alternative route, for walkers only, follows the Taf Fawr valley (as does the main A470 road), via Nant-ddu and the Storey Arms.

Offa's Dyke Path

The Offa's Dyke Path (p63) runs along the eastern fringe of the national park. The 17.5-mile section from Pandy (north of Abergavenny) to Hay-on-Wye offers splendid high-level walking with great views. It makes a great two-day outing; start from Abergavenny and follow the first part of the Beacons Way to Llanthony, where you can spend the night (10 miles), then climb back up to the ridge and continue on the Offa's Dyke Path to Hay-on-Wye (12 miles).

CYCLING & MOUNTAIN BIKING

The 55-mile Taff Trail from Cardiff to Brecon is the best known cycle route in the park, passing through some great scenery between Merthyr Tydfil and Brecon. Other waymarked cycle routes on minor roads include Abergavenny to Hay-on-Wye via the Vale of Ewyas,

and Hay to Brecon via Talgarth. Cycle hire is available in Brecon and Abergavenny.

There are many excellent off-road mountain-biking routes in the park, including a series of graded and waymarked trails laid out by the national park authority. These are detailed in a map and guidebook pack, *Mountain Biking in the Brecon Beacons* (£7), available from the National Park Visitor Centre, tourist offices and at www.mtbbreconbeacons.co.uk.

Sleeping

The website of the **Association of Bunkhouse Operators** (☎ 07071-780259; www.hostelswales.com) has a full listing of independent bunkhouses in the national park area; a leaflet with the same information is available from tourist offices.

The park also has five YHA/HI youth hostels (www.yha.org.uk). From west to east they are:
Llanddeusant Youth Hostel (☎ 0870 770 5930; Old Red Lion, Llanddeusant; dm £11; ⊙ Easter–Oct) A tree-shaded former inn nestled next to a 14th-century church, on the western fringes of Black Mountain.
Llwyn-y-Celyn Youth Hostel (☎ 0870 770 5936; Libanus; dm £14; ⊙ Easter–Oct) An 18th-century farmhouse in 15 acres of woodland, 7 miles south of Brecon. Handy for climbing Pen-y-Fan.
Ty'n-y-Caeau Youth Hostel (☎ 0870 770 5718; Groesffordd, Brecon; dm £14; ⊙ year-round) Lovely Victorian farmhouse 2 miles east of Brecon.

CLIMBING PEN-Y-FAN

One of the most popular hikes in the national park is the ascent of Pen-y-Fan (886m), the highest peak in the Brecon Beacons (around 120,000 people each year make the climb). The shortest route to the summit begins at the Pont ar Daf car park on the A470, 10 miles southwest of Brecon. It's a steep but straightforward slog up a deeply eroded path (now paved with natural stone) to the summit of Corn Du (873m), followed by a short dip and final ascent to Pen-y-Fan (4.5 miles round trip; allow three hours). A slightly longer (5.5 miles round trip) but just as crowded path starts at the Storey Arms outdoor centre, a mile to the north. The X4 Cardiff–Merthyr Tydfil–Brecon–Abergavenny bus and the Beacons bus (B1, B3, B6 and B9) stop at the Storey Arms. (Be aware the Storey Arms is not a pub!)

You can avoid the crowds by choosing one of the longer routes on the north side of the mountain, which also have the advantage of more interesting views on the way up. The best starting point is the Cwm Gwdi car park, at the end of a minor road 3.5 miles southwest of Brecon. From here, you follow a path along the crest of the Cefn Cwm Llwch ridge, with great views of the neighbouring peaks, with a final steep scramble up to the summit. The round trip from the car park is 7 miles; allow three to four hours. Starting and finishing in Brecon, the total distance is 14 miles.

Remember that Pen-y-Fan is a serious mountain – the weather can change rapidly, and people have to be rescued here every year. Wear hiking boots and take warm clothes, waterproofs, and a map and compass. You can get advice and weather forecasts at the **National Park Visitor Centre** (☎ 01874-623366; www.breconbeacons.org; Libanus). Weather forecasts are also available on ☎ 0870 900 0100 and at www.meto.gov.uk/outdoor/mountainsafety.

Danywenallt Youth Hostel (☎ 0870 770 6136; Talybont-on-Usk; dm £17.50; ✸ year-round) Converted farmhouse nestling beneath the dam of Talybont Reservoir, halfway between Brecon and Crickhowell.

Capel-y-Ffin Youth Hostel (☎ 0870 770 5748; Capel-y-Ffin, Llanthony; dm £11; ✸ year-round) A former hill farm in a remote setting near the head of the Vale of Ewyas.

Camping anywhere in the national park, even on open land, requires the permission of the farmer or landowner; all camping is prohibited on National Trust land. Tourist offices have lists of camping grounds with full facilities.

Getting There & Around

BUS

Most regional buses to and around the national park are operated by Stagecoach, with a few by local operators; for timetable information call **Traveline** (☎ 0870 608 2608; www.traveline-cymru .org.uk). You can pick up a national park time-table booklet at information offices. Some useful routes are listed in the table below. Most of these routes have no Sunday services, though – for travel on Sundays and bank holidays, you'll need to take the Beacons Bus and Beacons Roundabout services (see below).

Useful rail services are limited to Cardiff–Merthyr Tydfil, Cardiff–Newport–Abergavenny, and Swansea–Llandeilo–Llandovery (roughly hourly, Monday to Saturday; Sunday services are less frequent).

The **Beacons Bus** (☎ 01873-853254; www.visitbreacon beacons.com) is a network of special tourist bus services that operates on Sundays and bank holidays from late May to mid-September. You can pick up a leaflet with route map and time-tables at any tourist office. There is also a leaf-let, *One Way Walks with Beacons Bus*, detailing

BEACONS BUS ROUTES		
Route	Destination/s	Frequency (daily)
B1	Cardiff–Merthyr Tydfil–Brecon	1
B2	Swansea–Dan-yr-Ogof–Brecon	1
B3	Bridgend–Penderyn–Brecon	1
B4	Newport–Abergavenny–Brecon	1
B5	Brecon–National Park Visitor Centre	6
B6	Roundabout Service	4
B7	Hay-on-Wye–Llanfihangel Crucorney	3
B8	Brecon–Crickhowell–Abergavenny	2
B9	Porthcawl–Merthyr Tydfil–Brecon	1
B10	Carmarthen–Llandeilo–Brecon	1
B11	Brecon–Hay-on-Wye	1

walks accessible from the bus routes. Two of the services (B1 and B8) can carry bicycles.

On the circular routes B6 (also called the Beacons Roundabout) and B7 you can get on and off at any point. The B6 route takes in Brecon, the National Park Visitor Centre, the Storey Arms, Garwnant Forest Centre, Brecon Mountain Railway and Talybont-on-Usk. You can buy an all-day ticket (adult/child £6.50/4, bike £2.50) on the first Beacons Bus you board, which then remains valid all day on all other services. There are also cheaper single fares.

ABERGAVENNY (Y-FENNI)

☎ 01873 / pop 14,000

The handsome market town of Abergavenny is set amid shapely, tree-fringed hills on the eastern edge of Brecon Beacons National Park. Its ancient name, Y-Fenni (uh-*ven*-ni; Welsh for 'place of the smiths') was given to a stream that empties into the River Usk here, and later anglicised to Gavenny (Abergavenny means 'mouth of the Gavenny').

The Romans established Gobannium Fort, exactly a day's march from their garrison at Caerleon (p108), near Newport, and stayed from AD 57 to 400. But the town grew in importance after a Marcher lord, Hamelin

BUS SERVICES IN THE BRECON BEACONS		
Service	Destination/s	Frequency (daily)
X4	Cardiff–Merthyr Tydfil–Abergavenny	every 30min
G14	Llandovery–Brecon	6
X43	Merthyr Tydfil–Brecon-Abergavenny	7
63	Swansea–Craig-y-Nos–Brecon	3
704	Llandrindod Wells–Brecon	7

de Ballon, built a castle here around 1100. Today it thrives as a market, shopping and tourist centre.

Abergavenny makes a fine base for walks in the surrounding hills, and is one of only two towns providing rail access to the national park (the other is Merthyr Tydfil). The area has several excellent restaurants, and the annual Abergavenny Food Festival is a world-famous event.

Orientation

The tourist office is next to the bus station, a few minutes' walk southeast of the town centre; the train station is a further half a mile walk along Monmouth Rd and Station

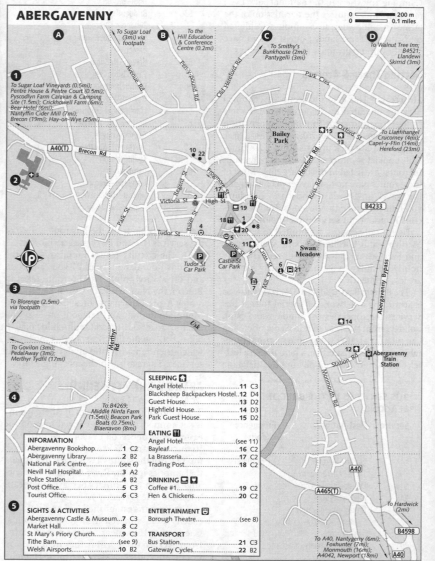

ABERGAVENNY

SLEEPING 🛏
Angel Hotel...................................11 C3
Blacksheep Backpackers Hostel..12 D4
Guest House................................13 D2
Highfield House...........................14 D3
Park Guest House.........................15 D2

EATING 🍴
Angel Hotel...........................(see 11)
Bayleaf..16 C2
La Brasseria.................................17 C2
Trading Post................................18 C2

DRINKING 🍷 🍺
Coffee #1....................................19 C2
Hen & Chickens..........................20 C2

ENTERTAINMENT 🎭
Borough Theatre.....................(see 8)

TRANSPORT
Bus Station.................................21 C3
Gateway Cycles..........................22 B2

INFORMATION
Abergavenny Bookshop................1 C2
Abergavenny Library......................2 B2
National Park Centre................(see 6)
Nevill Hall Hospital........................3 A2
Police Station.................................4 B2
Post Office.....................................5 C3
Tourist Office.................................6 C3

SIGHTS & ACTIVITIES
Abergavenny Castle & Museum.....7 C3
Market Hall....................................8 C2
St Mary's Priory Church.................9 C3
Tithe Barn.................................(see 9)
Welsh Airsports...........................10 B2

Rd. There are convenient central car parks on Tudor St and Castle St.

Information

Abergavenny Bookshop (☎ 850380; 1 High St) Local interest books, Ordnance Survey maps.

Abergavenny Library (☎ 735980; Baker St; ⏱ 9.30am-5.30pm Mon & Fri, 10am-5.30pm Tue, 9.30am-5pm Wed, 9.30am-8pm Thu, 9.30am-1pm Sat) Free internet access.

Nevill Hall Hospital (☎ 732732; Brecon Rd) With 24-hour emergency service.

Police Station (☎ 852273; Tudor St)

Post Office (Castle St)

Tourist Office (☎ 857588; www.abergavenny.co.uk; Swan Meadow, Cross St; ⏱ 9.30am-5.30pm Apr-Oct, 10am-4pm Nov-Mar) Also houses a national park visitor centre.

Sights

The modest-looking **St Mary's Priory Church** (☎ 853168; www.stmarys-priory.org; Hereford Rd; admission free, donation requested; ⏱ 10am-noon & 2-4pm Mon-Sat, 2-4pm Sun) has been described as 'the Westminster Abbey of South Wales', because of the remarkable treasury of aristocratic tombs that lies within. The church was founded as part of a Benedictine priory around the time the castle was built (1100), but the present building dates mainly from the 14th century, with many 19th-century additions and alterations. There's always a volunteer warden around to answer questions.

The oldest memorial, dating from around 1325, is a graceful, worn, carved-oak effigy of Sir John de Hastings II, who was probably responsible for the church's 14th-century restoration. In the northern transept is one of the most important medieval carvings in Europe – a monumental 15th-century wooden representation of the biblical figure of Jesse. It was the base of what must have been a mighty altarpiece showing the lineage of Jesus.

The Herbert Chapel is packed with recumbent effigies. Most depict members of the Herbert family, starting with Sir William ap Thomas, founder of Raglan Castle (p115), and his wife Gwladys – Sir William's feet rest on a lion that looks like it was modelled on a sheep. The oak choir stalls were carved in the 15th century (note the lively misericords and the little dragons at the ends).

The huge medieval **tithe barn** next to the church is being restored as a heritage and arts centre, and will also be used as a venue during the food festival (see p128).

Not much remains of **Abergavenny Castle** except for an impressive stretch of curtain wall on either side of the gatehouse on the northwest side. Elsewhere, the ruins of towers and fragments of wall peek out from among the trees. Frequently besieged but never taken, the castle was wrecked by royalist forces in 1645 during the Civil War in order to keep it out of parliamentary hands, and it has gone largely untouched since then.

The castle keep, converted into a hunting lodge by the Victorians, now houses the small but perfectly formed **Abergavenny Museum** (☎ 854282; Castle St; admission free; ⏱ 11am-1pm & 2-5pm Mon-Sat Mar-Oct, 11am-1pm & 2-4pm Mon-Sat Nov-Feb). It tells the history of the castle and the town, and includes re-creations of a Victorian Welsh farmhouse kitchen, a saddlery workshop, and Basil Jones' grocery shop. The latter was transferred intact when it closed in the 1980s and makes a fascinating display, with many items dating back to the 1930s and '40s.

The 19th-century **Market Hall** (☎ 735811; www.abergavennymarket.co.uk; Cross St) is a lively place, hosting a general market (food, drink, clothes, household goods) on Tuesday, Friday and Saturday, a flea market (bric-a-brac, collectables, secondhand goods) on Wednesday, regular weekend crafts and antiques fairs, and a farmers market on the fourth Thursday of each month.

On the western edge of town are the **Sugar Loaf Vineyards** (☎ 853066; ⏱ 10.30am-5pm Mon-Sat, noon-5pm Sun May-Oct, 10.30am-5pm Tue-Sat, noon-5pm Sun Mar & Apr, 11am-4pm Tue-Sat, noon-4pm Sun Nov-24 Dec), established in 1992 and producing around 12,000 bottles per year of award-winning Welsh wine. You can take a self-guided tour before sampling the goods at the café and gift shop.

Activities

WALKING

Abergavenny sits amid three glacially sculpted hills – **Ysgyryd Fawr** (Skirrid; 486m) to the northeast; **Sugar Loaf**, (596m) to the northwest; and the **Blorenge** (559m) to the southwest. Each has rewarding walks and fine views of the Usk Valley and the Black Mountains.

Easiest of the three is the cone-shaped **Sugar Loaf**, which offers a 9-mile return trip from the centre of town to the summit via heath, woodland and the superb viewpoint of Mynydd Llanwenarth. You can cheat by driving to a car park about halfway up on Mynydd

Llanwenarth; from here it's a 4-mile round trip. Head west on the A40, and at the edge of town turn right for Sugar Loaf Vineyards, then go left at the next two junctions.

Although the summit of the **Blorenge** is closer to town – the round trip is only 5 miles – it is a much steeper and more strenuous outing, and good walking boots are recommended. Cross the bridge over the Usk on Merthyr Rd and immediately turn right and follow the lane past the cemetery and under the main road. Cross the B4269 road in Llanfoist and follow the lane beside the church until it bends left; continue through a tunnel under the canal, and then follow a steep path straight uphill (a former tramroad that carried coal down to the canal). When you emerge from the woods, there is a final steep climb up an obvious path to the summit.

For more leisurely walks, you can follow easy paths along the banks of the River Usk, or explore the towpath of the Monmouthshire and Brecon Canal, which passes a mile southwest of the town.

You can buy a booklet called *Walks from Abergavenny* (£2) from the tourist office. There are also various guided walks on offer – again, ask at the tourist office.

BOATING

The Monmouthshire and Brecon Canal runs along the foot of the Blorenge mountain, southwest of town. You can take to the water with **Beacon Park Boats** (☎ 858277; www.beaconparkboats.com; The Boathouse, Llanfoist; ☯ 10am-6pm Mar-Oct), which rents out electric-powered boats (up to six persons) for £50 a day (£65 in July and August). In a day, you can cruise south to Goytre Wharf, or north to Llangattock and back.

PARAGLIDING

The Blorenge, rising above Abergavenny to the southwest, is one of Britain's finest paragliding and hang-gliding sites. In fact, it is so important that the Southeast Wales Hang-Gliding and Paragliding Club purchased the mountain in 1998. Several records have been set from here, and the mountain regularly hosts competition events.

Welsh Airsports (☎ 950910; www.welshairsports.com; Frogmore St) offers instruction in paragliding seven days a week, weather permitting – a one-day course costs £150.

Courses

Franco Taruschio (who founded the Walnut Tree Inn) and Lindy Wildsmith run one-/two-day cookery courses at the **Hill Education & Conference Centre** (☎ 333777; www.conferencecentrewales.co.uk; Pen-y-Pound) teaching Italian cooking with Welsh ingredients. Courses run once or twice a month, and cost £80/180 excluding accommodation.

Festivals

Abergavenny Food Festival (☎ 851643; www.abergavennyfoodfestival.co.uk) is the most high-profile foodie event in Wales and has lots of demonstrations, competitions, courses and stalls. The two-day event is held on the third weekend in September.

Sleeping
BUDGET

Pyscodlyn Farm Caravan & Camping Site (☎ 853271; www.pyscodlyncaravanpark.com; Llanwenarth Citra; sites per tent £4-12) This sheltered, grassy camping ground is beside the River Usk, 2 miles west of Abergavenny on the A40.

Smithy's Bunkhouse (☎ 853432; www.smithysbunkhouse.com; Lower House Farm, Pantygelli; sites per person £3, dm £8.50-9.50) Another independent bunkhouse with two comfortable 12-bed dorms plus laundry, kitchen and common room, this one on a working farm on the edge of the Black Mountains. It's 2 miles north of town along Old Hereford Rd; at Pantygelli turn right down the track opposite the Crown Inn.

Middle Ninfa Farm (☎ 854662; www.middleninfa.co.uk; Llanellen; sites per person £3, dm £10-12) Back-to-nature farm on the flanks of the Blorenge, with a comfortable six-bed bunkhouse and camping space for three tents. It's 2 miles south of Abergavenny – take the B4269 south from Llanfoist and go steeply up the first road on the right.

Blacksheep Backpackers (☎ 859125; www.blacksheepbackpackers.com; 24 Station Rd; dm/d £14/30; ☐) This independent hostel is across the street from the train station. It has a homey, cheerful atmosphere, comfy beds and a bar and pool room (generally not too noisy). Facilities include kitchen, TV lounge and mountain bike hire.

Guest House (☎ 854823; theguesthouseabergavenny@hotmail.com; 2 Oxford St; s/d from £25/45; Ⓟ) This family-friendly B&B with cheerful, flouncy rooms has a special treat for kids in the garden – a mini-menagerie of pigs, rabbits and chickens. There's a drying area for wet hiking gear, and hearty breakfasts (including vegetarian) to set you up for the day.

MIDRANGE

Park Guest House (☎ 853715; www.parkguesthouse.co.uk; 36 Hereford Rd; s/d £35/50; P) The seven bedrooms in this large former farmhouse are bright and cheerful, each with comfy duvets, pot plants and a chair for reading. Three are en suite; those with shared bathroom cost £25/40.

Highfield House (☎ 852371; www.highfieldabergavenny .co.uk; 6 Belmont Rd; s/d £36/58) A handsome Victorian villa set in spacious landscaped gardens, the Highfield has three comfortable, en suite bedrooms named after local castles, and enjoys a peaceful location not far from the town centre with views toward the Sugarloaf hill.

Pentre Court Guest House (☎ 853545; www.pentre court.com; Brecon Rd; d £50-70; 🐾) A splendid, rambling Georgian country house, the Pentre Court is packed with polished antiques and period furniture, with four-poster beds and plush sofas in the bedrooms, and a heated swimming pool and sun terrace in three acres of manicured gardens. One drawback – credit and debit cards are not accepted.

TOP END

Angel Hotel (☎ 857121; www.angelhotelabergavenny.com; 15 Cross St; s/d/tr from £60/85/105; P) Abergavenny's top hotel is housed in a fine Georgian building that was once a famous coaching inn. Recently refurbished, the bedrooms are stylish and understated, with clean lines and neutral colours set off with a touch of blue. Deluxe rooms (£100 to £120) have designer Villeroy and Boch bathrooms, and there's one bedroom with a four-poster bed. Note that rooms overlooking the street can be a bit noisy on Friday and Saturday nights.

Eating & Drinking

Trading Post (☎ 855448; 14 Nevill St; mains £3-8; 🕙 9.30am-5pm Mon-Sat) Housed in a 16th-century town house that was formerly the Cow Inn (check out the carved cow's heads on the outside), the Trading Post is a pleasantly old-fashioned café serving a wide range of teas and coffees as well as a bistro menu of light meals.

Bayleaf (☎ 851212; 7 Market St; mains £6-9; 🕙 6-11pm Tue-Thu & Sun, 6-11.30pm Fri & Sat) Abergavenny's best curry house, the Bayleaf specialises in Northern Indian and Bangladeshi cuisine, with dishes such as *gustaba* (a hot and sour lamb curry) and *aam achari* chicken (cooked in mango chutney).

La Brasseria (☎ 737937; Lewis' Lane; mains £8-13) This lively little bistro has a warm, sunny Mediterranean vibe, with a French-inspired menu that includes the likes of garlic mushrooms, roast duck (with chunky, homemade chips), and roast sea bream.

Angel Hotel (☎ 857121; 15 Cross St; mains £8-15) The Angel offers a choice of eating options, from an informal meal in front of the log fire in the bar, to the sophisticated restaurant with its crisp white linen and attentive service, to a romantic dinner in the candle-lit courtyard. The menu makes the most of local produce – the roast lamb is tender and succulent – and there's an excellent wine list.

Coffee #1 (☎ 737800; 14 High St) Wales' answer to Starbucks is a cosy nook of dark wood, brown leather and chilled music, and offers an extensive menu of organic and Fairtrade espresso, cappuccino and latte.

Hen & Chickens (☎ 853613; 7 Flannel St) A traditional real-ale pub tucked down a pedestrianised alley, the Hen & Chickens hosts live jazz sessions on Sunday afternoons (outside when it's sunny), and fortnightly folk music.

See also the boxed text, p130, for restaurants in the surrounding area.

Entertainment

The small **Borough Theatre** (☎ 850805; www.borough theatreabergavenny.co.uk; Cross St) in the Town Hall stages a varied programme of drama, opera, dance, comedy and music; the Beatles played here in 1963.

St Mary's Priory Church has regular evening choral concerts.

Getting There & Away

Stagecoach bus X3 runs to Abergavenny from Cardiff (£4, 1½ hours, hourly Monday to Saturday); five per day continue to Hereford (£4.50, one hour) in England. Sixty-Sixty bus X43 runs from Merthyr Tydfil to Abergavenny (£6, 1¾ hours, every two hours Monday to Saturday, twice on Sunday) via Brecon and Crickhowell.

The Beacons Bus (route B4) links Abergavenny with Brecon and Newport (p125).

There are trains from Cardiff (£8.20, 40 minutes, at least hourly Monday to Saturday, eight Sunday) to Abergavenny via Newport, continuing to Hereford (£6.20, 25 minutes).

Getting Around

You can rent bikes from **Gateway Cycles** (☎ 858519; 32 Frogmore St) in the town centre, and

EATING OUT & ABOUT

The countryside around Abergavenny is dotted with some of the best places to eat in South Wales. Here are five of the best within easy reach of the town:

Bear Hotel (☎ 01873-810408; Beaufort St, Crickhowell; mains £7-16) A fine old coaching inn with low-ceilinged rooms, stone fireplaces, blackened timber beams and antique furniture, the Bear serves top-quality bar meals as well as having a more formal restaurant. The menu ranges from heart-warming home cooking (sausages and mash with onion gravy, faggots with peas and chips) to the finest Black beef steaks and Welsh seafood. The Bear is in Crickhowell, 6.5 miles west of Abergavenny.

Nantyffin Cider Mill (☎ 01873-810775; Brecon Rd, Crickhowell; mains £8-15, 2-/3-course set menu £13/17; 🕑 closed Mon) One of the pioneers of fine dining in South Wales, this 16th-century drovers' inn takes great pride in using local produce (much of it from a farm just 5 miles down the road). The dining room is a stylish blend of bare stone, exposed roof beams, designer chairs and white table linen, while simple, unfussy dishes such as confit of lamb with garlic and rosemary sauce, or rib-eye steak with tarragon butter, allow the quality of the food to shine through. The Nantyffin is 7 miles west of Abergavenny, off the A40 just past Crickhowell.

Hardwick (☎ 01873-854220; Old Raglan Rd, Abergavenny; mains £12-16; 🕑 noon-3pm Tue-Sun, 6-10pm Tue-Sat) The Hardwick is a traditional pub-style restaurant with old stone fireplace, low ceiling beams and terracotta floor tiles. The combination of an ex-Walnut Tree chef and a gloriously unpretentious menu, from leek and potato soup to corned beef hash to juicy roast pork with perfect, crisp crackling, make for a delightful dining experience. The Hardwick is 2 miles south of Abergavenny on the B4598.

Walnut Tree Inn (☎ 01873-852797; Llandewi Skirrid; mains £10-20; 🕑 closed Sun dinner, all day Mon) Established by Franco Taruschio in 1963, the legendary Walnut Tree Inn remains one of Wales' finest restaurants. The produce is Welsh but the cuisine is Italian, with dishes such as crab tart, roast gnocchi with wild mushrooms, pan-fried sea bass with plum sauce, and shoulder of lamb roasted to pink and juicy perfection. The Walnut Tree is 3 miles northeast of Abergavenny on the B4521.

Foxhunter (☎ 01873-881101; Nant-y-Derry; mains £14-19; 🕑 closed Mon) An old Victorian pub with flagstone floors and wood-burning stoves that's had an elegant contemporary makeover, the Foxhunter brings an adventurous approach to fresh, seasonal produce with dishes such as sautéed duck liver and foie gras on toasted brioche, brown trout with *beurre blanc* (white butter sauce), sorrel and wild garlic, and (in season) deep-fried wild elvers (baby eels from the River Wye) with wild garlic mayonnaise. The Foxhunter is 7 miles south of Abergavenny, just east of the A4042.

from **PedalAway** (☎ 830219; www.pedalaway.co.uk), 3 miles west of Abergavenny near Govilon. Rates range from £10 to £30 per day, depending on type and features.

Local taxi companies include **Lewis Taxis** (☎ 854140) and **Station Taxis** (☎ 857233).

AROUND ABERGAVENNY
Crickhowell (Crughywel)
☎ 01873 / pop 2800

This prosperous, picturesque, flower-bedecked village on the Abergavenny to Brecon road is named after the distinctive flat-topped Crug Hywel (Table Mountain) that rises to the north. There's not a lot to see in town, but it's a pleasant place for lunch or an overnight stop.

At research time, the **tourist office** (☎ 812105; Beaufort Chambers, Beaufort St) was scheduled to move across the street to the newly renovated Market Hall.

SIGHTS & ACTIVITIES
The town grew up around the Norman motte (mound) and bailey castle and the nearby fording place on the River Usk. All that remains of the **castle** is a few tumbledown towers beside the High St, but the ford was superseded by an elegant 17th-century **stone bridge**, leading to the neighbouring village of Llangattock; it's famous for having 12 arches on one side, and 13 on the other.

You can hike to the top of **Crug Hywel** (Hywel's Rock; 451m), better known as Table Mountain (3 miles round trip); the tourist office has a leaflet showing the route. The summit is occupied by the remains of an Iron Age fort.

The Crickhowell area is perfect horse-riding country. **Golden Castle Riding Stables** (☎ 812649; www.golden-castle.co.uk), across the river in Llangattock, offers pony trekking, hacking, trail riding and children's activity days.

There's salmon and trout **fishing** on the River Usk; the Gliffaes Hotel beats are open to nonresidents for £22 to £30 a day.

SLEEPING
Riverside Caravan Park (☎ 810397; New Rd; sites per tent/person/car £3/2/2; ☽ Mar-Sep) The Riverside is well kept and very central, next to the bridge, but it's small and can get a bit crowded in high summer.

Greenhill Villas (☎ 811177; www.greenhillvillas.com; 2 Greenhill Villas, Beaufort St; s/d from £30/40) On the main road at the east end of town, this handsome town house presses all the right buttons, with bedside reading lamps, big fluffy towels and an armchair in each bedroom.

Dragon Hotel (☎ 810362; www.dragonhotel.co.uk; 47 High St; s/d from £45/60; P) Though set in an 18th century listed building, the Dragon has a more modern feel than the Bear (see opposite) – the 15 bedrooms boast crisp, clean design with pine furniture, bold colours, and wi-fi access.

Tŷ Gwyn (☎ 811625; Brecon Rd; d £55) Tŷ Gwyn is a lovely old Georgian country house with three spacious en suite rooms. It's only two minutes' walk from the town centre, and it was once the home of the Regency architect John Nash.

Bear Hotel (☎ 810408; www.bearhotel.co.uk; Brecon Rd; s/d from £58/77; P) The Bear is a local institution, a fine old coaching inn with a range of chintzy, old-fashioned rooms, the more expensive ones with four-posters and Jacuzzis. See also the boxed text, opposite.

Gliffaes Hotel (☎ 730371; www.gliffaeshotel.com; Gliffaes Rd; s/d from £75/137) This Victorian country-house hotel, set in thickly wooded grounds on the banks of the Usk, has the sort of plush, luxurious rooms that you could happily spend all day in. The more expensive ones have beautiful views across the valley. It's about 4 miles northwest of Crickhowell, off the A40.

EATING & DRINKING
Cheese Press (☎ 811122; 18 High St; snacks £2-5; ☽ 9.30am-4.15pm Mon, Tue & Thu-Sat, 9.30am-1.30pm Wed, 10.30am-4pm Sun) This pleasant tearoom is perched above a craft shop, a great place for a cuppa, a cake and a read of the papers.

Bridge End Inn (☎ 810338; Bridge St) The pub by the bridge is all timber beams and angling paraphernalia; it serves a range of real ales,

SOUTHEAST WALES & BRECON BEACONS

LOCAL VOICES *Jessica Bridgeman*

Name? Jessica Bridgeman.

Occupation? With my husband Glyn and our business partner Sean Gerrard, we run the Nantyffin Cider Mill, Peterstone Court Hotel and Manor Hotel near Brecon.

Where are you from? I grew up on Glaisfer Uchaf Farm, a 100-acre hill farm up in the Brecon Beacons. When I was a kid there was always work to be done and the whole family was involved – gathering the sheep from the mountain, feeding the calves, stone-picking the fields ready for hay-making, shearing and dipping the sheep, feeding, bedding and mucking out the animals during the winter. It was a great time – the farm was a so energetic and alive.

How did you get into the hotel/restaurant business? The farm started to struggle in the 1980s. My sister, my younger brother and I all worked for a year or so on the farm when we left school, but there was no way we could earn any money and my sister and I both moved to other jobs. We opened the Nantyffin Cider Mill in 1991 and moved back to the area, buying my grandparents' house off Dad to stop the farm going bankrupt. The farm was a shadow of its former self, as if all the stuffing had been knocked out of it. But Dad was determined that he wouldn't lose the farm – and so was I. There had to be a way forward.

So what did you do? We had talked many times about the farm supplying meat to our restaurants. Sean (who's still head chef of the Nantyffin) has always been passionate about sourcing food locally – he was banging this drum long before it became the 'in' thing to do. Slowly the farm produced a wider range of meat than just lamb – pork came on line, followed by chicken, duck, guinea fowl and finally beef. The farm now supplies not only our businesses but also sells locally to private customers and they do the farmers' markets every week.

The biggest impact all this has made? Well both my dad and my brother are now able to work full time on the farm – something, if we're honest, we didn't think would ever happen again. My brother's children (and mine) are being brought up on a busy, energetic and positive farm with the way of life and the values that were so important to us as children.

including Hancocks and Speckled Hen, and has a riverside beer garden across the road.

The Gliffaes Hotel does a sumptuous afternoon tea. See also the Bear Hotel and Nantyffin Cider Mill in the boxed text, p130.

GETTING THERE & AWAY

Crickhowell is served by the Beacons Bus routes B4 and B8, and bus X43 (see p129).

Tretower Court & Castle

Originally the home of the Vaughan family, **Tretower Court & Castle** (Cadw; ☎ 01874-730279; adult/child £2.90/2.50; ☺ 10am-5pm Tue-Sun Apr-Sep, 10am-4pm Tue-Sun Oct-Mar) gives you two historic buildings for the price of one – the sturdy circular tower of a Norman motte-and-bailey castle, and a 15th-century manor house with a fine medieval garden. Together they illustrate the transition from military stronghold to country house that took place in late medieval times. Staff deliver talks on the medieval garden on certain Saturdays from May to August (ask for dates at a tourist office), and there are occasional performances of Shakespeare plays in the manor house courtyard.

Tretower is 3 miles northwest of Crickhowell on the A479.

BLACK MOUNTAINS

The hills that stretch northward from Abergavenny to Hay-on-Wye, bordered by the A479 road to the west and the English border to the east, are known as the Black Mountains (not to be confused with the Black Mountain, singular, Mynydd Du in Welsh, at the western end of the Brecon Beacons National Park). The hills are bleak and wild and largely uninhabited, making this a popular walking area; the highest summit is Waun Fach (811m). The Offa's Dyke Path runs along the easternmost ridge between Pandy and Hay-on-Wye (see p63).

Llanfihangel Crucorney

The name of this little village, 4.5 miles north of Abergavenny, means 'Church of St Michael at the Corner of the Rock'. It's famous as the home of the **Skirrid Mountain Inn** (☎ 01873-890258; www.skirridmountaininn.co.uk; mains £8-9), said to be the oldest pub in Wales. From the early 12th century until the 17th century this was a courthouse as well as an inn, where almost 200 prisoners were hanged – you can still see rope marks on one of the beams. It serves

decent pub grub, and has three rooms offering B&B (doubles £85).

The inn makes a good base camp or finishing point for an ascent of **Ysgyryd Fawr** (Skirrid; 486m), the steep-sided peak to the south; it's a 4-mile round trip from pub to summit. Alternatively you can follow the Beacons Way hiking trail from Abergavenny over Skirrid and down to the pub.

Vale of Ewyas

The scenic and secluded valley of the River Honddu runs through the heart of the Black Mountains from Llanfihangel Crucorney to the 542m-high Gospel Pass, which leads down to Hay-on-Wye. It's a magical place, with only a very narrow, single-track road running along it, best explored on foot, bike or horseback.

Just west of the entrance to the valley, halfway up a hillside on a narrow country lane, is the remote and beautiful **Partrishow Church**. Part Norman and part medieval, this tiny church contains a remarkable, finely carved wooden rood screen and loft, dating from around 1500. On the walls are medieval frescoes of biblical texts, coats of arms, and a red-ochre skeleton bearing hourglass and scythe – the figure of Death. The church is usually open; leave a donation in the box.

Halfway along the valley lie the atmospheric ruins of the 13th-century **Llanthony Priory** (always open), set among grasslands and wooded hills by the River Honddu. Though not as grand as Tintern Abbey, the setting is even more romantic; JMW Turner painted the scene in 1794.

ACTIVITIES

Court Farm (☎ 01873-890359; www.llanthony.co.uk; half-/full day beginners £18/36, experienced £24/42), next door to Llanthony Priory and the Abbey Hotel, offers **pony trekking** and hacking. Half-day rides begin at 10am and 2pm.

There are lots of **walking** possibilities. From Llanthony, several paths lead up to the top of the Hatterall ridge to the east; it's a stiff climb, but straightforward (2 to 3 miles round trip). For a more ambitious hike, follow the ridge north for 4 miles then descend to Vision Farm, then back along the valley road to Llanthony (9 miles round trip).

SLEEPING & EATING

Barn B&B (☎ 01873-890477; www.thebarn-wales.co.uk; Pen-y-Maes, Capel-y-Ffin; s/d £25/50) The Barn is a warm and welcoming B&B in a delightful setting at the head of the valley, with stunning views from the conservatory-cum-breakfast room.

Abbey Hotel (☎ 01873-890487; www.llanthonyprioryhotel .co.uk; Llanthony; s/d £40/65) Seemingly growing out of the priory ruins, and incorporating some of the original medieval buildings, the Abbey Hotel is wonderfully atmospheric, with four-poster beds, stone spiral staircases and rooms squeezed into turrets; there are only five rooms, so book ahead. The vaulted cellars house a cosy bar that serves good pub lunches. Meals are available for £7 to £9.

There's bunkhouse accommodation at Court Farm, next to Llanthony Priory, and at **Capel-y-Ffin Youth Hostel** (☎ 0870 770 5748; Capel-y-Ffin, Llanthony; dm £11; ☉ year-round) near the head of the valley. There are also several basic camp sites in the valley.

GETTING THERE & AWAY
Beacons Bus B7 – also called the Offa's Dyke Flyer – runs on Sundays and bank holidays from late May to mid-September, following a circular route from Hay-on-Wye to Llanfi-hangel Crucorney via Capel-y-Ffin (30 minutes, three daily) and Llanthony (45 minutes), returning via Longtown and Craswall on the English side of the border. There is no other public transport.

BRECON (ABERHONDDU)
☎ 01874 / pop 7000
The handsome stone market town of Brecon stands at the meeting of the River Usk and the River Honddu. For centuries the town thrived as a centre of wool production and weaving; today it's the main transport hub for the national park and a natural base for exploring the surrounding countryside.

An Iron Age hill fort on Pen-y-Crug, northwest of town, and the remains of a Roman camp at Y Gaer, to the west, testifies to the site's antiquity. After the Romans, the area was ruled by the Irish-born king Bry-chan, who married into a Welsh royal house in the 5th century. The town takes its name from him, and his kingdom, Brycheiniog (anglicised to Brecknock), gave its name to the old county of Brecknockshire. Merthyr Tydfil was named for Brychan's daughter, St Tudful.

It was not until Norman times that Brecon began to burgeon. The local Welsh prince, Rhys ap Tewdwr, was defeated in 1093 by Bernard de Newmarch, a Norman lord, who then built the town's castle and church (which later became a cathedral).

Orientation
The main bus stop is on the Bulwark, the town's main street, next to St Mary's Church. The tourist office is on the town's main car park, a short walk north through Bethel Square Shopping Centre.

Information
Andrew Morton Books (☎ 620086; 7 Lion St) Staggering selection of fiction, nonfiction and local interest books. There's another branch at 10-11 Lion Yard.
Brecon Cyber Café (☎ 621912; 10 Lion St; ☉ 10am-5pm Mon-Sat; per 30 min £2.50)
Brecon Hospital (☎ 622443; Cerrigcochion Rd)
Brecon Library (Ship St; ☉ 9.30am-5pm Mon & Wed-Fri, 9.30am-7pm Tue, 9.30am-1pm Sat) Free internet access.
Police Station (☎ 0845 330 2000; Lion St)
Post Office (Co-op Supermarket, Lion St; ☉ 8.30am-5.30pm Mon-Fri, 8.30am-7.30pm Sat, 9.30am-4pm Sun)
Tourist Office (☎ 622485; Cattle Market car park; ☉ 9.30am-5.30pm Mon-Sat, 10am-4pm Sun) See also the National Park Visitor Centre (p123), 5 miles southwest of Brecon.

Sights
There's not a great deal to see in town – Brecon is more a base for exploring the surrounding hills – but there are a couple of sights for rainy days.

Behind the stolid neoclassical exterior of the former Shire Hall is the impressive **Brecknock Museum & Art Gallery** (☎ 624121; Captain's Walk; adult/child £1/50p; ☉ 10am-5pm Tue-Fri, 10am-1pm & 2-5pm Sat year-round, noon-5pm Sun Apr-Sep only). Exhibits include a 1200-year-old dugout canoe found at Llangorse Lake, a complete Victorian as-size court complete with a stilted recording of court pronouncements, and that favourite of Welsh museums, a re-created Welsh kitchen. Also featured are the archaeology, history and natural history of the Brecon area, and an art gallery with changing exhibits.

The **South Wales Borderers Museum** (☎ 613310; www.rrw.org.uk; The Barracks; adult/child £3/free; ☉ 10am-5pm Mon-Fri year-round, 10am-4pm Sat & bank holidays Easter-Sep) commemorates the history of the Royal Regiment of Wales, which is based in Brecon. Many of the soldiers are Gurkhas, often to be seen in their civvies around the town. The highlight is the Zulu War Room – the regiment's predecessor fought in the 1879 Anglo-Zulu war in South Africa, inspiration for the 1964 film *Zulu* starring Michael

Caine. The fascinating collection of artefacts recalls the defence of Rorke's Drift, when 150 Welsh soldiers held out against 4000 Zulu warriors.

Brecon Cathedral (☎ 623857; Cathedral Cl), perched on a hill above the River Honddu, was founded as part of a Benedictine monastery in 1093, though little remains of the Norman structure except the font and parts of the nave. At the western end of the nave, just inside the door, is a stone cresset (an ancient lighting device), the only one in Wales; the 30 cups carved into the stone slab once held oil for the cathedral's lamps. The nave is draped with regimental banners from the Zulu wars (the cathedral contains the regimental chapel of the South Wales Borderers). In the cathedral

grounds is a **Heritage Centre** (☎ 625222; admission free; ☷ 10am-4.30pm Mon-Sat Apr-Dec) and gift shop housed in a restored 15th-century tithe barn. The cathedral hosts regular choral concerts.

What little remains of Brecon's Norman **castle** was incorporated into the Castle of Brecon Hotel. Across the road from the hotel is the original Norman motte, capped by the ivy-clad **Ely Tower** (not open to the public).

Brecon is the northern terminus of the **Monmouthshire & Brecon Canal**, built between 1799 and 1812 for the movement of coal, iron ore, limestone and agricultural goods. The 33 miles from Brecon to Pontypool is back in business moving tourists around, and the busiest section is around Brecon. The canal basin is 400m south of the town centre.

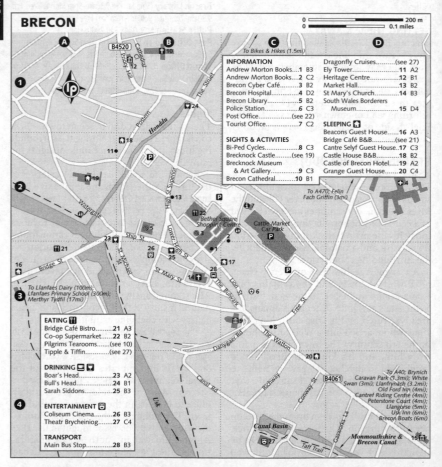

BRECON

INFORMATION		Dragonfly Cruises..........(see 27)
Andrew Morton Books....**1** B3		Ely Tower......................**11** A2
Andrew Morton Books....**2** C2		Heritage Centre.............**12** B1
Brecon Cyber Café.........**3** B2		Market Hall...................**13** B2
Brecon Hospital.............**4** D2		St Mary's Church............**14** B3
Brecon Library...............**5** B2		South Wales Borderers
Police Station................**6** C3		Museum....................**15** D4
Post Office.................(see 22)		
Tourist Office.................**7** C2		SLEEPING
		Beacons Guest House......**16** A3
SIGHTS & ACTIVITIES		Bridge Café B&B...........(see 21)
Bi-Ped Cycles.................**8** C3		Cantre Selyf Guest House..**17** C3
Brecknock Castle.........(see 19)		Castle House B&B............**18** B2
Brecknock Museum		Castle of Brecon Hotel....**19** A2
& Art Gallery.............**9** C3		Grange Guest House.......**20** C4
Brecon Cathedral..........**10** B1		

EATING
Bridge Café Bistro.........**21** A3
Co-op Supermarket.....**22** B2
Pilgrims Tearooms.......(see 10)
Tipple & Tiffin............(see 27)

DRINKING
Boar's Head..................**23** A2
Bull's Head...................**24** B1
Sarah Siddons.............**25** B3

ENTERTAINMENT
Coliseum Cinema.........**26** B3
Theatr Brycheiniog........**27** C4

TRANSPORT
Main Bus Stop.............**28** B3

Activities

WALKING

The conical hill of **Pen-y-Crug** (331m), capped by an Iron Age hill fort, rises to the northwest of the town, and makes a good objective for a short hike (2.5 miles round trip). There's a superb view of the Brecon Beacons from the summit.

A peaceful 8.5-mile walk along the towpath of the Monmouthshire & Brecon Canal leads to the picturesque village of **Talybont-on-Usk**. You can return on the X43 bus from Abergavenny to Brecon, or the Beacons Bus B4, B6 or B8.

For information on climbing Pen-y-Fan, see the boxed text, p124.

The tourist office sells a national park booklet, *Walks in the Brecon Area*.

CYCLING & MOUNTAIN BIKING

There are lots of opportunities for both on-road cycle-touring and off-road mountain biking around Brecon; the National Park Visitor Centre at Libanus (p123) has information on routes, some of which begin at the centre itself.

The classic off-road route in the Brecon Beacons is the **Gap Road**, a 24-mile loop from Brecon that takes in a high pass through the hills close to Pen-y-Fan, a descent through Talybont-on-Usk and a final easy return stretch along the Monmouthshire & Brecon Canal. Ask for details at Brecon tourist office or the National Park Visitor Centre.

At the beginning of September, Brecon hosts the annual **Brecon Beast** (www.breconbeast.co.uk) mountain-bike race, a gruelling 68-mile off-road event that starts and finishes in the town.

You can rent bikes at the following places:
Bikes & Hikes (☎ 610071; www.bikesandhikes.co.uk; 1 Warle Cottage, near Llandew) Rental per half-/full day £11/16; also runs guided trips.
Bi-Ped Cycles (☎ 622296; www.bipedcycles.co.uk; 10 Ship St) Rental per half-/full day £10/15; can also arrange guided rides for £30 per guide.

HORSE RIDING

The **Cantref Riding Centre** (☎ 665233; www.cantref.com; Upper Cantref Farm, Llanfrynach; per hr/half-/full day £10/20/40) offers pony trekking and hacking, and also runs two- to five-day guided treks into the Brecon Beacons.

BOATING

Dragonfly Cruises (☎ 685222; www.dragonfly-cruises.co.uk; adult/child £6/4; ☼ Apr-Oct), based in the canal basin in Brecon, runs 2½-hour canal boat trips; there are departures once or twice daily on Wednesday, Saturday and Sunday (as well as Thursday in July, plus Tuesday, Thursday and Friday in August).

If you prefer the self-drive experience, **Brecon Boats** (☎ 676401; Travellers Rest Inn, Talybont-on-Usk; ☼ Apr-Oct) hires out boats by the hour, charging £20/40/50 for 1/4/6 hours. They're at Talybont-on-Usk, southeast of Brecon (about 6 miles by road or 8.5 miles along the towpath).

Festivals

On the second weekend in August, the town hosts the **Brecon Jazz Festival** (www.breconjazz.co.uk), one of Europe's leading jazz events, attracting thousands of fans for a long, laid-back party. Accommodation is hard to find at this busy time, although open areas all over town become makeshift camping grounds. Previous headlining acts have included Sonny Rollins, Courtney Pine, Dr John, and George Melly (who has a house nearby).

The annual **Brecon Beacons Food Festival** (☎ 624979; www.breconbeaconsfoodfestival.com) takes place on the first Saturday in October, and is centred on the Market Hall.

Sleeping

BUDGET

Cantref Riding Centre (☎ 665233; www.cantref.com; Upper Cantref Farm, Llanfrynach; sites per person £3.50, dm £11.50) In a ravishing setting overlooking the hills, this family-run riding centre has two comfortable bunkhouses and a camping ground. It's 2 miles south of Brecon on foot, or 4 miles by car – take the A40 towards Abergavenny, then the B4558 towards Llanfrynach.

Brynich Caravan Park (☎ 623325; www.brynich.co.uk; Brynich; sites per tent & car plus 2 people £14-16; ☼ Apr-Oct) About 1.5 miles east of Brecon, Brynich is a cut above the usual camping ground with disabled access, an indoor children's play park, adventure playground, and an impressive barn restaurant.

Bridge Café B&B (☎ 622024; www.bridgecafe.co.uk; 7 Bridge St; s/d from £20/40; ☼ closed Nov-Jan) Owned by keen mountain-bikers and hill walkers who can advise on local activities, the Bridge has three plain but comfortable bedrooms with down-filled duvets and crisp cotton sheets. Bike storage is available. See also Bridge Café Bistro under Eating.

Grange Guest House (☎ 624038; 22 The Watton; s/d £35/48; P) A spacious Victorian town house

SOUTHEAST WALES &
BRECON BEACONS

with leafy gardens, the Grange is only a few minutes' stroll from both town centre and canal. Hikers, cyclists and motorbikers are welcome, and there's secure storage for bikes. Rooms with shared bathroom are £28/40.

MIDRANGE

Beacons Guest House (☎ 623339; www.beacons.brecon .co.uk; 16 Bridge St; s/d £40/52) Set in a former farmhouse with a Georgian frontage, the Beacons is just across the river from the town centre. As well as a couple of sprucely decorated rooms in the main house, there are a couple of self-contained suites, suitable for families, in the old barn and cottage out the back.

Castle House B&B (☎ 623343; www.castle-house.co.uk; The Postern; s/d £40/60) Located on a quiet back street close to the town centre, the Castle is a smartly renovated Victorian town house attractively furnished with period pieces and a pleasant lounge/dining room with leather sofas and a wood-burning stove. The 'dragon sausages' (made with pork, leek and a touch of chilli) add a bit of spice to breakfast!

Castle of Brecon Hotel (☎ 624611; www.breconcastle .co.uk; Castle Sq; s/d from £50/60) Built into the ruined walls of Brecknock Castle, this grand old hotel is getting a bit creaky but is still good value. It's worth splashing out for the spacious, south-facing deluxe rooms (singles/doubles £74/85), which have four-poster beds and great views of the Brecon Beacons.

Cantre Selyf Guest House (☎ 622904; www.cantre selyf.co.uk; 5 Lion St; s/d £48/72; **P**) This elegant Georgian town house, right in the middle of Brecon, has atmospheric period décor and furnishings, including plaster mouldings, original fireplaces and cast-iron bedsteads.

TOP END

Felin Fach Griffin (☎ 620111; www.eatdrinksleep.ltd.uk; Felin Fach; d £98-125) The Griffin prides itself on simplicity and quality: there are no chintz or floral patterns here, just neutral décor with a splash of colour to set off antique four-poster beds equipped with goose-down pillows and duvets. It also has a highly rated restaurant (see the boxed text, opposite). The Griffin is 5 miles northeast of Brecon, just off the A470.

Eating & Drinking

Most of the quality eating places in town are cafés that close around 5pm or 6pm. For an evening meal, you'll have to try a bar meal at one of the pubs (generally 6.30pm to 8.30pm),

or head for one of the out-of-town places recommended in the boxed text, opposite.

Pilgrims Tearooms (☎ 610610; Brecon Cathedral Cl; mains £3-7; 🕑 10am-5pm, lunch noon-2.30pm) The café in the cathedral grounds is housed in a tithe barn-style building, with outdoor tables beside a herb garden. The menu includes home-baked bread, salads, jacket potatoes and daily specials, and a Sunday lunch of roast lamb, beef or chicken.

Bridge Café Bistro (☎ 622024; www.bridgecafe.co.uk; 7 Bridge St; mains £4-7; 🕑 food served 11am-6pm) A great little bistro with a rustic, farmhouse kitchen look, the Bridge serves simple, home-cooked dishes using fresh, seasonal, organic produce, from onion soup to lamb stew, falafel to mushroom stroganoff. It also serves organic beer, wine and cider, and Welsh-made Brecon gin and Penderyn whisky.

Tipple & Tiffin (☎ 611622; Theatr Brycheiniog, Canal Wharf; mains £6-8; 🕑 noon-2.30pm & 7-9pm Mon-Sat) The restaurant attached to Brecon's theatre has outdoor tables beside the canal basin, and serves fresh, tasty fare such as game sausages and mash with onion gravy, and pasta with vegetable ragout.

Bull's Head (☎ 622044; The Struet; mains £7-9) Probably the best real-ale pub in town, with Evan Evans beer from Llandeilo and a range of guest ales, the Bull's Head is cosy, quiet and friendly. It also serves very good pub grub (until 9pm Monday to Friday, and 8pm weekends).

Boar's Head (Ship St) The Boar's Head is a lively local pub, with sofas in the back room and the full range of Breconshire Brewery real ales on tap. There's a sunny beer garden overlooking the river, and regular live music.

Llanfaes Dairy (☎ 625892; Bridge St) The local dairy has a café that serves fresh-ground Italian coffee, and homemade ice cream in a wide range of flavours.

Self-caterers can stock up at the **Co-op Supermarket** (Lion St; 🕑 8am-9pm Mon-Sat, 10am-4pm Sun).

Entertainment

Theatr Brycheiniog (☎ 611622; www.theatrbrycheiniog .co.uk; Canal Rd) The canalside theatre complex is the town's main venue for drama, comedy and music. It also has an exhibition centre.

Coliseum Cinema (☎ 622501; Wheat St; adult/child £5.50/4.50) The Coliseum is a refreshingly old-fashioned family cinema with two screens. As well as mainstream films, the local film society shows art-house films on Monday evenings.

Brecon Male Voice Choir (Llanfaes Primary School, Orchard St; 🕑 7.30-9.30pm Fri) For a few booming harmo-

TOP NOSH

The countryside around Brecon is dotted with pubs and restaurants that take great pride in using local Welsh produce that is fresh, seasonal and often organic. Here's our pick of the best:

Felin Fach Griffin (☎ 01874-620111; Felin Fach; mains £10-17; ☿ closed Mon lunch) With a string of awards as long as its extensive wine list, the Griffin offers gourmet dining in a relaxed and unpretentious setting. Open fires, leather sofas and timber beams create a comfortable atmosphere, while the kitchen makes the most of local fish, meat and game (they even grow their own veggies), serving dishes such as roast venison with braised red cabbage, wild mushroom risotto with sherry butter, and steak with braised leeks, chips and Béarnaise sauce. The Griffin is 5 miles northeast of Brecon on the A470.

Old Ford Inn (☎ 01874-665220; Llanhamlach; mains £7-12) The Old Ford is an old-fashioned country pub with weathered oak beams, stone fireplace and a range of well-looked-after real ales. You can eat in the bar, or opt for a more formal meal in the farmhouse-kitchen-style restaurant. Llanhamlach is on the A40, 4 miles southeast of Brecon

Usk Inn (☎ 01874-676251; Talybont-on-Usk; 2-/3-course dinner £20/25) This appealing Victorian country inn, close to the Brecon Canal, serves hearty local fare such as twice-cooked lamb shank with minted rosemary jus; ricotta cheese and basil ravioli with creamy tomato and spinach sauce; and seafood dishes such as swordfish fillet with a sesame crust. There's also an excellent three-course Sunday lunch for £15, served noon to 3pm. The Usk Inn is 6 miles southeast of Brecon on the B4558.

White Swan (☎ 01874-665276; Llanfrynach; mains £13-16) A traditional village inn that offers a candle-lit dining room with old wood floors, a bar with comfortably worn leather sofas and armchairs, and a beautiful garden terrace. The White Swan is a great place to relax after a walk along the canal or a hike in the Brecon Beacons. The menu emphasises Welsh lamb, beef and venison, with daily fish and vegetarian specials. Llanfrynach is 3.5 miles southeast of Brecon off the B4558.

SOUTHEAST WALES &
BRECON BEACONS

nies, head to the practice sessions of the Brecon Male Voice Choir; visitors are welcome.

Getting There & Away

Sixty-Sixty bus X43 runs from Cardiff to Brecon (£4, 1½ hours, five daily Monday to Saturday, one on Sunday) via Merthyr Tydfil (40 minutes, six daily Monday to Saturday, two on Sunday). The same service continues from Brecon to Crickhowell and Abergavenny (£4, 50 minutes, six daily Monday to Saturday, no Sunday service). All the Beacons Bus routes (see p125) converge on Brecon.

Stagecoach bus 63 links Brecon with Swansea (£4, 1½ hours, three daily Monday to Saturday) via Dan-yr-Ogof Showcaves. For Llandovery, take bus 714 (£4, 40 minutes, six daily Monday to Saturday), and for Newtown (£8, two hours, six daily Monday to Saturday) via Builth Wells and Llandrindod Wells take Stagecoach bus 704.

AROUND BRECON
Llangorse Lake

Reed-fringed Llangorse Lake (Llyn Syfaddan), to the east of Brecon, may be Wales' second-largest natural lake (after Llyn Tegid), but it's barely more than a mile long and half a mile wide. Close to the northern shore is a **crannog**, a lake dwelling built on an artificial island. Such dwellings or refuges were used from the late Bronze Age until early medieval times. Tree-ring dating shows that this one (of which only the base remains) was built around AD 900, probably by the royal house of Brycheiniog. Among the artefacts found here was a dugout canoe, now on display in Brecon's Brecknock Museum; other finds can be seen at the National Museum & Gallery of Wales in Cardiff (p86). There's a reconstruction of a crannog house on the shore at Lakeside Caravan Park.

ACTIVITIES

The lake is the national park's main water sports venue, with facilities for sailing, windsurfing, canoeing and water-skiing. **Lakeside Caravan Park** (☎ 01874-658226; www.llangors.com; Llangorse), on the north shore, rents rowing boats year-round for £8 per hour; Canadian canoes for £7 per half-hour (April to September); Wayfarer sailing dinghies for £16 per hour; and bicycles for £10/14 per half-/full-day.

Set on a hillside above the eastern end of Llangorse Lake is the **Llangorse Multi-Activity Centre** (☎ 658272; www.activityuk.com; Gilfach Farm, Llangorse; ☿ 9am-5pm). It offers a range of adventure

SOUTHEAST WALES &
BRECON BEACONS

AUTHOR'S CHOICE

An elegant Georgian manor house overlooking the River Usk, **Peterstone Court** (☎ 01874-665387; www.peterstone-court.com; Llanhamlach, near Brecon; s/d from £80/90; **P**)) enjoys a fantastic location with views across the valley to the peaks of Cribyn and Pen-y-Fan. Despite the country house setting the atmosphere is relaxed and informal, the oak floors, marble fireplaces, antique furniture and leather armchairs set off with fresh flowers and modern art. The bedrooms are large and luxurious, with crisp bed linen and comfy mattresses, while the restaurant is one of the best in the area. The basement leisure suite contains a candle-lit meditation room, four-seater sauna, Jacuzzi and gym, with a whole range of spa treatments on offer. Outside, there's a heated pool, and wooden decks with mountain views, and you're only a few yards from the hiking and biking trails along the river and the Monmouthshire & Brecon Canal. The hotel is 3 miles southeast of Brecon, just off the A40.

---

activities, the most popular of which is an outdoor aerial assault course that involves clambering up cargo nets, balancing along logs, swinging on tyres and zipping through the air on a 100m long ropeway (£18 for two hours). There's also an indoor facility with artificial rock-climbing walls, a log climb, abseil area, rope bridge and even an artificial caving area. A one-hour climbing 'taster' session costs £12.

The centre also offers pony trekking (£21 for two hours), horse riding (£26 for two hours), and gentle pony rides for kids aged four to seven years (£7), as well as three- to five-day riding holidays in the Brecon Beacons and Black Mountains.

SLEEPING

The **Lakeside Caravan Park** (☎ 01874-658226; www .llangors.com; Llangorse; sites per person £4.25-5.25) runs a well-appointed camp site, and there is a range of places to stay that can be arranged at Llangorse Activity Centre, from **Pen-Y-Bryn Guest House** (☎ 658606; d from £45), which offers B&B in a farmhouse in Llangorse village, to bunkhouse accommodation (£13 to £15.50 per person) and camping (£4 per person) at the centre itself.

GETTING THERE & AWAY

Llangorse Lake is 6 miles east of Brecon. The Postbus service from the Bulwark in Brecon stops in Llangorse village (30 minutes, one daily Monday to Friday), as does Beacons Bus route B11.

FFOREST FAWR & BLACK MOUNTAIN

The **Fforest Fawr** (Great Forest), once a Norman hunting ground, is now a Unesco geopark famous for its varied landscapes, ranging from bleak moorland to flower-flecked limestone pavement and lush wooded ravines choked with moss and greenery.

Near the isolated village of **Ystradfellte** lies a series of dramatic waterfalls, the finest being Sgwd-yr-Eira (Fall of Snow) where you can actually walk behind the waterfall. The **Waterfalls Walk** is a 9.5-mile circuit that takes in Sgwd-yr-Eira and seven other waterfalls, beginning and ending at the car park in Ystradfellte – ask for a leaflet with a map at the small shop in the village. Take special care – the footpaths can be slippery, and there are several steep, stony sections.

Just a mile south of the car park, along a signposted trail, the River Mellte disappears into **Porth-yr-Ogof** (Door to the Cave), the biggest cave entrance in Britain (3m high and 20m wide), only to reappear 100m further south.

If the weather's a bit cold and wet, you can warm up with a shot of whisky from **Penderyn Distillery** (☎ 01685-813300; www.welsh-whisky.co.uk), in the village of Penderyn, 4 miles south of Ystradfellte. Opened in 2004, the distillery produces Brecon Gin, Brecon Five Vodka and Merlyn Cream Liqueur as well as Penderyn single malt whisky. There are plans to build a visitor centre, which is scheduled to open in September 2007. A Welsh on the rocks, anyone?

The limestone plateau of the southern Fforest Fawr around the upper reaches of the River Tawe is riddled with some of the largest and most complex cave systems in Britain. Most can be visited only by experienced cavers, but the **Dan-yr-Ogof caves** (☎ 01639-730801; www.showcaves .co.uk; adult/child £10/6.50; ☺ 10am-4pm Apr-Oct, last entry to caves 3pm), near the Craig-y-Nos Country Park, are open to the public. The highlight of the 1.5-mile self-guided tour is the **Cathedral Cave**, a high-domed chamber with a lake fed by two waterfalls that pour from openings. Nearby is the **Bone Cave**, where 42 Bronze Age skeletons were discovered. The admission fee also gives entry to various other attractions on site, including a museum, a reconstructed Iron Age farm, a prehistoric theme park filled with life-sized fibreglass dinosaurs, a shire-horse centre, and even a dry ski slope. The caves are just off the A4067 north of Abercraf, 20 miles south of Brecon.

Beneath the hillside to the east of Dan-yr-Ogof lies the twisting maze of subterranean chambers known as **Ogof Ffynnon Ddu** (Cave of the Black Spring), the deepest and third-longest cave system in the UK (308m deep, with 31 miles of passages). This one is for expert potholers only, but you can explore it virtually at www.ogof.net.

Black Mountain, the western section of the national park, contains the wildest, loneliest and least visited walking country. Its finest feature is the sweeping escarpment of **Fan Brycheiniog** (802m), which rises steeply above the scenic glacial lakes of Llyn y Fan Fach and Llyn y Fan Fawr. It can be climbed from the Llanddeusant Youth Hostel (p124); the round trip is 12 miles.

Carreg Cennen Castle, in the far southwestern corner of the national park, is best approached from Llandeilo; see p158.

Getting There & Away

Stagecoach bus 63 between Swansea and Brecon stops at Dan-yr-Ogof (three per day Monday to Saturday). Beacons Bus B2 links Brecon and Swansea with Dan-yr-Ogof; B3 goes from Brecon to Penderyn. There is no public transport to Ystradfellte or Llanddeusant.

Swansea, the Gower & Carmarthenshire

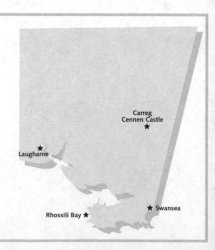

This corner of the country, between the valleys of Glamorgan and the rocky shores of Pembrokeshire, will forever be associated with Dylan Thomas. The wild boy of Welsh poetry was born in Swansea, Wales' city by the bay, a town busy pulling itself up by the bootstraps as it reinvents itself for the 21st century. By turns pretty and gritty, it offers an intriguing blend of seaside setting and big-city sophistication, with the new National Waterfront Museum as the jewel in its crown.

Swansea is the gateway to the Gower Peninsula, a compact compendium of coastal delights, from the golden-sand expanses of scenic Three Cliffs Bay to the pounding surf and wind-blown ridge-walking at Rhossili. Gower is the region's outdoor playground, offering easy coastal hiking, safe summer swimming, and some of the best surfing in the UK.

Carmarthenshire is too often passed by in the headlong rush towards the delights of neighbouring Pembrokeshire, but it's worth slowing down for a look. The county promotes itself as the 'Garden of Wales', and there are gardens aplenty to visit – from the formal walled gardens of Aberglasney to the magnificent National Botanic Garden with its spectacular, Norman Foster–designed glasshouse dome.

The rural hinterland of eastern Carmarthenshire brushes against the upland fringes of the Brecon Beacons National Park, where the craggy splendour of Carreg Cennen Castle rises above a jigsaw of limestone valleys, while down on the coast you can wander along the 'heron-priested shore' of the Taf estuary and visit the Boathouse, where Dylan Thomas wrote some of his finest work.

SWANSEA, THE GOWER & CARMARTHENSHIRE

HIGHLIGHTS

- Learning about Swansea's fascinating history at the superb **National Waterfront Museum** (p143)

- Enjoying the best of Welsh seafood in the **restaurants** (p147) of Swansea and the Mumbles

- Watching the surf break on the majestic sweep of **Rhossili Bay** (p154) at the tip of the Gower Peninsula

- Gazing at the views that inspired Dylan Thomas at **Laugharne** (p160)

- Taking in the expansive views from the hilltop site of **Carreg Cennen Castle** (p157)

Carreg
Cennen Castle ★

★
Laugharne

★ Swansea

Rhossili Bay ★

ACTIVITIES

The extensive coast and rolling inland valleys in this region provide an ideal environment for all sorts of outdoor fun. Sea kayaking, surfing, walking, horse riding, bird-watching and boating are just some of the pursuits available.

GETTING AROUND

The region's major bus operators are **First Cymru** (☎ 01792-572255; www.firstcymru.co.uk), **Roy Brown's Coaches** (☎ 01982-552597; www.roybrowns coaches.co.uk), **Pullman Coaches** (☎ 01792-851569; www .pullman-coaches.co.uk) and **Silcox Coaches** (☎ 01646-683143; www.silcoxcoaches.co.uk). For timetable information, call **Traveline** (☎ 0870 608 2 608; www .traveline-cymru.org.uk).

The West Wales Rover Ticket (adult/child £6/4) allows unlimited travel for one day on regional buses and on a few services to/from Swansea and Mid-Wales (but not Silcox, Postbus or National Express services, nor the No 100 Cardiff–Swansea shuttle).

Two railway lines run from Swansea – one through Mid-Wales skirting the Brecon Beacons (the Heart of Wales line) and the other via Carmarthen to Pembroke Dock, Haverfordwest and Fishguard. For route maps and timetables, see www.arrivatrainswales.co.uk.

SWANSEA (ABERTAWE)

☎ 01792 / pop 223,300

Dylan Thomas called Swansea an 'ugly, lovely town', and that remains a fair description today. Wales' second-largest city enjoys a stunning setting on the 5-mile sweep of Swansea Bay, but suffers from a less than stunning town centre, the result of unimaginative rebuilding after WWII bombing. But Swansea makes up for its visual shortcomings with a visceral charm that, if not able to out-dazzle more handsome places, can at least out-stare them.

In the National Waterfront Museum the city has one of the most exciting museum developments in Britain; it also has a superb Dylan Thomas Centre, a long seafront stretching down to the picturesque suburb of the Mumbles, and the glorious Gower Peninsula on its doorstep.

HISTORY

Swansea's Welsh name, Abertawe, describes its location at the mouth of the Tawe, where the river empties into Swansea Bay. The Vikings named the area Sveins Ey (Swein's Island), probably referring to the sandbank in the mouth of the River Tawe.

The Normans built a castle here, but Swansea didn't really get into its stride until the Industrial Revolution, when it developed into an important copper-smelting centre. Ore was first shipped in from Cornwall, across the Bristol Channel, but by the 19th century it was arriving from Chile, Cuba and the USA, in return for Welsh coal.

By the 20th century, however, the city's industrial base had declined, although Swansea's oil refinery and smaller factories were still judged a worthy target by the Luftwaffe, which devastated the city centre in 1941. The insensitive rebuilding of the city's heart did not do much for its recovery, but in recent years, with the opening of the new National Waterfront Museum, a sparkling marina, and a thriving restaurant and bar scene, Swansea's future is looking more lovely than ugly.

ORIENTATION

The compact city centre clusters around Castle Sq and pedestrianised Oxford St on the west bank of the River Tawe, with the redeveloped docklands of the Maritime Quarter to its southeast. The bus station and neighbouring tourist office are on the western edge of the city centre, next to the Quadrant shopping centre. The train station is 600m north of Castle Sq along Castle St and High St.

The suburb of Uplands, where many of the city's guesthouses are found, is a mile west of the city centre, along Mansel St and Walter Rd. From the southern edge of the city centre, Oystermouth Rd runs for 5 miles west and then south along the broad sweep of Swansea Bay to the seaside resort of the Mumbles.

INFORMATION
Bookshops

Dylan's Books (☎ 463 980; www.dylan-thomas-books .com; Dylan Thomas Centre, Somerset Pl; ☯ 10am-4.30pm) All of Thomas' works, plus biographies, CDs of *Under Milk Wood* etc.

Dylans Book Store (☎ 655255; 23 King Edward Rd) Antiquarian and secondhand books; Thomas 1st editions, collectors items.

Siop Tŷ Tawe (☎ 460906; 9 Christina St) Welsh-language books.

Waterstone's (☎ 463567; 17 Oxford St; ☯ 9.30am-5.30pm Mon-Sat, 10.30am-4.30pm Sun) Good selection of local interest books, maps and guides.

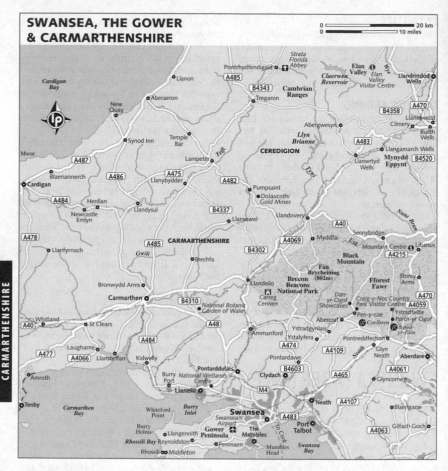

SWANSEA, THE GOWER & CARMARTHENSHIRE

Disabled Travellers

Swansea Shopmobility (☎ 461785; St David's Sq, off Princess Way; ☒ 9am-4.30pm Mon-Sat) Provides wheelchairs and electric scooters for a small fee.

Internet Access

County Library (☎ 516757; Alexandra Rd; ☒ 9.30am-6pm Mon-Wed, 9.30am-5pm Thu & Sat, 9.30am-7pm Fri) Free internet access.

Crossfire (☎ 461144; 46 Princess Way; per hr £2.40; ☒ 10am-7pm) Internet access, plus printing, CD burning etc.

Laundry

Lendart Laundrette (☎ 644682; 91 Bryn-y-Mor Rd)

Uplands Laundrette (☎ 644238; 73 Uplands Cres)

Medical & Emergency Services

Morriston Hospital (☎ 702222; Heol Maes Eglwys, Morriston) Accident and emergency department, 5 miles north of the city centre.

Police Station (☎ 456999; Grove Pl)

Money

Loads of banks dot the streets between the Kingsway and the Quadrant Shopping Centre. All have ATMs.

Post

Main Post Office (WH Smith, 37 the Quadrant Shopping Centre; ☒ 9am-5.30pm Mon-Sat)

Uplands Post Office (25 Uplands Cres, Uplands; ☒ 9am-1pm Mon-Fri, 9am-12.30pm Sat)

Tourist Information

Mumbles Tourist Office (☎ 361302; www.mumblestic
.co.uk; Methodist Church, Mumbles Rd; ☒ 10am-5pm
Mon-Sat year-round, noon-5pm Jul & Aug)
Swansea Tourist Office (☎ 468321; www.visitswansea
bay.com; Plymouth St; ☒ 9.30am-5.30pm Mon-Sat year-
round,10am-4pm Sun Easter-Sep) Can book accommodation
and has walking and cycling information.

SIGHTS

Swansea's city centre and Maritime Quarter,
and the new SA1 district on the east bank of
the Tawe, are undergoing a major redevelopment that plans to transform the city by 2020;
during that time building sites and road works
will be a feature of any visit.

WWII bombing flattened much of central
Swansea, which was rebuilt as a rather soulless
retail development in the 1960s, '70s and '80s.
What little remains of Georgian and Victorian
Swansea stretches from Wind St and York
St to Somerset Pl and Cambrian Way in the
Maritime Quarter; this is the most attractive
part of the city centre.

City Centre

The ruins of 14th-century **Swansea Castle**
(closed to the public) stand on the east side
of Castle Sq, hemmed in by modern buildings
and dwarfed by the gleaming blue skyscraper
of the BT Tower. The castle was mostly destroyed by Cromwell in 1647, but had a brief
lease of life as a prison in the 19th century.

Housed in an elegant Italianate building
in the north of the city centre, the **Glynn Vivian
Art Gallery** (☎ 516900; www.swansea.gov.uk/glynnvivian;
Alexandra Rd; admission free; ☒ 10am-5pm Tue-Sun) displays a wide range of Welsh art – Richard Wilson's evocative landscapes, haunting works
by Gwen John, bold portraits by her brother
Augustus, and a whole room devoted to the
more contemporary Ceri Richards. There
are also fine works by Walter Sickert, Wyndham Lewis, Stanley Spencer and John Nash,
alongside multimedia temporary exhibitions.
There's also a collection of ceramics.

A huge glass pyramid parked between the
Parc Tawe Shopping Centre and the river contains **Plantasia** (☎ 474555; www.plantasia.org; Parc Tawe
Link Rd; adult/child £3.30/2.30; ☒ 10am-5pm), a botanical exhibition containing hundreds of species
of exotic plants, plus attendant insects, rep-
tiles, tropical fish, birds and tamarin monkeys.
A coffee shop and range of kids' activities
make it a popular rainy-day retreat.

Maritime Quarter

The area around the former docks to the southeast of the city centre was originally redeveloped as a residential area in the 1980s – low-rise
red- and yellow-brick apartment blocks with
blue-painted steel balconies that are beginning
to look a little tired now. The South Dock and
the Tawe Basin (enclosed by a smaller version
of Cardiff Bay's tidal barrage) are now busy mar-
inas, surrounded by bars, restaurants and cafés,
and the odd bit of public art – there's a seated
statue of Dylan Thomas, and the old sailor with
the bell nearby is the fictional Captain Cat from
Thomas's play *Under Milk Wood*.

The process of regeneration is still going on,
with a big new commercial complex – the SA1
Waterfront development – on the far bank of
the river, linked to the Maritime Quarter by
the graceful swoop of the spectacular new **Sail
Bridge**. The 26-storey Marina Tower, under
construction at the time of research, will be
the tallest building in the city.

The Maritime Quarter's flagship attraction
is the **National Waterfront Museum** (☎ 638950; www
.waterfrontmuseum.co.uk; admission free; ☒ 10am-5pm),
housed partly in a 1901 dockside warehouse
(formerly the Industrial and Maritime Museum) and partly in a stunning modern extension built from glass and slate. A series of
themed exhibition galleries covers the history
of Welsh industry and innovation, making
much use of interactive computer screens and
audiovisual presentations. The effect can be
a bit overwhelming – at times you feel as if
you're being bombarded from all directions
with moving images, scrolling text, speech and
sound effects – but there is a lot of interesting
stuff here.

Highlights include the *People* exhibit, which
brings whole communities back to life by using
the records from the 1851 census to tell the stories of real Swansea people, and the Sea gallery,
with its tales of Cape Horner clipper ships and
how Swansea became the 19th-century copper
capital of the world. Best of all is the Industrial
Hall, where computers give way to real, historic
artefacts from Welsh coal pits, iron works, copper smelters, gold mines and slate quarries.

It would be hard to find a more complete contrast to the Waterfront Museum than the gloriously old-fashioned **Swansea Museum** (☎ 653763;
Victoria Rd; admission free; ☒ 10am-5pm Tue-Sun) – Dylan
Thomas referred to it as 'the museum which
should have *been* in a museum'. Founded in
1834, it remains charmingly low-tech, from

SWANSEA

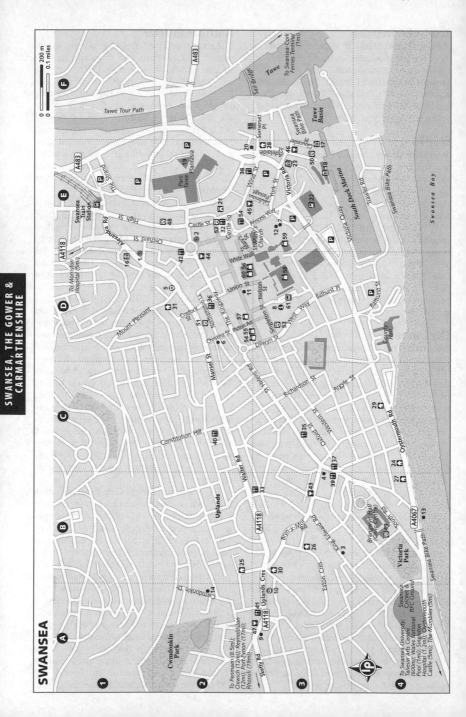

the eccentric Cabinet of Curiosities to the glass cases of archaeological finds from Gower caves, all explained in laminated notes stuck in ringbinders. Pride of place goes to the Mummy of Hor, which has been here since 1887 – a fascinating video in the display room explains the process of its repair and conservation.

The **Dylan Thomas Centre** (☎ 463980; www.dylanthomas.org; Somerset Pl; admission free; ☉ 10am-4.30pm), housed in the former Guildhall, contains an absorbing exhibition on the poet's life and work; entitled *Man and Myth*, it pulls no punches in examining the propensity of 'the most quoted author after Shakespeare' for puffing up his own myth. The centre also contains a bookshop, restaurant and café.

Set in a converted 19th-century seamen's chapel, the **Mission Gallery** (☎ 652016; Gloucester Pl; admission free; ☉ 11am-5pm) stages some of Swansea's most striking exhibitions of contemporary art. It is also a commercial gallery, selling glass, ceramics, jewellery and textiles by Welsh artists and designers, as well as paintings, posters and prints.

West of the Centre

Swansea University is in the suburb of Sketty, halfway between the city centre and the Mumbles, and possesses the UK's biggest collection of Egyptian antiquities outside the British Museum. Opened to the public in 1998, the volunteer-run **Egypt Centre** (☎ 295960; www.swan .ac.uk/egypt; Taliesin Arts Centre, Singleton Park, Mumbles Rd; admission free; ☉ 10am-4pm Tue-Sat) displays a fascinating collection of everyday ancient Egyptian artefacts, ranging from a 4000-year-old razor and cosmetic trays to a mummified crocodile.

The Mumbles

The Mumbles, strung out along the shoreline at the southern end of Swansea Bay, has been Swansea's seaside retreat since 1807, when the Oystermouth Railway was opened. Built for transporting coal, the horse-drawn carriages were soon converted for paying customers, and the Mumbles train became the first passenger railway service in the world.

The name Mumbles – which becomes a vowel-free zone in Welsh, Y Mwmbwls – is a legacy of French seamen who nicknamed the twin rounded rocks at the tip of the headland *Les Mamelles* – 'the breasts'.

The Mumbles is a mile-long strip of pastel-painted houses, pubs and restaurants, with a promenade walk and a Victorian pier at the far end. Built in 1898, **Mumbles Pier** (☎ 365220; www.mumbles-pier.co.uk; Mumbles Rd) was recently renovated; the pavilion now houses an amusement arcade, ten-pin bowling, and a brand new ice-rink, and there's a private, sandy beach down below.

Little remains of the old fishing village of Oystermouth, except the majestic ruin of

SWANSEA, THE GOWER & CARMARTHENSHIRE

INFORMATION		SLEEPING 🏠		DRINKING 🍸 🍷	
County Library	1 D1	Beachcomber Hotel	24 C4	Bryn-y-Mor	43 B3
Crossfire	2 E2	Christmas Pie B&B	25 B2	Mambo	44 D2
Dylan's Books	(see 15)	Crescent Guest House	26 B3	No Sign Bar	45 E2
Dylans Book Store	3 B3	Leonardo's Guest House	27 B4	Queen's Hotel	46 E3
Lendart Laundrette	4 B3	Morgans Hotel	28 E3	Uplands Tavern	47 A3
Main Post Office	(see 58)	Oyster Hotel	29 C4		
Police Station	5 D2	White House Hotel	30 B3	ENTERTAINMENT 🎭	
Siop Ty Tawe	6 D2	Windsor Lodge Hotel	31 D2	Bar Creation & Club	
Swansea Shopmobility	7 E3			Eden	48 E2
Swansea Tourist Office	8 D3	EATING 🍴		Brangwyn Hall	49 B4
Uplands Laundrette	9 A3	Bella Napoli	32 E2	Dylan Thomas Theatre	50 E3
Uplands Post Office	10 A3	Bizzie Lizzie's Bistro	33 B3	Escape	51 D2
Waterstone's	11 D2	Chelsea Café	34 E2	Monkey Bar	52 E2
		Didier & Stephanie	35 C3	Swansea Grand Theatre	53 D3
SIGHTS & ACTIVITIES		Dylan's Books 'n' Bites	(see 15)		
Action Bikes	12 E3	Govinda's	36 D2	SHOPPING 🛍	
Bay Watersports	13 B4	Joe's Ice Cream Parlour	37 C3	Derricks Music	54 D2
Cwmdonkin Drive (Dylan Thomas's		La Braseria	38 E2	Hobo's	55 D2
Birthplace)	14 A2	Miah's	39 B3	Musiquarium	56 D2
Dylan Thomas Centre	15 F2	Morgans Restaurant	(see 28)	Nucleus	57 D2
Glynn Vivian Art Gallery	16 D1	Retreat	40 C2	Quadrant Shopping Centre	58 D3
Mission Gallery	17 E3	Vietnam	41 A3	St David's Shopping Centre	59 E3
National Waterfront Museum	18 E3	Wild Swan	42 D2	Swansea Market	60 D2
Plantasia	19 E2				
Rainbow Sailing School	20 D2			TRANSPORT	
Swansea Castle	21 E2	Swansea Leisure Centre	22 E3	Central Bus Station	61 D3
		Swansea Museum	23 E3		

Oystermouth Castle (☎ 635436; adult/child £1.20/60p; Castle Ave; ☼ 11am-5pm Apr-Sep), once the stronghold of the Norman lords of Gower, but now the focus of summer mock medieval battles and Shakespeare performances. There's a fine view to enjoy over Swansea Bay from the battlements.

Newly fashionable in recent years, with gourmet restaurants vying for trade along the promenade, the Mumbles got a boost to its reputation when its most famous daughter, Hollywood actress Catherine Zeta-Jones, built a £2 million luxury mansion at Limeslade, on the south side of the peninsula.

For transport to the Mumbles, see p151.

ACTIVITIES
Walking & Cycling
You can walk or cycle along the **Swansea Bike Path**, a pleasingly flat 5-mile waterfront trail that runs from the Maritime Quarter to the Mumbles. The **Tawe Tour** is another 5-mile trail, running northwards along the River Tawe, past former industrial sites, to Morriston. You can get free booklets and maps from the tourist office.

From the parking area beyond Mumbles Head (continue along Mumbles Rd, past the pier), you can hike along a clifftop path for a mile to **Langland Bay**, and on for another mile to **Caswell Bay**; both are popular swimming and surfing beaches. You can return to the Mumbles waterfront by walking back along Caswell Rd, Langland Rd and Newton Rd.

Action Bikes (☎ 464640; 5 St David's Sq; ☼ 9am-5.30pm Mon-Sat, 11am-4pm Sun) rents bikes for £15 per day.

Swimming
The shiny new **Wales National Pool** (☎ 513513; www.walesnationalpoolswansea.co.uk; Sketty Lane, Sketty; adult/child £3.40/2.30) is the only 50m swimming pool in Wales; it's open for lane-swimming only during the week, but on Saturday and Sunday the 25m training pool is open for recreational swimming sessions from 1pm to 3pm, and kids' fun sessions from 3pm to 5pm.

Swansea Leisure Centre, closed down in 2003, was being given a total makeover at the time of research, and is scheduled to re-open in 2008 as an indoor water park, with swimming and paddling pools, hydroslides, wave pools, water-rides and, the icing on the cake, Europe's first indoor surfing centre.

Water Sports
You can hire surf-skis and windsurfers at **Bay Watersports** (☎ 534858; www.baywatersports .co.uk; Oystermouth Rd; ☼ May-Oct); a two-person surf-ski costs £12 for an hour. You can also get windsurfing lessons (1½-hour beginner's session £20). Opening times depend on tides and weather.

You can go **surfing** at Langland and Caswell bays, near the Mumbles – get advice and hire gear from **Nucleus** (☎ 361525; 75 Newton Rd, Mumbles); hire of a board and wetsuit for a half-/full-day costs £10/16.

If the sight of all those yachts in the marina has tempted you to have a go at sailing, **Rainbow Sailing School** (☎ 0844 545 7575; www .rainbowsailingschool.com; 5 Prospect Pl, Maritime Quarter; ☼ 9am-4pm Mon-Fri) offers taster days that are suitable for families and beginners who have no previous experience of sailing (£75 per person, minimum of three people).

FESTIVALS & EVENTS
From May to September, the waterfront from the city round to the Mumbles is taken over by the **Swansea Bay Summer Festival** (www.swanseabay festival.net), a smorgasbord of shows, fun fairs, carnivals, music, exhibitions, children's events and smaller festivals, including the **Swansea Film Festival** (www.swanseafilmfestival.com) in June, and the **Mumbles Beer Festival** (☎ 363391) in August.

The cultural celebrations continue with the **Swansea Festival of Music and the Arts** (www .swanseafestival.co.uk) in the first three weeks of October, with classical concerts, drama, lectures and exhibitions, swiftly followed by the **Dylan Thomas Festival** (☎ 463980; www.dylanthomasfestival .org), which celebrates Swansea's most famous son with poetry readings, talks, films and performances, and is held from 27 October (his birthday) to 9 November (the date he died).

Escape into the Park (www.escapefestival.com) is Wales' biggest outdoor dance-music festival, a one-day event featuring lots of different tents with big-name DJs enthusing the crowd. It takes place in August at Singleton Park (next to Swansea University campus), and tickets cost around £35.

SLEEPING
Most of Swansea's midrange accommodation is in Uplands, along Oystermouth Rd and in Mumbles; the city centre options are mostly chain hotels and more expensive independent hotels.

City Centre

Windsor Lodge Hotel (☎ 642158; www.windsor-lodge
.co.uk; Mount Pleasant; s/d from £50/65; **P**) Could do
with a bit of TLC, and some of the rooms,
especially the singles, are a bit cramped, but
the elegant Georgian building, fresh, modern
décor and quiet but central location make the
Windsor a decent choice.

Morgans Hotel (☎ 484848; www.morganshotel.co.uk;
Somerset Pl; d £125-250; **P**) The city's first boutique
hotel, set in the gorgeous red-brick and Portland stone former Ports Authority building,
Morgans combines historic elegance with contemporary design, and a high pamper factor –
Egyptian cotton bed linen, suede curtains, big
bathrobes, flat-screen TVs. It has a great restaurant and a lovely champagne bar, too.

West of the Centre

Christmas Pie B&B (☎ 480266; www.christmaspie.co.uk;
2 Mirador Cres; s/d £30/60; **P**) The name suggests
something warm and comforting, and this
suburban villa does not disappoint – hospita-
ble owners, three tastefully decorated en suite
bedrooms, vases of fresh flowers and an out-
of-the-ordinary, vegetarian-friendly breakfast
menu (kidney bean and sun-dried tomato sausages, anyone?).

Crescent Guest House (☎ 466814; www.crescentguest
house.co.uk; 132 Eaton Cres; s/d from £40/60; **P**) The
Crescent has a great location, perched on a
slope with great views from the lounge across
the rooftops to Swansea Bay. The bedrooms
are clean and comfortable, and the couple who
run the place are a fount of knowledge about
local attractions.

White House Hotel (☎ 473856; www.thewhitehouse
hotel.co.uk; 4 Nyanza Tce; s/d from £42/72) It seems like
nothing is too much trouble at this friendly,
flower-bedecked hotel – staff are only too
pleased to help out with any query or request.
The nine rooms are smart and well equipped;
even the smallish singles feel more like cosy,
well-designed ship's cabins than cramped
hotel rooms.

Leonardo's Guest House (☎ 470163; www.leonardos
guesthouse.co.uk; 380 Oystermouth Rd; s/d from £43/56)
Leonardo's is one of the best in the long strip
of seafront guesthouses on Oystermouth Rd,
with a warm welcome and recently redeco-
rated rooms in bright, sunny colours. Five
of the nine bedrooms enjoy sea views over
Swansea Bay.

Other places worth considering on Oystermouth Rd include:

Oyster Hotel (☎ 654345; oysterhotel@yahoo.co.uk; 262
Oystermouth Rd; s/d from £27/34)

Beachcomber Hotel (☎ 651380; www.beachcomber
hotel.co.uk; 364 Oystermouth Rd; s/d from £25/40)

The Mumbles

Coast House (☎ 368702; 708 Mumbles Rd; s/d from £35/50)
Ask for one of the 1st-floor front bedrooms at
this spick-and-span seafront guesthouse – the
décor leans toward the chintzy, floral look, but
the views from the big bay windows more than
compensate for any Laura Ashley overload.

Alexandra House (☎ 406406; www.alexandra-house
.com; 366 Mumbles Rd; s/d from £40/55; **P**) On the
promenade just north of Mumbles village,
this terraced Victorian house goes for the old-
fashioned look, with grandfather clock and
crystal chandeliers in the lounge, and flowery
bedspreads and lacy frills in the bedrooms.

Tides Reach Guest House (☎ 404877; 388 Mumbles
Rd; www.tidesreachguesthouse.com; s/d £50/65) From the
colourful hanging baskets outside the door
to the polished furniture and fresh flowers
throughout the house, this place exudes an
air of homey comfort. Several rooms have sea
views, as does the cosy lounge with its leather
sofas and armchairs.

Patricks with Rooms (☎ 360199; www.patrickswith
rooms.com; 638 Mumbles Rd; d £105) That rarest of
things, a child-friendly boutique hotel, Patricks
has eight individually styled designer bedrooms
in bold contemporary colours, with art on the
walls, fluffy robes and roll-top baths in the en
suites, and sea views from the windows.

EATING

Swansea has an impressive range of eateries,
clustered around Wind St, along St Helen's
Rd (chock-a-block with curry houses) and
out at the Mumbles.

City Centre

Govinda's (☎ 468469; 8 Cradock St; mains £4-6; ☯ noon-
3pm Mon-Thu, noon-6pm Fri & Sat) This sparkling restaurant specialises in vegetarian and vegan
cuisine using locally sourced organic produce.
The menu ranges from Indian samosa, dhal
and vegetable curry, to veggie lasagne, nut
burger and vegan cheesecake. It's run by Hare
Krishna, but there's no proselytising.

Dylan's Books'n'Bites (☎ 463980; Dylan Thomas
Centre, Somerset Pl; mains £3-8; ☯ café 10am-4.30pm,
lunch noon-2pm) Armchairs and tables scattered
among the bookshelves in the Dylan Thomas
Centre bookshop make an agreeable spot for

a coffee and a read. The lunch menu includes homemade soup and sandwiches, plus dishes from the more formal restaurant upstairs.

Wild Swan (☎ 472121; 14 Orchard St; mains £6-9) Swansea's best Cantonese restaurant is sumptuously decked out with red leather sofas, delicate Chinese screens, and even a pond filled with koi carp. The menu covers all the classics from stir-fried squid with black bean sauce to aromatic crispy duck.

Bella Napoli (☎ 644611; 66 Wind St; mains £6-14; ☒ noon-2.30pm & 5.30-11pm Tue-Fri, noon-11pm Sat & Sun) This cheery little southern Italian restaurant serves up classic pizza and pasta dishes, and is staffed by cheeky waiters who occasionally burst into song. Children are welcome.

La Braseria (☎ 469683; 28 Wind St; mains £8-15; ☒ noon-2.30pm & 7-11.30pm Mon-Sat) Having gained a reputation as a favourite hang-out of the Swansea glitterati (Catherine Zeta-Jones is a fan), this place is enormously popular, often packed solid at weekends. It's a Spanish bodega-style place, with a global menu ranging from beef satay to local lobster.

Chelsea Café (☎ 464068; 17 St Mary's St; mains £10-15; ☒ noon-2.30pm & 7-11.30pm Mon-Sat) Golden yellow tablecloths and dark-red banquettes against wood-panelled walls and a red-brick chimney breast make for a snug dining room at this popular restaurant. Check the blackboard specials for filo-pastry parcels filled with prawns, squat lobster tails, cockles and laver bread, and roast loin of lamb with a smoked bacon, date and rosemary jus.

Morgans Restaurant (☎ 484848; Morgans Hotel, Somerset Pl; mains £15-20) The grand former boardroom of the British Ports Authority building (now Morgans Hotel) is the setting for this sophisticated restaurant, all crisp white table linen and designer chairs with a single rose on each table. Relax with a G&T in the candle-lit bar before choosing from a menu that runs from asparagus, sage and orange risotto to seared fillet of sea bass with vanilla bean sauce.

West of the Centre

Joe's Ice Cream Parlour (☎ 653880; 85 St Helen's Rd; ice creams £1.20-3; ☒ 11am-9pm Mon-Fri, noon-8pm Sat & Sun) Joe's, established in 1922, is a Swansea institution, serving traditional fruit sundaes and knickerbocker glory, or just a dish of delicious buttery vanilla ice cream with a crisp wafer and a choice of toppings. There are two other branches – in the Parc Tawe Shopping

Centre in the city centre, and at 524 Mumbles Rd in the Mumbles.

Retreat (☎ 457880; 2 Humphrey St, Uplands; mains £3-5; ☒ noon-7.30pm Tue-Fri, noon-6pm Sat) Part of an incense-perfumed holistic centre, this New Age vegetarian and vegan café serves a range of healthy salads and sandwiches, as well as some naughtier dishes, including a delicious dairy-free chocolate fudge brownie.

Vietnam (☎ 650929; 36 Uplands Cres, Uplands; mains £6-9) Rather girly red, pink and white décor here, but it's a firm favourite with the local Asian community so the kitchen must be doing something right. Authentic Vietnamese dishes such as *bo bia* (rice-paper rolls with peanut sauce) and *thit vit quay* (roast duck with rice).

Miah's (☎ 466244; 137-138 St Helen's Rd, Uplands; mains £6-10; ☒ noon-2pm & 6pm-midnight Mon-Sat, noon-midnight Sun) Housed in a beautifully converted church with bare stone walls, exposed roof beams and tables ranged around a mezzanine at half-height, Miah's is a cut above the six-pints-and-a-curry type of Indian restaurant. The tandoori trout is exquisite.

Bizzie Lizzie's Bistro (☎ 473379; 55 Walter Rd, Uplands; mains £8-14; ☒ closed Sat lunch & all day Sun) A warmly lit basement with country-kitchen pine furniture and green-and-white check tablecloths, decorated with bric-a-brac and old street signs, Bizzie's has a half-vegetarian, half-carnivore menu – whichever you are, go for the delicious nut roast with chilli and tomato sauce.

Didier & Stephanie (☎ 655603; 56 St Helen's Rd, Uplands; mains £9-18; ☒ closed Mon) An intimate and relaxed French restaurant run by the eponymous Gallic duo. Didier and Stephanie combine classic French dishes, such as saddle of rabbit with mustard sauce with more adventurous offerings, such as a starter of seared foie gras with mango ice cream.

The Mumbles

Mermaid Restaurant & Coffee Lounge (☎ 367744; 686 Mumbles Rd; mains £7-15, 2-course lunch £10; ☒ closed Sun & Mon dinner) A bright décor of blond wood and fresh flowers complement the menu of fresh local produce, home-baked bread, good wine and real ale. The Mermaid is famous for its slow-roast salt-marsh lamb from the Gower Peninsula, and a kids' menu where everything is freshly prepared – no frozen chicken nuggets here. The building was once the Mermaid Hotel, a favourite haunt of Dylan Thomas.

Knights Restaurant (☎ 363184; 614 Mumbles Rd; mains £14-16) Seafood is the speciality of the house at this intimate and elegant waterfront restaurant (chef Michael Knight is a favourite of Michael Douglas and Catherine Zeta-Jones). Local crab, sea bass, salmon and Dover sole make regular appearances on the menu, as does sewin (wild sea trout) in season. The monkfish with bacon, leeks and brandy sauce is recommended.

698 (☎ 361616; 698 Mumbles Rd; mains £15-20; ✆ 10am-11pm) A very stylish bistro and coffee lounge with a modern European menu; try pan-fried scallops on pea purée to start, followed by grilled fillet steak with creamy mash and a wild mushroom jus. The 698 is also family-friendly, with highchairs, baby-changing facilities, and books and toys to borrow.

DRINKING
Swansea's main boozing strip is Wind St (pronounced to rhyme with 'blind', as in drunk), and on Friday and Saturday nights it can be a bit of a zoo; however, there are one or two bars where you can have a conversation that doesn't require shouting.

City Centre
No Sign Bar (☎ 465300; 56 Wind St) Once frequented by Dylan Thomas (it appears as the Wine Vaults in his story *The Followers*), the No Sign stands out as the only vaguely traditional bar left on Wind St, a long narrow haven of dark-wood panelling, friendly staff and decent beer. How long will it survive?

Mambo (☎ 456620; 46 The Kingsway) A Latin American–themed cocktail bar, serving margaritas (made with Patron tequila) by the glass or the pitcher, amid a swirl of mosaics and Latino music.

Queen's Hotel (☎ 521531; Gloucester Pl) This is an old-fashioned corner pub with polished mahogany and brass bar, old tiles and a range of cask-conditioned beers on tap, including Theakston's Old Peculier.

West of the Centre
Uplands Tavern (☎ 458242; 42 Uplands Cres) A classic student pub, big and brassy with reasonably priced beer (Greene King Abbott real ale), a poolroom, and live music – folk, rock, blues, country – five nights a week, open-mic night on Tuesday. Yet another place where Dylan Thomas used to hang out.

Bryn-y-Mor (☎ 466650; 17 Bryn-y-Mor Rd) Another friendly local that's popular with students, the Bryn-y-Mor has cheap beer, pool tables,

large-screen TV, a decent jukebox and service with a smile.

The Mumbles
The famous Mumbles Mile – a pub crawl through the bars between Newton Rd and Bracelet Bay – is not what it once was; most of the old pubs have succumbed to pumping house music and boisterous crowds of alcopop-fuelled teens.

One place worth seeking out is the **Park Inn** (☎ 366738; 23 Park St), set a block inland from the promenade and away from the crowds (coming out of the tourist office, turn left, then left again into Dunns Lane, and again into Park St; the pub's at the far end). It's a friendly local serving real ale, where any music you hear will be knocked out on the pub piano.

ENTERTAINMENT
Nightclubs
Check out *Buzz* magazine (available from bars or the tourist office) for what's-on listings of clubs and live music venues.

Monkey Bar (☎ 480822; 13 Castle St; ✆ 11am-2am or 3am, club nights from 9pm, food served 11am-5.30pm) An organic, vegetarian café-bar by day, with chunky tables, big sofas, modern art and cool tunes, this funky little venue transforms after dark into Swansea's best alternative club, where weekend DJs play drum and bass, hip hop, dub, reggae, salsa and world music.

Escape (☎ 652854; www.escapegroup.com; Northampton Lane; ✆ from 10pm) This is Swansea's mainstream house club, with touring DJs pumping it up every Saturday. The venue occasionally stages live bands too.

Bar Creation & Club Eden (☎ 410964; www.gay swansea.co.uk; 233 High St; bar ✆ noon-11pm daily, club ✆ 10pm-2.30am Tue & Wed, 10pm-3.30am Thu, 10pm-4.30am Fri & Sat, 9pm-1.20am Sun) One of the biggest gay venues in Wales, this bar and club combo stages a packed programme of club nights, drag acts, film screenings and cabaret shows.

Theatre & Music
Swansea Grand Theatre (☎ 475715; www.swanseagrand .co.uk; Singleton St) The town's largest theatre stages a mixed programme of ballet, opera, musicals, pantomimes and a regular comedy club.

Dylan Thomas Theatre (☎ 473238; www.dylan thomastheatre.org.uk; Gloucester Pl) Home to the Swansea Little Theatre Company, an amateur dramatics group of which DT was once a member. The company puts on productions of classic plays by Shakespeare, Oscar Wilde and Arthur Miller, among others, as well as the occasional performance of your man's *Under Milk Wood*.

Taliesin Arts Centre (☎ 602060; www.taliesinarts centre.co.uk; Singleton Park, Mumbles Rd) Part of the University of Wales, Swansea, this vibrant arts centre has a programme of contemporary, international music, theatre, dance and film.

Brangwyn Hall (☎ 635489; Guildhall Rd South) This handsome Art Deco hall, decorated with colourful painted panels by 1930s artist Frank Brangwyn, hosts choral and orchestral performances.

SHOPPING

Most of Swansea's retail therapy is crammed into the vast, soulless shopping centres of the Quadrant, St David's Centre and Parc Tawe.

Nucleus (☎ 466616; 230 Oxford St) A surf, snow and skate shop with a good range of T-shirts, shoes and skatewear, as well as boards, wetsuits and bags.

Musiquarium (☎ 465256; 61 Swansea Market) A great source for alternative music CDs and vinyl, with a wide range of indie, rock, funk, soul, country, folk, jazz, blues, R&B and punk.

Derricks Music (☎ 654226; 221 Oxford St) A good, varied CD shop and gig-ticket outlet.

Hobo's (☎ 654586; 214 Oxford St) Sells groovy secondhand '60s and '70s clothing, and is a good place to find out about local music events.

Swansea Market (entrances on White Walls & Union St; ⏰ closed Sun) Dates from 1830, and sells fresh fish, meat, cheese and vegetables, as well as clothing, books, music and hardware.

GETTING THERE & AWAY
Boat

Swansea Cork Ferries (☎ 456116; www.swanseacorkferries .com; King's Dock) sails to Cork (Ireland) four to six times per week; the 10-hour trip costs £23 to £34 for foot passengers, £85 to £199 for a standard car, one way. The ferry terminal is a mile east of the centre, on the east side of the river mouth.

Bus

First bus 100 is a shuttle service between Swansea and Cardiff (£4, one hour, every 30 to 45 minutes Monday to Saturday, five daily Sunday). Stagecoach bus 63 links Swansea with Brecon (£4, 1½ hours, three daily Monday to Saturday) via Dan-yr-Ogof Showcaves.

National Express coach 508 runs direct from London (Victoria station) to Swansea (£22, 4½ hours, twice daily), continuing to Carmarthen, Tenby, Pembroke and Haverfordwest. National Express also runs coach 528 from Swansea to Haverfordwest (£8, 2¼ hours, one per day).

Train

There are direct trains to Swansea from Cardiff (£4, one hour, every 45 minutes Monday to Saturday, every two hours Sunday), Tenby (£10, 1½ hours, seven daily Monday to Saturday, one on Sunday) and Haverfordwest (£10, 1½ hours, every two hours).

Swansea is the southern terminus of the scenic Heart of Wales line (www.heart-of-wales .co.uk), which runs across southern Mid-

---

THE DYLAN THOMAS TRAIL

There are several sites in Swansea and southwest Wales associated with the poet Dylan Thomas. The tourist office and the Dylan Thomas Centre have various maps, leaflets and booklets describing self-guided walks and trails, though many of the places mentioned no longer exist.

Here is a list of the major sites with something to see, or an exhibition to visit.

5 Cwmdonkin Drive, Swansea The unassuming terraced house where Thomas was born in 1914, and where he wrote two-thirds of his poetry. At the time of writing, the house had recently been purchased and the new owners intend to restore it and open it to the public.

Dylan Thomas Theatre, Swansea The present home of the amateur theatrical company of which Thomas was once a member (see p149).

Dylan Thomas Centre, Swansea Exhibition on Thomas' work and life (see p145).

New Quay, Cardiganshire Thomas and his wife Caitlin lived here for nine months in 1944–45, and the fictional Llareggub in *Under Milk Wood* was partly based on New Quay.

Boathouse, Laugharne The house where Thomas lived from 1949 until his death; the Boathouse is now home to a museum and exhibition (see p161).

St Martin's Church, Laugharne Both Thomas and his wife are buried in the cemetery here (see p161).

Wales to Shrewsbury in England, passing through Llandeilo (£5, one hour), Llandovery (£5.50, 1¼ hours) and Llandrindod Wells (£8.30, 1¾ hours, four daily Monday to Saturday, two on Sunday).

GETTING AROUND
Bus
First Cymru runs local services between Swansea and the Mumbles (£2, every 15 minutes, half-hourly on Monday to Saturday, hourly on Sunday). A Swansea Bay Day Ticket offers all-day bus travel in the Swansea and Mumbles area for £3.60 (£3 if bought after 10am). Buy a ticket from the driver.

During summer the **Swansea Bay Rider** (☎ 635436), a toy-town road-train, runs between Swansea and the Mumbles.

A new Swansea Metro rapid transit bus route will start operating in late 2008, linking the train station, bus station, Swansea University and the Mumbles.

Taxi
Try **Yellow Cabs** (☎ 644446). It costs about £10 to go from the train station to the Mumbles.

GOWER PENINSULA

☎ 01792
With its grey limestone cliffs, sweeping butterscotch-coloured beaches and pounding surf, the Gower Peninsula (Y Gŵyr) feels like a little chunk of the Pembrokeshire coast tacked onto Swansea's back yard.

A 15-mile long thumb of land stretching westward from the Mumbles, Gower was designated the UK's first official Area of Outstanding Natural Beauty (AONB) in 1956. The National Trust (NT) owns about three-quarters of the coast and, although there is no continuously waymarked path, you can hike almost the entire length of the coastline. The peninsula also has the best surfing in Wales outside Pembrokeshire.

The main family beaches, patrolled by lifeguards during the summer, are Langland Bay, Caswell Bay and Port Eynon. The most impressive, and most popular with surfers, is the magnificent 3-mile sweep of Rhossili Bay at the far end of the peninsula. Much of Gower's northern coast is salt marsh that faces the Burry Inlet, an important area for wading birds and wildfowl.

Information
The Swansea and Mumbles tourist offices (p143) provide information and advice on Gower, including accommodation listings and bus timetables. The NT runs a good, year-round visitor centre at Rhossili, which is stocked with informative leaflets on walking and wildlife.

Tide tables are important here – at high water many beaches shrink to a narrow strip of sand or shingle, and some coastal walks become impossible; surf conditions also depend on the state of the tide. You can pick up tide tables at tourist offices, or check them online at www.bbc.co.uk/weather/coast/tides/wales.shtml.

Gower is covered by both the OS Landranger map 159 and the OS Explorer 164.

Activities
WALKING
There are dozens of excellent walks in Gower, from clifftop coastal paths to inland heath. Tourist offices stock leaflets and maps, plus half a dozen dedicated walking guidebooks (see www.visitswanseabay.com/walking).

The National Trust website (www.nationaltrust.org.uk) also has five downloadable walks – go to the Rhossili Visitor Centre page and click on the Walks link.

The **Gower Way** is a waymarked footpath that runs for 35 miles from the ancient hill fort of Penlle'r Castell (on a minor road 10 miles north of Swansea) to Rhossili, along the central spine of the peninsula. There are three leaflets (£1.05 each) describing the route, available from tourist offices. The final section, from Penmaen to Rhossili via the ridge of Cefn Bryn, Reynoldston and Old Henllys (10 miles) makes a good one-day walk.

HORSE RIDING
The rural byways and bridleways of Gower are ideal territory for exploring on horseback. Several places offer pony trekking and hacking, with rates around £22/35 a half-/full day, including **Parc-Le-Breos Pony Trekking** (☎ 371636; www.parc-le-breos.co.uk; Parc-Le-Breos House, Parkmill).

SURFING
The Gower Peninsula has several good surf beaches, notably Llangennith, which is one of the best beaches in Wales for beginners. You can take lessons with the **Welsh Surfing Federation School** (☎ 386426; www.wsfsurfschool.co.uk; The Croft, Llangennith); a half-day session costs £25.

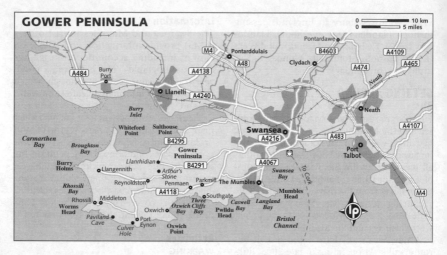

GOWER PENINSULA

You can check surf conditions online at www.gowerlive.co.uk.

Getting There & Around

Bus services in the Gower Peninsula are operated by First and Pullman Coaches. For route and timetable information, call **Traveline** (☎ 0870 608 2 608; www.traveline-cymru.org.uk) or pick up a timetable booklet from a tourist information centre.

Frequent buses cover pretty much the whole peninsula, running hourly Monday to Saturday and every two hours on Sunday. The most useful routes for visitors, departing from Swansea bus station, include 14 (to Pennard Cliffs via Bishopston), and 118 (to Rhossili via Uplands, Parkmill, Penmaen, Oxwich, Port Eynon and Reynoldston).

You can buy a Swansea Bay Day Ticket (First buses) or Gower Day Explorer Ticket (Pullman buses) for £3.50, gaining unlimited travel on both companies' services for a day.

SOUTH COAST
Mumbles Head to Three Cliffs Bay

Going west from Mumbles Head there are two small bays, **Langland Bay** and **Caswell Bay**, shingly at high tide but exposing acres of golden sand at low water; both are easily reached from Swansea and are popular with families and surfers. About 500m west of Caswell along the coast path is beautiful **Brandy Cove**, a tiny secluded beach away from the crowds.

West again is **Pwlldu Bay**, a shingle beach backed by a wooded ravine known as Bish-

opston Valley; you can walk there from Bishopston village (1.5 miles).

From Pwlldu Head the limestone **Pennard Cliffs**, honeycombed with caves, stretch westwards for 2 miles to Three Cliffs Bay. Halfway along is the National Trust's Pennard Cliffs car park (a little confusingly, it's in the village of **Southgate**, not Pennard; the Pennard Cliffs bus stop is also here). The car park is the starting point for scenic coastal walks east to Pwlldu (1.5 miles), and west to Three Cliffs Bay (1 mile).

Next to the car park is the **Three Cliffs Coffee Shop** (☎ 233230; 68 Southgate Rd, Southgate; ☀ 9am-6pm daily), which has good cakes, coffee and ice cream.

Three Cliffs Bay is named for the triple-pointed crag, pierced by a natural arch, that guards its eastern point. It is regularly voted one of the most beautiful beaches in Britain, even though the sand disappears completely at high tide.

The only way to get there is on foot. The most scenic approach is along the Pennard Cliffs, but you can also walk in from Parkmill village (1 mile), either along the valley of Pennard Pill, or along the edge of the golf course to the east via the ruins of Pennard Castle.

It is dangerous to swim here at high tide, because of river currents, but safe at low tide. The triple-pointed crag is a popular rock-climbing site.

Parkmill

The village of Parkmill is home to the **Gower Heritage Centre** (☎ 371206; www.gowerheritagecentre.co.uk; Parkmill; adult/child £3.95/2.80; ☀ 10am-5.30pm

Apr-Sep, 10am-4.30pm Oct-Mar), housed in a restored watermill, with a café, puppet theatre, craft centre, farm and fish pond. It's Gower's main rainy-day option for kids.

Penmaen

On **Penmaen Burrows**, the headland on the western side of Three Cliffs Bay, are the remains of a medieval church and the buried remains of a Viking village known as Steadworlango, fragments of a Norman tower, a huge Neolithic burial chamber and a limekiln used until a century ago for the production of quicklime fertiliser. Access is on foot from Penmaen.

Parc-le-Breos (☎ 371636; www.parc-le-breos.co.uk; Penmaen; B&B per person £29; P), set in its own private estate north of the main road, offers accommodation in a Victorian hunting lodge, with log fires in winter. It's also a pony-trekking centre (see p151).

Nicholaston Farm Caravan & Camping Site (☎ 37109; www.nicholastonfarm.co.uk; Penmaen; sites per 2 people, tent & car £10-12; Apr-Oct) is a working farm at the western end of Penmaen, a short walk from beaches at Tor Bay and Three Cliffs Bay.

Oxwich Bay

Oxwich Bay is a windy, 2.5-mile-long curve of sand backed by dunes. Road access and a large car park (£2) make it popular with families and water sports enthusiasts (no lifeguard, though).

Set on a hillside above the beach is the Cadw-operated (Cadw is the Welsh historic monuments agency) stately grey ruin of **Oxwich Castle** (☎ 390359; Oxwich Castle Farm; adult/child £2.50/2; 10am-5pm Apr-Sep), less a castle and more a sumptuous 16th-century, mock-military Tudor mansion.

Behind the beach lies **Oxwich Nature Reserve**, an area of salt and freshwater marshes, oak and ash woodlands, and dunes; it is home to a variety of birdlife and dune plants.

Euphoria Sailing (☎ 0870 770 2890; www.euphoria sailing.co.uk; Watersports4:all Beach Club, Oxwich Bay) runs water-skiing and wake-boarding sessions (£40), and rents out sailing dinghies (£30 an hour) and kayaks (£10 an hour).

SLEEPING & EATING

Oxwich Camping Park (☎ 390777; Oxwich; sites per tent & 2 people £6-11; Mar-Oct) This park has a good location at the top of the hill above the bay with views along the beach.

Woodside Guest House (☎ 390791; Woodside, Oxwich; s/d from £38/50; P) In the village centre, Woodside is close to the beach and nature reserve.

Oxwich Bay Hotel (☎ 390329; www.oxwichbayhotel.co .uk; Oxwich Bay; s/d from £55/66; P) This hotel is right on the beach – you can have a drink or a meal overlooking the sands – and has plush rooms with big windows and sea views. It serves snacks and bar meals and also has a formal restaurant (mains £12 to £16).

Port Eynon

The three-quarter-mile stretch of dunes at Port Eynon is Gower's busiest beach (in summer, at least), with half a dozen camping and caravan sites nearby. It's safe for swimming.

Gower Coast Adventures (☎ 250440; www.gower coastadventures.co.uk; adult/child £24/16) runs two-hour speedboat trips to Worms Head from Port Eynon beach (you have to paddle out to the boat).

Around the southern point of the bay is **Culver Hole**, a curious stone structure built into a gash in the cliff. Legend has it that it was a smugglers' hiding place, but the mundane truth is that it served as a dovecote (pigeons were a valuable food source in medieval times; the name comes from Old English *culufre*, meaning 'dove'). It's quite tricky to find – the easiest route is signposted from the youth hostel – and is only accessible for three hours either side of low tide; make sure you don't get caught out by the rising waters.

The coastal walk west from Port Eynon to Rhossili (7 miles) is the wildest and most dramatic part of the Gower coast, and fairly rough going. Halfway along is **Paviland Cave** (see the boxed text the Red Lady of Paviland Cave, p154).

SLEEPING & EATING

Port Eynon Youth Hostel (YHA; ☎ 0870 770 5998; Old Lifeboat House; dm £14; year-round) This is a former lifeboat station with a stunning beachside location, and the warden is a mine of information on the local area.

Carreglwyd Park (☎ 390795; www.porteynon.com; The Seafront; sites per tent & 2 people £15; Mar-Dec) Perched above the western end of the beach, with good views along the coast.

Culver House Hotel (☎ 390755; www.culverhousehotel .co.uk; Port Eynon; s/d from £40/66) A lovely old country house just 100m from the beach; rooms 7 and 10, both with balconies, have the best sea views. It doesn't have a restaurant, but

SWANSEA, THE GOWER & CARMARTHENSHIRE

THE RED LADY OF PAVILAND CAVE

Halfway along the Gower coast between Port Eynon and Rhossili is Paviland Cave, where in 1823 the Reverend William Buckland discovered a Stone Age human skeleton dyed with red ochre. As he also found jewellery buried along with the bones, the good Reverend assumed the deceased must be a woman. Being also a devout Christian, he believed she must date from the Roman era, as she could not be older than the biblical flood. The 'Red Lady', as the skeleton became known, was therefore a Roman prostitute or witch, according to Buckland.

Modern analysis shows that the Red Lady was actually a man – possibly a tribal chief – who died, aged around 21, some 29,000 years ago. His are the oldest human remains yet found in the UK; you can see a replica of his skeleton and burial in Swansea Museum.

---

you can eat at the nearby **Ship Inn** (☎ 390204; Port Eynon; mains £4-7).

WEST GOWER
Rhossili Bay

The western end of the Gower Peninsula bears the full brunt of Atlantic storms, whose waves have carved out some of Wales' most dramatic coastal scenery in the form of Rhossili Bay. The waves also make this one of Wales' best and most popular surfing beaches.

The dramatic 3-mile sweep of golden sand is backed by the steep slopes of **Rhossili Down** (193m), a humpbacked, heather-covered ridge whose updraughts create perfect soaring conditions for hang-gliders and paragliders. On the summit are numerous Iron Age earthworks, a burial chamber called Sweyne's Howes and the remains of a WWII radar station. At its foot, behind the beach, is the Warren, the sand-buried remains of an old village. At low tide the stark, ghostly ribs of the *Helvetica*, a Norwegian barque wrecked in a storm in 1887, protrude from the sand in the middle of the beach.

Access to the beach is via a path leading next to the Worms Head Hotel, across from the car park. Swimming at the beach is dangerous if there is any surf.

RHOSSILI VILLAGE

The National Trust's **Rhossili Visitor Centre** (☎ 390707; Coastguard Cottages; admission free; ☺ 10.30am-5.30pm Apr-Oct, 11am-4pm Wed-Sun Nov-Mar), at the downhill end of the car park, has information on local walks and wildlife. There are good hikes out to the headland overlooking Worms Head (1 mile), and up to the summit of Rhossili Down (a very steep half a mile).

South of the village is the **Viel** (pronounced 'vile'), a rare survival of a patchwork of strip-fields first laid out in medieval times.

The **Bay Bistro & Coffee House** (☎ 390519; ☺ 10am-5pm) does good coffee, cakes and light meals.

The neighbouring **Worms Head Hotel** (☎ 390512; www.thewormshead.co.uk; s/d from £53/70) trades mostly on its incredible views of Worms Head and the beach, but is overpriced in terms of the standard of accommodation.

WORMS HEAD

The southern extremity of Rhossili Bay is guarded by Worms Head (from the Old English *wurm*, meaning 'dragon' – the rocks present a snaking, Loch Ness–monster profile). There is a four-hour window of opportunity (two hours either side of low tide) when you can walk out across a causeway and along the narrow crest of the Outer Head to the furthest point of land. There are seals around the rocks, and the cliffs are thick with razorbills, guillemots, kittiwakes, fulmars and puffins during nesting season (April to July).

Pay close attention to the tides – tide tables are posted at the Rhossili Visitor Centre – as people are regularly rescued after being cut off by the rising waters. Among those who have spent a cold, nervous half-night trapped there was the young Dylan Thomas, as he relates in the story 'Who Do You Wish Was with Us?', from *Portrait of the Artist as a Young Dog*. If you do get stuck, do not try to wade or swim back. Currents are fierce and the rocks treacherous.

Llangennith

The northern end of Rhossili Bay is one of the best surfing beaches in Britain. Behind it is the pretty village of Llangennith, the hub of the surfie social scene.

PJ's Surfshop (☎ 386669; www.pjsurfshop.co.uk) owned by Pete Jones, the ex-European surf champion, stocks all the gear you'll need, and

---

LOVESPOONS

All over Wales, craft shops turn out wooden spoons with contorted handles in a variety of different designs, at a speed that would have left their original makers – village lads with their eyes on a lady – gawking in astonishment. The carving of these spoons seems to date back to the 17th century, when they were made by men to give to women to mark the start of a courtship.

Various symbols were carved into the spoons; the meanings of a few of them are as follows:

Anchor I'm home to stay; you can count on me.

Balls in a cage, links in a chain Captured love, together forever; the number of balls or links may correspond to the number of children desired, or the number of years already spent together.

Bell Marriage.

Celtic cross Faith; marriage.

Double spoon Side by side forever.

Flowers Love and affection; courtship.

Horseshoe Good luck; happiness.

Key, lock, little house My house is yours.

One heart My heart is yours.

Two hearts We feel the same way about one another.

Vines, trees, leaves Our love is growing.

Wheel I will work for you.

If you want to see carving in progress, the St Fagan's National History Museum (see p104) can usually oblige. Any number of shops will be happy to sell you the finished product.

---

rents out wetsuits (£9 per day), surfboards (£9 per day) and bodyboards (£5 per day).

SLEEPING & EATING

Hillend Campsite (☎ 386204; sites per 2 people, tent & car £15; ☉ Easter-Oct) As close to the beach as you can get. The on-site Eddy's Restaurant has brilliant views, and rustles up breakfast for under a fiver, and dinner for £7 or £8.

Bremmel Cottage (☎ 386308; s/d from £20/30; **P**) Another surfer-friendly place, this pretty little cottage is like a warren, with appealing attic rooms.

College House (☎ 386214; s/d £30/50) Down the lane between PJ's and the church, this is a charming B&B in a lovely house decorated with sculptures and paintings. The garden backs onto the church.

The centre of the village's social life is the **King's Head** (☎ 386212; mains £5-12), which serves real ales and home-cooked bar meals, including a good range of vegetarian dishes.

CENTRAL & NORTH GOWER

In complete contrast to the south coast, Gower's northern fringe is a series of salt marshes and mud flats, not much to look at but an important wildlife habitat. This coast also produces some of the region's most famous foodstuffs: Gower lamb, whose diet of salt-marsh vegetation imparts a distinct and delicious flavour; and Penclawdd cockles, harvested from the mud flats at the eastern end of the coast.

Arthur's Stone

Cefn Bryn is the name for the Gower's breezy, 186m-high central uplands. On the summit moor, north of the minor road from Reynoldston to Llanrhidian, is a 25-tonne quartz boulder, the fallen capstone of a Neolithic burial chamber known as Arthur's Stone (Coeten Arthur). In legend it's a pebble that Arthur removed from his boot and flung across the Burry Inlet on his way to the fateful Battle of Camlan. Local lore also says that a woman who crawls around the stone at midnight during the full moon would be joined by her lover – if he was faithful.

The view from the top is fantastic – you can see out to the edges of the Gower in every direction, and on a clear day you can see south to Lundy Island and the Devon and Somerset coast. It's a great spot to watch the sunset.

The **King Arthur Hotel** (☎ 390775; www.king arthurhotel.co.uk; Higher Green, Reynoldston; s/d from £55/65; mains £6-14) in Reynoldston has a lovely, old-fashioned, wood-panelled bar with open fires, and serves real ales and excellent pub grub. The hotel bedrooms are attractively decorated in shades of cream and burgundy, and there's a romantic 18th-century cottage too (self-catering or B&B).

CARMARTHENSHIRE

Castle-dotted Carmarthenshire has gentle valleys, deep-green woods and a sandy, sweeping coast. Playing second fiddle to its dramatic western neighbour, Pembrokeshire, it remains much quieter and less explored.

CARMARTHEN (CAERFYRDDIN)

☎ 01267 / pop 14,600

Carmarthenshire's handsome county town is where legend locates the birthplace of Merlin, the famous wizard of the Arthurian legends. An oak tree planted in 1660 for Charles II's coronation came to be called 'Merlin's Tree' and was linked to a prophecy that its death would mean curtains for the town. But the tree died peacefully in the 1970s and the town still thrives. Pieces of the tree are kept under glass at the Carmarthenshire County Museum.

The town centre is on the northern bank of the River Tywi (often anglicised to Towy). The **tourist office** (☎ 231557; 113 Lammas St; ☯ 10am-5.30pm Mon-Sat Apr-Sep, 10am-4.30pm Mon-Sat Oct-Mar) is on the main street, a block west of the main bus stop on Blue St. The train station is 300m south, across the river.

Sights

The hulking **county hall**, above the River Tywi bridge, was designed in the 18th century – apparently as a jail – by John Nash, better known for Buckingham Palace. It's on the site of Carmarthen's Norman Castle (destroyed in the Civil War, though there are a few remnants just west of the County Hall).

Housed in a former art college, **Oriel Myrddin** (Merlin Gallery; ☎ 222775; Church Lane; admission free; ☯ 10am-5pm Mon-Sat) stages changing exhibitions of contemporary arts and crafts. Opposite is the **King Street Gallery** (☎ 267652; King St; ☯ 10am-4pm Mon-Sat), which has a selection of works by local artists.

Sleeping & Eating

Y Dderwen Fach (☎ 234193; 98 Priory St; s/d from £20/39) Set in an interesting old town house northeast of the centre, this is a basic, no-frills B&B but is centrally located, welcoming and good value.

Boar's Head (☎ 222789; www.boarsheadhotel.com; 120 Lammas St; s/d £45/55; Ⓟ) This fine old coaching inn offers family-friendly B&B accommodation, with highchairs, cots and baby monitors available. There's also a special master bedroom with a four-poster bed (£75).

Falcon Hotel (☎ 237152; www.falconcarmarthen .co.uk; Lammas St; s/d from £45/55) A small, family-run hotel, the Falcon has a traditional, old-fashioned feel and a convenient location on the main street.

Café at No 4 Queen St (☎ 220461; 4 Queen St; mains £3.50-7; ☯ 9am-5pm Mon-Sat) This chic little corner café right in the middle of Carmarthen brews the best coffee in town and serves fantastic home-made cakes and scones as well as soups, salads, sandwiches and daily specials.

Quayside Brasserie (☎ 223000; the Quay; 2-course lunch £9, mains £10-15; ☯ closed Sun) A popular restaurant with an outdoor terrace overlooking the river, the Quayside has a farmhouse look indoors, and an inventive menu with the accent on seafood – grilled sea bass with sweet potato and coriander mash, or *paupiettes* (thin rolls) of plaice with Gower cockles.

Getting There & Away

First bus X11 runs from Carmarthen to Swansea (£5, 1½ hours, every 30 minutes Monday to Saturday), and the 460 goes to Cardigan (£4, 1½ hours, eight daily Monday to Saturday). Silcox bus 322 runs from Haverfordwest (£5, one hour, three daily Monday to Saturday). There are no Sunday services on these routes.

The Traws–Cambria bus service X40 (Cardiff to Aberystwyth) passes through daily, as does National Express service 508/528 (Haverfordwest–Swansea–London).

The Beacons Bus (see p125) route B10 links Carmarthen with Brecon.

Trains run between Carmarthen and Cardiff (£12, two hours, six daily) and also west to Fishguard, Tenby, Pembroke, Haverfordwest and Milford Haven.

AROUND CARMARTHEN

Gwili Steam Railway

The standard-gauge **Gwili Steam Railway** (☎ 01267-230666; www.gwili-railway.co.uk; adult/child £5.50/3) runs along the lovely Gwili valley, departing from Bronwydd Arms, 3 miles north of Carmarthen on the A484. It runs daily in August, on Wednesday and Sunday in June and July, and on holidays at other times of the year – check the website or Carmarthen tourist office for further details.

Carmarthenshire County Museum

Located in the country-house setting of the former bishop's palace, the **Carmarthenshire County Museum** (☎ 228696; Abergwili; admission free; ☻ 10am-4.30pm Mon-Sat) is a musty emporium of archaeology, Egyptology, pottery and paintings, with re-creations of a Victorian schoolroom and an 18th-century kitchen and parlour.

The museum is 2 miles east of Carmarthen on the A40. Take First bus 280 or 281 (12 minutes, six daily Monday to Saturday) and get off at the Abergwili Church stop.

National Botanic Garden of Wales

Concealed in the rolling Tywi valley countryside to the east of Carmarthen, the lavish **National Botanic Garden of Wales** (☎ 01558-667148; www .gardenofwales.org.uk; Llanarthne; adult/under 5yr/5-16yr £7.50/ free/2.50; ☻ 10am-6pm Apr-Oct, 10am-4.30pm Nov-Mar) are twice the size of London's Kew Gardens. Formerly an aristocratic estate, the garden has a wide range of plant habitats, from lakes and bogs to woodland and heath, with lots of decorative areas too – there's a walled garden, a Japanese garden and an apothecaries' garden – and educational exhibits on plant medicine and organic farming. The centrepiece is the **Great Glasshouse**, a huge glass dome designed by Norman Foster, which houses a display of endangered plants from all over the world.

Opened in 2000, the garden is still a work in progress, with new features being added every year. The latest addition is a tropical glasshouse in the walled garden for the display of plants from warmer climates.

The garden is 8 miles east of Carmarthen; take the A48 out of town (signposted Swansea and the M4) and after 8 miles take the B4310 on the left (signposted Nantgaredig), then follow the signs to the garden.

LLANDEILO

☎ 01558 / pop 3000

Llandeilo is a small, quiet town with grand Victorian and Georgian buildings lining a couple of narrow, hilly streets centred on the parish church of St Teilo. The surrounding region was once dominated by large country estates and, though they have long gone, the deer, parkland trees and agricultural character of the landscape are their legacy.

A good place to stay or eat at is the **Cawdor Arms** (☎ 823500; www.thecawdor.com; Rhosmaen St; d £65-200; **P**), a grand, spacious 18th-century

inn. It has old-fashioned rooms, some of which are finished off with chaise longues, and does formal food (mains £13 to £17), with good two- or three-course Sunday lunches.

Also serving good food, with various theme nights, is the **Capel Bach Bistro** (☎ 822765; 62 Rhosmaen St; mains £11-17; ☻ closed Sun), with a menu of fresh fish, vegetarian and vegan dishes.

Llandeilo is on the Heart of Wales railway line. Bus 280 between Carmarthen and Llandovery stops here.

AROUND LLANDEILO
Dinefwr Park

National Trust–run **Dinefwr Park** (☎ 01558-824512; Llandeilo, park only adult/child £3/1.50, park & house £5/2.50; ☻ 11am-5pm Thu-Mon Apr-Oct) is an 18th-century landscaped estate to the west of Llandeilo, home to fallow deer and a herd of rare White Park cattle. At the centre of the estate is the great 17th-century manor of **Newton House**, made over with a Victorian façade in the 19th century. It is still in the process of being restored – the plan is to show what life was like for both masters and servants. In the meantime there are various exhibitions in the main house, including one on Newton's incarnation as a WWII hospital.

Striking **Dinefwr Castle** is set on a hilltop in the southern corner of the estate and has fantastic views across the Tywi to the foothills of the Black Mountain. It dates from the 13th century, and in the 17th century it was converted into a picturesque feature. There are several marked walking routes around the grounds, a number of which are accessible to disabled visitors.

Bus 280 that runs between Carmarthen and Llandeilo stops here.

Aberglasney House & Gardens

Wandering through the formal walled gardens of **Aberglasney House** (☎ 01558-668998; www.aberglas ney.org; Llangathen; adult/child £6/3; ☻ 10am-6pm Apr-Sep, 10.30am-4pm Oct-Mar) feels a bit like walking into a Jane Austen novel. They date back to the 17th century and contain the only example of a cloister built solely as a garden decoration. There's also a pool garden, a 250-year-old yew tunnel and a 'wild' garden in the bluebell woods to the west. Several derelict rooms in the central courtyard of the house have been converted into a glass-roofed atrium garden full of subtropical plants such as orchids, palms and cycads.

Aberglasney is in the village of Llangathen, 3 miles west of Llandeilo. Bus 280 between

Carmarthen and Llandeilo stops on the main A40 road, 500m north of the village.

Carreg Cennen Castle

Perched atop a steep limestone crag high above the River Cennen, **Carreg Cennen Castle** (Cadw; ☎ 01558-822291; Tir y Castell Farm, Trapp; adult/child £3.50/3; 9.30am-6.30pm Apr-Oct, 9.30am-4pm Nov-Mar) is one of the most spectacularly situated fortresses in Wales, visible for miles in every direction.

So remote that it never played much of a military role, Carreg Cennen nevertheless fulfilled its role as a symbol of the power and pride of the Welsh princes. There was probably a stronghold here in the time of Rhys ap Gruffydd, ruler of the kingdom of Deheubarth, who in the 12th century reversed many of the territorial gains of the Normans. This castle, and others at Lord Rhys' royal seat of Dinefwr and at Dryslwyn, would have faced down the Tywi valley towards the Norman castle at Carmarthen. The castle you see today, however, was built at the end of the 13th century in the course of Edward I's conquest of Wales. It was not wrecked in battle, but dismantled in 1462 by Yorkists during the Wars of the Roses.

The steep uphill walk from the car park to the castle is rewarded with inspirational views over endless waves of rippling green hills. The inner ward, defended by two drawbridges and three gate-towers, is lined with the remains of water cisterns, kitchens and a great hall. The most unusual feature is the **Cliff Gallery**, a stone-vaulted passage running along the top of the sheer southern cliff, which leads down to a long, narrow, natural cave whose entrance was used as a dovecote. The cave goes a long way back, so bring a torch, or hire one from the ticket office, if you want to explore.

The castle is 4 miles southeast of Llandeilo. Take the A483 south across the river, and turn left in the village of Ffairrach, then fork right after you pass under the railway; 3 miles further on, turn left just before the bridge over the River Cennen.

LLANDOVERY (LLANYMDDYFRI)

☎ 01550 / pop 2870

Llandovery is an attractive market town that makes a good base for exploring the western fringes of the Brecon Beacons National Park (p123). The name means 'the church among the waters', and the town is indeed surrounded by rivers, sitting at the meeting place of three valleys: the Tywi, the Bran and the Gwydderig.

Once an important assembly point for drovers taking their cattle towards the border and English markets, the Bank of the Black Ox – one of the first independent Welsh banks – was established here by a wealthy cattle merchant.

Orientation & Information

The **tourist office** (☎ 720693; Kings Rd; 10am-1pm & 1.45-5.30pm Easter-Oct, 10am-1pm & 1.45-4pm Mon-Sat, 2-4pm Sun Nov-Easter) is beside the castle car park, a block west of the bus stop, and about 600m southeast of the train station.

Sights

Above the tourist office is the excellent **Heritage Centre** (☎ 720693; Kings Rd; admission free; same as tourist office), which has interesting displays on drovers and the Black Ox bank, local legends, the Heart of Wales Railway and the history of the town.

Across the car park rises the shattered stump of the motte-and-bailey **Llandovery Castle**, built in 1116. It changed hands many times between the Normans and Welsh, and between one Welsh prince and another, taking a severe beating in the process; it was finally left to decay after Owain Glyndŵr had a go at it in 1403. It's now home to a stainless-steel statue commemorating Llywelyn ap Gruffydd Fychan, who refused to take Henry IV to Owain Glyndŵr's base and paid with his life.

The town's Victorian market hall now houses **Dinefwr Craft Centre**, which has a couple of shops selling local handicrafts, oak furniture and Welsh lovespoons.

Sleeping & Eating

Cwmgwyn Farm (☎ 720410; www.cwmgwyn-holidays.co.uk; Llangadog Rd; s/d £30/50; P) A working 17th-century farm 2 miles southwest of Llandovery, Cwmgwyn has a lovely location high above the River Tywi. The three bedrooms are big and bright, with polished mahogany and exposed roof beams, and there's an oak-beamed lounge with leather sofa and open fire.

Drovers B&B (☎ 721115; 9 Market Sq; s/d from £35/50; P) This attractive Georgian house, on the town's main square, creates a comfortably old-fashioned feel with its ancient stone hearth, antique furniture and rose-patterned bedrooms. There's a licensed bar and you can take breakfast in front of a roaring fire in winter.

Kings Head Inn (☎ 720393; 1 Market Sq; s/d from £55/75) An ancient coaching inn with blazing log fires and sagging oak-beamed ceilings, the Kings Head has four comfortable en suite rooms and serves a predictable but tasty menu of pub grub (mains £6 to £16), from chicken pie to scampi to grilled steak. The bar also pours a decent pint of Old Speckled Hen real ale.

Red Lion (☎ 720813; Market Sq) This real-ale pub has remained pretty much unchanged for the 100 years it's been in the family – spartan, eccentric and resolutely traditional. There's no bar; the elderly landlord serves beer from a jug, filled from the barrels in the kitchen. Opening hours depend on the landlord's whim – usually 5.30pm to 8.30pm on Friday and noon to 8.30pm on Saturday.

Getting There & Away

Roy Brown bus 714 goes to Llandovery from Brecon (£4, 40 minutes, six daily Monday to Saturday), while First bus 280 and 281 comes from Carmarthen (1¾ hours, six daily Monday to Saturday). Coming from Swansea, change at Llandeilo. The Beacons Bus (see p125) route B10 also serves Llandovery.

Llandovery is on the Heart of Wales railway line, serviced by at least three trains daily (there are fewer on Sunday). Links include Llanwrtyd Wells (£2.10, 30 minutes), Llandrindod Wells (£5.50, one hour) and Swansea (£8.10, 1½ hours).

AROUND LLANDOVERY
Dolaucothi Gold Mines

Set in a beautiful wooded estate, the **Dolaucothi Gold Mines** (NT; ☎ 01558-650177; Pumsaint, Llanwrda; adult/child £3.40/1.70; ☾ 10am-5pm Apr-Oct) are on the site of the only known Roman gold mine in the UK. The Romans left around AD 120, but the locals carried on for a couple of hundred more years. Mining recommenced with the Victorians, and by the time the mine was finally closed down in 1938 the works employed more than 200 men.

The exhibition and the mining machinery above ground are interesting, but the main attraction is the chance to go underground on a guided tour of the old mine workings (adult/child £3.80/1.90 extra). Back at the surface, there's a sediment-filled water trough where you can try your hand at panning for gold – don't get your hopes up though!

The mines are 5 miles northwest of Llandovery on the A482.

CARMARTHENSHIRE COAST
National Wetlands Centre

Set on the northern shore of the Burry Inlet, across from the Gower Peninsula, the **National Wetlands Centre** (☎ 01554-741087;

THE PHYSICIANS OF MYDDFAI

About 8 miles southeast of Llandovery, nestled beneath the high escarpment of the Black Mountain, is a tiny lake called **Llyn y Fan Fach** (Lake of the Little Peak), said to be haunted by fairies. In the mid-13th century, a young man grazing his cattle beside the lake saw a woman, the loveliest he had ever seen, sitting on the surface of the water, combing her hair. He fell madly in love with her, coaxed her to shore with some bread and begged her to marry him. Her fairy father agreed, on the condition that if the young man struck her as many as three times she would return to the fairy world. As dowry she brought a herd of magic cows and for years the couple lived happily near Myddfai, raising three healthy sons.

Naturally the three-strikes-and-you're-out story ends badly. After three slaps – for making them late to a christening, for weeping at a wedding and laughing at a funeral, she and her cattle returned forever to the lake.

Her sons often returned to the lake and one day their mother appeared. She handed the eldest, Rhiwallon, a leather bag containing the secrets of the lake's medicinal wild plants, and informed him that he should heal the sick.

From this point, legend merges with fact. Historical records confirm that Rhiwallon and his sons Cadwgan, Gruffydd and Einion were well-known 13th-century physicians, and their descendants continued the tradition. The last of the line to practise was Rhys Williams in the 18th century.

The Pant-y-Meddygon, or 'Physicians' Valley', on Mynydd Myddfai is still rich in bog plants, herbs and lichens, and is well worth visiting for the scenery alone; ask at Llandovery tourist office for details of walks.

DYLAN THOMAS

Dylan Thomas is a towering figure in the Welsh literary landscape, one of those poets who seemed to embody what a poet should be – chaotic, dramatic, drunk, tragic and comic, with a life as full-blown as his revelry in language. Unfashionable since his death, he is yet an overwhelming presence, much loved, and the author of extraordinary poetry. His work, although written in English, is of the bardic tradition – written to be read aloud, thunderous, often humorous, with a lyrical sense of music that echoes the sound of the Welsh voice.

Like the other great 20th-century Welsh poet RS Thomas (see p42), much of his work is about Wales, inspired by places where he wrote and lived. Although Thomas travelled in New York and Iran, and also lived in London and Oxford, he wrote only when at home in Wales; his writings are an endless source of quotations on the country that seduced, amused and repelled him. He wrote, 'the land of my forefathers, they can keep it' (from a letter in the Dylan Thomas Centre, Swansea).

Born in Swansea in 1914, he lived an itinerant life, shifting from town to town in search of cheap accommodation and to escape debt. He married Caitlin Macnamara (a former dancer, and lover of Augustus John) in 1936 but had numerous, infamous affairs. Margaret Thomas, who was married to the historian AJP Taylor, was one of his admirers and paid his Boathouse rent (mysteriously enough, AJP detested him). His actorish inclinations sat well with drama: during a stay in New Quay (also one of the models for Llareggub in *Under Milk Wood*) between 1944 and 1945, he was shot at by a jealous local captain.

Thomas was also a promiscuous pub-goer, honing the habit that eventually killed him in an astonishing number of Welsh locals. By 1946 he had become an immense commercial success, making regular book tours to America, but his marriage was suffering. In December 1952 his father died – his failing health had inspired one of Thomas' most resonant poems.

Less than a year later, a period of depression while in New York ended in a heavy drinking spell, and he died shortly after his 39th birthday. His widow, Caitlin, died in 1994. The two are buried in Laugharne.

www.wwt.org.uk; Llanelli Centre, Penclacwydd; adult/child £5.50/3.50; ☯ 9.30am-5pm Apr-Sep, 9.30am-4.30pm Oct-May) is one of the most important feeding grounds in Wales for waders and waterfowl. The big attraction for bird watchers is the resident population of little egret, whose numbers have increased from a solitary pair in 1995 to around 400. Winter is the most spectacular season, when up to 60,000 birds converge on the salt marsh and mud flats; species include whooper swan, greylag goose, gadwall, wigeon, teal and black-tailed godwit. There are plenty of hides and observation points, and you can hire binoculars if you don't have your own. There's also a café and a kids play area.

The centre is a mile east of Llanelli and 5 miles northwest of Swansea.

Kidwelly Castle

The small town of Kidwelly, at the mouth of the River Gwendraeth Fach, is dominated by the impressive pigeon-inhabited remains of **Kidwelly Castle** (Cadw; ☎ 01554-890104; Castle St, Kidwelly; adult/child £2.90/2.50; ☯ 9.30am-6pm Jun-Sep, 9.30am-5pm Apr, May & Oct, 9.30am-4pm Mon-Sat & 11am-4pm Sun Nov-Feb), a forbidding grey eminence that

rises above a narrow waterway dotted with gliding swans. It was founded in 1106, but most of the system of towers and curtain walls was built by the Normans in the 13th century in reaction to Welsh uprisings.

Laugharne (Lacharn)

☎ 01994 / pop 2940

This sleepy little village (pronounced 'larn') – Dylan Thomas described it as a 'timeless, mild, beguiling island of a town' – sits above the glittering, tide-washed shores of the Taf Estuary, overlooked by the dramatic ruins of a Norman castle.

Thomas lived here for the last four years of his life, during which time he produced some of his most inspired work, including *Under Milk Wood*; the town is one of the inspirations for the play's fictional village of Llareggub (which spells 'bugger all' backwards). On Thomas' first visit he described it as the 'strangest town in Wales', but returned repeatedly throughout his restless life. Many Dylan fans make a pilgrimage here to see the Boathouse where he lived, Brown's Hotel where he drank (he used to give the pub telephone number as his contact number) and the churchyard where he's buried.

You can get tourist information at **Corran Books** (☎ 427444; King St).

SIGHTS & ACTIVITIES

The waterfront car park in the centre of town is overlooked by the ruins of **Laugharne Castle** (Cadw; ☎ 427906; adult/child £2.90/2.50; ☷ 10am-5pm Apr-Sep), which was converted into a Tudor mansion in the 16th century. It was landscaped with lawns and gardens in Victorian times, and the adjoining Castle House was leased by Richard Hughes, author of *High Wind in Jamaica*. Hughes was a friend of Dylan Thomas, who sometimes wrote in the little gazebo looking out over the estuary.

Except at high tide, you can follow a path around the castle and along the shoreline, then up some stairs to a lane that leads to the **Dylan Thomas Boathouse** (☎ 427420; www.dylanthomasboat house.com; Dylan's Walk; adult/child £3.50/1.75; ☷ 10am-5.30pm May-Oct, 10.30am-3.30pm Nov-Apr), where the poet lived from 1949 to 1953 with his wife Caitlin and their three children. It's a beautiful setting, looking out over the estuary with its 'heron-priested shore', silent except for the long, liquid call of the curlew and the urgent 'pleep pleep pleep' of the oystercatcher, birds which appear in Thomas' poetry of that time.

The parlour of the Boathouse has been restored to its 1950s appearance, with recordings of the poet reading his own works in that distinctive, booming voice, and the desk that once belonged to Thomas' schoolmaster father. Upstairs are photographs, manuscripts, a short video about his life, and his death mask, which once belonged to Richard Burton, while downstairs is a coffee shop.

Along the lane from the Boathouse is a replica of the old shed where Thomas did most of his writing. It looks as if he has just popped out, with screwed-up pieces of paper littered around, a curiously prominent copy of *Lives of the Great Poisoners,* and the table facing out to sea where he sat and wrote *Under Milk Wood* and poems such as 'Over Sir John's Hill' (which describes the view) and 'Do Not Go Gentle into That Good Night', which he wrote as his father was dying.

Thomas and his widow Caitlin are buried in a grave marked by a simple white, wooden cross, in the churchyard of **St Martin's Church**, on the northern edge of the town.

Dylan's Walk is a scenic 2-mile loop that continues north along the shore beyond the Boathouse, then turns inland past a 17th-century farm and back via St Martin's Church. It's clearly signposted.

The week-long **Laugharne Festival** (☎ 427689) takes place every three years at the beginning of August, with plays, poetry readings, art exhibitions, a carnival and *Under Milk Wood* guided walks. The next one will be in 2009.

SLEEPING & EATING

Swan Cottage (☎ 472409; 20 Gosport St; s/d from £25/43; Ⓟ) Just the one spacious, en-suite double room in this attractive modern house, where you can enjoy breakfast served on the garden patio with a view of the castle.

Hurst House (☎ 427417; www.hurst-house.co.uk; East Marsh; d from £150) Having recently had a £5 million makeover, you would expect this converted Georgian farm on the salt-marsh flats south of Laugharne to be luxurious. And it is, but in a comfortable, laid-back, self-indulgent kind of way; rooms have big beds, bold colours and roll-top baths; there is massage therapy on tap, and a convivial, clubbish lounge bar with bare floorboards, leather armchairs, open fire and grand piano. The romantic, candle-lit restaurant (four-course dinner £39) specialises in all things Welsh, from laver bread to salt-marsh lamb.

New Three Mariners (☎ 427426; Victoria St; mains £5-9) Owned by the same proprietor as Hurst House, this place feels like a cross between a designer bar and an old-fashioned local, with slate floors, leather sofas and grey-painted woodwork, but also a jukebox, dartboard and poker machine. It serves posh pub grub, including fish and chips and chilli con carne.

Brown's Hotel (☎ 427320; King St) The old pub where Dylan Thomas was once a regular customer – barely changed since the 1950s – was up for sale at the time of writing. Fingers crossed that whoever buys it doesn't turn it into a theme pub.

GETTING THERE & AWAY

First Cymru bus 222 runs from Carmarthen to Laugharne (£3, 30 minutes, eight daily Monday to Saturday). From Swansea you'll have to change at either Carmarthen or St Clears.

Pembrokeshire

Like a little corner of California transplanted to Wales, Pembrokeshire is where the west meets the sea in a welter of surf and golden sand, a scenic extravaganza of spectacular sea cliffs, seal-haunted islands and beautiful beaches.

Among the top-three sunniest places in the UK, this wave-lashed western promontory is one of the most popular holiday destinations in the country. Traditional bucket-and-spade seaside resorts like Tenby and Broad Haven alternate with picturesque harbour villages such as Solva and Porthgain, interspersed with long stretches of remote, roadless coastline frequented only by walkers and wildlife.

Almost one-third of the county, including all of the coastline, is protected within the Pembrokeshire Coast National Park – a 200-mile-long adventure playground famous for its surfing, sea kayaking, coasteering and rock climbing. And then there's the Pembrokeshire Coast Path, a 186-mile roller coaster of a long-distance trail that will sort out the hardcore hikers from the Sunday-afternoon strollers. The park is also a haven for wildlife; it's home to dolphins, porpoises, seals and sea birds, including the world's largest colony of Manx shearwaters.

There are historical attractions too, from the imposing medieval castles at Pembroke, Carew and Manorbier to the age-worn cathedral and Bishop's Palace of St David's – the smallest city in Britain and the cradle of Welsh Christianity. To the north rise the rounded ridges of the Mynydd Preseli, source of the Stonehenge bluestones, which watches over a mysterious prehistoric landscape that includes the dolmen (Neolithic burial chamber) of Pentre Ifan, the biggest megalithic monument in Wales.

HIGHLIGHTS

- Striding out along the dramatic clifftop paths around **St David's Head** (p189)
- Enjoying a picnic above the golden sands of **Barafundle Bay** (p170)
- Going dolphin-spotting in the waters off **Skomer Island** (p183)
- Catching your first wave at **Whitesands Bay** (p189)
- Contemplating centuries past at **St David's Cathedral** (p184)

St David's Head
St David's Cathedral
Whitesands Bay
Skomer Island
Barafundle Bay

PEMBROKESHIRE COAST NATIONAL PARK

The Pembrokeshire Coast National Park (Parc Cenedlaethol Arfordir Sir Benfro), established in 1952, takes in almost the entire coast of Pembrokeshire and its offshore islands, as well as the moorland hills of Mynydd Preseli in the north. Its many attractions include a scenic coastline of rugged cliffs with fantastically folded rock formations interspersed with some of the best beaches in Wales, and a profusion of wildlife – Pembrokeshire's sea cliffs and islands support huge breeding populations of sea birds, while seals, dolphins, porpoises and whales are frequently spotted in coastal waters.

The park is also a focus for activities, from hiking and bird-watching to high-adrenaline sports such as surfing, coasteering, sea kayaking and rock climbing.

INFORMATION

There are three national park visitor centres – in Tenby, St David's and Newport – and a dozen tourist offices scattered across Pembrokeshire. Pick up a copy of *Coast to Coast* (online at www.visitpembrokeshirecoast.com), the park's free annual newspaper, which has lots of information on park attractions, a calendar of events and details of park-organised activities, including guided walks, themed

PEMBROKESHIRE

tours, cycling trips, pony treks, island cruises, canoe trips and minibus tours. The National Park Authority's website (www.pcnpa.org.uk) is also packed with useful information.

ACTIVITIES

The centres listed here offer a range of activities and adventure sports for individual travellers, as well as residential group-based programmes. Activities include coasteering, sea kayaking, mountain biking, surfing, coastal hiking, horse riding, rock climbing and abseiling. Both places have their own accommodation and bar, supply healthy food and will collect you from the train or bus station. Typical prices are around £45/85 for a half-/full-day adventure, and £190 for an all-inclusive weekend.

Preseli Venture (☎ 01348-837709; www.preseliventure .com; Parcynole Fach, Mathry, Haverfordwest) Off the A487 between St David's and Fishguard.

TYF Adventure (☎ 01437-721611, 0800 132588; www .tyf.com; 1 High St, St David's)

Walking

The 186-mile Pembrokeshire Coast Path is one of the most beautiful long-distance walks in Britain; see p197 for more details. If you don't feel up to the full 14- or 15-day hike, there are lots of opportunities for short walks along various sections of the trail.

If you have only limited time, recommended one-day stretches include from Dale to Martin's Haven, and Caerfai to Whitesands Bay, close to St David's. Various shuttle buses serve the route in summer, allowing you to walk short sections and return to your starting point.

From April to October, National Park rangers lead a variety of guided walks; a full day costs £4, and events are listed in *Coast to Coast*. In May-June there is a 14-day guided walk of the entire path ☎ 0845-345 7275 costing £180. For baggage-carrying services see right.

The national park website (www.pcnpa.org .uk) has an excellent online walking guide, listing more than 200 walks ranging from easy strolls to 10-mile hikes; you can search by difficulty, distance and region, then print out a map and route description.

Cycling

Bikes are not allowed on the Pembrokeshire Coast Path, but there are plenty of quiet lanes and bridleways through isolated hamlets and deep woods, and some coastal tracks. Summer traffic on A-roads, especially the A487 in the north, can make cycling hazardous, so stick to unclassified roads or B-roads.

Parts of Lôn Geltaidd (the Celtic Trail), passes through Pembrokeshire; see p60 for more on the national cycling network. There are bike-hire places in many of the major villages and towns.

Water Sports

Pembrokeshire has some of Britain's best surfing at beaches such as Tenby South, Manorbier, Freshwater West and West Dale Bay in the south, and at Broad Haven, Newgale and Whitesands Bay in the west. Windsurfing and kite surfing are also popular. There are several surf schools where you can take lessons.

First pioneered on the Pembrokeshire coast, coasteering is a bit of a superhero sport – equipped with wetsuit, flotation jacket and helmet, you make your way along the coastal cliffs by a combination of climbing, traversing, scrambling, cliff jumping and swimming.

The western tip of the coast is one of the UK's finest sea-kayaking areas. Beginners can enjoy coastal trips starting from calm harbours and bays.

Pony Trekking & Horse Riding

The Pembrokeshire coast is a fantastic area for riding – along beaches, across open moorland, along wooded bridleways or down quiet country lanes – and there are a dozen stables in or near the national park; see *Coast to Coast* for listings.

Rock Climbing

Pembrokeshire can boast some of the finest sea-cliff climbing in Britain, with routes of all grades, mostly on limestone. The biggest concentration of classic routes is near Bosherston in South Pembrokeshire, from Stack Rocks near St Govan's Head to Stackpole Head. The main climbers' hang-out is Ye Olde Worlde Café (Ma Weston's; p170) in Bosherston. For full coverage of routes and access, get the two-volume *Climbers Club Guide to Pembrokeshire* (£22).

TOURS

Organised tours and walks are listed in *Coast to Coast*. The following organisations offer organised walking holidays, and/or can arrange baggage transfer if you want to hike the Coast Path without carrying a heavy pack.

Celtic Trails (☎ 01600-860846; www.pembrokeshire
coastpath.com; PO Box 11, Chepstow NP16 6DZ) Offers
flexible self-guided walking holidays along the Coast Path,
from three- to 13- days, staying in B&Bs.
Greenways Holidays (☎ 5501834-862109; www
.greenwaysholidays.com; Old School, Station Rd, Narberth)
Organised walking and cycling tours.
Tony's Taxis (☎ 01437-720931; www.tonystaxis.net;
Maes Dewi, St David's) Provides a luggage transfer service
covering the area from Little Haven to Fishguard.

SLEEPING
There are nine YHA/HI hostels in the national park (at Manorbier, Penycwm, Marloes Sands, Broad Haven, St David's, Trefin,
Pwll Deri, Newport and Poppit Sands), and
a couple of independent hostels at Fishguard
and Porthgain.

With the permission of the landowner or
farmer, it's possible to camp almost anywhere,
although not on National Trust (NT) land.

GETTING AROUND
In addition to the main, year-round bus
routes, there is a range of special bus services (some of them summer only, some year-
round), with names such as Poppit Rocket,
Strumble Shuttle and Celtic Coaster, aimed
at walkers and other visitors to the Pembrokeshire coast. For routes and timetables, see
www.pembrokeshiregreenways.co.uk. Tourist
offices give out free timetable booklets listing
all the bus services of use to visitors.

Trains are only useful for travel from Swansea to Fishguard, Tenby and Pembroke.

SOUTH PEMBROKESHIRE

TENBY (DINBYCH Y PYSGOD)
☎ 01834 / pop 4900
With its pastel-painted Georgian houses,
picturesque boat-crowded harbour and long
sandy beaches, Tenby is a typical bucket-and-
spade, ice-cream-and-candy-floss seaside
resort.

The town has avoided being taken over by
either amusement arcades or terminal twee-
ness, although in summer its population swells
massively. On summer weekends it can get
pretty lively, with the pubs spilling over with
boisterous, beery lads wolf-whistling at gangs
of girls out on hens nights, while out of season
it reverts to a sedate resort full of retired couples walking the dog on the beach.

The Pembrokeshire Coast Path (p197) runs
through Tenby and, as the biggest town in
the national park, it's a major stopover for
walkers.

History
Originally a Norman stronghold, Tenby
flourished in the 15th century as a centre for
the textile trade, exporting cloth in exchange
for salt and wine. Clothmaking declined in
the 18th century, but the town soon reinvented itself as a fashionable watering place.
The arrival of the railway in the 19th century sealed its future as a resort, and William
Paxton (owner of the Middleton estate in
Carmarthenshire, now home to the National
Botanic Garden of Wales, p157) developed
a saltwater spa here. Anxiety over a possible
French invasion of Milford Haven led to the
construction in 1869 of a fort on St Catherine's Island.

Among those who have taken inspiration
or rest here are Horatio Nelson, Sir William
and Lady Hamilton, Jane Austen, George
Eliot, JMW Turner, Beatrix Potter and Roald
Dahl. The artist Augustus John was born here,
and he and his sister Gwen lived here during
their early life.

Orientation
The town's main landmark is the prominent
headland of Castle Hill, site of the Norman
stronghold. Tenby harbour lies to its west,
with the old town rising steeply above it. The
old town is bounded to the west by the city
walls, which run north–south along South Pde
and St Florence Pde.

The bus station is next to the tourist office
and main car park on upper Park Rd, 100m
west of the old town walls; the train station
is 300m west.

Parking can be a struggle, especially in July
and August when vehicles are barred from the
town centre. During this period, free shuttle
buses run to the town centre from the Salterns
and North Beach car parks, on the A4139 and
A478 respectively.

Information
Cofion (Bridge St) Interesting secondhand bookshop.
National Park Visitor Centre (South Pde; ☺ 10am-
5.30pm Apr-Oct)
Police station (☎ 842303; Warren St)
Post office (Warren St)
Tenby Book Shop (Tudor Sq)

Tenby Cottage Hospital (☎ 842040; Trafalgar Rd) Southwest of the centre.
Tourist Office (☎ 842002; Unit 2, Upper Park Rd; ☺ 10am-5.30pm Jun-Sep, 10am-4pm Mon-Sat Oct-May)
Webb Computers (☎ 844101; 17 Warren St; ☺ 9am-5pm Mon-Sat; per hr £1) Internet access.

Sights
OLD TENBY
Tenby's oldest buildings are found on the Dickensian steep-stepped Quay Hill. You can visit the handsomely restored **Tudor Merchant's House** (NT; ☎ 842279; Quay Hill; adult/child £2.50/1.20; ☺ 10am-5pm Mon, Tue, Thu-Sat, 1-5pm Sun Apr-Sep, 10am-3pm Mon, Tue, Thu & Fri, noon-3pm Sun Oct), the town house of a late-15th-century merchant, which boasts late-medieval frescoes.

The graceful arched roof of **St Mary's Church** is dotted with charming wooden bosses, mainly dating from the 15th century and carved into flowers, cheeky faces, mythical beasts, fish and even a mermaid holding a comb and mirror. There's a memorial here to Robert Recorde, a local 16th-century writer and mathematician who invented the 'equals' sign. The young Henry Tudor was hidden here before fleeing to Brittany. It's thought that he left by means of a tunnel into the cellars under Mayor Thomas White's house across the road (where Boots is now).

CASTLE HILL & ST CATHERINE'S ISLAND
William Paxton built his saltwater baths above the harbour in what is now **Laston House** (1 Castle

Sq). The Greek writing on the pediment translates as the optimistic 'The sea will wash away all the evils of man'. Beyond here, a path leads out past the old and new **RNLI lifeboat stations** and around the Castle Hill headland. On top of the hill are the ruins of the Norman castle, a memorial to Prince Albert and a fine view over the coast.

The path leads to **Tenby Museum & Art Gallery** (☎ 842809; Castle Hill; adult/child £2.50/1.20; ☿ 10am-5pm Mar-Dec, 10am-5pm Mon-Fri Feb, closed Christmas–end Jan), which covers the town's development from a fishing village into a 19th-century seaside resort bigger than Blackpool, with interesting exhibits ranging from delicate Roman vases to a Victorian antiquarian's study. There's also a re-created pirate's cell and a gallery of paintings by Augustus and Gwen John.

At low tide you can walk across the sand to **St Catherine's Island**, but it's a long, cold wait if you get trapped by the tide – check tide tables in *Coast to Coast*, at any newsagent or ask at the tourist office. The Victorian fort on the island is closed to the public.

CALDEY ISLAND
Boat trips run from Tenby harbour to **Caldey Island** (☎ 844453; www.caldey-island.co.uk; adult/child £9/5; ☿ 10am-5pm Mon-Fri Apr-Oct), home to lots of grey seals and sea birds, and a red-topped, whitewashed monastery that houses a community of around 20 Cistercian monks. The monks live an austere life but make various luxurious products for sale, including perfume (based on the island's wildflowers), shortbread and chocolate, and do so well that they now employ people from the mainland.

There are twice-daily guided tours of the monastery and great walks around the island, with good views from the lighthouse. Make sure you visit the old priory and St Illtyd's Church, with its oddly shaped steeple. Inside is a stone with inscriptions in ogham (an ancient Celtic script).

Boats to Caldey Island depart half-hourly from the harbour at high tide and from Castle Beach at low tide. Tickets are sold from a kiosk at the harbour slipway.

Little **St Margaret's Island** at the western tip of Caldey is a nature reserve (landings are prohibited); it's home to grey seals and also Wales' biggest colony of cormorants.

The **Catalina** (☎ 843545; adult/child £6/3; ☿ Apr-Oct), a vessel that can carry up to 120 passengers, offers 1¼-hour cruises around Caldey Island and St Margaret's Island (without landing) to view birds and seals; in July and August there are also two-hour sunset cruises.

Activities
Guided walks of Tenby's historical sites are run by **Town Trails** (☎ 845841; www.guidedtourswales .co.uk; adult/child £3.75/2.75; ☿ Mon-Sat mid-Jun–mid-Sep). There are 1¼- to 1½-hour walks, with themes such as ghosts or pirates.

Tenby Watersports (☎ 843553; Castle Slipway) arranges water-skiing, wakeboarding, speedboat rides and kayak hire. Keen surfers should head to Tenby South Beach, which offers some of the best breaks in Pembrokeshire.

Tenby Fishing (☎ 07974 623542; www.tenbyfishing .co.uk) offers sea-angling trips to fish for mackerel in the waters around Caldey Island (£8 per person); all tackle is supplied, and the trips are suitable for kids. Book your trips at the kiosk next to the Caldey Island ticket kiosk.

You can rent bikes from **Tenby Cycles** (☎ 845573; The Norton; ☿ 9.30am-5.30pm Mon-Sat) for £10 a day.

Festivals
The **Tenby Arts Festival** (☎ 843839; www.tenbyartsfest .co.uk) runs for a week in late September, with street performers, poetry, classical-music concerts, samba bands, kite flying, sand-sculpture competitions, choirs and dancing.

Sleeping
Tenby is overflowing with guesthouses and B&Bs, but be sure to book ahead in summer. It can be difficult to find a single room (unless you pay the price of a double), or to book for just one night on a weekend (owners want to let the room for the whole weekend).

Rowston Holiday Park (☎ 842178; www.rowston -holiday-park.co.uk; New Hedges; sites per tent £10-15; ☿ Apr-Sep) There are dozens of caravan and camping sites around Tenby, but this is one of the more attractive ones, just 1.5 miles north of Tenby and only 600m from the coastal path and a sandy beach.

Boulston Cottage Guest House (☎ 843289; 29 Trafalgar Rd; r per person £20-25) Nothing special in the décor stakes, but this little guesthouse, run by a cheerful Spanish-Italian couple, is one of the best budget places in town.

Croyland Guest House (☎ 843880; www.thecroyland .co.uk; 10 Deer Park, Greenhill Rd; r per person £20-30; **P**) Pine furniture and bold colours – burgundy, purple, green – make this pleasant and friendly guesthouse stand out from the crowd. The

PEMBROKESHIRE

rooms are a little cramped, but are good value and close to the centre.

Myrtle House (☎ 842508; St Mary's St; r per person £28-40; **P**) A great location a few metres from the steps down to Castle Beach; tastefully decorated spacious rooms, great breakfasts and a friendly, helpful owner make this late-Georgian house an attractive place to stay.

Ivy Bank (☎ 842311; www.ivybanktenby.co.uk; Harding St; s/d from £30/60) Swagged curtains, tasselled lamp shades and busy-patterned wallpapers are the order of the day in this traditional – and very comfortable – Victorian B&B, close to the train station and about five minutes' walk from the old town.

Panorama Hotel (☎ 844976; www.tenby-hotel.co.uk; The Esplanade; r per person £35-50) Location, location, location – the pastel décor and floral bedspreads may be standard for Tenby, but the stunning panorama over South Beach and Caldey Island is not. It's worth forking out a few extra quid for a room with a sea view.

Bridge House (☎ 843893; Bridge St; d from £55; ☾ Apr-Oct) This well-kept, whitewashed Georgian house enjoys a top spot overlooking the harbour and has beautifully restored rooms set off by antique furniture. Ask for one of the rooms at the front to make the most of that view.

Rebleen Guest House (☎ 844175; www.rebleen.co .uk; Southcliffe St; d £55-75) This Victorian terraced house, just 300m from the old town, eschews traditional seaside chintz and frilliness for a cleaner, more modern décor of pale pastels and creams with a floral motif.

Eating

No 25 Café (☎ 842544; 25 High St; mains £2-6; ☾ 10am-5pm) An appealing café with marble tables and bentwood chairs, No 25 uses home-baked bread and fresh local produce to create delicious sandwiches, along with good coffee, homemade soup and cakes. It has wi-fi access, too.

Nana's Restaurant (☎ 844536; Bridge St; mains £6-16; ☾ lunch & dinner Jun-Sep, varies Oct-May) Set in a Georgian house overlooking the harbour, Nana's specialises in authentic Italian cuisine, from antipasti (a spread of cured meats, cheeses and olives) to freshly prepared risotto to traditional thin and crispy pizza.

Reef Café (☎ 845258; Vernon House, St Julian's St; mains £12-15) This small and intimate Mediterranean-style bistro-restaurant offers a menu of imaginative seafood and pasta dishes, as well as tasty snacks, cakes and good coffee.

Pam Pam Restaurant (☎ 842946; 2 Tudor Sq; mains £12-17) Smartly decked out with dark wood tables and chairs set off by blue napkins and white walls covered in local artwork and photos, Pam Pam is a local institution and a much loved family restaurant that produces quality dishes such as Moroccan-style lamb chops and baked sea bass, alongside a children's menu of burgers and pasta dishes.

Plantagenet House (☎ 842350; Quay Hill, Tudor Sq; mains £13-22) Tenby's oldest building, tucked away in an alley, houses its most atmospheric restaurant, dominated by an immense Tudor chimney hearth (no less than 6m wide). It's a good place for a romantic, candle-lit dinner, with the menu ranging from seafood to organic beef. The lunch menu, which includes mussels, battered cod and chips, and bangers and mash, is good value.

Blue Ball Restaurant ☎ 843038; Upper Frog St; mains £15-20; ☾ lunch Tue-Sun, dinner Mon-Sat) Polished wood, old timber beams and exposed brickwork create a cosy, rustic atmosphere in what is probably Tenby's best restaurant. The menu makes good use of local produce, notably seafood – try the pan-fried gurnard (a sustainable local species) with champagne-chive cream sauce and saffron mashed potato.

For the best fish and chips in town, head to **D Fecci & Sons** (Lower Frog St), in business since 1935. The same family run the traditional **Fecci's Ice Cream Parlour** (St George's St).

There's a large **Somerfield supermarket** (Upper Park Rd; ☾ 8am-8pm Mon-Sat, 10am-4pm Sun) next to the bus station.

Drinking

There are around two dozen pubs crammed into the area around Tudor Sq, and the place can get pretty riotous on Friday and Saturday nights, with big groups of lads and lasses on pub crawls from one karaoke bar to the next.

Tenby House (☎ 842000; Tudor Sq) Tenby House is a lively hotel bar with cool tunes on Friday and Saturday nights, and a sunny, flower-bedecked courtyard for summer afternoon sessions.

Buccaneer Inn (☎ 842273; St Julian's St) The Buccaneer is a rugby pub, with a loud, up-for-it crowd on match weekends, but it also has the best beer garden in town and serves excellent pub grub.

Lifeboat Tavern (☎ 844948; Tudor Sq) Another appealing old pub set in a Georgian house, the Lifeboat has outdoor tables on the footpath, a beer garden at the back, and live folk and blues music at weekends.

AUTHOR'S CHOICE

If you fancy a spot of luxury after a hard day's hiking on the coast path, head for the **St Brides Spa Hotel** (☎ 01834-812304; www.stbridespahotel.com; St Bride's Hill, Saundersfoot; d £130-250; [P]) in Saundersfoot, a few miles north of Tenby. Pembrokeshire's first boutique hotel offers the chance to relax in the sauna or steam room, or lounge in the infinity-edge pool overlooking the harbour, before dining in the candle-lit clifftop restaurant (mains £16 to £23). The bedrooms are stylish and modern, with designer bedspreads, oak furniture and local artwork, while the bathrooms have polished limestone, roll-top baths and powerful showers. Rooms are graded Good, Better and Best, with or without a sea view – we recommend a Good Sea View (£180) as being the best trade-off between price and pampering.

Getting There & Away

Silcox Coaches bus 381 runs from Tenby to Haverfordwest (£3, one hour, hourly Monday to Saturday, one on Sunday), where you can change for buses to St David's and Fishguard. To get to Cardigan, take the 381 as far as Narberth and change to the 430 (one hour, two daily Monday to Saturday).

First Cymru bus 349 goes to Haverfordwest via Manorbier and Pembroke (£2.50, 40 minutes, hourly Monday to Saturday).

There's a direct train service to Tenby from Swansea (£10, 1½ hours, seven daily Monday to Saturday, one on Sunday), continuing to Pembroke.

SOUTH PEMBROKESHIRE COAST
Manorbier
☎ 01834 / pop 665

Manorbier (pronounced man-er-beer) is a little village of leafy, twisting lanes nestled above a lovely sandy beach. It's home to craggy, lichen-spotted **Manorbier Castle** (☎ 871394; Manorbier; adult/child £3.50/1.50; ☼ 10.30am-5.30pm Easter-Sep), the birthplace of the extraordinary Giraldus Cambrensis (Gerald of Wales). 'In all the broad lands of Wales, Manorbier is the best place by far,' he wrote. The castle starred in the 2003 film *I Capture the Castle*.

The castle buildings, ranging in era from the 12th to 19th centuries, are grouped around a pretty garden, with medieval music playing in the Great Hall. There's a murky dungeon, a smuggler's secret passage, and tableaux of wax figures in period costume – apparently rejects from Madame Tussaud's in London. Look out for the figure that was originally Prince Philip, now sporting a coat of chain mail.

Set on a working farm 1.5 miles west of the village, **Swanlake Bay Farm Guesthouse** (☎ 871204; swanlake@pembrokeshire.com; Westmoor, Manorbier; r per person £24-27; [P]) offers bright and cheery bedrooms in a Georgian farmhouse and converted coach house, just 10 minutes' walk from secluded Swanlake beach.

Manorbier Youth Hostel (YHA; ☎ 0870 770 5954; dm £14; ☼ Easter-Oct) is 1.5 miles east of the village centre, close to the beach at Skrinkle Haven, and is housed in a weirdly futuristic ex–Ministry of Defence building.

The **Castle Inn** (☎ 871268; Manorbier) is a classic village pub with a rhododendron-shaded beer garden, a jukebox and occasional guitar and fiddle sessions on weekend evenings.

Manorbier is 5.5 miles southwest of Tenby. First Cymru bus 349 between Tenby and Pembroke stops in the village. There's also a train station, a mile north of the village, served by trains from Swansea to Pembroke.

Bosherston & Stackpole Estate
☎ 01646

The National Trust's **Stackpole Estate** (☎ 661359; admission free; ☼ dawn-dusk) takes in 8 miles of coast, including two fine beaches, a wooded valley and a system of artificial ponds famous for their spectacular display of water lilies. Stackpole was the seat of the Campbells, earls of Cawdor, a family with local roots dating back to medieval times; in the church in nearby Cheriton are 14th-century effigies of Richard de Stackpole and his wife, and Lord Cawdor, who featured in the French invasion of Fishguard (see the Last Invasion of Britain, p193). In the 18th and 19th centuries they created this elegant park.

A car park in Bosherston village gives access to the famous **Bosherston Lily Ponds** (at their best in June), criss-crossed by a network of footpaths and wooden bridges; parts are accessible by wheelchair. The ponds are home to otters, herons and more than 20 species of dragonfly, while the ruins of the manor house are inhabited.

PEMBROKESHIRE

A mile southeast of Bosherston village is the beautiful golden beach of **Broadhaven South**, framed by grey limestone cliffs and pointed sea stacks.

The tiny harbour of **Stackpole Quay**, just over a mile east of the lily ponds, marks the point where pink and purple sandstone gives way to the massive grey limestone that dominates the South Pembrokeshire coast from here to Freshwater West. There's a National Trust car park with information leaflets, and a good tearoom.

A 10-minute walk south along the coast path from Stackpole Quay leads to **Barafundle Bay**, regularly voted one of Britain's most beautiful beaches. Scenic it certainly is, but its reputation has put paid to seclusion – on summer weekends it can get pretty crowded. Go on a weekday in spring, though, and you might have the place to yourself.

SLEEPING & EATING

Trefalen Farm (☎ 661643; Bosherston; r per person £25, sites per person £3) A mile southeast of Bosherston, near Broadhaven South beach, this 17th-century farmhouse offers B&B and a basic camp site.

St Petrox Caravan & Camping Site (☎ 683980; Old Rectory, St Petrox; sites per tent £5) Close to the church in St Petrox village, midway between Pembroke and Bosherston, this is a basic but attractive camp site with showers; fresh eggs, milk and bread are sold.

St Govan's Country Inn (☎ 661455; Bosherston; r per person £30) This friendly village pub in the centre of Bosherston has good B&B accommodation above a convivial bar decorated with hair-raising photos of rock climbs on the local sea cliffs; it's popular with climbers attracted by excellent curries and a range of real ales. Mains cost £5 to 9.

Ye Olde Worlde Café (☎ 661216; Bosherston; mains £2-5; ⏱ 9am-6.30pm, to 9pm Jul & Aug) Better known as Ma Weston's, this appealing café is set in an old, ivy-covered coastguard cottage. It's a popular hang-out for rock climbers, and serves hearty fried breakfasts, teacakes and crumpets.

Boathouse Tearoom (Stackpole Quay; mains £5-8; ⏱ Easter-Oct) A pleasant little café with outdoor tables in the courtyard, the Boathouse has a surprisingly upmarket menu that includes smoked duck salad and fresh crab sandwiches, as well as coffee, Devonshire teas and cakes.

GETTING THERE & AWAY

Bosherston is 5 miles south of Pembroke. The Coastal Cruiser (387/362) bus runs from Pembroke to Stackpole Quay and Bosherston (40 minutes, three daily, no Sunday service October to April).

St Govan's Head & Stack Rocks

The southern coast of Pembrokeshire around St Govan's Head boasts some of the most harshly beautiful coastline in the country, with sheer cliffs dropping 50m into churning, thrashing surf. Unfortunately, much of this coastline lies within the Ministry of Defence's Castlemartin firing range and is off limits to the public. Two minor roads run south to the coast at St Govan's Head and Stack Rocks; when the range is in use these roads are closed. You can check whether the roads, and the section of coast path that links them, are open by calling ☎ 01646-662287, or by checking the notices posted at the Olde Worlde Café in Bosherston.

From the car park at the end of the St Govan's Head road, steps hacked into the rock lead down to tiny **St Govan's Chapel**, wedged into a slot in the cliffs just out of reach of the sea. The chapel dates from the 5th or 6th century, and is named for an itinerant 6th-century Irish preacher. The story goes that one day, when he was set upon by thieves, the cliff conveniently opened and enfolded him, protecting him from his attackers; in gratitude he built this chapel on the spot. The waters from St Govan's well (now dried out), just below the chapel, were reputed to cure skin and eye complaints.

A 10-minute walk along the coast path to the west leads to a spectacular gash in the cliffs known as **Huntsman's Leap**, its vertical walls often dotted with rock climbers.

The car park at **Stack Rocks**, 3 miles to the west, gives access to even more spectacular cliff scenery, including the **Green Bridge of Wales**, the biggest natural arch in the country.

Freshwater West

Wild and windblown Freshwater West, a 2-mile strand of golden sand and silver shingle backed by acres of dunes, is Wales' best surfing beach, wide open to the Atlantic rollers; each year in September it hosts the Welsh National Surfing Championships. But beware – although it's great for surfing, big waves and powerful rips make it dangerous for swimming; several people have drowned here. The beach has year-round red-flag status – do not swim here!

Outer Reef Surf School (☎ 01646-680070; www.outer reefsurfschool.com; 11 Maidenwells, Pembroke) runs courses here, and at Newgale, Broadhaven and Manorbier; prices start at £25 for a two-hour beginner's session.

If you're hiking the Coast Path, be aware that the **Old Rectory** (☎ 01646-661677; www.theoldrectory web.com; Castlemartin; r per person £32), 2 miles east of Freshwater West, is the only accommodation between Bosherston and Angle. It also has meals (three-course dinner for £19).

Angle

Stuck at the western extremity of South Pembrokeshire, the village of Angle feels a long way off the beaten track. The main attraction is the tiny beach in **West Angle Bay**, which has great views across the mouth of Milford Haven to St Ann's Head, and offers good coastal walks with lots of rock pools to explore.

On the eastern edge of the village, right on the Coast Path, the **Castle Farm Camping Site** (☎ 01646-641220; per tent £5) offers very basic facilities for campers among the ruins.

Continue past the farm on a very rough road to find **Old Point House** (☎ 01646-641205; The Point; s/d £30/60), a 15th-century cottage part built with shipwreck timbers, which serves locally caught seafood (mains £8 to £13, open lunch and dinner, closed Tuesday November to March) and has four rooms overlooking the sea.

PEMBROKE (PENFRO)

☎ 01646 / pop 7400

Pembroke is not much more than a single street of neat Georgian and Victorian houses sitting beneath a whopping great castle – the oldest in west Wales, seat of the Tudor dynasty and birthplace of King Henry VII.

Arnulph de Montgomery (Arnulf of Montgomery) built a castle here in 1093. In 1154 local traders scored a coup when a Royal Act of Incorporation made it illegal to land goods anywhere in the Milford Haven waterway except at Pembroke (now Pembroke Dock). In 1648, during the Civil War, the castle was besieged for 48 days before it fell, after which Cromwell had the town walls demolished.

Orientation & Information

The 700m-long Main St stretches east from the prominent castle. The main bus stops are at the castle entrance and outside Somerfield supermarket on Main St. The train station is 800m east of the castle. Pembroke Dock is a separate town, 2 miles to the northwest.

Ferries from Rosslare in Ireland arrive at Pembroke Dock. Pembroke Dock has its own train station, two-thirds of a mile east from the ferry terminal.

Dragon Alley (☎ 621456; 63 Main St; ☷ 10am-5pm Tue-Sat; per hr £3) Internet access.

Pembroke Bookshop (☎ 685144; 73 Main St) Independent bookshop with a good selection of local maps and guides.

Pembroke Library (☎ 682973; 38 Main St; ☷ 10am-1pm Tue-Sat & 2-5pm Tue & Fri, 2-7pm Thu) Free internet access.

Tourist Office (☎ 622388; Common Rd; ☷ 10am-5.30pm Apr-Oct) Has a lively exhibition on the history of the town.

Sights

The spectacular and forbidding **Pembroke Castle** (☎ 681510; www.pembrokecastle.co.uk; Main St; adult/child £3.50/2.50; ☷ 9.30am-6pm Apr-Sep, 10am-5pm Mar & Oct, 10am-4pm Nov-Feb) was the home of the earls of Pembroke for over 300 years. A fort was established here in 1093 by Arnulph de Montgomery, but most of the present buildings date from the 12th and 13th centuries; the sinister, looming keep is the oldest part, built in 1200. Guided tours are available from May to August.

It's a great place for kids to explore – wall walks and passages run from tower to tower, and there are vivid exhibitions detailing the castle's history. In one, a tableau commemorates the birth here in 1456 of Henry Tudor, who defeated Richard III at the Battle of Bosworth Field in 1485 to become King Henry VII. One hundred steps lead to the top of the massive **keep**, where there are great views over the town.

Next to the keep is the **Dungeon Tower**, where you can peer down into the dank, dark prison cell. Nearby, with access through the Northern Hall, are steps down to the creepy **Wogan Cavern**, a massive natural cave that was partially walled in by the Normans and probably used as a store and boathouse.

Pembroke Dock, on the Cleddau River to the north of Pembroke, was once the site of a Royal Dockyard – between 1814 and 1926 more than 260 ships were built here for the Royal Navy. It also served as a Royal Air Force (RAF) base for flying boats during WWII and after. Today it's a ferry terminal and commercial port, but some of its history survives in the **Gun Tower Museum** (☎ 622246; adult/child £2/1; ☷ 10am-4pm Apr-Sep), housed in a 19th-century Martello tower that was built to defend the harbour from possible attack by French invaders. There was rather an unfair distribution of space here – 33 men slept in hammocks in

PEMBROKESHIRE

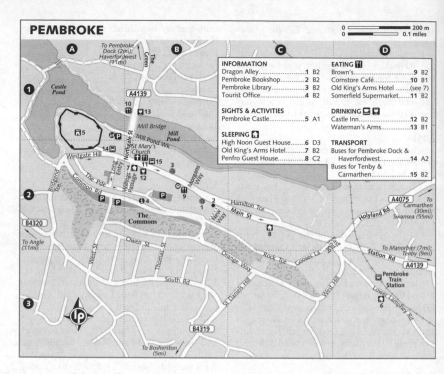

PEMBROKE

0 — 200 m
0 — 0.1 miles

INFORMATION
Dragon Alley.......................1 B2
Pembroke Bookshop............2 B2
Pembroke Library................3 B2
Tourist Office.......................4 B2

SIGHTS & ACTIVITIES
Pembroke Castle..................5 A1

SLEEPING
High Noon Guest House........6 D3
Old King's Arms Hotel..........7 B2
Penfro Guest House.............8 C2

EATING
Brown's.............................9 B2
Cornstore Café..................10 B1
Old King's Arms Hotel ....(see 7)
Somerfield Supermarket......11 B2

DRINKING
Castle Inn.........................12 B2
Waterman's Arms...............13 B1

TRANSPORT
Buses for Pembroke Dock &
   Haverfordwest...............14 A2
Buses for Tenby &
   Carmarthen...................15 B2

one room, while the officer got the other room all to himself. A walkway now runs from the shore but when the tower was in use the men had to lower a rope ladder for supplies.

Silcox buses 356 and 357 shuttle between Pembroke and Pembroke Dock (10 minutes, every 20 minutes Monday to Saturday) from opposite the castle entrance.

Sleeping

High Noon Guest House (☎ 683736; www.highnoon.co.uk; Lower Lamphey Rd; s/d from £20/46) Handy for Pembroke train station, and offering good value rather than atmosphere, this modern house has decent, though smallish, rooms with a pleasant garden terrace out back.

Old King's Arms Hotel (☎ 683611; www.oldkingsarms hotel.co.uk; Main St; s/d £40/70; P) The town's oldest inn, dating back to the 16th century, has unexceptional but well-appointed rooms, and a good restaurant.

Penfro Guest House (☎ 682753; www.penfro.co.uk; 111 Main St; s/d £55/65) Austerely elegant from the outside, this large Georgian town house is a delight inside, retaining many of its original 18th-century features, including 250-year-

old glass, Georgian wood panelling, moulded plaster ceilings and period fireplaces. Rooms are not en suite, as the owner has decided not to destroy original features. The Burgundy Room (£80) is the one to ask for – a huge double with a roll-top bath actually *in* the bedroom (toilet along the hall). You can take breakfast – cooked on an Aga, naturally – on a terrace overlooking the huge garden.

Eating & Drinking

Cornstore Café (☎ 684290; North Quay; mains £3-5; ☿ 10am-5pm) Housed in an 18th-century granary on the waterside, this café conjures up delicious lunches – daily specials include home-made soups and hot dishes such as lasagne – as well as Italian coffee, homemade cakes and dairy ice cream.

Brown's (☎ 682419; Main St; mains £3-10; ☿ 9am-5.30pm Mon-Sat) A splendidly time warped, 1960s greasy-spoon café, Brown's has upholstered booths lurking beyond the fish-and-chip counter, where you can tuck into sausage, egg and chips, washed down with a cup of tea.

(Continued on page 181)

History

Big Pit National Coal Museum (p122), Blaenavon

Bust of Lloyd George,
Lloyd George Museum (p268),
Llanystumdwy

Owain Glyndŵr Centre (p233), Machynlleth

Caerphilly Castle (p105), Caerphilly

People & Culture

JEFF MORGAN / ALAM

Rugby fans watch the Wales versus Ireland 2005 Grand Slam match (p40)

RICHARD H SMITH/LEBRECHT MUSIC
AND ARTS PHOTO LIBRARY / ALAMY

Opera singer, Bryn Terfel (p48),
as Falstaff

Chepstow Racecourse (p117), Monmouthshire

JEFF MORGAN / ALAMY

ROUGH GUIDES / ALAMY

Performance by a male voice choir (p50)

Café patrons, Cardiff Bay (p97)

NEIL SETCHFIELD

Ceremony at the National Eisteddfod (p47), Gwynedd

HOMER SYKES / ALAMY

Food & Drink

Bara brith (p71), a spicy fruit loaf

Laver bread (p70): boiled seaweed mixed with oatmeal

Cawl (p70), a broth of meat and vegetables

Caerphilly Cheese (p71)

Architecture

PATRICK HORTON

Low energy house at the Centre for
Alternative Technology (p234),
Machynlleth

CHRIS MELLOR

Conwy Castle (p289), Conwy

Menai Suspension Bridge (p287), near Bangor

PATRICK HORTON

Country

GRANT DIXC

Mt Snowdon (p237), Snowdonia National Park

An ancient stone bridge, Conwy (p288)

GREG GAWLOWS

Coast

South Stack Lighthouse (p284), Holyhead

DAVID TIPLING

Sailboats on the beach, Abersoch (p270)

DAVID TOMLINSON

Beach at Druidston Haven (p184), near Broad Haven, Pembrokeshire

JULIET COOMBE

Activities

White-water rafting, River Tryweryn (p246)

GARETH MCCORMACK

Hikers on Crib Goch, after scaling
Mt Snowdon (p239)

EOIN CLARKE

ANDERS BLOMQVIST

Rock climbers on ocean cliffs, Holyhead (p282)

Cycling (p238), Snowdonia National Park

DAVID LYONS / ALAMY

(Continued from page 172)

Old King's Arms Hotel (☎ 683611; Main St; mains £13-18) Dark timber beams, ochre walls and polished copperware lend a country kitchen atmosphere to the restaurant here, with local specialities such as braised lamb shank in red-wine sauce, pan-fried fillet of black beef with wild mushrooms, and daily seafood specials.

Waterman's Arms (☎ 682718; 2 The Green) This waterside pub has an outdoor terrace that's a suntrap on a summer afternoon, with fine views across the millpond to the castle.

Castle Inn (☎ 682883; 17 Main St) This snug local pub, all bare stone and horse brasses, is good for a quiet afternoon pint, but it fairly livens up in the evenings as a youngish crowd gathers for a night on the town.

Self-caterers can stock up at the **Somerfield supermarket** (6/10 Main St; ☒ 8am-8pm Mon-Sat, 10am-4pm Sun).

Getting There & Away
BOAT
For details of ferries between Pembroke and Rosslare (Ireland), see p324. The ferry terminal is in Pembroke Dock, 2 miles northwest of Pembroke town centre.

BUS
Note that Pembroke is not the same as Pembroke Dock. Some regional bus services go to one or the other but not both. Most buses heading from Pembroke town to Pembroke Dock and Haverfordwest depart from Westgate Hill near the castle entrance; those bound for Tenby and Carmarthen go from Main St outside Somerfield supermarket.

First Cymru bus 349 runs from Pembroke to Haverfordwest (45 minutes, hourly Monday to Saturday, three to five on Sunday) and, in the opposite direction, to Tenby (45 minutes).

The Coastal Cruiser (387) bus service runs in a loop south from Pembroke (three daily, no Sunday service October to April), taking in Angle, Bosherston, Stackpole Quay and Freshwater East.

TRAIN
There are direct trains from Swansea to Pembroke (£10, 2½ hours, every two hours Monday to Saturday, one on Sunday) and Pembroke Dock via Carmarthen and Tenby.

AROUND PEMBROKE
Looming romantically over the River Carew, its gaping windows reflected in the glassy water, craggy **Carew Castle** (☎ 01646-651782; www .carewcastle.com; Carew; adult/child £3/2; ☒ 10am-5pm Apr-Oct) is an impressive sight. These rambling limestone ruins range from functional 12th-century fortification (built by Gerald de Windsor, Henry I's constable of Pembroke) to Elizabethan country house.

Abandoned in 1690, the castle is now inhabited by a large number of bats, including the protected greater horseshoe bat. A summer programme of events includes battle re-enactments and open-air theatre. Near the castle entrance is the 11th-century **Carew Cross**, one of the oldest and grandest around – it's imposingly tall and covered in psychedelic Celtic squiggles. The castle ticket also gives you admission to **Carew Tidal Mill**, the only working tidal mill in Wales, built in Elizabethan times.

The nearby **Carew Inn** (☎ 01646-651267; Carew; mains £8-13) serves lunch and dinner, and has a beer garden overlooking the castle.

Carew is 4.5 miles east of Pembroke and 6 miles west of Tenby. First Cymru's 349 Pembroke–Tenby bus stops here.

WEST PEMBROKESHIRE

HAVERFORDWEST (HWLFFORDD)
☎ 01437 / pop 10,800
Haverfordwest is a bustling no-nonsense town, a thriving shopping centre and public transport hub. Though it retains some fine Georgian buildings, it lacks the prettiness and historic atmosphere of many of its Pembrokeshire neighbours. It grew up around a shallow spot on the Western Cleddau River where it was possible to ford the stream, and takes its name from the Old English term *haefer* (billy goat) – this was the western *haefer* ford, the place where drovers crossed the river with their goats.

Founded as a fortified Flemish settlement by the Norman Lord Gilbert de Clare in about 1110, its castle became the nucleus for a thriving market and its port remained important until the railway arrived in the mid-19th century.

Orientation
The old town centre is a compact maze of narrow streets and alleys between the two main road bridges over the river, with Castle Hill on the west bank. A one-way system runs

clockwise around the centre, on High St, Dew St, Bank St and Cartlett Rd.

The bus station and tourist office are on the east side of the river, close to the pedestrianised Old Bridge at the north end of the Riverside shopping centre. The train station is 400m east of the town centre, just off the A4067/A40 Narberth Rd.

Information

Haverfordwest Library (☎ 775244; Dew St; ☑ 9.30am-5pm Mon, Wed & Thu, 9.30am-7pm Tue & Fri, 9.30am-1pm Sat) Free internet access.
Police Station (☎ 763355; Merlin's Hill)
Post Office (12 Quay St)
Tourist Office (☎ 763110; Old Bridge St; ☑ 10am-5.30pm Apr-Oct, 10am-4pm Nov-Mar)
Withybush Hospital (☎ 764545; Fishguard Rd)

Sights

The meagre ruins of **Haverfordwest Castle** brood over the river above the Old Bridge. The castle survived an onslaught by Owain Glyndŵr in 1405, but according to one local story was abandoned by its Royalist garrison during the Civil War when its soldiers mistook a herd of cows for Roundheads.

Haverfordwest Town Museum (☎ 763087; adult/child £1/free; ☑ 10am-4pm Mon-Sat Apr-Oct) has an interesting display on the town's history, complete with a boil-ridden plague victim and an interesting section on local nicknames – a study has recorded 700 evocative endearments, such as Arse and Pockets, Drips and Stinko. The museum is housed in the old town jail in the castle's outer ward – it was here that the unsuccessful French invasion force was imprisoned in 1797 (see the Last Invasion of England, p193).

An excellent **farmers market** is held in the Riverside shopping centre every second Friday from 9am to 3pm.

Sleeping & Eating

College Guest House (☎ 763710; www.collegeguesthouse .com; 93 Hill St; s/d/tr £40/60/72; ☐) Set in a spacious Georgian townhouse close to the town centre, the College goes for the antique-pine-and-earthy-colours look, and has no fewer than eight en-suite rooms, including a family room with a double and two singles (£80).

Wilton House Hotel (☎ 760033; www.wiltonhouse hotel.com; 6 Quay St; s/d from £40/65) Another central place housed in a Georgian building, the Wilton House has bland but comfortable

modern rooms, and a decent restaurant that spills out into a large walled garden.

Georges (☎ 766683; 24 Market St; mains £5-8; ☑ 10am-5.30pm Mon-Sat) When it comes to places to eat, the Georges wins hands down – this cosy nook of stained glass and candlelight, lanterns and fairy lights, boasts a simple menu of home-cooked food, from seafood crêpe to steak-and-ale pie to sticky toffee pie with clotted cream. There's wine by the glass, and a separate menu for those with allergies or food intolerances.

Moon & Sixpence (☎ 767851; Swan Sq; mains £3-5; ☑ 9am-4.30pm Mon-Sat) Set in the top floor of a gift shop, this popular local café serves good coffee, cakes and pastries, salads, and pitta and tortilla sandwiches with a huge range of fillings.

Getting There & Away

BUS

Richards Brothers' bus 411 runs to St David's (£3.50, 40 minutes, hourly Monday to Saturday), while 412 runs to Fishguard (40 minutes, hourly Monday to Saturday); both stop at the train station as well as the bus station.

First Cymru's bus 349 goes to Pembroke (£3, 40 minutes, hourly Monday to Saturday, three to five Sunday) and Tenby (1½ hours). Silcox bus 322 runs to Carmarthen (£4.50, one hour, three daily Monday to Saturday).

National Express coach 508 runs direct from London Victoria (£26, seven hours, twice daily) to Haverfordwest via Chepstow, Swansea, Carmarthen, Tenby and Pembroke. National Express also runs coach 528 from Swansea to Haverfordwest (£8, 2¼ hours, one daily).

TRAIN

There are direct trains to Haverfordwest from Cardiff (£16, 2½ hours, every two hours) via Swansea (£10, 1½ hours).

WEST PEMBROKESHIRE COAST

St Bride's Bay (Bae Sain Ffraid) is the great scoop of coast cradled between the arms of the St Ann's Head and St David's Head peninsulas. Its west-facing shore is lined with some of the best beaches in Wales, and dotted with cute little villages.

All the villages and beaches around the bay can be reached using the Puffin Shuttle bus service, which runs from Haverfordwest to St David's via Martin's Haven, Little Haven, Broad Haven, Druidston, Newgale Beach and Solva (three daily Easter to September). The winter service runs on Tuesday, Thursday and Saturday only, and does not go to Martin's Haven.

St Ann's Head

The southern peninsula is much less frequented than crowded St David's, probably because of its proximity to the oil refineries of Milford Haven. But there is some great coastal walking to be enjoyed, notably out to St Ann's Head itself, and around **Wooltack Point** at the western tip of the peninsula.

At **Martin's Haven**, the tiny harbour that is the jumping-off point for boat trips to Skomer and Skokholm islands, you can visit **Lockley Lodge** (☺ 9.30am-12.15pm & 12.45-4.30pm Apr-Sep), a Wildlife Trust of South and West Wales visitor centre with remote-control TV screens that allow you to watch wildlife activity on Skomer.

Marloes Sands Youth Hostel (☎ 01646-636667; Runwayskiln, Marloes; dm £9.50; ☺ Easter-Oct) is housed in a group of National Trust–owned farm buildings near the Coast Path.

Skomer, Skokholm & Grassholm Islands

The rocky islands that lie in the turbulent, tide-ripped waters at the south end of St Bride's Bay are one of the richest wildlife environments in Britain. In the nesting season, Skomer and Skokholm islands are home to more than half a million sea birds, including guillemots, razorbills, puffins, storm petrels, and the world's largest colony of Manx shearwaters – 120,000 birds, 40% of the world population. These unusual birds nest in burrows, and after a day spent feeding at sea return to their nests under the cover of darkness.

Further offshore, on tiny Grassholm Island, is the third-largest gannet colony in the UK, with 32,500 breeding pairs. Grey seals are also plentiful on Skomer, especially in the pupping season (September).

Skomer and Skokholm Islands are nature reserves run by the **Wildlife Trust of South and West Wales** (WTSWW; ☎ 01437-765462; www.welshwildlife.org), while the surrounding waters are protected by Wales' only marine nature reserve. Boat trips to Skomer depart from Martin's Haven (adult/child £8/6) Tuesday to Sunday (plus bank holiday Mondays) from April to October, weather permitting, at 10am, 11am and noon, with return trips leaving the island between 3pm and 4pm. If you go ashore, there's also a landing fee of £6 for adults (children under 16 are free). These boat trips are first come, first served.

Grassholm is owned by the **Royal Society for the Protection of Birds** (RSPB; www.rspb.org.uk) and landing is not permitted, but from April to August **Dale Sailing Co** (☎ 01646-603123; www.dale-sailing.co.uk) runs three-hour, round-the-island trips (£25 per person) departing Martin's Haven at 2pm on Mondays only, on which you may also see seals, porpoises and dolphins.

From April to September Dale Sailing Co operates a range of boat trips out of Martin's Haven; for example, one-hour round-the-island trips (adult/child £8/6) with commentary, and an evening cruise (£10/7) that offers the opportunity to see (and hear – the noise can be deafening) the huge flocks of Manx shearwaters returning to their nests.

For keen bird-watchers, there is cottage and bunkhouse accommodation on Skomer and Skokholm (£175 per person for three nights, fully catered); you can book through www.welshwildlife.org.

Little Haven

Little Haven is Broad Haven's more upmarket neighbour, with a tiny shingle beach and a cluster of pastel-painted holiday cottages. The slipway is much used by local dive boats; if you're tempted, the **West Wales Dive Centre** (☎ 01437-781457; www.westwalesdivers.co.uk; Hasguard Cross) offers a one-day Discover Scuba course.

Nest Bistro (☎ 01437-781728; 12 Grove Pl; mains £12-16; ☺ 7-10pm Tue-Sat) is an informal little restaurant that specialises in locally caught seafood, including lobster, crab, sea bass, turbot and plaice.

Broad Haven

Broad Haven, tucked into the southern corner of St Bride's Bay, is a traditional bucket-and-spade family resort, with a sandy beach backed by tearooms, gift shops, and places selling rubber rings, water wings and boogie boards.

Haven Sports (☎ 01437-781354; www.havensports.co.uk; Marine Rd), at the south end of the prom behind the Galleon Inn, rents wetsuits, body boards and surfboards.

Broad Haven Youth Hostel (YHA; ☎ 0870 770 5728; dm £14; ☺ Easter-Oct) is a purpose-built hostel housed in a sprawling modern bungalow close to the beach.

Newgale Beach

Newgale is the biggest beach in St Bride's Bay. If the north end, next to Newgale village, is too busy, just walk south. It's one of the best beaches in South Wales for beginning surfers to

learn on, and you can hire surfboards, surf skis,
boogie boards and wetsuits from **Newsurf Hire
Centre** (☎ 01437-721398; www.newsurf.co.uk; Newgale).

ST DAVID'S (TYDDEWI)

☎ 01437 / pop 1800

Featured in the *Guinness Book of Records* as
the smallest city in the UK – population-wise
it's little more than an overgrown village – St
David's was awarded the title of 'city' courtesy
of its magnificent cathedral. Known in Welsh
as Tydewwi (the House of David), this is the
holiest site in Wales; birth- and burial-place of
the nation's patron saint, the cradle of Welsh
Christianity and a place of pilgrimage for
more than 1500 years.

St David founded a monastic community
here in the 6th century, only a short walk from
where he was born at St Non's Bay. In 1124,
Pope Calixtus II declared that two pilgrimages to St David's were the equivalent of one
to Rome, and three to St David's were equal
to one to Jerusalem. The cathedral has seen a
constant stream of visitors ever since.

Today, St David's attracts hordes of non
religious pilgrims too, drawn by the town's laid-
back vibe and the excellent hiking, surfing and
wildlife-watching in the surrounding area.

Orientation & Information

The centre of town is Cross Sq, with the cathedral 200m to the northwest. The main bus
stops are in New St and the National Park
Visitor Centre car park.

The main car park is at the eastern edge of
town, next to the tourist office (£3 a day). In
summer there's a free park-and-ride shuttle bus

(every 15 minutes from 10am to 4pm in July
and August, 11am to 3pm June and September)
from here to the Merrivale car park (with level
access to the cathedral and Bishop's Palace).
Bench Bar (☎ 721778; 11 High St; £1.50 per 30 min;
🕑 10am-8pm) Coffee bar with internet café and wi-fi
hotspot.
National Park Visitor Centre (☎ 720392; The Grove;
🕑 9.30am-5.30pm Easter-Oct, 10am-4pm Mon-Sat
Nov-Easter) A striking landscaped building next to the car
park, 350m east of the square; it includes a tourist office.
It will be relocated to town centre until summer 2008 for
building work.
National Trust Visitor Centre (☎ 720385; Captain's
House, High St; 🕑 10am-5.30pm Apr-Oct, 10am-4.30pm
Mon-Sat, 10am-3pm Sun Nov-Mar) Sells local-interest
books and guides to NT properties in Pembrokeshire.
Police Station (☎ 0845 330 2000; High St) Part-time
station; not always open.
Post Office (13 New St)
St David's Bookshop (5a The Pebbles; 🕑 11am-5pm
Mon-Sat) Sells local maps and guidebooks.

Sights
ST DAVID'S CATHEDRAL

Walking from the town centre into the cathedral precinct you pass through the 13th-
century gatehouse of **Porth y Twr** (adult/child £1/free;
🕑 10.30am-5.30pm Mon-Sat Jul-Sep, 11am-5pm Feb-Jun &
Oct), which houses an exhibition about St David
and the cathedral. There are some interesting
carved stones here, notably the 11th-century
Abraham Stone, carved with Celtic interlace
designs, which once marked the grave of Hedd
and Isaac, sons of Bishop Abraham, who was
murdered by Viking invaders in 1080.

Filling the valley beyond the gatehouse, **St
David's Cathedral** (www.stdavidscathedral.org.uk; donation invited; 🕑 8am-6pm, depending on services) is an
impressive sight. Massive and foursquare, its
multicoloured stones of purple, gold and green
mottled with lichen, it seems as much fortress
as church. Built on the site of a 6th-century

**TOP FIVE SURFING BEACHES IN
SOUTH WALES**

- Freshwater West (p170)
- Newgale (p183)
- Whitesands (p189)
- Manorbier (p169)
- Rhossili (p154)

chapel, the building you see dates mainly from the 12th to the 14th centuries. The valley site was chosen in the vain hope that the church would be hidden from Viking raiders, but it was ransacked at least seven times.

The sloping, boggy ground on which the cathedral sits caused problems, made worse by an earthquake in 1248. Extensive works were carried out in the 19th century by Sir George Gilbert Scott, architect of the Albert Memorial and St Pancras in London, to stabilise the building and repair damage caused by subsidence. The distinctive **west front**, with its four pointed towers of purple stone, dates from this period.

As you enter the **nave**, the oldest surviving part of the cathedral, the first things you notice are the sloping floor and the outward lean of the massive, purplish-grey pillars linked by semicircular Norman arches, a result of subsidence. Above is a richly carved 16th-century oak ceiling, adorned with pendants and bosses.

At the far end of the nave is a delicately carved 14th-century Gothic **pulpitum** (the screen wall between nave and choir), which bears a statue of St David dressed as a medieval bishop, and contains the tomb of Bishop

Henry Gower (died 1347), for whom the Bishop's Palace was built.

Beyond the pulpitum is the magnificent **choir**; check out the mischievous carved figures on the 16th-century misericords, one of which depicts pilgrims being seasick over the side of a boat. Don't forget to look up at the colourfully painted lantern tower above (those steel tie rods around the walls were installed in the 19th century to hold the structure together).

In a recess in the **Holy Trinity Chapel** at the east end of the cathedral is the object of all those religious pilgrimages – a simple oak casket that contains the bones of St David and St Justinian. The chapel ceiling is distinguished by superb fan vaulting dating from the early 16th century.

Lord Rhys ap Gruffydd, the greatest of the princes of South Wales, and his son Rhys Gryg are known to be buried in the cathedral, although their effigies in the south choir aisle date only from the 14th century. Gerald of Wales, an early rector of the cathedral, is said to be buried here; there is a gravestone, but scholars suggest he is buried at Lincolnshire Cathedral.

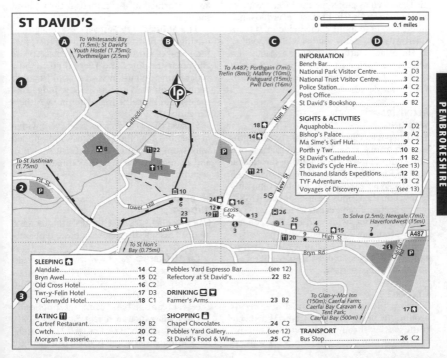

ST DAVID'S

0   200 m
0   0.1 miles

To Whitesands' Bay
(1.5mi); St David's
Youth Hostel (1.75mi);
Porthmelgan (2.5mi)

To A487; Porthgain (7mi);
Trefin (8mi); Mathry (10mi);
Fishguard (15mi);
Pwll Deri (16mi)

To St Justinian
(1.75mi)

Pit St

Cathedral Cl

Nun St

New St

Tower Hill

Cross
Sq

Goat St

High St

Bryn Rd

To St Non's
Bay (0.75mi)

To Solva (2.5mi); Newgale (7mi);
Haverfordwest (15mi)

A487

To Glan-y-Mor Inn
(150m); Caerfai Farm;
Caerfai Bay Caravan &
Tent Park;
Caerfai Bay (500m)

PEMBROKESHIRE

INFORMATION	
Bench Bar..1	C2
National Park Visitor Centre............2	D3
National Trust Visitor Centre..........3	C2
Police Station...................................4	C2
Post Office.......................................5	C2
St David's Bookshop.........................6	B2

SIGHTS & ACTIVITIES	
Aquaphobia......................................7	D2
Bishop's Palace.................................8	A2
Ma Sime's Surf Hut...........................9	C2
Porth y Twr....................................10	C2
St David's Cathedral.......................11	B2
St David's Cycle Hire...............(see 13)	
Thousand Islands Expeditions.........12	B2
TYF Adventure...............................13	C2
Voyages of Discovery................(see 13)	

SLEEPING	
Alandale...14	C2
Bryn Awel.......................................15	D2
Old Cross Hotel..............................16	C2
Twr-y-Felin Hotel...........................17	D3
Y Glennydd Hotel...........................18	C1

EATING	
Cartref Restaurant..........................19	B2
Cwtch...20	C2
Morgan's Brasserie.........................21	C2

Pebbles Yard Espresso Bar.........(see 12)	
Refectory at St David's...................22	B2

DRINKING	
Farmer's Arms................................23	B2

SHOPPING	
Chapel Chocolates..........................24	C2
Pebbles Yard Gallery.................(see 12)	
St David's Food & Wine..................25	C2

TRANSPORT	
Bus Stop...26	C2

You'll need at least half a day to do justice to the cathedral and the Bishop's Palace. In July and August there are 90-minute **guided tours** (☎ 720691; adult/child £4/1.20) at 2.30pm on Monday, Tuesday, Thursday and Friday; at other times, tours can be arranged in advance. The one led by the dean himself, a history and archaeology scholar, is recommended.

BISHOP'S PALACE
Across the river from the cathedral lies the **Bishop's Palace** (Cadw; adult/child £2.90/2.50; ☼ 9.30am-6pm Jun-Sep, 9.30am-5pm Apr, May & Oct, 9.30am-4pm Mon-Sat, 11am-4pm Sun Nov-Mar), a vast and stately ruin inhabited by noisy jackdaws. The scale of the building is eloquent testimony to the wealth and power of the medieval church. It was begun in the 12th century, at the same time as the cathedral, but its final, imposing form owes most to Henry Gower, bishop from 1327 to 1348.

Its most distinctive feature is the arcaded parapet that runs around the courtyard, decorated with a chequerboard pattern of purple and yellow stone blocks. The corbels that support the arches are richly adorned with a menagerie of carved figures – lions, monkeys, dogs and birds, as well as grotesque mythical creatures and human heads. The distinctive purple sandstone, also used in the cathedral, comes from Caerbwdy Bay, a mile southeast of St David's.

The palace courtyard provides a spectacular setting for open-air plays in summer; ask at the tourist office in the National Park Visitor Centre for details.

Activities
WALKING
You can put together coastal walks of all lengths starting from Caerfai Bay, three-quarters of a mile south of town, and following the coastal path to Porthclais (2 miles), St Justinian (6.5 miles) or Whitesands Bay (8.5 miles), returning to town on the Celtic Coaster bus (see p188).

The section from Porthclais to St Justinian is especially fine, with wild coastal scenery, plenty of wildlife (look out for seals, porpoises, sparrowhawks, choughs, gannets and cormorants) and views across turbulent Ramsey Sound to Ramsey Island.

CYCLING
There is pleasant cycling on minor roads around the peninsula – the Celtic Way cycle route passes through St David's – but no off-road action (the coast path is for walkers

only). You can rent bikes from **St David's Cycle Hire** (☎ 721911; 1 High St; per half-/full day £10/15), **Glan-y-Mor Inn** (☎ 721788; www.glan-y-mor.co.uk; Caerfai Rd; per day £5) or **Cycle Hire Pembrokeshire** (☎ 07875 775323; Trefochlyd Farm, Croesgoch; per day £12); the latter is on the A487 road 5 miles northeast of St David's.

OTHER ACTIVITIES
TYF Adventure (☎ 721611, 0800 132588; www.tyf.com; 1 High St) organises coasteering, surfing, sea-kayaking and rock-climbing trips, charging £45/85 for a half-/full-day.

Ma Sime's Surf Hut (☎ 720433; 28 High St) rents wetsuits, surfboards and body boards, and can arrange surf lessons with Whitesands Surf School (p189).

For details of boat trips to and around Ramsey Island see p188.

Festivals & Events
The **St David's Cathedral Festival** (www.stdavidscathedral .org.uk/festivals.htm) takes place over nine days, culminating on the Spring Bank Holiday weekend at the end of May, with classical music in the cathedral. Many other concerts are performed at the cathedral throughout the year.

The **St David's Arts Festival** (☎ 837034), held during the first two weeks in August, features Shakespeare at the Bishop's Palace, prose and poetry readings, and a very child-friendly programme. August also sees a sand-church competition at Whitesands Bay, judged by the dean of the cathedral (dates are weather-dependent).

St David's Day (1 March) is celebrated with a market and exhibition on Cross Sq, a guided walk from the National Park Visitor Centre and a choral Eucharist in the cathedral in the evening.

Sleeping
BUDGET
Glan-y-Mor Inn (☎ 721788; Caerfai Rd; sites per person from £5) This guesthouse has a basic tent-only camp site.

Caerfai Farm (☎ 720548; www.cawscaerfai.co.uk; sites per tent & 2 people £8-10; ☼ late-May–Sep) This is a tent-only site with fantastic sea views, set on an organic dairy farm where you can buy fresh cheese, bread and basic camping supplies.

Caerfai Bay Caravan & Tent Park (☎ 720274; www.caerfaibay.co.uk; sites per tent, car & 2 people £9-12) A 15-minute walk south of town (on the right at the end of Caerfai Rd), this large site has good facilities and great coastal views across St Brides Bay.

St David's Youth Hostel (YHA; ☎ 0870 770 6042; Llaethdy, Whitesands; dm £11; ☼ Easter-Oct) The youth hostel, tucked beneath Carn Llidi 2 miles northwest of town, is set in a former farmhouse, with snug dorms in the old cow sheds. It's close to the beach and coastal path at Whitesands Bay.

Bryn Awel (☎ 720082; www.brynawel-bb.co.uk; 45 High St; d £50) A pretty little terraced house on the main street, Bryn Awel has small but cosy rooms (all en suite). The owners are keen outdoors enthusiasts, and can advise on the best local spots for walking and bird-watching.

MIDRANGE

Y Glennydd Hotel (☎ 720576; www.yglennydd.co.uk; 51 Nun St; s/d from £30/55) This small, 10-room hotel feels more like a large B&B, with smallish, smartly decorated but unfussy bedrooms, a cosy lounge with 'mine-host' bar and nautical knick-knacks, and an attractive restaurant serving evening meals as well as breakfast.

Alandale (☎ 720404; 43 Nun St; s/d £33/65) A neat terraced house built in the 1880s for coastguard officers, the Alandale has a bright, cheerful atmosphere – ask for one of the rooms at the back, which are quieter and have good views over the countryside.

Twr-y-Felin Hotel (☎ 721678; www.tyf.com; Caerfai Rd; s/d £40/80; **P**) Set in a rambling old building (once a windmill – you can climb up into the old tower for some stupendous views) with a wood-panelled lobby, marble fireplaces and creaky-floored corridors, the Twr-y-Felin has a laid-back vibe – rooms with comfy mattresses and crisp cotton sheets (but no TVs), big healthy breakfasts (no fry-ups), and chilled, surf-dude staff (it's owned by TYF Adventure, p186).

Glan-y-Mor Inn (☎ 721788; www.glan-y-mor.co.uk; Caerfai Rd; d £50-70) This friendly guesthouse and bar, complete with beer garden and barbecue, has three comfortable double rooms; a family of five can squeeze into the largest. You can hire wetsuits, surfboards and body boards here, and even take surf lessons (£20 a session).

TOP END

Old Cross Hotel (☎ 720387; www.oldcrosshotel.co.uk; Cross Sq; s/d £62/105; **P**) An attractive, ivy-clad stone building set in a leafy garden on the main square, the Old Cross offers old-fashioned

service, plush (if unmemorable) rooms and afternoon tea in the garden.

Eating & Drinking

Pebbles Yard Espresso Bar (☎ 720122; The Pebbles; snacks £3-5; ☼ 9am-5.30pm Jul & Aug, 10am-5.30pm Sep-Jun) A cute little space, with butter-yellow walls, worn pine floors and basketwork chairs, this café is the place to read the papers over a cappuccino, or tuck into cakes and Devonshire teas. Art on the walls, and cool tunes on the sound system.

Refectory at St David's (☎ 721760; St David's Cathedral; mains £4-8; ☼ 10am-9pm Jul & Aug, 10am-6pm Apr-Jun, Sep & Oct, 11am-4pm Nov-Mar) Part of the ongoing restoration of the cathedral cloister, this stylish modern café has a lunch menu with a choice of sandwiches and hot dishes (at least two vegetarian dishes), as well as excellent coffee and home baking. Grab a table upstairs with a view of the cloister and garden.

Cartref Restaurant (☎ 720422; 22-23 Cross Sq; mains £10-13) A big barn of a place on the main square, the Cartref is a good family-friendly choice, with highchairs and kids menus, and plenty of choice for vegetarians. The food is hearty, mainstream stuff such as lasagne, burgers and steak pies.

Morgan's Brasserie (☎ 720508; 20 Nun St; mains £13-19; ☼ noon-2pm Fri-Sun, 6.30-10.30pm Thu-Mon) An elegant and intimate spot, with clean modern lines and an air of big-city sophistication, Morgan's turns out quality cuisine with a French touch, including local seafood specials and some gourmet vegetarian choices (how about leek and parsnip steamed pudding with herb and truffle gravy?).

Cwtch (☎ 720491; 22 High St; 2-/3-course dinner £20/25; ☼ 11am-2.30pm & 6-9.45pm Tue-Sat, noon-3pm Sun) Cwtch (pronounced 'cootch'; Welsh for 'cosy') lives up to its name, creating a snug atmosphere with the use of wood, warm colours and low lighting. The menu is big on local produce, from crab and asparagus to lamb, beef and sea bass. The signature fish pie is recommended.

Farmer's Arms (14 Goat St) One of the most popular pubs in the town, the Farmer's has real ale and Guinness on tap, and a good beer garden out back. It's a pleasant place to watch the sun go down on a summer's evening.

Shopping

Chapel Chocolates (The Pebbles) Chocoholics beware – the shelves in this shop are stacked floor to ceiling with more than 100 varieties of handmade Welsh chocolates, truffles and other confectionery.

Pebbles Yard Gallery (Cross Sq) This dinky little gallery sells works by local artists, as well as funky contemporary jewellery, handicrafts and creative toys for kids.

St David's Food & Wine (High St) Stock up on picnic supplies at this delicatessen, which specialises in local organic produce.

Getting There & Away

Richards Brothers bus 411 runs to St David's from Haverfordwest (£3.50, 45 minutes, hourly Monday to Saturday, every two hours Sunday) and to Fishguard (50 minutes, every two hours Monday to Saturday, one daily Sunday).

From Easter to September, the Puffin Shuttle (bus 400/315) goes around the coast three times each day, from St David's to Solva (15 minutes), Newgale Beach (30 minutes), Broad Haven (£2.20, 50 minutes), Dale (1¾ hours) and Milford Haven (2¼ hours) to Haverfordwest (2½ hours) and back again.

The Celtic Coaster (bus 403) shuttles from St David's to St Non's Bay, Porthclais, St Justinian and Whitesands Beach (hourly Easter to September); a return ticket costs £1, an all-day ticket is £2.

AROUND ST DAVID'S
Lower Solva
☎ 0147 / pop 1420

Lower Solva sits at the head of a picturesque, yacht-filled inlet, its single street lined with brightly painted, flower-laden cottages housing pretty B&Bs, art galleries, pubs and tearooms.

If sailing takes your fancy, you can enjoy a three-hour/full-day cruise aboard a 24ft yacht for £65/110 (up to three passengers) with **Solva Sailboats** (☎ 720972; 1 Maes-y-Forwen). It also rents sailing dinghies (£20 for two hours) and runs official Royal Yachting Association sailing courses.

The Puffin Shuttle bus (see above) calls here in summer; bus 411 between Haverfordwest and St David's also stops at Solva (hourly Monday to Saturday).

SLEEPING & EATING

Caleb's Cottage (☎ 721737; 7 Main St; s/d £35/50; ☯ Easter-Sep) Bold colours, local artworks and a warm, country-cottage atmosphere are the main attractions at this former fisherman's dwelling; the coast path is a mere 100m away.

Old Printing House (☎ 721603; 20 Main St; ☯ 9am-6pm Mar-Oct, 11am-5pm Dec & Feb) For homemade cakes and sumptuous Devonshire teas, head to this snug, bare-stone-and-timber-beams tearoom; it also has a gift shop, and has a couple of B&B rooms to let upstairs (£25 per person).

Old Pharmacy (☎ 720005; 5 Main St; mains £8-20; ☯ 5.30-10pm) This is the village's gastronomic highlight, with a cosy cottage atmosphere, outdoor tables in a riverside garden, and a menu of Solva lobster and crab, local organic beef and lamb, and decadent homemade desserts.

St Non's Bay

This scenic bay, three-quarters of a mile south of St David's, is the supposed birthplace of Wales' patron saint, and is named after his mother. A path from the parking area leads down to the 13th-century ruins of **St Non's Chapel**, passing a sacred spring that is said to have emerged at the moment of St David's birth. The shrine still attracts pilgrims, and the water is believed to have curative powers. Nearby is a modern chapel beside a clifftop Christian retreat centre.

Ramsey Island

Ramsey Island lies off St David's Head, ringed by dramatic sea cliffs and surrounded by an offshore armada of rocky islets and reefs known as the Bishops and Clerks. The island is an RSPB reserve famous for its large breeding population of choughs – glossy black birds with distinctive red bills and legs, members of the crow family – and for its grey seals. If you're here between late August and mid-November, you will also see seal pups.

You can reach the island by boat from the tiny harbour at St Justinian, 2 miles west of St David's. Longer boat trips run up to 20 miles offshore, to the edge of the Celtic Deep, to spot whales, porpoises and dolphins. What you'll see depends on the weather and the time of year; calm, clear conditions are best for sightings, and July to the September are the best months. Porpoises are seen on most trips, dolphins on four out of five, and there's a 40% chance of seeing whales. The most common whale species is the minke, but pilot whales, fin whales and killer whales have also been spotted.

Thousand Islands Expeditions (☎ 721721; www .thousandislands.co.uk; Cross Sq, St David's) is the only operator permitted by the RSPB to land daytrippers on Ramsey island (adult/child £14/7, including landing fee); there are two trips daily from April to October, each allowing

ST DAVID'S HEAD WALK

Begin at the Whitesands Bay car park (£2.50 per car in summer) and head north along the coastal path. After passing the secluded little beach at **Porthmelgan**, the path curves left and leads out to **St David's Head**. This promontory was fortified in prehistoric times, and you pass through the jumbled stones of an Iron Age rampart to find three oval rings of large rocks, the foundations of ancient huts. The tip of the headland is a series of rock and turf ledges, a great place for a picnic or a bit of wildlife-spotting – in summer you can see gannets diving into the sea offshore, and choughs soaring on the breeze above the cliffs.

Return to the gap in the rampart, and follow the obvious broad, grassy path through the heather, aiming at the middle of a long, low rocky outcrop on the skyline. As you get closer, it resolves into two outcrops; go past the smaller one (on your right), and behind it, to the right, you will find a Neolithic burial chamber known as **Coetan Arthur** (Arthur's Quoit).

Continue along the coastal path, climbing gently until you reach a cairn (marked 76m on OS map), then descend to where the path forks. The main coastal path strikes left along the clifftops, but bear right on a broad path through heather and bracken that descends into a shallow valley (there may be wild ponies grazing here). Cross the tiny stream and climb uphill on the dogleg path on the far side until it levels out on the shoulder of **Carn Hen**, then head steeply up to the left towards the summit of the hill, which is capped with the remains of a WWII radar station. The summit of **Carn Llidi** (181m) lies a few hundred metres further east. Here you can enjoy a panoramic view that takes in Whitesands Bay, Ramsey and Skomer Islands, the rocks and reefs of the Bishops and Clerks and, on a clear day, the coast of Ireland on the horizon. The tall lighthouse way out to sea is the Smalls.

Go down the old road from the radar station and follow it as it curves left and descends through Porthmawr Farm. At the main road, turn right to return to Whitesands car park. Total distance is 3.5 miles; allow two hours.

three hours on the island. It also runs two-hour trips around Ramsey and other islands by high-speed inflatable boat (£30/15), three-hour whale- and dolphin-spotting cruises around Grassholm Island (£50/25), and exciting one-hour jet-boat trips (£18/10).

Voyages of Discovery (☎ 720285, 0800 854367; www.ramseyisland.co.uk; 1 High St, St David's) and **Aquaphobia** (☎ 720471; www.aquaphobia-ramseyisland.co.uk; Grove Hotel, High St, St David's) offer similar trips.

Whitesands Bay

The mile-long strand of Whitesands Bay (Porth Mawr) is one of southwest Wales' best beaches, and a popular surfing spot. At extremely low tide you can see the wreck of a paddle tugboat that went aground here in 1882, and the fossil remains of a prehistoric forest.

If Whitesands is really busy – and it often is – you can escape the worst of the crowds by walking north along the coastal path for 10 to 15 minutes to the smaller, more secluded beach at **Porthmelgan**.

Whitesands Surf School (☎ 07789435670; www.whitesandssurfschool.co.uk) runs surfing lessons on the beach; a 2½-hour beginner's session costs £25, including equipment. You can book lessons

at **Ma Sime's Surf Hut** (☎ 720433; 28 High St) in St David's.

NORTH PEMBROKESHIRE

ST DAVID'S TO FISHGUARD

The coastline from St David's to Fishguard (and beyond) is less frequented than south and west Pembrokeshire, its coves and beaches mostly inaccessible by car. If you're only going to walk part of the Pembrokeshire Coast Path, this is an excellent section to tackle.

Porthgain

☎ 01348

For centuries the tiny harbour of Porthgain consisted of little more than a few sturdy cottages wedged into a rocky cove. In the mid-19th century it began to prosper as the port for shipping out slate quarried just down the coast at Abereiddy, and by the 1870s its own deposits of granite and fine clay had put it on the map as a source of building stone. The post-WWI slump burst the bubble, and the sturdy stone quays and overgrown brick storage 'bins' are all that remain.

Despite having been an industrial harbour, Porthgain is surprisingly picturesque and today it is home to a couple of art galleries and restaurants.

Porthgain is 8 miles northeast of St David's. The 411 St David's–Fishguard bus stops at Llanrhian, a mile inland (every two hours Monday to Saturday).

SLEEPING & EATING

Trefin Youth Hostel (YHA; ☎ 0870 770 6074; Fford-y-Afon; dm £11; ❂ Easter-Oct) This YHA hostel, set in a smartly refurbished former school building in the centre of the village, is two miles east of Trefin, half a mile inland from the Coast Path.

Caerhafod Lodge (☎ 837859; www.caerhafod.co.uk; Llanrhian; dm £13) About three-quarters of a mile southeast of Porthgain, Caerhafod is an excellent independent hostel in an old farm courtyard, with great views along the coast. Bike hire is available and dogs are welcome.

Sloop Inn (☎ 831449; Porthgain; mains £6-8; ❂ 9.30am-11pm, lunch noon-2.30pm, dinner 6-9.30pm) With wooden tables worn smooth by many a bended elbow, old photos of Porthgain in its industrial heyday, and interesting nautical clutter all over the place, the Sloop is a cosy and deservedly popular pub. It dishes up breakfast (to 11am) to hungry walkers, and serves excellent meals, including *moules mariniéres*, locally caught crab, Welsh beefsteaks and homemade lasagne.

Shed Wine Bar & Bistro (☎ 831518; Porthgain; mains lunch £10-17, dinner £20-23; ❂ noon-3pm & 6-11.30pm, tearoom 10am-4.30pm) Housed in a beautifully converted machine shop right by the little harbour, the Shed has grown into one of Pembrokeshire's finest seafood restaurants; the menu lists Porthgain crab and locally caught sea bass, gurnard, mullet and squid.

Strumble Head

At wild and rocky **Strumble Head**, the nearest point to Ireland, a lighthouse beams out its signal of four flashes every 15 seconds as the huge, high-speed catamaran ferries thunder past on their way from Fishguard to Rosslare. The headland makes a good vantage point for spotting whales and dolphins; below the parking area is a WWII lookout that now serves as a shelter for observing wildlife.

Two miles south of the headland is the scenic, cliff-bound cove of **Pwll Deri**, a good place for seal-watching, with the rocky summit of **Garn Fawr**, topped by an Iron Age fort, rising above it.

Little **Pwll Deri Youth Hostel** (YHA; ☎ 0870 770 6004; Castell Mawr, Trefasser; dm £11; ❂ Easter-Oct) enjoys a stunning location perched atop a 120m-high cliff overlooking the sea, perfectly placed for sunset with an immense panorama of coastal cliffs as far as St David's.

FISHGUARD (ABERGWAUN)
☎ 01348 / pop 3200

Fishguard, perched on a headland between its modern ferry port and former fishing harbour, is often overlooked by travellers, most of them passing through on their way to or from Ireland. But it's an appealing little town, with plenty of interest in the surrounding coast and countryside.

The Lower Town, next to the old fishing harbour, was used as a setting for the 1971 film version of *Under Milk Wood* with Richard Burton, Peter O'Toole and Elizabeth Taylor. It also featured (for all of two minutes) in the classic *Moby Dick* starring Gregory Peck.

This area was also the improbable setting for the last foreign invasion of Britain (see the boxed text the Last Invasion of Britain p193).

Orientation

Fishguard is split into three distinct areas. The main town sits on top of a raised headland west of the river mouth, and is centred on Market Sq, where the buses stop; to the east is the picturesque harbour of the Lower Town. The train station and ferry terminal lie a mile to the northwest of the town centre in Goodwick (Wdig; pronounced oo-dick).

Information

Fishguard Library (☎ 872694; High St; ❂ 9.30am-1pm Mon-Sat, 2-5pm Mon, Tue & Fri, 2-6.30pm Thu) Free internet access.

Health Centre (☎ 873041; Ropewalk)

Police Station (☎ 872835; Brodog Lane)

Post Office (West St)

Seaways Bookshop (12 West St) Selection of local books and maps, and an entertaining series of booklets on Pembrokeshire walks and history.

Tourist Office (☎ 873484; Town Hall, Market Sq; ❂ 10am-5.30pm Jun-Sep, 10am-5pm Mon-Sat Easter-May & Oct, 10am-4pm Mon-Sat Nov-Easter)

Tourist Office (☎ 874737; Ocean Lab, Goodwick; ❂ 10am-6pm Easter-Oct, 10am-4pm Nov-Easter; per hr £2) Internet access.

Sights

The **Royal Oak Inn** on Market Sq was the scene of the French surrender in 1797 (see the boxed text, the Last Invasion of Britain, p193), and the place has turned into something of an invasion museum, filled with memorabilia. In the parish churchyard behind the pub can be found the grave of local heroine Jemima Nicholas.

The **Ocean Lab** (☎ 874737; admission free; ♡ 10am-6pm Jul & Aug, 10am-5pm Easter-Jun, Sep & Oct; 10am-4pm Nov-Easter), on the waterfront near Goodwick, houses an exhibition on marine life and the environment. Aimed mainly at kids, it has various hands-on exhibits, as well as Oscar the mammoth skeleton, a soft play area and a café.

Activities

The **Marine Walk**, which follows the coast from the car park on the Parrog around to the Lower Town, offers great views over the old harbour and along the coast to Dinas Head.

The **Last Invasion Trail** is a circular, 14-mile cycle route that visits all the sites associated with the hapless invasion; a leaflet showing the route is available from the tourist offices. It's a rough and hilly outing, taking in the memorial at Carregwastad Point, Strumble Head, Garn Fawr and Tregwynt.

Celtic Diving (☎ 871938; www.celticdiving.co.uk; The Parrog, Goodwick) runs half-day scuba-diving taster sessions in its own practice pool (£65), and also offers PADI-certificated diving courses.

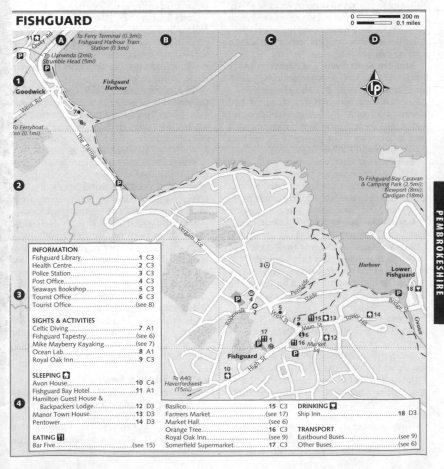

FISHGUARD

0 —————— 200 m
0 —————— 0.1 miles

PEMBROKESHIRE

INFORMATION	
Fishguard Library	1 C3
Health Centre	2 C3
Police Station	3 C3
Post Office	4 C3
Seaways Bookshop	5 C3
Tourist Office	6 C3
Tourist Office	(see 8)

SIGHTS & ACTIVITIES	
Celtic Diving	7 A1
Fishguard Tapestry	(see 6)
Mike Mayberry Kayaking	(see 7)
Ocean Lab	8 A1
Royal Oak Inn	9 C3

SLEEPING	
Avon House	10 C4
Fishguard Bay Hotel	11 A1
Hamilton Guest House & Backpackers Lodge	12 D3
Manor Town House	13 D3
Pentower	14 D3

EATING	
Bar Five	(see 15)

Basilico	15 C3
Farmers Market	(see 17)
Market Hall	(see 6)
Orange Tree	16 C3
Royal Oak Inn	(see 9)
Somerfield Supermarket	17 C3

DRINKING	
Ship Inn	18 D3

TRANSPORT	
Eastbound Buses	(see 9)
Other Buses	(see 6)

To Ferry Terminal (0.3mi); Fishguard Harbour Train Station (0.3mi)

To Llanwnda (2mi); Strumble Head (5mi)

Goodwick

Fishguard Harbour

Wern Rd

Quay Rd

The Parrog

To Ferryboat Inn (0.1mi)

Vergam Tce

Fishguard

To A40; Haverfordwest (15mi)

High St

Ropewalk

Penslade

Slade

West St

Main St

Market Sq

Tower Hill

Harbour

Lower Fishguard

Bridge St

Gwaun

To Fishguard Bay Caravan & Camping Park (2.5mi); Newport (8mi); Cardigan (18mi)

192 NORTH PEMBROKESHIRE •• Fishguard (Abergwaun)

Mike Mayberry Kayaking (☎ 874699; www.mikemay berrykayaking.co.uk) offers one-hour 'try it out' kayaking sessions (£10) for beginners, as well as instruction courses and guided kayaking tours for more experienced paddlers.

Festivals & Events

The International Music Festival (☎ 873612) takes place in the last week of July, with various classical concerts and choirs whooping it up in town.

There's music of another kind during the Fishguard Folk Festival (www.pembrokeshire-folk-music.co .uk), which is held over the Spring Bank Holiday weekend at the end of May.

Sleeping

Fishguard Bay Caravan & Camping Park (☎ 811415; www.fishguardbay.com; Garn Gelli; sites per tent, car & 2 people £11-17; ☼ Mar-Dec) This site is on the coastal path 2.5 miles east of town, perched on a headland overlooking the sea.

Hamilton Guest House & Backpackers Lodge (☎ 874797; www.hamiltonbackpackers.co.uk; 21 Hamilton St; dm/d/tr £14/36/48; P) The Hamilton is a homey and relaxed hostel with small, six-bed dorms, a kitchen, TV lounge, laundry and sauna. The owner knows Pembrokeshire well, and is happy to point you towards the best walks, pubs and eateries in the area.

Avon House (☎ 874476; www.avon-house.co.uk; 76 High St; s/d/tr £20/45/55) A decent budget B&B, Avon House has bright, smartly decorated rooms, albeit lacking in atmosphere. The family triple is en suite, and has a double and a single bed.

Manor Town House (☎ 873260; www.manortownhouse .com; Main St; r per person £33-40) This lovely old Georgian house is warm with the glow of polished mahogany and the scent of fresh flowers, and has a lovely garden terrace where you can sit in the evenings. Ask for one of the big rooms at the back with gorgeous views across the old harbour.

Pentower (☎ 874462; www.pentower.co.uk; Tower Hill; s/d £40/60) Another place that boasts fantastic sea views, Pentower was built on top of Tower Hill by Sir Evan Jones, the architect who designed the harbour. The house is filled with antique furniture and historic detail, and the bedrooms are large and luxurious – choose the turret room, where you can watch the boats come and go from the comfort of an armchair.

Ferryboat Inn (☎ 874747; www.ferryboatinn.co.uk; Manor Way, Goodwick; s/d £45/65; ☐ P) Although a touch bland looking on the outside, the Ferryboat has sleek, modern and stylish bedrooms with trendy taupe and chocolate-brown décor, and is only 500m from ferry and train station.

Fishguard Bay Hotel (☎ 873571; www.bayhotelfish guard.co.uk; Quay Rd, Goodwick; s/d from £54/75; P) A vast and rambling mansion of a place, this old-fashioned hotel has excellent views over the bay, and is where the film crew stayed during the shoot for Under Milk Wood in 1971. There's a large family room (£99) with a double and two bunk beds, and a deluxe double with four-poster beds and sea views (£95).

Eating & Drinking

Orange Tree (11 High St; snacks £2-3; ☼ 8am-5.30pm Mon-Sat) A delicatessen and takeaway sandwich place, the Orange Tree sells tasty baguettes and has a sit-in coffee shop (open from 10am).

Royal Oak Inn (☎ 872514; Market Sq; mains £6-13) Not only does this pub have an important place in Fishguard's history, but it also serves the best pub food in town and hosts a popular live folk night on Tuesday where musicians are welcome to join in.

Bar Five (☎ 875050; 5 Main St; mains £7-12) This Georgian town house has been converted into a den of designer furniture and contemporary touches, with outdoor dining on a terrace overlooking the harbour, and a bistro menu focused on fresh local produce, simply prepared.

Basilico (☎ 871845; 3 Main St; mains £10-13) A stylish and intimate little place with candlelight glinting off polished wood floors, Basilico serves fresh Italian cuisine, ranging from standard pasta dishes to gourmet seafood.

Ship Inn (Newport Rd) This is a lovely little pub with an open fire in winter and lots of memorabilia on the walls, including photos of Richard Burton filming Under Milk Wood outside (the street and nearby quay have not changed a bit).

To stock up on groceries, head for the Somerfield supermarket (High St). A general produce market is held every Thursday in the Market Hall (Market Sq), and there's a Farmers Market in the Somerfield car park every second Saturday in summer (in the Market Hall in winter).

Getting There & Away

Richards Brothers' bus 411 runs to Fishguard from St David's (£3, 50 minutes, every two hours Monday to Saturday, two or three Sunday); the 412 runs to Haverfordwest (40 minutes, hourly Monday to Saturday, two on Sunday) and Cardigan (£3, 40 minutes).

From Monday to Saturday there's one direct train a day from Cardiff to Fishguard Harbour (£16, 2¼ hours) via Llanelli; on Sunday there's a slower train (2¾ hours) that also calls in at Swansea and Carmarthen. Fishguard Harbour station is just a platform with no facilities; buy tickets on board the train.

For details of ferries to Ireland, see Transport, p324.

Getting Around

Bus 410 (half-hourly Monday to Saturday) runs a regular circuit from Market Sq to Goodwick and Fishguard Harbour.

AROUND FISHGUARD

Two miles northwest of Goodwick lies the tiny medieval church of **Llanwnda** (☎ 24hr), which has several pre-Norman carved stones, inscribed with crosses and Celtic designs, set into the walls. Inside, look up at the timber roof beams; at the far end of the third beam from the west (door) end, facing the altar, is a 15th-century carving of a tonsured monk's head.

Across the lane from the church, a wooden gate with a yellow waymark indicates the start of the footpath to **Carregwastad Point**, the site of the infamous 1797 invasion (see the Last Invasion of Britain, below), three-quarters of a mile away.

Running inland to the southeast of Fishguard is **Cwm Gwaun** (pronounced coom gwine), the valley of the River Gwaun. This narrow, wooded cleft, best explored on foot or

bicycle, feels strangely remote and mysterious. Famously, the inhabitants retain a soft spot for the Julian calendar (abandoned by the rest of Britain in 1752), which means that they celebrate New Year on 13 January.

Stop for a pint at the **Dyffryn Arms** (☎ 01348-881305; Pontfaen), better known as Bessie's, a rare old-fashioned pub where the landlady pours your beer from a jug filled straight from the barrel; no hand pumps here!

From May to September, the Preseli Green Dragon bus from Newport stops at the Dyffryn Arms (20 minutes, two daily Tuesday and Saturday).

NEWPORT (TREFDRAETH)

☎ 01239 / pop 1120

In stark contrast to the industrial city of Newport in Gwent, the Pembrokeshire Newport is a pretty cluster of flower-bedecked cottages huddled beneath a small Norman castle. It sits at the foot of Carn Ingli, a massive bump on the seaward side of the Preseli Hills, and in recent years has gained a reputation for the quality of its restaurants and guesthouses; Newport has been touted as Wales' answer to Padstow (a Cornish fishing village turned trendy gastronomic resort).

Newport makes a pleasant base for walks along the coastal path or south into the Preseli Hills, but it does get crowded in summer. At the northwest corner of the town is little Parrog Beach, dwarfed by Newport Sands (Traeth Mawr) across the river.

THE LAST INVASION OF BRITAIN

While Hastings in 1066 may get all the press, the last invasion of Britain was actually at Carregwastad Point, northwest of Fishguard, on 22 February 1797. The ragtag collection of 1400 French mercenaries and bailed convicts, led by an Irish-American named Colonel Tate, had intended to land at Bristol and march to Liverpool, keeping English troops occupied while France mounted an invasion of Ireland. But bad weather blew them ashore at Carregwastad, where after scrambling up a steep cliff, they set about looting the Pencaer peninsula for food and drink.

The invaders had hoped that the English peasants would rise up to join them in revolutionary fervour but, not surprisingly, their drunken pillaging didn't endear them to the locals, and the French were quickly seen off by volunteer 'yeoman' soldiers, the helpers included the people of Fishguard, including most famously, one Jemima Nicholas, who single-handedly captured 12 mercenaries armed with nothing more than a pitchfork.

The beleaguered Tate decided to surrender at a meeting in a house in Fishguard, now the Royal Oak Inn. A mere two days after their arrival, the invaders laid down their weapons at Goodwick and were sent off to the jail at Haverfordwest.

In 1997 Fishguard commemorated the bicentenary of the invasion with the creation by 76 local volunteers of a 30m tapestry. The **Fishguard Tapestry** (inspired by the Bayeux Tapestry, which recorded the Norman invasion at Hastings in 1066) is displayed in the Town Hall on Market Sq.

PEMBROKESHIRE

There's a **National Park Visitor Centre** (☎ 820912; 2 Bank Cottages, Long St; ☷ 10am-6pm Mon-Sat Easter-Oct) opposite the main car park, a block north of the main street.

Sights

The striking **Newport Castle** (now a private residence) was founded by a Norman nobleman called William FitzMartin – who was married to a daughter of Lord Rhys ap Gruffydd – after his father-in-law drove him out of nearby Nevern in 1191. Newport grew up around the castle, initially as a garrison town.

The **West Wales Eco Centre** (☎ 820235; www.ecocentre.org.uk; Lower St Mary's St; admission free; ☷ 9.30am-4.30pm Mon-Fri) is an environmental education and resource centre; the energy-efficient stone building has a photovoltaic array on the roof that generates up to 40% of the centre's electricity needs.

There's a little dolmen (Neolithic burial chamber) called **Carreg Coetan** right in town; it's northeast of the centre, about 200m along Pen-y-Bont on the left.

Activities

WALKING

If you keep walking past Carreg Coetan you come to an iron bridge over the **Nevern Estuary**, a haven for birdlife especially in winter. Cross the bridge and turn left for an easy walk along the shoreline to the sandy beach of **Newport Sands**.

There are lots of fine possibilities for longer walks around **Carn Ingli** (347m). You can climb to the summit from town – take Market St then Church St uphill, past the castle on your right. At a fork in the lane called College Sq, go right (uphill), following narrow tracks past a couple of farms and houses to reach a gate leading onto the open hillside. Work your way up on grassy paths to the summit, the site of an Iron Age hill fort, with great views of Newport Bay and Dinas Head (3.5 miles round trip).

CYCLING

The back roads south of Newport, around Carn Ingli and Cwm Gwaun, offer some of the loveliest on-road cycling in southwest Wales. You can rent a bike from **Newport Bike Hire** (☎ 820773; East St), based in the Whole Food Shop on the main street, with rates from £10/15 per half-/full day.

Sleeping

Morawelon Caravan & Camping Park (☎ 820565; Parrog Beach; sites per car, tent & 2 people £6.50-8.50) This pleasant grassy site overlooks the beach northwest of the town, with views across the river mouth to Newport Sands.

Trefdraeth Youth Hostel (YHA; ☎ 0870 770 6072; Lower St Mary's St; dm £12.50; ☷ Easter-Oct) Housed in a converted Victorian school next to the Eco Centre, this hostel is handy for the Coast Path, the beach and the town centre. It's closed during the day from 10am to 5pm.

Golden Lion Hotel (☎ 820321; www.goldenlionpembs .co.uk; East St; s/d £40/60) Bright, sunny décor, golden pine furniture and colourful flower arrangements make for a warm atmosphere in this appealing country inn. There's also a snug traditional bar with log fire, serving real ales, and a good restaurant (mains £8 to £14).

Soar Hill (☎ 820506; www.soarhilll.com; Cilgwyn Rd; s/d £40/70; ℗) Half a mile southeast of town (head up Bentick St, which becomes Cilgwyn Rd), Soar Hill is a 200-year-old house with a stunning hillside setting looking out over the Nevern Valley. The décor blends traditional and modern, with wood panelling and cast-iron fireplaces cheek-by-jowl with highback chairs and designer lampshades.

Llys Meddyg Guest House (☎ 820008; www.llys meddyg.com; East St; d £90; ▣) Housed in a lovely Georgian coaching inn, the 'Doctor's Court' has been beautifully restored and furnished with antiques. Bedrooms are large and bright, the lounge boasts leather sofas and a period fireplace, and there's a huge, secluded garden at the back. It's also one of the best places in town to eat.

Eating & Drinking

Café Fleur (☎ 820131; Market St; mains £4-6; ☷ 10am-8pm) This popular café goes for the rustic country-pine-and-terracotta-tile look, and serves tasty lunch dishes such as galettes, crepes, panini, soups and salads, as well as excellent coffee and cakes.

Morawelon Café Bar (☎ 820565; The Parrog; mains £8-15; ☷ 10am-5pm Apr-Oct, 10am-5pm Wed-Sun Dec-Mar, closed Nov) Down by the town beach, the Morawelon serves beer and wine as well as caffe lattes and herbal tea, and has a tempting lunch menu of local seafood dishes that includes hot buttered lobster. It also does a traditional roast lunch on Sundays.

Llys Meddyg Restaurant (☎ 820008; East St; mains £14-19) From the slate floor and leather armchairs in the bar to the modern art in the elegant dining room, this place oozes style. The food is superb, with the menu changing with the seasons and reflecting the best of local produce, from zesty Thai-style crab cakes with chilli and coriander to succulent marinated lamb.

Cnapan Country House (☎ 820575; East St; 2-/3-course dinner £22/28; ⏱ noon-2pm & 6.45-8.45pm, closed Sun lunch & Tue) The Cnapan has a more formal look than Llys Meddyg, with candlelight and crisp white linen tablecloths, but the service is friendly and relaxed. The menu is home-cooked comfort food from the chunky seafood chowder to the calorie-packed steamed marmalade pudding.

Getting There & Away

Richards Brothers' bus 412 runs from Fishguard to Newport (15 minutes, hourly Monday to Saturday, two on Sunday) and on to Cardigan (20 minutes).

From April to September, the Poppit Rocket bus 405 also runs from Newport to Fishguard and Cardigan (three daily), but takes the back roads via Moylgrove and Poppit Sands. The rest of the year it runs between Newport and Cardigan only (three daily Monday, Thursday and Saturday).

From May to September the **Preseli Green Dragon** (☎ 0845 602 7008; www.prta.co.uk) walkers' bus runs from Newport to Crymych via Cwm Gwaun and the back roads around the Preseli hills (two daily Tuesday and Saturday only). You need to book a seat at least an hour in advance; ask the tourist office for details.

AROUND NEWPORT

Dinas Island

The great wedge-shaped profile of Dinas Island juts out from the coast between Fishguard and Newport. It's not really an island, but is attached to the mainland by a neck of land, framed on either side by picturesque coves – the sandy strand of **Pwllgwaelod** to the west, and the rocky inlet of **Cwm-yr-Eglwys** to the east, where you can see the ruin of 12th-century St Brynach's Church, destroyed by the great storm of 1859.

The circuit of the headland (3.5 miles) makes an excellent walk, with the chance of spotting seals and dolphins from the 142m-high cliffs at Dinas Head, the northernmost point; a path across the neck between Pwllgwaelod and Cwm-yr-Eglwys allows you to return to your starting point.

Stop for lunch or a pint at the **Old Sailors** (☎ 01348-811491) at Pwllgwaelod, a former

haunt of Dylan Thomas; it serves fresh lobster and crab, and has outdoor tables.

Ceibwr Bay

Most of the 15 miles of coast between Newport and Cardigan is accessible only on foot. The one spot where a car or bike can get close is at the scenic, seal-haunted inlet of **Ceibwr Bay**, near the tiny hamlet of Moylgrove, reached via a maze of very narrow roads. A grassy platform near the road end, carpeted with sea pinks in summer, makes a great picnic spot.

The coastal scenery here is spectacular, with contorted cliffs to the north and a couple of sea stacks to the south. A half-mile walk south along the coast path leads to the **Witches' Cauldron**, a vast cliff-ringed, sea-filled hole caused by a cavern collapse.

There are no facilities at Ceibwr Bay. A mile inland is **Swn-y-Nant B&B** (☎ 01239-881244; www.moylegrove.co.uk; Moylgrove; r per person from £26), a modern house with a log fire and Rayburn stove; evening meals can be provided if you book in advance.

Nevern (Nanhyfer)

With its overgrown castle and atmospheric church, this little village 2 miles east of Newport makes a good objective for an easy walk. You approach the **Church of St Brynach** along a supremely gloomy alley of yew trees, estimated to be six centuries old; second on the right as you enter is the so-called bleeding yew, named after the curious reddish-brown sap that oozes from it. The beautifully melancholy churchyard dates from around the 6th century, predating the church.

Among the gravestones is a tall **Celtic cross**, one of the finest in Wales, decorated with interlace patterns and dating from the 10th or 11th century. According to tradition, the first cuckoo that sings each year in Pembrokeshire does so from atop this cross on St Brynach's Day (7 April).

Inside the church, the **Maglocunus Stone**, thought to date from the 5th century, forms a windowsill in the south transept. It is one of the few carved stones that bears an inscription in both Latin and ogham, and was instrumental in deciphering the meaning of ogham, an ancient Celtic script.

Pentre Ifan

The largest and best-preserved dolmen in Wales, Pentre Ifan is a 4500-year-old Neolithic

MYSTERY OF THE BLUESTONES

The only upland area in the Pembrokeshire Coast National Park is the **Preseli Hills** (Mynydd Preseli), rising to 536m at Foel Cwmcerwyn, the highest point. These hills are at the centre of a fascinating prehistoric landscape, scattered with hill forts, standing stones and burial chambers, and are famous as the source of the mysterious bluestones of Stonehenge.

There are 31 bluestone monoliths (plus 12 'stumps') at the centre of Stonehenge, each weighing around four tonnes, and how they were transported from Preseli to Salisbury Plain – a distance of 240 miles – is one of the great mysteries of the ancient world.

Geochemical analysis shows that the Stonehenge bluestones originated from outcrops around Carnmenyn and Carn Goedog at the eastern end of Mynydd Preseli. Stonehenge scholars have long been of the opinion that Preseli and the bluestones held some religious significance for the builders of Stonehenge, and that they laboriously dragged these monoliths down to the River Cleddau, then carried them by barge from Milford Haven, along the Bristol Channel and up the River Avon, then overland again to Salisbury Plain.

In 2000 a group of volunteers tried to re-enact this journey, using primitive technology to transport a single, three-tonne bluestone from Preseli to Stonehenge. They failed – having already resorted to the use of a lorry, a crane and modern roads, the stone slipped from its raft and sank just a few miles into the sea journey.

However, research published in the *Oxford Journal of Archaeology* in 2006 lends new support to an alternative theory that the bluestones were actually transported by Ice Age glaciers, and dumped around 40 miles to the west of the Stonehenge site by the melting ice some 12,000 years ago, where they were discovered by the prehistoric henge builders.

Whatever the truth, the Preseli hills provide some excellent walking country. An ancient track called the **Golden Road**, once part of a 5000-year-old trade route between Wessex and Ireland, runs along the crest of Mynydd Preseli, passing prehistoric cairns and the stone circle of Bedd Arthur.

The Preseli Green Dragon bus (see p195) will drop you at Crymych at the eastern end of the hills, allowing you to hike along the Golden Road to the car park at Bwlch Gwynt on the B4329 (7.5 miles), where you can catch the afternoon bus back to Newport.

burial chamber set on a remote hillside with superb views across the Preseli Hills and out to sea. The huge, 5m-long capstone, weighing more than 16 tonnes, is delicately poised on three tall, pointed, upright stones, made of the same bluestone that was used for the menhirs at Stonehenge.

The site is about 4 miles southeast of Newport, on a minor road south of the A487; it's signposted.

Castell Henllys

Some 2000 years ago there was a thriving Celtic settlement at what's now called Castell Henllys (Castle of the Prince's Court). Students from the University of York archaeology department have been digging and sifting at the site every summer since 1981, and have learned enough to build a remarkable re-creation of the settlement on its original foundations, complete with educated guesses about the clothing, tools, ceremonies and agricultural life of that time.

A visit to **Castell Henllys Iron Age Settlement** (☎ 01239-891319; www.castellhenllys.com; Felindre Farchog; adult/child £3/2; ☒ 10am-5pm Apr-Oct) is like travelling back in time. There are reconstructions of the settlement's buildings – four thatched roundhouses, animal pens, a smithy and a grain store. There are Iron Age breeds of livestock, craft demonstrations, Celtic festivals and other events that bring the settlement to life.

Castell Henllys is 4 miles east of Newport. Take the hourly Newport to Cardigan bus 412 and get off at the Melina Rd stop, from where it's a three-quarter-mile walk to Castell Henllys.

PEMBROKESHIRE

Pembrokeshire Coast Path

Duration	15 days
Distance	186 miles
Difficulty	moderate–demanding
Start	Amroth
Finish	St Dogmaels
Nearest Towns	Tenby (p165), Cardigan (p207)
Transport	train, bus

Summary Straddling the line where Wales drops suddenly into the sea, this is one of the most spectacular routes in Britain.

The rugged Pembrokeshire coast is what you would imagine the world would look like if God was a geology teacher. There are knobbly hills of volcanic rock, long thin inlets scoured by glacial meltwaters, and stratified limestone pushed up vertically and eroded into natural arches, blowholes and sea stacks. Stretches of towering red and grey cliff give way to perfect sandy beaches, only to resume around the headland painted black.

The Pembrokeshire Coast Path (PCP) was established in 1970, and takes you from popular holiday spots to long stretches where the only evidence of human existence are the ditches of numerous Celtic forts. In the south, Norman castles dominate many towns and villages, and once held the Celts at bay, creating a frontier that still exists today in the Landsker line (see p32).

The landscape allows for all kinds of outdoor pursuits, whether they are rock climbing, kayaking, surfing or stretching out on a towel with a trashy novel. Marine life is plentiful, and rare birds make the most of the remote cliffs, with peregrine falcons, red kites, buzzards, choughs, puffins and gannets to be spotted.

It's not all nature and beauty, however. Several military installations require long detours along roads, and two whole days are dominated by the heavy industry of Milford Haven. Still, other manmade structures redeem our impact somewhat – beautiful St David's with its delicate cathedral, haughty Pembroke Castle and the pastel-shaded cottages of Tenby.

PLANNING

We've suggested a south-to-north route, allowing an easy start in highly populated areas to build up to longer, more isolated stretches where you'll need to carry food with you. Some distances look deceptively short, but you must remember the endless steep ascents and descents where the trail crosses harbours and beaches. Referring to a tide table is essential if you want to avoid lengthy delays on a couple of sections.

The weather can be quite changeable, so bring wet-weather gear and something warm, even in the height of summer. During the school holidays it pays to book ahead, as B&Bs, hostels and camp sites fill up quickly. Between Whitesands and Fishguard, sleeping and eating options are especially limited.

When to Walk

In spring and early summer, wildflowers transform the route with an explosion of colour, and migratory birds are likely to be seen. The height of summer will tend to be dryer and more conducive to enjoying the numerous beaches on the route. Other mid- to late-summer advantages include migrating whales, flocks of butterflies and plenty of wild blackberries to snack on – a good payoff for walking in the heat. As you head into autumn, seals come ashore to give birth to their pups. Winter is generally more problematic, as many hostels and camp sites close from October until Easter, and buses are less frequent. Needless to say, walking around precipitous cliffs in the wind, rain and chill may not be the most enjoyable (or safest) experience.

Maps & Guides

The route is covered by Ordnance Survey (OS) Explorer 1:25,000 maps 35 *(North Pembrokeshire)* and 36 *(South Pembrokeshire)*. The official national trail guide, *Pembrokeshire Coast Path* by Brian John, includes the coastal section of these same maps, but is cheaper and more manageable, with detailed route descriptions, albeit running north to south. More useful is *The Pembrokeshire Coastal Path,* by Dennis Kelsall, which describes the routes in the preferred south-to-north direction, and includes detailed route descriptions, background information, line maps and an accommodation list. A series of 10 single-sheet trail cards (50p each), available from tourist offices and National Park Centres, cover the route, with basic maps pointing out sites of interest along the way.

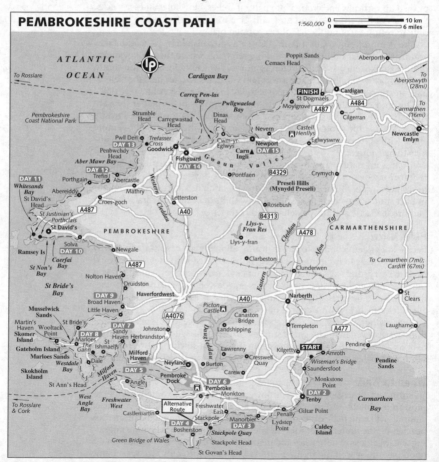

Day	From	To	Miles
1	Amroth	Tenby	7
2	Tenby	Manorbier	8.5
3	Manorbier	Bosherston	15
4	Bosherston	Angle	15
5	Angle	Pembroke	13.5
6	Pembroke	Sandy Haven	16
7	Sandy Haven	Marloes	14
8	Marloes	Broad Haven	13
9	Broad Haven	Solva	11
10	Solva	Whitesands	13
11	Whitesands	Trefin	12
12	Trefin	Pwll Deri	10
13	Pwll Deri	Fishguard	10
14	Fishguard	Newport	12.5
15	Newport	St Dogmaels	15.5

Information Sources

There are National Park Centres in St David's (p184), Newport (p193) and Tenby (p165), with maps, guidebooks and, most importantly the free *Coast to Coast* newspaper (online at www.visitpembrokeshirecoast.com). It contains bus timetables and tide tables, which are not just helpful – they're essential. The National Park website (www.pembrokeshirecoast.org.uk) is also incredibly useful, with accommodation listings and abundant advice for walkers.

THE WALK
Day 1: Amroth to Tenby
3–4 hours, 7 miles

Starting at a wide sandy beach, this short section is the perfect teaser for what's to come, allowing plenty of time for swimming and sightseeing.

A pair of bilingual brass plaques marks the beginning of the trail, near the eastern end of Amroth. Today's destination is clearly in sight, peering out behind rocky little Monkstone, which abuts the point at the south end of the bay. At low tide you can kick off your shoes and follow the shore all the way to Monkstone Point, although the official track takes the road and then follows the clifftops along what was once a railway track. Just over an hour away in Saundersfoot, there are places to eat and a **tourist office** (☎ 01834-813672) by the picturesque harbour.

The path continues through a wooded area, taking a short diversion down Monkstone Point before doubling back to come out into the fields near the large **Trevayne Farm Caravan & Camping Park** (☎ 01834-813402; www.camping-pembroke shire.co.uk; Monkstone; sites per person £4). From here there are a few sharp inclines, with ever nearer views of candy-striped **Tenby** (p165) along the way.

Day 2: Tenby to Manorbier
3½–4½ hours, 8.5 miles

Another brilliant day with breathtaking clifftop views. There are a number of steep climbs, but the distance is mercifully short.

Lose the shoes and enjoy the first mile along sandy South Beach. As you near the end you'll be able to spot whether the red flag is flying over Giltar Point. Don't get excited and break into the 'Internationale' – the revolution hasn't

---

WARNING

The Pembrokeshire Coast Path (PCP) is safe for sensible adult walkers, but parts of it are certainly not suitable for young children. At the time of writing, no-one has died on the path for 10 years, but fatal accidents have happened in the past. The path is quite narrow and often runs close to the top of sheer cliffs. Take great care, especially when you're tired, visibility is poor, the path is wet or there are high winds (when your backpack can turn into a sail).

Don't attempt to swim across river mouths and be aware that some beaches have strong undertows and rips. Particular care should be taken at Whitesands, Newgale, Freshwater West and Marloes Sands when the surf's up. Lifeguards patrol the areas between the flags every day during school holidays. Generally the beaches from Amroth to Tenby are the safest.

Don't pick up anything shiny in the military firing ranges, and definitely don't attempt to cross these zones when the red flags are flying, even if there's no guard to block your way.

Probably the most dangerous stretches are where the route follows roads with no footpath. A particularly treacherous area is near the grimly named Black Bridge on the way into Milford Haven. Take care also at Wiseman's Bridge, and between Little and Broad Havens. For these last two, you're safer crossing on the beach at low tide, but mind that you don't get cut off by the tide.

Don't attempt a short cut along any beach unless you're sure you can make it to the other side. If you get trapped, the best you can hope for is a sodden pack. At worst, you could be in real danger.

---

started. It just means that the military is using their firing range. Ordinarily the path takes you up around the clifftop, but when the flag is flying you're forced to make a diversion through the nearby village of **Penally**. This isn't all bad, as Penally has a pair of decent pubs and a church containing two Celtic crosses from the 10th and 11th centuries.

You'll eventually rejoin the cliff path to enjoy incredible views over **Caldey Island** (p167). Head down to caravan-covered Lydstep, about two hours from Tenby, before hooking up with the road at the other end of the beach, cutting across the point and regaining the cliffs as the path twists seriously close to sheer drops. Look out for the **Church Doors** limestone formation linking two beaches far below.

Soon you'll pass the futuristic grey-and-yellow Manorbier Youth Hostel (p169) – a cross between a space station and a motorway diner. It was once part of the military base that still occupies the neighbouring headland, where you're forced to make another detour away from the cliffs, returning high above the extraordinary red limestone ramparts of Presipe Beach.

It all builds to a spectacular finale, with the path heading alongside a number of sudden 20m-deep chasms. As you turn the corner and Manorbier comes into view, look out for **King's Quoit**, a Neolithic burial chamber fashioned from massive slabs of rock.

Day 3: Manorbier to Bosherston
5½–7 hours, 15 miles

A slightly longer day, continually alternating between sheer cliffs and sandy beaches. Lunch options are limited, so consider taking food with you.

From Manorbier it's an easy 3.5 miles to Freshwater East. While not the surfie haven of its western namesake, it's still a popular holiday destination. After another surging section of cliff you reach the tiny harbour of **Stackpole Quay** (p170), and then pass two massive arches, one big enough for large boats to pass through. From Stackpole Head you can look back proudly and survey your whole walk so far.

About 2 miles further on, you reach a bay called Broadhaven South (not to be confused with Broad Haven, your stopping point on Day 8), where the trail goes inland slightly and crosses a footbridge on the edge of the National

Trust's **Stackpole Estate** (p169). West of here is another military firing range and the trail divides; if there's no red flag you can take the path along the coast, past several natural rock arches, to St Govan's Head and visit the tiny 6th-century **St Govan's Chapel** (p170), set into the cliffs. From the chapel you follow a lane 1.5 miles north to reach the little village of Bosherston.

However, if the red flags are flying, you'll have to take a shortcut inland through the nature reserve (a very nice route in its own right), over foot-bridges and around long, thin lily ponds to reach **Bosherston** (p169).

Day 4: Bosherston to Angle
5½–7 hours, 15 miles
There are patches of wonderful coastal scenery, but prepare for some tedious road walking, courtesy of the British Army. For tips to avoid this, see p197.
Quite why the army needs to use some of the most beautiful parts of Britain's coast to test its killing power is anyone's guess. Much of the next stretch is a tank firing range, permanently off limits to the public. Other parts are open as long as firing isn't actually taking place. There's usually a schedule of the firing times posted in Ye Olde Worlde Café (p170) in Bosherton.

If you're lucky, you'll be able to head back down to St Govan's Chapel and continue the trail along the coast – a beautiful 3.5-mile stretch with numer-ous caves, blowholes and natural arches, including the much photographed **Green Bridge of Wales**. If you're unlucky and the red flags *are* flying, you'll have to take the road for an additional 3 miles west from Bosherton. But at Stack Rocks, red flags or not, you will have to turn inland and begin a 9-mile road walk. With ear-splitting detonations from the range, very little protection from passing vehicles and high hedgerows hiding much of the view, this is not an enjoyable diversion. The upside of this is that it does save you a few miles and gives you more incentive to wait for the bus.

You reach the coast again at spectacular **Freshwater West** (p170), beyond which the trail loops around the Angle Peninsula – another beautiful section with caves, tiny islands and little bays. At popular West Angle Bay you could easily cheat and follow the road for 10 minutes to the village of **Angle** (p171). Otherwise it's only an hour to Angle Point, where the path curves back into the village.

Day 5: Angle to Pembroke
5–6 hours, 13.5 miles
Today the scenery turns industrial and there's nowhere to get lunch.
As you enter the Milford Haven estuary, the castles and church steeples that have dominated this landscape since Norman times are now dwarfed by the massive towers and domes of modern oil refineries. When they're not spewing out black smoke there's something almost majestic about the scale of them – although the novelty may wear off after two full days of walking in their shadow.

The trail runs around Angle Bay and along the south bank of the estuary, alongside the vast Texaco refinery and past several tanker jetties. Your next highlight is the demolished power station, beyond which tracks, lanes and roads lead through medieval Monkton into **Pembroke** (p171).

Day 6: Pembroke to Sandy Haven
6–8 hours, 16 miles
The day starts urban and quickly becomes industrial. Make sure you check your tide tables before setting out, or you may find yourself taking a nasty detour.
The path takes you across the Pembroke River and round the backstreets of Pembroke Dock (a separate town), then over the large Cleddau Bridge, which does at least provide some views. Stay on the road until you cross a second bridge, before following the river back down into Neyland. If you're

camping, nearby **Shipping Farm** (☎ 01646-600286; Rose Market; sites per person £4) comes highly recommended. There's a large new gas terminal and a very dangerous section of pavement-deprived road before you cross the Black Bridge into the grim suburbs of Milford Haven. Beyond the docks there's a final section of grey suburban streets and, just for luck, another bloody gas terminal (Exxon) then – hooray! – you're back to the national park and the beautiful coast again. From here it's a short hop to Sandy Haven.

The little estuary of Sandy Haven can be crossed (using stepping stones) during the 2½ hours either side of low tide (a tide table is posted by the slipway on each side). At high tide it's a 4-mile detour via Herbrandston and Rickeston Bridge. At Herbrandston the **Taberna Inn** (☎ 01646-693498; s/d with shared bathroom £25/50) offers B&B (shared bathrooms) and food in a popular local pub (mains £10, open lunch and dinner).

Before the crossing, relaxed **Sandy Haven Camping Park** (☎ 01646-695899; www .sandyhavencampingpark.co.uk; sites per tent & 2 persons £9-11) has good facilities. On the west side of the estuary, close to the trail, **Skerryback Farm** (☎ 01646-636598; www.pfh.co.uk/skerryback; s/d incl breakfast £30/55) offers beds with en suites for weary walkers. Further towards St Ishmael's, **Bicton Farm** (☎ 01646-636215; jdllewellin@aol .com; s/tw with shared bathroom £20/46, d £50) is another good B&B option.

Day 7: Sandy Haven to Marloes
5–6½ hours, 14 miles

Today takes you back to nature, with more ragged cliffs and deserted sandy beaches, as the industrial plants dissolve into the distance.

From Sandy Haven there are 4 miles of fine clifftop walking to the Gann, another inlet that can only be crossed 3½ hours either side of low tide (otherwise it's a 2.5-mile detour via Mullock). The path leads into Dale, where you can grab a sandwich at the **Boathouse** (mains £2.50-5; ☺ breakfast & lunch) or a more substantial meal at the **Griffin Inn** (☎ 01646-636227; mains £4-12; ☺ lunch & dinner). A 10-minute walk through the village, past Dale castle, to Westdale Bay would save you 2½ hours, but cost you 5 miles of beautiful scenery around **St Ann's Head** (p183).

Two miles along the cliffs past Westdale Bay you'll see the remains of an abandoned **WWII airfield**. Above the impressive sweep of Marloes Sands, the sign to well-positioned Marloes Sands Youth Hostel (p183) is three-quarters of the way along the beach.

Day 8: Marloes to Broad Haven
4½–6 hours, 13 miles

A wonderful walk along dramatic clifftops, ending in an impressive beach.

Head back to Marloes Sands; at the end of the beach you pass Gateholm Island, a major Iron Age Celtic settlement where the remains of 130 hut circles have been found. You'll pass many such sites today – look out for the earthwork ramparts of promontory forts.

Martin's Haven, at the tip of the peninsula, is the base for **Skomer Island boat trips** (p183) and the office of the Skomer Marine Nature Reserve, with an interesting display on the underwater environment. Set into the wall next to the office is a **Celtic cross**, which may date to the 7th century.

Around the headland the cliffs change from red to black, and after an hour you'll reach Musselwick Sands. **St Bride's Haven** is a further 2 miles down the track, with the headland dominated by a Victorian faux castle, once owned by the barons of Kensington. A reasonably easy 5-mile stretch leads to Little Haven, separated by rocks from **Broad Haven** (p183). From the path you'll be able to assess the tide and decide whether to follow the busy road or cross via the beach.

Day 9: Broad Haven to Solva
4–5½ hours, 11 miles

Don't be fooled by the distance – today's no easy stroll. There are several steep climbs, but thankfully the scenery remains superb.

Ancient fortifications are even more evident today as you follow the cliffs up from the beach. After an hour you should reach the Druidstone Hotel (p184), a rambling old hotel and restaurant at the top of Druidston Haven. Just down from the hotel, what looks like a Bronze Age barrow turns out to be an ultramodern home dug into the earth.

A further 30 minutes will bring you to Nolton Haven, a former coal port with a pub by the beach. From here the trail gets really steep, sweeping up and down the cliffs towards beautiful 2.5-mile-long **Newgale Beach** (p183). Frustratingly, you can't get down to the beach until you've walked half its length on the undulating cliff path. **Newgale Camping Site** (☎ 01437-710253; www.newgalecampingsite .co.uk; sites per person £5) has well-kept facilities, and is perfectly positioned by the beach and the **Duke of Edinburgh** (☎ 01437-720586; mains £4-7; ☺ lunch & dinner).

As you pass over the bridge by the pub, you're crossing the Landsker Line (p32). From Newgale the trail climbs back onto the cliffs. The 5-mile walk to **Lower Solva** (p188) is along a rugged section with impressive rock formations.

Day 10: Solva to Whitesands
5–7 hours, 13 miles

The spectacular coastline takes a spiritual turn as you follow in the footsteps of Wales' patron saint.

From Solva, the trail climbs back onto the cliffs and the superb coastal scenery continues. After two hours you'll reach **Caerfai Bay**, a sheltered sandy beach with two wonderful walker-friendly camp sites (p186) right on the path.

Around the next headland is **St Non's Bay** (p188). If you're cutting inland to St David's for lunch, it's a 20-minute walk from here along the marked path through the fields.

Back on the PCP, another half-hour brings you to the tiny harbour of Porthclais. Continuing round the headland there are good views across to **Ramsey Island** (p188). The treacherous reefs close to the island are evocatively known as the Bitches; from the shore you can see and hear the tide rushing through the largest of them, the **Great Bitch**. Another easy 2 miles will bring you to the busy surf beach of **Whitesands Bay** (p189).

Day 11: Whitesands to Trefin
4½–6 hours, 12 miles

Wild St David's Head offers a rugged new landscape at the beginning of a beautiful but taxing walk with several steep ascents.

From Whitesands the trail quickly takes you to **St David's Head**, an untamed outcrop scattered with boulders and the remnants of an Iron Age fort, which is painted with streaks of yellow and purple flowers in summer. For the next 2 miles the only sign of human habitation is an ancient dolmen (Neolithic burial chamber); herds of horses roam around, adding to the primitive feel.

After an undulating 3½-hour walk, the beachside settlement of Abereiddy reveals ruins from the industrial age. Another half hour will bring you to **Porthgain** (p189), another former quarry town and now a quiet village with a quaint harbour. From here it's an easy hour to Trefin and a well-earned rest.

At Trefin you'll find **Prendergast Camping Park** (☎ 01348-831368; www.prendergast caravanpark.co.uk; sites per person £3.50), so well sheltered behind its hedges it's difficult to spot. The facilities are excellent and well-maintained, but you'll need to put a coin in the slot to get a hot shower. Relaxed and friendly **Hampton House**

(☎ 01348-837701; viv.kay@virgin.net; 2 Ffordd-y-Felin; s/d £25/50) has three simple rooms, and **Bryngarw Guest House** (☎ 01348-831221; www.bryngarwguesthouse.co.uk; Abercastle Rd; s/d £40/60) has some impressive sea views. The only dinner option is the **Ship Inn** (☎ 01348-831445; mains £7-15; ☾ lunch & dinner), serving typically uninspiring but hearty pub food.

Day 12: Trefin to Pwll Deri
3½–4½ hours, 10 miles

Today's walk is yet another wonderful experience, with cliffs, rock buttresses, pinnacles, islets, bays and beaches. It's tempered by a distinct paucity of eating and accommodation options.

From Trefin it's an easy 3 miles to Abercastle. Before you reach the small beach, take a short detour over the stiles to **Carreg Sampson**, a 5000-year-old burial chamber with a capstone over 5m long. After another 4 miles you'll reach sandy Aber Mawr Beach.

The headland of Penbwchdy is the beginning of one of the most impressive stretches of cliff on the whole path. If the weather is good you can see all the way back to St David's Head; if it's windy you may be thankful for the circular dry-stone shepherds' shelter here. Either way, it's a wild 40-minute walk to join the road above the bay of **Pwll Deri** (p190), where there's another stunning view back along the cliffs.

Day 13: Pwll Deri to Fishguard
3½–4½ hours, 10 miles

There's excellent cliff scenery and reasonably easy walking on this deserted section, but come prepared or you may be very hungry by the time you reach Goodwick.

From Pwll Deri the trail leads along the cliffs for 3 miles to the impressive promontory of **Strumble Head** (p190), marked by its famous lighthouse. A mile inland you can pitch a tent at **Tresinwen Farm** (☎ 01348-891238; sites per person £2). About 3 miles further on you reach Carregwastad Point, where the last invasion of Britain occurred some 200 years ago (see p193). Shortly after this, the small wooded valley of Cwm Felin comes as a surprise in this otherwise windswept landscape.

An hour later you round the headland, and with a sudden jolt there's Goodwick and behind it **Fishguard** (p190), the largest town since Milford Haven. The trail drops down to the port of Goodwick to come out by the ferry quay, then heads past a roundabout at the bottom of the hill. Along the waterfront there are a series of interesting historical plaques and mosaics illustrating the history of the area.

From here the trail climbs steeply up to the cliffs, skirting Fishguard. Stay with it until you reach a viewpoint overlooking Lower Fishguard, then go up Penslade St, which will bring you out on West St, very near the town centre.

Day 14: Fishguard to Newport
5–6 hours; 12.5 miles

There are superb views from the cliffs on this section, but only one lunch option.

Leaving Fishguard you follow the trail round picturesque Lower Fishguard, the location for the 1971 film of Dylan Thomas' *Under Milk Wood*, and then head out along the clifftops once again.

About 4 miles on, at the small bay of Pwllgwaelod, the Old Sailors (p195) is a good lunch stop. It's possible to take a short cut to Cwm-yr-Eglwys through the valley that almost divides Dinas Head from the mainland, but

don't be tempted – it's a wonderful walk along the coast and you might spot
seals and dolphins.

From Cwm-yr-Eglwys it's only 3 miles on to the Parrog, the old port of
Newport. From here, continue to follow the PCP through a small wooded
section; turn right at the fingerpost to the youth hostel and you'll hit the
centre of **Newport** (p193).

Day 15: Newport to St Dogmaels
6–8 hours, 15.5 miles

*We've saved the longest, steepest day till last – when those newly formed rocklike
thighs and buns of steel can best handle it. Grab a packed lunch and head for
the finish line, enjoying some of the best walking on the whole route.*

East of Newport Sands, the coast along the first half of this section is wild
and uninhabited, with numerous rock formations and caves. You may see
Atlantic grey seals on the rocks nearby. Onwards from **Ceibwr Bay** (p195)
is quite tough, but it's a wonderful roller-coasting finale, past sheer cliffs
reaching a height of 175m – the highest of the trail.

At Cemaes Head, stop and take stock. The end of the trail is nigh but
aesthetically this headland is the finish. So, turning your back on the cliffs,
follow the lane towards St Dogmaels and **Cardigan** (p207).

A mile past the beach of Poppit Sands you leave the national park and a
plaque on a wall seems like the end of the trail. Don't celebrate just yet. The actual end is a couple of miles further on, unmarked, near a carved wooden mermaid as you enter St Dogmaels village. Now you can pop the champagne!

Mid-Wales

Falling between Snowdonia to the north and the Brecon Beacons National Park to the south, Mid-Wales is something of a well-kept secret. This is Wales at its most thoroughly rural, a landscape of lakes, forests, lustrous green fields and small market towns. It's also thoroughly Welsh, with three out of five people speaking the mother tongue. In 1974, Brecknockshire, Radnorshire and Montgomeryshire were combined into the vast new county of Powys, while Cardiganshire kept its boundaries but got back its ancient name, Ceredigion.

Mid-Wales isn't a secret, however, to people seeking out a more environmentally aware existence or an alternative lifestyle. The scenery, space and laid-back feel have been attracting hippies since the 1970s, while the superb Centre for Alternative Technology, situated near Machynlleth, has become the focal point for Wales' green consciousness.

Elsewhere, the candyfloss-coloured university town and seaside resort of Aberystwyth has lots of student-powered fizz, and the trip from here to Devil's Bridge is one of Wales' best steam-train journeys. The lovely Heart of Wales railway line also crosses southern Powys, and this is fine walking, cycling and riding country.

The Mid-Wales cultural scene is also thriving, with Builth Wells the favourite of the old spa towns and home to both the excellent Wyeside Arts Centre and the annual Royal Welsh Show. Eccentric Llanwrtyd Wells, meanwhile, not only lies amid beautiful countryside, but also has established itself as Wales' capital of the quirky festival.

For information about Mid-Wales, see the website www.exploremidwales.com.

HIGHLIGHTS

- Save the planet by going green at the superb **Centre for Alternative Technology**, Machynlleth (p234)
- Take the pulse of the Mid-Wales cultural scene with a visit to the spa town of **Builth Wells** (p218)
- Revel in Welsh history with a stroll through the yew-laden terraces of Welshpool's **Powis Castle** (p228)
- Try snorkelling the bog or real ale wobbling at the increasingly wacky **Llanwrtyd Wells** (p216)
- Relive the age of steam with a ride out to Devil's Bridge on the narrow-gauge **Vale of Rheidol Railway** (p213)

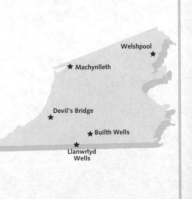

ACTIVITIES

This is unspoilt walking country, with Offa's Dyke Path National Trail, a 177-mile path that runs the length of the Welsh border, the best trail for walkers. Also popular is Wales' newest national trail, the 132-mile Glyndŵr's Way that forms a huge arc through Powys, stretching from Knighton to Machynlleth and back to Welshpool. It takes in some fine countryside and follows in the footsteps of the Welsh hero Owain Glyndŵr. The Cambrian Way is a major walking path that crosses Ceredigion. For more on these trails see p62.

For bikers, Lôn Las Cymru, the Welsh National Cycling Route (Sustrans Rte 8), drops down through the Cambrian Mountains and the Mid-Wales backroads, making it a dream for tourers on two wheels.

GETTING THERE & AROUND

The railway lines in Mid-Wales all run daily services, albeit often with reduced frequency on Sundays. The **Cambrian Line** (www.thecambrian line.co.uk) runs from Shrewsbury (England) to Aberystwyth via Machynlleth; the **Heart of Wales Line** (www.heart-of-wales.co.uk) runs from Shrewsbury to Swansea via Llandrindod Wells and Knighton.

Bus transport is patchy, especially in Powys, and services are rare on Sunday. Mid-Wales' major companies are **Arriva Cymru** (www.arrivabus.co .uk) based in Aberystwyth, and **Roy Brown's Coaches** (www.roybrownscoaches.co.uk) in Builth Wells.

For details of travel passes, see (p326).

CEREDIGION

CARDIGAN (ABERTEIFI)

☎ 01239 / pop 4200

With its long, festive main street rising from the river, and a colourful huddle of Georgian and Victorian houses clustered around the ruins of the old castle, Cardigan makes for a pleasant and picturesque stopover. Its position at the northern end of the Pembrokeshire Coastal Path sees plenty of hikers coming and going, but there are lots of gentler ways to pass the time, from relaxing on the beach at Poppit Sands, to watching for otters at the Welsh Wildlife Centre.

Aberteifi, the Welsh name for Cardigan, refers to the town's location at the mouth of the River Teifi. In Elizabethan times this was Wales' second most important port, and by the 18th century one of Britain's busiest seafaring centres. By the late 19th century, however, the railway was displacing sea transport, and the river began silting up.

Orientation & Information

The town centre lies on the northern bank of the River Teifi. From the main bus stop in Finch Sq, it's a 200m walk up Priory St to High St/Pendre, the town's main drag – turn right and then take the first left to find the tourist office.

Cardigan Library (☎ 612578; Pendre; 🕒 9.30am-6pm Mon-Fri, to 5pm Sat) Free internet access; on the top floor of the shopping arcade.

Cardigan Memorial Hospital (☎ 612214; Pont-y-Cleifion)

Intelligent Computers (🕒 9am-5.30pm Mon-Sat) Charges £1.50 per 30 minutes for internet access.

Police station (☎ 612209; Priory St)

Tourist office (☎ 613230; www.tourism.ceredigion.gov .uk; Bath House Rd; 🕒 10am-6pm Mon-Sat Jun-Aug, 10am-5pm Mon-Sat Sep-Jun) In the lobby of the Theatr Mwldan.

Sights

The shored-up and overgrown walls of **Cardigan Castle** make for a sorry sight. Long neglected by its private owner – a private house was built within the walls in the 19th century – the crumbling castle was purchased by Ceredigion Council in 2003; plans are under way to restore it and open it to the public. It holds an important place in Welsh culture, having been the venue for the first competitive National Eisteddfod (see p47), held in 1176 under the aegis of Lord Rhys ap Gruffydd.

Just across Cardigan Bridge from the town centre, **Cardigan Heritage Centre** (☎ 614404; Teifi Wharf; adult/child £2/1; 🕒 10am-5pm mid-Mar-Nov) is housed in a restored 18th-century granary on what was once one of the busiest quays in the port. It explores Cardigan's history from pre-Norman times to the present day, with interactive displays for kids and a riverside café.

The neo-Gothic **Guildhall** (High St) dates from 1860, and is now home to **Cardigan Market**. The field cannon outside commemorates the Charge of the Light Brigade in 1854, which was led by Lord Cardigan (after whom the button-up woollen sweater was named).

Activities

The **Pembrokeshire Coastal Path** (see p197) finishes in St Dogmaels, a mile west of Cardigan town centre. You can hike the final section of

MID-WALES

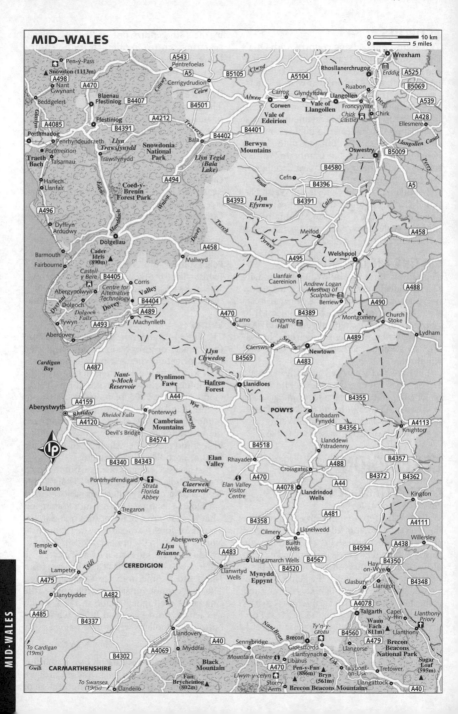

the coast path in reverse from Cardigan Bridge to Ceibwr Bay (9 miles) via Cemaes Head, then cut inland to Moylgrove village (1 mile) and return on the Poppit Rocket bus (see p165).

In the other direction, you can walk or cycle from Cardigan through the **Teifi Marshes** to the Welsh Wildlife Centre (see p210). Start from Finch Sq then head east along Pont-y-Cleifion to the roundabout and turn right, cross the bridge and descend the stairs on the right, then follow the trail east under the bridge (1 mile).

You can hire bikes from **New Image Bicycles** (☎ 621275; 29-30 Pendre) for £12/18 per half-day/day.

If you fancy taking to the river, head for **Heritage Canoes** (☎ 613961; www.heritagecanoes.co.uk) at the Welsh Wildlife Centre (p210). They offer guided canoe trips through Cilgerran Gorge on the River Teifi (adult/child £25/15 for 2½ hours).

Festivals & Events

The **Cardigan Festival of Walking** takes place over the first weekend in October, with themed walks around the area, plus talks, exhibitions and much quaffing of beer. There's also the one-day **Cardigan River & Food Festival** in the middle of August, with food stalls, cooking demonstrations, a summer pageant and boat races. For information on events in town call ☎ 615554.

A **farmers market** (🕙 10am-2pm) is held in Pendre Car Park in the Upper Market Hall of the Guildhall on the second and fourth Thursdays of the month, from April to December.

Sleeping

Nant y Croi Farm (☎ 614024; www.nant-y-croi.co.uk; Ferwig; sites per tent £10-15, B&B per person £25-30) This working farm, 4 miles north of Cardigan, offers B&B in the farmhouse, and camping on a site overlooking the sea. It has its own private cove, and is only 15 minutes' walk along the coastal path from the beach at Mwnt.

Poppit Sands Youth Hostel (☎ 0870 7705996; Sea View, Poppit; dm £14; 🕙 Easter-Oct) Tucked on a hillside overlooking the sweeping beach of Poppit Sands, this hostel is housed in a former inn close to the end of the Pembrokeshire Coastal Path. It's 3½ miles northwest of Cardigan; take bus 405 or 407 from Finch Sq to Poppit Sands, from where it's a half-mile walk.

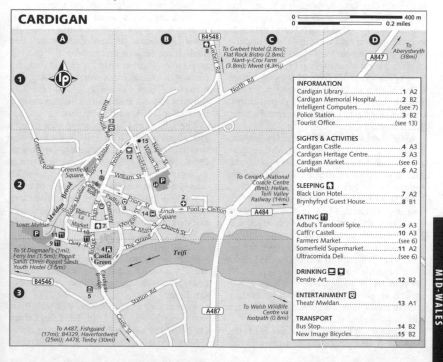

CARDIGAN

| INFORMATION |
| Cardigan Library.................................1 A2 |
| Cardigan Memorial Hospital...........2 B2 |
| Intelligent Computers.....................(see 7) |
| Police Station....................................3 B2 |
| Tourist Office...................................(see 13) |

| SIGHTS & ACTIVITIES |
| Cardigan Castle..................................4 A3 |
| Cardigan Heritage Centre................5 A3 |
| Cardigan Market..............................(see 6) |
| Guildhall...6 A2 |

| SLEEPING |
| Black Lion Hotel................................7 A2 |
| Brynhyfryd Guest House...................8 B1 |

| EATING |
| Adbul's Tandoori Spice.....................9 A3 |
| Caffi'r Castell....................................10 A3 |
| Farmers Market...............................(see 6) |
| Somerfield Supermarket..................11 A2 |
| Ultracomida Deli..............................(see 6) |

| DRINKING |
| Pendre Art...12 B2 |

| ENTERTAINMENT |
| Theatr Mwldan.................................13 A1 |

| TRANSPORT |
| Bus Stop..14 B2 |
| New Image Bicycles.........................15 B2 |

MID-WALES

Brynhyfryd Guest House (☎ 612861; g.arcus@btinternet .com; Park Place, Gwbert Rd; s/d £30/45) This large and long-established guesthouse is in a spacious Victorian villa less than ten minutes' walk northeast of the town centre; the hearty breakfast will set you up for the rest of the day.

Black Lion Hotel (☎ 612532; www.theblacklion cardigan.com; High St; s/d/t £40/60/90; **P**) A former coaching inn, the Black Lion has large, comfortable, pine-furnished rooms, some with timber beams and exposed stonework. There's also a family room that sleeps five (£120).

Gwbert Hotel (☎ 612638; www.gwberthotel.net; Gwbert-on-Sea; s/d from £50/80; **P**) With refurbished rooms decked out in stylish shades of cream, chocolate and red, stunning sea views (ask for room 3 or 4) and coastal walks beginning at the front door, the Gwbert – on the coast 3 miles north of town – makes a good out-of-town choice.

Eating & Drinking

Caffi'r Castell (☎ 621882; 26 Quay St; mains £2.50-5; ⏱ 9am-6pm) A deservedly busy little corner café, with sunny outdoor tables in summer, the Castell does good coffees, cakes and hot snacks.

Ultracomida Deli (Cardigan Market Hall, High St; mains £3-5; ⏱ deli 10am-4pm, café 10am-2.30pm Tue-Sat) This deli counter in the market hall serves hot panini, chunky Spanish tortilla and paella, as well as a perfect café latte made with organic Welsh milk. Sample local cheeses before you buy; it's a great place to shop for picnic food.

Ferry Inn (☎ 615172; Poppit Rd, St Dogmaels; mains £6-7) This is a snug old-fashioned pub overlooking the river on the road to Poppit Sands, with real ale, good food and a great deck for sunny days.

Abdul's Tandoori Spice (☎ 621416; 2 Royal Oak, Quay St; mains £6-10; ⏱ 5-11.45pm) Abdul's, which enjoys a loyal local following, is a cut above your usual curry house, with a warm and cosy atmosphere and consistently tasty tandoori dishes.

Flat Rock Bistro (☎ 612638; Gwbert Hotel, Gwbert-on-Sea; mains £8-15) Head three miles north to Gwbert for this stylish bistro with an outdoor terrace, great sea views and a menu of good seafood (roast sea bass with citrus butter), Welsh beef (fillet steak with stilton and port sauce) and a range of sandwiches and snacks.

Pendre Art (☎ 615151; 35 Pendre; ⏱ 10am-5pm Mon-Sat) This art gallery has an excellent coffee shop serving freshly ground Ferrari coffee and tea with home-baked scones.

For evening pub grub, your best bet is the **Black Lion Hotel** (see above). Self-caterers can shop at **Somerfield supermarket** (Lower Mwldan; ⏱ 8am-8pm Mon-Sat, 10am-4pm Sun).

Entertainment

Theatr Mwldan (☎ 621200; www.mwldan.co.uk; Bath House Rd) Located in the former slaughterhouse, Theatr Mwldan stages comedy, drama, dance, music and film, and has an art gallery and a good café. In the summer there are open-air productions.

Getting There & Away

Richards Brothers' bus 412 runs to Cardigan from Haverfordwest (£4, 1½ hours, hourly Monday to Saturday) and Fishguard (50 minutes). Richards Brothers' bus X50 goes to Aberystwyth (£4, 1½ hours, three daily Monday to Saturday).

AROUND CARDIGAN

The **Welsh Wildlife Centre** (☎ 01239-621600; admission free, parking £3; Visitor Centre ⏱ 10.30am-5pm Apr-Oct) is an interpretation centre for the Teifi Marshes Nature Reserve, just southeast of Cardigan. The reserve borders the River Teifi and features river, marsh and woodland habitats, and is a haven for birds, otters, badgers and butterflies.

There are several short waymarked trails, most of them wheelchair accessible. There are plans to improve the centre and install live feeds from remote cameras on the reserve and also on Skomer Island (p183) so that you can watch nesting birds without causing disturbance. There's also a shop and café. The centre is about a mile from Cardigan along a riverside path, or 4 miles by road.

The village of Cenarth occupies a picturesque spot on the River Teifi, at the foot of a stretch of rocky rapids. It's home to the **National Coracle Centre** (☎ 01239-710980; www.coracle-centre.co .uk; Cenarth; admission £3; ⏱ 10.30am-6pm Easter-Oct, 11am-4pm Thu-Sun Nov & Dec), a collection of coracles (small boats made of hide and wicker) from all over the world, along with exhibits and demonstrations showing how these fragile craft were made and used.

Cenarth is 8 miles southeast of Cardigan, and can be reached by taking First Cymru bus 460 (15 minutes, eight daily Monday to Saturday) from the main bus stop in Finch Sq, Cardigan.

Pocket-size steam locomotives puff their way along the wonderful little **Teifi Valley Railway** (☎ 01559-371077; www.teifivalleyrailway.co.uk; adult/child £5.50/3.50; ⏱ Apr-Oct), a 2-mile stretch of narrow-gauge line at Henllan (14 miles east of Cardigan). They run to a complicated timetable, so check on the website or with the Cardigan tourist office before making the trip.

First Cymru buses 460 and 461 run from Cardigan to Henllan (40 minutes, three daily Monday to Saturday).

ABERYSTWYTH

☎ 01970 / pop 12,000

Thanks to its status as one of the liveliest university towns in Wales, and its excellent range of options for eating out, drinking and taking in some great Welsh culture, Aberystwyth is an essential stop along the Ceredigion coast. It's a particularly buzzy town during term time and retains a cosmopolitan feel year-round. Alongside these facets of Aberystwyth life, the trappings of a stately Georgian seaside resort remain, with an impressive promenade skirted by a sweep of pastel-coloured buildings. Welsh is widely spoken here and locals are proud of their heritage.

When pub culture and student life get too much for you though, the quintessential Aberystwyth experience remains soaking up the sunset over Cardigan Bay and enjoying a moment's contemplation from the promenade.

History

Like many other towns in Wales, Aberystwyth is a product of Edward I's mania for castle-building. The now mainly ruined castle was erected in 1277; like many other castles in Wales it was captured by Owain Glyndŵr at the start of the 15th century and wrecked by Oliver Cromwell's forces during the Civil War. By the beginning of the 19th century, the town's walls and gates had completely disappeared.

The town developed a fishing industry, and silver and lead mining were also important here. With the arrival of the railway in 1864, it reinvented itself as a resort appealing to genteel Victorian sensibilities. In 1872 Aberystwyth was chosen as the site of the first college of the University of Wales, and in 1907 it became home to the National Library of Wales, a building which was dramatically but tastefully redeveloped following a £2.4 million investment grant from the Heritage Lottery Fund in 2001 (see p213).

Orientation

Aberystwyth sits where the River Rheidol and the smaller River Ystwyth empty into Cardigan Bay, at the end of the railway line that crosses Mid-Wales. Beaches make up the town's entire western side. The train station is located at the southeastern end of town at the bottom of Terrace Rd, a thoroughfare that dissects the town and leads directly to the North Sea seafront by means of a brisk 10-minute stroll.

Regional buses and National Express coaches stop just northeast of the train station on Alexandra Rd; a new stop for Traws-Cambria buses is located immediately east of the station forecourt.

Information

The **tourist office** (☎ 612125; cnr Terrace Rd & Bath St; ☽ 10am-5pm Mon-Sat Sep-Jun, 10am-6pm daily Jun-early Sep) is located downstairs in the same building as the Ceredigion Museum (see p213). This helpful office has a useful stock of maps and books on local history; staff can help to arrange accommodation.

All major UK banks have branches (with ATMs) on Great Darkgate St or around the corner on Terrace Rd. The **post office** (8 Great Darkgate St; ☽ 9am-5.30pm Mon-Fri, 9am-12.30pm Sat) has a foreign exchange facility. There's free internet access at the **library** (☎ 617464; Corporation St; ☽ 9.30am-8pm Mon-Fri, to 5pm Sat) and at the community-style centre, **Biognosis**, (☎ 636953; 21 Pier St; ☽ 10am-7pm Mon-Thu, to 5pm Fri), which charges £3 per hour (£2.50 per hour if you plug in your own laptop) and offers a raft of secretarial services, such as printing and fax.

Siop Y Pethe (Princess St) is a good, small bookshop with some Welsh language books and information on local folklore. **Galloway Bookshop** (Pier St) has an array of maps, guidebooks and novels.

The **University of Aberystwyth** (www.aber.ac.uk), with more than 7000 students, is split into two campuses – one at Penglais, about half a mile northeast up Penglais Rd (A487), and at Llanbadarn, a mile southeast of the centre.

Places to do your washing include **Maes-y-Môr** (Bath St; ☽ 8.30-9pm), which also offers budget accommodation, (see p213); **Wash 'n' Spin 'n' Dry** (Bridge St; ☽ 9-6pm) and **Laundrette** (75 North Pde; ☽ 9-7pm).

In case of emergency, **Bronglais Hospital** (☎ 623131; Caradoc Rd) is about 500m from the centre, off the A44; the **police station** (☎ 0845 3302000; Blvd St Brieuc) is two blocks south of the train station.

ABERYSTWYTH

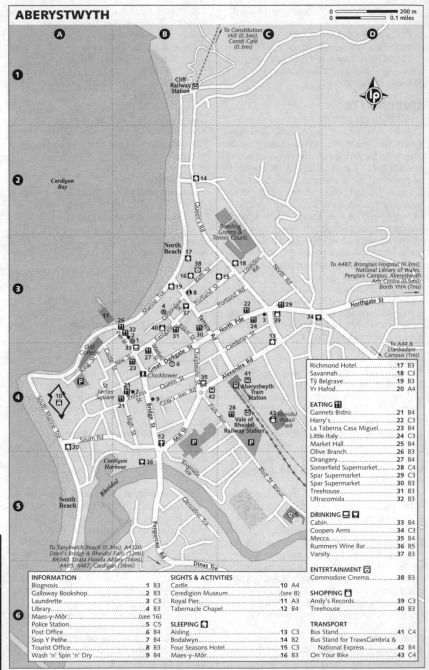

INFORMATION	
Biognosis................................1	B3
Galloway Bookshop................2	B3
Laundrette............................3	C3
Library..................................4	B3
Maes-y-Môr.......................(see 16)	
Police Station........................5	C5
Post Office............................6	B4
Siop Y Pethe.........................7	B4
Tourist Office.........................8	B3
Wash 'n' Spin 'n' Dry............9	B4

SIGHTS & ACTIVITIES	
Castle..................................10	A4
Ceredigion Museum...........(see 8)	
Royal Pier...........................11	A3
Tabernacle Chapel...............12	B4

SLEEPING	
Aisling.................................13	C3
Bodalwyn.............................14	B2
Four Seasons Hotel..............15	C3
Maes-y-Môr.........................16	B3

Richmond Hotel....................17	B3
Savannah.............................18	C3
Tŷ Belgrave..........................19	B3
Yr Hafod.............................20	A4

EATING	
Gannets Bistro......................21	B4
Harry's.................................22	C3
La Taberna Casa Miguel.......23	B4
Little Italy............................24	C3
Market Hall..........................25	B4
Olive Branch.........................26	B3
Orangery..............................27	B4
Somerfield Supermarket........28	C4
Spar Supermarket.................29	C3
Spar Supermarket.................30	B3
Treehouse............................31	B3
Ultracomida..........................32	B3

DRINKING	
Cabin...................................33	B4
Coopers Arms.......................34	C3
Mecca.................................35	B4
Rummers Wine Bar................36	B5
Varsity.................................37	B3

ENTERTAINMENT	
Commodore Cinema..............38	B3

SHOPPING	
Andy's Records.....................39	C3
Treehouse............................40	B3

TRANSPORT	
Bus Stand.............................41	C4
Bus Stand for TrawsCambria &	
National Express..................42	B4
On Your Bike........................43	C4

MID-WALES

Sights & Activities

ALONG THE WATERFRONT

A stroll along Marine Tce, the walkway overlooking North Beach, is the most genteel pursuit on offer and one that harks back to the town's erstwhile halcyon days as a Victorian resort. When you reach the bottom of the 1.5-mile prom, it's customary to kick the white bar, although the locals can't seem to explain the rationale behind this ritual.

North Beach is lined by faintly shabby Georgian hotels, albeit with a couple of notable exceptions. The top-heavy **Royal Pier** lumbers out to sea under the weight of its cheerfully tacky amusements arcade. North Beach is also the main swimming beach as South Beach has few facilities, although both beaches have lifeguards and an EU blue-flag rating. Many locals prefer the stony but emptier **Tanybwlch Beach**, just south of the harbour where the Rivers Rheidol and Ystwyth meet. It's a great spot for a bracing stroll and some terrific ozone-fuelled views.

The enigmatic, sparse ruins of the **castle** sit looking out to sea from the corner of the prom, which pivots and leads along South Beach – a more desolate, but still attractive seafront.

CONSTITUTION HILL

At the northern end of North Beach is Aberystwyth's headland, **Constitution Hill** (430ft). Victorian tourists enjoyed a stately ride to the summit from 1896 onwards, and you can too, on the trundling little **Cliff Railway** (☎ 617642; adult/child £2.50/1.50; ⏲ 10am-6pm Apr-Oct, 10am-5pm Nov-Mar), the UK's longest electric funicular and possibly the slowest too at a G-force-busting 4mph.

From the wind-blown balding hilltop there are tremendous, long coastal views – 60 miles from the Llŷn to Strumble Head – and you can spot 26 mountain peaks including Snowdon. The site has been redeveloped in recent years with new children's attractions, including gold panning and go-karts. The erstwhile Victorian tearooms have been rebuilt in line with environmental considerations and the resulting **Consti Café** (⏲ 10am-5pm Mon-Wed & Sun, to 9pm Thu-Sat; lunch specials around £5, steaks from £10) is a café by day and licensed steakhouse three nights per week. It also features displays of the wildlife you can spot on a, ahem, constitutional around the hill. One relic of the Victorian structure that survived the revamp is a **camera obscura** (an immense pinhole camera or projecting telescope) that allows you to see practically into the windows of the houses below.

VALE OF RHEIDOL RAILWAY

One of Aberystwyth's most popular attractions is a one-hour ride on the **narrow-gauge railway** (☎ 625819; www.rheidolrailway.co.uk; adult/child return £12.50, £3 each for first 2 children, £6.25 each additional child; 2 departures per day in low season, 4 in summer), one of the most scenic of Wales' many 'little trains'. Old steam locomotives, lovingly restored by volunteers, chug for almost 12 miles up the valley of the River Rheidol to Devil's Bridge (see above). The line opened in 1902 to bring lead and timber out of the valley; the engines were built by the Great Western Railway between 1923 and 1938.

NATIONAL LIBRARY

Half a mile east of town, the **National Library of Wales** (☎ 623800; www.llgc.org.uk; admission free; ⏲ 9.30am-5pm Mon-Sat) is an imposing hilltop spread of a building, with great views. It holds superb, intelligent, innovative exhibitions – at one of these, visitors were invited to graffiti their comments on the walls – and opened a new visitor centre in 2003. Founded in 1911, the library holds more than five million books in many languages – it's a copyright library so it has copies of every book published in the UK. Among its ancient manuscripts is the oldest existing Welsh text, the 12th-century *Black Book of Carmarthen*. The turn is off Penglais Rd, taking a right just beyond the hospital.

CEREDIGION MUSEUM

The **Ceredigion Museum** (☎ 633088; Terrace Rd; admission free; ⏲ 10am-5pm Mon-Sat), sharing a building with the tourist office, is located in the Coliseum, which opened in 1905 as a theatre and served as a cinema from 1932 onwards. It has a wonderful spacious, elegant interior, complete with stage, and features entertaining exhibitions on Aberystwyth's history – everything from pianos played for silent films to old chemist furnishings and hand-knitted woollen knickers.

Sleeping

Borth YHA (☎ 08707 705708; Morlais; dm adult/child £11.95/8.95; ⏲ mid-Mar–Oct) This Edwardian property situated at Borth, seven miles north of Aberystwyth along the B4572, is best known for its setting: overlooking Cardigan Bay and just a stone's throw from the beach with a blue-flag rating.

Maes-y-Môr (☎ 639270; 25 Bath St; dm £15) Yes, that is a laundrette. But don't be fooled: venture upstairs from the drying machine and there's a clean, bright and inviting independent hostel with 15 beds – it's the cheapest place to sleep in the city centre.

Savannah (☎ 651131; www.savannahguesthouse.co.uk; 27 Queen's Rd; s/d from £26/52) Central, cheap and relatively cheerful, this is the pick of the budget options for a bed in the heart of the city centre.

Aisling (☎ 626980; 21 Alexandra Rd; s/d £30/50; ✖) The closest B&B to the train station, Aisling (the name means 'a dream' in Irish Gallic) is a welcoming spot. The rooms may be a bit flowery but the Irish landlady is very knowledgeable about the local area.

Yr Hafod (☎ 617579; 1 South Marine Tce; s/d £30/50) The best of the B&Bs along this stretch of the seafront, this place has basic rooms but great sea views and friendly service.

Bodalwyn (☎ 612578; www.bodalwyn.co.uk; Queen's Rd; s/d/fm £45/65/80; ✖ P) This upmarket B&B in a handsome Edwardian house feels like a big, comfy family house. The rooms have tasteful fittings and the owners serve up a huge breakfast (with vegetarian options), making for an all-round comfortable stay – a touch of class while feeling right at home.

Four Seasons Hotel (☎ 612120; www.fourseasonshotel.uk.com; 50-54 Portland St; s/d £50/75) The sister property to Tŷ Belgrave is older and humbler, offering a comfortable midrange option, located down a quiet sidestreet.

Tŷ Belgrave (☎ 630553; www.tybelgravehouse.co.uk; Marine Tce; s/d/fm £50/75/80; ✖ P) The latest opening in town is also by far the smartest, with a very contemporary feel and good facilities – including wi-fi internet to cater for the business market. Rooms are tastefully decorated with a dash of funky boutique-hotel chic while a downstairs bar and lounge area is the place to take in the view across the bay from a comfy leather sofa.

Richmond Hotel (☎ 612201; www.richmondhotel.uk.com; 44-50 Marine Tce; s/d from £55/85) The Richmond is a typical seaside hotel with bay-fronted windows overlooking Cardigan Bay. Professional but plain, it's a good family option but these days lacks its former sparkle.

Eating

Ultra Comida (☎ 630686; Pier St; ⏲ 10-6pm Mon-Fri, to 5pm Sat) Spanish, French and Welsh produce are the mainstays of this excellent little deli. Currently it's only take-away fare, but the owners are planning an extension for a small restaurant to be added in 2007.

La Taberna Casa Miguel (☎ 627677; 1 New St; tapas £4 per dish, paella for 2 people £18; ⏲ 6.30-10pm Mon-Sat) Spanish cuisine and tapas are the house specials at this popular little eatery one block back from the pier.

Little Italy (☎ 625707; 51 North Pde; mains £8 ⏲ 5.45pm-late Mon-Fri, 10am-late Sat & Sun) With red-and-white chequered tablecloths, this is the cosy, wine-bottle-in-baskets kind of Italian eatery. It's also popular, with a big menu of traditional Italian favourites including good vegetarian options. There's also a decent Sunday lunch (£8). Main meals on other days are around the same price.

Orangery (☎ 617606; Market St; mains £10; ⏲ 10am-11pm) The smartest place in town brings a brand-new sense of style to Aberystwyth: think palm trees and wicker chairs arranged around chunky wooden tables strewn with newspapers, all located in the erstwhile Talbot Inn, a 19th-century coaching house. The space is divided between a restaurant, a cocktail bar with bar snacks (around £8) and a family room where children are welcome until 8pm. Quality produce and a lively feel add to the kudos.

Olive Branch (☎ 630572; 35 Pier St; mains £10; ⏲ 9.30am-10pm daily) A newcomer to the local dining scene, this Greek restaurant is open all day for fair-trade Arabic coffee, snack lunches (toasties around £2.50) and traditional Greek dinners with a mix of dips, spreads and hot and cold meze. If the fug gets too much downstairs, head up to the quieter, nonsmoking restaurant on the second floor.

Treehouse (☎ 615791; 14 Baker St; ⏲ 9.30am-5pm Mon-Sat) Located upstairs from an inviting food shop in an attractive Victorian house, this excellent organic restaurant uses locally grown produce. A wide menu of organic fare makes this one of the best places for lunch in town. It's sister venue is the Treehouse fair-trade shop (see opposite).

Gannets Bistro (☎ 617164; 7 St James Square; mains £12; ⏲ noon-2pm & 6-9.30pm Mon, Wed-Sat) A cheery, long-standing bistro, this bistro offers hearty food in huge portions, with lots of fresh fish, simply cooked. There are decent vegetarian options.

Harry's (☎ 612647; www.harrysaberystwyth.com; 40-46 North Pde; mains £12; ⏲ 6-10.30pm Mon-Sat) Candle-lit, warm and friendly, Harry's restaurant is a smart place, serving up an imaginative menu of tasty, well-presented meals to patrons in a relaxed bistro-style setting. Local fish is a house speciality and there's also a stylish bar area for a pre-prandial snifter. Upstairs is accommodation, with a maze of cheery and comfortable rooms for visitors (s/d £50/60).

For self-caterers, there are two **Spar supermarkets** (Northgate St & Terrace Rd) and a **Somerfield supermarket** is beside the train station.

A big **farmers market** (and crafts fair) clusters around the **Market Hall** (St James Square) on the third Friday of the month.

Drinking

Mecca (☎ 61288; 25 Chalybeale St; 🕑 9am-5.30pm Mon-Sat) This great little café serves up superb espressos and a range of specialty teas and coffees. Directly opposite, the Mecca shop is great for stocking up on caffeine-addict paraphernalia.

Cabin (☎ 617398; Pier St; 🕑 9.30-5pm Mon-Sat) A simple little coffee shop with lots of pictures of old film stars on the walls, this is a relaxed spot for coffees and snacks.

Varsity (☎ 615234; Portland St; 💻) Spacious, simple and student-friendly, Varsity has huge pipes running around the ceiling and big windows for watching activity on the street. It's packed on weekend nights and relaxing during the daytime when you can make the most of the free wi-fi internet.

Rummers Wine Bar (☎ 625177; Bridge St) Right by the river, this popular place has seats outside for summer nights, a friendly vibe and some live bands. Bar food is served evenings only.

Coopers Arms (☎ 624050; Northgate St) This popular, friendly pub is good for a pint and a chance to catch some live music.

Entertainment

One of the largest arts centres in Wales, **Aberystwyth Arts Centre** (☎ 623232; www.aberystwythartscentre.co.uk; Penglais Rd; box office 🕑 10am-8pm Mon-Sat, 1.30pm-5.30pm Sun) has excellent opera, drama, dance and concerts (all of which can also be booked at the tourist office), plus a bookshop, an art gallery and a good, albeit slightly uncomfortably stylish, café. The cinema in particular shows a good range of world and foreign-language cinema. The centre is half a mile east of the town centre.

Commodore Cinema (☎ 612421; www.commodorecinema.co.uk; Bath St) shows current mainstream releases in the evening and has a weekend matinee. There's even a bar here for a pre-flick beer.

Aberystwyth Male Voice Choir (Mill St; free entry) rehearses at the Tabernacle Chapel at 7.45pm most Thursdays, except during August.

Shopping

Andy's Records (☎ 624581; 4 Northgate St; 🕑 10am-5.30pm Mon-Sat) is a handy independent record shop that also sells gig tickets for bands at the university.

Treehouse (☎ 625116; www.treehousewales.co.uk; 3 Eastgate St; 🕑 9am-6pm Mon-Fri, 9am-5pm Sat) The sister property to the Treehouse deli and restaurant (opposite), this great little boutique specialises in organic and fair-trade homewares and baby goods.

Getting There & Away

BUS

Major bus connections include:

Arriva buses 550 and X50 to Cardigan (two hours, hourly), with a change of bus near New Quay.

Arriva buses 28 to Dolgellau (two hours 20 minutes, five daily Monday to Saturday) via Machynlleth (45 minutes, every two hours).

Arriva bus X32 to Bangor (three hours 15 minutes, four daily).

Arriva's TrawsCambria bus X40 goes to Cardiff (four hours, twice daily).

National Express coach 419 runs once daily to London (seven hours) via Birmingham (four hours).

TRAIN

Aberystwyth is the terminus of Arriva's Cambrian Coast railway line, which crosses Mid-Wales en route to Shrewsbury (£15.90, one hour 55 minutes) via Machynlleth (£3.80, 30 minutes). Services run every two hours (less frequently on Sunday). The Cambrian Coast line also runs to Pwllheli (£10, four hours, every two hours).

Getting Around

The quickest bus to/from the Penglais campus (five minutes, every 15 minutes) is Arriva's bus 501.

On Your Bike (☎ 626532; Craft, Rheidol Retail Park; 🕑 9am-5pm Mon-Sat) hires out mountain bikes from £12 a day.

AROUND ABERYSTWYTH

Devil's Bridge & Rheidol Falls

The dramatic **Devil's Bridge** (☎ 890233; adult/child £2.50/1.30; 🕑 9.45am-5pm Apr-Oct, other times access via Number 2 turnstile) spans the Rheidol Valley on the lush western slopes of the 2400ft Plynlimon Fawr (Pumlumon), source of the Rivers

Wye and Severn. Here the Rivers Mynach and Rheidol tumble together in a narrow gorge.

The Mynach is spanned by three famous stone bridges. The lowest and oldest is believed to have been built by the monks of Strata Florida Abbey before 1188. Just above the confluence, the Rheidol drops 90m in a series of spectacular waterfalls. Access to the waterfalls and the old bridges is from beside the topmost bridge, which is itself 300m downhill from the terminus of the Vale of Rheidol Railway. There are two possible walks: one, to view the three bridges, takes only 10 minutes; the other, a half-hour walk, descends 100 steps (Jacob's Ladder), crosses the Mynach and ascends the other side, passing what is said to have been a robbers' cave.

The Vale of Rheidol Railway (see p213) is the most delightful way to reach Devil's Bridge. An alternative is the new Rheidol Cycle Trail, a 22-mile, partly off-road trail that shadows and occasionally crisscrosses the A4120 through the Rheidol Valley.

Strata Florida Abbey
On an isolated, peaceful site southeast of Aberystwyth lies this 12th-century **Cistercian abbey** (☎ 01974-831261; adult/child £2/1.50; 🕑 10am-5pm Apr-Sep). The sparse ruins retain a simple, complete arch, with lines like thick rope, and there are two covered chapels with some 14th-century tiling. The Cistercians were a monastic order with roots in France, and the community at Strata Florida (Ystrad Fflur or 'Valley of the Flowers') was founded in 1164 by a Norman lord named Robert FitzStephen.

After Welsh resurgence in the southwest however, the independent, self-sufficient Cistercians won the support of the Welsh princes. Their abbeys also became a focus for literary activity and influence. The present site was established under Lord Rhys ap Gruffydd, and a number of princes of Deheubarth, as well as the great 14th-century poet Dafydd ap Gwilym, are buried here.

The site is a mile down a farm road from the village of Pontrhydfendigaid on the B4343; the village is 15 miles from Aberystwyth or 9.5 miles south of Devil's Bridge. Bus T21 (£2, 45 minutes) has four daily services Monday to Saturday from Aberystwyth, with four daily services Monday to Saturday running in the opposite direction from Pontrhydfendigaid.

SOUTHERN POWYS

LLANWRTYD WELLS (LLANWRTYD)
☎ 01591 / pop 800

Llanwrtyd (khlan-*oor*-tid) Wells is an odd little town: mostly deserted but, during one of its weird and wacky festivals, packed to the rafters with an influx of merrymakers. According to the *Guinness Book of Records*, it is the UK's smallest town – some local residents even claim that to cling onto this status there's a periodic cull.

The one certainty is that, despite its newfound status as the capital of wacky Wales, Llanwrtyd Wells is surrounded by beautiful walking, cycling and riding country with the Cambrian Mountains to the northwest and the Mynydd Eppynt to the southeast. When you're not outdoors, the festival of unorthodox events now extends to cover each month of the year.

Theophilus Evans, the local vicar, first discovered the healing properties of the Ffynon Droellwyd (Stinking Well) in 1732 and found it cured his scurvy. The popularity of the waters grew and Llanwrtyd became a spa town. Nowadays, however, its wells have been capped and, outside of the festivals, it's hard to find much by way of vital signs.

Orientation & Information
The town centre is Y Sgwar (The Square), the five-way intersection by the old bridge on which the A483 crosses the River Irfon. Virtually nothing in town is much more than a stone's throw away from here. The train station is a located half a mile south of the tourist office.

The independently run **tourist office** (☎ 610666; http://llanwrtyd-wells.powys.org.uk; Irfon Tce; 🕑 10am-6pm Mon, Wed-Sat) is staffed by volunteers and has been keeping erratic hours due to a shortage of staff. When it is open, they sell useful walking and cycling leaflets and offer free **internet access** (£2.50 per hr).

The police station is right next door and a Barclays Bank, directly opposite, is the only bank in town. There's no ATM.

Take your chances with **car parking** – there's a roadside space just over the bridge by the **post office** (🕑 9am-1pm & 2-5.30pm Mon-Fri, 9am-12.30pm Sat).

Activities
The hills around Llanwrtyd are crisscrossed with country lanes, bridlepaths and footpaths, with distractingly beautiful scenery – it's dream

---

THE BOG STAR

Twenty or so years ago, while mulling over a pint on how to encourage tourism in Llanwrtyd in the dark winter months, some citizens started an inspired roll call of unconventionality. The first of the town's unusual events was the **Man Versus Horse Marathon** in 1980. This has become an annual jamboree each June, and has resulted in some tense finishes – a two-legged runner won for the first time in 2004 (the prize is £25,000).

Very well subscribed are the **Real Ale Wobble** and **Real Ale Ramble** (on bikes and foot respectively), with pint rather than pit stops (both held annually in autumn).

At New Year, the ancient practice of parading a horse's skull from house to house while reciting Welsh poetry (the horse's jaw mouths the words) has been revived.

Most famous of all, however, is the **World Bog Snorkelling Championships**, which attracts an international field. Competitors are allowed snorkels and flippers to get along the 60-yard trench, but may not use conventional swimming strokes. There are prizes for the slowest time as well as the fastest. One runner-up said: 'It's an unforgiving sport, you get bitten by insects, very dirty, smelly and you are wet all day.' Another variation involves cycling through the bog trench (like trying to ride through treacle).

Many of these ideas were generated by Gordon Green, who ran the Neuadd Arms for 26 years. One future proposal is a race between a Celtic and Roman chariot, as part of the Saturnalia Roman Festival in January. Saturnalia currently involves, among other things, tucking into stuffed bull's testicles – a Roman treat.

---

territory for horse riders, mountain-bikers (with lots of forest trails) and ramblers.

The main activity operator in town is the **Red Kite Mountain Bike Centre** (☎ 610236; www .neuaddarmshotel.co.uk; Y Sgwar) based at the Neuadd Arms Hotel (see right), which runs walking, biking or pony trekking trips. Prices for an all-inclusive weekend start from £90 per person, based on full-board B&B accommodation and two days' guided biking.

Sleeping & Eating

Stonecroft Lodge (☎ 610327; www.stonecroft.co.uk; Dolecoed Rd; dm £14; bar meals £9; 🕙 5-11pm, meals noon-2.45pm Fri-Sun & 6.15-8.45pm daily) This independent, bunk-free hostel is located above a friendly, popular pub with something of a party vibe, real ales, live music and bar meals. There are 28 beds split over nine rooms, some of which are doubles or family rooms providing extra privacy; prices are hiked by a few pounds during events and bank holidays but all bedding is provided. The owner takes an active role in local events and also rents out a self-catering holiday cottage (from £500 for two nights).

Drovers Rest (☎ 610264; www.food-food-food.co.uk; Y Sgwar; s/d £25/48; café meals 🕙 10.30am-5.30pm, dinner 7.30-9.30pm) This restaurant with rooms is better known for the former than the latter with a snug little restaurant serving up the best of local fresh produce. By day it's a relaxed affair but in the evening the dinner is a grander, fine-dining

experience (from £25.95); Sunday roasts (12.30 to 2.30pm; from £10.50) are also excellent. The owners also run regular cooking classes – call for details of the next course.

Neuadd Arms Hotel (☎ 610236; www.neuaddarms hotel.co.uk; Y Sgwar; s/d £32/55; bar meals £6, set menu from £13.50) The town's big, central inn has basic B&B rooms in a creaky old place, but at least the bar has a roaring fire to keep out winter chills. Eating options are good, with the bar given over to bar meals and a more formal dining room serving a table d'hôte menu. It's also the base for activity weekends organised by the Red Kite Mountain Bike Centre (see left).

Lasswade (☎ 610515; www.lasswadehotel.co.uk; s/d from £50/70; ✗ ℗) The closest place to the train station, Lasswade is an Edwardian country-house-style property which has good green credentials given its pro-organic stance and nonsmoking policy. The rooms tend towards the floral but there are also some nice touches, such as a sauna and a drying room for walkers' kits. The decent breakfast is served in a conservatory area with great rural views.

Carlton House (☎ 610248; www.carltonrestaurant.co.uk; DoleCoed Rd; r £60-90; mains £23; 🕙 dinner Mon-Sat) This upscale restaurant with rooms has a boutique feel and a mantelpiece that positively groans under the strain of awards for its foodie achievements. The rooms are traditional and tasteful but it's the restaurant that attracts the greatest critical acclaim for its changing menu, imaginative use of local produce and impressive wine list. Ask about all-inclusive foodie breaks.

Getting There & Away

The best way to reach Llanwrtyd is on the Heart of Wales railway line, as spa guests did a century ago. Services run to Llandrindod Wells (£3.20, 30 minutes, four daily Monday to Saturday, one Sunday), and Swansea (£10.50, one hour 55 minutes).

There are scant useful bus services; ask the tourist office for details of rare local bus connections.

BUILTH WELLS (LLANFAIR-YM-MUALLT)

☎ 01982 / pop 2350

Builth (pronounced bilth) Wells is by far the most lively and worthwhile of the former spa towns, with a bustling, workaday feel. Once the playground of the Welsh working classes, today it's based around a few main streets and sits prettily on the river.

While there are few attractions per se, it's a good base for the area, particularly for walkers on the Wye Valley walk and bikers on the Lôn Las Cymru cycle route, with decent eating and dining options. Book well ahead, however, during the **Royal Welsh Agricultural Show** (www.rwas.co .uk), when farmers flock to the town for this annual event, held at the end of July. The show, which was founded in 1904, involves everything from livestock judging to lumberjack competitions. The event is organised by the **Royal Welsh Agricultural Society** (☎ 553683) and held at the Royal Welsh Showgrounds at Llanelwedd, just across the bridge over the River Wye.

There's a massive range of other events held there too, such as the **Bike Show** in May, when a grungy biker crowd roar into town, and the **Dog Show** in August, which attracts around 11,000 mutts.

Cilmery, two miles up the Llandovery road, is where Llywelyn ap Gruffydd, last of the Welsh Princes of Wales, was killed in a chance encounter with a lone English soldier in 1282. The spot is marked with a sad obelisk of Caernarfon granite.

Orientation and Information

The very helpful **tourist office** (☎ 553307; www .builth-wells.co.uk; The Grow; ☒ 9.30am-5pm Mon-Sat, 10am-4pm Sun Apr-Oct, 9.30am-4pm Mon-Fri, 10am-4pm Sat Nov-Mar) is located in the **car park** (£0.40 per hr)

by the 18th-century arched bridge, next to a distinctive statue of the Welsh black bull.

Buses stop behind the tourist office, but the nearest train station to Builth Wells is over two miles away: Builth Road station is on the Rhayader road (A470), and Cilmery station is up the Llandovery road (A483); a **taxi** (☎ 663630) from either costs about £3.

High St is the focal point of the action. The **post office** (☒ 8.30am-5.30pm Mon-Fri, 9am-1pm Sat), next door to the Spar supermarket on High St, has foreign exchange facilities. Banks line High St while the **library** (☒ 9.30am-1pm & 2-5pm Mon, Tue & Fri, 9.30am-1pm & 2-7pm Thu, 9.30am-12.30pm Sat), also on High St, has free internet access.

The **Solitaire laundrette** (20 West St; ☒ 11am-6pm Mon, Tue, Thu-Sat, noon-5pm Sun) is located just east of the Greyhound Hotel (see below).

For ordinance survey (OS) maps and information about local history, head for **Foreman's Emporium** (☎ 552034; 25 High St; ☒ 9am-5.30pm Mon-Sat).

Sleeping

Woodlands (☎ 552354; Hay Rd; s/d £35/50; P) A traditional Edwardian house, this place is set up a private driveway and five minutes further back along the main road from the Lion Hotel (see below). The four rooms, all en suite, offer simple home comforts at a budget price.

Greyhound Hotel (☎ 553255; www.thegreyhoundhotel .co.uk; 3 Garth Rd; s/d £55/75, bar meals £7; P) Situated at the northwest end of town by the Wesley Methodist Church, this is a stately pub with tidy rooms and decent bar food. Catch the local male voice choir rehearsal here on Monday nights (see opposite).

Lion Hotel (☎ 553311; www.lionhotelbuilthwells.com; 2 Broad St; s/d/fm £65/95/100; ☐ P) Recently given a major refit, this smart place now has a much more contemporary look and boasts some disabled-access rooms. The rooms are tastefully decorated, some with views of the River Wye, and the installation of wi-fi internet now attracts a business-traveller crowd. Foodwise the stakes have also been raised, so while the smoky bar area remains the locals' favourite, the dining room now offers both bar meals and finer dining options, with food served all day.

Eating

Cosy Corner (☎ 551700; 55 High St; ☒ 9am-5pm Mon-Sat) A simple tearoom with homemade cakes and coffees in an 18th-century, white-fronted building.

Calon Wen (☎ 07765-812739; 3 Groe St; mains £10; ☺ 10am-4pm Mon-Wed, 10am-10pm Thu-Sat, noon-3pm Sun) The newest opening in town makes for an interesting addition to the Builth dining scene: a South African café by day and bistro by night. The owners bring a touch of African panache to the menu – local produce meets African recipes – plus there's a daytime selection of homemade cakes, pastries and coffees. The menu changes every day.

Drawing Room (☎ 552493; www.the-drawing-room .co.uk; dinner & B&B from £95 per person per night; ▢ ✖ Ⓟ) Foodies flock to the boutique restaurant with rooms located four miles from Builth Wells along the A470. The quality of the cuisine is excellent, even award winning, albeit at a steep premium price. Problem is that at these prices you would expect a moderately friendly welcome – but sadly no. Great food if you can put up with the attitude.

For self caterers there's a **Spar supermarket** (☺ 8am-9pm daily) on High St.

Entertainment

The thriving **Wyeside Arts Centre** (☎ 552555; www .wyeside.co.uk; Castle St; ☺ box office noon-9pm Tue-Fri, 6-9pm Sat & Sun) is a great little venue with a bar, exhibitions, cinema and live shows. It's located where the A470 comes into the eastern end of town.

Getting There & Away

Roy Brown's Coaches bus 17 (alternate Saturdays) runs between Rhayader (45 minutes) and Cardiff (two hours).

Crossgates Coaches bus 21 runs services to/from Llandrindod Wells (25 minutes, two to four daily Monday to Saturday).

Crossgates Coaches & Roy Brown's Coaches run services to Rhayader (30 minutes, four daily Monday to Saturday).

Roy Brown's Coaches bus 55 runs services to Newtown (one hour 10 minutes, once daily).

It's best to check with the local tourist office for up-to-date bus timetables and prices, as these change from season to season, and services are often cut and rescheduled.

HAY-ON-WYE (Y GELLI)
☎ 01497 / pop 1500

Hay-on-Wye, the world's second-hand book capital, is a charmingly eccentric little town. Indeed, the town has many literary associations: Bruce Chatwin's *On the Black Hill* is set in the Black Mountains, and both Tom Maschler of Jonathan Cape and singer George Melly claimed that Chatwin wrote the book while staying with them here. Some of the film *American Werewolf in London* was shot nearby, around Hay Bluff; and Iain Sinclair's novel *Landor's Tower* takes a poetic poke at local booksellers.

More recently Hay has become synonymous with its **literature festival** (p222), which sees the small population swell to over 80,000 and an influx of big-name stars come to read form their latest tomes. The former US president, Bill Clinton, was a high-profile visitor in 2001 and christened the event 'The Woodstock of the mind'. Today the whole event is now sponsored by the *Guardian* newspaper and has become a major cultural event.

AUTHOR'S CHOICE

A 17th-century stone farmhouse in the Edw Valley, six miles from Builth Wells along the B467, **Cwm-Moel** (☎ 570271; Aberedw; r from £30; three-course meal £14) is a great spot to enjoy some famous Welsh hospitality and a chance to blow away the big-city cobwebs. But, unlike your communal garden rural Welsh bolthole, guests at Cwm-Moel have to – quite literally – sing for their supper.

The owner, Eleanor Madoc Davies, has over 30 years experience of teaching music and has been performing since the age of three, when she first formed a vocal harmony group with her sisters for the local eisteddfod. Recently she set up the seven-bed, family-run B&B and, while her husband, Mervyn, looks after the livestock at the farm down the road, she offers one-on-one vocal coaching in her dedicated music room. She offers a free half-hour singing assessment with lessons charged at £25 per hour thereafter – ask about B&B and singing package deals.

For guests in need of inspiration, she even takes groups to the see the Builth Male Voice Choir rehearse in an upstairs room of the Greyhound Hotel in Builth Wells (see opposite). The choir formed in 1968 as a rugby choir and now sing internationally. Practice is every Monday night; visitors are welcome to attend for free.

MID-WALES

Hay is also now synonymous with self-promotion, thanks mainly to the efforts of Richard Booth, the colourful, self-styled King of Hay (see boxed text opposite), who kick-started Hay literary aspirations when he opened the first bookshop in 1961. In 1971 Booth bought Hay Castle, complete with the Jacobean mansion built within its walls. The castle was damaged by a fire in 1977 and repair work is ongoing.

The small town centre is made up of narrow sloping lanes, peppered by interesting shops, and peopled by the differing types that such individuality and so many books tend to attract. Even outside of festival time, Hay has a vague Glastonbury-festival vibe, with more than its fair share of New-Age types attracted to soak up the alternative ambience. But while it's busy during the day, the evenings tend to be library-quiet – everyone must be reading.

If books are not your bag, Hay is also a great base for exploring the stunning Black Mountains. Indeed, Offa's Dyke and the Offa's Dyke Path run right through the centre of town.

History

Hay has had a tempestuous history, due to its borderlands position almost on the dividing line between England and Wales. In fact, at the time of the Norman conquest it was administered separately as English Hay (the town proper) and Welsh Hay (the countryside to the south and west).

Around 1200 William de Braose II, one of the Norman barons (marcher lords), built a castle here on the site of an earlier one. For the next three-and-a-half centuries Hay changed hands many times. Following the Tudor Acts of Union in 1536 and 1543 (see p32) it settled down as a market town, and by the 18th century it had become a centre of the flannel trade.

Orientation & Information

Hay's small centre contains the castle and most of the bookshops. The border with England runs along Dulas Brook, which crosses under Newport St just north of the centre. Buses stop near the tourist office on Oxford Rd and **car parking** is available (per hr 40p) in a panoramic car park also on Oxford Rd with great views across the surrounding countryside.

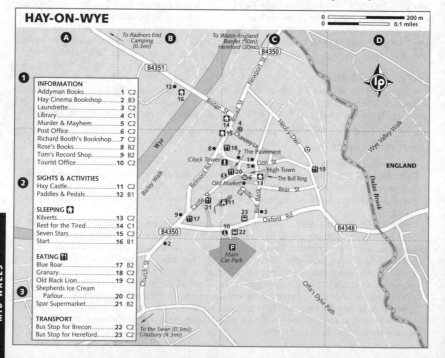

HAY-ON-WYE

0   200 m
0   0.1 miles

INFORMATION
Addyman Books...............1 C2
Hay Cinema Bookshop........2 B3
Laundrette...................3 C2
Library......................4 C1
Murder & Mayhem............5 C2
Post Office..................6 C2
Richard Booth's Bookshop....7 C2
Rose's Books.................8 B2
Tom's Record Shop...........9 B2
Tourist Office...............10 C2

SIGHTS & ACTIVITIES
Hay Castle...................11 C2
Paddles & Pedals.............12 B1

SLEEPING
Kilverts.....................13 C2
Rest for the Tired...........14 C1
Seven Stars..................15 C2
Start........................16 B1

EATING
Blue Boar....................17 B2
Granary......................18 C2
Old Black Lion...............19 C2
Shepherds Ice Cream
   Parlour....................20 C2
Spar Supermarket.............21 B2

TRANSPORT
Bus Stop for Brecon..........22 C2
Bus Stop for Hereford........23 C2

To Radnors End Camping (0.3mi)

To Wales–England Border (50m); Hereford (20mi)

B4350
B4351
B4350
B4348

Newport St
Broad St
Bridge St
Heol-y-Dwr
Wye Valley Walk

ENGLAND

Chancery La
The Pavement
Clock Tower
Lion St
Belmont Rd
Bailey Walk
High Town
The Bull Ring
Old Market
Bear St
Castle St
Bell Bank
Oxford Rd
Church St

Dulas Brook

Main Car Park

Offa's Dyke Path

To the Swan (0.3mi); Glasbury (4.3mi)

MID-WALES

The professional **tourist office** (☎ 820144; www
.hay-on-wye.co.uk; Oxford Rd; ◷ 10am-5pm Apr-Oct, 11am-
1pm & 2-4pm Nov-Mar) stocks a free guide and map
showing all of Hay's bookshops (most bookshops have the map, too). You can also access the internet here (75p per 30 minutes),
or there's free internet access at the **library**
(Chancery Lane; ◷ 10am-1pm & 2-5pm Thu & Fri, 9.30am-
1pm Sat, 10am-1pm, 2-4.30pm & 5-7pm Mon). Book fans
can look for particular books at www.book
search-at-hay.com.

There's also a **post office** (High Town; ◷ 9am-
1pm & 2-5.30pm Mon, Wed, Fri, 9am-5.30pm Thu, 9am-
12.30pm Tue & Sat) and a **laundrette** (Bell Bank;
◷ 8am-9pm Mon-Sat). Banks are located along
Castle St.

BOOKSHOPS

There are 30 bookshops in Hay, mostly stocking second-hand books – 400,000 in Richard
Booth's bookshop alone. Many bookshops
cover all subjects, while others concentrate on
one speciality. In addition, three bookbinders
base themselves locally. Bookshops generally
open 9.30am to 5.30pm with extended hours
during the festival.

Addyman Books (☎ 821136; www.hay-on-wyebooks
.com; 39 Lion St) Stocks books on all sorts of subjects, has a
sitting room upstairs and a sci-fi room.

Hay Cinema Bookshop (☎ 820071; www.haycinema
bookshop.co.uk; Castle St) In a converted cinema, this is a
cavernous place, stacked with tomes.

Murder & Mayhem (☎ 821613; 5 Lion St) Filled to the
brim with detective fiction, true crime and horror.

Richard Booth's Bookshop (☎ 820322; www.richard
booth.demon.co.uk; 44 Lion St) The most famous, and still
the best; has a sizable Anglo-Welsh literature section, and
a Wales travel section. Booth also runs bookshops in the
castle, covering subjects from hobbies to erotica. In the
castle grounds is an honesty bookshop (50p per book).

Rose's Books (☎ 820013; www.rosesbooks.com; 14
Broad St) Specialises in rare children's books.

Also worth a look is **Tom's Record Shop** (☎ 821590;
www.tomsrecords.com; 13 Castle St), which has some
books alongside new and second-hand records
and CDs.

Activities

For a change of pace, **Paddles & Pedals** (☎ 820604;
www.canoehire.co.uk) now run its business from a
portacabin in a field close to the Start B&B
(p222) and hires out **canoes and kayaks** (half/full
day £22.50/35 & £15/20 respectively) for river trips.
Don't be fooled by the name – there aren't
any bikes for rent.

In Glasbury, 4.5 miles southwest of Hay, **Black
Mountain Activities** (☎ 847897; www.blackmountain

RICHARD BOOTH, KING OF HAY

Richard Booth is a larger-than-life character and the dynamic force behind Hay's metamorphosis
from declining border town into eminent book capital. A provocative character, he's been called
a monarchist, anarchist, socialist and separatist. All of which have some element of truth, and he's
definitely a superb self-publicist. After graduating from Oxford he bought Hay's old fire station
and turned it into a second-hand bookshop. He bought whole libraries from all over the world
and sold in bulk to new universities. He's had setbacks, becoming bankrupt in 1984, but never
lost his instinct for a good story. He first hit the headlines when he offered books for burning
at £1.50 a car-boot load.

Booth established the world's largest bookshop in the old cinema (now moved to 44 Lion St,
and the largest bookshop in Hay) and owns the 900-year-old Hay Castle. His success attracted
other booksellers and nowadays 30 or so bookshops cover 2000 different categories.

The idea for a separate state blossomed during a liquid lunch in 1976. Booth announced
that Hay would declare independence on 1 April (April Fools' Day). Breconshire Council fiercely
dismissed the idea as a Booth publicity stunt, which…fuelled the publicity. On declaration day,
three TV stations, eight national newspapers and the world's press covered the event. Booth was
crowned king and the Hay navy sent a gunboat (a rowing boat) up the Wye, firing blanks from
a drainpipe. Many of the king's drinking pals gained cabinet posts.

All this comedy has a serious undercurrent, and Booth continues to campaign against the
causes of rural decline – with particular contempt reserved for rural development boards, supermarkets and factory farming.

Booth has suffered from some health problems recently, but is still very much around. The bookshop, however, has been put up for sale. At the time of writing, no buyer had come forward.

.co.uk; Three Cocks) offers other activities such as climbing, caving and mountain biking with prices from £55 per person per day. They do hire out mountain bikes (half-/full-day £15/25) as well as canoes (half-/full-day £20/30).

Festivals & Events

The 10-day **Hay Festival** (☎ 0870 9901299; www.hay festival.com; ❖ late May-early Jun), held annually, is like a literary Glastonbury, when anyone who's anyone in the world of words descends on the town. It is massively popular and entertaining, with readings, workshops, guest appearances, book signings and a subsidiary children's literature festival. Book accommodation very well in advance – the Swan (below) is currently booked out until 2012 at festival time.

Sleeping

Radnors End Camping (☎ 820780; fax 820780; adult/child £5/3.50; ❖ Mar-Oct) Located just half a mile northwest of Hay on the way to Clyro, this is a friendly, helpful place, with tucked-away small green fields. It's an ideal spot for walkers tackling the Offa's Dyke Path.

Rest for the Tired (☎ 820550; www.restforthetired .co.uk; 6 Broad St; s/d £35/50; ❖ Mar-Dec) The three en-suite rooms in the family house are simple but welcoming with basic facilities. The guesthouse is located just 25m before the river.

Start (☎ 821391; Bridge St; www.the-start.net; s/d £35/60; ✗) This slightly tucked-away little place boasts an unbeatable riverside setting, homely rooms in a renovated 18th-century house and a flagstone-floored breakfast room. The owner can advise on local activities and walks.

Seven Stars (☎ 820886; www.thesevenstars.co.uk; 11 Broad St; s/d £40/55) A well-appointed midrange guesthouse in a converted 16th-century house, the unique selling point of this place is the indoor pool and sauna, which is also open to nonresidents for £3.50. The comfortable rooms continue the sauna theme with wood-plank walls.

Swan (☎ 821188; www.swanathay.co.uk; s/d £77.50/120) The smartest place in town is currently undergoing a programme of refurbishment to create a more contemporary look. The rooms are comfortable and the dining room serves a good menu of upscale cuisine, but the hotel's slightly tired look should finally be banished after the revamp is completed in 2007.

Kilverts (☎ 821042; www.kilverts.co.uk; The Bull Ring; d/tw/fm £80/90/110; bar meals ❖ noon-2pm & 6.30-9pm; ✗) This two-star hotel at the heart of town has traditional if slightly worn rooms and a busy oak-beamed dining room for à la carte mains each evening.

Eating

Granary (☎ 820790; Broad St; snacks £6; ❖ 9.30am-6pm) This most popular café-style place in town is bustling and welcoming with streetside tables and a country-kitchen interior. It's child friendly and has an imaginative menu of daily snacks and light lunches, including lots of vegetarian choices: hard to beat for a meal that won't break the bank.

Blue Boar (☎ 820884; Oxford Rd; mains £11; ❖ 9.30am-11pm, lunch noon-2pm) This bar-cum-restaurant specialises in hearty, home-cooked fare and has an inventive range of dishes, from light bites, such as hummus and pitta bread (£4.95) to traditional Welsh stew.

Old Black Lion (☎ 820841; Lion St; www.oldblacklion .co.uk; mains around £11) Walkers, book-browsers and the literary glitterati all flock to this creaky, converted 17th-century inn, with heavy black beams and warm red walls. The town's best upmarket offering, it serves tiptop elaborate pub food and a fine pint of Old Black Lion ale. There's also B&B accommodation (s/d £50/85) in ten attractive rooms, with heavy wooden furniture.

For self caterers, there's a **Spar supermarket** (Castle St; ❖ 7.30am-10pm Mon-Fri, 8am-10pm Sat & Sun). Nobody should leave Hay without trying the ice cream from **Shepherds Ice Cream Parlour** (☎ 821898; 9 High Town; ❖ 9.30am-6pm Mon-Sat, 10am-5pm Sun) – it's made from sheep's milk for a lighter, smoother taste.

Getting There & Away

The main bus services include Stagecoach bus 39 to Hereford (one hour, five daily Monday to Saturday, three daily Sunday) and Brecon (45 minutes, five daily Monday to Saturday, two daily Sunday).

Yeomans Canyon's Travel Beacons bus 40 runs the same Brecon to Hereford via Hay-on-Wye route (six daily Monday to Saturday, two daily Sunday). Prices are subject to change, so it's best to check with the local tourist office.

The nearest train station to Hay is located 21 miles away in Hereford. To call a taxi, try **Border Taxis** (☎ 821266).

LLANDRINDOD WELLS (LLANDRINDOD)

☎ 01597 / pop 4500

Llandrindod (meaning Church of the Trinity) was once a fashionable spa town for taking the waters and, even today, retains an element of the splendid architecture of a Victorian and Edwardian resort, with large parks, wrought iron and red brick. However, Llandrindod has long since had its day and subsequently succumbed to torpidity.

Roman remains at nearby Castell Collen show that it wasn't the Victorians who first discovered the healthy effects of the local spring waters, but it was the arrival of the Central Wales railway (now the Heart of Wales railway line) in 1865 that brought visitors en masse.

On Wednesday businesses open for only half the day, while Friday is the market day.

Orientation & Information

The town sits on the eastern bank of the River Ithon with the A483 (as Temple St) and the railway line plunging right through the town centre. Between the two is the main shopping zone, Middleton St. Most regional buses stop outside the train station on Station Crescent.

The **tourist office** (☎ 822600; Automobile Palace, Temple St; ☼ 9.30am-5.30pm Mon-Sat), has moved to smart new premises in the same building as the National Cycle Collection. The office produces a useful series of pamphlets about day walks around the town, including the 2-mile circular spa walk

All major UK banks (with ATMs) are represented along Middleton St, and the **post office** (Station Cres; ☼ 9am-5.30pm Mon-Fri, 9am-12.30pm Sat) is located just south of the train station. You can access the internet for free at the **library** (☎ 826870; Beaufort Rd; ☼ 9.30am-5pm Mon, Tue & Fri, to 1pm Wed & Sat, to 7pm Thu) or pay for access at **Media Resource Centre** (☎ 822230; Oxford Rd; ☼ 9am-6pm Mon-Fri; per hour £3), a business and conference centre located 200m west of the train station.

The **Llandrindod Wells Memorial Hospital** (☎ 822951; Temple St) is just north of the centre and the **police station** (☎ 822227; High St) is just behind the train station. A **laundrette** (Temple St; ☼ 9am-5pm daily) is to be found at the southern end of Temple St.

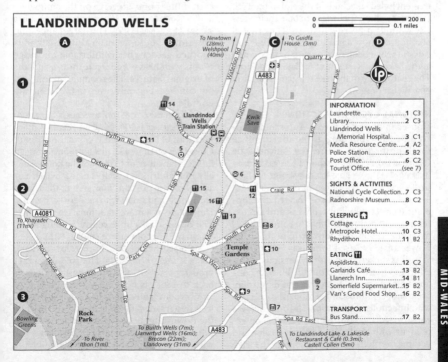

LLANDRINDOD WELLS

INFORMATION	
Laundrette	1 C3
Library	2 C3
Llandrindod Wells	
Memorial Hospital	3 C1
Media Resource Centre	4 A2
Police Station	5 B2
Post Office	6 C2
Tourist Office	(see 7)

SIGHTS & ACTIVITIES	
National Cycle Collection	7 C3
Radnorshire Museum	8 C2

SLEEPING 🛏	
Cottage	9 C3
Metropole Hotel	10 C3
Rhydithon	11 B2

EATING 🍴	
Aspidistra	12 C2
Garlands Café	13 B2
Llanerch Inn	14 B1
Somerfield Supermarket	15 B2
Van's Good Food Shop	16 B2

TRANSPORT	
Bus Stand	17 B2

MID-WALES

Sights

ROCK PARK

In 1670 the local spring was given the name the 'Well of the Blacksmith's Dingle', but it was not till the mid-18th century that its therapeutic qualities were discovered. An eminent German doctor had a variety of diseases, drank the waters and was cured, hence the spa became enormously popular. However, the allure of stinky water gradually diminished and it closed in 1972.

You can still soothe your nerves beside **Arlais Brook**, in serene forested, landscaped Rock Park. This is the site of the earliest spa development, though all that remains is the restored Rock Park Spa Pump Room and a small **complementary health centre** (☎ 822997) offering therapies such as massage and acupuncture. Fill your bottle at the Chalybeate Spring (donated to the public by the Lord of the Manor in 1879) beside the brook – apparently the water is good for treating gout, rheumatism, anaemia and more (chalybeate refers to its iron salts).

LLANDRINDOD LAKE

Just southeast of the centre is a sedately pretty, tree-encircled lake, built at the end of the 19th century to allow Victorians to take their exercise without appearing to do so. The original boathouse is now a private residence, but you can still rent a boat, fish for carp or take lunch at the Lakeside Restaurant & Café (opposite). The centrepiece of the lake is a giant sculpture of a Welsh dragon.

NATIONAL CYCLE COLLECTION

Housed in the Art Nouveau Automobile Palace, the same building as the tourist office south of the town centre, the **National Cycle Collection** (☎ 825531; www.cyclemuseum.org.uk; Temple St; adult/child £3/1; ⏰ 10am-4pm daily Mar-Oct, Tue, Thu & Sun Nov-Feb) has a collection of over 250 bikes. The exhibits show the two-wheeled development from clunky boneshakers and circus-reminiscent penny-farthings to bamboo bikes from the 1890s and the vertiginous 'Eiffel Tower' of 1899 (used to display billboards), as well as slicker, modern-day versions. Great effort has been made to put the bikes in context, with re-created Victorian and Edwardian cycle shops, photos and signboards – it's run with infectious enthusiasm. The building was constructed by Tom Norton, a local entrepreneur who started as a bicycle dealer and became the main Austin distributor. The trike

on which Norton used to ride to work is here, with a picture of him on it.

RADNORSHIRE MUSEUM

There's a small and rather low-key **museum** (Temple St; adult/child £1/0.50; ⏰ 10am-4pm Mon-Fri, 10am-5pm Sat & Sun) to fill you in on the local history of Llandrindod.

Festivals & Events

Llandrindod Wells comes over all historical during its **Victorian Festival** (☎ 823441), a week of 19th-century high jinks during the last full week before the August bank holiday. Just about everybody puts on period costumes, and transport is by horse and carriage.

There are also several **Jazz Weekends** (☎ 823700) at the Metropole Hotel, and a popular **Drama Festival** (☎ 825677) during the first full week of May, when amateur groups from all over the UK come to perform in competitions.

Sleeping

Rhydithon (☎ 822624; Dyffryn Rd; s/d from £30/50) Charmingly and cheerfully run, with spotless, comfy rooms, this a popular budget choice, even if the rooms do verge on the chintzy.

The **Cottage** (☎ 825435; www.thecottagebandb.co .uk; Spa Rd; s/d from £33/50) This large, appealing Edwardian house, set in an attractive flower-adorned garden, has comfortable midrange rooms with heavy wooden furniture and lots of original features. The rooms are traditional but comfortable; only seven of the rooms are en suite.

Guidfa House (☎ 851241; www.guidfa-house.co.uk; Crossgates; s/d from £48/70; ☒ P) Located 3 miles northeast of Llandrindod Wells in the village of Crossgates on the A483, this six-room Georgian house is far superior to most of the hotels actually in Llandrindod itself. There's wheelchair access on the ground floor and all the rooms are homely and smart with modern bathrooms. Downstairs is a more traditional guest lounge. The owner cooks up excellent evening meals Tuesday to Sunday (three courses £21).

Metropole Hotel (☎ 823700; www.metropole.co.uk; Temple St; s/d/fm £79/104/114) The sole upmarket property in town, this historic hostelry (it dates back to 1868) is now a three-star place with family rooms and disabled access. The interior feels rather faded, like much of the town, while the downstairs brasserie has been converted into the slightly incongruous Spencer's Bar with a glass streetside terrace. The hotel is increasingly aiming for the corporate meetings market and does well out of its leisure complex with a swimming pool and sauna.

Eating

Van's Good Food Shop (☎ 823079; Middleton St; ☯ 9am-5.30pm Mon, Tue, Thu & Fri, to 5pm Wed & Sat) This excellent vegetarian deli features the best of local produce with organic fruit, cheese and wine, plus it operates a strong ethical policy on their selection of featured produce.

Garlands Café (☎ 824132; Middleton St; ☯ 9am-5pm Mon-Fri, 9.30am-3pm Sat) A simple, cosy café with traditional snack food for morning coffees or a cheap lunch on the run.

Aspidistra (☎ 822949; Station Cres; ☯ 9am-4.30pm Mon, Tue, Thu-Sat, to 2pm Wed) An old-fashioned café with a time-warp feel, this place has floral tablecloths and lots of basic snack lunches; a strict nonsmoking policy is in force.

Lakeside Restaurant & Café (☎ 825679; The Lake; ☯ 10am-4pm daily) The nicest place in town for lunch is located southeast of the centre by Llandrindod Lake. There's a nice conservatory area, a terrace for outdoor dining and a changing menu of daily specials. It's café-style food, with soups, sandwiches and jacket potatoes all served with a smile.

Llanerch Inn (☎ 822086; www.llanerchinn.com; Llanerch Lane; bar meals ☯ noon-2pm & 6-9pm) It's mainly just bar food available outside of the café-style places and this 16th-century coaching inn (it's probably the town's oldest building) is the best of the mediocre bunch, serving tasty, good-value bar food, including big Welsh steaks.

For self-caterers there's a large **Somerfield supermarket** (8am-8pm Mon-Wed & Sat, to 9pm Thu & Fri, 10am-4pm Sun) with a car park just southwest of the train station.

Getting There & Around

Bus connections are very limited; it's best to check with the local tourist office for up-to-date timetables and prices. Crossgates runs bus 19 to/from Rhayader (25 minutes, five daily Monday to Saturday) and also the bus 21 service to/from Builth Wells (25 minutes, two to four daily Monday to Saturday).

The busiest local route is the TrawsCambria bus 704 from Brecon to Newtown; there are six daily services Monday to Saturday from Llandrindod Wells to Brecon (one hour) and Newtown (one hour).

Llandrindod Wells is on the Heart of Wales railway line, with services to Llanwrtyd Wells

(£3.20; 30 minutes, four trains daily – two on Sunday) and Swansea (£12.70, two hours 30 minutes).To get around, call a **taxi** (☎ 822877).

RHAYADER (RHAEADR)
☎ 01597 / pop 2000
Rhayader is a small and fairly uneventful livestock-market town revolving around a central crossroads marked by a towering war-memorial clock. It's a place that appeals to walkers visiting the nearby Elan Valley (see p227) and tackling the 136-mile Wye Valley Walk, which has its northern terminus at Plynlimon Fawr (2469ft), 29 miles northwest of Rhayader; 35 miles of the walking trail falls within Powys.

Rhayader is deserted on Thursdays when businesses trade for only half a day, but market day on Wednesdays attracts a crowd.

Orientation & Information
The town centre is focused around the clock tower at the intersection of North St (A470), East St (A44), South St (A470) and West St (B4518). The **tourist office** (☎ 810591; off North St; ☯ 10am-5pm daily May-Oct, Fri-Wed Nov-Apr) is just north of the tower and based within the Rhayader Leisure Centre. You can check your email for free at the **library** (West St; ☯ 10am-1pm & 2-4.30pm Mon, Wed & Fri, 10am-noon Sat).

There are banks dotted along East St, where you'll also find a **post office** (8.30am-5.30pm Mon-Fri, 8.30am-12.30pm Sat) and a **laundrette** (8.45am-5.30pm Mon-Sat).

Buses set you down at the Dark Lane **car park** (per hour 50p) opposite the tourist office. The nearest train station is situated 10 miles away at Llandrindod Wells.

Activities
The **Clive Powell Mountain Bike Centre** (☎ 811343; www.clivepowell-mtb.co.uk; West St) is run by Powell, a former cycling champion and coach. It is the venue in town for advice and equipment for a more active break. You can hire a mountain/off-road bike here (£20/15 per day, including helmet and puncture kit), and Powell runs a regular programme of so-called 'Dirty Weekends', activity weekends with all-inclusive prices and B&B from £160 per person, including two days of mountain biking on trails around the Elan Valley.

Sleeping
Wyeside Caravan & Camping Park (☎ 810183; Llangurig Rd; www.wyesidecamping.co.uk; sites per adult/child from

£4.50/1.50, caravan £9 per person) Located just a short walk from the centre of town, this is a relaxed, grassy site with lovely river views and lots of trees for caravans and tents.

Brynteg (☎ 810052; East St; s/d £20/40) A good-value budget place, with four plain and cosy rooms, Brynteg is simple but satisfying. The en suite double room has the best outlook with leafy, hill-filled views.

Liverpool House (☎ 810706; www.liverpoolhouse.co .uk; East St; s/d £25/40) This comfy nine-room guesthouse offers a friendly welcome, albeit with rather floral rooms. It's located just off the main intersection along East St.

Elan Valley Hotel (☎ 810448; www.elanvalley.co.uk; s/d £32.50/90) A former Victorian fishing lodge, this large white house in the peaceful Elan Valley is two miles outside of Rhayader on the B4518 – head out past the Triangle Inn. It's not an overly grand place but good for families. There has, however, been a change in management recently so call ahead to see if they are still running the popular Fungi Forays, wild mushroom breaks for true lovers of fungi, or check the website www.fungiforays.co.uk. The in-house restaurant serves bar meals from 7pm to 9pm (mains around £12) and does a decent Sunday lunch with roasts (noon to 2pm).

Brynafon Country House Hotel (☎ 810735; www .brynafon.co.uk; South St; s/d from £43/66) For more of a rural experience, this former workhouse has views of the River Wye and Elan Valley from its stately rooms. There's a range of rooms, some with four-poster beds, some with exposed beams, but all with leafy outlooks. The avocado-tree-canopied bar is popular with day-trippers; mains are around £8. A new attraction is the introduction of 'Plein Air' Painting Safaris that combine a weekend break with art classes – ask the owners for details.

Eating & Drinking

Strand (☎ 810564; East St; mains £6; ☼ 8.30am-5pm Mon-Fri, restaurant to 9pm) The best all-rounder in town is split between a simple café serving coffees and snacks on one side and a pricier restaurant for full meals and grills on the other. It's not complicated fare but it is good for families, with lunch boxes for kids available (£2.50).

Triangle Inn (☎ 810537; mains £7) This tiny 16th-century pub, located just over the bridge from the town centre, is the pick of the local places to eat and drink for its unique sense of character and history. In fact, it is so small that the toilets are located across the road, and the ceiling is so low that there's a trapdoor in the floor so that darts players can stand in a hole to throw their arrows. Bar meals are served from 6.30pm to 8.30pm and include daily specials.

Morgan's (☎ 810564; East St; mains £9) This is a cosy little bistro offering tasty alternatives to the abundance of local pub food, with some imaginative dishes such as grilled Wye trout and a stir-fry of local produce.

Café Cwmdauddwr (☎ 811343; West St; mains £10) This smart little licensed eatery, actually part of the Clive Powell Mountain Bike Centre (see p225) and housed in the erstwhile Cwmdaud-dwr Arms, an old pub dating back to 1650, is an excellent place with just six tables. The menu puts the emphasis on vegetarian and organic fare and there's a nonsmoking policy throughout. The mains menu changes on a daily basis, and there's always a selection of delicious deserts. A little gem.

For a pint, try the **Crown** (☎ 811099; North St; mains £8; ☼ bar food noon-2.15pm & 6-9.30pm Mon-Fri, noon-6pm Sat, Sun roasts noon-3pm only), an olde-worlde pub with bar food and real ales.

For self-caterers, there's a **Spar supermarket** (☼ 7am-10pm Mon-Sat, 7.30am-10pm Sun).

Getting There & Around

Crossgates Coaches run bus 019A/01 from Rhayader to Llandrindod Wells (30 minutes, five daily Monday to Saturday) and Builth Wells (30 minutes, one daily Monday to Saturday). Contact the local tourist office for up-to-date prices.

Around Rhayader

GIGRIN FARM RED KITE FEEDING STATION

There's been a dramatic Mid-Wales resurgence in the UK's threatened population of red kites (see p54), but these handsome raptors have not quite re-established themselves, so feeding programmes continue.

Red kites are fed at the **Gigrin Farm Red Kite Feeding Station** (☎ 810243; www.gigrin.co.uk; adult/child £3/1), a working farm on the A470 located half a mile south of Rhayader town centre (or one mile from the Wye Valley Walk). At 2pm GMT (3pm during summer daylight-saving time) meat scraps (from local butchers and a local abattoir) are spread on a field. Altogether anywhere from 12 to 300 kites may partake, though usually less than 20 at any one time. First come crows, then ravens, then the acrobatically swooping kites – often mugging the crows to get the meat – and later ravens and buzzards. You can watch from a wheelchair-accessible hide.

There's an interpretive centre, with information on red kites and other local wildlife, with recorded night-time footage of badgers, a camera overlooking the feeding site, and marked nature trails.

The appealing 350-year-old working farm, with beautiful wandering white peafowl, also has **camping** (tent/caravan £3/8 per person) and a cosy **B&B** (£30 per week) for up to four people.

ELAN VALLEY

The Elan Valley is filled with strikingly beautiful countryside, split by amazing Edwardian impositions of grey stone on the landscape. In the early 19th century, dams were built on the River Elan (pronounced ellen), west of Rhayader, mainly to provide a reliable water supply for the city of Birmingham. Around 100 people had to move, but only landowners received compensation. In 1952 a fourth, large dam was inaugurated on the tributary River Claerwen. Together their reservoirs now provide over 70 million gallons of water daily for Birmingham and parts of South and Mid-Wales.

Though not a project to warm Welsh hearts, the need to protect the 70-sq-mile watershed, called the Elan Valley Estate, has turned it and adjacent areas into an important wildlife conservation area. The dams and associated projects also produce some 4.2 megawatts of hydroelectric power.

Located just downstream of the lowest dam, three miles from Rhayader on the B4518, is Welsh Water's **Elan Valley Visitor Centre** (☎ 810898; admission free; ◷ 10am-5.30pm Mar-Oct) with an interesting exhibit on the water scheme, complete with photos of houses being swallowed up by the waters. There's also wildlife and local history, information on the frequent guided walks and bird-watching trips, and it also provides leaflets on the estate's 80 miles of nature trails and footpaths.

The Elan Valley Trail is an 8-mile traffic-free walking, horse riding and cycling path that mostly follows the line of the long-gone Birmingham Corporation Railway alongside the River Elan and its reservoirs. It starts just west of Rhayader at Cwmdauddwr.

KNIGHTON (TREF-Y-CLAWDD)
☎ 01547 / pop 3000

Pretty Knighton, just over the border from England, is a walking hub midway along the Offa's Dyke Path National Trail, and the starting point or terminus for the Glyndŵr's Way National Trail, which wends its way via Machynlleth to Welshpool (p228).

Knighton has seen its fortunes rise and fall with the coming of the railway and the growth of livestock farming, then the subsequent decline in population post WWII and failed attempts to turn it into a spa town.

One intriguing piece of local folklore suggests that until the mid-1800s it was possible for a man to obtain a divorce by 'selling' his wife at the square where today the clocktower stands proud. Husbands would bring their spouse to the square at the end of a rope; the last wife was 'sold' in 1842.

Knighton is a small town with limited facilities, making it a place to stop for lunch.

Orientation & Information

The town is centred around a handsome stone clock tower, which was built in 1872 on the main thoroughfare, Broad St. The train station is actually in England, five blocks to the northeast via Station Rd; buses stop by the community centre in Bowling Green Lane where there is also car parking.

The two-in-one **tourist office and Offa's Dyke Centre** (☎ 528753; West St; ◷ 9am-5.30pm Apr-Oct, 9am-5pm Mon-Fri Nov-Mar) is located three blocks west of the clock tower. The building houses the Offa's Dyke Centre and there's a large amount of information for walkers, see p62.

There are banks and a **post office** (◷ 9am-5.30pm Mon-Fri, 9am-12.30pm Sat) all located near the clock tower on Broad St, plus a **Spar supermarket** (◷ 7am-9pm). Knighton's **livestock market** (Station Rd) comes alive on Thursdays (and sometimes Friday).

Sights

Two miles southeast of town, the hilltop **Spaceguard Centre** (☎ 520247; www.spaceguarduk.com; adult/child £5/2.50; ◷ Wed-Sun, 1½-hr tours 10.30am, 2pm & 4pm), in the former Powys Observatory, is a centre for research into asteroids and comets. Tours take in the telescopes, tracking and planetarium shows.

Across Broad St and two blocks down Church St is **St Edward's Church**, with an unusual, rather stumpy 18th-century bell tower.

The traffic-free lane, The Narrows, also known as High St, rises steeply from the central clock tower.

Sleeping & Eating

Horse & Jockey Inn (☎ 520062; www.thehorseand jockeyinn.co.uk; Wylcwm Place; s/d £35/55; restaurant mains £10, bar mains £7; ☒ noon-2pm & 7-9pm) This former 14th-century coaching inn is now a pub-cum-restaurant and B&B with upscale accommodation and a broad menu of meals. The five en-suite rooms are smart and stylish with flat-screen TVs and modern fittings. The bar area has a cosy feel with a large open fire and meals, and by night, the adjoining restaurant serves hearty mains to satisfy every appetite.

Fleece House (☎ 520168; www.fleecehouse.co.uk; Market St; s/d £37/54) Situated at the top of The Narrows, this former 18th-century coaching inn has cosy rooms with cheery quilted features. It's a good base for tired walkers, with simple facilities.

Butterfingers (☎ 528692; 8 High St; ☒ 8.30am-4pm Mon-Fri, 9am-3pm Sat) is a simple little coffee shop for snacks and hot drinks on the go.

Getting There & Around

Knighton is one of the stops on the lovely Heart of Wales line, with at least three trains daily (fewer on Sunday) from Llandrindod Wells (£3, 35 minutes) and on to Shrewsbury (£6.30, 55 minutes).

NORTHERN POWYS

WELSHPOOL (TRALLWNG)

☎ 01938 / pop 6000

This little Severn Valley town was originally called Pool – after the 'pills', boggy, marshy ground (long since drained) along the nearby river. It was changed in 1835 to Welshpool, so nobody would get confused with Poole in Dorset.

It's a workaday little town with few distractions in the town centre proper and few inspiring options for people seeking to overnight. More compelling, however, are the peripheral sights, which are the big draw for visitors: the glorious Powis Castle, the narrow-gauge Welshpool and Llanfair Light Railway and, for the more open-minded, the supremely flamboyant, not to mention slightly incongruous, Andrew Logan Museum of Sculpture.

Orientation & Information

The centre of Welshpool is a four-way intersection called The Cross. From Raven Sq train station it's a 700m slog east down Raven St (and its extensions, Mount, Broad and High Sts) to The Cross, then left at Church St to reach the **tourist office** (☎ 552043; ☒ 9.30am-5pm Mon-Fri, 9am-4pm Sat & Sun Apr-Sep, irregular hr off season) located next to the Vicarage Gardens **car park** (per hr 40p). Regional buses stop on High St, about 400m from the tourist office; National Express coaches stop in front of the tourist office.

From The Cross, Welshpool's **police station** (☎ 552345; Severn St) is 300m east and the **Victoria Memorial Hospital** (☎ 553133; Salop Rd) just north. There's free internet access at the **library** (☎ 553001; ☒ 9.30am-7pm Mon, to 5pm Tue & Wed, to 1pm Thu & Sat, to 4pm Fri).

High Street is the place to find banks, a **laundrette** (☒ 9am-6pm Mon-Sat) and the **post office** (☒ 9am-5.30pm Mon-Fri, 9am-1pm Sat).

Sights

POWIS CASTLE & CLIVE MUSEUM

Cupped by magnificent gardens, the red-brick **Powis Castle** (☎ 551920; adult/child castle, museum & gardens £9/4.80, garden only £6.60/3.30; ☒ castle & museum 1-5pm Thu-Mon Apr–mid-Sep, 1-4pm Thu-Mon mid-Sep–end Oct, house 11am-4.30pm Thu-Mon Apr-Oct, garden 11am-5.30pm Thu-Mon Apr-Sep, 11am-4.30pm Thu-Mon Mar & Oct) rises up from its terraces as if floating on a fantastical bed of moss-green, massive, clipped yew trees. South of Welshpool, just under a mile from The Cross, it was originally constructed by Gruffydd ap Gwenwynwyn, prince of Powys, and subsequently enriched by generations of the Herbert and Clive families. Today it is operated by the National Trust (NT). The extravagant mural-covered, wood-panelled interior contains one of Wales' finest collections of furniture and paintings. The Clive Museum holds a fascinating and exquisite cache of jade, ivory, armour, textiles and other treasures brought back from India by Baron Clive (British conqueror of Bengal at the Battle of Plassey in 1757), allowing a rare insight into the lifestyle of early colonialists.

The baroque garden is peerless, dotted with ornamental lead statues, and features an orangery, formal gardens, wilderness, terraces and orchards.

WELSHPOOL & LLANFAIR LIGHT RAILWAY

This sturdy **narrow-gauge railway** (☎ 810441; www .wllr.org.uk; adult/child £10.50/5.25; ☒ three services daily

Apr-Oct) was completed in 1902 to help people bring their sheep and cattle to market. It runs up steep inclines and through the pretty Banwy Valley. The line was closed in 1956 but reopened four years later by enthusiastic volunteers.

Trains make the 8-mile journey from Raven Square Station to Llanfair Caereinion in 50 minutes and according to a complex timetable of regular services and special weekend events. There are also courses on offer in May, June and September to learn how to drive your very own steam engine – call for details.

MONTGOMERY CANAL

The Montgomery Canal originally ran for 35 miles starting at Newtown and ending at Frankton Junction in Shropshire, where it joined the Llangollen Canal. After sections of its banks burst in 1936 it lay abandoned until a group of volunteers and the British Waterways Board began repairing it in 1969. Today it is 38 miles long and is a centre for day-cruising and boating trips.

The **Heulwen Trust** (☎ 552563) is a charity that provides free **canal trips** (☸ Mon-Fri) for disabled people in an adapted narrow boat along the canal – call for details.

OTHER SIGHTS

Beside the canal wharf to the west of the town is the **Powysland Museum** (☎ 554656; adult/child £1/free; ☸ 11am-1pm & 2-5pm Mon-Tue, Thu & Fri, 10am-1pm & 2-5pm Sat & Sun May-Sep, 11am-2pm Sat Oct-Apr), marked outside by a big blue handbag – an Andy Hancock sculpture to commemorate the Queen's Jubilee. There's a football mobile by the same artist and also brilliant pillars painted by local schoolchildren and topped by carved birds. Inside, the museum tells the story of the canal and town, with great details – such as the Roman recipe for stuffed dormouse.

Festivals & Events

On the third Sunday in July, Welshpool becomes the unlikely venue for a one-day **Country & Western Music Festival** (☎ 552563) with spit roasts and line dancing, at the county showground near Powis Castle; proceeds benefit the Heulwen Trust (above).

Sleeping

Montgomery House (☎ 552693; 43 Salop Rd; s/d £30/45) This simple, friendly place is just 300m from the tourist office and has basic but comfortable rooms.

Royal Oak Hotel (☎ 552217; www.royaloakhotel.info; The Cross; s/d £65/94) By far the smartest place in town, this hotel with lots of history contained within its walls has recently undergone major refurbishment. The rooms have a stately feel while there are both tasty bar and restaurant meals, the latter served in a refined dining room.

Eating

Buttery (☎ 552658; 8 High St; ☸ 9.30am-4.30pm Mon, Tue, Thu-Sat) This nonsmoking traditional tearoom, set in an old timber-framed building, is a quiet spot for a last morning coffee or a light lunch.

Mermaid Inn (☎ 552027; 28 High St; mains £6) This timber-framed pub has been here for at least 200 years and serves up a menu of decent pub meals.

For self-caterers, there's a **Spar supermarket** (Church St; ☸ 7am-11pm Mon-Sat, 8am-10.30pm Sun) located opposite the tourist office and a **Morrisons supermarket** (Berriew Rd; ☸ 8am-8pm Mon-Wed & Sat, to 9pm Thu & Fri, 10am-4pm Sun) at the southern end of town.

Shopping

Ashmans Antiques & Old Lace (☎ 554505; Park Lane House, High St) This is a marvellous antique clothes shop, crammed with hats and ball gowns, and located right next door to the Buttery tearooms.

Coed-y-Dinas (☎ 555545; Home & Country Centre; 8.30am-5.30pm Mon-Sat, 10am-4pm Sun) is a major new development in old farm buildings of the Powys Castle estate. It stocks a huge array of crafts, household and local, organic fresh produce. It's also the base for new horse-drawn canal boat rides along the Montgomery Canal.

Getting There & Away

Arriva bus 75 runs to/from Shrewsbury (45 minutes, seven daily Monday to Saturday) and Newtown (35 minutes). National Express coach 420 stops daily en route from Telford and Shrewsbury to Aberystwyth.

Welshpool is on the Cambrian railway line from Shrewsbury (£3.70 single, 25 minutes), Machynlleth (£8.40, 50 minutes) and Aberystwyth (£8.70, 1½ hours), with services leaving every two hours (fewer on Sunday). Check with the local tourist office for prices.

Brooks Cycles (☎ 553582; 9 Severn St) charges £12.50 a day for mountain-bike hire.

AROUND WELSHPOOL
Andrew Logan Museum of Sculpture

Unlikely as the location is, this supremely flouncy and fascinating **sculpture museum** (☎ 01686-640689; www.andrewlogan.com; adult/child £3/1.50; ☼ noon-4pm Sat & Sun Jun-Sep) is devoted to the work of Andrew Logan. The building is actually a former squash court but, since Logan took over the space in 1991, it has played host to a very different display of physical prowess. Today, the museum is a glorious celebration of sequins and camp, with beautiful, frivolous, humorous artworks, including a huge cosmic egg made of fibreglass and a larger-than-life portrayal of fashion designer Zandra Rhodes.

There's a small café area on site for coffees and cakes, plus occasional workshops for children and families – call ahead for details.

The museum is situated five miles south of Welshpool in the tiny village of Berriew; take the Newtown bus 75 (15 minutes) to stop close to the entrance.

NEWTOWN (Y DRENEWYDD)
☎ 01686 / pop 10,000

This former mill town has lots of history but, as a destination, it's a pretty sleepy place these days – absolutely soporific on a Sunday – and one that trades increasingly on its past. The modern buildings are less attractive and the high street has a rather homogenised feel.

Newtown's big claim to fame is that Robert Owen, the factory reformer, founder of the cooperative movement and so-called 'father of Socialism', was born here in 1771, though he left at the age of 10 and only returned just before his death in 1858. Nevertheless, monuments to him now litter the town centre.

Newtown was also once the home of Welsh flannel, and a major UK textile centre. When competition began driving wages down, Wales' first Chartist meeting was held here in October 1838. Pryce Jones, the world's first-ever mail-order firm, got its start here, on the back of the textile trade. But by the end of the 19th century Newtown's boom days were over – and they've never been back. There are several small museums devoted to those long-gone salad days.

Newtown is almost the home of Laura Ashley (she opened her first shop in Carno, 10 miles west of the centre).

Orientation & Information

Newtown sits in a bend of the River Severn (Afon Hafren) alongside the Welshpool–Aberystwyth road. The centre is The Cross, at the intersection of Broad, High, Severn and Shortbridge Sts.

From the train station it's a 600m walk via Old Kerry Rd, Shortbridge St and The Cross, to the **tourist office** (☎ 625580; Back Lane; ☼ 9.30am-5pm Mon-Sat Oct-Feb, daily Mar-Sep). The Cross backs onto a large public **car park** (per hr 50p), where you'll also find the bus station.

Major UK banks dot The Cross and Broad St; you'll also find a **post office** (Broad St; ☼ 8.30am-5.30pm Mon-Fri, 8.30am-12.30pm Sat) and a **laundrette** (Severn St; ☼ 8am-8pm).

Sights

Textile Museum (☎ 622024; 5-7 Commercial St; admission free; ☼ 2-5pm Mon, Tue, Thu-Sat May-Sep) Located in former weavers' cottages and workshops, just north of the river, this museum has impressively re-created rooms to show what living conditions were like in the 1820s. Above the cottages are the workshops – as they were originally – depicting the children (and adults) of the time at work.

Oriel Davies Gallery (☎ 625041; www.orieldavies.org; The Park; admission free; ☒ 10am-5pm Mon-Sat), Beside the tourist office is this excellent gallery with temporary contemporary exhibitions. The good little café inside is also the best place to eat in town (see below).

South of the river, at the end of Church St, are the remains of the **Church of St Mary**, where Robert Owen is buried. The tiny **Robert Owen Museum** (☎ 626345; The Cross; admission free; ☒ 9.30am-noon & 2-3.30pm Mon-Fri, 9.30-11.30am Sat) is in the town-council building where they have made a little arts centre, and has some mementos and a biographical film.

The **WH Smith shop** (24 High St) looks much as it did when it first opened in 1927. Upstairs is a little company **museum** (☎ 626280; admission free; ☒ 9am-5.30pm), for stationery lovers.

A mound in the riverside park southwest of the tourist office is the remains of Newtown's 13th-century **castle**. The gorsedd stone circle in the park dates from the Royal National Eisteddfod of 1965.

Sleeping
Yesterdays (☎ 622644; Severn Square; s/d £30/45; ☒) A block east of The Cross, Yesterdays offers snug beamed rooms with plaid decoration. The building was a former temperance hotel and girl's boarding house before becoming a hotel. Downstairs is an excellent restaurant (open 6pm to 8pm Monday to Saturday, noon to 2pm Sat and Sun; mains £6.50 to £12) with a cottage-style ambience, offering traditional dishes such as Sunday roasts.

Plas Canol Guest House (☎ 625598; New Rd; s/d £35/50) The closest guesthouse to the train station, this is a simple place with basic en-suite rooms and all mod cons.

Eating
Oriel Davies Gallery (☎ 622288; snacks £5; ☒ 10am-4.30pm Mon-Sat) The gallery's in-house eatery is a bright and surprisingly good little café with lots of tasty lunch dishes, including plenty of vegetarian options, tapas and warming home-made soups.

Black Boy Hotel (☎ 626834; Broad St; lunch mains £6; bar meals ☒ noon-2.30pm & 6-9pm) Simple but hearty pub fare is the order of the day here. Better still, it's one of the few places that is actually open on a Sunday with an excellent, good-value Sunday carvery. It's also a good spot to

sink a pint away from the hubris of the High St chain pubs.

For self-caterers, there's a **Spar supermarket** (Broad St; ☒ 7am-11pm Mon-Sat, 8am-10pm Sun).

Getting There & Away
Arriva bus 522 runs to Newtown (one hour, four daily Mon to Sat); Red Dragon Travel bus 75 runs to Wrexham (one hour 15 minutes, one daily) via Welshpool (30 minutes).

Newtown is on the Cambrian main line, with trains every hour or two from Machynlleth (£6, 35 minutes), Aberystwyth (£8.70, one hour 15 minutes) and Shrewsbury (£4.50, 40 minutes).

Check with the local tourist office for prices.

AROUND NEWTOWN
Gregynog Hall
This splendid, 19th-century, mock-Tudor mansion was (from 1924) home of the Davies sisters, Gwendoline and Margaret, who are known for the extraordinary collection of paintings they bequeathed to the National Museum and Gallery of Wales (see p86). Their grandfather was David Davies, a sawyer who turned to mining and who, when prevented by the Bute family (see boxed text, p82) from exporting his coal from Cardiff, built his own docks at Barry and made a pile.

The sisters intended to make the house an arts centre, founding a fine-arts press in the stables and holding an annual Festival of Music and Poetry. In the 1960s the estate was given to the University of Wales, which uses it as a conference centre. Successor to the sisters' festival is the week-long **Gregynog Music Festival** (☎ 650224) held annually in mid-June, with operatic, choral, orchestral and instrumental music performed in the grounds of the house. The house, its interior largely unchanged since Margaret's death in 1963, opens for group tours by appointment.

Gregynog Hall is situated five miles north of Newtown on the B4389.

MACHYNLLETH
☎ 01654 / pop 2200
Small but perfectly formed, Machynlleth pivots around an overwrought clock tower at the heart of town. Edward I gave Machynlleth its charter as a market town in 1291 but it was Owain Glyndŵr setting up his parliament here in 1404 that put it on the historical map.

In recent years, however, Machynlleth has become better known as the green capital of Wales – thanks primarily to the burgeoning Centre for Alternative Technology (CAT; see p234), located 3 miles north of town. The centre has been a huge success and is now, by far, the attraction that keeps Machynlleth on the tourist map.

Following the hippie-chic lead of Byron Bay in Australia, if you want to get your runes read, take up yoga, or explore holistic dancing, Machynlleth is the ideal place for you. Better still, it's surrounded by some meltingly serene countryside to explore, particularly suited to mountain biking (opposite).

Orientation & Information

From the train station it's about 400m walk down Doll and Penrallt Sts to the centre, to the Castlereagh Clock Tower, which is also where buses set you down. The **car park** (per hr 40p) is situated parallel to Maengwyn St behind the library.

The **tourist office** (☎ 702401; Royal House, Penrallt St; 9.30am-5pm Mon-Sat, to 4pm Sun) has moved to a smart new centre. Staff will help visitors

with accommodation and information on local trails, plus the office has a good range of maps and books on local history. The **Machynlleth Book Shop** (Maengwyn St) also has a useful range of books and maps. For information about events around the region, check the free monthly flyer **Dyfi Diary** (☎ 761463; www.ecodyfi.org.uk).

There are banks located close to the clock tower, and a **post office** (Maengwyn St; 9.30am-5.30pm Mon-Fri; 9.30am-12.30pm Sat) located within the Spar supermarket. Internet access is free at the **library** (☎ 702322; Maengwyn St; 9.30am-1pm Mon-Wed, Fri & Sat, 2-7pm Mon & Fri, to 5pm Tue & Wed).

Nigel's Laundrette (8.30am-8pm Mon-Sat; 9am-8pm Sun) is located off Maengwyn St behind Maengwyn Café. In case of an emergency, contact the local **police** (☎ 702215; Doll St).

Sights

On Penrallt St is the town's only neoclassical building, the **Tabernacle**, a former Methodist chapel (1880) that's been restored and now forms part of the **Museum of Modern Art for Wales** (MOMA; ☎ 703355; www.momawales.org.uk; admission free; 10am-4pm Mon-Sat). Welsh artists exhibit here; there is a small permanent collection within

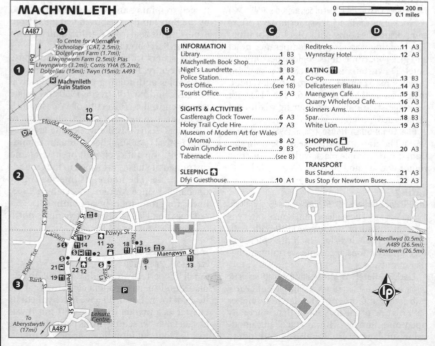

MACHYNLLETH

0 — 200 m
0 — 0.1 miles

INFORMATION
Library.................................1 B3
Machynlleth Book Shop.......2 A3
Nigel's Laundrette...............3 B3
Police Station......................4 A2
Post Office.....................(see 18)
Tourist Office......................5 A3

SIGHTS & ACTIVITIES
Castlereagh Clock Tower......6 A3
Holey Trail Cycle Hire..........7 A3
Museum of Modern Art for Wales
(Moma)............................8 A2
Owain Glyndŵr Centre.........9 B3
Tabernacle....................(see 8)

SLEEPING
Dfyi Guesthouse...............10 A1

Reditreks..........................11 A3
Wynnstay Hotel................12 A3

EATING
Co-op..............................13 B3
Delicatessen Blasau...........14 A3
Maengwyn Café................15 B3
Quarry Wholefood Café......16 A3
Skinners Arms...................17 A3
Spar................................18 B3
White Lion........................19 A3

SHOPPING
Spectrum Gallery...............20 A3

TRANSPORT
Bus Stand........................21 A3
Bus Stop for Newtown Buses...22 A3

To Centre for Alternative
Technology (CAT, 2.5mi);
Dolgelynen Farm (1.7mi);
Llwyngwern Farm (2.5mi); Plas
Llwyngwern (3.2mi); Corris YHA (5.2mi);
Dolgellau (15mi); Twyn (15mi); A493

Machynlleth Train Station

Ffordd Mynydd Griffiths

Brickfield St

Carslwn

Poplar Tce

Penrallt St

Powys St

Maengwyn St

Bank La

Penrhedyn St

Leisure Centre

To Maenllwyd (0.5mi);
A489 (26.5mi);
Newtown (26.5mi)

To Aberystwyth (17mi) A487

the white-walled galleries. The chapel has the feel of a courtroom, but has good acoustics and is a venue for concerts, theatre and talks.

At the western end of town is a rare example of a late-medieval Welsh townhouse, the **Owain Glyndŵr Centre** (☎ 702827; admission £1; ☯ Apr-Sep), with dry displays that nevertheless tell a rip-roaring story of the Welsh hero's fight for independence. This building was probably built somewhat later than Glyndŵr's parliament but is believed to closely resemble the former venue. At the time of writing it was undergoing refurbishment to re-open with a fresh look for summer 2007.

Activities
CYCLING
There are three waymarked routes from Machynlleth, the Mach 1, 2 and 3, which at 10, 14 and 19 miles respectively, are increasingly challenging, but nonetheless exciting, mountain-bike trails. Beginners should not attempt the Mach 3.

There's also a walking/cycling trail that leads off the A487, just north of the train station, and follows a countryside path, crossing the Millennium Bridge, to lead you towards the CAT by the greenest possible forms of transport.

Festivals & Events
The **Gŵyl Machynlleth** (Machynlleth Festival) takes place during the third week of August at the Tabernacle (see MOMA above), with music ranging from kids' stuff to jazz, plus a lively fringe festival.

Sleeping
Llwyngwern Farm (☎ 702492; Corris; caravan/tent £8/11; ☯ Apr-end Sep) An appealing farm-attached site is set in pretty countryside near the CAT 3 miles north of the town centre along the A487. The site has toilets and a shower block, plus facilities for electrical hook-ups.

Reditreks (☎ 702184; Powys St; www.reditreks.co.uk; dm £15) Mountain-bikers flock to this simple but satisfying hostel, owned and run by the people behind the Holey Trail Cycle Hire shop in town.

Dolgelynen Farm (☎ 702026; www.dolgelynenfarmhouse.co.uk; Pennal; s/d £30/60; ☯ Easter-Oct; ☒ P) This farmhouse has just three plain homely rooms and lovely views. Located on a working farm, follow the A487 from Machynlleth for half a mile. After crossing the Dyfi Bridge, take the first left-hand turn towards Tywyn (A493)

and the first turn left off this road – the farm lane entrance is signposted Dolgelynen.

Maenllwyd (☎ 702928, Newtown Rd; s/d £35/55; P) A large Victorian house with a preponderance of pale-pink rooms, it makes for a reliable midrange option – low on frills but welcoming and homely.

Dyfi Guesthouse (☎ 702562; www.dyfiguest.co.uk; s/d £40/60; ☒ P ☖) This is the closest B&B to the train station – it's just 200 metres away, but the owners will also pick you up if you call ahead. The modern bungalow-style accommodation is comfortable but the in-house ethos reflects the green nature of the town with great vegan-friendly organic breakfasts and disabled access.

Plas Llwyngwern (☎ 703970; Pantperthog; d/f £45/50) A very welcoming little place, located just 300 metres from the CAT to the north of the centre, it has huge rooms with fantastic views. The building is a grand old house dating from 1750 to 1850 with vast grounds for children to run wild.

Wynnstay Hotel (☎ 702941; www.wynnstay-hotel.com; Maengwyn St; s/d from £55/80, mains £14; ☯ meals noon-2pm & 6.30-9.30pm; ☒ P) This erstwhile Georgian coaching inn, dating from 1780, remains the best all-rounder in town and the only superior option for a few extra home comforts. The rooms are stylishly furnished with one room featuring a four-poster bed. Downstairs is given over to a rustic bar-eatery area, split between a deep-blue nonsmoking restaurant and a deep-red smoking bar. There are imaginative evening meals and a more informal pizzeria (around £8), which also offers takeaway.

Eating
There are lots of good cafés open during the day, but in the evening it's mainly pub food or takeaway on offer.

Maengwyn Café (☎ 702126; 57 Maengwyn St; mains £4; ☯ 8.30am-5pm Mon-Wed, Fri & Sat, 8.30am-4pm Thu, 9am-4pm Sun) Straightforward dishes and décor are the staples of this locals' café. It's simple fare at budget prices, but accordingly very low on frills.

Quarry Wholefood Café (☎ 702624; Maengwyn St; specials £6; ☯ 9am-4.30pm Mon-Sat, to 2pm Thu) Run by the same people that manage the CAT, this woody, gentle-paced place has delicious, wholesome vegetarian lunch specials, using mostly organic ingredients. It's also fantastically baby friendly with organic baby food on the menu, and changing facilities. The only

MID-WALES

downside to its popularity? Queuing for a table.

Skinners Arms (☎ 702354; Penrallt St; bar meals £7) Popular with locals, this has some of the best bar food in town, great Sunday roasts and local ales. It's a warm and cosy spot with a fireplace to ward off the winter chill.

White Lion (☎ 703455; Pentrehedyn St; www.white lionhotel.co.uk; mains £9) This big old inn offers good bar meals, served all day in big portions, plus there are lots of fish and vegetarian options.

Supermarkets include a **Spar** (Maengwyn St; h7am-11pm Mon-Sat, to 10.30pm Sun) and a **Co-op** (Maengwyn St; ☼ 8am-10pm Mon-Sat, 8am-4pm Sun). For more of a treat, **Delicatessen Blasau** (☎ 700410; Penrallt Rd; ☼ 8.30am-5.30pm Mon-Sat) is a superb little deli selling take-away sandwiches, organic produce and fair-trade supplies. Specialising in local produce, they have a huge selection of local wines, liqueurs, whiskies and chocolate.

The town's Wednesday **farmers market** (Maengwyn St) has been going on for over seven centuries and remains a lively affair.

Shopping

Machynlleth has a proud tradition of keeping local, independent shops alive with the main suspects all found along Maengwyn St. The **Spectrum Gallery** (☎ 702877; www.spectrumgallery .co.uk; Maengwyn Street; ☼ 10am-5pm Mon-Sat) is a particularly interesting little place with a range of arty crafts and design-led gifts. Keep a lookout for the all-seeing eye that keeps guard over the high street from the shop's façade.

Getting There & Away

The bus stand for CAT, Corris and Dolgellau is on Pentrehedyn St near the junction with Maengwyn St; buses to Aberystwyth stop opposite. Arriva bus 28 runs to Aberystwyth (35 minutes, six daily Monday to Saturday, two Sunday) and Dolgellau (35 minutes, eight daily Monday to Saturday, three Sunday). Buses to Newtown stop along Maengwyn St by the Red Lion pub; bus 522 runs to Newtown (one hour, four daily Monday to Saturday). Check prices with the local tourist office.

Machynlleth is on the Cambrian main line route across Mid-Wales, with services roughly every two hours from Aberystwyth (£3.80, 30 minutes) and Shrewsbury (£10, 1¼ hours). There are also three services on a Sunday. From Machynlleth the Cambrian Coaster runs up the coast to Pwllheli (£10,

two hours 25 minutes, seven times daily, one Sunday).

Getting Around

Holey Trail Cycle Hire (☎ 700411; www.theholeytrail.co .uk; 31 Maengwyn St; ☼ 10am-6pm Mon-Sat) hires out mountain bikes from half-/full-day £12/18; the staff is a mine of information on the local cycle trails. The owners also offer bike repairs and run the Reditreks bunkhouse.

AROUND MACHYNLLETH
Centre for Alternative Technology

The **Centre for Alternative Technology** (CAT; ☎ 705950; www.cat.org.uk; adult/child £8/4; ☼ 10am-5.30pm Apr-Oct; 10am-4.30pm Nov-Mar, closed first 2 weeks in Jan) is a pioneering environmental centre and the main catalyst for re-branding Machynlleth as the 'green capital of Wales'.

CAT was founded in 1974 – way ahead of its time – to test alternative technologies. Since then, the centre has gone from strength to strength as an ecologically driven laboratory and information source. The centre is a workers cooperative, with about 130 on-site workers and 15 full-time residents.

From the car park you ride 60m up to the site on a **funicular railway** (closed in winter), one of the steepest in the world. The two carriages are connected by a cable over a winding drum; water fills a tank beneath the upper one until it's heavier than the other, and they gently swap places. At the top you disembark by a small, scenic lake with great views across the Dyfi Valley.

To explore the whole site takes about two hours – take rainwear as it's primarily outdoors – and makes for a hugely educational experience for children and adults alike. A variety of displays deal with topics such as composting, solar energy and recycling. Indeed, the whole complex runs mainly on wind, water and solar power, and generates almost no waste. There are workshops and games for children during the school holidays and a vast programme of residential courses for adults throughout the year (course fees start from £30 per hour). Check the website for a range of CAT publications.

You can stay on site with B&B/full-board accommodation (from £22/36 per day), or in two eco-cabins (from £225 per week); the latter are aimed primarily at residential groups. The self-catering cabins are equipped with monitoring facilities, so groups can identify their energy input and output over the week.

LOCAL VOICES   *Paul Allen*

Green ideas are spreading across Mid-Wales. The Dyfi Valley has become one of the UK's leading areas for sustainable tourism, with mountain-bike trails, outdoor pursuits, local food producers, small independent shops, cafés and restaurants.

We like to think that the Centre for Alternative Technology (CAT) has been a major catalyst in this movement.

CAT was established 30 years ago when a bunch of young idealists colonised a derelict slate quarry near Machynlleth. While the outside world thought they were just hippies building houses, the group had a purpose both serious and joyful: to build a community with a lighter impact on the planet.

These young pioneers set out to develop new building and power technologies and test them through normal daily use. These now form a set of practical solutions to the major environmental problems facing the planet.

Today, we receive around 70,000 visitors a year to our 7-acre visitor centre. They enter via our dramatic water-powered cliff railway that carries them up a 60m slope to begin CAT's positive, solutions-driven experience. Interactive displays give a crash course in sustainable technologies and lifestyles. The visitor centre is powered mainly by wind, water and sun, and we recycle almost everything. This includes treating the deposits from visitors with an innovative reed-bed sewage system, returning the goodness to the soil as compost.

CAT's free information service deals with tens of thousands inquiries each year and is often the first port of call for people seeking data and advice. CAT also offers an annual programme of residential courses, taught by academics and other experts with many years' practical experience. Topics include: renewable energy, ecological building, sewage treatment, water supply, organic gardening, composting.

Paul Allen, Development Director, Centre for Alternative Technology

---

They have their own energy from renewable sources, water supply and sewage recycling systems.

Volunteer helpers are also welcome, but required to book ahead around October time – short-term stays are usually between March and September. Those with a more serious interest can book a free trial week, with the aim of staying as a long-term volunteer (a minimum of six months).

CAT is located 3 miles north of Machynlleth on the A487. Arriva bus X32 (five mins, eight daily Monday to Saturday, two on Sunday; £1.20 but price is subject to change) runs here en route to Corris, (see below). Arriving by bus, bicycle or train – not car – gets you a discount of £1.

Corris

This peaceful former slate village, located 5 miles north of Machynlleth, is surrounded by hills covered in tall pines.

Corris Railway (☎ 01654 761303; www.corris.co.uk; ☯ weekends & bank hols Apr-Oct) is a narrow-gauge railway built in the 1850s that once carried slate; it closed in 1948. It disintegrated and became overgrown, but enthusiasts began to rescue the line in 1966 and it re-opened for journeys in 2003. The return trip to Maespoeth takes 50 minutes, which includes a tour of the sheds.

Corris YHA (☎ 761686; Old School, Corris; d/f £13/43; ☯ Fri-Sun mid-Jan–mid-Feb & Nov–mid-Dec, daily mid-Feb–mid-Nov; ✕ Ⓟ) is a pioneering, energy-efficient independent hostel, housed in a grand greystone former school and set in the village of Corris amid some beautiful countryside. The hostel's vehemently green principles have won it awards, with low-energy light bulbs, organic produce and a strict recycling policy all de rigueur.

Arriva bus X32 from Machynlleth calls here (10 minutes, eight daily Monday to Saturday, two on Sunday, £1.20 but price subject to change).

MID-WALES

Snowdonia & the Llŷn

Snowdonia never ceases to inspire. From the spectacular mountain scenery to the welcoming Welsh hospitality in small villages among the peaks, Wales' rural heartland is one of the most attractive and visited areas of the country. It's not just about panoramas, however. Snowdonia is also a hub for activities, with walking, climbing and a new penchant for water sports the main drawcards.

Away from the hiking trails, there's the glorious Portmeirion, an Italianate village nestling on the North Wales coast; Edward I's formidable castles at Caernarfon and Harlech, part of a joint Unesco World Heritage Site with those at Beaumaris and Conwy; and lively hubs for active travellers at Betws-y-Coed and Bala.

The northwest is the most traditionally minded and heavily Welsh-speaking corner. Indeed, modern Gwynedd is more than 70% Welsh-speaking, while old Gwynedd was a stronghold of the Welsh princes. The Snowdon highlands sheltered Llywelyn ap Gruffydd in the 13th century and Owain Glyndŵr in the 15th during their struggles against the English.

With such a formidable mountain shield, it's little wonder that the Llŷn Peninsula has held with even greater confidence to old Welsh ways, making it the one of the lesser-known areas, but one worthy of discovery.

For more information about the region, check the website www.visitsnowdonia.info.

HIGHLIGHTS

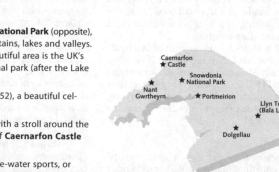

- Explore **Snowdonia National Park** (opposite), a crescendo of mountains, lakes and valleys. This dramatically beautiful area is the UK's second-largest national park (after the Lake District).

- Visit **Portmeirion** (p252), a beautiful celebration of kitsch

- Soak up the history with a stroll around the World Heritage Site of **Caernarfon Castle** (p254)

- Try your hand at white-water sports, or try to spot the monster of the lake at **Llyn Tegid** (p245)

- Stretch your legs around **Dolgellau** (p241), climbing Cader Idris or tackling the Precipice Walk

- Venture to the end of the earth and learn a new language in the process with a trip to the **Welsh Language & Heritage Centre** (p274) at Nant Gwrtheyrn

ACTIVITIES

One of the best regions in Wales for getting out and about, Snowdonia is prime climbing, cycling, mountain biking, walking, scrambling country, while the Llŷn is one of the best areas in Wales for water sports, including sailing (p256, p247), surfing (p270) and wakeboarding (p271). Just contemplating the list of activities could tire you out.

GETTING THERE & AROUND

The region's biggest bus operator is **Arriva Cymru** (www.arrivabus.co.uk) for bus connections between major towns; service is poor on Sundays. Most of the services to trailheads within Snowdonia National Park are operated by **Snowdon Sherpa** (www.gwynedd.gov.uk/bwsgwynedd), a park-run association of local companies, whose dedicated blue-liveried buses run on a network of routes around the park, making it easier for people to leave their cars outside the park. Buses run on fixed schedules every hour or two (less often on Sunday).

Railway travel is more important here than in many parts of the country, thanks to the **Cambrian Coast line** (www.thecambrianline.co.uk), which runs right down the coast from Pwthelli on the Llŷn Peninsula to Machynlleth in Mid-Wales; and the **Conwy Valley line** (www.conwyvalleyrailway.co .uk) in the north. The **Rheilffordd Ffestiniog Railway** (www.festrail.co.uk) links them.

For details of travel passes, see p326.

SNOWDONIA

SNOWDONIA NATIONAL PARK (PARC CENEDLAETHOL ERYRI)

Snowdonia National Park was founded in 1951 (Wales' first national park), primarily to keep the area from being loved to death. This is, after all, Wales' best-known and most heavily used national park, with the busiest part of the park around Mt Snowdon (1085m). Around 750,000 people climb, walk or take the train to the summit each year, and all those sturdy shoes make trail maintenance and repair a frantic job for park staff. The Snowdonia Society (see the boxed text Local Voices, p264) estimates that the park is visited an average of 10 million times each year.

The Welsh name for Snowdonia, the Snowdon highlands, is Eryri (eh-*ruh*-ree). The Welsh call Snowdon itself Yr Wyddfa (uhr-*with*-vuh), meaning Great Tomb – according

to legend a giant called Rita Gawr was slain here by King Arthur, and is buried at the summit (for more on King Arthur, see p77).

Like Wales' other national parks, this one is very lived-in, with sizeable towns at Dolgellau, Bala, Harlech and Betws-y-Coed. Two-thirds of the park is privately owned, with over three-quarters in use for raising sheep and beef cattle. While the most popular reason for visiting the park is to walk, you can also go climbing, white-water rafting, pony trekking, even windsurfing.

The park is the only home to two endangered species, an arctic/alpine plant called the Snowdon lily *(Lloydia seotina)* as well as the rainbow-coloured Snowdon beetle *(Chrysolina cerealis)*. The gwyniad is a species of whitefish found only in Llyn Tegid (Bala Lake), which also has probably the UK's only colony of glutinous snails *(Myxas glutinosa)*.

Orientation & Information

Although the focus is on Mt Snowdon, the park – some 35 miles east to west and over 50 miles north to south – extends all the way from Aberdovey to Conwy.

The park's **administrative head office** (☎ 01766-770274; www.eryri-npa.co.uk; Penrhyndeudraeth) is situated 4 miles east of Porthmadog, although it's not a public enquiries office. This office manages six local tourist offices, including Betws-y-Cod, Dolgellau, Beddgelert and Harlech, where you can pick up a copy of *Eryri/Snowdonia,* the park's free annual visitor newspaper, which includes information on getting around, park-organised walks and other activities.

The office also runs – under licence from the Met Office – its own 24-hour **weather service** (☎ 08709-000100; www.metoffice.gov.uk). Most tourist offices also display weather forecasts, as do several outdoors shops in the area.

Activities
WALKING & CLIMBING

Mt Snowdon (p239) is the main destination for walkers and Llanberis (p263) the favoured base. For climbers, Cader (or Cadair) Idris (p244), near Dolgellau, is the most popular and rises to 892m. Choose your time carefully to escape the crowds. There are gentler walks in the forests and hills around Betws-y-Coed (p260).

The park information centres and some tourist offices stock useful brochures on each of the six main routes up Snowdon, while Dolgellau and a few other offices have a similar set on the three main routes up Cader Idris.

Be prepared to deal with hostile conditions at any time of the year; the sudden appearance of low cloud and mist is common, even on days that start out clear and sunny. Never leave without food, drink, warm clothing and waterproofs, whatever the weather. Carry *and* know how to read the appropriate large-scale OS map for the area, and carry a compass at all times. Also be aware that even some walks described as easy may follow paths that go near very steep slopes and over loose scree – the Pyg Track up Snowdon, for example. If the weather turns for the worse, consider taking the train down.

There are dozens of private outfits offering guided or self-guided Snowdonia walks and

walking holidays, often with luggage transport; details of various organisations are listed throughout this chapter.

CYCLING & MOUNTAIN BIKING

There are good routes for cycling and mountain biking through **Coed Y Brenin Forest Park** (☎ 01341-422289), near Dolgellau, **Gwydyr Forest Park** (☎ 01492-640578), near Betws-y-Coed, and **Beddgelert Forest Park** (☎ 01492-640578).

Lôn Las Cymru, the Welsh National Cycle Route (Sustrans route 8; see p60), runs from Dolgellau, via Porthmadog and Criccieth, to Caernarfon and Bangor. Much of it runs alongside two county-built, dedicated walking and cycling paths on either side of Caernarfon.

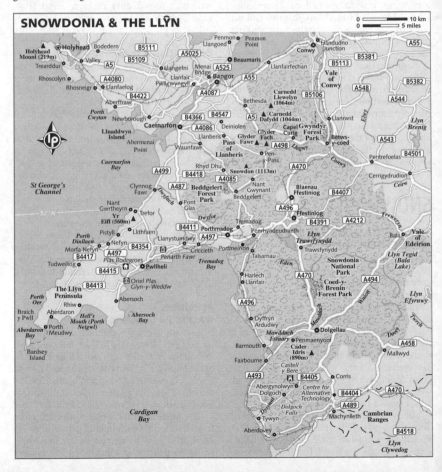

SNOWDONIA & THE LLŶN

The heavy use of bridleways (paths shared by walkers, cyclists and horse riders) for off-road cycling to the summit of Snowdon has led to erosion and fears for walkers' safety. Restrictions are now in place and cycling is not allowed from 10am to 5pm May to the end of September. Traffic on A-roads in summer can make cycling hazardous, so stick to B-roads or unclassified roads.

NARROW-GAUGE RAILWAY JOURNEYS

One of the attractions of this area is the large number of narrow-gauge railways, many of them originally built to haul slate out of the mountains. The scenic **Ffestiniog Railway** (p250) runs from Porthmadog up to Blaenau Ffestiniog; the rack-and-pinion **Snowdon Mountain Railway** (p265) from Llanberis goes to the summit of Snowdon; and the **Talyllyn Railway** (p243) from Tywyn heads inland to Abergynolwyn, on the southern side of Cader Idris.

For Getting There & Around information, see p237.

BARMOUTH (Y BERMO)

☎ 01341 / pop 2500

During summer Barmouth comes across as a typical kiss-me-quick seaside resort – all chip shops and dodgem cars. Out of season,

however, it has a very different feel, with a mellower vibe offsetting the brash neon of high summer. Whatever the season, this small town makes a good base for walkers, with its solid infrastructure for tourists.

Clinging to a headland at the mouth of the immense Mawddach Estuary and fronted by a vast breathtaking beach, Barmouth is a great place for getting your cobwebs blasted away by the salty wind, for views out to sea and back across the estuary to a tableau of Snowdon's peaks, and for breezy trips by ferry or fishing boat. Barmouth Bridge, Wales' only surviving wooden rail viaduct, spans the estuary, and has a fantastic pedestrian walkway across it. Behind the town rises Dinas Oleu, Wales' answer to the Rock of Gibraltar, the first property ever bequeathed to the National Trust (NT; in 1895) and an irresistible temptation for walkers.

Orientation & Information

The hub of the action is grouped along High St and into the Old Town along Church St. Buses stop on Jubilee Rd, right across Beach Rd from the train station, which anchors the bottom end of town at the tip of Station Rd and opposite the police station. Taxis wait outside the train station, and the main **car park** (per hr £0.50) is just behind the seafront.

SCALING SNOWDON

Views from Mt Snowdon are stupendous on a clear day, with the peak's fine ridges dropping away in great swoops to sheltered *cwms* (valleys) and deep lakes. Even on a gloomy day you could find yourself above the clouds. Be warned that midsummer weekends can be busy. Often it's just the summit, with its incongruously mundane café, that's really crowded, but you may also encounter queues across Crib Goch.

There are six main walking routes to the top. The easiest – and least interesting – is the **Llanberis Path**, heading southwards from Llanberis along the Snowdon Mountain Railway line (five hours up and back). Almost as easy, the shortest of all and the safest in winter, is the **Snowdon Ranger Path**, which leads northwards from the Snowdon Ranger Youth Hostel near Beddgelert (five hours).

From Pen-y-Pass YHA at the top of Llanberis Pass on the A4086, two tracks run westwards to the summit. The **Pyg Track** (5½ hours) is more interesting but involves some scrambling, while the **Miner's Track** (five hours) starts out gently but gets steeper. Pen-y-Pass has the advantage of starting higher up, but parking is limited.

The undemanding **Rhyd Ddu Path**, the least-used route, runs from the Caernarfon–Beddgelert road (five hours); the trailhead can be accessed from the Welsh Highland Railway station (see p256). The most challenging route is the Watkin Path, northwards from Nant Gwynant, 3 miles northeast of Beddgelert on the A498 (seven hours) – trailhead parking is plentiful.

For some fine variants on the trails see the Snowdonia chapter of Lonely Planet's *Walking in Britain*. The Snowdon Sherpa bus stops regularly at trailheads for all of these walks, and if all this sounds like far too much effort, hop on the Snowdon Mountain Railway all the way to the summit (see p265) – once it reopens in 2008.

The new and very professional **tourist office** (☎ 280787; ☒ 10am-6pm daily May-Sep, 9.30am-5pm daily Mar Apr & Oct, 9.30am-4pm Mon, Tue & Thu-Sat Nov-Mar) is now in the train station's concourse. It sells leaflets on local walks, train tickets for mainline connections and offers an accommodation service.

There's a **post office** (High St; ☒ 9.30am-5.30pm Mon-Sat, 9.30am-12.30pm Sat) inside Martin's newsagent; it is fringed by banks. The **Barmouth Laundry Centre** (High St; ☒ 8.30am-6.30pm) is on High St. There's free internet at the **library** (Talbot Sq; ☒ 10am-noon & 3-7pm Mon, 2-4pm Tue, 2-6pm Thu & Fri), located just behind the **police station** (Talbot Sq).

Sights

FAIRBOURNE
Nearby Fairbourne has a lovely, long beach, but little else to offer except a pleasant enough journey across the estuary. From April to September, regular **railway ferries** (adult/child return £2.50/1.50) make the five-minute crossing across the estuary to another sandy beach at Penrhyn Point to connect with Wales' only seaside narrow-gauge railway, the steam-hauled **Fairbourne & Barmouth Steam Railway** (☎ 250362; www.fairbournerailway.com; Beach Rd; adult/child £6.90/3.90; ☒ 3-8 services daily Apr-Sep plus occasional other services). The line heads south along the coast for 2.5 miles to Fairbourne, and was built in 1895 to move materials for the construction of Fairbourne village.

There's a restaurant at Penrhyn Point, and a café and the take-it-or-leave-it **Rowen Indoor Nature Centre** (☎ 250362; Fairbourne station; admission free; ☒ 10.30am-4.30pm). There is a mainline station for the Cambrian Coast train line at Fairbourne.

QUAYSIDE
The sweep of old Barmouth down by the quay is good for walks and blasts of fresh air. The ferry also departs from here for Penrhyn Point. The little round house is Ty Crwn, once a jail where drunk and disorderly sailors could cool off until morning.

Volunteers run the small **Barmouth Lifeboat Station** (☎ 281168; The Promenade; admission free; ☒ 10am-4pm), which tells many a brave rescue story.

MAWDDACH ESTUARY
The glorious Mawddach Estuary is a striking sight: a mass of water flooding out to sea, flanked by woodlands, wetlands and the romantic mountains of southern Snowdonia. Around its edge, the **Mawddach Trail** is an easy walk or cycle from Barmouth via Penmaen-

pool to Dolgellau – a distance of 11 miles with a marvellous stretch right across the estuary on the Barmouth Railway Bridge.

There are two Royal Society for the Protection of Birds (RSPB) reserves in the estuary valley, rich in oak wood, and popular haunts for herons, pied flycatchers, woodpeckers, ravens and buzzards, as well as dragonflies and butterflies. For more information, visit the **RSPB Information Centre** (☎ 422071; Penmaenpool; ☒ 11am-5pm May-Aug), which is housed in the old signal box adjacent to the George III Hotel and displays maps on reserve trails.

Activities
Apart from the Mawddach Trail (left), you can scramble up any one of several alleys running uphill off Church St and you'll find the town gets more and more vertical, with better and better views, and old houses nearly on top of one another.

Carry on up to a network of trails, all across 258m Dinas Oleu. Bear eastwards around the headland – on one of these paths or from the far end of Church St – to the popular **Panorama Walk**, which has the best of the estuary views. Alternatively, follow Church St onto the Barmouth Bridge and cross the estuary on its pedestrian walkway for wonderful views down the estuary; the latter forms part of the Mawddach Trail. For more details of walks, ask at the tourist office.

Biking excursions are available via **Snow Bikers** (☎ 430628; www.snowbikers.com), starting with a one-hour taster session (£18 per person). **RIB Rides** (☎ 281366; www.rib-rides.com) offers 30-minute bursts around the harbour (from £10 per person); the organisers also run the Richmond House guesthouse (opposite).

Festivals & Events
The international **Three Peaks Yacht Race** (☎ 280298; www.threepeaksyachtrace.co.uk), held in late June, has been an annual event for more than 25 years. Contestants sail to Caernarfon where two crew members run to the summit of Snowdon; then they sail to Whitehaven in England and run up Scaféll Pike; and finally to Fort William in Scotland, with another run up Ben Nevis – 390 nautical miles of sailing and 75 miles of fell running. The record so far is an astonishing two days, two hours and four minutes, achieved in 1998.

During the first three weekends in August, the **Barmouth Harbour Festival** features bands, street theatre, music, fireworks and more.

There's the **Barmouth Walking Festival** (www.bar mouthwalkingfestival.co.uk) in mid-September and an annual **Barmouth Arts Festival** (www.barmoutharts festival.co.uk) held in early September.

Sleeping

Aber House (☎ 280624; High St; s/d £30/55; ✗) From the outside, this regal 200-year-old house looks like a stately pile. Inside, the four rooms are comfortable, albeit a little on the chintzy side, but none have en suites. Still, the place has a homely feel and the owners cater for vegans and vegetarians at breakfast. Watch out for the aggressive dog.

Wavecrest Guesthouse (☎ 280330; 8 Marine Pde; s/d £30/60; ✗) There's a string of modest B&Bs along Marine Pde with sea views, but Wavecrest is a cut above the rest. The best rooms have sea views while recent refurbishment has brought some nice touches, such as under-floor heating and new flat-screen TVs with Freeview channels. The generous breakfast makes use of local, organic and fair-trade products.

Dros-y-Dwr (☎ 280284; www.barmouthbandb.co.uk; 6 Porkington Place; s/d £40/60; ✗) The favourite choice for hikers, bikers and walkers, this friendly little place (just three rooms, two en suite) has a drying room for wet kit and big vegetarian-friendly breakfasts. Best of all, however, is the tiny, deep-red library that overlooks the sea – pull up a chair, browse through a book and soak up the view.

Richmond House (☎ 281366; www.barmouthbedand breakfast.co.uk; High St; s/d/f £45/60/80; ✗ 🖳) The smartest place in town is a handsome town-house with a stylish interior and big, contemporary rooms. Thoughtful touches include in-room DVD players and free Kit-Kat biscuits supplied along with tea- and coffee-making facilities. There's wi-fi available and an attractive garden area for summer lounging on chunky, wooden furniture. The owners also organise boat trips (see opposite).

Eating & Drinking

Goodie's Coffee Shop (High St; meals around £5; ⏲ 11.30am-3.30pm) A simple café for teas and coffees all day, plus light lunches in a bright, cheery eatery.

Wannabe's (☎ 280820; King Edward St; meals around £5; ⏲ 9.30am-5pm Mon-Tue, Thu & Sat, 10am-4pm Sun; 🖳) This great, relaxed café is a cut above the average coffee shop with daily lunch specials and hot sandwiches served among leather sofas and daily newspapers. The owners also sell their homemade preserves, chutneys and

jams on the premises and there's internet access (£1 per 30 minutes).

Inglenook (☎ 280807; Harbour Lane; mains about £8) Set in a 17th-century building off Church St, this longstanding place is best for its seafood, notably lobster and crab.

Bistro (☎ 281009; Church St; mains around £10; ⏲ 6-9.30pm Thu-Tue; ✗) The top-end place in town is now completely nonsmoking and looking smart; it offers a broad menu of fresh local produce and a comprehensive wine list.

For a pint, feel the **Tal y Don** (☎ 280508; High St) and the **Royal Hotel** (☎ 281682; King Edward St) are both decent pubs serving a good selection of bar meals (mains around £12).

For self-caterers, there's a **Co-op supermarket** (⏲ 8am-10pm Mon-Sat, 10am-4pm Sun) by the train station and a **Spar supermarket** (⏲ 8am-11pm Mon-Sat, 9am-11pm Sun) on High St opposite Wannabe's.

Entertainment

The town's cultural life is concentrated on the small theatre-cum-arts centre **Theatr y Ddraig** (☎ 281697) with its occasional programme of cultural activities. Ask in the tourist office for more information.

Getting There & Away

Barmouth is the western terminus of Arriva's bus X94 inter-regional service from Wrexham (1½ hours) via Llangollen (1¼ hours) and Dolgellau (20 minutes, eight daily Monday to Saturday, three Sunday). Express Motors bus 38 runs to/from Blaenau Ffestiniog (one hour) and Porthmadog (one hour 20 minutes, three daily Monday to Saturday).

Barmouth is on the Cambrian Coast railway line, with trains from Machynlleth (single £5.80, 50 minutes, roughly hourly) and Porthmadog (£4.30, one hour 10 minutes, every two hours Monday to Saturday).

Mainline trains to Fairbourne (£1.50, 10 minutes) run regularly – take the train out there, then walk back over the bridge.

DOLGELLAU
☎ 01341 / pop 2800

Dolgellau is a place steeped in history with lots of historic architecture and a genteel feel. It's thought the Welsh hero Owain Glyndŵr met with fellow rebels here, although the likely venue (on Bridge St) is now derelict and forgotten.

The Dolgellau area also has historical links with the Society of Friends or Quaker movement (with its philosophy of direct communication with God, free of creeds, rites and clergy). After George Fox – the most influential exponent of the Friends' philosophy – made a visit in 1657, a Quaker community was founded here. Converts, from simple farmers to local gentry, were persecuted with vigour because their refusal to swear oaths – in particular to the king – was considered treasonous. Many eventually emigrated to William Penn's Quaker community in America.

Dolgellau was a regional centre for Wales' prosperous wool industry in the early 19th century. Many of the town's finest buildings, sturdy and unornamented, were built at that time, and the town centre hasn't changed all that much since. Local mills failed to keep pace with mass mechanisation, however, and decline set in after about 1800. The region bounced back when the Romantic Revival of the late-18th century made Wales' wild landscapes popular with genteel travellers. There was also, surprisingly, a gold rush here when waves of hopefuls descended to pan for gold.

Today, however, this grey-slate, charmingly gruff little market town relies on tour-ism. Dolgellau is an ideal base to climb Cader Idris (892m) or to explore the lovely Mawddach Estuary. Recently, the town has also smartened up its act with new and more sophisticated places to sleep and eat. It has a lively feel and enough facilities to make it a great base for activities in the Snowdonia National Park.

Orientation & Information

Dolgellau sits at the confluence of the River Wnion (a tributary of the Mawddach) and the smaller River Arran. The A470 passes just north of the town centre, which is located south of Bont Fawr (Big Bridge; built 1638).

Buses stop on Eldon Sq at the heart of town and there's a car park just south of the River Wnion, next to Bont Fawr. This is also the home to the efficient **Tourist Office & National Park Information Centre** (☎ 422888; Eldon Sq; 🕙 10am-5.30pm daily Apr-Oct, 10am-4.30pm Thu-Mon Oct-Mar). The office sells an excellent range of maps, local history books and leaflets charting the trails for a climbing excursion to Cader Idris (see the boxed text Climbing

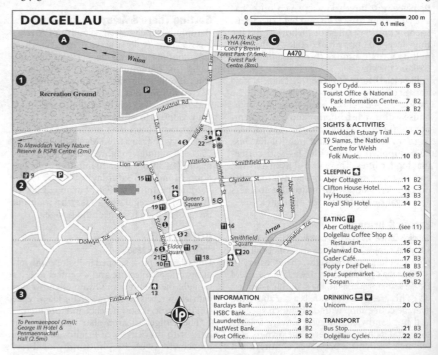

DOLGELLAU

0 _____ 200 m
0 _____ 0.1 miles

To A470; Kings YHA (4mi); Coed y Brenin Forest Park (7.5mi); Forest Park Centre (8mi)

A470

Wnion

Recreation Ground

Industrial Rd

Lôn Las

Bont Fawr

Bridge

To Mawddach Valley Nature Reserve & RSPB Centre (2mi)

Lion Yard

Lôn Las

Waterloo St

Smithfield St

Smithfield La

Glyndwr St

Marian Rd

Eldon Rd

Queen's Square

English Tce

Aber Wnion

Glyncaion Tce

Dolwyn Tce

Eldon Square

Smithfield Square

Arran

Finsbury Sq

To Penmaenpool (2mi); George III Hotel & Penmaennuchaf Hall (2.5mi)

Siop Y Dydd	6 B3
Tourist Office & National Park Information Centre	7 B2
Web	8 B2

SIGHTS & ACTIVITIES
Mawddach Estuary Trail	9 A2
Tŷ Siamas, the National Centre for Welsh Folk Music	10 B3

SLEEPING
Aber Cottage	11 B2
Clifton House Hotel	12 C3
Ivy House	13 B3
Royal Ship Hotel	14 B2

EATING
Aber Cottage	(see 11)
Dolgellau Coffee Shop & Restaurant	15 B2
Dylanwad Da	16 C2
Gader Café	17 B3
Popty r Dref Deli	18 B3
Spar Supermarket	(see 5)
Y Sospan	19 B2

DRINKING
Unicorn	20 C3

INFORMATION
Barclays Bank	1 B2
HSBC Bank	2 B2
Laundrette	3 B2
NatWest Bank	4 B2
Post Office	5 B2

TRANSPORT
Bus Stop	21 B3
Dolgellau Cycles	22 B2

IN THE AREA: TALYLLYN RAILWAY & TALYLLYN LAKE

The narrow-gauge **Talyllyn Railway** (☎ 01654-710472; www.talyllyn.co.uk; Wharf Station, Tywyn; adult/ 1 child with adult/child without adult £11/2/5.50; 2-8 services daily; Apr-Oct plus some seasonal excursions) was opened in 1865 to carry slate from the Bryn Eglwys quarries near Abergynolwyn. In 1950 the line was saved from closure by the world's first railway preservation society. It's one of Wales' most enchanting little railways and puffs for 7.3 scenic, steam-powered miles up the Fathew Valley to Abergynolwyn. There are five stations along the way, each with waymarked walking trails (and waterfalls at Dolgoch and Nant Gwernol); leaflets on these are available at the stations. Your ticket entitles you to all-day travel.

At the lower terminus of Tywyn Wharf, the **Narrow Gauge Railway Museum** (☎ 01654-710472; www.ngrm.org.uk; Wharf Station, Tywyn; adult/child £1/0.50; 11am-3pm Apr-Oct, plus extended hr when trains running) is one for the history buffs, with shiny narrow-gauge steam locomotives and the story of the volunteers who preserved the railway.

About 2 miles northeast of Abergynolwyn along the B4405 is **Talyllyn Lake**, a substantial and tranquil body of water edged by fields and hills and overlooked by Cadair Idris. It's stocked with trout and popular with anglers.

Cader Idris, p244). Upstairs there's a permanent **exhibition** (admission free) on the region's Quaker heritage in a suitably dour wood-panelled room.

If you find the tourist office closed, a small bookshop **Siop Y Dydd** (☎ 421133; Eldon Sq; 9.30am-5.30pm Mon-Fri) has maps and some local information. The **post office** (Smithfield St; 9.30am-5.30pm Mon-Fri, 9.30am-12.30pm Sat) is inside the town's Spar supermarket and there's also a **laundrette** (9am-7pm Wed-Mon) further along the same street. For internet access, head for the **Web** (☎ 422022; Smithfield St; per hr £3; 10am-5pm), which has wi-fi access, simple coffees and snacks.

The banks are sprinkled liberally around town, and include **HSBC** (Eldon Sq), **Barclays** (Lion St) and **NatWest** (Bridge St).

Sights

Tŷ Siamas, the National Centre for Welsh Folk Music (☎ 421800; www.tysiamas.com; Idris Hall, Eldon Sq) was under construction at the time of writing and due to open spring 2007. A major new attraction, it's the first centre of its kind in Wales and celebrates Dollgellau's hosting of the first ever Welsh folk festival in 1952. Idris Hall, the former market hall on Eldon Sq, will house the centre and the initial programme offers a mix of performance, exhibitions, workshops and facilities for tourists. The centre is named after Elis Sion Siamas, a harpist from Dolgellau who was the royal harpist to Queen Anne between 1702 and 1714. He was one of the first people to introduce the triple harp in Wales.

Activities
WALKING & CYCLING

The beautiful 11-mile **Mawddach Estuary Trail** is a flat (and in places wheelchair-accessible) path that's great for walking or cycling. Running through woods and past wetlands on the southern side of the Mawddach Estuary, it begins in town at the car park and runs past the **RSPB Information Centre** (☎ 01341-422071; Penmaenpool; 11am-5pm May-Aug), 2 miles west of Dolgellau.

The **Precipice Walk** is a 4-mile hike along a flat stretch running around the steep flanks of Moel Cynwch, which provides superb estuary views. The path starts near Cymer Abbey, a 13th-century ruin located 2 miles north of Dolgellau.

Festivals & Events

Sesiwn Fawr (☎ 0871 230 1314; www.sesiwnfawr.co.uk) is a three-day jamboree of Welsh folk music and beer that fills Dolgellau's main square on the third weekend in July. 'The Mighty Session' has lived up to its name – the festival has grown in stature in recent years and is now ticketed with an extensive sideline in family-friendly events and activities. During the festival, accommodation prices across Dolgellau are at a heavy premium.

Sleeping

Local legend says that anyone who spends the night on top of Cader Idris will awake either mad or a poet. If you would like something more conventional, there's a wide choice of accommodation available.

CLIMBING CADER IDRIS

Cader Idris (892m), or the 'Seat of Idris' (a legendary giant), is a hulking, menacing-looking mountain with the requisite mythology attached. It's said that Hounds of the Underworld fly around its peaks, and strange light effects are often sighted in the area. However, climbing it is less taxing than launching up Snowdon, and the reward is great views. The usual route is the **Dolgellau** or **Ty Nant Path**, southeastwards from Ty Nant Farm on the A493. The farm is 3 miles west of Dolgellau, just beyond Penmaenpool. It's a rocky but safe, straightforward route, taking about five hours there and back.

The easiest but longest route (5 miles each way, six hours return) is the **'Tywyn' or Llanfihangel y Pennant Path**, a gentle pony track that heads northeast from the hamlet of Llanfihangel y Pennant, joining the Ty Nant Path at the latter's midpoint. Llanfihangel is 1.5 miles from the terminus of the Talyllyn Railway (p243) at Abergynolwyn.

The shortest (3 miles) but steepest route is the **Minffordd Path**, running northwest from the Dol Idris car park, a few hundred metres down the B4405 from Minffordd, itself 6.5 miles from Dolgellau on the A487 Machynlleth road. This route, taking around five hours there and back, requires the most caution, especially on the way back down. Stout shoes are essential.

Before embarking on any climb, check for the latest information and weather conditions from the Dolgellau tourist office (p242). Inexperienced climbers should consult specialist advice before undertaking any activity.

Kings YHA (☎ 0870 7705900; adult/child £11.95/8.95; Easter-Oct) A great spot for peace, quiet and outdoor pursuits, this country-house hostel, northwest of Dolgellau, is gloriously remote – just don't expect a mobile phone signal. To get there, Arriva's bus 28 stops at Abergwynant, 1.5 miles west of Penmaenpool, from where it's a 1-mile walk south through a spooky wood.

Ivy House (☎ 422535; Finsbury Sq; s/d £37/58) This central, rather twee B&B in a grey-stone house, has six comfy rooms (four with en suites) and traditional facilities.

Aber Cottage (☎ 422460; www.abercottagegallery.com; Smithfield St; s/d £30/60; P ⊠ ▯) Just south of the bridge, this superior cottage-style guesthouse has spotless rooms and an efficient welcome on a year-round basis. The owners' artworks adorn the walls, lending a gallery feel to communal areas. Expect hearty breakfasts, served in the tearoom (see opposite), where a strict 'no chips or burgers' policy operates.

Royal Ship Hotel (☎ 422209; Queen's Sq; s/d £50/87.50) The décor of this 19th-century, ivy-covered coaching inn looks a bit faded while the communal areas are given over to serving bar meals with chips galore. It remains a centrally located staple in the midrange category, although new management could breathe life into an old dame past her prime.

Clifton House Hotel (☎ 422554; Smithfield Sq; s/d £50/70) Big changes are afoot at this central hotel, formerly the town jail. The new owners are promising a fresh new look for 2007

to transform the place from a simple B&B to more of a boutique hotel. The extensive refurbishment will not alter the wheelchair-accessible room downstairs and the cosy cellar restaurant, which opens to the public for lunch and dinner (mains around £10 to £15).

George III Hotel (☎ 422525; www.georgethethird.co .uk; Penmaenpool; s/d £60/98; bar meals noon-2pm & 6-9pm; P) All aboard for a trainspotter's dream – this quirky hotel is partly housed in the former waiting room, ticket office and station master's house of the old Cambrian Railway station. Rooms in the latter are rather small but cottage-style rooms, located on the former platform one, are superior. And if railway sleepers don't grab you, the view will: nine of the 11 rooms have fantastic vistas out across the Mawddach estuary, which is accessible via a 115-year-old toll bridge.

Penmaennuchaf Hall (☎ 422129; www.penhall.co .uk; Penmaenpool; s/d from £65/130; P) With imposing furnishings and elaborate gardens, this stately country-house hotel is the former pile of Bolton cotton magnate, James Leigh. It's an imposing setting and ideally placed for the country set, although it does feel a bit sniffy and formal for a casual weekend break. The 14 rooms have a lavish air with drapes and soft furnishings but also feature in-room mod cons such as CD players. Four-course dinners (£35) are available, and children over six years old are welcome; ask about midweek breaks and special promotions.

Eating & Drinking

Gader Café (☎ 423425; Eldon Sq; 9am-4pm) This is a straightforward, belly-filling café and bakery with good sandwiches.

Dolgellau Coffee Shop & Restaurant (☎ 423040; Lion St; mains around £6; 8am-5.30pm Mon-Fri, 8am-5pm Sat) No-frills toasties, breakfasts and a surprisingly large menu of vegetarian options are on offer at this big café-style place. It's nothing fancy, but family friendly for kids.

Y Sospan (☎ 423174; Queen's Sq; lunch specials around £4, bistro mains around £11; 9am-9.30pm Tue-Sun, 9am-5.30pm Mon) In the old town hall, book-lined and woody, this relaxed eatery is split between a small downstairs tearoom for coffees and lunches, and an upstairs wine bar bistro.

Aber Cottage (☎ 422460; Smithfield St; snacks £3-4; 10am-5pm, evening meals to order) Like stepping back into your grandmother's living room, this super-cosy tearoom–cum–gallery is big on knick-knacks and great food. It's best for lunch with homemade soup (£3) and sandwiches (£4), plus friendly service. It also offers B&B (see opposite).

Dylanwad Da (☎ 422870; 2 Smithfield St; mains around £14; 5-9pm Tue-Sat Jun-Sep) A long-standing favourite on the Snowdonia scene, this low-lit upscale eatery has a healthy wine list and an imaginative menu for a tasty dinner. For a caffeine hit on the run, it also now boasts a small coffee shop, **Ty Coffi** (10am-4pm).

Popty r Dref Deli (☎ 422507; Smithfield St) A fantastic deli for take-away sandwiches and one of the few left with the original bakery out the back. Support it to keep a rare example of local industry alive. The house speciality is the honey bun – be quick, they're usually sold out by 11am. For self-caterers, there's also the **Spar supermarket** (Smithfield St).

Unicorn (☎ 422742; Queen's Sq) For a pint, try the no-nonsense Unicorn to meet the locals over a real ale; it also has simple bar meals (around £6).

Getting There & Around

There are several Arriva Cymru bus services:
X32 or 2 To/from Caernarfon (1½ hours, three daily).
94 To/from Barmouth (20 minutes, seven daily Monday to Saturday and two on Sunday), continuing onto Bala (35 minutes).

You can hire a bike from **Dolgellau Cycles** (☎ 423332; Smithfield St; per half-/full day £13/20); the owner can help advise on local cycle routes.

AROUND DOLGELLAU
Mawddach Valley Nature Reserve

Set in oak woodlands along the northern side of the Mawddach Estuary, this **RSPB nature reserve** (admission free) is open year round. Permanent residents include ravens and buzzards, while spring visitors feature redstarts, wood warblers and pied flycatchers. There is a 2.5-mile trail and a wheelchair-accessible half-mile trail. The reserve is 2 miles west of Dolgellau on the A493. There's an **information centre** (☎ 01341-422071; 11am-5pm late-May–Aug) by the Penmaenpool toll bridge.

Coed y Brenin Forest Park

This woodland park, 7.5 miles north of Dolgellau, is laced with 25 miles of cycle trails – some of the best in Wales. It was all-purpose built with the help of the Forest Enterprise Wales. There are beginner and family routes, and it's also a venue for regular rallies. The **Forest Park Centre** (☎ 01341-440742; www.forestry.gov.uk/wales) is 8 miles north of Dolgellau on the A470 Blaenau Ffestiniog road. The centre produces an excellent leaflet with details of the various bike trails.

BALA (Y BALA)
☎ 01678 / pop 2000

The town of Bala is synonymous with beautiful **Llyn Tegid** (Bala Lake), which sits at the northeastern end of town and was formed during the last Ice Age when glaciers blocked up the valley of the River Dee (Afon Dyfrdwy) with debris. This is Wales' largest freshwater lake – 4 miles long, three-quarters of a mile wide and, in places, over 43m deep. The town, 18 miles northeast of Dolgellau, sits where the River Dee flows out of the lake and is joined by the River Tryweryn.

Bala is big on folk tales, (see the boxed text The Legend of Teggie, p246). One such tale, an alternative to the glacial version of events, says the valley was once the home of a cruel and dissolute prince named Tegid Foel. One night, at a banquet thrown by the prince, the harpist kept hearing a small bird urging him to flee the palace. He finally did so, fell asleep on a hilltop, and awoke at dawn to find the palace and principality drowned beneath the lake.

Bala was a centre for the Welsh wool industry during the 18th century but today it's better known as a gateway town to the Snowdonia National Park. It has also recently built a reputation as a centre for water sports. The tiny main street is often bustling with visitors in summer and increasingly dotted with adventure sports and outdoors shops. The proximity to the lake and availability of top-notch adventures makes it a very lively little place.

Though founded by the Normans in 1310, Bala today is staunchly Welsh and a predominantly Welsh-speaking town – about 80%. Local hero and MP Thomas Edward Ellis, the Liberal Member of Parliament elected in 1886, was a prominent contemporary of Lloyd George (see p36) in the movement towards an independent Wales at the end of the 19th century. One of Ellis' friends was Michael D Jones, founder of the Welsh colony in Patagonia.

Orientation & Information

The town is essentially one long street (the A494), called Pensarn Rd at the southwestern end, High St through the centre and Station Rd on the other side. The centre is the intersection of High and Tegid Sts, by the White Lion Royal Hotel; buses stop along High St.

The **tourist office** (☎ 521021; Pensarn Rd; ⏰ 10am-5.30pm Thu-Mon Apr-Oct, 10am-4pm Fri-Mon Nov-Mar) is about a third of a mile southwest of the centre and next to the leisure centre. There are banks along the high street, and a **post office** (High St; ⏰ 9.30am-5.30pm Mon-Fri, 9.30am-12.30pm Sat) opposite the White Lion Royal Hotel. **Café Cwpwrdd Cornel** (☎ 521851; 64-66 High St; per hr £3; ⏰ 9am-5pm), next to Barclays Bank, has internet access plus simple coffees and snacks.

The **car park** (per hr 50p) is behind the Rainbow's End café at the southern end of town.

Sights

BALA LAKE RAILWAY

The genteel narrow-gauge **Bala Lake Railway** (☎ 540666; www.bala-lake-railway.co.uk; adult/child return £7/3; ⏰ Apr-Oct) was opened in 1868 to link mainline stations at Bala and Dolgellau. In 1965 the entire route from Barmouth to Llangollen was shut down and Bala station was closed. Volunteers reopened the 4.5-mile stretch from Bala to Llanuwchllyn in 1971, with vintage locomotives departing from a little station at Penybont, half a mile from Bala town centre, off the B4391. There are now up to four daily services skirting the lake for a scenic 90-minute return journey.

Events

Wa! Bala (www.wabala.co.uk) is a music festival held annually in mid September in a similar vein to the Sesiwn Fawr Dolgellau (p243), with events based around a marquee at the northern end of town.

Activities

WHITE-WATER RAFTING

Due to the damming of the River Tryweryn in the 1960s, this and the River Dee are among the few Welsh rivers with fairly reliable white water – making for year-round opening. The **Canolfan Tryweryn National Whitewater Centre** (☎ 521083; www.ukrafting.co.uk; Frongoch; ⏰ 8.30am-7pm Sat & Sun, 8.30am-4pm Mon-Fri Dec–mid-Oct) runs skills and safety courses, and rafting trips on a 1.5-mile stretch of the Treweryn that is almost continuous class-III white water with class IV sections. The centre is 3.5 miles northwest of

---

THE LEGEND OF TEGGIE

The beast of Llyn Tegid, or Bala Lake, has been reported since at least the 1920s and has been variously likened to a crocodile or a small dinosaur. Affectionately known as Teggie, this Welsh answer to the Loch Ness Monster prompted a three-day search by a Japanese film crew in 1995, but their minisubmarine failed to find any sign of the elusive beast.

One man who claims to have seen the beastie from the deep, however, is local farmer Rhodri Jones, whose sheep farm extends to the lake's foreshore. 'One night in the summer of 2006 I was heading home from the fields when I saw something making concentric ripples. The lake was very still, pretty spooky in the dusk and the water was very calm. That's when I saw the top of a creature about the size of a crocodile moving through the water.'

Since then Jones has spoken to other local farmers and found that many of them have stories of mysterious sightings and evidence they have collected dating back over 60 years.

'Bala is a landlocked, volcanic lake and there are species of fish living there that are only to be found in the lake,' says Jones. 'I think there's something special about the waters, but we live in a narrow-minded world where people are afraid of the unexplained. Still, humanity always needs a mystery.'

Bala on the A4212. Bookings are best made at least two days in advance, and are subject to cancellation in the event of insufficient releases from the dam – call to check the day before. New weekend adventure breaks offer multi-activity packages, such as the High Slide (combining rafting with canyoning). Prices are from £138 per person, including B&B – ask about midweek discounts.

The owners will help advise on local accommodation options and the site boasts a **café** (8.30am-7pm Sat & Sun, to 4pm Mon-Fri) for snacks between activities.

OTHER ACTIVITIES

Bala Adventure & Watersports Centre (/fax 521059; www.balawatersports.com; Foreshore, Pensarn Rd) is a one-stop activity and retail centre, located behind the tourist office by the lakeshore. Courses include windsurfing, sailing, canoeing, white-water rafting, mountain biking, rock-climbing and abseiling trips (prices for all courses start from £33/55 per half-/full day). Gear rental is also available.

Yr Afan (521888; 33 High St; 9.30am-5.30pm Mon-Sat) is a friendly outdoor shop, which also helps to arrange canyoning courses.

Sleeping

Bala Backpackers (521700; www.bala-backpackers.co.uk; 32 Tegid St; dm Sun-Thu/Fri/Sat £10/11/12, breakfast £3;) This popular backpackers' hang-out is low on frills but big on budget facilities and makes no pretence otherwise. The beds are all singles with bedding provided and laid out in large rooms divided by curtains for greater privacy. The best beds are located in the upstairs dorm, which is lighter and airier than those downstairs. There's a drying room, a communal kitchen and a TV lounge. Note: the owner enforces a strict no smoking policy and a midnight curfew.

Glanllyn (540227; www.glanllyn.com; sites per tent/caravan £12/15; mid-Mar–Oct) A well-appointed camp site and caravan park 3 miles out on the A494 Dolgellau road and also close to the lake, this is the pick of the local budget options.

Cynwyd YHA (0870 7705786; The Old Mill, Cynwyd; adult/child £13.95/9.95; May-Sep) This is the nearest hostel, some 10 miles northeast of Bala on the A494 and B4401. Built in a former wool mill by a river, it has basic facilities and is favoured by walkers and bikers. Arriva bus X94 provides the nearest public transport link.

Abercelyn Country House (521109; www.abercelyn .co.uk; Llanycil; s/d £35/70) Located on the A494 Bala

to Dolgellau Rd, 1 mile from the centre of Bala, this B&B is not the easiest to spot (clue: look out for the squirrel), but it's worth the effort. Stylish rooms, a homely atmosphere and a lovely setting in gardens with a gurgling brook make this a great midrange option. Ask about special offers for hire of the self-catering cottage.

White Lion Royal Hotel (520314; www.welsh -historic-inns.com; 61 High St; s/d/f from £70/95/110) The grand old dame in town is a stately affair, refurbished in 2005 for a fresh look, but retaining its sense of history: Queen Victoria once stayed here and George Borrow wrote in *Wild Wales* (see Travel Literature, p20) that his breakfast here was the finest of any in his 1854 walking tour of Wales. The rooms are refined while the gloriously characterful lounge bar (with lots of Welsh cats in hats and dark-wood carved settles) serves decent bar meals. It's also a sister property to the Black Boy Inn (p257) in Caernarfon.

Eating

Rainbow's End (521937; High St; 9am-5.30pm Mon-Sat, 10am-5pm Sun) For a coffee on the go, this friendly little café serves basic coffee and snacks above a craft shop.

Caffi'r Cyfnod (521260; High St; 9am-5pm Mon-Sat, 10am-4pm Sun) The oldest café in Bala is a regular place for breakfasts and cheap snacks with a slightly stuck-in-time feel.

Y Tyfnod (521260; High St; 8.30am-6pm Mon-Wed & Fri, to 8pm Thu, to 7.30pm Sat, to 6.30pm Sun) Snacks, leather sofas, Sunday papers and good coffee are a winning formula at this laid-back, central café. It's a nice little spot to watch the world go by.

Ty Coffi (9am-5pm; snacks around £4) Offers snacks, coffees and pavement tables at an adjacent building, and is a popular spot for families pushing buggies.

Plas Coch Hotel (520309; www.plascoch.com; High St; mains around £7; bar meals noon-2pm & 6-9pm) This large pub on the main drag has an extensive menu of tasty bar meals and lots of fish and grill mains, plus vegetarian options.

Plas-yn-Dre Restaurant (521256; High St; mains £8.95-15.95; noon-2pm & 6.30-9.30pm) The décor in this smart eatery is a tasteful take on country-kitchen chic, finished with soft-leather chairs. The menu has lots of interesting Welsh dishes, including fresh Menai mussels, plus lots of traditional choices for a hearty dinner.

For self-caterers there's a **Somerfield supermarket** (High St; 8am-8pm Mon-Wed & Sat, 8am-9pm Thu & Fri, 10am-4pm Sun) to stock up on supplies.

SNOWDONIA & THE LLŶN

Getting There & Around

The main connection through Bala is Arriva Cymru's bus X94, which runs daily from Barmouth (40 minutes) to Wrexham (2½ hours) with seven daily services Monday to Saturday, and three Sunday, passing through Bala.

Roberts Cycles (☎ 520252; High St; per day £16), about 200m northeast of the White Lion Royal Hotel, rents out mountain bikes.

HARLECH

☎ 01766 / pop 2000

Sleepy Harlech is best known for the mighty, grey-stone towers of its castle, framed by gleaming Tremadog Bay and with the mountains of Snowdonia as a backdrop. Some sort of fortified structure has probably surmounted the rock since Iron Age times, but Edward I removed all traces when he commissioned the construction of the castle. Harlech was also the destination of the ships of Matholwch, who sailed with his armies from Ireland in the tales of the *Mabinogion* (see p75 for details of this book).

Today Harlech is a small town with a smattering of antique shops, but it lacks overall infrastructure. Most visitors come for the castle and a stroll on the beach in fine weather. It's not such a good base, however, so grab a coffee, visit the castle, and then best move on.

Orientation & Information

The town's oldest area, along High St and home to the majority of facilities for tourists, is located uphill and to the north of the castle. From the train station it's a strenuous 20-minute climb on one of several stepped tracks up to High St, or about half a mile by road. Buses stop by the car park situated opposite the Weary Walkers café, from where the castle is just a few minutes' walk north along High St.

The **tourist office** (☎ 780658; High St; ⌚ 9.30am-5.30pm Apr-Oct) is on High St next to the Harlech Emporium, a gloriously retro old sweetshop. There's also a small **post office** (High St; ⌚ 9.30am-5.30pm Mon-Fri, ⌚ 9.30am-5pm Sat), a HSBC bank with ATM and a **Spar supermarket** (High St; ⌚ 8am-8pm Mon-Sat, 9am-8pm Sun).

Sights & Activities

Harlech Castle (☎ 780552; adult/child £3.50/3; ⌚ 9.30am-5pm Apr, May & Oct, 9.30am-6pm Jun-Sep, 9.30am-4pm Mon-Sat, 11am-4pm Sun Nov-Mar) is an intimidating yet spectacular building. Edward I finished it in 1289, the southernmost of his 'iron ring' of

fortresses designed to keep the Welsh firmly beneath his boot.

Despite its might, the storybook fortress has been called the Castle of Lost Causes because it has been lucklessly defended so many times. Owain Glyndŵr captured it after a long siege in 1404. He is said to have been crowned Prince of Wales during one of his parliaments in the town, before envoys from Scotland, France and Spain. He was in turn besieged here by the future Henry V.

During the Wars of the Roses the castle is said to have held out against a siege for seven years and was the last Lancastrian stronghold to fall. The siege inspired the popular Welsh hymn *Men of Harlech*, which is still sung today with patriotic gusto. The castle was again besieged in the Civil War, finally giving in to Cromwell's forces in 1647.

The grey sandstone castle's massive, twin-towered gatehouse and outer walls are still intact, and make the place seem impregnable even now. You can climb the gloomy towers onto the ramparts. The finest exterior view (with Snowdon as a backdrop) is a few minutes' walk back past the adjacent car park.

Today Harlech castle joins its contemporaries at Caernarfon (p255), Conwy (p289) and Beaumaris (p278) as a Unesco World Heritage Site.

Sleeping

Castle Hotel (☎ 780529; www.harlechcastlehotel.co.uk; Castle Sq; s/d £35/60) Located directly opposite the castle, this hotel props up the budget end of the market with rather old-fashioned two-star accommodation. The best of the rooms are 3 and 4, which look straight out at the castle's gatehouse. For the price, the location is superb.

Byrdir House (☎ 780316; www.byrdir.com; High St; d/tw £63/69, with shared bathroom £24/48) Newly refurbished, this welcoming place next to the church has given its otherwise simple B&B rooms a fresher, more modern look. It's at the bottom end of town and popular with the walking crowd.

Castle Cottage (☎ 780479; www.castlecottageharlech.co.uk; s/d from £65/90; ⌚ Dec-Oct; Ⓟ ☒) An excellent restaurant with rooms, this place is a cleat cut above anything else in town. The rooms are spacious in a contemporary style with exposed beams, in-room DVD players and a bowl of fresh fruit for each guest. The restaurant focuses on fresh local produce and an imaginative menu, including lots of local seafood –

try the Barmouth lobster. You can enjoy a three-course dinner here from £29.

Eating

Weary Walker (☎ 780751; High St; mains around £5; ☾ 9am-5pm May-Sep, 10am-4pm Oct-Apr) Bacon butties and mugs of coffee are the preferred fodder for walkers, hikers and outdoors types at this small but friendly little spot. There's a daily lunch menu.

Cemlyn Restaurant (☎ 780425; High St; ☾ 10am-5pm Tue-Sun; ✗) Good views and a delicate-coloured interior are the trademarks of this small non-smoking teashop. It's simple fare overall – but try the Welsh rarebit for a tasty snack (£4.20).

Plas Café (☎ 780204; High St; lunches around £5, mains £17; ☾ noon-2pm & 6-9pm) Boasting the finest view of any restaurant in town – across to the castle and down to the sea – the Plas Café has its best vantage point from the outside terrace. It has sandwich lunches and hearty dinner mains.

Castle Restaurant (☎ 780416; Castle Sq; lunches around £5, mains £12; ☾ 10.30am-9pm) Right by the castle, this more refined place has a cosy feel and broad menu of traditional fare for light lunches and dinner. It's the smartest option in town for those looking for a treat.

Entertainment

Theatr Ardudwy (☎ 780667; www.theatrardudwy.com; box office ☾ 9.30am-5.30pm Mon-Thu, 9.30am-5pm Fri, plus 1hr prior to any live event) With films, dance, theatre and music, Theatr Ardudwy is a lively arts centre.

Getting There & Away

Arriva's bus 38 comes from Barmouth (30 minutes, 16 daily Monday to Saturday, three services on Sunday) and heads onto Blaenau Ffestiniog (40 minutes, 12 daily Monday to Saturday).

Trains run on the scenic Cambrian Coast line to Harlech from Machynlleth (£7.50, one hour 20 minutes) and Porthmadog (£2.10, 40 minutes) every two hours or so.

PORTHMADOG

☎ 01766 / pop 5000

Given its abundance of transport options, Porthmadog (port-*mad*-uk) is a good base for exploring the Snowdonia National Park. The town itself may not be the most aesthetically spectacular place, but it does retain a busy, workaday feel with the hub of the action strung out along the bustling High St, which runs for half a mile through the middle of town.

The town was founded by an 1821 Act of Parliament granting permission to slate magnate William Alexander Madocks – after whom the town is named – to reclaim estuary land and create a new harbour.

Madocks had begun by laying a mile-long causeway called The Cob across Traeth Mawr, the estuary at the mouth of River Glaslyn. Some 400 hectares of wetland habitat behind The Cob was drained and turned into farmland. The resulting causeway provided the route Madocks needed to transport slate on the new Ffestiniog Railway down to the new port.

In the 1870s it was estimated that over a thousand vessels per year departed from the harbour and, at the peak of 1873, over 116,000 tons of Blaenau Ffestiniog slate left Porthmadog for ports around the world.

Today Porthmadog is the southern terminus for one of Wales' finest narrow-gauge train journeys, the **Rheilffordd Ffestiniog Railway** (p250). It's also a popular, not to mention slightly cheaper, place to stay for visitors to the village of Portmeirion (p252), a fantasy-style pocket of *la dolce vita* Italy in North Wales.

Porthmadog is proud of its status as a bastion for small, local businesses with several shops and the local cinema all privately owned by members of the local community.

Orientation & Information

The Cob is the only direct road to Porthmadog from the southeast. It's subject to major traffic congestion in summer after a much-vaunted bypass failed to materialise. The Ffestiniog Railway station and the Welsh Highland Railway station top and tail the town at the southern and northern ends of High St respectively.

The **tourist office** (☎ 512981; High St; ☾ 10am-5pm Thu-Tue Nov-Mar, 10am-6pm Apr-Oct, 9.30am-6pm daily Jul & Aug) is a busy little office located at the intersection of The Cob and High St. Banks are located along High St near the intersection with Bank Pl, as is the **post office** (☾ 8.45am-5.45pm Mon-Fri, 8.45am-12.30pm Sat).

Free internet access is available at the **library** (☎ 514091; Chapel St; ☾ 10am-noon Mon-Sat, 2-6pm Mon-Tue & Fri, to 4pm Wed). **Browsers Bookshop** (☎ 512066; 73 High St; ☾ 9am-5.30pm Mon-Sat) has a good selection of books and maps for walkers and fans of local history. To wash your kit post hike, try **Madog Laundrette** (34 Snowdon St; ☾ 9am-7pm).

The **police station** (☎ 512226; High St) is centrally located; the nearest hospital is currently

SNOWDONIA & THE LLŶN

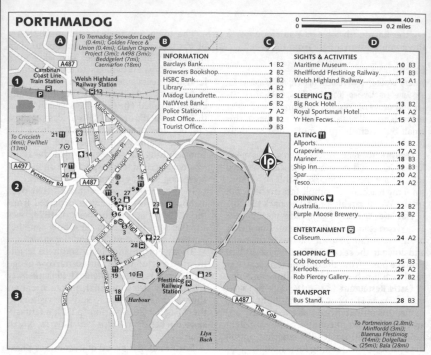

PORTHMADOG

0 ————— 400 m
0 ————— 0.2 miles

INFORMATION
Barclays Bank...................................1 B2
Browsers Bookshop...........................2 B2
HSBC Bank.......................................3 B2
Library..4 B2
Madog Laundrette.............................5 B2
NatWest Bank...................................6 B2
Police Station....................................7 A2
Post Office..8 B2
Tourist Office....................................9 B3

SIGHTS & ACTIVITIES
Maritime Museum............................10 B3
Rheilffordd Ffestiniog Railway..........11 B3
Welsh Highland Railway...................12 A1

SLEEPING 🛏
Big Rock Hotel.................................13 B2
Royal Sportsman Hotel.....................14 A2
Yr Hen Fecws...................................15 A3

EATING 🍴
Allports..16 B2
Grapevine..17 B3
Mariner..18 B3
Ship Inn...19 B3
Spar...20 A2
Tesco...21 A2

DRINKING 🍷
Australia...22 B3
Purple Moose Brewery......................23 B2

ENTERTAINMENT 🎭
Coliseum..24 A2

SHOPPING 🛍
Cob Records.....................................25 B3
Kerfoots..26 A2
Rob Piercey Gallery..........................27 B2

TRANSPORT
Bus Stand..28 B3

To Tremadog; Snowdon Lodge (0.4mi); Golden Fleece & Union (0.4mi); Glaslyn Osprey Project (3mi); A498 (3mi); Beddgelert (7mi); Caernarfon (18mi)

To Criccieth (4mi); Pwllheli (13mi)

To Portmeirion (2.8mi); Minffordd (3mi); Blaenau Ffestiniog (14mi); Dolgellau (25mi); Bala (28mi)

---

in Minffordd, 3 miles east, although a new hospital was under construction in Porthmadog at the time of writing.

Sights
RHEILFFORDD FFESTINIOG RAILWAY & WELSH HIGHLAND RAILWAY
The **Rheilffordd Ffestiniog Railway** (☎ 516000; www.festrail.co.uk; all-day rover ticket adult/concession £16.50/13.20) is a fantastic, twisting and precipitous 13.5-mile narrow-gauge railway that was built between 1832 and 1836 to haul slate down to Porthmadog from the mines at Blaenau Ffestiniog. Horse-drawn wagons were replaced in the 1860s by steam locomotives and the line was opened up as a passenger service. Saved from years of neglect, it is one of Wales' most spectacular and beautiful narrow-gauge journeys. Because it links the Cambrian Coast and Conwy Valley main lines, it also serves as a serious passenger transport option. Nearly all services are steam-hauled. A standard all-day rover ticket offers unlimited travel.

The same company also runs the sibling **Welsh Highland Railway** (☎ 513402; www.whr.co.uk; all-day ticket adult/child £4.95/2.95) from Porthmadog

to Pen-y-Mount, and Caernarfon to Rhyd Ddu (for more information, see p256). Extensions to the network to Blaenau Ffestiniog and Porthmadog are planned for completion by 2009 for links to Snowdonia National Park.

Both railways organise regular events and showcases. A combined three-in-one ticket (adult/child £30/24) is available for use across the whole network.

OTHER SIGHTS
The **Glaslyn Osprey Project** (www.rspb.org.uk; ☼ Apr-Aug) is the newest attraction in the area. It was founded after a pair of ospreys, regular visitors to Wales on migration from Africa, first nested near Porthmadog in 2004. A round-the-clock protection scheme now operates during the breeding season while a public viewing site is open at Pont Croesor with telescopes and live footage from the nest-cams. The project is located on the B4410, a turning off the A498 Tremadog road.

Next to the tourist office, the tiny **Maritime Museum** (☎ 513736; adult/child £1.50/0.75; ☼ 11am-5pm Jun-Sep) has a low-key pocket history of the highs and lows of topsail schooners and other sailing ships in a wharf-side slate shed.

Sleeping

Yr Hen Fecws (☎ 514625; www.henfecws.com; 16 Lombard St; s/d from £42/59) In the midrange B&B market, this welcoming restaurant with rooms is hard to beat. The seven en-suite rooms are simply decorated but have feature exposed-slate walls and fireplaces. Downstairs, the inviting restaurant, all red walls and dark wood floors, serves traditional evening meals from 6pm to 10pm.

Big Rock Cafe & Hotel (☎ 512098; www.bigrockcafe .co.uk; 71 High St; s/d/f £35/65/90; P 🔔) A new arrival in town with a very contemporary feel compared to the more traditional local B&Bs, Big Rock is a family-friendly guesthouse with eight en-suite rooms. Downstairs, the owners run a café (open 9.30am to 5pm, Monday to Saturday; open to 7pm Wednesdays and Fridays) with fair-trade products and lots of smoothies. The owners take an interest in Christian faith issues.

Royal Sportsman Hotel (☎ 512015; www.royalsports man.co.uk; 131 High St; s/d £48/74; P) Some of the rooms in this traditional pub feel a bit old-fashioned and frayed around the edges, but the hotel docs offer a great base for exploring the area. The building is full of character, having been constructed in 1862 as a coaching inn. Ask about promotional deals and special breaks. There's also an inhouse restaurant

(mains around £16), which serves bar meals from noon to 2.30pm and 6pm to 9pm Monday to Saturday.

Eating

Grapevine (☎ 514230; 152 High St; mains £8-14; 🕙 8am-9pm Mon & Wed-Sat, to 5pm Tue, 11am-4pm Sun) A no-frills spot with a sun terrace out deck, this welcoming locals' place offers snack lunches, traditional mains and a kid's menu for families.

Ship Inn (☎ 512990; 14 Lombard St; mains around £8; 🕙 noon-2pm & 5-9.30pm Mon-Sat, noon-2.30pm Sun) A great local pub with a traditional feel and decent real ales, the Ship Inn has a wide menu of hearty pub fare, including speciality grills and curries.

Mariner (☎ 512569; 10 Cornhill) A very small BYO eatery by the harbour, the Mariner is a café by day and a restaurant specialising in fresh fish by night. The tables outside are an attractive feature on sunny evenings.

For self-caterers there are two supermarkets in Porthmadog: **Tesco** (High St; 🕙 8am-8pm Mon-Sat, 10am-4pm Sun) and **Spar** (95 High St; 🕙 7am-11pm). For a traditional fish supper, **Allports** (☎ 512589; 38 Snowdon St; 🕙 11.30am-10pm Mon-Sat, noon-10pm Sun) is an award-winning fish 'n' chip shop with a local following.

A PINT OF PORTHMADOG'S FINEST

The **Purple Moose Brewery** (☎ 515571; www.purplemoose.co.uk; Madoc St) is one of approximately 30 microbreweries across Wales. From humble beginnings the venture is now very much a working business with a small staff of four and contacts to supply pubs across North Wales from Anglesey to Harlech. In August 2006 the Snowdonia Ale won the Society of Independent Brewers (SIBA) award for Champion Beer.

Brewing started in June 2005 with a one-off special pale ale at 3.5%. The brewery now produces three standard beers in both cask conditioned and bottle conditioned formats: Snowdonia Ale (3.6%), Madog's Ale (3.7%) and Glaslyn Ale (4.2%). During the winter they also produce Dark Side of the Moose (4.6%). The Madog is a traditional bitter, while the Snowdonia and Glaslyn are more refreshing ales with a fruity, hoppy aroma and a lighter, golden-brown hue.

The founder, Lawrence Washington, originally hails from Cheltenham but was a long-time volunteer on the local Ffestiniog Railway. As such, he decided to set up the business in Porthmadog, relying on the support of friends from the local community. Today the brewery produces 360 gallons per brew with two to three brews per week.

'There has been very little in the way of enterprising local breweries in Wales for years, hence very little choice,' explains Washington. 'We basically realised that people were thirsty for more options aside from Bass and Brains and set out to fill a niche in the market.'

Currently there is a small brewery shop with memorabilia and souvenirs. The team plans to develop this into a visitor's attraction with exhibitions and information about the brewing process in the next few years.

For information about Penderyn, Wales' only whisky distillery, based just south of Brecon, see p71.

Drinking & Entertainment

Australia (☎ 510931; 31 High St) For a pint, Australia is a lively, rough-and-ready place with simple bar meals (noon to 8pm daily).

Coliseum (☎ 512108; High St) A classic, old-fashioned picture house showing the latest releases.

Shopping

The most famous local institution is **Kerfoots** (☎ 512256; www.kerfoots.com; 138-140 High St; ⏰ 9.30am-5.30pm Mon-Sat, 10am-4pm Sun), an independent department store, established 1874, with a range of household goods. There's also a useful little **coffee shop** (⏰ 10am-5pm Mon-Sat, 10.15am-3.30pm Sun).

The **Rob Piercey Gallery** (☎ 513833; Snowdon St; ⏰ 10am-5pm Mon-Sat, to 12.30pm Wed Oct-Mar) showcases the work of Piercey, a local artist and member of the Watercolour Society of Wales, who specialises in mountain landscapes.

Cob Records (☎ 512170; www.cobrecords.com; Britannia Tce; ⏰ 9am-5.30pm Mon-Sat, noon-5pm Sun) is a great little independent record shop with a healthy collection of Welsh bands and music (for more on music, see p46).

Getting There & Away

The Snowdon Sherpa bus provides useful links to Snowdon trailheads and elsewhere. Bus S97 runs to Betws-y-Coed via Beddgelert and Pen-Y-Pass; buses stop along High St by the park. National Express coach 545 passes through daily at 8am en route to London via Llandudno, Bangor and Caernarfon; coaches stop by Tesco at the north end of town.

Express Motors bus 1 runs roughly hourly (fewer on Sunday) from Blaenau Ffestiniog (30 minutes) to Bangor (one hour) via Caernarfon (50 minutes). Arriva bus 3 runs to Pwllheli (every 20 minutes, 40 minutes) via Criceth (25 minutes) for connections across the Llŷn Peninsula.

Arriva's TrawsCambria coach X32 leaves daily at 10.20am for Aberystwyth (2¼ hours) and runs onto Cardiff (seven hours); it stops along High St outside the Australia pub.

Porthmadog is on the Cambrian Coast line with trains to Machynlleth (£8.60, two hours, every two hours) and Pwllheli (£3, 30 minutes, every two hours).

AROUND PORTHMADOG
Portmeirion
☎ 01766

Set on its own tranquil peninsula on the Snowdonia coast, **Portmeirion village** (www.portmeirion-village.com; adult/child £6.50/3.50; ⏰ 9am-5.30pm) is a gingerbread, cake-decoration collection of buildings with a heavy Italian influence. Founded in 1926 by the late Welsh architect Sir Clough Williams-Ellis, it's located 5 miles from Plas Brondanw, his ancestral home. Clough collected bits and pieces from disintegrating stately mansions to create this weird

---

IN THE AREA: TREMADOG

While Porthmadog has several places to stay and eat, a couple of the best options in the area are actually located about half a mile further along the A487 in the attractive little village of Tremadog. It feels like an extension to Porthmadog but is actually a separate village with a small post office and Spar supermarket grouped around the handsome town square.

One of the best local sleeping options is **Snowdon Lodge** (☎ 515354; www.snowdonlodge.co.uk; Lawrence House, Church St; dm/d/f £15/35/58; P ✗), a four-star-rated independent hostel. Run by travellers for travellers, the building is actually the house where TE Lawrence (Lawrence of Arabia) was born on August 16, 1888. In 1896 the Lawrence family moved to Oxford, but the house is still recognised for its importance by the TE Lawrence Society. It's a friendly spot and a great base for organising activities in the area (the owners can advise on local options and operators), while communal areas encourage guests to socialise and swap Snowdonia tips. The rooms are mainly dorms but some private and family rooms are also available; a continental breakfast is included in the price. All bedding is provided, there's an in-house café and a bar, and bike hire is available (£15).

For something to eat, one of the best options is the **Golden Fleece** (☎ 512421; Market Sq; mains around £8; food ⏰ noon-2pm & 7-9pm) in Tremadog's main square. It's an inviting and friendly little pub with real ales, some decent pub grub, an open fire for cold nights and a sunny courtyard for balmy days. This is a great spot to sample a pint of the local microbrewery ale from the Purple Moose Brewery (see the boxed text A Pint of Porthmadog's Finest, p251). There are live acoustic music sessions on Tuesdays and occasional live bands.

and wonderful seaside townscape. There's glorious attention to detail and absurdity in each and every one of the nooks and crannies.

The project was completed in two phases – 1926–1939 and 1954–1976, when it was deemed to be finished. Clough reached the ripe old age of 90 years old at this time and had designed and built many of the constructions himself. The buildings are all listed and the whole site is today a Conservation Area. It celebrated its 80th anniversary in 2006.

Clough's lifelong concern was with the whimsical and intriguing nature of architecture, his *raison d'être* to demonstrate how a naturally beautiful site could be developed without defiling it. His life's work now stands as a testament to beauty, something he described as 'that strange necessity'. He died in 1978, having campaigned for the environment throughout his life. He was a founder member of the Council for the Protection of Rural Wales in 1928 and served as its president for 20 years.

An **audio-visual show** (10am-5.30pm), just off the central piazza to the right of the Arc de Triomph, has a commentary by Sir Clough Williams-Ellis himself. A series of brochures, leaflets and plans are available for collection from the Tollgate.

Today the grounds are open daily; guests staying in the two Portmeirion hotels are admitted free. There are seven **shops** (9am-5.30pm) around the village, selling books, souvenirs and some basic supplies. Also available is Portmeirion pottery, the famous pottery designed by Susan, Sir Clough's daughter, which bears the Portmeirion label, even though these days it's made in Stoke-on-Trent (England).

The village formed the ideally surreal stage set for the 1960s cult TV series, *The Prisoner*, which was filmed here from 1966 to '67; it still draws fans of the show in droves with *Prisoner* conventions held annually in March. The **Prisoner Information Centre** (9am-5.30pm Apr-Oct) has a raft of memorabilia for hard-core fans, who no doubt receive a frisson of excitement from knowing that the centre is housed in what was No 6's cottage – buy the souvenir DVD for an explanation. More recently the village was the setting for the hugely popular TV series, *Cold Feet*. The giant Plaster of Paris Buddha, located just off the piazza, also featured in the 1958 film, *The Inn of the Sixth Happiness*, starring Ingrid Bergman (for more on film sets in Wales, see the boxed text the North Wales Film & Television Trail, p303).

SLEEPING

You can live the dream and overnight within the village. The management company has three options for accommodation:

Portmeirion Hotel (770000; www.portmeirion -village.com; s/d/ste £155/188/209) The original hotel, dating from 1926, has an impressive guest book – HG Wells, Bertrand Russell and Noel Coward all stayed here. The latter was suitably inspired to pen the novel *Blithe Spirit* after a sojourn in the Watch House. The 14 rooms are all individually styled to different themes and ooze a sense of whimsy and history, even if the décor reflects the vaguely psychedelic nature of the surrounds. Ask about low-season promotional deals. A fine-dining-style evening meal is served in the formal dining room for a hefty supplement.

Castell Deudraeth (770000; www.portmeirion -village.com; r £175-245; P) Opened in 2001 as a more contemporary alternative to the traditional Portmeirion Hotel, Castell Deudraeth lies just outside the village but is connected by a free shuttle bus service. It was extensively refurbished following a fire but retains the fairytale castle design. The 11 rooms are a blend of contemporary chic and gadget heaven with apartment-style design dominated by a flat-screen entertainment system. There's a less formal grill restaurant with a menu of modern British (and Welsh) staples, plus a busy bar area for cocktails. Of the two hotels, this is better suited to families, with children welcome in the restaurant.

Self-catering cottages (770000; www.portmeirion -village.com; per week £695-1124) There is a range of 26 self-catering cottages and apartments in the village, all of them individually styled with names like Mermaid, White Horses and Angel, dotted around in eccentric nooks and crannies. They are hired out according to a complex series of rates for weekly, weekend or midweek stays. Facilities and size vary considerably between the properties; check the website for the latest promotional rates and deals.

EATING

Town Hall (10am-5pm Mon-Sat, noon-3pm Sun) A simple, café-style restaurant for self-service lunches and coffees, although the food can be a bit hit and miss.

GETTING THERE & AWAY

Portmeirion village is located about 2 miles east of Porthmadog and 1 mile off the road – an

LOCAL VOICES

I've spent 30 years working in Gwyllt Gardens in Portmeirion village and have seen how the colours and designs have changed over the years – the best time for colour is April and May. We are a team of 12 gardeners, now working over 70 acres of woodland with the gardens stretching to 120 acres in total.

The gardens have a unique fairytale-like quality about them. We're on the Gulf Stream here, so we can grow more exotic plants. This is not just a botanic garden. It's constantly developing, so the plan now is to create more one-off events and foster more winter colours. Susan Williams-Ellis, Clough's daughter, adds new designs to the gardens inspired by new themes.

The diversity of species is huge: more than 200 species of rhododendrons, 60 varieties of camellias and 40 varieties of magnolias. There's a lot of fauna too: badgers, foxes, rabbits and ospreys are all common sights.

Of course, these days Portmeirion is as famous as a TV location as it is for the displays of flora. I was here when the TV crew was filming the 1960s TV series, *The Prisoner*, and I just remember spending all my time sweeping up after them as they were a bunch of chain smokers. I was also here when they were filming the TV series *Cold Feet* too. It's great to see Portmeirion getting recognition but, for me, the village will always be about exploring the gardens through the seasons.

Arwel Hughes, head gardener, Gwyllt Gardens, Portmeirion village

Portmeirion village produces two leaflets for walks in the Gwyllt Gardens: the Tree Trail and Woodland Garden Walk. Collect them from the Tollgate.

easy stroll from Porthmadog's tourist office (p249). Williams bus 99B has two daily services at 9.55am and 1.05pm to cover the 10-minute journey to the site from Porthmadog.

CAERNARFON
☎ 01286 / pop 4000

Caernarfon, situated 9 miles from Bangor between the gleaming swell of the Menai Strait and the deep-purple mountains of Snowdonia, is home to Wales' most magnificent castle, a looming, fantastical World Heritage Site built by Edward I as a medieval show of strength. Following the efforts of the former Welsh prime minister, David Lloyd George (see the boxed text, p36), the castle was designated as the venue for the 1911 and 1969 investitures of the Prince of Wales, the latter focusing the attention of the world to Caernarfon when Prince Charles, the current heir to the British throne, had his investiture broadcast live on TV.

Given the town's crucial historical importance, the pervading downbeat feel of the town comes as something of a disappointment. There is a tangible sense of history in the streets around the castle, and within the walled town, cobbled and lined by fine Georgian buildings, but many shopfronts are boarded up and Caernarfon has a rather down-at-heel feel. Only the new arts centre, Galeri Caernarfon (p257) brings a breath of fresh air to the town's cultural life.

Caernarfon has traditionally been the heartland of the Welsh Nationalist movement and remains a defiantly Welsh-speaking enclave that preserves its traditional language and culture with pride. Indeed, about 70% of locals speak Welsh as their first language.

Orientation & Information

The historical heart of Caernarfon is enclosed within stout 14th-century walls, just to the north of the castle, beside the River Seiont (where it empties into the Menai Strait). The centre of modern Caernarfon is just east of the castle, at Castle Sq (Y Maes). The main shopping area is pedestrianised Pool St, running east from Castle Sq. Buses stop at stands along Penllyn, two blocks north of Pool St. The terminus of the Welsh Highland Railway is two blocks southeast of the **Slate Quay car park** (per day £3).

The **tourist office** (☎ 672232; Castle Ditch; ☼ 9.30am-5pm Apr-Oct, 10am-4.30pm Mon-Sat Nov-Mar), opposite the castle's main entrance, the King's Gate, incorporates the Pendeitsh Gallery, which showcases crafts from the **Parc Glynllifon craft centre** (☎ 830222; adult/child £3/1), located 6 miles southwest of Caernarfon on the A499.

All the major banks have branches around Castle Sq, where the **post office** (☼ 9am-5.30 Mon-Fri, 9am-12.30pm Sat) is also located. The **library** (Bangor St; ☼ 9.30am-7pm Mon-Tue & Thu- Fri, to 1pm Wed & Sat) has free internet access, while the **Dylan Thomas Café**

(☎ 678777; 4 Bangor St; ☼ 9.30am-5.30pm Mon-Tue & Thu, to 6.30pm Wed, to 7pm Fri, to 5pm Sat) offers internet access (£0.50 per 10 mins) and wi-fi access for laptop carriers (£5 per day) along with a simple café, which has a vague aroma of old socks.

Pete's Launderette (☎ 678395; 10 Skiner St) is northeast of Castle Sq. The **police station** (☎ 673333; Maesincla Lane) is half a mile east of the town centre, while the nearest accident-and-emergency service is at Bangor's **Gwynedd Hospital** (☎ 01248-384384), approximately 9 miles east.

Sights
CAERNARFON CASTLE
One of the world's greatest medieval castles, majestic **Caernarfon Castle** (☎ 677617; adult/child/family £4.90/4.50/15; ☼ 9.30am-5pm Apr-May & Oct, 9.30am-

6pm Jun-Sep, 9.30am-4pm Mon-Sat & 11am-4pm Sun Nov-Mar) was built between 1283 and 1330 as a military stronghold, a seat of government and a royal palace. Like the other royal strongholds, it was designed and mainly supervised by Master James of St George, but the brief and scale were extraordinary. Inspired by the dream of Macsen Wledig recounted in the *Mabinogion*, Caernarfon echoes the 5th-century walls of Constantinople, with colour-banded masonry and polygonal towers, instead of the traditional round towers and turrets.

Despite its fairytale aspect it is thoroughly fortified with a series of murder holes and a sophisticated arrangement of multiple arrow slits. It repelled Owain Glyndŵr's army in 1404 with a garrison of only 28 men, and resisted

three sieges during the Civil War before surrender to Cromwell's army in 1646. Finest of all is the **Eagle Tower**, on whose turrets you can spot the weathered eagle from which it gets its name, and where stone helmeted figures were intended to swell the garrison's numbers.

A year after construction of the building was begun, Edward I's second son was born here, becoming heir to the throne four months later when his elder brother died. To consolidate Edward's power he was made Prince of Wales in 1301, and his much-eroded statue is over the **King's Gate**. He came to a very nasty end via a red-hot poker, but this did not destroy the title. However, the first investiture that took place here, rather than in London, wasn't until 1911 – of the rather less ill-fated Edward VIII. Although initiated by the Welsh prime minister, David Lloyd George, it incensed the largely Nationalist local population.

There is an exhibition plus cinematic glimpse of the 1969 investiture of today's Prince of Wales in the **North East Tower** (that time Nationalists tried to blow up his train). In the **Queen's Tower** (named after Edward I's wife Eleanor) is the vivid **Museum of the Royal Welsh Fusiliers** (free admission with castle ticket); poets Robert Graves and Siegfried Sassoon both served in the brigade.

SEGONTIUM

Just east of the centre, the excavated foundations of the **Segontium Roman Fort** (☎ 675625; ⏱ 10am-4.30pm Tue-Sun) represent the westernmost Roman legionary fort of the Roman Empire. Overlooking the Menai Strait, the fort dates back to AD 77, when Caesar Julius Agricola completed the Roman conquest of Wales by capturing the Isle of Anglesey. It was designed to accommodate a force of up to 1000 infantrymen, and coins recovered from the site indicate that it was an active garrison until AD 394 – a reflection of the crucial strategic position.

The one-site museum explains the background to complement the stark remains. The site is located about half a mile along Llanbelig Rd (A4085), which crosses through the middle of it.

WELSH HIGHLAND RAILWAY

The narrow-gauge **Welsh Highland Railway** (☎ 677018; www.festrail.co.uk; all-day Rover ticket adult/child £16.50/13.20; 2-5 daily services, selected days Apr-Oct), the sister service to the Rheilffordd Ffestiniog Railway, is an amalgamation of several late-19th-century railways used for carrying slate.

The line opened for passenger traffic in 1923 but closed just 14 years later. It was saved by volunteers and reopened as a tourist attraction in 1997, currently running to **Rhyd Ddu**, from where several trails lead up Snowdon, making the train a major link for walkers. Extensions to the network to Blaenau Ffestiniog and Porthmadog are planned for completion by 2009 for links to Snowdonia National Park.

Activities

The excellent **Plas Menai, The National Watersports Centre** (☎ 01248-670964; www.plasmenai.co.uk), 3 miles out along the A487 towards Bangor, offers a year-round range of water-based courses for all interests and ability levels – from sailing to power-boating, plus multi-activity courses suitable for families and youth groups. Advance reservations are mandatory. The centre also offers on-site accommodation with en suite B&B (rooms £30) and a bunkhouse (dorms £20).

The tourist office has a brochure-map of Gwynedd recreational cycle routes, established by Gwynedd Council along disused railway lines. Three of these are based around Caernarfon: the 12-mile **Lôn Eifion** running south to Bryncir (starting near the Welsh Highland Railway station); the 4.5-mile **Lôn Las Menai** along the Menai Strait to the village of Y Felinheli; and the 4-mile **Lôn Gwyfrai** to the village of Waunfawr. See p258 for details of bike hire.

The pleasure boat **Queen of the Sea** (☎ 672772; ⏱ May-Oct; adult/child £5/3.50) offers five daily, 40-minute tours up and down the Menai Strait from Slate Quay, beside the castle. For something with more of an adrenaline kick, **Menai Ventures** (☎ 674540; www.ribride.co.uk; RIB rides adult/child £17/13; ⏱ 9am-5pm Mon-Sat, 10am-3pm Sun May-Sep) offers one-hour RIB (rigid inflatable boat) rides and arranges water sports activities for groups – enquire for details. All activities depend on current tidal conditions.

Sleeping

Cadnant Valley Camping & Caravan Park (☎ 673196; www.cwmcadnantvalley.co.uk; sites per adult/tent £2/4; ⏱ Mar–end Oct) Located half a mile east of the castle along the A4086 Llanberis road, this leafy park has a good range of facilities, including a children's play area and disabled-access toilets.

Plas Gwyn Caravan Park (☎ 672619; www.plasgwyn.co.uk; Llanrug; from £11.50, sites per tent plus £2 per adult) This quiet family-run site, set in the grounds of an imposing Georgian house, has good facilities and a peaceful setting. From Caernarfon, take the A4086, signposted Llanberis, for 3 miles – the park is situated on the right before entering Llanrug.

Totters (☎ 672963; www.totters.co.uk; Plas Porth Yr Aur; 2 High St; dm/r £14/16; ☒) Modern, clean and very welcoming, this excellent independent hostel is the best-value place to stay in town by a country mile. In addition to traveller-friendly facilities, the 14th-century arched basement hosts a long table that gives a sense of history to guests' dinner parties. In addition to dorms, there's a two-bed family-friendly attic apartment with TV and bathroom (£20 per person).

Cartref (☎ 677392; www.cartref-caernarfon.co.uk; 23 Market St; s/d £35/60; ☒ ☐) New owners have brought a fresh look to this attractive 18th-century townhouse. In addition to restoring original features, such as slate fireplaces, wi-fi internet adds extra appeal for the business traveller. Ask about group and off-season deals.

Caer Menai (☎ 672612; www.caermenai.co.uk; 15 Church St; d/f £60/80; ☒ ☒) A former county school building, dating from 1894, this pale-yellow Georgian building has been a guesthouse since 1974. The seven en-suite rooms are comfortable, if a little old-fashioned, and some are suitable for families.

Bron Menai (☎ 675589; www.bronmenai.co.uk; North Rd; s/d £55/70; ☒ ☒) A cut above the average B&B, this smart, family place has six en-suite rooms with tasteful features and a few nice homely touches. The owners have run the guesthouse for over 20 years and are full of tips for visiting the local area.

Celtic Royal Hotel (☎ 674477; www.celtic-royal.co.uk; Bangor St; s/d from £77/93) This grand old Georgian building resembles a stately home with its impressive entrance hall. It certainly targets the high rollers with a leisure club, buzzy Havana bar–cum–bistro, plus specialist facilities for conferences. Given the formal atmosphere, however, this is definitely one for the older, more genteel visitor, rather than families or young couples.

Eating

Y Tebot Bach (☎ 678444; 13 Castle St; cakes £1, sandwiches £5; ☒ 10.30am-5pm Tue-Sat) The nicest of the many tearooms around the castle, this tiny place for a light bite has a cosy, living-room feel, homemade cakes and sandwiches.

Café Macsen (☎ 676464; 11 Castle Sq; mains around £7; ☒ 10am-4.30pm Mon-Sat, 10am-4pm Sun) A simple but airy café with marble tables, it offers the stock-in-trade all-day breakfasts and sandwiches, as well as some reliable mains. While the food may be simple, the place is cleaner and friendlier than other cafés in the block.

Molly's (☎ 673238; Hole in the Wall St; mains from £9; ☒ noon-2.30pm & 5.30-9pm Wed-Sun) An arty café bar for snack-style meals. It specialises in creative recipes using local fish.

Stones Bistro (☎ 671152; 4 Hole in the Wall St; mains £10.50-14; ☒ 6pm-late Tue-Sat) Housed in what was a 17th-century temperance house, this French-style bistro is open only for dinner with speciality roast lamb and some decent options for vegetarians.

Black Boy Inn (☎ 673604; Northgate St; mains around £12; ☒ bar meals 11am-9pm Mon-Sat, noon-9pm Sun) This 15th-century inn, rammed with original features and divided into a series of snug, small rooms, has good bar meals – try the farmhouse basket (£6.50) for a hearty lunch. The hotel also offers B&B accommodation (rooms with shared/private bathroom £35/60).

Molly's Restaurant (Castle St; ☒ 6.30-10pm Wed-Sat) This is a more formal spot for dinner than the flagship café Molly's.

Y Pantri Cymraeg (☎ 678884; Castle Sq; ☒ 9am-5pm Mon-Sat) A tiny deli with supplies of Welsh wines and chocolate, plus other local specialities.

There's a **Spar supermarket** (Castle Sq; ☒ 7am-11pm); a farmers market sprawls across Castle Sq every Saturday and, in summer, on Monday too.

Drinking & Entertainment

Galeri Caernarfon (☎ 685222; www.galericaernarfon.com; Victoria Dock; box office ☒ 9.30am-5.30pm Mon-Fri, 10am-4pm Sat, plus during events; ☒ ☒ ☒) Caernarfon's cultural scene has been dramatically boosted by the 2005 opening of this excellent multi-purpose arts centre, which hosts exhibitions, theatre, film and events. Check the programme for details. The in-house **DOC café bar** (☒ 10.30am-8.30pm Mon-Sat, 10.30am-5.30pm Sun) has day-round snacks and pre-event suppers.

Anglesey Arms (☎ 672158; The Promenade; bar meals ☒ noon-8.30pm) For a pint, the Anglesey Arms down by the water is your best bet, especially with outside seating in summer offering a great harbour view for a sundowner. The owners also run a floating restaurant in summer in the harbour (mains around £6).

Shopping

Na-Nôg (☎ 676946; www.na-nog.com; Castle Sq; ☒ 9am-5pm Mon-Sat) This little music, DVD and book shop is devoted to Welsh-language material for culture vultures keen to explore material in Welsh.

Getting There & Away

With the exception of the Welsh Highland Railway (p256), Caernarfon has no train service, though bus services are plentiful:

Arriva Cymru Bus 5/X5 runs from Bangor (30 minutes, every 20 minutes Monday to Saturday, hourly Sunday) and from Llandudno (1½ hours, every 30 minutes Monday to Saturday, hourly Sunday).

Express Motors Bus 1 runs to Porthmadog (45 minutes, hourly Monday to Saturday) and onto Blaenau Ffestiniog (1¼ hours).

Snowdon Sherpa Bus S4 to Beddgelert.

Getting Around

Bikes are available for hire from **Beics Menai** (☎ 676804; 1 Slate Quay; adult/child £16/9; ⏰ 9.30am-5pm); the owner can also advise on local cycle routes.

BEDDGELERT

☎ 01766 / pop 500

The charming little community of Beddgelert is a conservation village at the heart of the Snowdonia National Park. The rough greystone buildings, overlooking the trickling river with its ivy-covered bridge, come alive in spring when flowers festoon the village – hence Beddgelert is a regular prize-winner in the 'Britain in Bloom' competition. Scenes from Mark Robson's 1958 film, *The Inn of the Sixth Happiness,* starring Ingrid Bergman, were shot here.

Beddgelert, meaning 'Gelert's Grave', is allegedly named after the folk tale of the 13th-century Welsh prince, Llewelyn, whose faithful dog was killed by its owner because he thought it had savaged his baby son. In truth, Gelert had actually killed the wolf that was attacking the baby. The grave is now just a short walk from the village along a riverside trail and, according to the tombstone: 'The prince filled with remorse is said never to have smiled again. He buried Gelert here. The spot he called Beddgelert.'

Today the grave is a major attraction but, some locals suggest that the dog's grave was the invention of a canny 19th-century hotelier to boost visitor numbers. More likely the name refers to Celert, a 5th-century missionary preacher from Ireland, who is thought to have founded a church here.

Orientation & Information

The hub of the village is the ancient bridge, where the rivers Colwyn and Glaslyn meet and the roads split for Caernarfon and Capel Curig. Most of the sleeping and eating options are strung out along the main street. The **tourist office** (☎ 890615; Canolfan Hebog; ⏰ 9.30am-5.30pm daily Easter-Oct, 9.30am-4.30pm Fri-Sun Nov-Mar) is at the southern end of the village, close to the short-stay **car park** (per hr 40p).

There's a **post office** (⏰ 7.15am-1pm & 2-5.30pm Mon-Thu, 7.15am-1pm Fri, 8am-6pm Sat, 8am-noon Sun) with a bureau de change, but no banks or grocery store.

Sights

At the heart of the village, **Tŷ Isaf** (☎ 510129; admission free; ⏰ 1-4pm Wed-Sun) is managed by the National Trust. The oldest house in Beddgelert, Tŷ Isaf has a tiny exhibition showcasing traditional village life in the 19th century.

A mile east of the village, the Gwynany Valley features the hill **Dinas Emrys** where the legendary King Vortigern – son-in-law of the last Roman ruler, Magnus Maximus – tried to build a castle. According to folklore, the young wizard Merlin liberated two dragons in a cavern under the hill, a white one representing the Saxons and a red one representing the Welsh, and prophesied that they'd fight until the red dragon was triumphant. The act was the spiritual birth of the Welsh nation and the two dragons have apparently been at each other's throats ever since (for more on Merlin, see p78).

Across the road from Dinas Emrys is the **Sygun Copper Mine** (☎ 890595; www.syguncoppermine .co.uk; adult/child £8/6; ⏰ 9.30am-5pm Apr-Oct), which was mined from Roman times, but especially in the 19th century. It was abandoned in 1903, later onverted into a museum and now boasts an audio-visual underground tour that evokes the life of Victorian miners.

Sleeping

Beddgelert Forest Campsite (☎ 890288; sites per tent/ caravan £13-16; ⏰ mid-Dec—end Oct; ♿) Well-equipped and well-situated, this forest site 1 mile west of Beddgelert on the A4085 Caernarfon road has a log cabin and adventure playground for children.

Snowdon Ranger YHA (☎ 01286-650391; Rhyd Ddu; adult/child £12/9) On the A4085, 5 miles north of Beddgelert, at the trailhead for the Snowdon Ranger Path up Snowdon, this former inn, full of character, is perfect for walkers and has its own adjoining beach. The Snowdon Sherpa bus S4 from Caernarfon passes by the door with connections to Bangor.

Bryn Gwynant YHA (☎ 890251; Nantgwynant; adult/ child £12/9) Four miles east of Beddgelert, this walkers' staple overlooks Llyn Gwynant and Snowdon, and is set in an early Victorian mansion. The Watkin Path trailhead for Snowdon begins less than 1 mile from the hostel and leads into incredible mountain scenery.

Near the bridge, there's a group of B&Bs similar in style and price.

Plas Gwyn (☎ 890215; Beddgelert; www.plas-gwyn .com; s/d £25/50) Try Plas Gwyn, a 19th-century red-granite house with high-ceilinged rooms and some original features. A hearty cooked breakfast is served in the dining room with views across the river.

Plas Colwyn (☎ 890458; Beddgelert; www.plascolwyn .co.uk; s/d £27/54; P ✕) The slightly smarter Plas Colwyn, a 17th-century house with river and mountain views, offers traditional rooms (some of them with original fireplaces) and a homely atmosphere.

Tanronnen Inn (☎ 890347; Beddgelert; s/d £55/100) Following a recent refit, this traditional coaching inn has smart, albeit slightly formal rooms at the top end of the scale. Set in an attractive location, it's right at the heart of the village. Bar meals are also available from noon to 2pm and 7pm to 8.30pm.

Eating

Beddgelert Bistro & Antique Shop (☎ 890543; Beddgelert; mains around £12; ☷ noon-5pm & 7-9pm) Beside the bridge, this tearoom-style place is divided between several small rooms with exposed flagstone walls. It has snack meals and – rather incongruously – a range of fondues.

Café Glandwr & Glandwr Ices (☎ 890339; Beddgelert; ☷ 9am-9pm Apr-Sep, 10am-5pm Oct-Mar; ♿) The busiest place in the village! This excellent ice-cream parlour serves a huge array of home-made flavours and is now joined by an annexe family restaurant with a café-style menu. You don't have to love pizza to eat here – but it helps.

Lyn's Café (☎ 890374; Beddgelert; meals £6-8; ☷ 10am-7pm Mon-Fri, to 8pm Sat & Sun; ♿) A good family-friendly all-rounder, Lyn's is split between a restaurant serving big breakfasts and Sunday roasts, and a tearoom round the back with seats by the river for simple snacks.

Getting There & Around

Beddgelert is served by the Snowdon Sherpa bus S4 from Caernarfon and the S97 from Porthmadog to Betws-y-Coed.

Beics Beddgelert (☎ 890434; www.beddgelertbikes.co .uk; adult/child per day £18/17), located 2 miles north on the A4085 and close to the entrance to the Beddgelert Forest Campsite, rents out mountain bikes, tandems and child seats.

AROUND BEDDGELERT
Blaenau Ffestiniog
☎ 01766

Slate was the basis of Snowdonia's wealth in the 19th century. Most of the slate used to keep English houses dry came from Wales, and most of that came either from the quarries of Bethesda or the mines of Blaenau Ffestiniog. However, only about 10% of mined slate is usable, so for every ton that goes to the factory, nine tons are left as rubble.

Despite being in the very centre of Snowdonia National Park, the grey mountains of mine waste that surround Blaenau Ffestiniog prevented it from being officially included in the park – a slap in the face for this impoverished town, in the days before Wales' industrial sites were recognised as part of its heritage.

Today, although slate mining continues on a small scale, Blaenau (*blay*-nyc) struggles to survive as a tourist town, selling the history of the slate industry and of the Ffestiniog Railway (which has its northern terminus here). The town has a deeply mournful feel about it and an amazing sparsity of any worthwhile sleeping and eating options. If you're not interested in slate or rail heritage, then frankly there's little here to distract you.

SIGHTS

Blaenau's main attraction, the **Llechwedd Slate Caverns** (☎ 830306; www.llechwedd-slate-caverns.co.uk; either ride adult/child £8.95/6.75, both rides £13.50/9.50; ☷ from 10am daily, last tour 5.15pm Mar-Sep, 4.15pm Oct-Feb) offer a chance to descend into a real slate mine and get a sense of what the working life was like. There are two tours; the best is the 25-minute Deep Mine tour, including a descent on the UK's steepest passenger railway and a walk through 10 multimedia sequences, which guide you through the Victorian mining experience. If you can't manage a lot of steps, go for the Miner's Tramway Tour, a ride through the huge 1846 network of tunnels, caverns and Victorian tableaux. The site is just under a mile north of town on the A470 Betws-y-Coed road.

Riding the **Rheilffordd Ffestiniog Railway** (☎ 516024; www.festrail.co.uk; all-day Rover ticket to/from Porthmadog adult/concession £16.50/13.20), one of Wales' finest narrow-gauge railways, remains the main reason for visiting Blaenau. The Ffestiniog Railway Company is the oldest independent railway company in the world, and was established by Act of Parliament in 1832. The 13.5-mile line, built in the 1830s to haul slate to the port at Porthmadog (p250), is now an important link between the Conwy Valley and Cambrian Coast main lines. Frequency ranges from two to a high-summer maximum of six trains daily from April to October (45 minutes).

BETWS-Y-COED
☎ 01690 / pop 900

If you're looking for a base with an Alpine feel from which to explore Snowdonia National Park, the bustling little village of Betws-y-Coed *(bet-us-ee-coyd)* stands out as a natural option. It boasts a dramatic setting above an inky river, is engulfed in the verdant leafiness of the Gwydyr Forest and benefits from a position near the junction of three river valleys: the Lledr meets the Conwy and, about 1 mile south of the centre, they join the Llugwy. Betws-y-Coed takes its name (which means 'sanctuary in the wood') from the 14th-century St Michael's Church at the heart of town.

The town has blossomed as Wales' most popular inland resort since Victorian days when a group of countryside painters founded an artistic community to record the diversity of the landscape. The arrival of the railway in 1868 cemented its popularity and today Betws-y-Coed is as busy with families and coach parties as with walkers.

Activities are its stock-in-trade, however, with outdoor-activity shops strung out along the A5, the London–Holyhead highway that forms the main thoroughfare. The rivers Conwy and Llugwy are rich with salmon in autumn while water sports and skiing are best organised through the nearby Plas y Brenin National Mountain Centre (p263).

Orientation & Information
Betws-y-Coed is essentially centred around the A5 (known locally as the Holyhead Rd) with buses stopping at the end of Station Rd by the **short-stay car park** (per 3hr £1).

The excellent **National Park Information Centre** (☎ 710426; www.betws-y-coed.co.uk; Royal Oak Stables; ☉ 9.30am-5.30pm Apr-Oct, 9.30am-4.30pm Nov-Mar) is the hub for tourist information in the area with a comprehensive array of books and maps. The adjoining, free exhibition on Snowdonia National Park includes a virtual-reality helicopter ride over Snowdon. For specialist references for walkers, climbers and cyclists, call into **Ultimate Outdoors** (☎ 710555; www.ultimateoutdoors.co.uk; Holyhead Rd; ☉ 9.30am-6.30pm May-Sep, 9.30am-5.30pm Mon-Thu, to 6.30pm Fri & Sat Oct-Apr), an adventure shop with a huge range of equipment.

The **post office** (Holyhead Rd; ☉ 9am-5.30pm Mon-Fri, 9am-12.30pm Sat) is located within a **Londis convenience store** (☉ 8am-9pm), while the only bank in town is the close-by **HSBC** (Holyhead Rd).

You can access the internet at the **Cotswold Rock Bottom Shop** (Holyhead Rd; per 30min £1).

Sights
The main draw here is the surrounding landscape, with **Swallow Falls** (viewing platform £1), located 2 miles northwest of town, the main natural tourist trap. But there's also a raft of quieter day walks close by (see below).

In the tiny town centre, the 14th-century **St Michael's Church** is across the train tracks – the National Park Information Centre has a key, as does the **Conwy Valley Railway Museum** (☎ 710568; adult/child £1.50/0.80; ☉ 10am-5pm), which also arranges miniature steam train rides for families – the 1-mile round trip costs £1.50. Less compelling is the rather fusty **Betws-y-Coed Motor Museum** (☎ 710760; adult/child £1.50/1; ☉ 10am-6pm Apr-Oct) with vintage models of Aston Martin, Bentley, MG and various racing cars for enthusiasts.

Activities
WALKING & CYCLING
The 28-sq-mile **Gwydyr Forest**, planted since the 1920s with oak, beech and larch, encircles Betws-y-Coed to the west and south. At its heart, the **Gwydyr Forest Park**, laced with walking trails and boasting a designated cycle track, is an ideal spot for a day's walking close to town, though it gets very muddy in wet weather.

The **Forestry Commission** (www.forestry.gov.uk) publishes a brochure with 13 graded walks across a variety of distances; it's available from the National Park Information Centre for £2.

PONY TREKKING & HORSE RIDING
Located 6 miles east of Betws-y-Coed at Penmachno, **Ty Coch Farm** (☎ 760248; rides per hr/half-day

£17/30) arranges rides through the Gwydyr Forest for novice and regular riders alike. It also offers a pub ride for £36, lasting around four hours and stopping off for a pint at a couple of local pubs along the way.

Sleeping

Riverside Camping & Caravan Park (☎ 710310; Old Church Rd; sites per adult/child £6/3; ☼ Mar-Oct) This well-appointed site has tent and caravan pitches and hot showers. The owners operate a strict noise curfew after 10pm and bookings are highly recommended at peak times.

Betws-y-Coed (Swallow Falls) YHA (☎ 710796; adult/child £14/10) Two miles west of town and opposite the trail leading down to Swallow Falls (opposite), this year-round hostel is part

of a bustling traveller hub with camping, a restaurant and self-catering facilities. While facilities are excellent, it's aimed at serious walkers rather than families with children. The Snowdon Sherpa bus S2 runs out here every 30 minutes from Betws-y-Coed train station.

Ferns (☎ 710587; www.ferns-guesthouse.co.uk; Holyhead Rd; s £38 d £50-60) New owners have taken over this four-star-rated B&B at the heart of the village and introduced 'fry up'-free healthy breakfasts using local produce. The rooms are comfortable with some nice, homely touches.

Afon View (☎ 710726; www.afon-view.co.uk; Holyhead Rd; s/d/f £31/60/80; P ✗) Traditional but homely, with a few frilly touches for Laura Ashley fans, this Victorian property has seven en-suite rooms and is set back from the main road in a

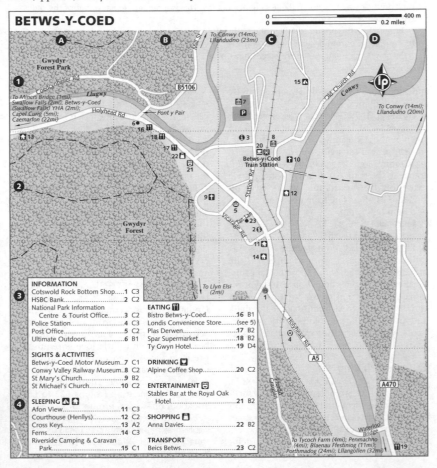

BETWS-Y-COED

To Conwy (14mi); Llandudno (23mi)
To Minors Bridge (3mi); Swallow Falls (2mi); Betws-y-Coed (Swallow Falls) YHA (2mi); Capel Curig (5mi); Caernarfon (22mi)
To Conwy (14mi); Llandudno (20mi)
To Llyn Elsi (2mi)
To Tycoch Farm (4mi); Penmachno (4mi); Blaenau Ffestiniog (11mi); Porthmadog (24mi); Llangollen (32mi)

INFORMATION
Cotswold Rock Bottom Shop.....1 C3
HSBC Bank...............................2 C2
National Park Information
  Centre & Tourist Office........3 C2
Police Station...........................4 C3
Post Office...............................5 C2
Ultimate Outdoors....................6 B1

SIGHTS & ACTIVITIES
Betws-y-Coed Motor Museum..7 C1
Conwy Valley Railway Museum.8 C2
St Mary's Church......................9 B2
St Michael's Church................10 C2

SLEEPING
Afon View..............................11 C3
Courthouse (Henllys)..............12 C2
Cross Keys..............................13 A2
Ferns.....................................14 C3
Riverside Camping & Caravan
  Park...................................15 C1

EATING
Bistro Betws-y-Coed...............16 B1
Londis Convenience Store....(see 5)
Plas Derwen...........................17 B2
Spar Supermarket...................18 B2
Ty Gwyn Hotel.......................19 D4

DRINKING
Alpine Coffee Shop.................20 C2

ENTERTAINMENT
Stables Bar at the Royal Oak
  Hotel.................................21 B2

SHOPPING
Anna Davies...........................22 B2

TRANSPORT
Beics Betws............................23 C2

A DAY WALK AROUND BETWS-Y-COED

Starting from the car park behind the National Park Information Centre in Betws-y-Coed, this 4-mile circular walk is an easy stroll suitable for families. The walk draws on the unique location of the town at the convergence of the Conwy and Llugwy rivers.

From the tourist office the footpath passes the Motor Museum to the point where the Llugwy and Conwy rivers meet. Take a right and follow the Conwy, passing some large stepping stones, the oldest crossing point of the Conwy.

Back on the main road, follow the left-hand fork, which leads to the 14th-century church of St Michael, now used only for funerals. Cross the Conwy by the white suspension bridge built in 1930 and follow the path through the fields to the main road. Then head south along the A470 until you come to Waterloo Bridge. Built in 1815 and known locally as 'iron bridge', it spans 32m and is inscribed thus: 'This arch was constructed in the same year as the battle of Waterloo was fought'. Take a right over the bridge and follow the main road through the village. At the stone-built Pont y Pair, the 'Bridge of the Cauldron', cross the river, taking the left path alongside the river Llugwy – keep to the river side.

After about 1 mile you will come to the Miners' Bridge, so called as this was the route miners took on their way to work in the lead mines nearby. This is a modern replacement of the oldest crossing of the Llugwy.

Either cross the bridge to follow the path to the main road, where you turn left to get back to the village, or retrace your steps alongside the river.

For more information, see www.eryri-npa.gov.uk.

---

quiet location. The friendly owner can advise on local activities.

Cross Keys (☎ 710334; www.crosskeyssnowdonia.co.uk; Holyhead Rd; s/d £40/70; ✕) About half a mile from town on the A5 heading west to Capel Curig, this simple but satisfying pub has decent en-suite rooms, some accessible via a separate entrance to the main bar area in a cottage-style extension. Downstairs the owners serve up standard bar-food fare from noon to 12.30pm and 6pm to 8.30pm.

Courthouse (Henllys) (☎ 710534; www.guesthouse-snowdonia.co.uk; Old Church Rd; s/d £36/80; ✕) Nine individually styled rooms feature in this traditional guesthouse; the most popular is the old judge's quarters with exposed oak beams. Formerly the town's courthouse, today it retains its connection to the legal profession with its treasure-trove interior of memorabilia and artefacts. The guest lounge offers a particularly, ahem, arresting experience with its fine collection of police helmets.

Eating & Drinking

Plas Derwen (☎ 710388; Holyhead Rd; light meals £4; 🕙 10am-5pm) A very modern and airy café serving lunches and light meals, plus a full afternoon tea (£6.50). A few tables overlook the main street for an al fresco morning coffee and the owners have introduced a couple of modern, tasteful rooms upstairs for B&B (rooms £25).

Alpine Coffee Shop (☎ 710747; Train Station Complex; snacks £5; 🕙 8.30am-5.30pm) Grab a bite at this excellent, friendly little café, which serves toasted sandwiches and snacks. Unusually, it also boasts a huge tea menu with 25 varieties, including the 'world's rarest tea' at £8.50 per pot. Unfortunately, after all that tea, there's no toilet – use the public loo in the nearby car park.

Bistro Betws-y-Coed (☎ 710328; www.bistrobetws-y-coed; mains £15; Holyhead Rd; 🕙 noon-3pm & 6.30-9pm) The sister property to Bistro Conwy (p291), this smart new eatery is one of the best places for an evening meal, with a menu of traditional Welsh dishes and daily specials. Reservations are often mandatory at weekends and during peak season.

Ty Gwyn Hotel (☎ 710383; www.tygwynhotel.co.uk; bar meals £8, mains £15; meals 🕙 noon-2pm & 6.30-9pm) Under new management, this 17th-century coaching inn (it dates from 1636) oozes character from every one of its numerous exposed beams, although a little love is required to preserve the ambience. The menu focuses on hearty, meaty mains but lighter bar-style meals are also available. The owners also offer B&B accommodation (rooms £22 to £50) – ask about off-season promotions.

For self-caterers, there's a **Spar supermarket** (Holyhead Rd; 🕙 8am-10pm) and a **Londis convenience store** (Holyhead Rd; 🕙 8am-10pm) to stock up on basic supplies.

Entertainment

Stables Bar (☎ 710219; www.royaloakhotel.net; Royal Oak Hotel, Holyhead Rd) There's live jazz on Thursday nights and a male voice choir in residence every other Friday as well as cheap bar meals (from £7), dinner and B&B accommodation packages (from £57.50 per person).

Shopping

Anna Davies (☎ 710292; www.annadavies.co.uk; Holyhead Rd; ⏰ 9am-5.30pm Mon-Fri, 10am-6pm Sat & Sun) A local institution, the Anna Davies department store sells crafts and household goods, and celebrated its 50 years of service in 2006.

Getting There & Away

The most scenic journey to Betws-y-Coed is by train, with six daily services (three on Sundays) from Llandudno Junction (£4, 30 minutes) and onto Blaenau Ffestiniog (£3.30, 30 minutes) on the **Conwy Valley Line** (www.conwyvalleyrailway.co.uk).

Snowdon Sherpa runs bus S2 from Llandudno and S6 from Llanberis to Capel Curig via Betws-y-Coed, stopping outside the train station.

Arriva's bus 84 runs three daily services to Llandudno Junction (35 minutes); bus X19 runs four daily services (two on Sundays) to Llangollen (one hour).

Getting Around

Beics Betws (☎ 710766; www.bikewales.co.uk; Tan Lan) can advise on local cycling trails and hires a range of mountain bikes from £14/18 per half-/full day. Ask about full-suspension and free-ride bike prices.

AROUND BETWS-Y-COED
Capel Curig
☎ 01690 / pop 190

Tiny Capel Curig, 5 miles west of Betws-y-Coed with a population of less than 200 people, is one of Snowdonia's oldest hill stations, and has long been a centre for walkers, climbers and other outdoor junkies. A scattered village at the heart of soaring, heady scenery and ringed by looming mountains, Capel Curig has two primary claims to fame.

Ugly House (☎ 720287; ⏰ 9.30am-5.30pm Easter-Oct; admission £1) is a historic property with an educational centre for children and a wildlife garden. More crucially, the property is home to the **Snowdonia Society** (www.snowdonia-society.org.uk), a charity working to protect and enhance Snowdonia National Park (see the boxed text Local

Voices, p264). The origins of the house make for great local folklore. One yarn suggests it was built in 1475 by two local bandits as their hideout; another states that, because Welsh law in the Middle Ages said that any man who built on common land and had smoke coming out of the chimney by daybreak could stake a claim for the freehold as far as he could throw an axe around the property, the outlaws claimed the place as their own after some axe-throwing practice. The Snowdonia Society rescued the property from dereliction and turned it into their headquarters in 1988 following painstaking renovations by a team of dedicated volunteers.

The **Plas y Brenin National Mountain Centre** (☎ 720214; www.pyb.co.uk), at the western edge of the village, is a multiactivity centre with excellent facilities and a huge array of residential, year-round courses, ranging from basic rock climbing to summer and winter mountaineering, and professional development and teaching qualifications. Advance bookings are required. The management can arrange local B&B accommodation and offer simple in-house dorm rooms (£20). There's a communal bar area to meet other students and regular talks cover related topics on Monday, Tuesday and Saturday evenings at 8pm. Taster days runs throughout the year with an introduction to three activities for £30.

For cheap sleeping options, there is a youth hostel in the local area open year-round, but call ahead to check availability. **Capel Curig YHA** (☎ 0870 7705746; Plas Curig; adult/child £16/12.50) is very much a walkers' hang-out (with great views across to the Snowdon Horseshoe), but has limited access with its entrance up a very steep track. Snowdon Sherpa bus S2 runs close by – ask the driver to shout when approaching the junction with the A4086. Call ahead to check opening times off season.

The liveliest spot to head for after dark is **Bryn Tyrch** (☎ 720223; www.bryntyrch-hotel.co.uk), the most popular pub in the village. It has log fires in winter, bar meals, including lots of vegetarian and vegan options (mains around £9), and B&B in cosy rooms (singles/doubles £45/65).

LLANBERIS
☎ 01286 / pop 2000

Llanberis is a magnet for walkers and climbers, with lots of rugged, fleece-wearing trekkers relishing hearty meals and pub post mortems of the day's activities. While not the most

LOCAL VOICES

Nowhere in the UK can offer such diverse scenery as the Snowdonia National Park: majestic mountain tops (15 over 3000ft), 23 miles of stunning coastline, shimmering lakes, tranquil valleys dotted with ancient woodland, moorland and an abundance of wildlife can all be found within the park's 823 sq miles. The lure of the scenery is irresistible and each year the equivalent of 11 million day visits are made to the oldest and largest national park in Wales.

The park has the twin aims of conserving the landscape, while encouraging the public's enjoyment. With growing visitor numbers, reconciling these aims can be difficult.

The Snowdonia Society, a charitable organisation, has been passionately working to protect and enhance the park for some 40 years through a range of innovative and imaginative projects. Their Sustainable Energy and Tourism Project (SEAT) is all about working with visitors and tourism businesses to reduce the industry's impact on the park's fragile environment.

Visiting such a delicate environment will always have some negative impact – but we can all play a part to lessen this. Why not leave the car behind? Take the time to travel and enjoy the views on foot or bike, or make use of the Snowdon Sherpa buses and local trains. Or join volunteers to use traditional techniques and materials to restore footpaths and prevent erosion. Help the environment and local economy and reward yourself with the scrumptious fruit of this living landscape with a locally produced meal. At the end of your day take a shower instead of a bath – you'll save lots of water which looks much better in the rivers and lakes!

The society is working with local tourism businesses to encourage them to reduce, reuse and recycle the amount of resources they use and to use local products. When booking accommodation look out for environmental hallmarks such as the Green Dragon Accreditation or the Society's Green Snowdonia Tourism Award – you can then rest assured that you're playing your part in protecting this spectacular region.

Dan James, Operations Director, The Snowdonia Society (www.snowdonia-society.org.uk)

attractive town, it's a popular and busy base from which to explore Snowdonia, especially in July and August when room space is at a premium.

The town was originally built to house workers in the Dinorwig slate quarry, whose massive waste tips are hard to miss as you approach from the east – despite the fact the quarry shut down in 1969. While tourism is the cornerstone of Llanberis life these days, the town still wears its industrial heritage on its sleeve with pride. Indeed, Dinorwig, which once boasted the largest artificial cavern in the world, has now become part of Europe's biggest pumped-storage power station. Some of the old quarry workshops have been reincarnated as a museum of the slate industry, and the narrow-gauge railway that once hauled slate to the coast now tootles along Llyn Padarn.

Orientation & Information

Llanberis straddles the A4086 with nearly all the points of interest spread out along the High St, which runs parallel to it. Across the A4086 are the village's two lakes, Llyn Padarn and Llyn Peris. The Snowdon Mountain Railway has its base at the southern end of town while **car parking** (per hr 40p) is available at sites close to Electric Mountain (opposite). Buses stop along the High St at request stops.

The High St is the hub of the action with a helpful **tourist office** (☎ 870765; 41 High St; ✆ 9am-5pm Fri-Wed Apr-Oct, Mon-Wed, Fri & Sat Nov-Mar), a **post office** (✆ 9.30am-5.30pm Mon-Fri, 9.30am-12.30pm Sat) across the street and a series of banks.

To tap into the travellers' and walkers' network, **Pete's Eats** (☎ 870117; www.petes-eats.co.uk; 40 High St; ✆ 9am-9pm Jul & Aug, 9am-8pm Apr-Jun & Sep, 9am-6.30pm Mon-Fri, 8am-8pm Sat & Sun Oct-Mar) has a huge noticeboard, a book exchange, a map and guidebook room, and – when it's actually working – some computers for internet access (50p initial charge, then 5p per minute); see also above.

Joe Brown (☎ 870327; www.joebrownonline.co.uk; ✆ 9am-6pm Mon-Sat, 9am-5pm Sun), a climbing shop selling all things outdoors, has a notice board that includes gear for sale and accommodation, plus three-day forecasts and lots of information or advice for walkers.

Swigoda Sebon (54 High St; service wash £5.50; ✆ 9am-5.30pm Mon-Fri) has a service wash to clean post-walking kit.

Sights

SNOWDON MOUNTAIN RAILWAY

Opened in 1896, the **Snowdon Mountain Railway** (☎ 0870 4580033; www.snowdonrailway.co.uk; ☺ 9am-5pm Mar-Oct) is the UK's highest and only public rack-and-pinion railway. It will take you up to the summit of Snowdon (1085m) with the minimum of effort – the 5-mile journey takes an hour. Seven vintage steam and four modern diesel locomotives haul carriages up and down; departures are weather-dependent and summer queues can be long.

However, the railway is currently undergoing major construction work, and trains will only run to **Clogwyn station** (adult/child £11/7), at a height of 762m, throughout 2007 and into 2008. A new summit station, complete with a café and new attractions, is due to open in time for the summer season 2008.

ELECTRIC MOUNTAIN

The Dinorwig pumped-storage power station is the largest scheme of its kind in Europe. Located deep below Elidir mountain, its construction required one million tonnes of concrete, 200,000 tonnes of cement and 4500 tonnes of steel. The power station uses surplus energy to pump water from Llyn Peris up to Marchlyn Reservoir. When half the population switches on their kettles for tea during a TV ad break, the water is released to fall through underground turbines. Dinorwig's reversible pump/turbines are capable of reaching maximum generation in less than 16 seconds.

Electric Mountain (☎ 870636; www.electricmountain .co.uk; ☺ 10.30am-4.30pm Wed-Sun Feb, Mar, Nov & Dec, daily Apr, May, Sep & Oct, 9.30am-4.30pm Jun-Aug), the power station's visitor centre, has free interactive exhibits on the history of hydropower. An interesting **guided tour** (adult/child £7/3.50; every 30min Jun-Aug, by reservation otherwise) into the underground power station also starts from here; advance bookings are essential.

The centre is also home to Connections Café (p266) and **Techniquest** (www.techniquest.org; adult/child £3.20/2.20; ☺ 10.30am-4.30pm May-Nov), a child-friendly science museum with hands-on exhibits and an interactive science theatre show.

The centre is located where High St joins the A4086, about a third of a mile south of the tourist office.

WELSH SLATE MUSEUM

The **Welsh Slate Museum** (☎ 870630; www.museum wales.ac.uk/en/slate; admission free; ☺ 10am-5pm Apr-Oct,

10am-4pm Sun-Fri Nov-Apr), inside the Victorian workshops beside Llyn Padarn, brings the local slate industry alive. It features a huge working water wheel, reconstructed workers' cottages (furnished as they would have been between 1860 and 1969 when the quarries closed), demonstrations on splitting slate into tiles and a 3D-presentation on working in a quarry.

The turn-off is located along the A4086 between the Electric Mountain exhibition centre and the Snowdon Mountain Railway station.

RHEILFFORDD LLYN PADARN LLANBERIS LAKE RAILWAY

This little tourist **train** (☎ 870549; www.lake-railway .co.uk; adult/child £6/4; ☺ 4-10 services daily mid-Mar-Oct plus occasional special services; ♿) departs on a 5-mile return jaunt beside Llyn Padarn, part of the route (though not the same track) used from 1843 to 1961 to haul slate to port on the Menai Strait. It's a tame but scenic one-hour return trip through Padarn Country Park to the terminus at Penllyn, with scenic mountain views en route; there's a wheelchair-adapted carriage.

The terminus station is located across the A4086 towards Llyn Peris and opposite the Snowdon Railway station, with a second station by the Welsh Slate Museum.

Activities

Beacon Climbing Centre (☎ 650045; Ceunant; www .beaconclimbing.com; ☺ 11am-10pm Mon-Fri, 10am-10pm Sat & Sun) is a large indoor climbing centre with over 100 climbs to learn and the chance to hone your skills; it's 5 miles west of Llanberis, off the A4086. There are also 90-minute taster sessions for one to three people for £45 per person.

Boulder Adventures (☎ 870556; www.boulder adventures.co.uk; Bryn Du Mountain Centre; half-/full-day courses £26/42) offers a range of activities, including kayaking, canoeing, climbing, abseiling and mountain walking, plus activities for small groups and families, in a spacious Victorian property. Communal hostel-style facilities are good with on-site B&B (dorm beds £14).

Llanberis Lake Cruises (☎ 671156; adult/child £5/3.50; ☺ 11am-5pm May-Oct) runs scenic 45-minute boat trips on Llyn Padarn aboard the *Snowdon Star*; the boat sails from the Padarn Country Park jetty near the Welsh Slate Museum car park.

Sleeping

Llanberis YHA (☎ 0870 7705928; Llwyn Celyn; adult/child £14/10; ☺ daily Easter-Oct, Fri & Sat Nov-Mar) Originally a quarry manager's house, this hostel is a haven for walkers, hikers and outdoor pursuits with self-catering facilities and a drying room. It's half a mile southwest of town.

Pen-y-Pass YHA (☎ 0870 7705990; Nantgwynant; adult/child £14/10; ☒ daily Easter-Oct, Fri & Sat Nov-Mar) Superbly situated 5.5 miles up the A4086 atop Llanberis Pass, this hostel was once the haunt of Victorian climbers – George Mallory of Everest fame once stayed here on his early climbing trips to Wales. Given the prestigious history, it's now a natural base for climbers on the Snowdon pilgrimage, or for those exploring the surrounding mountains. Transport connections are provided by the Snowdon Sherpa service, with various services passing close by.

Snowdon House (☎ 870284; www.snowdonhouse.co .uk; 3 Gwastadnant; camping/dm £5/10, cottages per week up to £590) Three miles towards Pen-y-Pass at Nant Peris, this traveller hang-out makes up for its lack of welcome with its range of budget alternatives. The smarter cottage option accommodates up to nine people with central heating and a fitted kitchen.

Jesse James' Bunkhouse (☎ 870521; Penisa'r Waun; dm £10-30; ☒) Located about 3 miles out of Llanberis on the A4244 Bangor road, this budget hostel has been a popular walkers' base since 1966. The eponymous Jesse, a retired mountain guide, is full of useful advice and believes in a keep-it-simple ethos: bring a sleeping bag and food, everything else is provided.

Alpine Lodge (☎ 870294; www.alpinelodgehotel .co.uk; 1 High St; r per person £28-37.50; P) With lodge-style accommodation in an attractive setting, the Alpine has rooms with balconies and great views across the mountains. The décor is simple and modern, although the so-called 'luxury lodges' offer a few more home comforts.

Bron-y-Graig (☎ 872073; www.bronygraig.co.uk; Capel Coch; r per person from £32) About 150m off High St (turn at the Spar supermarket), this picturesque Victorian guesthouse, with its own little garden, has three well-equipped rooms. The breakfast menu includes options for vegetarians and vegans.

Dolafon (☎ 870993; www.dolafon.com; High St; s £28, d £56-75; ☒) Set back from the road, this imposing 19th-century house offers a series of very traditional rooms, most of them with en suites. The hearty breakfast includes vegetarian options and, if you need a lie in after a long walk, continental breakfasts can be delivered to the room.

Plas Coch (☎ 872122; www.plas-coch.co.uk; High St; s/d £31/62; ☒ ▢ ☒ ☒) With a warm welcome and a homely feel, this excellent upper-scale guesthouse is the most family-friendly in town. The owners have also adapted one ground-floor room for disabled and wheelchair access, plus installed wi-fi access. Prices include a huge and hearty breakfast, which draws on local and organic produce.

Quality Hotel Snowdonia (☎ 870253; www.hotels -snowdonia.com; s/d £70/110) Formerly known as the Royal Victoria Hotel, this property has undergone changes in management and decoration recently. It remains the top-end property in town and is set in a suitably stately, grand building, although the rooms do still feel rather old-fashioned. In-house facilities cater increasingly for the group and conference markets.

Eating & Drinking

Connections Café (☎ 873024; www.electricmountain.co.uk; ☒ 10.30am-4.30pm Wed-Sun Feb, Mar, Nov & Dec, 10.30am-4.30pm daily Apr, May, Sep & Oct, 9.30am-4.30pm Jun-Aug) A welcoming, child-friendly café for coffees, snacks and simple daily specials set within the Electric Mountain visitor centre (p265).

AUTHOR'S CHOICE

Pen-y-Gwyrd (☎ 870211; www.pyg.co.uk; Nant Gwynant; s/d £35/45; bar meals ☒ noon-2pm & 7.30-9.30pm) For a unique place to sleep, this amazing old hotel gives a great sense of living history without sacrificing on comforts. The 1953 Everest team used the inn as a training base, and memorabilia from their stay – including their signatures on the ceiling of the dining room – lends the place the atmosphere of a private museum. You can even re-create the scene as guests gather round a large communal dining table for evening meals.

The rooms are very traditional with hefty wooden furniture, while the bathrooms feature free-standing baths with huge Victorian taps. The hotel is 5 miles southeast of Llanberis over the Llanberis Pass at the junction of the A498 and A4086. A little gem.

Saffran (☎ 871777; High St; ⏰ 9.30am-5.30pm Mon-Sat, 11am-4.30pm Sun) An organic deli selling takeaway organic foodstuffs, including soups and sandwiches. The shop is also home to a giant noticeboard which helps visitors tap into the local network of organic producers.

Pete's Eats (☎ 870117; www.petes-eats.co.uk; 40 High St; meals £4-6; ⏰ 9am-9pm Jul & Aug, 9am-8pm Apr-Jun & Sep, 9am-6.30pm Mon-Fri, 8am-8pm Sat & Sun Oct-Mar) This place is a local institution, a crowded (expect queues), bright café where hikers and climbers swap tips over monster portions in a hostel-like environment. Mostly it's big breakfasts (around £4) and meals with chips, but the extensive menu does offer the odd imaginative daily special, such as spinach and chick pea curry (£6). Huge portions, terrible service. The owners also offer basic bunkhouse accommodation (dorm beds £12).

Peak Restaurant (☎ 872777; High St; mains around £12; ⏰ 11.30am-4pm Thu & Fri, 7-9.30pm Wed-Fri, 6-9.30pm Sat, 4.30-8pm Sun) Looking smarter and fresher after expansion and refurbishment, this popular spot continues to serve the best dinners in town with hearty mains at dinner and snack-style lunches.

Y Bistro (☎ 871278; www.ybistro.co.uk; 45 High St; mains around £16; ⏰ 7-10.30pm) This inviting dinner-only restaurant has a good range of favourite Welsh dishes with a rustic-French twist, such as roasted Anglesey pheasant with bread sauce. It's one of the few places in town with a nod to fine dining; bookings are strongly advised.

Along High St there's a **Spar Supermarket** (⏰ 8am-8pm) for self caterers.

Heights Hotel (☎ 871179; 74 High St; www.heights hotel.co.uk; bar meals ⏰ noon-9pm) In the evenings, climbers and walkers head for the bar at the Heights Hotel, a pub with bar meals, music and – wait for it – its own climbing wall. The owners also offer basic B&B accommodation (singles/doubles £35/55).

Getting There & Away

KMP's bus 88 runs from Llanberis to Bangor (one hour, hourly, no Sunday service) via Caernarfon (25 minutes, eight services Sunday); bus 9 follows a similar route but runs from Bangor onto Llandudno (two hours, hourly, no Sunday service).

The Snowdon Sherpa bus S1 connects Llanberis with Pen-y-Pass, where you can connect with all the other Sherpa services.

THE LLŶN

Jutting out from the mountains of Snowdonia, the Llŷn Peninsula is a long, narrow, green-patchwork finger of land jutting into the sea, some 25 miles long and averaging 8 miles in width. The Llŷn and the Isle of Anglesey were the last places on the Roman and Norman itineraries, and both areas maintain a strong sense of a separate identity, although the Llŷn remains far more untouched compared to Anglesey today. Over the centuries the heaviest footfalls have been those of pilgrims on their way to holy Bardsey Island.

Criccieth is a sedate family resort, Abersoch a big water sports draw and Pwllheli, the biggest town, the main railway hub of the peninsula. The latter is also home to the only official tourist office on the peninsula. The land is peaceful and largely undeveloped, with 70 miles of wildlife-rich coastline (much of it in the hands of the National Trust, and almost 80% of it designated an Area of Outstanding Natural Beauty). It offers quiet walking and cycling, some excellent beaches and a handful of small fishing villages. Welsh is the language of everyday life. Indeed, as places go, this is about as Welsh as it gets.

CRICCIETH
☎ 01766 / pop 1800
This genteel slow-moving seaside town sits above a sweep of sand-and-stone beach and is about 5 miles west of Porthmadog. The town is topped off by a small high-up castle, is a good spot for brisk seafront walks and it also makes a low-key base for exploring the surrounding countryside.

Orientation & Information
The town's focal point is Y Maes, a wide square on the High St, the A497 Porthmadog–Pwllheli road. The seaside road running parallel to High St is Castle St. There's parking space on the opposite side of High St behind the Lion Hotel (p268) and the train station is about two blocks west down the A497.

There is no longer a tourist office, although **Roots** (☎ 523564; 46 High St; ⏰ 10am-5pm Mon-Sat Apr-Oct, Tue-Sat Nov-Mar), a Christian bookshop, now acts as the de-facto tourist office. It has OS maps and offers internet access (50p to connect, then 5p per min). You can also fill your water bottle for free here.

Along High St, you can find a HSBC bank with ATM, a small **Spar supermarket** (☯ 8am-8pm Mon-Sat, 9am-6pm Sun) and a **post office** (☯ 9am-5.30pm Mon-Fri, 9.30am-12.30pm Sat).

Sights

Criccieth Castle (☎ 522227; adult/child £2.90/2.40; ☯ 10am-6pm Jun-Sep, to 5pm Apr, May & Oct, 9.30am-4pm Fri-Sun Nov-Mar) is still considered Welsh – it was taken by force and enlarged by Edward I in 1283, but established between 1230 and 1240 by Llewelyn ap Iorwerth (Llewelyn the Great). Little remains of the castle, but it's in a fantastic position, with views stretching along the southern coast and across Tremadog Bay to Harlech. The castle's fate was sealed when, in 1404, the Welsh leader, Owain Glyndŵr, captured and burnt the castle. Today there is a small but informative exhibition centre at the ticket office.

Festivals & Events

The week-long **Criccieth Festival** (☎ 522778) is an eclectic sampler of art, lectures, walks, drama, jazz and classical music in venues around the town in the second half of June each year.

Sleeping

Lion Hotel (☎ 522460; www.lionhotelcriccieth.co.uk; Y Maes; s/d from £35/60) One block northwest of Y Maes, this large, 46-room hotel has views of the castle and sea, and is also a good mid-range option. Family friendly, it has bar meals (served from noon to 8.30pm daily), a beer garden for summer days and a penchant for hosting murder mystery weekends.

Moelwyn (☎ 522500; www.themoelwyn.co.uk; 27-29 Mona Tce; s/d £40/60) Two blocks southeast of Y Maes, this serene smart restaurant with rooms is a friendly spot. There are only six en-suite rooms, although sea views are a bonus. The owners serve a hearty dinner (from 6.30pm to 9.30pm) in a restaurant with Tiffany-coloured walls and cream tablecloths.

Bron Eifion (☎ 522385; www.broneifion.co.uk; s/d from £60/80) A country-house hotel with fabulously formal gardens, grand old Bron Eifion has been taken over by new management and refurbished with flat-screen TVs and less chintz to give it a fresher, cleaner look. Check out the chunky wooden furniture now gracing all the rooms – it was all imported from Brazil. The hotel is half a mile from Criccieth, off the A497 towards Pwllheli.

Eating & Drinking

Café Cust (Y Maes; ☯ 10am-6pm) For a snack on the go, this is a simple café for coffees and sandwiches.

Poachers Restaurant (☎ 522512; 66 High St; mains around £10; ☯ noon-2pm Wed-Sun, 6-9pm daily) A popular local eatery, Poachers has a menu with an international flavour and a suitably pleasant setting. Try the good-value three-course dinner (£13.95).

Prince of Wales (☎ 522556; Y Maes; ✗) The liveliest pub in town, with local ales and decent bar meals (served from noon to 9.30pm).

Getting There & Away

Express Motors bus 1 runs from Blaenau Ffestiniog (40 minutes, every two hours Monday to Saturday) via Porthmadog (10 minutes). Arriva's bus 3 passes by en route from Porthmadog (13 minutes, half-hourly Monday to Saturday, every two hours Sunday), and from Pwllheli (25 minutes).

National Express coach 545 from Pwllheli stops by Y Maes daily at 7.45am en route to London (11 hours) via Birmingham (eight hours).

AROUND CRICCIETH

The village of **Llanystumdwy** is the boyhood home and final resting place of David Lloyd George, one of Wales' finest ever political statesmen, and the British prime minister from 1916 to 1922 (see the boxed text, p36). There's a small **Lloyd George Museum** (☎ 522071; ☯ 10.30am-5pm Mon-Fri Apr & May, Mon-Sat Jun, daily Jul-Sep, 11am-4pm Mon-Fri Oct), which gives an idea of the man and to some extent illustrates the tension between his nationality and position, through photos, posters and personal effects. Highgate, the house he grew up in, is 50m away, and his grave is about 150m away on the other side of the car park – the memorial is designed by Clough Williams-Ellis, the creator of Portmeirion (p252). There's a new interactive children's area for families inside the museum.

The turn-off to the village is to be found 1.5 miles west of Criccieth on the A497. The Porthmadog–Pwllheli bus (bus 3) stops here (half-hourly Monday to Saturday, every two hours on Sunday).

PWLLHELI

☎ 01758 / pop 4000

The largest town and transport hub of the peninsula, Pwllheli (poolth-*heh*-lee; meaning 'salt-water pool') is 13 miles from Porth-madog and 8 miles from Criccieth. Despite its hub status, it's not a particularly attractive or well served town to overnight. It has narrow, cobbled streets and loads of pubs, but lacks the infrastructure for holidaymakers of other places on the peninsula. It's best to stop at the tourist office to stock up on information – then move on.

Pwllheli is a passionately Welsh town (it was here in 1925 that Plaid Cymru, the Welsh National Party, was founded, though the building is long gone) and Welsh is still widely spoken. As such, you'll get further here with Welsh street names than English ones – for example Stryd Fawr instead of High St, and Ffordd-y-Cob rather than Embankment Rd.

Orientation & Information

The train station, bus stands and harbour are all within a block of one another just south of Y Maes, the main square. Pwllheli is the terminus of the Cambrian Coast railway from Machynlleth and the train station is two blocks south of High St, with the bus station tucked one block further west. A large **Co-op supermarket** (8am-10pm Mon-Sat, 10am-4pm Sun) dominates the station area, with parking available in its extensive car park overlooking the railway line.

The **tourist office** (☎ 613000; Station Sq; 10.30am-4.30pm Mon-Wed, Fri & Sat Nov-Mar, 9am-5pm Apr-Oct), just east of the train station, has everything you'll need to know about the peninsula, including information on walks and a brochure detailing the walks around Llŷn Coastal Path. Free internet access is available at the **library** (☎ 612089; Stryd Penlan; 10am-1pm Tue, Thu & Sat, 10am-1pm & 2-7pm Mon & Wed, 2-5pm Fri). There's a **post office** (9.30am-5.30pm Mon-Fri, 9.30am-1pm Sat) opposite the Co-op and banks located along High St.

Activities

Operators based in or around Pwllheli offer the following activities:
Bardsey Ferry Service (☎ 07814-128620; www .enllicharter.me.uk; adult/child £30/18) Has daily departures to Bardsey Island (depending on the weather) with departures from Pwllheli harbour at 8.45am.
Judy B (☎ 01691-650223) Arranges deep-sea fishing trips.
Pathfinder Activities (☎ 01766-810909; www.path findersnowdonia.co.uk; The Coach House, Pencaenewydd) Runs outdoors navigation courses, plus abseiling and canoeing.

Sleeping

If you do find yourself stuck in town for the night, there are a few good options to choose from.
Rhosydd (☎ 612956; Golf Rd; s/d £20/30) This basic B&B, located three blocks southwest of Y Maes, is a friendly spot with very traditional fittings and furnishings.
Crown Hotel (☎ 612664; High St; s/d £40/60;) A smarter midrange option, this pub-hotel offers free wi-fi internet for laptop carriers. Make sure to ask for a room on one of the upper floors, however, to avoid the thump of the jukebox from the public bar and watch out for the noisy plumbing. There's a decent in-house restaurant with bar meals (from noon to 2.30pm and 6pm to 9.30pm).

Eating

Coffee Bean Emporium Graffi (☎ 613143; High St; 9.30am-5pm Mon-Sat;) A useful spot for a caffeine fix and a pastry, with a huge range of fair-trade speciality coffees.
Barn (☎ 613800; Goal St; meals £6.95; 10.30am-9pm) Simple but satisfying, this family restaurant has a big menu of traditional favourites, plus daily specials and a busy Sunday carvery with all the trimmings.
Taro Deg (☎ 701271; Lon Dywod; lunch/dinner mains £5/8; 9am-4.30pm Mon-Thu, 9am-9pm Fri & Sat) Stylish yet nice and relaxed, this café-cum-bistro offers newspapers to browse and a thoughtful menu, featuring organic local produce. Coffees and pastries are served all day while it takes on a more intimate feel for dinner.
Ship Inn (☎ 740521; Llanbedrog; bar meals noon-9pm) A popular, family-friendly pub about 3 miles out of Pwllheli off the A499, the Ship Inn is well worth the drive. Great, hearty bar meals with lots of daily specials make this place the stand-out for bar food in the area.
Esi Café Bar (☎ 701321; Station Sq; mains around £15; 10am-2.30pm & 6pm-late Mon-Sat) This new stylish addition to the dining scene has a contemporary restaurant downstairs and a bar area upstairs, the latter open late for post-prandial snifters into the early hours.
Pili Palas (☎ 612248; 2-4 Goal St; mains around £15; 10am-3.30pm & 6.30-9pm Tue-Sat) A welcome addition to the restaurant scene, this great little eatery has friendly service and upmarket but affordable fare. By day the menu has light bites, such as hot ciabatta, while the evening menu boasts traditional hearty mains. Bookings recommended.

SNOWDONIA & THE LLŶN

AUTHOR'S CHOICE

Plas Bodegroes (☎ 612363; www.bodegroes.co.uk; s/d from £50/100; ⊗ Mar-Nov) This slick, highly professional restaurant with rooms is a rare treat in the area, boasting a Michelin star for its elegant, pistachio-coloured dining room. Set in a stately Georgian Manor House with flower-strewn and immaculately coiffeured gardens, it's a romantic spot for couples and welcoming to families seeking a special weekend break. The rooms are richly and stylishly decorated, with lots of wooden antique furniture, while the fine-dining restaurant specialises in using the best fresh local produce. The latter is also open to nonresidents, serving a four-course dinner (£40) and a Sunday lunch (£17).

The hotel is 2 miles from Pwllheli, heading west along the A497. Take the turn-off for the B4415 and then follow the long twisting drive to the property. Ask about promotional rates for midweek breaks (two nights, dinner, B&B) available from Tuesday to Friday.

Entertainment

Neuadd Dwyfor (☎ 704088; Stryd Penlan) Sharing a building with the library, it shows the latest films.

Getting There & Away

Trains come from Machynlleth via Porthmadog (single £10.40, 25 minutes, every two or three hours Monday to Saturday, one Sunday).

The main bus services to Pwllheli include Arriva's bus 3 from Porthmadog (40 minutes, half-hourly, six Sunday services) and Clynnog A Trefor's bus 12 from Caernarfon (45 minutes, hourly, three Sunday services).

AROUND PWLLHELI
Oriel Plas Glyn-y-Weddw

This **art gallery** (☎ 740763; Llandbedrog; www.oriel .uk; admission free; ⊗ 11am-5pm Wed-Mon, daily Jul & Aug) is housed in a great Victorian Gothic mansion and set in green wooded grounds. The interior has exposed beams and stained glass, and shows changing exhibitions of Welsh artists that are always worth a look. There's also a nice little café and gift shop set in a conservatory area overlooking the grounds.

The gallery is 4 miles west of Pwllheli off the A497. You can also take bus 18 between Pwllheli and Abersoch (25 minutes, roughly hourly Monday to Saturday, four services Sunday) – ask to be let off at Llandbedrog. Nearby is the NT-owned Llandbedrog beach for a bracing blast of fresh air.

ABERSOCH & AROUND

☎ 01758 / pop 1000

Abersoch comes alive in summer with a 30,000-person influx from the sailing and surfing crowd. Packed in high season, it's a virtual ghost town in winter. Edged by gentle blue-green hills, the town's main attraction is its beaches and waves and today it's the Llŷn's premier water sports centre. Surfers head for the Atlantic swell at **Porth Neigwl (Hell's Mouth)** and Porth Ceiriad, while sailors, windsurfers and boaters prefer the gentle waters of Abersoch Bay.

Orientation & Information

Most of the action is spread out along the main drag, Lon Pen Cei. Buses stop along this street, while **car parking** (per day £3.50) is available at the top end of town close to the strip of B&Bs.

There's a small and independently run **tourist office** (☎ 712929; www.abersochtouristinfo .co.uk; Lon Pen Cei; ⊗ 10.30am-4.30pm daily in summer), which is friendly and helpful; it also offers internet access (£2.50 per 30 minutes). On the main street there's a **Londis convenience store** (⊗ 7.30am-10pm), a **post office** (⊗ 9.30am-12.30pm & 1.30-5.30pm Mon, Tue, Thu & Fri, 9.30am-12.30pm Wed & Sat) and various banks.

Activities

West Coast Surf Shop (☎ 713067; www.westcoastsurf .co.uk; Main St; ⊗ 9am-5pm) offers half-day surf lessons (£27.50, including equipment) year-round; the course is approved by the British Surfing Association (BSA).

Offaxis (☎ 713407; www.offaxis.co.uk; Lon Engan St; ⊗ 9am-5pm Apr-Oct) is another outdoors-cum-surf shop, which specialises in wakeboarding classes (£30 per 15-minute session) and surfing lessons (£30 per half-day), with both prices including equipment. Surfboard and wakeboard rental starts at £10 per day.

Abersoch Sailing School (☎ 712963; www.abersoch sailingschool.co.uk; Main Beach; ⊗ Mar–end Oct) has sailing, power-boating and windsurfing classes with small-group tuition.

Events

The popular **jazz festival** (www.abersochjazzfestival
.com) is held at various venues around town
during the second weekend of June. **Wakestock**
(www.wakestock.co.uk), Europe's largest wakeboard
festival, features competitions and two nights
of DJs and live music, and is held each year
from mid- to the end of July.

Sleeping

Sgubor Unnos, aka The Bunkhouse (☎ 713527; www
.tanrallt.com; dm adult/child £15/7) Located 1 mile from
Abersoch, this no-frills place offers budget
bunkhouse accommodation with two four-
bed and one six-bed dorms, plus a communal
kitchen and laundry. The owners also run **land
hovercraft rides** (per 30min £50; ☯ Apr-Sep).

Tudor Court Hotel (☎ 713354; www.tudorcourt.com;
d £65.50; ☯ Mar-Oct) A two-star midrange hotel,
close to the car park at the top end of town,
the Tudor Court has comfortable rooms with
few frills.

Riverside (www.riversideabersoch.co.uk; s/d £68/110;
☯ Mar-Oct) This place has undergone major
renovations to give it a fresher, smarter look,
although it's rather pricey for what you get.
Family rooms are available.

At the time of writing there were plans to
open a new five-star property just outside
Abersoch, to be run by the owners of Plas
Bodegroes (opposite). Check with the tourist
office for more information.

Eating & Drinking

Abersoch Café (☎ 713433; High St; ☯ 9am-5pm) This
is a cheap and cheerful coffee shop for snacks
and drinks. Next door, **Abersoch Deli** (☎ 713456;
☯ 9am-5pm) is a great little spot for eat-in or
take-away sandwiches.

Fresh Bar & Grill (☎ 710033; www.fresh-abersoch.co
.uk; High St; ☯ from 6pm) The ultimate surfer's
hang-out, this place has beanbags, a TV area
and a regular clientele of surfer dudes. The
food is of high quality, though the service is
rather slow. Think wraps and fries at lunch
(around £4) and more hearty dinners in the
evening. Surf gear is optional.

Angelina (☎ 712353; High St; mains £8-14 ☯ from
6pm) A traditional, well-established Italian place that specialises in fish mains and
pasta, this is Abersoch's smartest option for
dinner.

Vaynol Arms (☎ 712776) For a pint, head for
the Vaynol Arms, which has real ales, simple
bar snacks and wi-fi access.

Shopping

Hideaway Bookstore (☎ 711 0002; 4 High St; ☯ 10am-
5.30pm) A book and craft shop with a nice range
of children's books to offer some blessed relief
from the relentless onslaught of surf shops.

Getting There & Away

Arriva's bus 18 runs to Abersoch from Pwllheli (25 minutes, roughly hourly Monday to
Saturday, four services Sunday).

ABERDARON & AROUND
☎ 01758 / pop 1000

Aberdaron is an ends-of-the-earth kind of
place on the northwestern tip of the Llŷn Peninsula with whitewashed, windswept houses
contemplating Aberdaron Bay. This is where
Welsh poet RS Thomas was the local minister
from 1967 to 1978, and the desolate chapel, **St
Hywyn's Church** (☯ 10am-5pm Apr-Oct, to 4pm Nov-Mar),
set above the pebble beach, seems an appropriate setting for his bleak, furious poetry (see
the boxed text Poet, Priest & Patriot, p43). The
church was restored in 2006 and today has lots
of information about local history.

At the heart of the village, there's a tiny
village shop (☯ 8am-8pm Mon-Sat, from 9am Sun) and
a Spar supermarket with a **post office** (☯ 8am-
9pm). **Car parking** (per 2hr £2) is available on open
ground just before the bridge.

Sights

The little **Gwylan Islands** in the bay are North
Wales' most important puffin-breeding site.
At wind-blasted Braich-y-Pwll, the Llŷn's
westernmost mainland point, the National
Trust has a small information post in an old
coast-guard hut, open most weekends from
Easter to September, and there are amazing
views to Bardsey Island (p272) and from here.
Inland are strip fields that preserve many of
the patterns of ancient land-use.

Just north of Aberdaron at Porthor are the
Whistling Sands, a crescent-shaped beach whose
sand squeals unnervingly when you walk on
it. From here it's a 2-mile coastal walk west via
the twin headlands of Dinas Bach and Dinas
Fawr to the cove of Porth Orion.

On the heights near the hamlet of Rhiw,
5 miles east of Aberdaron, is **Plas-yn-Rhiw**
(☎ 780219; adult/child house & garden £3.40/1.70, garden
only £2.20/1.10; ☯ noon-5pm Thu-Mon Apr–mid-May, Wed-
Mon mid-May–Sep, Sat & Sun only Oct) A 17th-century
Welsh manor house restored by three sisters
in the 1930s and '40s, Plas-yn-Rhiw features

ornamental gardens that are a startling contrast to the surrounding moorland. The property is today managed by the National Trust.

Activities

To follow in the footsteps of the pilgrims, **Edge of Wales Walk** (☎ 760652; www.edgeofwaleswalk.co.uk), a cooperative of local residents, will help to arrange a 47-mile, self-guided walking tour around the peninsula and Bardsey Island, based around a new extension to the Llŷn coastal path that opened in 2005.

Sleeping & Eating

Ty Newydd Hotel (☎ 760207; s/d Oct-Mar £35/55, Apr-Sep £40/65) Right on the beach, this hotel is a friendly place with spacious rooms featuring exposed brickwork; the ones with sea views over the broad sweep of beach and sea are best.

Ship Hotel (☎ 760204; www.theshiphotelaberdaron.co .uk; d/f £68/75) A pub-hotel with a decent in-house restaurant (mains around £8), this place has comfortable rooms, some with sea views.

Y Gegin Fawr (The Big Kitchen; ☼ 9am-6pm) A little thick-walled café with tiny windows, next to Ty Newydd at the centre of the village. It was built around 1300 so the saints could claim a meal before heading over to Bardsey Island as part of their pilgrimage. Today it serves up basic coffees – and it's service very much without a smile. Ask the owners for the latest ferry information.

Getting There & Away

Arriva bus 17 runs to Aberdaron from Pwllheli (40 minutes, every hour or two Monday to Saturday).

BARDSEY ISLAND (YNYS ENLLI)

This mysterious island, 2 miles long and 2 miles off the tip of the Llŷn, is a magical place, its otherworldliness emphasised by its ancient name: the Isle of 20,000 Saints. In the 6th or 7th century the obscure St Cadfan founded a monastery here, giving shelter to Celts fleeing the Saxon invaders. Medieval pilgrims followed in their wake and, at a time when journeys from Britain to Italy were long, perilous and beyond the means of most people, the Pope decreed that three pilgrimages to Bardsey would have the same value as one to Rome. A Celtic cross amidst the Abbey ruins commemorates the 20,000 pilgrims who came here to die – the 20,000 saints that give the island its ancient name.

To add to its mythical status, it is one of many candidates for the Isle of Avalon, where King Arthur is alleged to have been taken after the Battle of Camlann. Other legends say the wizard Merlin is asleep in a glass castle on the island.

The island's Welsh name means 'Isle of the Currents', a reference to the treacherous tidal surges in Bardsey Sound, which doubtless convinced medieval visitors that their lives were indeed in God's hands.

Most modern pilgrims to Bardsey are sea-bird-watchers (the island is home to an important colony of Manx shearwaters), although there are also some 6th-century **carved stones** and the remains of a 13th-century **abbey tower**.

The **Bardsey Island Trust** (☎ 0845 8112233; www .enlli.org; boat trips adult/child £25/15), which looks after the island, organises boat trips from Porth Meudwy, the closest harbour to the island. There are up to three daily departures at 10am, 11am and noon, according to tidal conditions. The boat trip takes 30 minutes, and the fare includes 3½ hours on the island. Book tickets through the **Bardsey Ferry Service** (☎ 128620).

NEFYN

☎ 01758 / pop 800

The north coast of the Llŷn feels supremely remote with a handful of small villages and a few quiet sweeping beaches. The village of Nefyn is a sleepy spot with a tiny post office and a Spar supermarket.

St Beuno was to North Wales what St David was to the south of the country, and there's a tiny church dedicated to him – one of the peninsula's many stopovers for medieval pilgrims – at the hamlet of Pistyll, 2 miles east of Nefyn (another St Beuno church is further up the coast at Clynnog Fawr). A few miles on from Pistyll are the 100m sea cliffs of **Carreg y Llam**, a major North Wales sea-bird site, with huge colonies of razorbills, guillemots and kittiwakes.

Sleeping & Eating

Caeau Capel Hotel (☎ 720240; www.caeaucapelhotel.com; Rhodfa'r Môr; s/d £40/75) Former Prime Minister, Clement Atlee, often used to stay here when it was a family house. Today it's a characterful but slightly faded, old-fashioned place located towards the beach and signposted from the village's main street. Ask about off-season promotional rates.

Nanhoron Arms (☎ 720203; Ffordd Dewi Sant; s/d/d £42/72/85) Large and modern with a rather chain-

---

LOCAL VOICES

The village of Nant Gwrtheyrn as you see it today was formed when companies began excavating granite from the surrounding mountains during the 19th century. In 1861, Port Nant quarry was opened by the Kneeshaw and Lupton company from Liverpool. The granite, which was used for road building, was carried straight from the quarry by ships sailing to Liverpool, Manchester, Birkenhead and some the world over.

In 1878 Nant Gwrtheyrn village was built to house the quarry workers, but the quarries closed after the Second World War and slowly the villagers left, leaving empty buildings behind which soon became derelict.

The first Welsh Language Act was passed in 1967. This meant that Welsh now had to be given a status equal to that of English when it came to providing public services. This resulted in more and more adults learning Welsh as a second language because of the need for bilingual workers in the public sector.

In July 1978, the Nant Gwrtheyrn Trust, set up by the local doctor, Dr Carl Clowes, succeeded in buying the derelict village from Amey Roadstone Company, the then owners, for the sum of £25,000, with the aim of turning it into a residential centre for learning the Welsh language. Because the village had been empty for so long (with a lack of electricity, running water and sewerage), there was a tremendous amount of work to be done to re-build the village.

The years that followed saw individuals and societies the length and breadth of Wales raising hundreds of thousands of pounds to enable the restoration work. Since the first course was held in 1982, thousands have flocked to Nant Gwrtheyrn Welsh Language & Heritage Centre to learn one of Europe's oldest living languages.

Eleri Williams, Marketing Manager, Welsh Language & Heritage Centre

---

hotel feel, the Nanhoron Arms has a good raft of services, including a decent in-house restaurant. The latter is particularly popular for its Sunday carvery (three courses £11.50).

MORFA NEFYN
☎ 01758
Tiny Morfa Nefyn is based around the NT-run **car park** (£3, free to NT members), where there's a small information kiosk giving weather advice. This is the trailhead for walks and access to the nearby golf course. It's a more attractive base than Nefyn, with a wild feel and a couple of good options for sleeping and eating.

For food, try **Cliffs Inn** (☎ 720356; bar meals ⏰ noon-9pm), a decent lunch spot with great panoramic views from the conservatory eating area and generous Sunday roasts. The owners also offer self-catering accommodation (weekly rates from £295 per week according to the number of people) in three studios close to the hotel.

It's hard to believe that the little crescent of sand at **Porth Dinllaen** – now owned in its entirety by the National Trust – was once a busy cargo, shipbuilding and herring port, the only safe haven on the peninsula's north coast. Indeed, it was eyed up by slate magnate William Madocks as a possible home for ferries to Ireland, but in 1839 the House of Commons gave that job to Holyhead. Today, the beach is known for gloriously bracing beach strolls. The most agreeable way to get here is on foot along the beach and via part of the golf course – it's a 1-mile walk west from Morfa Nefyn's car park.

Reward yourself upon arrival with a drink at **Ty Coch Inn** (☎ 720498; ☎ lunch noon-2.30pm), a tremendously photogenic pub with a dramatic beach-side location. The pub has been used as a film set (see p303) and today is popular with walkers and families for its daily specials, such as Bay Crab (£8).

AROUND MORFA NEFYN
☎ 01758
Heading away from Porth Dinllaen, a good place to overnight is **Llys Olwen** (☎ 720493; www.llysolwen.co.uk; s/d £26/52), an impressive former Victorian sea captain's residence. The rooms are large and have big windows that overlook fields and gardens, but none have en suites – they just have washbasins. What makes the place stand out is that the friendly owner prepares all her own bread and yoghurt and serves great home-cooked meals every evening. Dinner is also open to non-residents, with three freshly cooked courses from £19.

For a lunchtime bar meal, try **Y Bryncynan** (☎ 720879; bar meals ☷ noon-9pm), a great place with a traditional but not overdone feel, real ales and huge portions of tasty bar meals, including vegetarian and children's options.

From Morfa Nefyn, the B4417 leads onto the village of **Llithfaen** (it's signposted Welsh Language & Heritage Centre), the access point to the former 'ghost village' of Nant Gwrtheyrn.

Nant Gwrtheyrn was brought back from the dead when it was bought and restored as the home of the **Welsh Language & Heritage Centre** (☎ 750334; www.nantgwrtheyrn.org; heritage centre ☷ 11am-4pm daily Jun-Aug, Mon-Fri Sep-May). The centre is reached from the village of Llithfaen by following a path down a steep valley. According to tradition it is here that the semi-mythical Celtic King Vortigern is buried. You

can also drive down – but take it very slowly and be extremely careful.

The heritage centre has a small but very compelling exhibition on the history of the Welsh language, while the centre offers a range of residential courses (prices from £245 for three days full-board) to study Welsh language and literature, including B&B accommodation at homely little grey-stone cottages on the site. During August, it offers half-day taster courses (adult/child/family £4/2/10) to get a basic grasp of a few key phrases. Even if you don't take a course, it's a magical place – eerily quiet but tranquil and ideal for a walk along the cliffs with an end-of-the-world feel.

Caffi Meinir (☎ 750442; ☷ 10.30am-4.30pm) has light meals and coffees served daily during summer and during courses at other times.

Anglesey & the North Coast

The far north of Wales may not be the region most synonymous with tourism but it actually boasts some of the best hidden gems. Walking enthusiasts are particularly well catered for, with the scenic Isle of Anglesey Coastal Path an appealing new option, while fans of adventure sports can indulge in the burgeoning sports scene around Llandudno's West Shore and Llangollen.

Joined to the mainland by two monumental bridges, Anglesey is very different physically from the biblical splendour of neighbouring Snowdonia. This is where Britain's Celts made their last stand against the Romans, and the island is nicknamed Mother of Wales. The island offers a scenic surprise of gentle green slopes, ringed by dramatic sea cliffs and bays, and small windswept settlements. It has a greater concentration of prehistoric sites than anywhere else in Wales. All too many people zip through on the thundering Bangor–Holyhead road for ferries to Ireland, but get off this well-beaten track and you'll be rewarded with some of the quietest, most remote and timeless places in the country.

The North Coast, meanwhile, is home to some prime examples of Welsh heritage. The splendid castle at Conwy has been listed by Unesco as a World Heritage Site, while Bangor is an impressive centre of learning and numerous historic properties are scattered throughout the region. It's the contemporary culture, however, that has been making all the running in recent times. The Victorian resort town of Llandudno, overshadowed by the Great Orme, is shifting demographics to attract a younger, thrill-seeking crowd, while the friendly little town of Llangollen now hosts a major Fringe Festival each summer – a small-scale but highly rewarding answer to Edinburgh's annual culture fest.

For more information about Anglesey, check www.islandofchoice.com; for more information about the North Wales borderlands, check the website www.borderlands.co.uk.

HIGHLIGHTS

- Explore **Beaumaris** (p278), a charming Georgian town that has reinvented itself as the style and dining hub of Anglesey

- Tackle a leg of the new Isle of **Anglesey Coastal Path** (p280), which starts in Holyhead, and explore the hidden coves and sandy beaches en route

- Get active at **Llandudno** (p292), a former genteel resort reborn as a location for adventure sports

- Take a canal boat ride across the spectacular **Pontcysyllte Aqueduct** (p299), near Llangollen, then head into town for the Fringe Festival

- Stretch your legs with a walk through the **Clwydian Ranges** (p302) and scale the summit of Moel Famau for a view across North Wales

ACTIVITIES

Diversity is the word to describe the choices in this part of Wales. Coastal watersports are available at Holyhead (p290) with boating also possible around Conwy (p290) and Beaumaris (p279). Inland, Llangollen has become a white-water centre (p300) and also offers kayaking and quad biking trips. You can walk and yet still avoid the crowds by heading off into the Clwydian Ranges (p302), and the new circular coastal path around Anglesey (p280) links delightful little villages from its starting point at Holyhead. There's also climbing near Holyhead and cycling is popular; try the Lôn Las Cymru Route (p60). There are nine golf courses on the island and four biking trails, plus course and game fishing.

The king of the walking trails, however, is the Offa's Dyke National Trail, which begins amid the faded seaside glamour of tiny Prestatyn's Central Beach. The **Offa's Dyke Path & Tourist Office** (☎ 01745-889092; Central Beach; ☻ 9am-5.30pm Apr-Sep) is located here, and has everything you ever need to know about the path all the way to Chepstow (p116) in the south.

GETTING THERE & AROUND

The **North Wales Coast Line** (www.nwrail.org.uk) from Chester (England) to Holyhead provides easy access to the coastal towns, including Llandudno and Conwy, and via Bangor across Anglesey to the Irish ferries hub at Holyhead. The **Conwy Valley Line** (www.conwyvalleyrailway.co.uk) between Llandudno and Blaenau Ffestiniog via Betws-y-Coed allows rail access through the heart of the Snowdonia National Park.

The bulk of bus services in the region are run by **Arriva Wales** (www.arrivabus.co.uk); other useful operators include GHA, Arriva Cymru and Bryn Melyn.

For details of travel passes, see p326.

THE ISLE OF ANGLESEY (YNYS MÔN)

A parcel of green, gently rolling land that's cut off not only by the sea but also by the mountains of Snowdonia, it's not surprising that Anglesey has a singular character. This was the Celts' last refuge in Britain against the Roman advance, so it's got a fair claim to

---

THE DRUIDS

Mysterious and magical, the druidic mystique is assisted by a lack of evidence – they wrote nothing down about their beliefs. It is known that they had charge of Celtic religion and ritual, and were educators and healers as well as political advisors, so were vastly influential. However, the main sources of information about this spiritual aristocracy are Roman scholars, whose accounts are seen through an adversarial glass. The Romans are coloured as a civilising force, and the Celts and druids as bloodthirsty and keen on human sacrifice.

Around 400 druidic gods are known, mainly pertaining to localised cults. Ceremonies were very important, and druids had to undergo 20 years of training. Like Hindus, they believed in reincarnation; Julius Caesar, whose writings on his wars in Gaul in 59–51 BC are one of the main sources on the druids, thought that this accounted for the Celts' bravery in war.

Resistance to the Romans was powered by druidic influence in Britain – hence the Roman antagonism. Anglesey was a major seat of druidic learning because of its strategic placement between Wales, Ireland and France, and was the last place to fall to the Romans. According to the Roman historian Tacitus, when the Romans attacked Anglesey in AD 61, they were terrified by the resident wild women and holy fanatics who greeted them with howls and prayers, and found the altars there covered in the blood of prisoners. The conquerors did all they could to impress their culture on the locals, but the result was inevitably a mix of new and old beliefs.

Druidism became a fashionable interest in the 18th century, and the Welsh poetic tradition is believed to stem from the druids. In 1820 Edward Williams created druidic ceremonies to be performed during the annual Eisteddfod, which accounts for many of the long beards and solemn ceremonies still in evidence at this festival of poetry and literature today.

Their influence did not only permeate poetry and politics: it's said that the tradition of kissing under the mistletoe at Christmas comes from druidic beliefs, as mistletoe was an herb used during childbirth and symbolised fertility.

being the Welsh heartland. Gerald of Wales quoted the ancient name for the island 'Môn mam Cymru' (Mother of Wales) at the end of the 12th century. Its geography has also given it links with other nations across the Irish Sea.

Inhabited for at least 10,000 years, there is an intense concentration of Neolithic burial sites here. The finest is the burial mound Bryn Celli Ddu (p282), but the one in the most dramatic and evocative setting, above crashing waves on a deserted headland, is Barclodiad y Gawres (p282).

The Celts are thought to have arrived on the island around 500 BC. Their artistic and metalworking skills have been confirmed by a famously rich cache of iron tools, slave-chains, jewellery and other objects (now in Cardiff's National Museum Wales, p86) found at the bottom of Llyn Cerrig Bach in west Anglesey. The Romans finally conquered the island around AD 60.

Anglesey, at 276 sq miles, is the largest island in Wales and England. It has for centuries been North Wales' breadbasket, and still produces more than its share of cereal crops

and beef. In addition to farming, its inhabitants have relied on smuggling, copper and coal mining and quarrying, as well as fishing, for their income.

The island was only linked to the mainland in 1826, when Thomas Telford built the handsome Menai Bridge, the first ever heavy-duty iron suspension bridge. A mile away is the Britannia Bridge, designed by Robert Stephenson (whose father, George Stephenson, developed the steam-powered *Rocket,* the first passenger locomotive) and opened in 1850. This now bears most of the traffic, including the train line between Bangor and Holyhead. Bangor (p285) is the transport hub for the easiest access to the island.

This is the flattest part of Wales, rising to just 219m at Holyhead Mountain, but the coast offers rugged cliffs, some excellent beaches, and coastal water sports at Beaumaris and Holyhead. Beaumaris (p278) is the best base on the island with the greatest array of sleeping and eating options. The only official tourist office on the island is located at 'Llanfair PG' (p281), the town with the inordinately long name but little else.

ANGLESEY & THE NORTH COAST

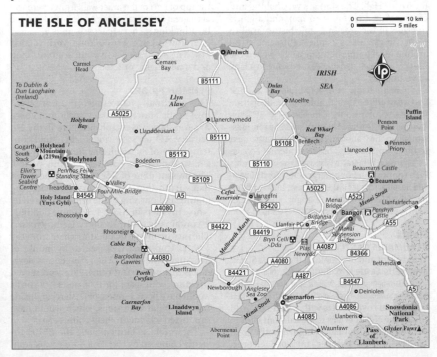

THE ISLE OF ANGLESEY

BEAUMARIS (BIWMARES)

☎ 01248 / pop 2000

Beaumaris has always been the island's principal town and chief port. Today it is a picturesque collection of grandiose, flaking pastel Georgian buildings, with a wonderful waterfront location, looking across to Snowdonia. Busy by day but quiet by night, it has a buoyant feel and lots of infrastructure for tourists, plus a slew of upmarket new openings, including galleries and boutiques. From Beaumaris, it's just 7 miles to Bangor and a 30-minute drive to Holyhead. Traditionally, the superb, fairytale castle, which James of St George built here for Edward I, has been the main draw, but as Beaumaris reinvents itself for a new generation of tourism, it has blossomed as a centre for sailing, walking and water sports.

Orientation & Information

Castle St is the main thoroughfare with most services strung out along the street; buses from Bangor also drop passengers here.

There's no official tourist office but there is an **information kiosk** (☎ 810040; Castle St; 10.30am-4.45pm Mon-Thu Apr-Sep) run by the volunteers in the Town Hall. The staff are very helpful and can provide a useful town map and a guide to walks in the area (a 2-mile history trail to Nant Meigan and a 2-mile sightseeing stroll around local points of interest). However, the kiosk is often closed at weekends due to a lack of volunteers.

There are banks with ATMs along Castle St and a **post office** (Church St), although both operate rather irregular hours. The **library** (☎ 810659; 4-7pm Mon, 10am-1pm Tue & Thu, 10am-1pm & 2-5pm Fri, 10am-noon Sat), in the Canolfan community centre next to the council offices, has free internet access.

There's a **laundrette** (Margaret St) beside Sarah's Deli (opposite). For emergencies, **Ysbyty Gwynedd Hospital** (☎ 384424) is nearest, located back over the Menai Bridge in Bangor, and you can contact **North Wales Police** (☎ 0845 6071002).

Sights

BEAUMARIS CASTLE

Windswept and overlooking the Menai Strait, **Beaumaris Castle** (☎ 810361; adult/child £3.50/3; ⏰ 9.30am-6pm Jun-Sep, 9.30am-5pm Apr, May & Oct, 9.30am-4pm Mon-Sat, 11am-4pm Sun Nov-Mar) is the last of the great royal castles with which Edward I ringed the North Wales seaboard from Flint to Aberystwyth. Originally designed by the great military architect, Master James of St George,

with work running continuously between 1295 and 1330 on the level marshy ground from which it gets its name ('Beau Mareys' means beautiful marsh), the castle is a great unfinished masterpiece of military architecture. The reason? The money ran out before the fortifications reached their full height.

Nevertheless, Beaumaris is the most technically perfect castle in Great Britain – the symmetry of its concentric 'walls within walls' is more perfect than any of the earlier strongholds. The plans included four successive lines of fortifications and no less than 14 major obstacles to any potential attacker.

Today it is a World Heritage–listed site and managed by Cadw (the Welsh historic monuments agency). The effect may seem more picturesque than menacing, but the massive gates with their murder holes (which were used to pour boiling oil on invaders), belie this. It's particularly intriguing to explore the wall passages that link the towers, leading to watching and domestic chambers, latrines (not in use) and to the secluded semi-octagonal chapel royal, where you can still just see traces of its former bright decoration. There is a great walk along the top of part of the inner wall, from where you get a great view both of the castle layout and the breathtaking scenery that surrounds it.

Following recent restoration work, there is now a new entrance with a little souvenir shop and a new ticket office.

PENMON PRIORY

This spiritual, picturesque group of buildings nestle above a striking section of coast. A monastery was established here in the 6th century AD by St Seiriol, a friend and contemporary of St Scybi. The nearby holy well is also thought to date back to this period. The present stone of **St Seiriols Church**, however, dates from the 10th century following the looting and burning of the original church by Norse invaders in AD 971. A simple building, it contains two 11th-century Celtic crosses. The nearby monastic buildings date from the 13th century, and were settled by monks of the Augustine order. The 17th-century **dovecote** is the most extraordinary well-preserved structure, with space for 1000 nests – the birds would have been a source of fresh meat. Inside is a 12ft pillar with steps, which would have supported a ladder to help collect eggs.

The priory is located along the B5109 towards Llangoed by car; it's a 4-mile walk from

Beaumaris, heading northeast along the Isle of Anglesey Coastal Path (see the boxed text Walking the Isle of Anglesey Coastal Path, p280).

OTHER SIGHTS

The sensation and pathos of some of the trials that took place at **Beaumaris Courthouse** (☎ 811691; www.angleseyheritage.co.uk; adult/child £2/1.50; 10.30am-5pm Apr-Sep) over 300 years adds to the atmosphere of this small, plain building (1614), where you can retrace the prisoner's journey to the dock. For example, a sentence was handed down here on Hugh Hughes to be whipped through the streets of four towns on the island for stealing food. Hammer-beam roof, benches and fittings of the perfidiously picturesque courtroom are all the original ones. The spiky railings that divide the court from the public were added in the early 19th century, as was the octagonal grand jury room.

Appropriately, the same ticket will get you into the **gaol** (☎ 810921; 10.30am-5pm Apr-Sep). Built in 1829 by Joseph Hansom (of the cab fame), this is a massive, grey, forbidding witness to Victorian law and order. Its tread wheel (designed for hard-labour prisoners) is the only one in Britain still in place. A nursery above the women's workroom has a slit in the floor through which mothers could, by pulling a rope, rock their babies' cradles without stopping work. Cells are as tiny, and the punishment cell is a windowless, pitch-dark hell hole. In contrast, the condemned cell has a fireplace – a rare (and last-minute) sign of comfort. Executions were huge local attractions (that even had souvenirs), but happily there were only ever two.

The **Museum of Childhood Memories** (☎ 712498; 1 Castle St; adult/child £4/2.25; 10.30am-4.45pm Mon-Sat, noon-4.15pm Sun Apr-Oct), opposite the castle, is one for nostalgia fans. It's an entertaining exercise in celebrating a bygone age with doll houses, clockwork toys, teddy bears, a rocking horse and Disney characters among the exhibits. There's a little souvenir shop next door.

Activities

BOAT TRIPS

Rising out of the sea off the east coast, **Puffin Island** is inhabited by a few puffins and plenty of seals. Operators run summer cruises from Beaumaris pier out here or along the Menai Strait. **Starida Sea Services** (☎ 810251; www.starida.co .uk) runs trips from a kiosk at the entrance to the pier with one-hour Puffin Island or Menai

Strait cruises (adult/child £5/4) on 60-seater boats, or sea-fishing trips (from adult/child £15/10 for two hours), including equipment.

Sleeping

Mountfield (☎ 810380; s/d from £40/60) This handsome 1930s villa is 230m northeast of the Courthouse and opposite the bowling green. All rooms have en suites and good views of the Menai Strait and castle.

Bishopsgate House & Restaurant (☎ 810302; www .bishopsgatehousehotel.co.uk; 54 Castle St; s/d £55/80) Set in a fine Georgian building, the three-star Bishopsgate is elegantly decorated. While rooms are fairly standard, the in-house restaurant serves up a hearty dinner (three courses £16.95) and Sunday roasts (12.30pm to 2.30pm).

Cleifiog B&B (☎ 811507; www.cleifiogbandb.co.uk; Townsend; s/d from £45/65) This new addition to the town's accommodation scene is a little gem: a charismatic townhouse that oozes with character and boasts superb views of the Menai Straits. A former monk's hospice, it's just 275m southeast of Castle St. There are only three rooms but they're all stylishly designed, while the breakfast has healthy options and draws on the best local produce. Great stuff.

Ye Olde Bulls Head Inn (☎ 810329; www.bullsheadinn .co.uk; Castle St; s/4 poster/ste £98.50/112/116) Dating back to 1472, when it was the borough posting-house, Ye Olde Bulls Head once hosted Charles Dickens, and today the bedrooms are all named after his characters. Samuel Johnson was another literary great who kipped here. By far the most stylish and smart option in town, the inn's rooms are modern but tastefully decorated with lots of dark-wood furniture and rustic, autumnal hues. There is an excellent fine-dining restaurant, the **Loft** (7-10pm Mon-Sat; 3-course dinner £35), and the more informal **Brasserie** (noon-2pm & 6-9pm), which is a little kinder on the wallet. Even if you don't stay the night, stop off for a pint of the guest ale in the cosy house bar, set around a roaring log fire.

Eating & Drinking

Sarah's Deli (☎ 811534; 11 Church St; 9am-5.30pm Mon-Sat Apr-Oct, to 5pm Nov-Mar) This excellent local deli has a huge range of local and international produce, including house specialities of homemade quiche, mezze and tapas. There are great hot paninis to take away, plus hampers if you're splashing out.

Neptune Café Bar (☎ 812990; Castle St; mains around £10; restaurant noon-2pm & 6-9.30pm) Don't be put off by the initial chip-shop look: while downstairs is a take-away chippie, upstairs is a smart restaurant specialising in fish mains such as mussels with fennel and garlic.

Pier House Café (☎ 810321; The Front; specials around £10; ☖ 9.30am-4pm Mon-Fri, to 5pm Sat & Sun, to 8.30pm daily Jul & Aug) A bright and breezy café right on the seafront with plenty of alfresco tables to soak up the view, this licensed eatery specialises in fresh fish dishes. There are also big breakfasts and imaginative specials (around £10), such as prawn and chorizo salad. It's a good spot for a sundowner.

Courtyard (☎ 810565; www.courtyardcuisine.com; Regent House, Church St; mains £14.50-21; ☖ 11.30am-3pm & 6-9pm; ☖) Another new, upscale opening,

WALKING THE ISLE OF ANGLESEY COASTAL PATH

In 2006, the inauguration of a major new walking route, the Isle of Anglesey Coastal Path (www.angleseycoastalpath.co.uk), confirmed the island's status as one of the greatest walking destinations in Wales. The new 125-mile coastal walking path, backed by a £1.4m investment from the EU and The Welsh Development Agency, falls within a designated Area of Outstanding Natural Beauty that covers 95% of the coast. The full trail, a 12-day walk appealing to all ability ranges and reaching a maximum altitude of just 219m, passes through a changing landscape of farmland, coastal heath, salt-marsh, cliffs, beaches and even a National Nature Reserve. There are 20 towns and villages along the route of the path.

The trail has its official start/end point at St Cybi's Church (p283) in Holyhead, but the 12 stages can be tackled as individual day hikes, ranging from seven to 13 miles per day. The path is marked with distinctive yellow signs, featuring the Arctic turn, and aims to attract up to 300,000 walkers per year. Some of the stages, particularly the far northern trails from Cemeas Bay to Church Bay, make for bracing strolls against a dramatic backdrop of wild, wind-swept scenery.

Setting out on an introductory walk from Beaumaris, it's an easy 4-mile stroll to Penmon Priory, which is still a working church (p278). From here a path leads north to Penmon Point with great views across to Puffin Island. There's a £2 fee if you arrive by car and a small café with toilets – the only official toilet stop on this leg of the coastal path.

From Penmon, the trail heads towards Llanddona, a 5.5-mile stretch, more inland and comprised of country lanes, which passes Bwrdd Arthur (Arthur's Table), a pre-Roman fortress from around 3000 BC. This is the highest point on the eastern side of the island with spectacular views across to Snowdonia. Llanddona is a Blue Flag beach for bathing (a maritime or freshwater recreational beach that has met stringent quality standards during the whole of the previous bathing season). It is better known, however, for the local folk tale, which tells of the flame-haired Llanddona witches who were washed ashore in the 16th century and settled here.

The last stretch of the day is a tiring 2-mile yomp along the shoreline, but with a major incentive: a celebratory beer at the **Ship Inn, Red Wharf Bay** (☎ 852568; bar meals ☖ noon-2pm & 6-9pm). The best place to overnight is nearby Benllech, where **Hafod** (☎ 853092; Almwch Rd; s/d £40/60) is a traditional B&B in an old Edwardian house. For dinner that night, try the **Seaview Restaurant** (☎ 853406; 3-course dinner £11.95), or the **Water's Edge Restaurant** (☎ 852005; 3-course dinner £15.50).

Further along Moelfre is one of the prettiest harbour villages on the east coast, but has witnessed some spectacular wrecks on its shore with the *Royal Charter* sinking off the coast in 1859 and losing 495 lives. Today it is home to the **Seawatch Centre** (☎ 410277; admission free; ☖ 11am-5pm Tue-Sat, 1-5pm Sun Apr-Sep), a testament to the importance of the sea to the people of Anglesey. Overlooking the sea is a statue to local coxwain Richard Evans, who won the first Royal National Lifeboat Institute (RNLI) gold medal in 1959 for a rescue in winds of up to 104mph. He won a second gold medal in 1966 for a daring rescue in winds of 127mph and was named 'Man of the Year' in 1967.

Walkers should equip themselves with a copy of the *OS Explorer Maps 262 (west coast)* and *263 (east coast)* before setting out. In the event of an emergency, contact the **North Wales Police** (☎ 0845 607 1002).

To book a full package, including self-guided walks, accommodation and transport between trailheads, contact **Anglesey Walking Holidays** (☎ 713611; www.angleseywalkingholidays.com), which can arrange trips from £50 per person per day, according to the standard of B&B you choose to book.

this sleek and stylish restaurant has modern European fare in a very contemporary setting. Main dishes include fish and meat specials, plus there are special menus for both vegetarians and children.

For self-caterers, there's a **Spar supermarket** (Castle St; 🕑 7am-11pm) and the **Castle Bakery** (🕑 9am-5pm) for pastries on the go.

Getting There & Around
Arriva buses 53, 57 and 58 run regular services from Bangor (30 minutes, half-hourly Monday to Saturday).

You can hire bikes at the **Iorwerth Rowlands Centre** (☎ 811508; full/half-day £16/9; 🕑 9am-5pm Mon-Thu, to 4pm Fri).

LLANFAIRPWLLGWYNGYLLGOGERYCH-WYRNDROBWLLLLANTYSILIOGOGOGOCH
☎ 01248 / pop 2500
Coach parties are drawn like moths to a light to this nondescript little village on the A5 simply because it has a very long and very famous name, which means 'St Mary's Church in the Hollow of the White Hazel near a Rapid Whirlpool and the Church of St Tysilio near the Red Cave'. It was dreamt up in the 19th century to get the tourists in. And it worked.

The previous name, Llanfairpwllgwyngyll, would have been hard enough. Locals call it 'Llanfairpwll' and most tourist and transport officials call it 'Llanfair PG'. You should too. The village was the site of Anglesey's first train station (built 1848) and still remains a request stop on the Bangor–Holyhead mainline – you can even buy a large platform ticket as a souvenir.

Llanfair PG is not a place to overnight. The first ever Women's Institute in the whole of the UK and Channel Islands opened here in 1915; little has happened since.

Orientation & Information
The village is a one-horse town strung out along Holyhead Rd. The local **tourist office** (☎ 713177; www.anglesey.gov.uk; 🕑 9.30am-5.30pm Mon-Sat, 10am-5pm Sun Apr-Oct, to 5pm daily Nov-Mar), the only official one on the island, is an excellent source of information on Anglesey. It is located across the car park from the train station, in one corner of a gift-shop complex that has a service-station vibe.

There is a **post office** (🕑 9am-12.30pm & 1.30-5.30pm Mon, Tue, Thu & Fri, to 12.30pm Wed & Sat) on Holyhead Rd, and a Somerfield supermarket at the western end of town.

Sights
Arriving on the island via the Britannia Bridge, the road passes the 1817 **Marquess of Anglesey's Tower** (ticket office ☎ 714393; adult/child £1.50/75p; 🕑 9am-5pm). This commemorates Wellington's right-hand man at the 1815 Battle of Waterloo, Henry William Paget of Plas Newydd, who lost a leg at the end of the battle. You can climb the 115 steps up to the base to enjoy great views across the island.

The old station building has now been converted to the **Oriel Tŷ Gorsaf** (☎ 717876; Station Rd; 🕑 9am-5pm Mon-Sat), an art gallery showcasing Welsh and international glass artists. The shop also has a big range of art books and magazines.

Sleeping & Eating
Penrhos Arms (☎ 714892; Holyhead Rd; bar meals around £9; 🕑 noon-2pm & 6-9pm) is a simple place located opposite the tourist office.

Getting There & Away
Numerous bus routes from Bangor stop by here, including Arriva buses 4, 9, 42, 43, 44 and 47 (20 minutes).

Mainline trains from Holyhead (£4.90, 40 minutes) and Bangor (£1.80, eight minutes) stop here every two hours. Note: Llanfair PG is a request stop.

SOUTHERN ANGLESEY
☎ 01248
Plas Newydd
Looking out over steeply falling lawns to the Menai Strait and way across Snowdonia, **Plas Newydd** (☎ 71495; adult/child £6/3, garden only £4/2; 🕑 noon-5pm, garden 11am-5.30pm Sat-Wed Apr-Oct) is a National Trust (NT)–run, 18th-century Gothic masterpiece. The home of the first Marquess of Anglesey, who commanded the cavalry during the 1815 battle of Waterloo, it was built by the architect James Wyatt. The music room and the grand-hall staircase are splendid, but most stunning of all are Rex Whistler's great *trompe l'oeil* dreamscape murals in the former dining room – a busy fantasy version of the views from the house, painted with towns, castles and boats from all over Europe and all ages. Close to one of the fireplaces there is even a portrait of the artist himself, sweeping up leaves.

ANGLESEY & THE NORTH COAST

For a ghoulish frisson, the section devoted to the Military Museum has an array of relics, including the wooden leg of the first marquess (one of the first articulated limbs ever made) and the blood-spattered, shot-ridden trousers from Waterloo in which he lost the original leg.

Bryn Celli Ddu

This atmospheric burial chamber, in which archaeologists found the remains of Stone Age people, forms one of Anglesey's most important Neolithic monuments. At the centre is a stone chamber roofed by two huge capstones, which was originally covered by a mound of earth. Take a torch and note the spiral design carved into one wall of the inner chamber (this is a reproduction; the original is in Cardiff's National Museum Wales, p86).

You can reach the site by tramping through fields from a car park located on the A4080, just west of Plas Newydd and 2 miles west of Llanfair PG.

Anglesey Sea Zoo

The zoo (☎ 430411; www.angleseyseazoo.co.uk; Brynsiencyn; adult/child £6/5; ☾ 10am-6pm Apr-Oct, 11am-4pm mid-Feb–Mar) has shallow pools imaginatively displaying local marine life. There's a lobster hatchery and sea horse–conservation project as well as common sharks, a re-created wreck and a crashing wave exhibit.

The zoo is 7 miles southwest of Llanfair PG on the A4080. Bus 42 from Bangor runs to the entrance (25 minutes), but with a limited service.

Barclodiad y Gawres

This Neolithic site has an incredible setting. It's on top of a rocky sea cliff, overlooking crashing surf, near a small sandy bay. The burial chamber has a long entrance flanked by upright stones, a cross-shaped inner chamber and several side-chambers. This site (whose name translates as 'The Giantess' Apronful') includes some remarkable upright stones bearing spiral and zigzag designs; it seems the chamber was used for ceremonial functions rather than burial ones. The actual mound seen today is a reconstruction of the original.

The site is just off the A4080, about 1 mile south of the village of Llanfaelog. Stop in at Wayside Stores (Llanfaelog) for the key (£5 deposit) and bring a torch.

Porth Cwyfan

From Aberffraw village on the A4080, a lane runs for 1.5 miles down to this dramatic location, a small, wind-blasted cove. On a small, walled island is the so-called 'Church in the Sea', the **Church of St Cwyfan**, which dates back to the 12th century. There's a disused military camp on the far shore.

In a converted farm building in Aberffraw itself there's a little **Coastal Heritage Centre** run by the North Wales Wildlife Trust, with exhibits on local flora, fauna and marine ecology, and a small café.

HOLYHEAD (CAERGYBI)
☎ 01407 / pop 13,000

In its day Holyhead was the terminus of the London to Holyhead road (today the A5), which was created by the Act of Union in 1801 and completed in 1826 by Thomas Telford to enable the mail coaches to make the 286-mile journey in good condition. Today the ferry port of Holyhead has seen better days: a grey and listless little town, its sole function is as a hub for ferry traffic to Ireland – more than 2.5 million passengers per year pass through here. There have been numerous initiatives to clean up the town centre – many without much success. However, the latest project, the redevelopment of the marina area around the sailing club, hopes to capture some of the seafaring charm of the waterfront when completed in 2007.

To see a more attractive side of Holyhead, strike out to explore the surrounding area, which features a beautiful, rocky coastline with huge colonies of sea birds, an observation centre run by the Royal Society for the Protection of Birds (RSPB), a two-century-old lighthouse and the foundations of Stone Age dwellings.

The port and surrounding area are actually separated from the west coast of Anglesey proper by sandbanks and a narrow channel on **Holy Island** (Ynys Gybi), a 7-mile stretch of land. It's 'Holy' because this was the territory of St Cybi, a well-travelled monk thought to have lived in the 6th century. Arriving in North Wales fresh from a pilgrimage to Jerusalem, he was granted land for a monastic settlement by King Maelgwyn of Gwynedd. Indeed, Holyhead's Welsh name Caergybi means 'Cybi's Fort'.

Orientation & Information

The A55 and the North Coast railway line both reach a terminus at the Holyhead train station, located at the southern tip of the Inner Harbour.

There are two ferry terminals on the inner harbour: **Terminal 1** is connected to the train station for all foot passengers, and some buses stop here too; **Terminal 2** is the hub for car passengers. North of the inner harbour on the Salt Island peninsula (via a dedicated bridge and roadway), **Terminal 3** is reserved for Irish Ferries. A free shuttle-bus service runs all day for foot passengers between Terminals 1 and 3. A new footbridge, The Celtic Gateway, is due to open in 2007, linking Terminal 1 with the pedestrian area along Market St.

The town's **tourist office** (☎ 762622; ☼ 8.30am-6pm) is in Terminal 1. Boston St is home to the major banks and the **post office** (☼ 9am-5.30pm Mon-Fri, 9am-12.30pm Sat), which offers a bureau de change service.

You can access the internet for free at the **library** (☎ 762917; Newry St; ☼ 10am-5pm Mon, to 7pm Tue & Thu-Fri, 9.30am-12.30pm Sat); the internet room closes noon to 1pm. The **Internet Café** (Victoria Tce; per hr £2; ☼ 9am-5pm Mon-Sat, 11am-4pm Sun) offers basic snacks and lunches, but the main draw is a bank of computers for fast internet access.

There's a basic **laundrette** (☎ 765391; ☼ 9am-5pm Mon-Sat) off Thomas St in the **short-stay car park** (per hr 40p). Buses stop on Victoria Rd and at the Summer Hill Bus Terminal.

Sights

Overlooking the ferry port from Holyhead Mountain are the recognisable remains of a 4th-century **Roman fort**, from which the town got its Welsh name. It was built as a defence against the Saxons and is one of only a handful remaining in the British Isles. Three of its corner towers are still more or less standing, while the fourth is a restoration.

A Celtic monastic settlement from the 6th century, Holyhead is also the site of the **Church of St Cybi**, begun in the 13th century, and of the ancient chapel of **Eglwys-y-Bedd**, which legend says was built over St Cybi's grave.

The refurbished **Holyhead Maritime Museum** (☎ 769745; Newry Beach; adult/child £2.50/1; ☼ 10am-5pm), located in what is believed to be the oldest lifeboat house in Wales (c 1858), has model ships, photographs and exhibits on Holyhead's maritime history from Roman

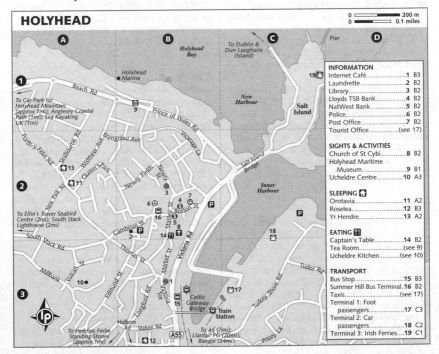

HOLYHEAD

| 0 | 200 m |
| 0 | 0.1 miles |

INFORMATION	
Internet Café............................1	B3
Laundrette................................2	B2
Library......................................3	B2
Lloyds TSB Bank.......................4	B2
NatWest Bank...........................5	B2
Police.......................................6	B2
Post Office................................7	B2
Tourist Office....................(see 17)	

SIGHTS & ACTIVITIES	
Church of St Cybi.....................8	B2
Holyhead Maritime	
Museum...............................9	B1
Ucheldre Centre.....................10	A3

SLEEPING	
Orotavia.................................11	A2
Roselea..................................12	B3
Yr Hendre...............................13	A2

EATING	
Captain's Table........................14	B2
Tea Room........................(see 9)	
Ucheldre Kitchen..............(see 10)	

TRANSPORT	
Bus Stop.................................15	B3
Summer Hill Bus Terminal..16	B2
Taxis..............................(see 17)	
Terminal 1: Foot	
passengers..........................17	C3
Terminal 2: Car	
passengers..........................18	C2
Terminal 3: Irish Ferries.........19	C1

times onwards. The new café/bistro (right) is an excellent place to eat.

Ucheldre Centre (☎ 763361; www.ucheldre.org; Millbank; admission free; ☼ 10am-5pm Mon-Sat, 2-5pm Sun; **P** ⃠) is the town's most compelling attraction – a marvellous arts centre housed in a former convent chapel, with films, live music, drama and dance, plus exhibitions and a good licensed restaurant (right). It's a great family-friendly venue with something for all ages.

West of town is **Holyhead Mountain** (219m), the highest point on Anglesey. At its summit are a prehistoric hill-fort called **Caer-y-Twr** and the remains of a 19th-century semaphore station. On a clear day you can see Ireland and the Isle of Man. From a car park at the end of Beach Rd a footpath winds round the mountain; the best access to the site is on the western side. The former Breakwater quarry was converted in 1990 and now forms the mountain's **Breakwater Country Park** (☎ 752428), an ideal picnic spot and vantage point for wildlife spotters.

Further west, you feel as if you've reached the end of the world, with a cliff overlooking crashing waves and the lone **South Stack Lighthouse** (☎ 763207; www.trinityhouse.co.uk; tours ☼ 10.30am-5.30pm Apr-Sep). Located down 400 steep steps and across a narrow bridge over a deep-water channel, the lighthouse was built for £12,000 and the station's oil lamps were first lit in February 1809. It was withdrawn from service in 1984 and is today managed from the Trinity House Operations Centre in Harwich.

Just off the road above the lighthouse, the RSPB-run **Ellin's Tower Seabird Centre** (☎ 764973; Plas Nico; ☼ 11am-5pm Apr-Sep) is the ideal place to look down at the island's choughs, fulmars, kittiwakes, guillemots, razorbills, gulls and, from about mid-April to July, puffins. Follow South Stack Rd for about 2 miles to a car park – it is located at the road's end, where there is also a café.

Activities

The tourist office has a series of brochures with details of walks to sites of historical and archaeological interest in the area. These should be used in conjunction with *OS Explorer maps 262* and *263*. Holyhead is also the starting point for the 311-mile **Lôn Las Cymru** (p60), the Welsh National Cycle Route through the heart of Wales.

Sea Kayaking UK (☎ 765550; Newry Beach Rd; www.seakayakinguk.com) is a kayak manufacturer in Holyhead, which offers weekend residential sea-kayaking courses for £155 (including full-board accommodation).

Sleeping

There have been some reports about unscrupulous B&B owners in Holyhead taking advantage of travellers stranded by late or missed ferries. Don't just knock on the first door you find.

Orotavia (☎ 760259; www.orotavia.co.uk; 66 Walthew Ave, s/d with shared bathroom £20/45) This bright, simple place is a good option for travellers on more of a budget. The rooms share a bathroom but do have washbasins and a few nice, homely touches, such as tea-making facilities. The friendly owners will arrange to pick up ferry passengers.

Roselea (☎ 764391; www.roseleaguesthouse.co.uk; 26 Holborn Rd; s/d with shared bathroom £25/40; ⃠) A very simple place with just two rooms, neither of them with en suites. It's very handy for the ferry terminal and train station (a three-minute walk over the bridge) and does a decent cooked breakfast to start the day.

Yr Hendre (☎ 762929; www.yr-hendre.net; Porth-y-Felin Rd; s/d £35/60; **P** ⃠) This four-star-rated B&B is something of a local institution and still a cut above the others. Professionally run and homely, the rooms are tastefully decorated – and some feature sea views and flat-screen TVs. A daily breakfast buffet includes local organic produce and healthy options.

Eating

Captain's Table (Market St; snacks £2-5; ☼ 9am-5pm Mon-Sat) Formerly the home of Captain J McGregor Skinner, this simple café is where the locals now eat. It's just for basic snacks but the bacon sandwich is tasty and cheap. Try eating downstairs to avoid the fug of cigarette smoke.

Tea Room at Holyhead Maritime Museum (☎ 769745; Newry Beach; snacks £2-6; ☼ 1-9pm Tue-Sat, to 5pm Sun & Mon) A smart welcoming bistro with a decent range of snack lunches and more filling dinners, all served up on an alfresco decking area with great views across the marina development.

Ucheldre Kitchen (☎ 763361; Ucheldre Centre; ☼ 10am-4.30pm Mon-Fri, 2-4.30pm Sun) Part of Holyhead's excellent arts centre, this relaxed, family-friendly spot is ideal for lunch or coffee.

Getting There & Away

Arriva bus 4/X4 runs to/from Bangor (1½ hours, half-hourly Monday to Saturday); bus 44 (bi-hourly, five daily) runs on Sunday.

Train services run roughly hourly along the North Coast Line via Bangor to Chester (£16.40; 1¾ hours). Services to London run on the Virgin West Coast mainline (4½ hours, five daily Monday to Saturday, two Sunday). Check www.virgintrains.co.uk for details.

Both **Irish Ferries** (☎ 08705 171717; www.irishferries .com) and **Stena Line** (☎ 08705 421126; www.stenaline .co.uk) operate ferry services to Ireland from Holyhead. Irish Ferries has two daily slow ferries (3¼ hours) and two fast services (one hour 50 minutes). Stena has twice-daily services from Dublin for car passengers (3¼ hours) and four daily services from Dun Laoghaire for foot passengers (1¾ hours). Check the websites for promotional offers. Check websites for details.

THE NORTH COAST

The North Coast is packed with variety, from castles and walled towns to Victorian piers and neon-flanked amusements. Bangor is a handsome university town along the coast with a youthful spark (at least during term time). Beyond is Conwy, an extraordinary walled city

that has one of Wales' World Heritage Site castles. Out on a fingernail of land is Llandudno, a stately Victorian resort busily maintaining its popularity into the 21st century. From here the North Coast serves as a holiday playground for much of the English North and Midlands, with long beaches stacked with caravan parks. But it's worth venturing along the less-travelled inland roads for a true taste of the North.

BANGOR
☎ 01248 / pop 12,000
Bangor is one of the campus centres of the University of Wales and the town's population practically doubles during term time when an influx of 12,000-odd students makes this one of the most important centres of learning in Wales. The town itself will win no beauty contests and relies rather heavily on its raucous student-night drinks promotions to foster a sense of nightlife.

Bangor is a major transport hub, however, with a raft of onward connections to Anglesey and Snowdonia, making it a useful place to break your journey before continuing onwards.

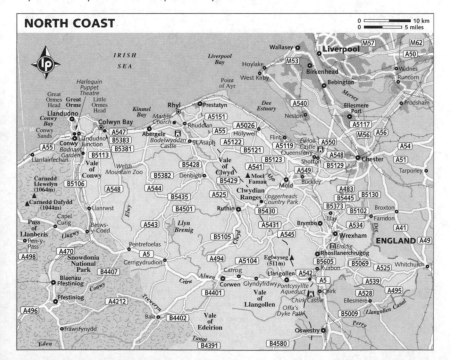

NORTH COAST

The first settlement of Bangor was probably a monastery established in AD 525 by St Deiniol, and the small, lopsided, proud cathedral named after him is the town's main attraction today. Bangor was also a popular destination in Victorian times and retains lots of solid red-brick buildings from that period, particularly on the waterside bluffs, where a fanciful pier – wrought-iron, turreted and long – stretches out into the Menai Strait.

Orientation & Information

From Bangor's train station it's about a half-mile northeast along Deiniol Rd to the tourist office, and another block northeast onto the bus station on Garth Rd. Most of the **University of Wales, Bangor** (☎ 351151) buildings are located along Deiniol Rd. Running parallel is High St, the main shopping street centred around the clock tower and home to all the main banks. A major new shopping development, the **Menai Shopping Centre**, was under construction at the time of writing, promising a vast retail mall just behind the bus station.

The **tourist office** (☎ 352786; Deiniol Rd; ⏰ 9.30am-1pm & 2-4.30pm Mon-Fri Apr-Oct) can help with any accommodation bookings. On Bangor Pier, there's a small **tourist information kiosk** (⏰ 10am-4.30pm) run by the council. The tourist office produces the booklet *Town Walks in Bangor* with three options for day walks around town, of which the Millennium Walk is the lengthiest but most compelling route to uncover aspects of local history.

The **post office** (Gwynedd Rd; ⏰ 9am-5.30pm Mon-Fri, 9am-12.30pm Sat) is opposite the police station, with the tourist office located just southwest along Deiniol Rd, and has a bureau de change. The **library** (☎ 600737; Gwynedd Rd; ⏰ 9.30am-7pm Mon-Tue & Thu-Fri, to 1pm Wed & Sat) offers free internet access. The bookshop **Bookland** (High St) has some maps and a photocopying service.

The **police station** (☎ 370333) is opposite the tourist office while **Gwynedd Hospital** (☎ 384384; Penrhos Rd), located 2.3 miles southwest of the centre, is the nearest place for emergencies.

Sights
BANGOR CATHEDRAL
Also called the **Cathedral Church of St Deiniol**, the cathedral – surprisingly squat, partly due to lack of cash for a central spire – occupies one of

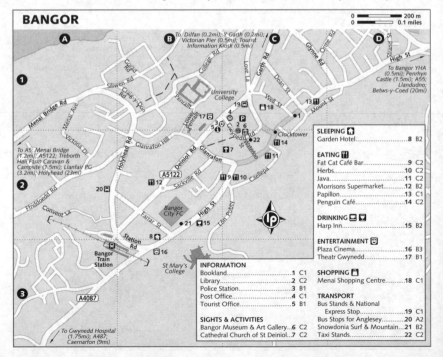

BANGOR

0 — 200 m
0 — 0.1 miles

SLEEPING	
Garden Hotel	**8** B2

EATING	
Fat Cat Café Bar	**9** C2
Herbs	**10** C2
Java	**11** C2
Morrisons Supermarket	**12** B2
Papillon	**13** C1
Penguin Café	**14** C2

DRINKING	
Harp Inn	**15** C2

ENTERTAINMENT	
Plaza Cinema	**16** B3
Theatr Gwynedd	**17** B1

SHOPPING	
Menai Shopping Centre	**18** B2

TRANSPORT	
Bus Stands & National Express Stop	**19** C1
Bus Stops for Anglesey	**20** A2
Snowdonia Surf & Mountain	**21** B2
Taxi Stands	**22** C2

INFORMATION	
Bookland	**1** C1
Library	**2** C2
Police Station	**3** B1
Post Office	**4** C1
Tourist Office	**5** B1

SIGHTS & ACTIVITIES	
Bangor Museum & Art Gallery	**6** C2
Cathedral Church of St Deiniol	**7** C2

the oldest ecclesiastical sites in Britain. A more recent claim to fame is the boy singer turned presenter Aled Jones, who was a choirboy here. Dedicated to St Deiniol, who founded a cell here in AD 525 and who was consecrated as bishop in AD 546, the cathedral's earliest traces are of a 12th-century stone building, while some of what you see today is based on reconstruction work in the late 13th century. Responsibility for damage can be blamed on King John, whose men also burned the city, seized the bishop and ransomed him for 200 falcons. Further ravages took place at the turn of the 15th century, during the Glyndŵr rebellion (p31), and two centuries later Cromwell's men used the cathedral as a stable.

Aside from the 15th-century end tower, much of the architecture you can see today is due to a sensitive reconstruction by the eminent Victorian architect Sir George Gilbert Scott from 1870–80. He used fragments of the medieval building to restore arches and transept windows, and had copies made of some of the floor tiles now in the chancel and Lady chapel. The highlight, facing the northern entrance, is a late-15th-century, almost life-sized oak carving of Christ, seated and shackled in the moments before his crucifixion. Don't miss the touching 14th-century Eva's tombstone, with its meticulous carving of her medieval clothes; the mice are the signature of the main woodcarver, Robert Thompson.

VICTORIAN PIER
Built in 1896, the **Victorian pier** (adult/child 25p/10p; 9am-9pm Mon-Fri, 10am-9pm Sat & Sun), with its fanciful Oriental kiosks, is a lovely place for a stroll, stretching 450m out into the Menai Strait – seemingly almost to Anglesey. In the distance you can see Thomas Telford's handsome **Menai Suspension Bridge**. There are several small shops, a café and you can fish here (permits £2/1 per adult/child).

PENRHYN CASTLE
About 1.5 miles east of town, **Penrhyn Castle** (☎ 353084; adult/child/family £8/4/20, grounds only adult/child £5.40/2.70; castle noon-5pm Wed-Mon Mar-Jun & Sep-Oct, 11am-5pm Jul & Aug, grounds open 1hr earlier) is a fine example of neo-Norman architecture set in beautiful grounds with parkland and wooded walks. Managed by the NT today, it was built between 1820 and 1845 on the spoils of Welsh slate and Jamaican sugar, and designed by Thomas Hopper for the wealthy Pennant family.

It's a vast, extravagant place, with a great hall modelled on Durham Cathedral in England, rooms full of Hopper's mock-Norman furniture, stained glass and hand-painted wallpaper – not to mention a one-tonne slate bed built for Queen Victoria. The lofty grand staircase took 10 years to build while adjacent stable blocks are home to several galleries and mini-museums.

Arriva bus 5 (10 minutes, every 20 minutes) runs out there from the Garth Rd bus station.

BANGOR MUSEUM & ART GALLERY
This **museum** (☎ 353368; Ffordd Gwynedd; admission free; 12.30-4.30pm Tue-Fri, 10.30am-4.30pm Sat) is small in scale and not consistently well labelled, but it does offer some potent evocations of past lives in Bangor and the surrounding countryside. The furniture display boasts some glorious Welsh dressers and a colossal 17th-century dower chest. A gruesome mantrap shows that feeding the family wasn't always a doddle. Upstairs, a compact but very-well-labelled archaeological exhibition takes you from Palaeolithic to medieval times. It's most worthwhile if you are visiting nearby sites.

Sleeping
Treborth Hall Farm Caravan & Campsite (☎ 364104; Treborth Rd; sites per tent/caravan £7/10) About 2 miles west of town and just west of the Menai Bridge, this is a spacious, well-appointed site next to a farmhouse and surrounded by trees.

Bangor YHA (☎ 353516; Tan-y-Bryn; dm with/without breakfast £17.45/13.50, ste £36.95; reception 7.30am-10.30pm, hostel Tue-Sat Mar & Nov—mid-Feb, daily Apr-Oct) This large grey-stone Victorian house, with views of Penrhyn Castle, is located 0.8 miles east of the centre, just off the A5122 Llandegai road. Evening meals are served from 5.30pm to 8pm in the dining hall and the hostel is now open to nonmembers. Take Arriva bus 5 or 9 (every 15 minutes) from outside the train station to opposite the hostel's driveway.

There's a cluster of B&Bs on Garth Rd. They're all much the same but there are a couple of good options.

Dilfan (☎ 353030; s/d/f £25/50/65; P) An unfussy spot with standard B&B décor, this place recently changed hands and the new owners are planning refurbishment.

Y Garth (☎ 362277; r per person £25; P) Recently refurbished, this no-frills place offers negotiable rates for children under 11. The best room is No 6 with a little patio.

ANGLESEY & THE NORTH COAST

Garden Hotel (☎ 362189; www.gardenhotel.co.uk; 1 High St; s/d £49/37; **P**) The closest hotel to the train station, this 12-room place is run by a Chinese family. The rooms may be fairly standard, but at least you'll never go hungry – the owners also run an on-site Cantonese restaurant and the adjacent Garden Oriental Spice Shop, with exotic ingredients from Asia.

Eating & Drinking

Penguin Café (☎ 362036; 260 High St; snacks £2-6) This simple but satisfying café has a small menu, including breakfasts (until 11am) and home-made pizzas to eat in or take away.

Herbs (☎ 351249; 162 High St; lunch specials £6.50) A relaxed café for lunch with simple but hearty, homemade fare, such as soups, sandwiches and daily specials.

Harp Inn (☎ 361817; High St; meals ☎ noon-3pm & 6-9pm Sun-Thu, noon-8pm Fri & Sat) The pick of the pubs in town has real ales and decent, unpretentious bar meals, all served in homely surroundings. There's also live music on Thursday evenings.

Fat Cat Café Bar (☎ 370445; 161 High St; mains £8-12) A bustling bar with big leather sofas, pumping music and a younger, out-for-a-laugh crowd. The Sunday chill-out session has roasts from noon to 4pm.

Java (☎ 361652; off High St; mains around £10; food served ✆ 10am-3pm Mon-Sat, 6-9pm Thu-Sat; 🖳) Located above a skate and surf shop, this is a funky, laid-back bar/eatery with wooden tables and floorboards, good music and an incongruous but welcome array of international dishes. There's also internet access (£1 per 20 minutes).

Papillon (☎ 360248; www.papillonrestaurant.org.uk; 347a High St; sandwiches from £2.20; ✆ 10am-3pm & 6.30-10pm Mon-Sat) An excellent deli-cum-café with a Mediterranean motif and an ethical policy of donating tips to international aid projects, this is Bangor's best place to eat by far. Aside from tapas, special deals include an express set lunch (£5.50) and all-you-can-eat Italian night on Wednesdays (£8.95).

Entertainment

Theatr Gwynedd (☎ 351708; www.theatrgwynedd.co.uk; Deiniol Rd; box office ✆ 9.30am-1.30pm & 2.30-5pm Mon-Fri, from 10.30am Sat, to 8pm during performances) Associated to the university, this excellent performing arts venue is one of four theatres in Wales with its own resident acting company. The ever-changing programme features a full schedule of drama (both Welsh- and English-language), dance, musicals and new-release films.

Plaza Cinema (☎ 0871 2233441; High St) The Plaza has a half-price deal on Wednesdays if you can ignore the fleapit surroundings.

Getting There & Away

Arriva's bus 5/X5 runs from Caernarfon (30 minutes, every 20 minutes Monday to Saturday, hourly Sunday) and from Llandudno (one hour, every 20 minutes Monday to Saturday, hourly Sunday).

The Snowdon Sherpa S6 route runs from Bangor to Capel Curig (20 minutes, three daily Monday to Saturday, one Sunday) and onto Llanwrst (90 minutes, two daily Monday to Saturday) for the heart of the national park.

Arriva bus 4/44 connects Bangor with Holyhead (one hour 10 minutes, every 30 minutes Monday to Friday, bi-hourly Sunday).

Bangor is also the terminus of Arriva's Traws-Cambria bus X32 route to Aberystwyth (3¼ hours, bi-hourly) via Dolgellau (one hour 50 minutes).

National Express bus 545 is a once daily direct service to London (nine hours) running via Llandudno and Chester.

Bangor is accessible from London's Euston station using Virgin Trains' West Coast mainline (3½ hours). See www.virgintrains.co.uk for details. Bangor also lies on Arriva's North Coast line from Chester (£13.50; one hour 10 minutes, hourly).

Getting Around

Snowdonia Surf & Mountain (☎ 354321; 75 High St; per day £25; ✆ 9.30am-12.30pm & 1.30-5.30pm Mon-Tue & Thu-Fri, to 5pm Sat) rents out mountain bikes.

CONWY

☎ 01492 / pop 4000

Conwy feels a bit like old Wales: it's all love-spoons and teashops. Conwy Castle, a Unesco-designated cultural treasure, is an essential part of Welsh heritage and the 0.8 mile-stroll around the castle walls gives an evocative insight into the era of Edward I, when the monarch planted an iron ring of fortifications around the coast to keep the Welsh in order.

The town itself, however, feels rather stuck in the past, with the castle the main attraction and an eerie quiet after the day-trippers head home in the late afternoon. Conwy remains the most complete walled town and castle in Britain, so come for the day but consider making your base elsewhere, notably nearby Llandudno (p292).

At the time of writing, extensive redevelopment of the harbour area was set to continue long term, bringing chaos and disruption to the run-down waterfront.

Orientation & Information

Conwy is edged by the Conwy Estuary and situated just half a mile beyond the boundaries of the Snowdonia National Park.

The town is centred on Lancaster Sq. The small and rather unprepared **tourist office** (☎ 592248; ☼ 9.30am-5pm Apr-May, 9.30am-6pm Jun-Sep, 9.30am-5pm Oct, 9.30am-4pm Mon-Sat, 11am-4pm Sun Nov-Mar) is swamped by enquiries in high season from its kiosk location within the Conwy Castle Visitors Centre, just west of the **Vicarage Gardens short-stay car park** (per hr 70p).

There's free internet access at the **library** (☎ 596242; Castle St; ☼ 10am-5.30pm Mon & Thu-Fri, to 7pm Tue, to 1pm Sat). The **post office** (☼ 8.30am-5pm Mon & Tue, 9am-5.30pm Wed-Fri, 9am-1.30pm Sat) is located on Lancaster Sq, also home to the **HSBC bank**; other banks include **NatWest** (Castle St) and a **Barclays** (High St).

The **Bookshop** (☎ 592137; 21 High St) has some information on local history.

Sights

CONWY CASTLE & WALLS

Rising from a rocky outcrop with commanding views across the estuary and Snowdonia National Park, **Conwy Castle** (☎ 592358; adult/child £4.50/4; ☼ 9.30am-5pm Apr-May, 9.30am-6pm Jun-Sep, 9.30am-5pm Oct, 9.30am-4pm Mon-Sat & 11am-4pm Sun

CONWY

0 —————————— 200 m
0 —————————— 0.1 miles

INFORMATION
Barclays Bank.........................**1** B3
Bookshop...............................**2** B3
HSBC Bank.............................**3** B3
Library....................................**4** C3
NatWest Bank........................**5** C3
Post Office.............................**6** B3
Tourist Office.........................**7** C3

SIGHTS & ACTIVITIES
Aberconwy House...................**8** B3
Conwy Butterfly Jungle...........**9** B2
Conwy Castle.......................**10** C2
Conwy River Trips.................**11** C2

Plas Mawr.............................**12** B3
Royal Cambrian Academy......**13** B3
St Mary's Church...................**14** B3
Smallest House in Great Britain....**15** B2

SLEEPING 🛏
Castle Hotel..........................**16** B3
Gwynfryn...............................**17** B3
Town House...........................**18** B3

EATING 🍴
Alfredo Restaurant................**19** B3
Amelies..................................**20** B3
Bistro Conwy.........................**21** B3

Bridge Inn.............................**22** C3
Edwards of Conwy.................**23** B3
Press Room...........................**24** C3
Spar Supermarket.................**25** B3
Tower Coffee House...............**26** C3

SHOPPING 🛍
Conwy Outdoor Shop.............**27** C3
Potter's Gallery.....................**28** B3

TRANSPORT
Bus Stop................................**29** C3
Bus Stop................................**30** B3
Vicarage Gardens Car Park....**31** C3

To Bangor (15mi);
Caernarfon (22mi)

Bangor Rd

A547

Town Ditch Rd

Berry St

Lower Gate St

Chapel St

Crown La

Upper Gate St

York St

Lancaster Square

High St

Castle St

Conwy Quay

River Conwy

To Llandudno Junction
Train Station (1mi);
A470 (1.5mi);
Llandudno (4mi);
Bodnant Garden (8mi)

A547

Conwy Rd

Conwy Suspension Bridge

Rosemary La

Conwy Train Station

Church St

Rosehill St

Castle Square

To Conwy
YHA (0.3mi);
Old Rectory
Country House (1mi)

To B5106;
Conwy Touring Park
(1mi); Rowen; Ty
Gwyn Hotel; Rowen YHA (4mi)

Nov-Mar) may look like a fairytale construction. But it's very much solid, with eight fierce, slightly tapered towers of coarse dark stone and four additional turrets poking from the interior. The castle took just five years (1283–87) to build, with 1500 workers helping at the height of construction, and remains today one of the greatest examples of medieval military architecture in the UK. After the Civil War in the 17th century, it fell into disrepair and the Council of State ordered it to be partially pulled down.

Inside it's more tumbledown than its Unesco partner at Caernarfon (p255), and smaller and simpler in design, but it's still a great place to explore, with layers of ramparts, towers and passages offering a combination of claustrophobic enclosures and awesome views across the walled town and estuary. The grand ruins of the royal apartments and chapel, and the towering shell of the 10m roofless Great Hall are impressive despite their state of disrepair.

In contrast the town walls are fully intact, with 22 towers and three original gateways; you can walk along many sections.

CONWY SUSPENSION BRIDGE
With its Gothic turrets, Thomas Telford's handsome **suspension bridge** (☎ 573282; adult/child £1/50p; ☼ 11am-5pm) looks, at first glance, like an extension to Conwy Castle. It was completed, however, in 1826, the same year as Telford's other milestone bridge over the Menai Strait – both of them intended to speed the movement of people and goods from London to Holyhead. Like its Menai cousin, it was eclipsed a quarter of a century later by an adjacent steel bridge designed by Robert Stephenson (who also designed the arch where the railway punctures the old town walls). The Conwy suspension bridge is now pedestrian and you can visit its restored tollhouse, furnished as it was over a century ago.

OTHER SIGHTS
Plas Mawr (☎ 580167; High St; adult/child £4.90/4.50; ☼ 9.30am-5pm Tue-Sun Apr-May & Sep, to 6pm Tue-Sun Jun-Aug, to 4pm Oct Tue-Sun) is the UK's finest surviving Elizabethan townhouse. It was completed in 1585 for the Welsh merchant and courtier Robert Wynn, and the lavish decoration is testament to his social standing. Rugged, whitewashed outer walls give way to a lavish interior: the painted plasterwork is extraordinarily vivid, while the decorated ceilings

and friezes dance with colour and life. A new, free audio tour of the house describes the restoration and the life of the Tudor gentry. A combined ticket with Conwy Castle costs £7/6/22 per adult/child/family.

The very rare, timber-and-plaster **Aberconwy House** (☎ 592246; Castle St; adult/child £3/1.50; ☼ 11am-5pm Apr-Oct) is the town's oldest medieval merchant's house, dating from around 1300. Today managed by the NT, it has been a coffee house, temperance hotel, bakery and antique shop, but remains startlingly well preserved. An audio-visual presentation shows daily life from different periods of history.

Wales' top art institute, the **Royal Cambrian Academy** (☎ 593413; www.rcaconwy.org; Crown Lane; admission free; ☼ 11am-5pm Tue-Sat, 1-4.30pm Sun) is in a stylish building with an impressive white-walled gallery that has a full programme of exhibitions by members, plus visiting shows from the National Museum Wales and elsewhere. The academy hosts an excellent arts festival every August with free workshops and events.

The small riverside quay is currently being redeveloped and its attractions are less than compelling. The **Smallest House in Great Britain** (☎ 593484; Lower Gate St; adult/child £1/0.50; ☼ 10am-9pm Jul-Aug, 10am-6pm Apr-Jun) is a curiosity with dimensions of 72 by 122 inches and a mention in the *Guinness Book of Records*.

More appealing is **Conwy Butterfly Jungle** (☎ 593149; www.conwy-butterfly.co.uk; adult/child £4/3; ☼ 10am-5.30pm Wed-Mon May-Sep, 10am-4pm Mar-Oct), a nature park with displays of exotic flora and fauna.

Activities
BOAT TRIPS
Conwy River Trips (☎ 592830; www.conwyboats.co.uk) runs 30-minute sightseeing and nature-watching trips from the harbour, both out through the estuary and upstream into the Conwy Valley (adult/child £4.50/3). However, note that the River Conwy is tidal here, so the timetable varies. Sailing courses and boat hire are available from **Conwy School of Yachting** (☎ 572999; www.conwy-yachting.com) at the harbour.

Sleeping
Conwy Touring Park (☎ 592856; www.conwytouringpark.com; site per tent/caravan £10.85/15.86) A spacious park, 1.5 miles south of Conwy on the B5106, this is a green and well-appointed site with great views across to Snowdonia and a good range of services.

Conwy YHA (☎ 593571; Larkhill, Sychnant Pass Rd; dm adult/child £15.50/10.95, r £40/31; ☺ daily Feb-Oct, Fri-Sun Nov-Jan; ☒) Located one third of a mile from the centre, this ultra-modern hostel has a raft of services – from a restaurant (breakfast/dinner £3.95/7.90) to an observation desk. There are disabled facilities and family rooms. Ask about low-season promotional deals.

Rowen YHA (☎ 650089; Rhiw Farm, Rowen; adult/child £10.95/8.50; ☺ Easter-Sep) This farmhouse property set near the rustic village of Rowen is very much a walkers' hang-out. There are only self catering facilities and access is very limited via a steep, narrow lane and best tackled by a 4WD. You can also get here by catching Arriva bus 19 between Llandudno and Llanberis.

Town House (☎ 596454; www.thetownhousebb .co.uk; 18 Rosehill St; d/tw £55/60) Simple but homely, this six-room place boasts a quiet but central location. The guesthouse closes in December and January.

Gwynfryn (☎ 576733; www.gwynfrynbandb.co.uk; 4 York Pl; r £55/70) This Victorian property has been newly refurbished with some nice, thoughtful touches, such as in-room fridges and DVDs. The five rooms are all individually styled in different colours and breakfast is served in the secluded garden during summer. The best rooms to be found for families are on the top floor.

Castle Hotel (☎ 582800; www.castlewales.co.uk; High St; s/d/ste £75/75/92.50) On the site of a former Cistercian abbey, this historic coaching inn turned country-house hotel has characterful rooms (one of them, the Wynn Suite, features a carved four-poster dating from 1570). Children are welcome but may not appreciate the formal ambience.

Old Rectory Country House (☎ 580611; www .oldrectorycountryhouse.co.uk; r £99-169; ☒ ☒) With a fantastic setting and panoramic views across the Conwy Estuary and a hidden-away Georgian country retreat feel, this place is just over a mile south of Conwy on the A470. The rooms feature modern bathrooms but suffer slightly old-fashioned decoration, and will appeal to those seeking a more traditional, environment full of character. The Walnut Room is the best for views of the castle. The hotel was traditionally renowned for its high standards of cuisine but, as the owners approach retirement age, it now offers rooms on a purely B&B basis with a minimum two-night stay.

Eating

Tower Coffee House (snacks £2-5) An airy café with great views across the estuary to Deganwy. Downstairs there's a rather incongruous dungeon-style area – watch out for the shrunken head.

Press Room (☎ 592242; 3 Rosehill St, snacks £2-6, meals £8-12; ☺ 10.30am-5pm & 7-11pm daily Apr-Oct, Wed-Sun Nov-Mar) An arty café that is great for a coffee stop and lunches, this place has real South American coffee, funky artworks on the walls, a menu of tasty café fare and a garden area for alfresco elevenses. It's just by the entrance to the castle and also serves evening meals Thursday to Saturday.

Bridge Inn (☎ 573482; Rosehill St) For a pub meal, the Bridge has food all day, daily specials and Sunday roasts, albeit in a slightly rough-around-the-edges setting.

Ty Gwyn Hotel (☎ 650232; Rowen; meals £5-7; ☺ Sat & Sun lunch, Tue-Sat dinner) This pub, 5 miles southwest of Conwy in the village of Rowen, has a gorgeous riverside garden and simple pub food with homemade curries and bar meals. Try to time a visit with the practice session for the local male voice choir, held each Friday at 9pm.

Alfredo Restaurant (☎ 592381; Lancaster Sq; set menu £14.50) This local institution is now becoming rather tired looking, but it continues to serve up family favourites, such as pizzas (£7 to £8), pastas (£6.25 to £8.25) and meaty mains with an Italian twist (£11 to £14).

Amelies (☎ 583142; 10 High St) Recently refurbished and renamed after the Audrey Tautou film, this is one of the few decent places in town for lunch; it also offers tasty homemade cakes and coffees.

Bistro Conwy (☎ 596326; www.bistroconwy.com; Chapel St; mains around £15; ☺ 6.30-9pm Mon-Sat) It may not be the cheapest in town, but this intimate little bistro with a cosy ambience and an attractive setting in a secluded little red-brick cottage offers modern and traditional Welsh cooking. Vegetarians will feel particularly well served by the broad menu.

For self-caterers, try the **Spar supermarket** (High St) and **Edwards Of Conwy** (☎ 592443; www .edwardsofconwy.co.uk; High St), an award winning butcher-cum-deli with pies and hot meals to take away.

Shopping

Conwy Outdoor Shop (☎ 593390; www.conwyoutdoor .co.uk; 9 Castle St; ☺ 9am-5.30pm Mon-Sat) This useful,

ANGLESEY & THE NORTH COAST

friendly store has kit for sale and advice on local activities, and will arrange bike hire for £16 per day.

Potter's Gallery (☎ 593590; www.northwalespotters.co .uk; 1 High St; ⦿ 10am-5pm) Run by members of North Wales Potters, the gallery showcases ceramic works and promotes understanding of studio ceramics.

Getting There & Away

The Castle St bus stop is the hub for Arriva bus 5/5X, which runs to Llandudno (20 minutes, every 20 minutes Monday to Saturday, hourly Sunday), KMP bus 9/9A to Llandudno (every 20 to 40 minutes Monday to Saturday) and Arriva bus X19 to Llangollen (1¾ hours, every 2½ hours Monday to Saturday, two services Sunday).

The train station bus stop is the hub for KMP bus 9/9A to Bangor (40 minutes, every 30 minutes Monday to Saturday) and Arriva Bus 5 to Bangor (40 minutes, hourly Monday to Saturday).

Conwy is on the North Coast Line, although Llandudno Junction, a 15-minute walk west of Conwy across the river, is the nearest mainline station for inter-city connections. There are trains hourly to Llandudno Junction (£1.70, three minutes).

AROUND CONWY
Bodnant Garden

One of the UK's most splendid gardens and noted for its botanical collections, **Bodnant Garden** (☎ 01492-650460; www.bodnantgarden.co.uk; Tal-y-Cafn; ⦿ 10am-5pm Mar-Nov, plant centre 10am-5pm year round) is 8 miles south of Conwy off the A470. Landscaped in 1875, it boasts commanding views across the Conwy Valley to the peaks of Snowdonia. The gardens are a riot of rhododendrons, camellias and magnolias in spring; of roses and water lilies in summer; and of hydrangeas and turning leaves in autumn. Best of all is the laburnum arch, a 50m tunnel of blooms at its best from mid-May to June.

Arriva's bus 25 passes by hourly from Llandudno; from Conwy you have to change at Llandudno Junction.

LLANDUDNO
☎ 01492 / pop 22,000

Llandudno is a thriving seaside resort and Wales' largest. The twin humps of the ancient mountains, the Great Orme and Little Orme, loom over the graceful Victorian wedding-cake architecture of the seafront buildings that line the sweeping prom for a full mile. The town seethes with tourists of all ages in summer and is now increasingly attracting a new generation of adventure seekers throughout the year with the West Shore developing as a centre for extreme sports. The town also makes a good base for walkers, with just 27 miles from Llandudno to Llanberis at the foot of Mt Snowdon (p239).

Developed as an upmarket Victorian holiday town, it has retained much of its 19th-century atmosphere – only the kiss-me-quick tackiness of the pier lets the side down. In the town itself, a host of new guesthouses and restaurants have helped to bolster Llandudno's upmarket aspirations. Today there are over 200 hotels and guesthouses in town and they do a roaring trade in summer. Travel writer Bill Bryson was even moved to describe it as his 'favourite seaside resort'.

In 1861 the Liddell family, whose daughter was Lewis Carroll's model for the main character of *Alice's Adventures in Wonderland,* summered in the house that is now the St Tudno Hotel (p295). Their legacy is marked with a statue of the White Rabbit on the West Shore.

Orientation & Information

The town straddles its own peninsula, with Llandudno Bay and North Shore Beach to the northeast and Conwy Bay and West Shore Beach to the southwest. The entrance to town from the A470 is now marked by a huge retail shopping area, Parc Llandudno, with a giant Asda supermarket. There's a problem finding car parking in town, so try to park up here and walk in, or take your chances along the promenade.

The train station is three blocks south of Mostyn St, the main thoroughfare; buses and National Express coaches stop on Mostyn St. The new **tourist office** (☎ 876413; www.visitlland udno.org.uk; Mostyn St; ⦿ 9am-5pm Mon-Sat Nov-Mar, 9am-5.30pm Mon-Sat & 9.30am-4.30pm Sun Apr-Oct) has moved into a purpose-built area in the **library building** (☎ 574020; ⦿ 9am-6pm Mon, Tue & Fri, 10am-5pm Wed, 9am-7pm Thu, 9.30am-1pm Sat), where you'll also find free internet access.

The post office and all major banks are along Mostyn St. **Bubbles Laundrette** (25 Brookes St; per load £7.50; ⦿ 8.30am-5pm Mon-Sat) has a service wash.

The **police station** (☎ 517171) is one block east of the train station; **Llandudno General Hospital** (☎ 860066) is almost 1 mile south of the centre.

Sights

GREAT ORME

Llandudno is dominated by the spectacular 207m **Great Orme** (Y Gogarth), yet there's hardly a clue from town as to what's there. Apparently 'Orme' is Norse for worm or sea serpent, a reference to its snaky shape. This ancient hill offers some of the best views in Wales (excellent for sunset), which on a clear day will take in the peaks of Snowdonia, the Isle of Man and even Ireland. There are some spectacular walks, several Neolithic sites, an encyclopedia of flowers, and clouds of moths, butterflies and sea birds. There's even a herd of around 150 Kashmir mountain goats (the original pair were given by Queen Victoria). The more adventurous (and expert) go climbing around Marine Dr, but it's not for beginners.

The entire headland is a country park with its own **visitor centre** (☎ 874151; www.conwy.gov.uk /countryside; ⏰ 9.30am-5pm mid-Mar–Oct), and a designated Site of Special Scientific Interest (SSSI). The centre organises two-hour guided walks of the headland every Sunday from May to September, plus the summit complex has picnic tables, a café and gift shop.

The **Great Orme Tramway** (☎ 575275; www.great ormetramway.com; Victoria Tramway Station; adult/child return £4.80/3.40; ⏰ every 20min 10am-6pm mid-Mar–Oct), at the top of Church Walks, takes you up the steep incline in an original 1902 tramcar. It's one of only three cable-operated trams in the world (the other two are in equally glamorous Lisbon and

LLANDUDNO

0 — 400 m
0 — 0.2 miles

INFORMATION
Barclays Bank.................................**1** B2
Bubbles Laundrette.........................**2** B3
Library..(see 7)
Lloyds TSB Bank.............................**3** B2
NatWest Bank................................**4** B2
Police Station.................................**5** C3
Post Office.....................................**6** C3
Tourist Office.................................**7** B2

SIGHTS & ACTIVITIES
Alice in Wonderland Centre.............**8** C3
Cable Car Terminus........................**9** B1
Great Orme Tramway.....................**10** A1
Home Front Experience...................**11** A2
John Nike Leisuresport....................**12** B1
Llandudno Museum.......................**13** A2
Llandudno Pier.............................**14** B1
Oriel Mostyn Gallery.....................**15** C3

SLEEPING
Abbey Lodge.................................**16** A2
Escape B&B...................................**17** A1
Hawarden Villa..............................**18** B2
Hilary Hotel...................................**19** A3
Imperial Hotel................................**20** C2
Llandudno Hostel...........................**21** B3
Lynton House................................**22** B1
Osborne House..............................**23** B1
Plas Madoc...................................**24** A1
St Tudno Hotel..............................**25** B1

EATING
Asda Supermarket..........................**26** C3
Canolfan Victoria Shopping Centre...**27** B2
Fat Cat Café Bar............................**28** B1
Fountains Bar & Café......................**29** A1

Greenery.......................................**30** B2
Hambone Food Hall........................**31** B2
Londis...**32** B1
Londis...**33** B1
Moulin Rouge Café.........................**34** A1
Number 1 Bistro.............................**35** A1
Richard's Bistro..............................**36** A1
Romeo Ristorante Italiano...............**37** B2

DRINKING
King's Head...................................**38** A1
Nineteen.......................................**39** B2

Ottakar's......................................**40** B2

ENTERTAINMENT
Venue Cymru.................................**41** D3

SHOPPING
Parc Llandudno Retail Park.............**42** C3

TRANSPORT
National Express & Regional Buses...**43** C3
Snowdon Sherpa & Local Buses.......**44** B2
Taxis...**45** B3

San Francisco). There's also a **cable car** (☎ 877205; www.llandudnocablecar.co.uk; £5 return), the longest in Britain, that runs from Happy Valley, above the pier (subject to the weather) and completes the journey to the summit in 18 minutes.

Halfway up the tramline is **Great Orme Mines** (☎ 870447; www.greatormemines.info; adult/child/family £5.30/3.50/5; ☺ 10am-5pm Feb–end Oct), a Bronze Age copper mine that was possibly one of the most important sources of the metal during that era. It's the oldest Bronze Age copper mine in the world that's open to visitors (the *Guinness Book of Records* confirms this). Take the self-guided tour to explore 4 miles of 3500-year-old tunnels.

LLANDUDNO PIER

This Victorian pier stalks an impressive and genteel 670m into the sea. It was first built in 1857 but collapsed in a storm two years later. Construction of the current pier was begun in 1877; its main use was as a disembarkation point for passengers from Isle of Man steamers (these are long gone). Damaged by fire in the 1990s it has risen again, but its downmarket seaside amusements are a far cry from its Victorian halcyon days.

OTHER SIGHTS

Oriel Mostyn Gallery (☎ 879201; www.mostyn.org; 12 Vaughan St; admission free; ☺ 10am-5pm Mon-Sat) is North Wales' leading venue for contemporary art with fine, adventurous exhibitions in a striking white interior; there are also short art workshops, an excellent craft shop and a café. In 2008, a new expanded gallery will be unveiled.

Home Front Experience (☎ 871032; New St; adult/child £3/2; ☺ 10am-4.30pm Mon-Sat, 11am-3pm Sun Mar-Oct) is a small museum that looks at life at home during WWII, and offers visitors the chance to try out an air-raid shelter.

The 'real Alice' holidayed in Llandudno, and the connection has led the town to adopt Lewis Carroll. However tenuous the link, the **Alice in Wonderland Centre** (☎ 860082; www.wonderland.co.uk; 3-4 Trinity Sq; adult/child £2.95/2.50; ☺ 10am-5pm Mon-Sat year round, to 4pm Sun Apr-Oct), with models inspired by the books, is a good one to entertain kids with on a rainy day.

Llandudno Museum (☎ 876517; 17-19 Gloddaeth St; adult/child £1.50/75p; ☺ 10.30am-1pm & 2-5pm Tue-Sat, 2.15-5pm Sun Apr-Oct, 1.30-4.30pm Tue-Sat Nov-Mar) presents local history through an assortment of artefacts and explores themes such as the development of the town as a holiday resort.

Activities

Turbulence (☎ 08456 589656; www.ukkiting.com; 148 Conwy Rd, Llandudno Junction) is the local specialist for adrenaline sports with kite surfing, kite buggying and kite landboarding the main activities. You can arrange lessons from the shop in Llandudno Junction, which also sells outdoors gear.

If you prefer the downhill type of speed, **John Nike Leisuresport** (☎ 874707; www.jnll.co.uk; Wyddfyd Rd, Great Orme) is an artificial ski slope with year-round skiing, snowboarding and to-boggan tuition. Ski lessons start from £21/13 per adult/child per session.

Festivals & Events

Llandudno's biggest event is its **Victorian Extravaganza** (www.victorian-extravaganza.co.uk), held over the early-May bank-holiday weekend, with many streets closed off for steam engines, parades, a funfair and more.

For the more adventure-minded, **Kitejam** (www.kitejam.co.uk) is an adventure sports festival held each year in mid-September on the West Shore. It is organised by the people behind Turbulence (see above).

Sleeping

Llandudno Hostel (☎ 877430; www.llandudnohostel .co.uk; 14 Charlton St; dm £15, breakfast £3) There may be no camping facilities in the immediate area, but there is an excellent independently run hostel for a genuine budget option. It's open year round, is friendly and there's even an en-suite room (£36) if you want some privacy. The owners are very knowledgeable about local activities and attractions.

Hawarden Villa (☎ 860447; 27 Chapel St; s/d £22.50/45; P ⊠) Central and friendly, Hawarden Villa has modest but good-value en-suite rooms and traditional fry-up breakfasts. Evening meals are available for £10 and single guests are made to feel welcome.

Hilary Hotel (☎ 875623; www.thehilaryguesthouse -llandudno.co.uk; 32 St David's Rd; s/d £35/58; P ⊠) This large guesthouse has comfortable rooms on a quiet sidestreet. It's a decent midrange option, but aims at over-25s only and does not welcome children or families. Ask the owners about their massage and reflexology services.

Lynton House (☎ 875057; www.lyntonhousellandudno .co.uk; 80 Church Walks; s/d £35/58; P ⊠) Close to the pier and the tramway, this modest place has rooms with whirlpool baths and floral walls; there are three four-poster rooms.

Plas Madoc (☎ 876514; www.plasmadocguesthouse .co.uk; 60 Church Walks; s/d £45/60; Ⓟ 🗙) This place used to be a fully vegetarian and vegan guesthouse. New owners have now taken over and also cater to nonvegetarian guests, but they do maintain the soya milk and free-range eggs tradition for those who request it. The five en-suite rooms are very contemporary with a clean, airy feel and a small in-room library of DVDs to watch.

Abbey Lodge (☎ 878042; 14 Abbey Rd; s/d £45/75; Ⓟ 🗙 💻) A cut above the average seaside guesthouse, this smart, Victorian-style lodge is set in a well-attended garden, pays close attention to detail. The four en-suite rooms feature big, iron-framed beds and marble bathrooms with tubs. The owners are taking an increasingly green policy towards running the place and cater for more corporate clients since installing free wi-fi internet. A good breakfast is served around a large communal table.

Lighthouse (☎ 876819; www.lighthouse-llandudno.co .uk; Marine Dr; s/d from £70/140) Head to bed in the lighthouse, an amazing castle-like structure atop a sheer 100m cliff at the end of the Great Orme promontory. Decorated like a ship on the inside, it has three rooms with bath and binoculars, and breathes living history. Book ahead; you'll have a better chance of a room on a weekday.

Imperial Hotel (☎ 877466; www.theimperial.co.uk; The Promenade; s/d/f £110/140/220; Ⓟ 🗙 ♿) Now privately owned by the Classic British Hotels group, this is the pick of the old-school seafront hotels and has recently benefited from a major refurbishment that has introduced two disabled rooms. It's a sprawling behemoth of a place with large, comfortable rooms, although back-facing rooms are a bit dark. Facilities include a health club and the hotel caters increasingly for the conference market.

Escape B&B (☎ 877776; www.escapebandb.co.uk; 48 Church Walks; r midweek £75, weekends £105; Ⓟ 🗙 💻) This place is very much in vogue for its funky interior, but suffers from style-over-substance syndrome and fails to offer much of a welcome. Children are definitely not catered for but the owner is planning a new familyfriendly property nearby for 2007.

St Tudno Hotel (☎ 874411; www.st-tudno.co.uk; 16 North Pde; s/d from £85/110) A small, award-winning Victorian hotel on the seafront, St Tudno has rooms that are prim yet bold, with lots of colours and big whirlpool baths. They're a bit small at the price, however. The in-house restaurant is one of the best in town, attracting a well-to-do crowd of visiting dignitaries. A seven-course tasting menu costs £49.50.

Osborne House (☎ 860330; www.osbornehouse.com; 17 North Pde; ste £145-175; Ⓟ) Lavish and finely furnished, this Victorian townhouse on the promenade offers large elegant suites with Egyptian-cotton sheets, DVD, wide-screen TV and fireplace. The stylish in-house restaurant serves a three-course express menu (£17.95) and three-course Sunday lunch (£13.50) among other main meals. Food is served from 10.30am to 10pm Monday to Saturday, and to 9pm on Sunday.

Eating & Drinking

Nineteen (☎ 873333; 19 Lloyd St; 🕑 9am-5pm Mon-Sat) This relaxed little coffee bar specialises in smoothies, juices, coffees and snacks with big comfy sofas and a jazz-music background.

Ottakar's (☎ 873040; 37-38 Mostyn St; 🕑 9am-5.30pm Mon-Sat, 10.30am-4.30pm Sun) The best bookshop in

ANGLESEY & THE NORTH COAST

AUTHOR'S CHOICE

Bodysgallen Hall (☎ 584466; www.bodysgallen.com; s/d/ste £125/175/375; food 🕑 12.30-1.45pm & 7.30-9.30pm) A stately country-house hotel set in verdant gardens, Bodysgallen Hall is just 2 miles south of Llandudno on the A470. The historic house dates mainly from the 17th century and is a treasure trove of antiques, artefacts and traditions, with a sense of history engrained into every wood-beamed roof. Overall it's the little touches that make the place stand out, such as the silver tea strainer for afternoon tea. Food is served from 12.30pm to 1.45pm and 7.30pm to 9.30pm. The owners also produce a tree brochure tracing a route through the grounds with panoramic views across to Conwy Castle. Meanwhile, in the grounds, a very contemporary spa has a range of specialist treatments – from a primal radiance spa facial to a detoxifying algae wrap. Ask about promotional rates for spa breaks and winter weekends. Beware: this is not a child-friendly hotel and under 12s are positively frowned upon. While the restaurant is open to nonguests, this is not the place to bring the family.

town has a great little café upstairs serving fair-trade coffee, a perfect complement to a browse through the nearby travel section.

Moulin Rouge Café (104 Upper Mostyn St) A simple café for drinks and snacks, plus it has internet facilities – spend £3 and get 20 minutes of free internet access.

Hambone Food Hall (☎ 860084; Lloyd St; ☼ 9.30am-5.30pm Mon-Sat) A fantastic little deli with eat-in or take-away sandwiches, salads and drinks.

Fat Cat Café Bar (☎ 871844; 149 Upper Mostyn St) The sister property to the Bangor venue (p288), the local member of the Fat Cat chain serves up beers and pub food in a modern café-bar setting.

Fountains Bar & Café (☎ 875600; 114 Upper Mostyn St) This high-ceilinged café-bar serves beers, wines and cocktails, plus a good menu of pub-style food, including wraps and burgers. Try the house special – a hot beef and onion baguette (£5.95).

Greenery (☎ 877193; Lloyd St; mains around £5; ☼ 7.30am-5pm Mon-Sat, to 10pm Jul & Aug; ♿) With plastic greenery and green tables, this is a no-frills, family-friendly, all-round eatery for snacks, mains, vegetarian options and a kid's menu. Good value and no-nonsense stuff.

Romeo Ristorante Italiano (☎ 877777; 25 Lloyd St; fish specials around £15) With plastic-looking plants and red tablecloths, this friendly local Italian eatery serves pizzas, pasta and lasagne. Try the fish specials.

Richard's Bistro (☎ 875315; 7 Church Walks; ☼ 5.30pm-late Tue-Sat) An upmarket bistro for dinner, this stylish little place offers heavy dishes featuring lots of game and adventurous combinations of flavours.

Number 1 Bistro (☎ 875424; Old Rd; ☼ 5.30-9.30pm Mon-Sat) There's a touch of France about this stylish, dark-red, woody bistro with an imaginative menu including venison and ostrich, plus lots of fresh fish. The early evening set menu offers two/three courses for £12/15 before 6.30pm.

For self-caterers there are two **Londis supermarkets** (Madoc St & Upper Mostyn St) as well as various coffee bars and snack joints in the **Canolfan Victoria Shopping Centre** (Mostyn St; ☼ 9am-5.30pm Mon-Sat).

Upper Mostyn St is the place to head to for nightlife, with a slew of late-night venues.

King's Head (☎ 877993; Old Rd) For a quieter pint, try the King's Head. Overlooking the tramway station, this Victorian pub is one of the oldest in town and also serves decent bar meals.

Entertainment

Venue Cymru (☎ 872000; www.nwtheatre.co.uk; The Promenade; ☼ box office 9.30am-8.30pm Mon-Sat plus prior to performances) has recently undergone an expansion programme and is now one of North Wales' leading performance venues. It offers everything from West End musicals to the Welsh National Opera, plus dance, drama, comedy, pop and classical music, on the UK's second-biggest stage (after Brighton). There's even a free shuttle bus service available – call the box office for details.

Cineworld Llandudno (☎ 08712 002000; www.cineworld.co.uk) is a major cinema complex close to Llandudno Junction train station.

Getting There & Away

BUS

KMP Coaches' bus 9/9A runs from Llandudno to Bangor (55 minutes, every 30 minutes Monday to Saturday) and Menai Bridge (two hours). Arriva's bus 5/5X runs from Llandudno to Caernarfon (1¾ hours, every 30 minutes, hourly Sunday) via Conwy (25 minutes).

Connections to/from Snowdonia are run by the Snowdon Sherpa service: route S2 arrives via Llandudno Junction (four daily Monday to Saturday) from Betws-y-Coed and Llanberis.

National Express coach 545 passes through Llandudno twice daily to London (about nine hours) via Chester, and from Pwllheli, Porthmadog, Caernarfon and Bangor; coaches stop at the Mostyn Broadway coach station.

TRAIN

The Conwy Valley line from Llandudno and Llandudno Junction (£1.70, eight minutes) heads to Blaenau Ffestiniog (£5.50, 1¼ hours, every two hours) via Betws-y-Coed (single £4.10, 45 minutes, at least five times daily Monday to Saturday).

Arriva Trains Wales has direct services from Llandudno to Manchester (£20.10, 2¼ hours, 15 daily) via Chester (£11.70, one hour). For other destinations on the London–Holyhead mainline, change trains at Llandudno Junction, which is £3 by taxi from Llandudno station.

Llandudno Junction is served by Virgin Trains direct from London's Euston station (from £15.50, 3½ hours), with more options if you change at Crewe. Trains also run to Holyhead (see p284).

Getting Around
Snowdonia Cycle Hire (☎ 878771; www.snowdonia cyclehire.co.uk; per half-/full day £11/16) offers bicycle hire and will deliver and collect within 6 miles.

Taxis (☎ 878787) are waiting outside the train station.

AROUND LLANDUDNO
Four miles east of Llandudno at Rhos-on-Sea, the **Harlequin Puppet Theatre** (☎ 548166; www.puppets .inuk.com; The Promenade; adult/child £5/4; ☾ shows 3pm daily during school holidays; 3pm Mon-Wed & Fri plus 8pm Wed during summer holidays) is the UK's only permanent marionette theatre.

Six miles east at Colwyn Bay the **Welsh Mountain Zoo** (☎ 532938; www.welshmountainzoo.org; adult/ child/family £7.75/5.50/23.40; ☾ 9.30am-5pm Mar-Oct, to 4pm Nov-Feb) is a good day out for families, with a range of animals from bears to tigers amid attractive gardens. There's also a new condor house in collaboration with a conservation project from Ecuador.

LLANGOLLEN
☎ 01978 / pop 3500
Set in the scenic Vale of Llangollen and featuring the River Dee as its gurgling heart, Llangollen is a slightly odd blend of cultured cool and gritty realism, perfectly illustrated by its culinary options, which range from foodie-friendly places to avoid-at-all-costs greasy spoons. The vale was part of the London to Holyhead stagecoach route in the 18th and 19th centuries, when the road ran through the middle of the town (now Bridge and Church Sts).

Traditionally Llangollen was a favourite day-trip destination for tourists in search of culture and Devonshire teas. In recent times, however, the town has made efforts to smooth over its rougher edges by building the profile of its increasingly respected Fringe Festival and celebrating the cachet it enjoys as host to the International Musical Eisteddfod, a six-day jamboree of music and dance that attracts folk groups from all over the world.

What's more, the abundance of walking trails and a growing array of activity-based excursions reflect the way that Llangollen is changing as a destination – and it is all the more interesting for it.

Orientation & Information
Llangollen sits astride the River Dee (Afon Dyfrdwy), about 6 miles by road from the English border; the nearest big town is 11

miles away in Wrexham. The A5 road, successor to the stagecoach route, skirts the southern edge of town, while the Llangollen Canal is a stone's throw from the river on the other side. The town is easily navigable on foot and bus connections stop on Market St opposite the **short-stay car park** (per hr 40p).

The town's excellent **tourist office** (☎ 860828; The Chapel, Castle St; ☾ 9.30am-5.30pm) is housed in the former chapel that also contains the **library** (☾ 9.30am-7pm Mon, to 5.30pm Tue, Wed & Fri, to 12.30pm Sat Apr-Oct, 9.30am-5pm Fri-Wed Nov-Mar), where you may access the internet for free. There are regular art exhibitions staged here and the building also houses the Fringe box office during the festival.

Around town there are bank branches of **Barclays** (Castle St), **NatWest** (Castle St) and **HSBC** (Bridge St). The **post office** (Castle St; ☾ 9am-5.30pm Mon-Fri, to 12.30pm Sat) is opposite the NatWest bank. The **Blue Bay Laundrette** (Regent St; per load £4.70; ☾ 9am-6pm Mon-Sat) offers a service wash.

The **police station** (☎ 860222; Parade St) is round the block from the tourist office. There's a small **Cottage Hospital** (☎ 860226; Abbey Rd); the nearest accident and emergency services are in Wrexham, 11 miles away.

The mannerly **Court Yard Books** (☾ 9am-5.30pm Mon-Sat) is down an alleyway in the Courtyard pedestrian area among a slew of knick-knacks shops.

Sights
PLAS NEWYDD
The Ladies of Llangollen lived at **Plas Newydd** (☎ 861314; adult/child £3/2; ☾ 10am-5pm Apr-Oct) for almost half a century. Lady Eleanor Butler and Miss Sarah Ponsonby transformed the house into their own private romantic hybrid of Gothic and Tudor styles, complete with stained-glass windows, carved-oak panels and formal gardens. English and Welsh audio guides are now included in the ticket price and a new educational centre with an artist-in-residence is now based in the grounds. The house is a quarter of a mile southeast of the tourist office. Don't confuse this place with the stately home of the same name on Anglesey (p281).

VALLE CRUCIS ABBEY
Located at the foot of the Horseshoe Pass, the dignified ruins of the **Valle Crucis Abbey** (☎ 860326; adult/child £2.50/2; ☾ 10am-5pm Apr-Sep) represent one of Wales' last Cistercian

monasteries. Founded in 1201 by Madog ap Gruffydd, ruler of Northern Powys, its serene setting and now largely Gothic form (including a huge rose window) predates its more famous sibling at Tintern (p115). It suffered several fires during the Middle Ages – partly at the hands of Edward I, following the abbot's support for Llywelyn ap Gruffudd – and then later during the Owain Glyndŵr uprising.

Things looked up in the 15th century, and the buildings were extended. In 1525 the estate was valued and found to be the second-richest abbey in Wales, but it was one of the first abbeys to be closed by King Henry VIII in 1536. Dissolution and robbery accelerated the building's ruin. The 13th-century west front of the abbey church still stands, retaining a beautifully carved doorway and impressive remains of the transepts and presbytery. Best preserved of all is the east range, rebuilt in the late 14th century, and the vaulting arches of the chapter house.

The site is 2 miles from Llangollen on the A542 with no bus connections.

LLANGOLLEN CANAL

In the 18th century canals and the horse-drawn barge were the most efficient way of hauling goods over long distances but, with the advent of the railway, most of them fell into disrepair. The Llangollen Canal fared better than most because it was used, for years more, to carry drinking water from the River Dee to the Hurleston Reservoir in Cheshire.

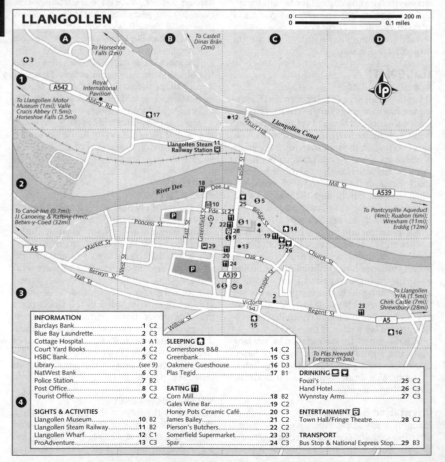

LLANGOLLEN

0   200 m
0   0.1 miles

To Plas Newydd Entrance (0.2mi)

Today it's again in use, carrying visitors up and down the Vale of Llangollen. In addition, the old towpaths offer miles of peaceful, traffic-free walking. And the canal itself is part of the attraction, thanks to the great civil engineer Thomas Telford (1757–1834).

To collect water for the canal from the River Dee, Telford designed an elegant curving weir called **Horseshoe Falls**. The adjacent riverbank is a tranquil picnic spot. It's about 2.5 miles west of Llangollen. You can get there on foot along the canal towpath via the Llangollen Steam Railway (a 15-minute walk from Berwyn station), on bus 98, or by car along the A542 (turn left onto the B5103 after about 1.5 miles).

However, Telford's real masterpiece is the **Pontcysyllte Aqueduct**, completed in 1805 to carry the canal over the Dee. At 316m long and 38m high, it is perhaps the most spectacular piece of engineering on the entire UK canal system and the highest canal aqueduct ever built. The first stone of the aqueduct, which connected the rivers Severn, Mersey and Dee at the height of the Industrial Revolution, was laid in 1795.

More recently it was nominated by the government as a World Heritage Site. If accepted by Unesco, the aqueduct will join Stonehenge and the Tower of London on the list of 27 World Heritage Sites in Britain.

The aqueduct is about 4 miles east of Llangollen, near the village of Froncysyllte – walk along the towpath, or drive out on the A539 Ruabon road.

Llangollen Wharf (☎ 860702; Wharf Hill; www.horsedrawnboats.co.uk) arranges two options: a short excursion on the canal by **horse-drawn narrow boat** (adult/child £4.50/2.50, 45min return; ☼ 11am-4.30pm Apr-Oct) and **motorised narrow-boat trips** (adult/child £9/7, 2hr; ☼ from 12.15pm Apr-Oct). Trip options include travelling one way from Llangollen to Froncysllte, a return from Froncysllte to Bryn Howel crossing the aqueduct, or a single to Llangollen Wharf – you can combine any of these trips to travel by boat there and back. Return transport to Llangollen is provided where necessary. Only the horse-drawn narrow boats are wheelchair accessible. You can also hire self-steer boats from £100 per day.

LLANGOLLEN RAILWAY

The delightful standard-gauge **Llangollen Railway** (☎ 860979, timetable 860951; www.llangollen-railway.co.uk; adult/child/senior £8/4/6, 80min return) was once part of the Ruabon to Barmouth main line. Closed down in 1968, it was brought back to life seven years later by keen volunteers, and now runs on an 8-mile stretch up the valley from Llangollen via Berwyn (near Horseshoe Falls) to Glyndyfrdwy and Carrog.

Departures run year round, with a minimum of three departures per day between 11am and 3pm, and there are a variety of special events throughout the year (for example, steam-drawn trips with mince pies at Christmas and a heritage diesel railcar weekend in early spring).

The station is just across the river from the town centre and tickets are sold in the station café.

CASTELL DINAS BRÂN

A spectacular hill-top site, 229m above the Dee Valley and to the north of Llangollen, Dinas

---

THE LADIES OF LLANGOLLEN

The Right Honourable Lady Eleanor Butler and Miss Sarah Ponsonby, the 'Ladies of Llangollen', lived in Plas Newydd from 1780 to 1829 with their maid, Mary Carryl. They had fallen in love in Ireland, but their aristocratic Anglo-Irish families discouraged the relationship. In a desperate bid to be allowed to live together the women eloped to Wales, disguised as men, and set up home in Llangollen to devote themselves to 'friendship, celibacy and the knitting of stockings'.

Their romantic friendship became well known yet respected, and they were visited by many national figures of the day, including the Duke of Wellington, the Duke of Gloucester, William Wordsworth and Sir Walter Scott. Wordsworth called them 'sisters in love, a love allowed to climb, even on this earth above the reach of time'. He was less accepting of Plas Newydd itself, however, which he described as 'a low-browed cot'.

The ladies' relationship with their maid, Mary, was also close – most unusual for those days. Mary managed to buy the freehold of Plas Newydd, and left it to them when she died. They erected a large monument to her in the graveyard at the Church of St Collen on Bridge St, where they are also buried. Lady Eleanor died in 1829; Sarah Ponsonby was reunited with her soulmate just two years later.

Brân marks the remnants of an Iron Age fort and the tumbledown ruins of a castle whose history is shrouded in mystery. It may have been built in the late 12th century by Madog ap Gruffydd, the Welsh chieftain credited with the building of nearby Valle Crucis Abbey (p297). The castle fell to the forces of Edward I in 1277 and remained in English hands for two centuries, after which it went to ruin.

The attraction for visitors today is the fantastic panorama – northeast to the limestone escarpments of Eglwyseg Mountain, southwest to the rounded Berwyn Mountains, west to Snowdonia and east into the flattening Marches. The site is an exhilarating but strenuous 45-minute walk up from near Llangollen Wharf, taking the marked footpath at the north end of the canal bridge. Offa's Dyke Path also passes within a mile of Llangollen on the far side of Dinas Brân and crosses the Pontcysyllte Aqueduct.

OTHER SIGHTS

The **Llangollen Museum** (☎ 862862; www.llangollen museum.org.uk; admission free; ꙮ 10am-5pm Thu-Tue, 1-5pm Wed) has a small collection for fans of local history.

About a mile out of town on the A542 at Pentrefelin is the **Llangollen Motor Museum** (☎ 860324; www.llangollenmotormuseum.co.uk; adult/child £3/1; ꙮ 10am-5pm Tue-Sun Mar-Oct), featuring over 30 classic vehicles from the 1920s to the 1970s, a 1950s garage with pumps, and the owner's living room.

Activities

For walkers, branded signs around town mark out the new **Llangollen History Trail**, a 6-mile, or four-hour, circular trail following the history of the town and the surrounding Dee Valley. For a longer stroll, the **Dee Valley Way** is a 15-mile trail split into five sections that follows the course of the River Dee from Corwen to Llangollen. Allow 1½ days to cover the whole trail.

Both walks offer a chance to spot local fauna, such as birds of prey. Arm yourself with a copy of *OS Explorer Map 255* before setting out and see www.deevalleywalks.com for details of both walks.

For fans of water sports, Llangollen is an increasingly popular activity centre. In town, **ProAdventure** (☎ 861912; www.proadventure.co.uk; 23 Castle St) has kit for sale and offers a range of courses, including a white-water kayaking taster day (from £90), a rock climbing day (from £80) and family adventure days (from £220).

Less than a mile west of Llangollen on the A5, **JJ Canoeing & Rafting** (☎ 860763; www.jjraftcanoe .com; Mile End Mill, Berwyn Rd) offers a range of activities and instruction year round, such as canoeing (from £95 per day), kayak instruction (from £40 per two hours) and gorge walking (from £40 per day). You can bring your own equipment and use the river for a £5 water fee.

Festivals & Events

The **International Musical Eisteddfod** (☎ 862000; www.international-eisteddfod.co.uk) celebrated its 60th anniversary in 2006. Dylan Thomas praised the first event, declaring that the 'town sang and danced, as though it was right.' It now takes place in the Royal International Pavilion, a purpose-built pavilion just less than a mile northwest of the centre, for six days each July. It's a massive, multilingual affair, with over 12,000 performers from over 50 countries and crowds of more than 150,000 people.

The **Llangollen Fringe Festival** (☎ 860600; www .llangollenfringe.co.uk) has grown in stature to something akin to a mini version of the famous Edinburgh Fringe Festival. The event enters its 10th year in 2007 with talks, poetry, music and theatre, the majority of performances taking place at the **Town Hall** (Castle St).

Sleeping

Llangollen YHA (☎ 860330; Tyndwr Rd; dm full-board £24.95) This hostel now only caters for groups and offers a set-price all-in deal. It's a great setting in an old Victorian manor house and is surrounded by woodland, but it's rather a slog on foot at 2 miles southeast of town. A taxi to the hostel costs £4.

Plas Tegid (☎ 861013; Abbey Rd; s/d with shared bathroom £25/50; ꙮ Easter–end Sep) A welcoming place with simple, good-value rooms during the high season only.

Greenbank (☎ 861835; www.greenbank.uk.com; Victoria Sq; s/d/annex used as 2 doubles £30/50/100) Walk into Greenbank and first impressions are positive: there's a cosy private dining room for group dinner parties. Upstairs the threadbare aesthetics are less inviting. But for simple rooms close to town, this place does well out of groups coming for local activities and sports, especially for its two annexed cottages, where groups can split the cost. The B&B runs an appealing steakhouse in the evenings with mains and à la carte specials from around £10.

Cornerstones B&B (☎ 861569; www.cornerstones -guesthouse.co.uk; 15 Bridge St; s/d/f £35/60/75; P ✕) For an intimate but relaxed stay, this converted 16th-century house has three individually styled rooms with sloping floorboards and oak beams. The River Room is a double with views overlooking the River Dee while The Suite comes with a sofa bed suitable for conversion to a family room. Some nice homely touches, such as in-room DVDs and big, cooked breakfasts, give this place the edge.

Oakmere Guesthouse (☎ 861126; www.oakmere .llangollen.co.uk; Regent St; s/d £45/60) Set back from the A5 Shrewsbury Rd, along a genteel gravel drive, this charismatic Victorian property in a refined setting is a little on the formal side. The rooms are comfortable but best of all is a cheery conservatory area with views across the well-groomed gardens.

Eating

Honey Pots Ceramic Café (☎ 869008; www.honeypots .com; 18 Castle St; ♿) Excellent little café with an artistic motif: upstairs you can paint your own pot over coffee for £3.50, plus the cost of the pottery – excellent for families. There are also hand-painted pots for sale.

Corn Mill (☎ 869555; Dee Lane; mains £7.45-14.75; ⏱ noon-9.30pm) With its young, buzzy feel, excellent riverside location, and stripped floorboards and exposed stone walls, the Corn Mill has the broadest appeal in town. The water mill still turns at the heart of this converted mill while an outdoor deck above the river makes a great lunch spot in summer. The food is superior fare with the odd tasty surprise, such as a range of desert wines and enticing vegetarian options.

Gales Wine Bar (☎ 860089; www.galesofllangollen.co .uk; 18 Bridge St; mains around £10; ⏱ lunch & dinner Mon-Sat; ✕) With 30 years of history as a wine bar and a 100-strong wine list that spans the globe, this wood-lined eatery, with a huge log burner, is a friendly and popular spot with a relaxed feel. Inventive mains make the most of local produce with daily changing menus based around lamb, steaks and fish. The owners also accommodation (singles/doubles £50/60) in comfortable rooms with a continental breakfast.

Pierson's Butchers (☎ 860650; Castle St) sells hot food and the adjacent delicatessen, **James Bailey** (☎ 860617; Castle St) has home-made pies – try a Welsh Oggie (a meat, potato and onion pasty).

For self-caterers, there's a **Somerfield supermarket** (Regent St; ⏱ 8am-8pm Mon-Thu & Sat, to 9pm Fri, 10am-4pm Sun).

Drinking & Entertainment

Fouzi's (☎ 861340; Castle St) This espresso bar with a few Italian-influenced snacks in the newly revamped Royal Hotel complex is a simple but useful drop-in for a caffeine fix.

Wynnstay Arms (☎ 860710; Bridge St; bar meals ⏱ noon-8.30pm Mon-Sat; ♿) The liveliest pub is the Wynnstay Arms, with real ales, a beer garden, bar menus friendly to vegetarians and children, and Sunday roasts served from noon to 4pm.

Hand Hotel (☎ 861616; Bridge St) This place hosts the Llangollen Male Voice Choir each Friday evening. Head to the bar around 9pm and catch them in full voice over a pint of Plessey Bitter.

Shopping

Tuesday is market day, with produce, handicrafts and more in the car park on Market St.

Getting There & Away

Bryn Melyn bus X5 and GHA Coaches 555 run every 15 minutes to/from Wrexham (30 minutes) via Ruabon (15 minutes) from Monday to Saturday; Arriva's 5A service and GHA X94 runs 10 and two services respectively, with roughly hourly departures on Sundays.

National Express coach 420 runs daily from Llangollen to London via Birmingham and Shrewsbury, leaving at 7.45am – you can buy tickets at the tourist office.

Llangollen's train station serves the Llangollen Railway (see p299) only. The nearest main-line station is at Ruabon, 6 miles east on the Shrewsbury–Chester mainline.

AROUND LLANGOLLEN
Chirk Castle

Southeast of Llangollen near the English border, **Chirk Castle** (☎ 01691-777701; adult/child £7/3.50, garden only £4.50/2.20; castle ⏱ noon-5pm Mar-Sep, to 4pm Oct, gardens 10am-6pm Mar-Sep, to 5pm Oct) is a NT property with sweeping views over the English borderlands. This handsome Marcher fortress (built in 1310) was bought in 1595 by the Myddelton family, who adapted it for more comfortable living and still live there today. It has fine formal gardens, with sculpted hedges lining the pathways and a farm shop with estate and local produce.

The castle is 2 miles west of Chirk village, itself 6 miles from Llangollen.

Erddig

The Yorke family home for over two centuries (until 1973), **Erddig** (☎ 01978-355314; adult/

child/family £8/4/20, grounds only £5/2.50/12.50; ☿ house noon-5pm Sat-Wed Apr-Sep, plus noon-5pm Thu Jul & Aug, noon-4pm Sat-Wed Oct & Mar, garden 11am-5pm Sat-Wed late Mar–early Apr & Oct, 11am-6pm Sat-Wed Apr-Jun & Sep, 10am-6pm Sat-Thu Jul & Aug, 11am-4pm Sat & Sun Nov & Dec) gives an unusually illuminating look into the life of the British upper classes in the 19th century, and perhaps the best insight in the UK into the 'upstairs-downstairs' relationship that existed between masters and their servants.

The Yorkes were known for the respect with which they treated their servants. Below the stairs are portraits and photographs of servants through the years, and a collection of household appliances of the time.

Today the property is managed by the NT with much of the family's original furniture on display in the fine staterooms and the numerous outbuildings home to a variety of displays and shops. A formal walled garden has been restored in Victorian style and features rare fruit trees, a canal and the National Ivy Collection. Complete with two café-style restaurants and extensive woodland walks, it makes a good family outing.

Erddig is about 12 miles northeast of Llangollen in the village of Rhostyllen, signposted off the A483.

OTHER NORTH COAST HIGHLIGHTS

This area of the coastline, with its wall-to-wall caravan sites, fish and chips shops and run-down seaside resorts, does not put Wales' best face forward. But following the North Coast train line from Chester (England) to Holyhead (Anglesey) does reveal a few hidden gems. Don't bother stopping at the tacky seaside resorts along the way, but instead seek out these worthwhile diversions from the journey.

Ewloe Castle

One of the great Welsh castles, **Ewloe Castle** (Cadw; Wepre Park; admission free) is hidden away in a hollow, making it come as quite a surprise when you stumble upon it – unusual in a country where most castles dominate hilltops. You walk through the woods to find the honey-and-red-coloured ruins – making for an unusually serene site. Most likely built in the middle of the 13th century by Llywelyn ap Gruffydd, you can make out the D-shaped Great Tower that was typical of Welsh castles of that era. The eerily remote location may account for the strange phenomena that have been reported here, such as mysterious lights, the sound of marching men and ghostly singing.

A WALK IN THE CLWYDIAN RANGES

Most walkers tend to rush on past the Clwydian Ranges in their haste to get to Snowdonia, making it a lesser known area for walking. But it's very manageable with well-marked paths and ideal for a half- to full-day's walking from nearby bases such as Llandudno or Llangollen. Many of the walks are less than 8 miles and some criss-cross the Offa's Dyke Path, verging mainly on the western side of the designated Area of Outstanding Natural Beauty.

The trailhead for many of the walks is best accessed from the **car park** (per day £5) at the **Loggerheads Country Park Centre** (☿ 10am-4.30pm Sat, Sun & school holidays, 10am-4pm at other times), which is located on the A494 Mold to Ruthin Rd.

One of the best walks is an easy and well-marked 5-mile romp up Moel Famau (555m), the highest point on the Clwydian Ranges. The Jubilee Tour, the ruined monument at the top of Moel Famau, was built in 1810 for the 50th jubilee of King George III and offers a spectacular 360° view across the Northwest from Liverpool to the Cheshire Plains. From the summit there are also clear views over to Snowdonia and Cadar Idris. The original monument, a 35m obelisk, was the first Egyptian-style monument to be built in Britain.

The walk ends in the pretty village of Cilcain at the **White Horse** (bar meals ☿ noon-2pm & 7-9pm), a converted 16th-century coaching inn, and the ideal place to rest up, although the selection of beers is disappointing. The pub featured in the film _Hilary and Jackie_ as a location shoot for some interior scenes and is now marked as part of the North Wales Film & Television Trail (see the boxed text, opposite).

From Cilcain the 2-mile Leete path is a woodland trail leading back to Loggerheads Country Park Centre – cross over the bridge at the bottom of the village and it's signposted on the right-hand side.

THE NORTH WALES FILM & TELEVISION TRAIL

It all started with the filming of the *Inn of the Sixth Happiness* in 1958 in Beddgelert. The film, starring Ingrid Bergman and Burt Kwok (better known for his role in the *Pink Panther*), blazed a trail for other filmmakers and stars to follow. Kwok returned to Beddgelert in 2004 to unveil the first of the film plaques in the main street and, hence, the North Wales Film & Television Trail was born.

Today nine plaques trace a route across North Wales that follows in the footsteps of the stars. A further 20 plaques are planned along the trail that stretches from Llandudno to Blaenau Ffestioniog via Menai Bridge in Anglesey. Big-name stars who have graced the trail include Angelina Jolie in Snowdonia (*Tomb Raider 2 – Lara Croft and the Cradle of Life;* 2003), Emily Watson and Rachel Griffiths in Cilcain, near Mold (*Hilary and Jackie;* 1998) and David Tenant and Peter O'Toole at Chirk Castle (*Casanova;* 2005). There's even a plaque in Llanberis in memory of Sid James and Kenneth Williams (*Carry On Up The Khyber;* 1968).

In recent years Wales has become a popular location for film and TV directors, and tourism officials identified the trail as a way to boost tourism, especially in the often-overlooked North Wales borderlands region. The Wales Screen Commission is responsible for the Film & Television Trail, while the Movie Map was commissioned by Tourism Partnership North Wales. It's estimated that the North Wales initiative will lead to film buffs boosting the region's economy by an extra £1 million annually, with many visitors coming from the United States.

The locations link together to form a route across North Wales. See regional chapters for details of local transport and check the website www.moviemapnw.co.uk for a full list of the locations of the plaques. For more details, see www.walesscreencommission.co.uk.

The castle is situated off the A55. The nearest train station is at Shotton, on the North Coast line.

Bodelwyddan Castle

This Welsh outpost of the **National Portrait Gallery** (NPG; ☎ 01745-584060; www.bodelwyddan-castle.co.uk; adult/child £5/2; ☼ 10.30am-5pm daily Jul-Sep, 10.30am-5pm Tue-Thu Mar-Jul & Sep, 10.30am-4pm Thu, Sat & Sun Jan-Mar & Nov-Dec) occupies a magnificent limestone-turreted house set in parkland. Nineteenth-century life is brought alive here, with much of the house built between 1800 and 1852 and the building designed by architects including Joseph Hansom of Hansom cab renown. The building houses exhibits from London's Victoria and Albert Museum and from the 19th-century collection of the NPG as well as many contemporary pieces.

The 1st-floor galleries have been refurbished and now house intriguing temporary exhibits.

Across the road is the distinctive landmark of the white **Marble Church** with its towering 62m spire that looms over the region. The interior is characterised by the marble arcades that give the church its name, while the churchyard tells a story of local men and international victims of WWII.

The castle and church are both situated on the A55 Expressway from Chester to Bangor, or the nearest train station is Rhyll on the North Coast line.

ANGLESEY & THE NORTH COAST

Directory

CONTENTS

PRACTICALITIES

- Wales uses the metric system for weights and measures. However, speed and distance are measured in miles, and pubs still pull pints.

- Wales uses the PAL video system (incompatible with both the French SECAM system and the North American and Japanese NTSC system).

- Recharge your mobile with a three-pin (square) adaptor plugged into the 240V AC, 50Hz electricity supply.

- Flick through the popular *Daily Post* or the *Western Mail,* Wales' only national English-language daily newspaper.

- For the low-down on what's happening around the country, try the magazines *Cambria, Planet,* or *Golwg* (Vision).

- Tune in to BBC Radio Wales (103.9FM) for English-language news and features, or BBC Radio Cymru (a range of frequencies between 103.5FM and 105FM) for the Welsh-language version.

- Sianel Pedwar Cymru (S4C) is the national Welsh-language broadcaster.

ACCOMMODATION

Where accommodation listings in this book are broken down by price, we have used the following breakdown, based on two people sharing a double room: budget (less than £25 per person); midrange (£25 to £50 per person); and top-end (more than £50 per person).

Budget accommodation includes camp sites, bunkhouses and hostels as well as cheaper B&Bs and guesthouses without private bathrooms or with limited facilities. Midrange options include costlier B&Bs, hotels, pubs, inns and university accommodation. Here visitors receive a private bathroom, tea-and-coffee-making facilities, TV and phone.

Top-end listings, many of them converted castles and mansions, include Wales' best hotels. In these places the service and facilities should be exemplary. The worst-value accommodation tends to be in big towns, and cheap B&Bs are rare in city centres. Single rooms seem to be in short supply everywhere.

Grading

VisitWales (www.visitwales.com), the national tourist board, operates a grading system based on facilities and quality of service. Participating hostels, hotels, guesthouses, B&Bs and camp sites usually display their star-rating. In practice, however, there's variability within each classification, and some one-star guesthouses are better than the three-star hotel around the block.

Some excellent B&Bs don't participate in the system at all because they have to pay to do

BOOK ACCOMMODATION ONLINE

For more accommodation reviews and rec-
ommendations by Lonely Planet authors,
check out the online booking service at
www.lonelyplanet.com. You'll find the true,
insider lowdown on the best places to stay.
Reviews are thorough and independent.
Best of all, you can book online.

so. Tourist offices rarely mention good non-
participating places, or may simply dismiss
them as 'not approved'. In the end, actually
seeing a place and talking to the owner will
give the best clue as to what to expect.

It's worth ordering a copy of VisitWales'
annually updated accommodation guide
through its website. Although listed establishments are VisitWales-approved it's worth
keeping in mind that the descriptions are actually provided by the proprietors.

For online information about accommodation, try www.stayinwales.co.uk or www.wales
directory.co.uk.

Reservations

It is essential to book ahead for Easter and
Christmas, and for the peak season (mid-May
to mid-September), especially July and August,
which are the busiest months. Outside peak
season room rates are often reduced and special offers may be available – it's always worth
asking. In most city hotels rates are reduced at
weekends, when there are no business people
to fill the rooms.

Most tourist offices will book accommodation for you for a £2 fee plus a 10% deposit
(the latter is then deducted from your accommodation bill). For the same charge, most can
also book your next two nights' accommodation anywhere in the UK, under the Book-A-
Bed-Ahead (BABA) scheme. Outside opening
hours, many tourist offices put up a list of local
places with beds available as of closing time.

B&Bs & Guesthouses

Almost anywhere you go in Wales you'll
find reasonably priced, comfortable B&Bs –
essentially just private houses with bedrooms
to let, with prices from around £20 to £40 per
person. Outside Cardiff, Swansea and Snowdonia, you're unlikely to have to pay more than
£30, even in high season. Some of the finest
and most family-friendly B&Bs are in rural

farmhouses, used to the muddy boots and appetites of walkers, cyclists and climbers.

Guesthouses, which are often just large
converted houses with half a dozen rooms, are
an extension of the B&B idea. Prices are a little
higher than at B&Bs and in general they're
less personal and more like small hotels, but
without the same level of service.

Both B&Bs and guesthouses usually have
central heating, TV, tea-and-coffee-making
facilities and a wash basin. Better places have
at least some rooms with private bathrooms.
Double rooms will often have twin beds, so
you don't have to be too familiar to share.
Breakfast generally offers a choice between
an artery-clogging concoction of fried eggs,
bacon, sausages and tomatoes – enough to
fill you for most of the day – or a healthier
alternative of cereal, fruit and yoghurt.

Camping & Caravan Parks

Free camping is rarely possible in Wales but
there are plenty of camp sites around the
country, concentrated in the national parks
and along the coast. Most camp sites have
reasonable facilities, though quality can vary
widely and some can be tricky to reach without your own transport.

Local tourist offices will have information
on nearby sites, as well as free catalogues of
camp sites all around their region. VisitWales
lists approved caravan and camp sites in their
accommodation guide *Where to Stay,* which
you can order online. Other useful references
are the website of the **Royal Automobile Club** (RAC;
www.rac.co.uk) and its publication *Camping and
Caravanning in Britain.*

Expect to pay between £8 and £15 a night
for two people plus a tent, although on some
basic sites prices may be lower, especially in
the off season. Most sites are only open from
March or April to October, so phone before
going out of your way at other times.

For more information, try the following
organisations' websites:

Camping & Caravanning Club (☎ 0845 130 7632;
www.campingandcaravanningclub.co.uk) The annual membership fee of £33 is good value for campers. The club runs
many of its own sites and has a guide to several thousand
others across Europe where members can get discounts.

Campsites (www.campsites.co.uk) Provides listings and
links to websites where you can make online bookings for
camp sites.

Forestry Commission (☎ 0845 130 8223; www.forest
holidays.co.uk) Information on camping in forest sites.

DIRECTORY

Freedom Park Holidays (www.freedom-hols.co.uk)
Lists all VisitWales-approved sites.

Home Swaps

An economical accommodation option is swapping houses. Agencies specialising in organising a house swap typically charge anywhere between £30 and £115 to join and advertise your property. For more information, try www.home base-hols.com, or www.homelink.org.uk.

Hostels

Wales has a great variety of youth hostels, both independent and affiliated with the International Youth Hostel Federation (IYHF), and you don't have to be young or single to use them.

Youth Hostel Association (YHA; ☎ 0870 770 8868; www.yha.org.uk) hostels tend to be in rural areas, or in town suburbs, have daytime lockouts and 11pm curfews. Independent hostels are generally much more relaxed about these matters and are usually close to the city centre. A few even have small licensed bars.

Nightly rates for a dorm bed range from about £10 to £18 for adults; for under-18s YHA hostels charge around 70% of the adult rate. Holders of Wales Flexipass travel passes (see p326) get a £1 discount at YHA hostels. Bed linen is generally included in the price.

You'll need a Hostelling International (HI) card to stay at YHA hostels; you can purchase one on the YHA website, or over the phone if you're in a hurry. If you don't get a card before you leave home, you can join through a system of 'welcome stamps', available at most hostels: a £2 stamp is purchased at each of your first six hostels, after which you become a member.

In general, it's a good idea to call ahead and check availability at hostels, and it's essential at peak holiday times.

For more information, pick up a copy of the *Independent Hostel Guide* at tourist offices or bookshops and try the websites of **Hostels Wales** (www.hostelswales.com) and **Hostels of Europe** (www.hostelseurope.com).

Hotels

The term 'hotel' is used with abandon in Wales, and may refer to anything from a pub to a castle. In general, hotels tend to have a reception desk, room service and other extras such as a licensed bar. Many offer weekend-break and other promotional rates, so if you're booking ahead, ask if they offer any discounts.

The very best hotels are magnificent places, often with restaurants to match. In rural areas you'll find country-house hotels set in vast grounds, and castles complete with crenellated battlements, grand staircases, oak panelling and the obligatory rows of stags' heads. For such places you can pay from £75 to more than £120 per person.

A new breed of boutique hotel has also emerged, offering individually styled designer rooms, clublike bars filled with leather sofas, top-quality restaurants and a range of spa treatments.

Three websites with select lists of atmospheric accommodation are **Wales in Style** (www.walesinstyle.com), **Great Little Places** (www.wales.little-places.co.uk) and **Welsh Rarebits** (www.welsh.rarebits.co.uk).

Pubs & Inns

Many country pubs offer midrange accommodation, though they vary widely in quality. Staying in a pub or inn can be good fun as it places you at the hub of the community, but they can be noisy; they aren't always ideal for solo women travellers, as they are often a male-dominated environment, where a single woman might attract unwanted attention. They usually have a lounge where

---

CAMPING BARNS & BUNKHOUSES

Camping barns and their more comfortable brothers, bunkhouses, primarily cater to walkers and are often in spectacular settings but with little public-transport access and few places close by to go for a bite or a beer. Bunkhouses generally have dormitory accommodation, hot showers, drying rooms, stoves for heating and cooking, and usually a social area of some sort. You're expected to bring your own sleeping bag and food supplies, and to generally look after yourself. The majority of those in Wales are in or around the Brecon Beacons National Park. Bunkhouses tend to get block-booked by groups in summer, but can usually accommodate individuals during the week and outside peak season. Expect to pay about £10 to £15 in the best places. For a listing of Welsh bunkhouses, check out www.hostelswales.com.

RESTAURANTS WITH ROOMS

A burgeoning new concept in Wales is the **restaurant with rooms** (www.restaurantswith rooms.net). It's a unique combination of gourmet food and a small number of lovingly decorated rooms, generally overseen by an owner/chef who's dedicated to the cause of bringing good food to the discerning. With accommodation only a staircase away you can sit back, relax and really enjoy your meal – without the need of a designated driver.

---

cheap meals are served; some also have decent restaurants.

Slightly more upscale from pubs are former coaching inns, offering what Brits like to call an 'olde-worlde atmosphere'. But the atmosphere at such places tends to inflate the prices, and you're best to check out the room no matter how elegant the front desk looks.

Rental Accommodation

There's plenty of rental accommodation around Wales, much of it of a high standard; a cottage for four can cost as little as £400 per week. Outside weekends and July and August, it's not essential to book a long way ahead, in which case the nearest tourist office can often help you find a place. The variety of cottages on offer means there's something to suit most visitors – traditional stone farmhouses, tiny quaint cottages, cleverly converted farm buildings, gracious manor houses and seaside hideaways. Quality and service are on the up, and you can even arrange an upmarket package with helicopter transfers, catering and someone to unpack for you at your smart, designer property.

For something special the **National Trust** (NT; ☎ 0870 458 4422; www.nationaltrustcottages.co.uk) has some really splendid rural properties that are let as holiday cottages. Similarly stunning rentals are offered by the **Landmark Trust** (☎ 01628-825925; www.landmarktrust.co.uk), an architectural charity that rescues unique old buildings, often in conjunction with the NT, and supports the work by renting them out.

For other properties, check out the following websites:

www.breconcottages.com For the Brecon Beacons area.
www.coastalcottages.co.uk Pembrokeshire options.
www.qualitycottages.co.uk Covers all of Wales.

www.ruralretreats.co.uk Properties in the three Welsh national parks and the rest of the UK.
www.sts-holidays.co.uk Sea and mountain cottages in Snowdonia.
www.wales-holidays.co.uk Covers all of Wales.

Resorts

Wales' attempts at resorts are rather low-key by international standards. Llandudno in the north and Tenby in the south are as close as Wales comes to palm trees and promenades. At both, development is understated and there are no vast condo complexes or international hotels. It's more Victoriana and blue rinse than tequilas and casinos, and many are blighted by vast windswept caravan parks. Llandudno is popular year-round and has a graceful air and some great beaches. Tenby is slightly trendier and attracts a young surfing crowd as well as the bus tours. For more information, see www.britishresorts.co.uk.

University Accommodation

Many University of Wales campuses offer student rooms to visitors during the holidays usually for three weeks over Easter and Christmas and from late June to late September. Rooms tend to be comfortable, functional singles, and many come with private bathrooms. Aberystwyth and Swansea have the greatest choice of rooms. Full-board, half-board, B&B and self-catering options are available. A B&B option normally costs from £22 to £28 per person.

For more information, contact **Venuemasters** (☎ 0114-249 3090; www.venuemasters.co.uk).

ACTIVITIES

Despite the weather, Wales is a great place for outdoor pursuits. Check the Outdoor Activities chapter (p58) for details.

THE END OF DRY SUNDAY

'Dry Sunday', the prohibition against drinking alcohol on the Sabbath, dates back more than two centuries to the time of religious revivals. Regular campaigns were mounted in the 20th century that called for an end to the tradition, but the first Welsh districts to vote for an end to the practice only did so in the 1970s. It was 1995 before the last of them, Dwyfor (essentially all of the Llŷn), went 'wet'.

BUSINESS HOURS

Offices are generally open from 9am to 5pm weekdays, and banks from 9.30am to 4.30pm. Shops generally stay open until 5.30pm or 6pm and most open all day on Saturday. An increasing number of shops also open on Sunday, from 11am to 4pm. Late-night shopping (to 8pm) is usually on Thursday or Friday.

Cafés tend to be open from 9am to 5pm Monday to Saturday, while restaurants generally open from noon to 2pm and also 6pm to 10pm. Pubs and bars usually open at around 11am and close at 11pm (10.30pm on Sunday). Many pubs in larger towns have late licences and stay open until 2am from Thursday to Saturday.

Many businesses in small and country towns have a weekly early-closing day – it's different in each region of the country, but is usually Tuesday, Wednesday or Thursday afternoon – though not all shops honour it. Early-closing is more common in winter.

If someone tells you a place (eg a shop, café or restaurant) opens daily, they almost always mean 'daily except Sunday'.

See also Post (p316) and Tourist Information (p317).

CHILDREN

Forward planning and a bit of research generally make for a much smoother ride when travelling with children.

In Wales most hotels, B&Bs and restaurants offer a warm welcome to families, but to avoid hassle confirm this when you book. Also pick up a copy of VisitWales' free brochure, *A View of Wales,* which gives plenty of helpful tips and ideas for family holidays and activities.

Wales presents no major health risks for children, other than cold, wet mountains and the occasional hot and sunny beach. For more general and wide-ranging suggestions for keeping children healthy and entertained, pick up Lonely Planet's *Travel with Children,* and talk to fellow travellers with kids for the best up-to-the-minute advice.

Practicalities

Generally, cafés and middle- and lower-bracket restaurants are quite tolerant of children and have highchairs. Many pubs have gardens with playgrounds and children's menus and most hotels and B&Bs can rustle up a baby cot or heat a bottle.

Baby-changing facilities are available in most supermarkets, bigger train stations, motorway service stations and at major attractions. Some trains also offer separate family carriages, where you needn't cringe when your tots enjoy themselves at high volume. If you're hiring a car and need a baby or booster seat, specify this at the time of booking.

Sights & Activities

Preschool children usually get into museums and other sights for free, and those aged up to about 16 get in for one-half to two-thirds of the adult price.

There are lots of friendly farm parks and zoos where children can help with feeding and get to know the animals, as well as loads of coastal amusements, and hundreds of fascinating castles and ruins worth exploring.

For older children, multiactivity centres, horse-riding schools and some excellent interactive museums should provide ample entertainment without boring you to tears. In the Cardiff area in particular you can go mad on museums, which have some excellent programmes for children. Heritage parks and industrial sights can also be real winners, and they offer the chance to go into mines, pan for gold and explore workers cottages. The Centre for Alternative Technology (p234) is also worth a detour for its sheer joy of discovery.

Wales also has some great natural attractions for children, including massive caves in the Brecon Beacons; incredible beaches along the coast, most of which have plenty of fun activities and adventure sports for children; and resorts with plenty of distractions in Rhyl, Llandudno (p292) and Tenby (p165).

If you fancy seeing animals in the wild, the best bet is going on a boat tour from the Pembrokeshire coast, where you can spot seals, dolphins and whales. Also worth considering is a trip through stunning scenery on one of the country's many preserved steam railways.

For more information on activities for kids, take a look at our Wales for Kids itinerary (p27), or visit the Wales page of www.travelforkids.com.

CLIMATE CHARTS

No-one goes to Wales looking for a tan, but it's not all rain clouds and gloomy days. October to January are the wettest months and although it can rain at any time of year, summers are generally mild and fresh with average temperatures just below 20°C. In general, the coast is the driest part of the country and

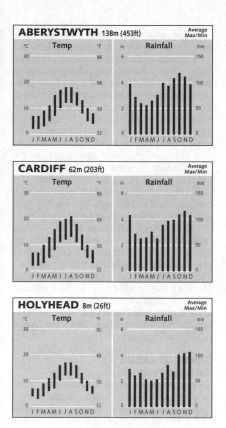

the mountains the wettest. Mt Snowdon gets several weeks of the white stuff per year, while the Cambrian Mountains and Brecon Beacons get about half that amount.

The weather in Wales is unpredictable, and conditions can change within a matter of hours, so if you're out and about, be prepared!

For more information, see p18.

COURSES
Welsh Language
The obvious subject for courses in Wales – and one you'd be hard-pressed to study anywhere else – is the Welsh language. Courses are taught throughout the country from March to September, including three- and four-day family courses, weekend and week-long intensives, and residential courses for those prepared to spend one to six weeks immersed in the language. Most immersion courses are based on a programme called Wlpan (*ool*-pahn), an

adopted Hebrew word for the Hebrew-language programme on which they're based.

Major centres include the **University of Wales** (www.wales.ac.uk) campuses at **Aberystwyth** (www .aber.ac.uk), **Bangor** (www.bangor.ac.uk), **Cardiff** (www .cf.ac.uk) and **Swansea** (www.swan.ac.uk); there are other educational centres at Abergavenny, Builth Wells, Conwy, Dolgellau, Fishguard, Harlech, Mold, Newport and Pontypridd.

The **Welsh Language Board** (Bwrdd yr Iaith Gymraeg; ☎ 029-2087 8000; www.bwrdd-yr-iaith.org.uk) publishes a leaflet with details of summer and residential courses available. The year-round **Welsh Language and Heritage Centre** (Nant Gwrtheyrn; ☎ 01758-750334; www.nantgwr.com), in the Welsh-speaking heartland of the Llŷn, caters for all levels and is ideal for families and individuals who are looking to spend time in Snowdonia. Typical prices at the Welsh Language and Heritage Centre for a five-day course range from £275 (for nonresidential) to £395 (includes full board). A one-week taster course through **Cardiff University** (☎ 029-2087 4710; www.caerdydd .ac.uk/cymraeg/canolfan) will cost you £10 to £22.

For those keen to plug into the language before arriving, there are online beginners' courses available through **Cardiff University** (www.cs.cf.ac.uk/fun/welsh). And if you're really keen and you live in North America you can take a course at home with the **Welsh Studies Institute of North America** (www.madog.org).

Other Courses
For courses dealing with the outdoors, see the Outdoor Activities chapter (p58). Check out the following websites for a range of different courses:

www.aberystwythartscentre.co.uk Residential courses in stone carving and ceramics at Aberystwyth.

www.bucklandhall.co.uk Holistic lifestyle workshops and courses in the Brecon Beacons.

www.cat.org.uk Wide range of residential courses, from eco-renovation to the art of composting, at the Centre for Alternative Technology.

www.eryri-npa.gov.uk Offers various autumn and winter courses in Snowdonia, including art, history, folklore, photography and jewellery-making.

www.oriel.org.uk Arts-related courses, from watercolours to glass-making, at the Llŷn Peninsula.

www.shamanism.co.uk Residential courses on shamanism, which take place at a wilderness camp.

www.tynewydd.org Creative writing courses in a communal setting near Criccieth.

www.uksurvivalschool.co.uk Learn survival skills during a wild weekend in the Brecon Beacons.

CUSTOMS
Duty-Free Goods
Travellers arriving in the UK from the EU can bring into the country up to 3200 cigarettes (only 200 cigarettes if arriving from the Czech Republic, Estonia, Hungary, Latvia, Lithuania, Poland, Slovakia or Slovenia), 400 cigarillos, 200 cigars, 3kg of smoking tobacco, 10L of spirits, 20L of fortified wine (eg port or sherry), 90L of wine and 110L of beer, provided the goods are for personal use only.

Travellers arriving from outside the EU can bring in, duty-free, a maximum of 200 cigarettes *or* 100 cigarillos *or* 50 cigars *or* 250g of tobacco; 2L of still table wine; 1L of spirits *or* 2L of fortified wine, sparkling wine or liqueurs; 60mL of perfume; 250mL of eau de toilette; and £145 worth of all other goods (including gifts and souvenirs). Anything over this limit must be declared to customs officers. People under 17 do not get the alcohol and tobacco allowances.

For details of prohibited and restricted goods (such as meat, milk and other animal products), and quarantine regulations, see the website of **HM Customs & Excise** (www.hmrc.gov.uk).

Pets
The UK has draconian pet-quarantine policies to protect its rabies-free status. The Pet Travel Scheme (PETS) allows dogs and cats from a number of European countries to travel to the UK without going into quarantine. The animals must not have been outside those countries in the previous six months; they must also have an identity microchip implanted, and must have various vaccinations, tests and certifications. Other animals and all animals from outside these countries must be placed in quarantine for six months.

For more information on bringing your pet to the UK, contact your nearest UK embassy or consulate or check out the website www.defra.gov.uk/animalh/quarantine/index.htm.

DANGERS & ANNOYANCES
Wales is a pretty safe place to travel, but use your common sense when it comes to hitching, or walking in city centres at night. If you're unlucky enough to encounter a brawl outside a pub at closing time, just give it a wide berth. In general you'll receive a warm welcome all across Wales, but outside the main cities the population is overwhelmingly white and, although racists are a small minority, there have been some reports of unpleasant incidents.

The obvious things to guard are your passport, travel documents, tickets and money, and it's a good idea to bring a padlock for hostel lockers. Don't leave valuables lying around in your hotel or B&B room and never leave valuables in a car, especially overnight, even in rural locations. Look for secure parking near tourist offices and national-park visitor centres, otherwise while you're discovering the countryside someone else may be exploring the contents of your glove compartment. Report thefts to the police and ask for a statement otherwise your travel-insurance company won't pay out.

In Wales never assume that just because it's midsummer it will be warm and dry. The general wetness aside, it's even more important to treat the Brecon Beacons and Snowdonia National Parks with respect. Mist can drop with a startling suddenness, leaving you dangerously chilled and disoriented.

Never venture onto the heights without checking the weather forecast and without being sensibly clad and equipped, and always make sure someone knows where you're heading. For more information, see Hypothermia (p332) and Walking (p62).

DISCOUNT CARDS
Heritage Passes
Several passes offer good value to anyone keen to see a number of the castles, stately homes, ruined abbeys and other properties owned by Wales' heritage trusts, Cadw and the NT. See p318 for details.

Hostel Cards
If you're travelling on a budget, YHA or Hostelling International (HI) membership is a must. Membership costs £15.95/22.95 for an individual/family. There are around 40 hostels in Wales, and members are also eligible for all sorts of discounts on travel, attractions and purchases. See p306 for more information about hostelling in Wales.

Senior Cards
Travellers aged 60 and over get 50% off standard National Express bus fares with a routesixty card (www.nationalexpress.com), and 30% off most rail fares with a **Senior Railcard** (www.rail card.co.uk; £20).

Many attractions have lower admission prices for those aged over 60 or 65 (sometimes as low as 55 for women); it's always worth asking even if it's not posted.

Student & Youth Cards

The most useful of these is the **International Student Identity Card** (ISIC; www.isiccard.com; £7), issued to full-time students aged 12 years and over. It provides cheap or free admission to museums and sights, inexpensive meals in some student restaurants and discounts on many forms of transport.

If you're aged under 26 but not a student, you can apply for an **International Youth Travel Card** (IYTC/GO25/Euro26; www.euro26.org), which gives much the same discounts as the ISIC.

Student unions, hostelling organisations and student travel agencies issue both cards.

Travel Cards

If you plan to do a lot of travelling by bus or train, Wales offers some good-value travel passes, especially those marketed under the name Flexipass (see p326). Most local bus operators also offer day and family passes.

EMBASSIES & CONSULATES
UK Embassies Abroad

Overseas embassies and high commissions represent the UK, of which Wales is a part. Some are listed below; if you need the details of others, consult the website of the Foreign & Commonwealth Office (www.fco.gov.uk).

Australia (High Commission; ☎ 02-6270 6666; www.brit aus.net; Commonwealth Ave, Yarralumla, Canberra, ACT 2600)

Canada (High Commission; ☎ 613-237 1530; www .britainincanada.org; 80 Elgin St, Ottawa, Ontario K1P 5K7)

France (Embassy; ☎ 01 44 51 31 00; www.amb-grande bretagne.fr; 35 rue du Faubourg St Honoré, 75383 Paris)

Germany (Embassy; ☎ 030-20457-0; www.britisch ebotschaft.de; Wilhelmstrasse 70, 10117 Berlin)

Ireland (Embassy; ☎ 01 205 3700; www.britishembassy .ie; 29 Merrion Rd, Ballsbridge, Dublin 4)

Japan (Embassy; ☎ 03-5211 1100; www.uknow.or.jp; 1 Ichiban-cho, Chiyoda-ku, Tokyo 102-8381)

Netherlands (Embassy; ☎ 070-4270 427; www.britain .nl; Lange Voorhout 10, 2514 ED, The Hague)

New Zealand (High Commission; ☎ 04-924 2888; www.britain.org.nz; 44 Hill St, Wellington)

South Africa (High Commission; ☎ 012 421 7500; www.britain.org.za; 255 Hill St, Arcadia, 0002 Pretoria)

USA (Embassy; ☎ 202-588 7800; www.britainusa.com; 3100 Massachusetts Ave NW, Washington DC 20008)

Embassies & Consulates in the UK

It's important to realise what your own embassy (ie the embassy of the country of which you are a citizen) can and can't do to help you if you get into trouble.

Generally speaking, it won't be much help if the trouble you're in is remotely your own fault; remember that you're bound by the laws of the country you're in. Your embassy will not be sympathetic if you end up in jail after committing a crime locally, even if such actions are legal in your own country.

In genuine emergencies you might get some assistance, but only if other channels have been exhausted. For example, if you need to get home urgently, a free ticket home is exceedingly unlikely – the embassy would expect you to have insurance. If you have all of your money and documents stolen, the embassy might assist with getting a new passport, but a loan for onward travel is generally out of the question.

There are a handful of foreign consular offices in Cardiff, including the following:

Canada (☎ 2044 9635; c/o St John Cymru Wales, Beignon Close, Ocean Way, Cardiff CF24 5PB)

Ireland (☎ 029-2066 2000; Brunel House, 2 Fitzalan Rd, Cardiff CF24 0EB)

Italy (☎ 029-2034 1757; 1st fl, 14 Museum Pl, Cardiff CF10 3BH)

Netherlands (☎ 0871 226 0180; c/o Sam Smith Travel, 55 High St, Cowbridge, Cardiff CF71 7AE)

For the embassies or high commissions of most other countries, you'll have to go to London. Some foreign missions in London include the following:

Australia (☎ 020-7379 4334; www.australia.org.uk; Australia House, Strand, WC2B 4LA)

Canada (☎ 020-7258 6600; www.dfait-maeci.gc.ca /canadaeuropa/united_kingdom; 1 Grosvenor Sq, W1K 4AB)

France (☎ 020-7073 1000; www.ambafrance-uk.org; 58 Knightsbridge, SW1X 7JT)

Germany (☎ 020-7824 1300; www.london-diplo.de; 23 Belgrave Sq, SW1X 8PZ)

Ireland (☎ 020-7235 2171; fax 7245 6961; 17 Grosvenor Pl, SW1X 7HR)

Netherlands (☎ 020-7590 3200; www.netherlands -embassy.org.uk; 38 Hyde Park Gate, SW7 5DP)

New Zealand (☎ 020-7930 8422; www.nzembassy.com; New Zealand House, 80 Haymarket, SW1Y 4TQ)

South Africa (☎ 020-7451 7299; www.southafrica house.com; South Africa House, Trafalgar Sq, WC2N 5DP)

USA (☎ 020-7499 9000; www.usembassy.org.uk; 24 Grosvenor Sq, W1A 1AE)

FESTIVALS & EVENTS

Wales' biggest annual cultural events are its *eisteddfodau* (gatherings; singular *eisteddfod*), described on p47. They range from little village songfests to vast annual gatherings, of which there are three:

International Musical Eisteddfod (www.internation aleisteddfod.co.uk)

Royal National Eisteddfod of Wales (www.eisteddfod .org.uk)

Urdd Eisteddfod (www.urdd.org)

Other events to look out for include summer theatre performances at many of the castles and other properties managed by **Cadw** (www.cadw.wales .gov.uk), and ecofriendly **Festival of the Countryside** (www.foc.org.uk, www.thingstodo.org.uk) events – including fairs, art workshops and exhibitions, guided walks and wildlife watching – all promoting environmentally sensitive tourism in Wales.

There are hundreds of events in Wales throughout the year. The following list details some of the larger events; see the regional chapters for information on local celebrations.

March
Six Nations Rugby Championship (Millennium Stadium, Cardiff) The highlight of the Welsh rugby calendar. Match dates vary.

St David's Day Celebrations on 1 March all over the country in honour of the patron saint of Wales.

May
Urdd Eisteddfod (Youth Eisteddfod; www.urdd.org; changing venues) The largest youth festival of performing arts in Europe held over six days late in May or early June.

St David's Cathedral Festival (www.stdavidscathedral .org.uk; St David's) Festival of classical music with a grandiose backdrop held on the Spring Bank Holiday weekend.

Hay Festival (www.hayfestival.co.uk; Hay-on-Wye) Bookworms break for this one-week festival of literature.

June
Man vs Horse Marathon (Llanwrtyd Wells) Two legs versus four legs in this lunatic cross-country dash to win £25,000; a two-legged runner won for the first time in 2004. First Saturday in June.

Cardiff Singer of the World (www.bbc.co.uk/cardiff singer) International songsters compete in Cardiff. Takes place in odd-numbered years only.

July
International Musical Eisteddfod (www.inter national-eisteddfod.co.uk, www.llangollenfringe.co.uk; Llangollen) Swinging international music fest with an eclectic fringe held for six days in early July.

Morris in the Forest (Llanwrtyd Wells) Offbeat festival of morris dancing, ceilidhs, walks and workshops. Three-day weekend in early July.

Sesiwn Fawr Festival (www.sesiwnfawr.com; Dolgellau) Free Celtic folk festival. Third weekend in July.

Ras yr Wyddfa (www.snowdonrace.com; Llanberis) This one-day race up Snowdon is only for the truly hardy. Late July.

Royal Welsh Show (www.rwas.co.uk; Builth Wells) Sniff out the prize bullocks at Wales' biggest farm and livestock show. One week, late July.

Fishguard International Music Festival (www.fish guardfestival.org.uk; Fishguard) From chamber and orchestral to choirs and jazz. One week, late July.

Big Cheese (www.caerphilly.gov.uk/bigcheese; Caerphilly) Street theatre, folk dancing, medieval costumes and food – including some smelly cheeses. Last weekend in July.

August
Cardiff Festival (www.cardiff-festival.com; Cardiff) Europe's biggest free arts festival, with street theatre and music around the city. Two weeks culminating on the first weekend in August.

Royal National Eisteddfod (www.eisteddfod.org.uk; changing venues) The largest and oldest celebration of Welsh culture, with a fabulous fringe. Eight days in early August.

Brecon Jazz Festival (www.breconjazz.co.uk; Brecon) Smoky sounds at one of Europe's leading jazz festivals. One weekend in mid-August.

Race the Train (www.racethetrain.co.uk; Tywyn) Quirky all-terrain race pitting man against steam train. Saturday in mid-August.

Victorian Festival (www.victorianfestival.co.uk; Llandrindod Wells) Family fun and Victorian dress-ups at this week-long festival. Mid-to-late August.

World Bog Snorkelling Championships (www .worldbogsnork.com; Llanwrtyd Wells) Competitors submerge themselves in the murky bog waters for a 110m swim and their five minutes of fame. You can also try it on a mountain bike…Summer Bank Holiday Monday.

Faenol Festival (www.brynfest.com; near Bangor) An unlikely world-class mix of rock, pop and opera. Three days in late August.

September
North Wales Hot Air Balloon Festival (Llangollen) Hot air hits the skies in this blow-up bonanza. First weekend in September.

Tenby Arts Festival (www.tenbyartsfest.co.uk; Tenby) Street theatre, samba bands, classical and pop concerts. Nine days in late September.

Abergavenny Food Festival (www.abergavenny foodfestival.com; Abergavenny) All the ingredients to satisfy any gourmet – or just a sweet tooth. One weekend towards the end of September.

October
Swansea Festival (www.swanseabayfestival.net; Swansea) Drama, opera, film, ballet, jazz and classical music. Three weeks.

November
Mid-Wales Beer Festival (Llanwrtyd Wells) Scores of real ale in the town's pubs, plus beer-fuelled off-road foot and cycle races, including the Real Ale Wobble. One and a half weeks.
International Film Festival of Wales (www.iffw.co.uk; Cardiff) Art-house, indie and blockbuster films go head to head in the capital's cinemas. One week.

FOOD
Where eating listings in this book have been subdivided on price, we have used three categories based on the price of a main course at dinner: budget (mostly cafés and cheaper restaurants where main courses cost less than £7); midrange (from £7 to £15); top-end (more than £15).

For more information on the culinary delights of Wales, see p70.

GAY & LESBIAN TRAVELLERS
In general, Wales is tolerant of homosexuality; certainly it's possible for people to acknowledge their homosexuality in a way that would have been unthinkable 20 years ago. But tolerance only goes so far, as a glance at any tabloid newspaper will confirm. The age of consent for homosexual sex is 16.

Cardiff and Swansea both have active gay and lesbian scenes, and there are small above-the-parapet gay communities in Newport and in the university towns of Aberystwyth and Bangor, although overt displays of affection may not be wise beyond acknowledged venues. These two University of Wales campuses also have limited but regular social events for gay and lesbian students (and visitors) and have lesbian/gay/bisexual student officers who can be contacted for information and help. Aberystwyth also has a gay and bisexual hotline. See under those towns for further information.

Wales' biggest gay/lesbian/bisexual bash is the extravagant Cardiff Mardi Gras festival held in late August or early September (p93).

For more general information try the following sites.
Border Women (www.borderwomen.org.uk) Information, support and events for lesbians on the English–Welsh border.
Diva (www.divamag.co.uk) British lesbian magazine.
Gay Times (www.gaytimes.co.uk) British gay periodical.

Gay Wales (www.gaywales.co.uk) The best Wales-specific resource, with news, events, listings and helplines.
Lesbian & Gay Switchboard (☎ 020-7837 7324; www.llgs.org.uk; 🕑 24hr) London resource that can help with most inquiries.
Pink UK (www.pinkuk.com) UK-wide gay and lesbian resource.

HOLIDAYS
Public Holidays
Most banks, businesses, a few museums and other places of interest are closed on public holidays. A 'bank holiday' is a weekday closure that is defined generically (eg the first Monday of May) rather than associated with a particular calendar date or religious festival.

Wales' official public holidays are:
New Year's Day 1 January
Good Friday March/April
Easter Monday March/April
May Day Bank Holiday First Monday in May
Spring Bank Holiday Last Monday in May
Summer Bank Holiday Last Monday in August
Christmas Day 25 December
Boxing Day/St Stephen's Day 26 December

If New Year's Day, Christmas Day or Boxing Day falls on a weekend, the following Monday is also a bank holiday. Most museums and attractions in Wales close on Christmas and Boxing Day but stay open for the other holidays. Exceptions are those that normally close on Sunday. Some smaller museums close on Monday and/or Tuesday.

School Holidays
Peak holiday times in Wales coincide with the school holidays, notably Christmas and New Year, Easter, six weeks in July and August and two one-week midterm breaks (one in April and one in October). During these times it's essential to book accommodation in advance and be prepared for crowds at most attractions.

INSURANCE
However you're travelling, make sure you take out a comprehensive travel insurance policy that covers you for medical expenses, luggage theft or loss and for cancellation of (or delays in) your travel arrangements. When choosing a policy, check whether the insurance company will make payments directly to providers or reimburse you later for overseas health expenditures.

DIRECTORY

The international travel policies handled by STA Travel and other student travel organisations are usually good value. Some policies offer lower and higher medical-expense options; unless you're eligible for free NHS treatment (see p331), go for as much as you can afford.

Paying for your ticket with a credit card often provides limited travel-accident insurance (ie it covers accidental death, loss of limbs or permanent total disablement). You may be able to reclaim the payment if the operator doesn't deliver.

It's a good idea to photocopy all your important documents (including your travel insurance policy) before you leave home. Leave one copy with someone at home and keep another with you, separate from the originals.

INTERNET ACCESS

If you're travelling in Wales with a laptop, you should be able to connect to the internet via a hotel-room phone socket for the cost of a local call by registering with an internet roaming service such as **MaGlobe** (www.maglobe.com). Many upmarket hotels offer in-room internet connections via RJ-11 Ethernet sockets or wi-fi. For help and information on getting online from hotel rooms, see www.kropla.com.

There is an ever-increasing number of wi-fi hot spots around Wales where you can access the internet with a wi-fi-enabled laptop, including McDonald's restaurants, Starbucks coffee shops, and anywhere within 50m of blue-topped BT internet payphones; you can search for wi-fi hot spots on www.jiwire.com.

If you don't have a laptop, the best places to check email and surf the internet in Wales are public libraries – almost every town and village in the country has at least a couple of computer terminals devoted to the internet, and they are mostly free to use.

Internet cafés also exist in the cities and larger towns and generally charge around £2 to £5 per hour. Always check the minimum charge, though, before you settle in – it's sometimes not worth the 10 minutes it takes to check your emails.

Remember that many of the larger tourist offices across the country have internet access too.

LEGAL MATTERS

Police have the power to detain anyone suspected of having committed an offence punishable by imprisonment (including drugs

LEGAL AGE
Legal age requirements in Wales are the same as those for the rest of the UK.
■ Buying alcohol – 18
■ Buying tobacco – 16
■ Driving – 17 (16 for a moped)
■ Heterosexual and homosexual sex – 16
■ Marriage – 16
■ Voting – 18

offences) for up to six hours. They can search you, take photographs and fingerprints, and question you. You are legally required to provide your correct name and address – not doing so, or giving false details, is an offence – but you are not obliged to answer any other questions. After six hours, the police must either formally charge you or let you go. If you are detained and/or arrested, you have the right to inform a lawyer and one other person, though you have no right to actually see the lawyer or to make a telephone call. If you don't know a lawyer, the police will inform the duty solicitor for you.

In the wake of September 11, the UK parliament passed the *Anti-Terrorism, Crime and Security Act 2001*. The legislation makes it possible for the government to detain foreigners suspected of terrorist activities, without trial. Since the London Underground and bus bombings in July 2005, further laws are being considered.

Possession of a small amount of cannabis is an offence punishable by a fine, but possession of a larger amount of cannabis, or any amount of harder drugs, is much more serious, with a sentence of up to 14 years in prison. Police have the right to search anyone they suspect of possessing drugs.

You're allowed to have a maximum blood-alcohol level of 35mg/100mL when driving. Traffic offences (illegal parking, speeding etc) often incur a fine for which you're usually allowed 30 to 60 days to pay.

MAPS

Two useful countrywide maps, updated annually by VisitWales, are available at nearly every tourist office. The *Wales Tourist Map* presents all major roads and major sights, national parks, towns with tourist offices (and a list of those open in winter), several town plans, and suggested car tours. The free *Wales Bus, Rail and Tourist Map and Guide* manages to map just about every bus and train route in Wales that has more than about three services per week, plus the essentials of bus, train and ferry connections into Wales, as well as tables of frequencies and information numbers.

Free regional transport booklets, with complete maps and timetables, are also available at tourist offices, and train stations stock free timetables provided by each train operator.

For walkers and cyclists, it's essential to have a good map before setting off on any trip. Most tourist offices and local bookshops stock maps produced by the UK's national mapping agency, the **Ordnance Survey** (OS; www.ordnancesurvey .co.uk), which cover their regions, including the useful 1:50,000 Landranger series and the excruciatingly detailed 1:25,000 Explorer series. OS Pathfinder Walking Guides cover short walks in popular areas, and Outdoor Leisure maps cover the national parks, both at 1:25,000.

For motoring, look for the OS Routemaster series at 1:250,000. A to Z publishes 1:200,000 *North Wales* and *South Wales* road maps, with useful detailed town indexes.

Maps can be ordered online at the OS website or from www.amazon.co.uk.

MONEY

Wales uses the pound sterling (£), and the same major banks as the rest of the UK. There are 1p, 2p, 5p, 10p, 20p, 50p, £1 and £2 coins and £5, £10, £20 and £50 notes.

Most banks and larger post offices can change foreign currency; US dollars and euros are the easiest currencies to change and will get the best rates. For exchange rates, see the inside front cover.

Whichever way you decide to carry your money, it makes sense to keep most of it in a money belt and an emergency stash somewhere else.

ATMs

Nearly all banks in Wales have ATMs linked to international systems such as Cirrus, Maestro or Plus. An increasing number of ATMs, especially ones you find in shops, make a charge for withdrawal (at least £1.50).

Credit Cards

Various cards including Visa, MasterCard, American Express (Amex) and Diners Club are widely accepted in Wales, although small businesses such as B&Bs prefer cash. If your credit card is lost or stolen contact the relevant provider.
Amex (☎ 01273-696933)
Diners Club (☎ 0870 190 0011)
MasterCard (☎ 0800 964767)
Visa (☎ 0800 891725)

Tipping

In general, when you eat in a restaurant you should leave a tip of at least 10% unless the service was unsatisfactory. Waiting staff are often paid derisory wages on the assumption that the money will be supplemented by tips. If the bill already includes a service charge (usually 10%), you needn't add a further tip. Tipping in bars is not customary.

Taxis in Wales are expensive, and drivers rarely expect a tip unless they have gone out of their way to help you.

Travellers Cheques

Travellers cheques issued by Amex, Thomas Cook and Visa are widely recognised. Eurocheques are not commonly used in the UK and many places refuse to accept them. Keep a record of the numbers of your cheques and which cheques you have cashed, so if they're lost or stolen you'll be able to tell the issuing agency which cheques have gone. Keep this list separate from the cheques themselves. If they are lost or stolen contact the relevant issuer.
Amex (☎ 0800 521313)
Thomas Cook (☎ 0800 622101)
Visa (☎ 0800 895078)

PHOTOGRAPHY & VIDEO

Print film is available just about everywhere, but for slide film you'll have to go to a specialist photo shop. With dull, overcast conditions common, high-speed film (ISO 200 or ISO 400) is useful. Try to get out in the early morning or just before sunset for the gentlest light.

You can buy Mini-DV cassettes and memory cards for digital cameras at branches of Currys Digital, Dixons, Jessops, and specialist photgraphy shops.

For expert guidance pick up a copy of Lonely Planet's *Travel Photography: A Guide to Taking Better Pictures,* by Richard I'Anson.

Get some practice with your video camera before recording that holiday of a lifetime. Be particularly careful to assess the effect of background noise on the soundtrack.

Many tourist attractions charge for taking photos or prohibit photography altogether.

Use of a flash is frequently forbidden in order to protect delicate pictures and fabrics. Video cameras are often disallowed because of the inconvenience they can cause to other visitors.

POST

Mail sent within the UK can go either 1st or 2nd class. First-class mail is faster (normally next-day delivery) and more expensive (32p for a letter up to 100g) than 2nd-class mail (23p); rates depend on the size as well as weight of the letter or packet.

Airmail postcards/letters (60g) to European countries cost 44/83p; to South Africa, the USA and Canada 50p/£1.51; and Australia and New Zealand 50p/£1.66. An airmail letter generally takes five days to get to the USA or Canada and a week to Australia or New Zealand.

If you don't have a permanent address, mail can be sent to poste restante in the town or city where you're staying. Amex offices also hold card-holders' mail for free.

Post office hours vary, but most open from 9am to 5.30pm on weekdays and 9am to 12.30pm on Saturday.

SHOPPING
Crafts

The recent revival of craft industries in centres all over Wales has provided plentiful shopping fodder for visitors with a yen for anything from carved-wood dressers to ceramics, knitwear, tartan and lace. As well as the craft boom there's hardly a visitor attraction left now that doesn't have its own shop selling commemorative T-shirts, pencils, stationery, books, key rings, flags and souvenir fudge. Even the industrial sites have got in on the act, hawking repro miner's lamps and coal sculptures. Prices are often high, and quality variable, but among the furry red dragons you may just spot that ideal souvenir or gift.

VAT Refunds

Value-added tax (VAT) is a 17.5% sales tax that is levied on all goods and services in the UK except fresh food, books, newspapers and children's clothes. Non-EU citizens can claim a refund of VAT paid on most goods bought within the EU, which can make for a considerable saving.

The VAT Retail Export Scheme is voluntary and not all shops participate; look for a blue Tax-Free Shopping sign in the window. Different shops may have different minimum-purchase conditions (normally around £40).

On purchase of goods and presentation of your passport, participating shops will give you a special form called VAT 407. This form must be presented at customs, along with the goods and sales receipts, when you depart the country (VAT-free goods can't be posted or shipped home). After customs has stamped the form, you can hand it in to a refund desk (several companies offer a centralised refund service, and have desks at major UK airports) for an immediate cash refund, or mail it back to the shop for a refund by cheque (an administration fee may be charged). Alternatively, if you use a credit card for the purchases, you can ask to have your VAT refund credited to your credit-card account.

For further details, check out the website of **HM Revenue & Customs** (www.hmrc.gov.uk), call the **National Advice Centre** (☎ 0845 010 9000) or pick up the leaflet *Notice 704 – VAT Retail Exports,* available from all customs arrival points throughout the UK. For examples of centralised refund services, see www.globalrefund.com and www.premiertaxfree.com.

TELEPHONE

Wales' country code (☎ 44) is the same as that of the rest of the UK; to call from abroad, dial your country's international access code, then 44, then the area code (dropping the initial 0) followed by the phone number. To dial out of the UK, phone 00 before the country code.

Public Phones

You'll see two types of phone booth in Wales: one takes money (and doesn't give change), while the other uses prepaid phone cards and credit cards. Some phones accept both coins and cards. The minimum charge is 20p.

All phones come with reasonably clear instructions in several languages. British Telecom (BT) offers phonecards for £3, £5, £10 and £20; they're widely available from retailers, including post offices and newsagents.

Mobile Phones

Codes for mobile phones usually begin with ☎ 07. The UK uses the GSM 900/1800 network, which covers the rest of Europe, Australia and New Zealand, but isn't compatible with the North American GSM 1900 (though some North Americans have GSM 1900/900

SPECIAL-RATE UK PHONE CODES

☎ 0500	toll-free
☎ 0800	toll-free
☎ 0808	toll-free
☎ 07	mobile phone (far more expensive to call than a landline)
☎ 0845	local-call rate applies
☎ 0870	national-call rate applies
☎ 09	premium-rate numbers (60p to £1 per minute)
☎ 00	international access code

phones that work in the UK). If you have a GSM phone, check with your service provider about using it in the UK, and beware of calls being routed internationally (very expensive for a 'local' call). You can also rent a mobile phone – ask a tourist office for details – or buy a 'pay-as-you-go' UK SIM card for as little as £10.

TIME
All of the UK is on GMT/UTC in winter and GMT/UTC plus one hour during summer. Clocks are set forward by an hour on the last Sunday in March and set back on the last Sunday in October.

See the time-zone world map (p350) for information on time differences in other parts of the world.

TOURIST INFORMATION
The national tourist board, **VisitWales** (☎ 029-2049 9909; www.visitwales.co.uk; Brunel House, 2 Fitzalan Rd, Cardiff CF24 4QZ), deals with postal, telephone and email inquiries only.

Every town of any size in Wales has its own tourist office, usually run by the local council. In towns in and around one of Wales' three national parks, the tourist office may be run by the park.

You can book accommodation anywhere in Wales using the Book-A-Bed-Ahead (BABA) scheme; you'll have to pay a £2 fee and a 10% deposit, which is then deducted from the cost of your accommodation.

TRAVELLERS WITH DISABILITIES
For many disabled travellers, Wales is a strange mix of user-friendliness and unfriendliness. Most new buildings are accessible to wheelchair users, so large new hotels and modern tourist attractions are usually fine.

However, most B&Bs and guesthouses are in hard-to-adapt older buildings. This means that travellers with mobility problems may pay more for accommodation than their able-bodied fellows.

It's a similar story with public transport. Newer buses sometimes have steps that lower for easier access, as do trains, but it's always wise to check before setting out. Most tourist offices, tourist attractions and public buildings reserve parking spaces for the disabled near the entrance. Most tourist offices in Wales are wheelchair accessible, have counter sections at wheelchair height and have information on accessibility in their particular area.

Many ticket offices and banks are fitted with hearing loops to assist the hearing impaired; look for the ear logo.

VisitWales publishes useful information on accommodation for people with disabilities in its *Where to Stay* guide, which is available at tourist offices and online at www.visitwales .co.uk.

The NT has its own *Access Guide* (downloadable as a pdf file from www.nationaltrust.org .uk) and offers free admission at all sites for companions of the disabled. Cadw, the Welsh historic monument agency, allows wheelchair users and the visually impaired (and their companions) free entry to all monuments.

For more detailed information contact the following organisations:

Disability Wales (☎ 029-2088 7352; www.disability wales.org) The national association of disability groups in Wales is a good source of information.

Holiday Care Service (☎ 0845 124 9971; www .holidaycare.org.uk) Publishes a wide range of regional accommodation guides, and can offer general advice.

Royal Association for Disability & Rehabilitation (Radar; ☎ 020-7250 3222; www.radar.org.uk) Publishes an annually updated survey, *Holidays in Britain & Ireland; A Guide for Disabled People.*

Royal National Institute for the Blind (RNIB; ☎ 0845 766 9999; www.rnib.org.uk) RNIB's holiday service provides general and more detailed information for the visually impaired. It also produces a guidebook of hotels recommended by visually impaired people, which is available in large print, Braille, on tape and on disc.

Shopmobility (☎ 08456 444 442; www.justmobility .co.uk/shop) UK-wide scheme under which wheelchairs and electric scooters are available in some towns at central points for access to shopping areas. The scheme is run as a charity in Cardiff; in other Welsh towns – including Swansea, Newport, Merthyr Tydfil and Wrexham – it's council-run, with modest rental fees.

DIRECTORY

USEFUL ORGANISATIONS

Membership of Cadw (pronounced *ka*-doo; Welsh for 'to preserve'), which is the Welsh historic monuments agency, and/or the National Trust (NT) is worth considering, especially if you're going to be in Wales for a while. Both care for hundreds of spectacular sites, and membership allows you to visit for free. You can join at any staffed Cadw or NT site, by post or phone, or online.

In this book, a Cadw or NT property is indicated using one of these names in parenthesis, preceding the telephone number.

Cadw (☎ 0800 074 3121; www.cadw.wales.gov.uk; Freepost CF1142/9, Cardiff CF24 5GZ) A year's membership costs £32 for individuals, and £55 for a family (two adults plus all children under 16). Wheelchair users and the visually impaired, together with their assisting companion, are admitted free of charge to all Cadw monuments.

National Trust (☎ 0870 458 4000; www.nationaltrust .org.uk; PO Box 39, Warrington WA5 7WD) A year's membership costs £40.50 for an individual, and £73 for a family.

For visitors who are unlikely to be in the country for more than a few weeks, Cadw sells a three-/seven-day Explorer Pass for £10.50/17 per person, £17.50/28 for two people or £25/35 for a family, which entitles you to free entry to all Cadw attractions. Typical admission fees are around £2.50 to £3.50, so you'd have to plan on visiting four or more sites to make the three-day pass worthwhile.

The **Great British Heritage Pass** (www.gbheritage pass.com) gives free access to almost 600 properties under the care of Cadw, NT (and NT Scotland), Historic Scotland and English Heritage. A four-/seven-/15-/30-day pass costs £28/39/52/70 irrespective of age, but it's available only to non-British citizens. You can buy the pass online, and in the UK at many international airports and seaports (though none in Wales), from VisitBritain's Visitor Information Centre in London, and from Cardiff and Caernarfon tourist offices.

VISAS

No visas are required if you arrive in Wales from within the UK. If you arrive directly from any other country, British regulations apply.

At present, citizens of Australia, Canada, New Zealand, South Africa and the USA are given 'leave to enter' the UK at their point of arrival for up to six months, but are prohibited from working. If you're a citizen of the EU, you don't need a visa to enter the country and may live and work freely. Visa regulations are always subject to change, however; so check with your local British embassy, high commission or consulate before leaving home. For more information, see www.ukvisas.gov.uk.

To extend your stay in the UK, contact the **Home Office, Immigration & Nationality Directorate** (☎ 0870 606 7766; www.ind.homeoffice.gov.uk; Lunar House, 40 Wellesley Rd, Croydon, London CR9 2BY) *before* your existing permit expires. You'll need to send your passport with your application.

WOMEN TRAVELLERS

Women will find Wales to be a fairly enlightened place. In 2003 the Welsh National Assembly became the first legislative body in the world to have equal numbers of men and women and, although the country has a particularly strong patriarchal tradition, things are gradually beginning to change on the domestic front as well.

Gender roles were deeply ingrained in the Welsh psyche for many years; men were the breadwinners who put in long, hard days at the mine or on the land, while women stayed at home and looked after the children and the house.

The decline in agriculture and the closure of the pits has meant that there's been a very gradual process of change; however, liberated attitudes to independent women arrived later and took longer to take hold in Wales than in most other European countries. Women in Wales have now taken over most of the jobs in light manufacturing and in call centres, and traditional opinions about the role of women have all but died out.

Women travellers shouldn't encounter any problems in Wales, though they should use common sense in larger cities, especially at night. There's nothing to stop women going into pubs alone, although not everyone likes doing this. It may cause a few curious glances or a brief conversation but in general it's very rarely a problem.

Should you suffer an attack, Rape Crisis Centres can offer support. There are two in Wales:

New Pathways Rape and Sexual Abuse Support Service (☎ 01685 350099; www.newpathways.co.uk; Willow House, 57-58 Lower Thomas Street, Merthyr Tydfil CF47 0DA)

Rape & Sexual Abuse Support Centre North Wales (☎ 01286 669266; PO Box 87, Caernarfon, Gwynedd LL55 9AA)

WORK
Finding Work

Unemployment levels in Wales are hovering at around 5%, though there are some pockets of higher unemployment around the country. If you're prepared to work at menial jobs for long hours and relatively low pay, you should have little problem finding work, but you'll have a hard time saving anything on the minimum wage of £5.05 per hour (£4.25 for those aged 18 to 21), and if you're working 'under the table' no-one's obliged to pay you even that.

Low-paid seasonal work is available in the tourist industry, usually in restaurants and pubs. This was once the domain of Australian, South African and New Zealand travellers but the 2004 enlargement of the EU has seen many of these jobs taken up by young people arriving from Eastern Europe.

Professionals stand a higher chance of finding better-paid work. Check the job boards at the following websites before you leave home and register with several recruitment agencies when you arrive. It may also help to regularly check the government-operated Jobcentres in most large towns.

For details on all aspects of short-term work, pick up *Work Your Way Around the World,* by Susan Griffith.

Good job-search websites include www.fish 4jobs.co.uk; www.gojobsite.co.uk; www.job search.co.uk; and www.monsterwales.com.

Work Permits

EU nationals don't need a permit to work in the UK, but everyone else does. If you're not a EU national and the main purpose of your visit is to work, you must be sponsored by a British company.

If you're a citizen of a Commonwealth country and aged 17 to 30, however, you can apply for entry to the UK under the Working Holidaymaker Scheme, which allows you to spend up to two years in the UK and take work that is 'incidental' to a holiday. Working holiday entry certificates are not granted on arrival in the UK – you must apply to the nearest UK mission overseas – and you cannot switch from being a visitor to a working holiday-maker. When you apply you must satisfy the authorities that you have the means to pay for a return or onward journey and that you will be able to maintain yourself without recourse to public funds. After 12 months on the scheme you can switch to work-permit employment if you can find a sponsor. See www.ukvisas.gov.uk for full details.

US citizens aged 18 to 25 and full-time students at US universities (who have a green card) can get a six-month work permit through **British Universities North America Club** (www.bunac.org).

If you have any queries once you're in the UK, contact the **Immigration & Nationality Directorate** (☎ 0870 606 7766; www.ind.homeoffice.gov.uk; Lunar House, 40 Wellesley Rd, Croydon CR2 2BY).

Volunteer Work

There's plenty of opportunity to do volunteer work in Wales and it can be a great way to meet people and get to know some locals. For more information, contact the following organisations:

Centre for Alternative Technology (www.cat.org.uk) Long-term volunteer opportunities at Europe's premiere ecocentre.

European Youth Programme (www.britishcouncil .org/education) Runs a similar system to the International Voluntary Service.

International Voluntary Service (www.ivs-gb.org.uk) Runs short- and long-term projects that change annually. There may be some in Wales at the time of your visit.

National Trust (www.nationaltrust.org.uk) 'Working holidays' of two to 10 days include archaeological work, dry-stone walling and construction work on historic properties.

Willing Workers on Organic Farms (www.wwoof.org .uk) Free board and lodging in return for work on organic farms.

Youth Hostel Association (www.yha.org.uk) Volunteer to be a warden at a youth hostel.

Transport

TRANSPORT

GETTING THERE & AWAY

ENTERING THE COUNTRY

Passports must be valid for at least three months after your UK trip. Citizens of EU countries *might* only require an identity card.

Wales has an international airport at Cardiff, but the vast bulk of international connections (and the best bargains) come through London. International seaports at Swansea, Pembroke Dock, Fishguard and Holyhead have regular passenger services to and from the Republic of Ireland; otherwise, sea connections from continental Europe go through English ports.

There are no border controls between England and Wales; however if you're driving to South Wales on the M4 motorway you'll have to pay a toll as you enter the country over the Severn Bridge (to the amusement of many, it's free to leave). See p318 for details of visas.

AIR
Airports & Airlines

Wales' main international airport is **Cardiff International Airport** (☎ 01446-711111; www.cwlfly .com). There are scheduled flights into Cardiff from Canada, a handful of European cities, and several cities in England, Scotland and Ireland, plus loads of charter flights from European, Middle Eastern, North African and Caribbean destinations.

THINGS CHANGE...

The information in this chapter is particularly vulnerable to change. Check directly with the airline or a travel agent to make sure you understand how a fare (and ticket you may buy) works and be aware of the security requirements for international travel. Shop carefully. The details given in this chapter should be regarded as pointers and are not a substitute for your own careful, up-to-date research.

Just over the border in England (some 45 miles from Cardiff) is **Bristol International Airport** (☎ 0870 121 2747; www.bristolairport.co.uk), which serves a variety of UK domestic routes and also has flights to European destinations. Manchester and Birmingham also have international connections and are convenient for quick access to Mid- or North Wales.

Most of the world's major airlines fly to Heathrow and Gatwick airports in London. Many flights from European centres go to London City, Stansted or Luton airports. It's easiest to travel overland to Wales from Heathrow and Gatwick (see p322).

For flights to Cardiff (and Bristol) from European destinations, the main scheduled airlines serving Cardiff International Airport are the best source if you're looking for cheap fares. The airlines and their phone numbers in the UK are listed below.

Aer Arann (☎ 0800 587 2324; www.aerarann .com)

Air Southwest (☎ 0870 241 8202; www.air southwest.com)

bmibaby (☎ 0870 264 2229; www.bmibaby.com)

Eastern Airways (☎ 08703 669 100; www.eastern airways.com)

Excel (☎ 0870 169 0169; www.xl.com)

KLM UK (☎ 0870 507 4074; www.klmuk.com)

Thomsonfly (☎ 0870 1900 737; www.thomson fly.com)

Zoom (☎ 0870 240 0055; www.flyzoom.com)

Many of the low-cost airlines send an email notification to members when there is a promotional fare available on certain routes, so

TRANSPORT

CLIMATE CHANGE & TRAVEL

Climate change is a serious threat to the ecosystems that humans rely upon, and air travel is the fastest-growing contributor to the problem. Lonely Planet regards travel, overall, as a global benefit, but believes we all have a responsibility to limit our personal impact on global warming.

Flying & Climate Change

Pretty much every form of motor transport generates CO_2 (the main cause of human-induced climate change) but planes are far and away the worst offenders, not just because of the sheer distances they allow us to travel, but because they release greenhouse gases high into the atmosphere. The statistics are frightening: two people taking a return flight between Europe and the US will contribute as much to climate change as an average household's gas and electricity consumption over a whole year.

Carbon Offset Schemes

Climatecare.org and other websites use 'carbon calculators' that allow travellers to offset the greenhouse gases they are responsible for with contributions to energy-saving projects and other climate-friendly initiatives in the developing world – including projects in India, Honduras, Kazakhstan and Uganda.

Lonely Planet, together with Rough Guides and other concerned partners in the travel industry, supports the carbon offset scheme run by climatecare.org. Lonely Planet offsets all of its staff and author travel.

For more information check out our website: www.lonelyplanet.com.

---

it may be worth registering as a member in advance of your trip. The following websites are best for finding flights to London.

- www.bestfares.com
- www.cheaptickets.com
- www.ebookers.com
- www.expedia.com
- www.flycheap.com
- www.opodo.com
- www.priceline.com
- www.skyscanner.net

Australia & New Zealand

Many airlines compete on flights between Australia and New Zealand and the UK and there is a wide range of fares. Round-the-World (RTW) tickets are often real bargains and can sometimes work out cheaper than a straightforward return ticket.

Expect to pay anything from A$2000 to A$3000. It's also possible to fly into Amsterdam; adding a connecting flight from there to Cardiff should only add around A$100 to the cost of the ticket.

STA Travel (☎ 1300 733 035; www.statravel.com.au) has offices in all major cities and on many university campuses. **Flight Centre** (☎ 131 133 Australiawide; www.flightcentre.com.au) has dozens of offices throughout Australia and New Zealand.

Canada & the USA

Zoom Airlines has two flights a week direct from Toronto to Cardiff. There are no direct scheduled flights from the USA to Wales, but KLM offers a connection via Amsterdam, and Aer Arann via Dublin.

Also, a limited number of charter flights operate during the summer season; your travel agent will be the best place to inquire. Heavy competition on transatlantic routes into London makes it cheapest to fly there and then continue to Wales by bus or train, but there are also scheduled flights to Manchester and Birmingham.

Fares from the East Coast can cost as low as US$350; fares from the West Coast are about US$100 to US$150 higher. Travel time from New York is approximately seven hours.

In the USA there are discount-travel agencies (known as consolidators) that sell cut-price tickets on scheduled carriers; they can be found by looking in the *Yellow Pages* or in major newspapers. The Sunday travel sections of the *New York Times, San Francisco Chronicle-Examiner, Los Angeles Times* or the *Chicago Tribune* list cheap fares, as do the travel sections of the *Globe and Mail, Toronto Star, Montreal Gazette* and *Vancouver Sun.*

TRANSPORT

AIRPORT CONNECTIONS TO WALES

Each London airport has shuttle services into London for onward connections to Wales. To catch a bus to Mid- and North Wales, first get yourself to Victoria station; there are direct trains to Victoria from Gatwick, while flightline buses go there from Stansted and bus 757 goes from Luton. **National Express** (☎ 0870 580 8080; www.nationalexpress.co.uk) has regular bus services throughout the day and night from both Heathrow and Gatwick direct to South Wales (including Newport, Cardiff and Swansea). Heathrow–Cardiff (3½ hours) costs £35 one way, and Gatwick–Cardiff (4½ hours) is £39.

To catch a train to Wales from London you'll need to get to either Paddington station (for South Wales) or Euston station (for Mid- and North Wales). Trains from Heathrow run direct to Paddington. From Gatwick you can also catch a train west to Reading (which has easy train connections to South Wales).

All other international airports in the UK have shuttle services of some kind into the city centre. For more on long-distance buses and trains into Wales, see p325 and p328.

RECOMMENDED TRAVEL AGENCIES
Canada
Canadian Affair (☎ 1877 8FLY2UK; www.canadian affair.com) This agency sells cheap one-way fares to British cities.
Skylink (☎ 1800 759 5465)
STA Travel (☎ 1888 427 5639)
Travel Cuts (☎ 1866-246 9762; www.travel cuts.com)

US
Skylink (☎ 1800 247 6659; www.skylinkus.com)
STA Travel (☎ 1800 781 4040; www.statravel.com)
Worldtrek Travel (☎ 1800 243 1723; www.world trek.com)

Continental Europe
Cardiff has direct scheduled flights from the following European cities: Prague, Lorient, Amsterdam and Geneva.

For Bristol, **Easyjet** (www.easyjet.com) flies from Prague, Rome, Venice, Faro, Alicante, Barcelona, Valencia, Malaga and Palma, Nice, Paris, Toulouse, Berlin, Hamburg, Amsterdam and Krakow.

There are also flights to Bristol from Brussels and Frankfurt. Alternatively, there are connections to London from all over Europe.

RECOMMENDED TRAVEL AGENCIES
France
Go Voyages (☎ 08 92 89 18 32; www.govoyages .com)
Nouvelles Frontières (☎ 08 25 00 07 47; www.nouvelles -frontieres.fr)
OTU Voyages (☎ 01 55 82 32 32; www.otu.fr)
Voyageurs du Monde (☎ 08 92 23 56 56; www.vdm .com)

Germany
Just Travel (☎ 089-747 3330; www.justtravel.de)
STA Travel (☎ 069-743 032 92; www.statravel.de)

Italy
CTS Viaggi (☎ 199-501 150; www.cts.it)
Travel Price (☎ 199-400 466; www.travelprice.it)

Netherlands
Air Fair (☎ 0900-7 717 717; www.airfair.nl)
NBBS Reizen (☎ 0900-10 20 300; www.nbbs.nl)

UK & Ireland
No-frills air carriers offer reduced-price tickets on flights from Wales to other parts of the UK and to Ireland. The carrier bmibaby flies to Belfast, Edinburgh and Glasgow; Air Southwest flies to Manchester; Eastern Airways to Newcastle; and Aer Arann to Dublin, Galway and Cork.

Prices on all these flights vary considerably depending on the day and even time of day you fly, so it's worth checking the websites (p320) regularly.

Discount air travel is big business in London. If you are looking for a cheap ticket from the UK, note that cheap international fares often appear in the weekend broadsheet papers and, in London, in the *Evening Standard, Time Out* and the free *TNT* magazine. Bargain ticket agencies for tickets include the following:
Flight Centre (☎ 0870 499 0040; www.flightcentre .co.uk)
Saga (☎ 0800 414 525; www.saga.co.uk) Air-fare bargains for the over-50s.
STA Travel (☎ 0871 2 300 040; www.statravel.co.uk)
Trailfinders (☎ 0845 054 6060; www.trailfinders.com)
Travel Bag (☎ 0800 082 5000; www.travelbag.co.uk)

LAND
England & Scotland
BUS
Compared to trains, buses are slower but cheaper, and serve a greater variety of destinations.

National Express (☎ 0870 580 8080; www.nationalexpress.co.uk) is the largest national network and has frequent services between most major cities.

Megabus (☎ 0900 160 0900; www.megabus.com) has one-way fares from London to Cardiff from as little as £6.

The table below shows some direct bus routes to Wales from England and Scotland, with approximate one-way fares.

BUSES TO WALES

Journey	Fare	Duration	Frequency (Mon-Sat)
Birmingham-Aberystwyth	£22	4hr	1/day
Birmingham-Cardiff	£21	2½hr	8/day
Bristol-Cardiff	£7	1¼hr	7/day
Edinburgh-Wrexham	£34	11½hr	1/day
London-Aberystwyth	£27	7hr	2/day
London-Cardiff	£19	3¼hr	10/day
Manchester-Llandudno	£13	4hr	1/day
Shrewsbury-Aberystwyth	£16	2¼hr	1/day

TRAIN
Fast train services run to Cardiff from London (Paddington), Bristol, Birmingham, York and Newcastle. You can also take the train to Mid-Wales (including Welshpool and Machynlleth) or North Wales (including Llandudno, Bangor and Holyhead; or Porthmadog and Pwllheli) from London (Euston) via Birmingham.

Trains in the UK are privatised and expensive in comparison to the rest of Europe. The fare structure is bewildering but in general the cheapest tickets are those bought well in advance of the date of travel.

Train timetables and fares are available from **National Rail** (☎ 08457 48 49 50; www.nationalrail.co.uk, www.thetrainline.com).

The following table shows some sample routes with standard one-way fares.

TRAINS TO WALES

Journey	Fare	Duration	Frequency (Mon-Sat)
Birmingham-Aberystwyth	£19	3hr	7/day
Birmingham-Cardiff	£29	2hr	15/day
Bristol-Cardiff	£10	40min	4/hr
London (Paddington)-Cardiff	£68	2hr	2/hr
London (Euston)-Aberystwyth	£87	4¾hr	7/day
London-Llandudno	£94	3¾hr	2/day
Newcastle-Cardiff	£86	5¼hr	2/hr

Continental Europe
BUS
Travelling by bus from Europe can be a slow, painful process and with so many cheap flights available it isn't always cost effective either. You can book a bus ticket right through to Wales via London with **Eurolines** (www.eurolines.com), Europe's largest international bus network.

Another possibility is **Busabout** (www.busabout.com), a hop-on, hop-off network linking some 70 European cities. Buses run from April to October, but the only UK stop is in London.

TRAIN
All rail connections from continental Europe to Wales will pass through London. The high-speed passenger service **Eurostar** (☎ 08705 186 186 in the UK, ☎ 0892 35 35 39 in France; www.eurostar.com) links London (Waterloo) with Paris (Gare du Nord) or Brussels. From November 2007, Eurostar trains will use the new St Pancras International rail terminal.

Cheaper rail connections involve a Channel crossing by ferry or SeaCat (see p324).

TRANSPORT

TRANSPORT

SEAPORT CONNECTIONS TO WALES

Nearly all seaports in southeast England have shuttle services into London or other transport centres for onward connections to Wales. See opposite or p328 for details on getting to Wales from London.

Dover Shuttle bus to Dover Priory train station; from there train to London's Charing Cross station.

Folkestone Taxi to Folkestone Central train station; from there train to London's Charing Cross station.

Harwich Adjacent to Harwich Parkeston Quay train station, with services to London's Liverpool Street station.

Newhaven Train to London's Victoria station.

Plymouth Taxi to Plymouth train station; from there direct trains to Newport and Cardiff.

Poole Shuttle bus to Poole train station; from there train to Southampton and direct trains to Newport and Cardiff.

Portsmouth Shuttle bus to Portsmouth Harbour train station; and from there direct trains to Newport and Cardiff, or taxi to Portsmouth coach station with connections to London's Victoria coach station.

Other international seaports in the UK have shuttle services or taxis into the city centre.

SEA

All direct ferry crossings to Wales are from Ireland. There are four routes: Dublin and Dun Laoghaire to Holyhead (1½ to 3¼ hours); Rosslare to Pembroke Dock (four hours); Rosslare to Fishguard (two to 3½ hours); and Cork to Swansea (10 hours).

Fares vary considerably (depending on the season, day, time and length of stay) and some return fares don't cost much more than a one-way ticket.

It's worth keeping an eye out for promotional fares that can reduce the cost considerably. International Student Identity Card (ISIC) holders and HI members qualify for a discount on the normal fare.

The following companies operate ferries between Ireland and Wales:

Irish Ferries (☎ 08705 17 17 17; www.irishferries.com) Ferry and fast-boat services from Dublin to Holyhead, and ferry services from Rosslare to Pembroke Dock.

Stena Line (☎ 08705 70 70 70; www.stenaline.com) Ferry services from Dublin to Holyhead and fast-boat services from Dun Laoghaire to Holyhead and Rosslare to Fishguard.

Swansea Cork Ferries (Swansea ☎ 01792-456116, Cork ☎ 021-483 6000; www.swanseacorkferries.com) Ferry services from Swansea to Cork.

Typical one-way fares for a peak-season crossing are in the region of €30 to €50 for a foot passenger, and €150 to €200 for a car and driver, plus €22 per extra passenger.

Ferries to England

There's a bewildering array of ferry services to England from continental Europe, including services from Denmark, Germany and the Netherlands to Harwich; a service from

Belgium to Dover; and a service from France to Dover, Newhaven, Poole, Portsmouth and Plymouth. Check out www.directferries.co.uk or www.ferrybooker.com.

GETTING AROUND

It's worth considering car hire for at least part of your trip to Wales, as getting around the country by public transport can be a bit of a challenge. Regional coordination of transport services is limited, nonstop bus services are almost nonexistent and many remote areas are not served by any transport at all. But if you aren't in a hurry, you can patch together an odyssey by taking public transport and perhaps the odd taxi ride, Postbus trip, walk or bicycle journey.

Buses are nearly always the cheapest way to get around but you may be able to snare a bargain on the trains if you're lucky. For information on services your best bet is the local tourist office, where you'll be able to pick up maps, timetables, and a copy of the free and indispensable *Wales Bus, Rail and Tourist Map and Guide.*

For up-to-date information on public transport throughout Wales call **Traveline** (☎ 0870 608 2608; www.traveline.org.uk).

BICYCLE

Rural Wales is a great place for cycling enthusiasts; traffic on back roads is limited, there are loads of multiuse trails and three long-distance cycling routes as part of Sustrans' National Cycle Network. Distances are generally short. For long-distance travel around Wales, though, the hilly and often mountainous terrain is mostly for experienced cycle tourers.

In the larger towns and cities, there are few cycle lanes and there is also a general disrespect for cyclists by motorists. Bike theft can also be a major problem in urban areas; try to keep your bike in a secure area (many guest houses and hotels offer secure bicycle storage).

For more information on cycling around Wales, see p59.

Purchase & Hire
All large towns have bicycle shops where you can buy a bike on arrival; you may even be able to negotiate a deal for the shop to buy the bike back later.

Most sizable or tourist towns in Wales have at least one shop where you can hire bikes for around £10 to £15 per day for a tourer and between £17 and £25 for a full-suspension mountain bike. Many hire outfits will require you to make a deposit of about £50 for a tourer and up to £100 for a top-of-the-line mean machine.

Transporting Your Bicycle
Bikes can be taken on most trains, although there is limited space for them. On most train services in Wales it's compulsory to make a reservation for your bike at least 24 hours in advance; there is a small charge for this on some routes. On others, bikes are carried free as long as there is space available; if not, you're stuck. Timetables usually have an 'R' symbol above each service on which a reservation is necessary.

Arriva Trains Wales (www.arrivatrainswales.co.uk), which operates most rail services in Wales, publishes an annual guide called *Cycling by Train*. It's also available for download from the website.

BUS
Long-distance bus services are thin on the ground in Wales, but half-a-dozen longer routes (run by a range of operators) have been gathered under the banner of the **TrawsCambria** (www.traws cambria.info) network. The routes on this network include Bangor to Aberystwyth, Aberystwyth to Cardiff, Aberystwyth to Cardigan and Brecon to Newtown.

However, most longer bus journeys have to be cobbled together from a web of routes operated by some 70 private bus companies across the country. **Traveline Cymru** (☎ 0870 608 2608; www .traveline-cymru.org.uk) is the one-stop shop for all bus route and timetable information.

The biggest bus operators in Wales:
Arriva Cymru (☎ 08701 201 088; www.arrivabus.co.uk) Services in North and West Wales.
First Cymru (☎ 01792-572255; www.firstcymru.co.uk) Services in southwest Wales.
National Express (☎ 0870 580 8080; www.national express.com) UK-wide services.
Stagecoach (www.stagecoachbus.com/southwales) Services in southeast Wales.

Bus Passes
Apart from the combined bus and rail Flexipasses (see p326), there are lots of regional and local one-day and one-week passes, but many are only worthwhile if you're planning to do a lot of travelling.

For example, the FirstWeek South & West Wales pass (adult/child £22/10) gives unlimited travel for seven days on all First bus services in South and West Wales. The First-Day Swansea Bay pass (adult/child £3.60/2) gives unlimited travel for a day (on the day of purchase only) on First and Pullman buses in Swansea and the Gower Peninsula. You can buy these passes in Swansea bus station, or from the driver on any First bus.

The West Wales Rover pass (adult/child £6/4) allows unlimited travel for one day on most local bus services in Carmarthenshire, Pembrokeshire and Ceredigion. The Red Rover (adult/child £4.95/2.45) is valid for one

BUSES WITHIN WALES			
Route	**Fare**	**Duration**	**Frequency (Mon-Sat)**
Bangor-Caernarfon	£3	25min	2/hr
Barmouth-Wrexham	£5	2½hr	1/hr
Cardiff-Abergavenny	£4	1½hr	1/hr
Cardigan-Aberystwyth	£4	½hr	3/day
Swansea-Brecon	£4	1½hr	3/day
Swansea-Haverfordwest	£8	2¼hr	3/day
Welshpool-Aberystwyth	£11	1¾hr	1/day

TRANSPORT

day on buses 1 to 99 in Gwynedd and the Isle of Anglesey in northwest Wales. The Stagecoach Explorer (adult/child £5.50/3.50) gives unlimited travel for one day on all Stagecoach services in South Wales. Again, you can buy these tickets from the driver; for full details, ask at a tourist office.

If you're planning to travel throughout the UK, National Express has a variety of passes and discount cards, including options for senior travellers. Details are available online at www.nationalexpress.com.

Costs

Bus travel is much cheaper than train travel and return fares cost only 15% more than a one-way fare. See table, p325, for costs; the details relate to approximate one-way fares.

National Park Bus Services

Each of Wales' national-park authorities runs or organises dedicated bus services aimed at walkers and cyclists trying to get around the parks. Many routes include transport for bicycles. These services are described in more detail in the regional chapters.

Postbus

For an authentic look at rural Wales, travel with the **Royal Mail Postbus** (☎ 0845 774 0740; www.post bus.royalmail.com). You won't get anywhere fast,

but you'll get a unique insight into rural Wales. The services are often the only means of public transport in remote parts of Mid-Wales. Buses carry between four and 10 passengers, and can be hailed anywhere en route. Fares range from 40p to £4.

CAR & MOTORCYCLE

If you want to see the more remote regions of Wales or cram in as much as possible in a short time, travelling by car or motorcycle is the easiest way to go. Petrol, however, is expensive – about 90p per litre at the time of research.

Getting around North or South Wales is easy, but elsewhere roads are considerably slower, especially in the mountains and through Mid-Wales. To get from the northeast to the southeast, it's quickest to go via England. Rural roads are often single-track affairs with passing places only at intervals, and they can be treacherous in winter.

Wales can be a dream for motorcyclists, with good-quality winding roads and stunning scenery. Just make sure your wet-weather gear is up to scratch.

In built-up areas be sure to check the parking restrictions as traffic wardens and clampers can be merciless.

The main motoring organisations in the UK include the following:

TRAVEL PASSES

If you're planning a whirlwind tour of Wales by public transport, getting a **Flexipass** (www .walesflexipass.co.uk) is a good idea. Passes allow free travel in Wales and adjacent areas of England, on all rail routes and nearly all intercity bus routes.

The passes also get you discounts at Youth Hostels Association (YHA) and HI hostels in Wales; free or discounted travel on heritage railways; discount on admission to several properties owned by the National Trust and Cadw; and a discount for Guide Friday's Cardiff, Llandudno and Conwy tours.

The passes, with high/low season prices (high season is from mid-May to late September):

Freedom of South Wales Flexi Rover Seven days of bus travel plus any three days of train travel (within the seven-day period) in South Wales (£35/30).

Freedom of Wales 4-in-8 Flexipass Eight days of bus travel plus any four days of train travel throughout Wales (£55/45).

Freedom of Wales 8-in-15 Flexipass Fifteen days of bus travel plus any eight days of train travel throughout Wales (£92/75).

North & Mid Wales Rover Any three days of bus and train travel within a seven-day period in North and Mid-Wales (£30 year-round).

Those aged between five and 15 and Senior Railcard holders get one-third off the flexipass prices. Passes can be bought online, at all staffed train stations and rail-accredited travel agencies in Wales, a number of tourist offices, and YHA/HI hostels in Bangor, Cardiff, Chester, Conwy and Llangollen in Wales (as well as Bath, Bristol, Shrewsbury and Liverpool in England).

Auto-Cycle Union (☎ 01788-566400; www.acu.org.uk)
Automobile Association (AA; ☎ 0800 085 2721; www.theaa.co.uk)
Bike Tours UK (www.biketours-uk.com) For information on motorcycle touring.
Royal Automobile Club (RAC; ☎ 08705 722 722; www.rac.co.uk)

Driving Licence

Non-UK driving licences are legal for 12 months from the date you last entered the UK and usually allow you to hire a car for three months. However, if you don't hold an EU licence, it may be a good idea to get an International Driving Permit (IDP) from your home automobile association before you leave.

You should carry your driving licence with you at all times.

Hire

Hire cars are expensive in the UK, and you'll often get a better rate by taking advantage of package deals booked in advance. The best deals can usually be found on the internet. To hire a car, drivers must usually be between 23 and 65 years of age – outside these limits

special conditions or insurance requirements may apply. You will also need a credit card to make an advance booking and act as a deposit.

For a compact car, expect to pay in the region of £135 a week (including insurance etc). Most cars are manual; automatic cars are available but they're generally more expensive to hire. If you need a baby chair or booster seat specify this at the time of booking.

Some agencies in the UK:

Alamo (☎ 0870 400 4562; www.alamo.co.uk)
Avis (☎ 0870 608 6363; www.avis.co.uk)
Budget (☎ 0844 581 2231; www.budget.co.uk)
Europcar (☎ 0845 758 5375; www.europcar.co.uk)
Fast Quote (☎ 0870 900 0533; www.fastquotecarhire.co.uk)
Hertz (☎ 0870 844 8844; www.hertz.co.uk)
Holiday Autos (☎ 0870 400 4461; www.holidayautos.co.uk)

Insurance

If you are bringing your own vehicle from abroad, make sure you check that your insurance will cover you in the UK. In the

TRANSPORT

ROAD DISTANCES (km)

	Abergavenny	Aberystwyth	Bangor	Cardiff	Dolgellau	Fishguard	Holyhead	Llandrindod Wells	Llandudno	Newtown	Pembroke	Swansea	Wrexham
Abergavenny	---												
Aberystwyth	80	---											
Bangor	155	86	---										
Cardiff	42	110	185	---									
Dolgellau	103	34	53	133	---								
Fishguard	115	57	144	110	91	---							
Holyhead	174	105	25	205	72	163	---						
Llandrindod Wells	41	45	118	71	64	103	138	---					
Llandudno	154	85	23	228	51	142	43	121	---				
Newtown	67	43	93	97	40	98	112	26	91	---			
Pembroke	102	84	171	97	118	27	190	90	169	116	---		
Swansea	49	78	164	41	112	71	184	68	163	94	58	---	
Wrexham	105	83	66	140	52	140	87	69	48	43	159	137	---

TRANSPORT

UK, third-party insurance is a minimum requirement. If you're renting a car, check the fine print – policies can vary widely and the cheapest hire rates often include an excess (for which you are liable in the event of an accident) of up to £800.

HITCHING

Hitching is never entirely safe anywhere, and we don't recommend it. Travellers who hitch should understand that they are taking a small but potentially serious risk. Travel in pairs and let someone know where you are planning to go. Women hitching on their own should be extremely careful when choosing lifts – if in doubt, don't get in.

It's against the law to hitch on motorways or the immediate slip roads (access ramps); make a sign and use approach roads, roundabouts, or service stations instead.

TOURS

Scores of local and regional outfits offer walking, cycling and multiactivity tours. Many are mentioned in Outdoor Activities (p58) and more appear in the destination chapters.

For a fun way to see Wales and to meet new people, several companies offer minibus tours of the country, in which there are a variety of possible routes and activities on offer.

For more information try the following organisations.

Bus Wales (☎ 0800 328 0284; www.buswales.co.uk) Offers three-day tours, including Snowdonia, Brecon Beacons, Wye Valley and Gower Surf and Beach. Aimed at independent travellers, backpackers and students.

Bushwakkers (☎ 01874-636552; www.bushwakkers.co.uk) Weekend horse riding and canoeing adventure trips to Wales by minibus; mostly for the under-35s.

Dragon Tours (☎ 01874-658124; www.dragonbackpackertours.co.uk) Tours to off-the-beaten-track destinations. Aimed at under-35s.

Shaggy Sheep (☎ 01267-281202; www.shaggysheep.com) Jump-on, jump-off tours of the Brecon Beacons, Pembrokeshire coast and Snowdonia, as well as surfing and other activity weekends. Aimed at young backpackers.

The following international companies offer UK tours or packages with a Wales component.

British Travel International (www.britishtravel.com) Aimed at travellers over 50.

Contiki (www.contiki.com) Mostly for the under-35s.

Haggis Tours (www.radicaltravel.com) Aimed at the youth market.

Home at First (www.homeatfirst.com) Tours suited to over-50s.

Insight (www.insightvacations.com) Caters for the over-50s market.

Roadtrip (www.roadtrip.co.uk) Tours will appeal to under-35s.

Saga Holidays (www.saga.co.uk) Holidays for the over-50s.

Wales Countryside Holidays (www.holidays-in-wales.com) Tours for all age groups.

TRAIN

Like the rest of the UK, the Welsh rail network has been privatised; almost all train services in Wales are run by **Arriva** (www.arrivatrainswales.co.uk), except for the London (Paddington)–Cardiff–Swansea route (operated by First Great Western) and the London (Euston)–Chester–Holyhead route (Virgin Trains).

The **National Rail Enquiry Service** (☎ 08457 484950; www.nationalrail.co.uk) provides centralised timetable information for all train operators in the UK, and allows you to buy tickets and make reservations by phone using a credit card. You can buy tickets online through www.thetrainline.com, though you'll need a UK address to register with the site.

To a large extent, trains along Wales' north and south coasts serve to link the English rail network with seaports at Swansea, Pembroke Dock, Fishguard and Holyhead. But there are some fine rail journeys across the middle of the country, and an amazing number of 'heritage' railways (mainly steam and narrow-gauge), survivors of an earlier era.

Wales' most beautiful railway journeys fan out from Shrewsbury in England: the Heart of Wales line through southern Mid-Wales, the Cambrian line across northern Mid-Wales to Aberystwyth, and its spectacular branch line up the coast and along the Llŷn. Another gem is the Conwy Valley line down through Snowdonia. Each trip is worth the fare just for the scenery and the hypnotic, clickety-clack pace.

Classes

There are two classes of rail travel in the UK: 1st class and what is referred to as 'standard' class. First class costs about 30% to 50% more than standard and, except on very crowded trains, simply isn't worth the extra money.

Costs

You can just roll up to a station and buy a standard single (one-way) or return ticket any time, but this is often the most expensive way to go. Each train-operating company sets its own fares and has its own discount schemes, and passengers can only use their tickets on services operated by the company that issued the ticket.

TRANSPORT

TRAIN ROUTES

You might find that the same journey will have a different fare depending on whether you buy it at the station, over the phone or on the internet. The system is so bizarre that in some cases two singles are cheaper than a return ticket, and even a one-way journey can be cheaper if you split it into two (ie if you're going from A to C, it can be cheaper to buy a single from A to B, and another single from B to C; go figure). If you have the time, it's worth playing around with various combinations on www.thetrainline.com.

The cheapest fares have advance-purchase and minimum-stay requirements, as well as limited availability. Children under five travel free; those aged between five and 15 pay half-price for most tickets. However, when travelling with children it is almost always worth buying a Family Railcard (right). See table below for approximate one-way fares for various train journeys:

TRAINS WITHIN WALES

Journey	Fare	Duration	Frequency (Mon-Sat)
Swansea-Llandrindod Wells	£8	1¾hr	4/day
Cardiff-Haverfordwest	£16	2½hr	7/day
Welshpool-Aberystwyth	£9	1½hr	7/day
Machynlleth-Pwllheli	£10	2¼hr	6/day
Llandudno-Blaenau Ffestiniog	£6	1¼hr	5/day

The main fare classifications include:

Apex For outward and return journeys not on the same day, but at fixed times and dates; it's the cheapest long-term return ticket, but must be booked well in advance and has limited availability.

Cheap Day Return For outward and return journeys on the same day, with restricted outward travel time (eg only after 9.30am); often costs barely more than a single. A great deal for day-trippers.

Open Return For outward travel on a stated day and return on any day within a month.

Saver Open return but with no travel allowed during weekday peak-traffic periods.

SuperSaver Open return but with no travel allowed during weekday peak-traffic periods, nor on Friday at any time, nor on certain other high-traffic days (eg during the Christmas and Easter holidays).

Train Passes

BritRail passes are not cost effective for travel in Wales unless you plan to make a very fleeting visit. They're available only to non-Brits and must be bought overseas. Most larger overseas travel agencies will have details. The following local passes will be more useful. See also p326.

These passes allow unlimited one-day rail travel on weekdays after 9am and on all weekends and holidays:

Cambrian Coaster Day Ranger (£7) Pwllheli–Machynlleth–Aberystwyth.

Heart of Wales Two Day Rover (£20) Shrewsbury–Llandrindod Wells–Swansea.

North & Mid-Wales Day Ranger (£20) Anywhere within circle formed by Aberystwyth–Shrewsbury–Prestatyn–Holyhead–Pwllheli–Aberystwyth.

RAILCARDS

Railcards are valid for one year and entitle the holder to discounts of up to 30% on most rail (and some ferry) fares in the UK. Most train stations have application forms or you can apply online at www.railcard.co.uk; note that processing for some cards can take up to two weeks. Railcards are accepted by all operating companies.

Disabled Person's Railcard (£18) Applies to its holder and one person accompanying them.

Family Railcard (£20) A great bargain – it allows discounts for up to four adults travelling together (only one needs to hold a card), and a 60% discount on children's fares.

Senior Railcard (£20) For anyone aged over 60.

Young Person's Railcard (£20) For those aged between 16 and 25, or a full-time UK student of any age.

Health

CONTENTS

Travel health largely depends on predeparture preparations, day-to-day health care while travelling and how you handle any medical problem or emergency that does develop. Wales is a healthy place to travel. Hygiene standards are high and there are no unusual diseases to worry about.

Stomach upsets are the most likely travel health problem (between 30% and 50% of travellers in a two-week stay experience this), but the majority of these upsets will be relatively minor.

BEFORE YOU GO

Make sure you're healthy before you start travelling. If you are going on a long trip make sure your teeth are OK and if you wear glasses take your prescription.

If you require medication, you should take along the packaging that shows its generic name, rather than the brand, which will make getting replacements easier and cheaper. To avoid any problems, it's also wise to have a legible prescription or doctor's letter to show that you legally use the medication.

INSURANCE

Make sure you have adequate health insurance. Find out in advance if your insurance plan will make payments directly to providers or reimburse you later for overseas health costs. The former is generally preferable, as it doesn't require you to pay out of pocket. See right for details of who is eligible for free health services.

RECOMMENDED VACCINATIONS

Although no immunisations are required, it's recommended that everyone keep up to date with diphtheria, tetanus and polio vaccinations.

IN WALES

AVAILABILITY & COST OF HEALTH CARE

Reciprocal arrangements with the UK allow residents of Australia, New Zealand and several other countries to receive free emergency medical treatment and subsidised dental care through the National Health Service (NHS); they can use hospital emergency departments, general practitioners (GPs) and dentists. Long-term visitors from Australia, New Zealand and certain other countries who have the proper documentation will receive care under the NHS by registering with a specific practice near where they live. EU nationals can obtain free emergency treatment on presentation of a European Health Insurance Card (EHIC).

Travel insurance, however, is advisable as it offers greater flexibility in where and how you're treated, and covers expenses for an ambulance and repatriation that won't be picked up by the NHS. Regardless of nationality, anyone with a medical emergency that requires a doctor's attention will not be refused treatment.

All blood donations in the UK are screened.

Chemists

Chemists (pharmacies) can advise on minor ailments such as sore throats, coughs and earache. There's always one local chemist open somewhere at any hour; other chemists should display details in their window or doorway (or you can look in a local newspaper). All standard medications are readily available either over the counter or on prescription.

ENVIRONMENTAL HAZARDS
Diarrhoea

A change of water, food or climate can cause the runs; diarrhoea caused by contaminated food or water is more serious. Dehydration is the main danger with any diarrhoea, particularly in children or the elderly, and it can occur quite quickly. Fluid replacement (at least equal to the volume being lost) is the most important thing to remember. Weak black tea with a little sugar, soda water, or soft drinks allowed to go flat and diluted 50% with clean water are all good. With severe diarrhoea, a rehydrating solution is preferable to replace minerals and salts lost. Keep drinking small amounts often and stick to a bland diet as you recover.

Heat Exhaustion
Wales may not seem like a place to worry about heat exhaustion, but it's not entirely unknown. Dehydration or salt deficiency can cause heat exhaustion. If you're in hot conditions and/or exerting yourself make sure you drink sufficient nonalcoholic liquids. Salt deficiency is characterised by fatigue, lethargy, headaches, giddiness and muscle cramps.

Hypothermia
Too much cold can be just as dangerous as too much heat. In much of Wales you should always be prepared for cold, wet or windy conditions, even if you're just out walking or hitching. Every year people set out for walks and end up in trouble when the weather suddenly changes.

To help prevent hypothermia dress in layers; silk, wool and some of the new artificial fibres are all good insulating materials. A hat is important as much heat is lost through the head. A strong, waterproof outer layer is essential, and a space blanket is wise for emergencies. Carry basic supplies, including fluid to drink and food containing simple sugars to generate heat quickly.

Symptoms of hypothermia are exhaustion, numb skin (particularly toes and fingers), shivering, slurred speech, irrational or violent behaviour, lethargy, stumbling, dizzy spells, muscle cramps and violent bursts of energy. Irrationality may take the form of sufferers claiming they are warm and trying to take off their clothes.

To treat mild hypothermia, first get the person out of the wind and/or rain, remove their clothing if it's wet and replace it with dry, warm clothing. Give them hot liquids – not alcohol – and some high-kilojoule, easily digestible food. Do not rub victims; instead, allow them to slowly warm themselves. The early recognition and treatment of mild hypothermia is the only way to prevent severe hypothermia, which is a critical condition.

Motion Sickness
Eating lightly before and during a trip will reduce the chances of motion sickness. If you're prone to motion sickness, try to find a place that minimises disturbance – near the wing on aircraft, close to midships on boats, near the centre on buses. Fresh air usually helps; reading and cigarette smoke don't. Commercial motion-sickness preparations, which can cause drowsiness, have to be taken before the trip commences; when you're feeling sick it's too late. Ginger (available in capsule form) and peppermint (including mint-flavoured sweets) are effective natural preventatives.

Insect Bites & Stings
Bee and wasp stings are usually painful rather than dangerous. However, in people who are allergic to them, severe breathing difficulties may occur and require urgent medical care. Calamine lotion or Stingose spray will give relief, and ice packs will reduce the pain and swelling.

Midges – small blood-sucking flies – and clegs (horseflies) can be a problem during summer, especially in North Wales. Bring mosquito repellent, some antihistamine tablets and a head net. Always check all over your body if you've been walking through a potentially tick-infested area as ticks can cause skin infections and other more serious diseases. To remove a tick, press down around the tick's head with tweezers, grab the head and gently pull upwards.

Sunburn
Even in Wales, including when there's cloud cover, it's possible to get sunburned surprisingly quickly – especially if you're on water, snow or ice. Use 15-plus sunscreen, wear a hat, and cover up with a long-sleeved shirt and trousers.

Water
Tap water is always safe unless there's a sign to the contrary (eg on trains). Don't drink straight from a stream – you can never be certain there are no people or cattle upstream.

TRAVELLING WITH CHILDREN
Make sure the children are up-to-date with routine vaccinations, and discuss possible travel vaccines well before departure as some

vaccines are not suitable for children under a year. See also Lonely Planet's *Travel with Children*, by Cathy Lanigan.

WOMEN'S HEALTH

In the UK, the contraceptive pill is only available on prescription. Emergency contraception (the morning-after pill; actually effective for up to 72 hours after unprotected sex) is now available over the counter in many chemists, but it's expensive at around £20. It's also free on prescription. Most big towns have a Well Woman Clinic that can advise on general health issues.

HEALTH

Language

CONTENTS

You can get by almost anywhere in Wales these days without speaking Welsh (although that probably won't be the case in a generation!). Nevertheless, anyone who's serious about getting to grips with Welsh people and their culture will find the ability to speak basic Welsh immeasurably valuable right now.

Beginners will find lots of resources on the Welsh language, including videotapes, teach-yourself books and CD-ROMs; you can even learn Welsh on the internet. For information on courses – including learning by correspondence – see p309.

The Welsh language belongs to the Celtic branch of the Indo-European language family. Closely related to Breton and Cornish, and more distantly to Irish, Scottish and Manx, it's the strongest Celtic language both in terms of numbers of speakers (over 500,000) and place in society.

PRONUNCIATION

All letters in Welsh are pronounced and the stress is usually on the second-last syllable. Letters are pronounced as in English, except for those listed below.

Vowels

Vowels can be long or short. Those marked with a circumflex (eg **ê**) are always long and those with a grave accent (eg **è**) short.

a	short as in 'map'; long as in 'farm'
e	short as in 'pen'; long as in 'there'
i	short as in 'bit'; long as in 'police'
o	short as in 'box'; long as in 'bore'
u	as **i** (short and long)
w	short as the 'oo' in 'book'; long as the 'oo' in 'spook'

y	as **i** (short or long); sometimes as the 'a' in 'about', especially in common one-syllable words like *y, yr, fy, dy* and *yn*

In words of one syllable, vowels followed by two consonants are short – eg *corff* (body). If a one-syllable word ends in **p**, **t**, **c**, **m** or **ng**, the vowel is short – eg *llong* (ship). If it ends in **b**, **d**, **g**, **f**, **dd**, **ff**, **th**, **ch**, or **s**, the vowel is long – eg *bad* (boat) – as is any vowel at the end of a one-syllable word, such as *pla* (plague).

In words of more than one syllable, all unstressed vowels are short, as in the first and final vowels of *cariadon* (lovers). Stressed vowels can be long or short and in general follow the rules for vowels in monosyllables.

Diphthongs

ae/ai/au	as the 'y' in 'my'
aw	as the 'ow' in 'cow'
ei/eu/ey	as the 'ay' in 'day'
ew	as a short 'e' followed by 'oo'
iw/uw/yw	as the 'ew' in 'few'
oe/oi	as 'oy' in 'boy'
ow	as the 'ow' in 'tow'
wy	sometimes as 'uey' (as in 'chop suey'); sometimes as the 'wi' in 'wing' (especially after g)

Consonants

The combinations **ch**, **dd**, **ff**, **ng**, **ll**, **ph**, **rh** and **th** count as single consonants in Welsh.

c	always as 'k'
ch	as the 'ch' in Scottish loch
dd	as the 'th' in 'this'
ff	as the 'f' in 'fork'
g	always as the 'g' in 'garden', not as in 'gentle'
ng	as the 'ng' in 'sing'
ll	as 'hl' (put the tongue in the position for 'l' and breathe out)
ph	as 'f'
r	rolled, as in Spanish or Italian
rh	pronounced as 'hr'
s	always as in 'so', never as in 'rose'
si	as the 'sh' in 'shop'
th	always as the 'th' in 'thin'

LANGUAGE

CONVERSATION & ESSENTIALS

Hello.
Sut mae.   sit mai

Good morning.
Bore da.   bo-rre dah

Good afternoon.
Prynhawn da.   pruhn-hown dah

Good evening.
Noswaith dda.   noss-waith thah

Goodnight.
Nos da.   nohs dah

See you (later).
Wela i chi (wedyn).   wel-ah ee khee (we-din)

Goodbye.
Hwyl fawr.   hueyl vowrr

Please.
Os gwelwch in dda.   os gwel-ookh uhn thah

Thank you (very much).
Diolch (in fawr iawn).   dee-olkh (uhn vowrr yown)

You're welcome.
Croeso.   kroy-ssoh

Excuse me.
Esgusodwch fi.   ess-gi-so-dookh vee

Sorry/Excuse me/Forgive me.
Mae'n ddrwg gyda fi.   main thrroog guh-da vee

Don't mention it.
Peidiwch â sôn.   payd-yookh ah sohn

Yes.
Oes.   oyss

No.
Nac oes.   nag oyss

How are you?
Sut ydych chi?   sit uh-deekh khee?

(Very) well.
(Da) iawn.   (dah) yown

What's your name?
Beth yw eich enw chi?   beth yu uhch en-oo khee?

My name's...
Fy enw i yw...   ne-noo ee yu...

Where are you from?
O ble ydych chi'n dod?   oh ble uh-deekh kheen dohd?

I'm from...
Dw i'n dod o...   doo een dohd oh...

LANGUAGE DIFFICULTIES

I don't understand.
Dw i ddim in deall.
doo ee thim uhn deh-ahhl

How do you say...?
Sut mae dweud...?
sit mai dwayd...?

What's this called in Welsh?
Beth yw hwn in Gymraeg?
beth yu hoon uhn guhm-raig?

PLACE NAMES

Welsh place names are often based on words that describe a landmark or a feature of the countryside.

aber	ab-berr	estuary
afon	a-von	river
bach	bahkh	small
bro	broh	vale
bryn	brin	hill
caer	kairr	fort
capel	ka-pl	chapel
carreg	karr-ek	stone
clwn	kloon	meadow
coed	koyd	wood/forest
cwm	koom	valley
dinas	dee-nass	hill fortress
eglwys	eglueyss	church
fach	vahkh	small
fawr	vowrr	big
ffordd	forth	road
glan	glahn	shore
glyn	glin	valley
isa (f)	issa	lower
llan	hlan	church/enclosure
llyn	hlin	lake
maes	maiss	field
mawr	mowrr	big
mynydd	muhneeth	mountain
nant	nahnt	valley/stream
ogof	o-gov	cave
pen	pen	head/top/end
plas	plahss	hall/mansion
pont	pont	bridge
rhos	hross	moor/marsh
twr	toorr	tower
tŷ	tee	house
uchaf	ikhav	upper
ynys	uh-niss	island/holm

DAYS & MONTHS

Monday	*dydd Llun*	deeth hleen
Tuesday	*dydd Mawrth*	deeth mowrrth
Wednesday	*dydd Mercher*	deeth merr-kherr
Thursday	*dydd Iau*	deeth yigh
Friday	*dydd Gwener*	deeth gwen-err
Saturday	*dydd Sadwrn*	deeth sad-oorrn
Sunday	*dydd Sul*	deeth seel

Some names for months are borrowed from Latin; others are native Welsh.

January	*Ionawr*	yon-owrr
February	*Chwefror*	khwe-vrrohrr
March	*Mawrth*	mowrrth

April	*Ebrill*	eh-brihl
May	*Mai*	mai
June	*Mehefin*	me-he-vin
	(lit: the middle of summer)	
July	*Gorffennaf*	gor-fen-ahv
	(lit: the end of summer)	
August	*Awst*	owst
September	*Medi*	med-dee
	(lit: reaping)	
October	*Hydref*	huh-drev
	(the rutting season, lit: stag roaring)	
November	*Tachwedd*	tahkh-weth
	(the time for slaughtering animals before winter, lit: slaughter)	
December	*Rhagfyr*	hrag-virr
	(the shortest day, lit: before short)	

NUMBERS

0	*dim*	dim
1	*un*	een
2	*dau/dwy* (f)	dy/duey
3	*tri/tair* (f)	tree/tairr
4	*pedwar/pedair* (f)	ped-wahrr/ped-airr
5	*pump*	pimp
6	*chwech*	khwekh
7	*saith*	saith
8	*wyth*	ueyth
9	*naw*	now
10	*deg*	dehg

Glossary

For some additional, specifically Welsh, words and roots, see Place Names, p335, and p73.

AONB – Area of Outstanding Natural Beauty

BABA – Book-A-Bed-Ahead scheme
bitter – beer
bridleway – path that can be used by walkers, horse riders and cyclists
BTA – British Tourist Authority

cadair – stronghold or chair (Welsh)
Cadw – Welsh historic monuments agency (Welsh)
castell – castle (Welsh)
coasteering – making your way around the coastline by climbing, jumping, swimming and scrambling
cromlech – burial chamber (Welsh)
cwm – valley (Welsh)
Cymraeg – Welsh (language, not person) (Welsh)
Cymraes – Welsh female (Welsh)
Cymro – Welsh male (Welsh)
Cymru – Wales (Welsh)

din – fort (Welsh)
dolmen – chambered tomb

EH – English Heritage
eisteddfod – session; festival in which competitions are held in music, poetry, drama and the fine arts (Welsh); plural eisteddfodau

Gymraeg – Welsh (Welsh)

HI – Hostelling International
hotel – accommodation with food and bar, not always open to passing trade

inn – pub with accommodation

lager – light-bodied beer
Landsker line – boundary between Welsh-speaking and English-speaking areas in southwest Wales

laver bread – boiled seaweed mixed with oatmeal

merthyr – burial place of a saint (Welsh)
midge – a tiny, biting fly

National Assembly – National (Welsh) Assembly; devolved regional government of Wales, in power since 1999
newydd – new (Welsh)
NMGW – National Museums and Galleries of Wales
NT – National Trust

OS – Ordnance Survey

pint – measure (of beer)
pistyll – waterfall (Welsh)
postbus – minibus, operated by the Royal Mail, which follows postal delivery routes
pwll – pool (Welsh)

rhiw – slope (Welsh)
RSPB – Royal Society for the Protection of Birds

sarnie – sandwich
sewin – sea trout
SSSI – Site of Special Scientific Interest
Sustrans – sustainable-transport charity encouraging people to walk, cycle and use public transport

tafern – pub (Welsh)
towpath – a path running beside a river or canal
tre – town (Welsh)

urdd – youth (Welsh)

VAT – value-added tax, levied on most goods and services; currently 17.5%

way – long-distance trail
WTB – Wales Tourist Board

y, yr – the, of the (Welsh)
YHA – Youth Hostels Association

Behind the Scenes

THIS BOOK

This 3rd edition of Lonely Planet's *Wales* guide was updated by David Atkinson and Neil Wilson. The 1st edition was written by John King. The 2nd edition was written by Abigail Hole and Etain O'Carroll. This guidebook was commissioned in Lonely Planet's London office, and produced by the following:

Commissioning Editor Clifton Wilkinson
Coordinating Editor Amy Thomas
Coordinating Cartographer Csanad Csutoros
Coordinating Layout Designer Jacqui Saunders
Managing Editor Bruce Evans
Managing Cartographer Mark Griffiths
Assisting Editors Justin Flynn, David Carroll, Susie Ashworth
Proofreaders Susan Paterson, Elisa Arduca, Laura Stansfeld
Assisting Cartographers Anita Banh, Julie Dodkins, Helen Rowley
Cover Designer Jane Hart
Project Managers Glenn van der Knijff, Eoin Dunlevy
Language Content Coordinator Quentin Frayne

Thanks to Yvonne Byron, Melanie Dankel, Sally Darmody, Ryan Evans, Liz Heynes, Chris Lee Ack, Wayne Murphy, Trent Paton, Suzannah Shwer, Tamsin Wilson and Celia Wood

THANKS
DAVID ATKINSON
Many thanks to Lowri Jones and Glenda Davies at VisitWales for their valuable assistance. Cheers also to co-author Neil Wilson and the LP team for making this a smooth and professional assignment. Finally, grateful thanks to my family members that accompanied me on parts of the journey and hopefully enjoyed the ride, especially little Maya, who added yet another new country to her tally before even turning one year old.

NEIL WILSON
Many thanks to Lowri Jones at VisitWales, Frank Sheahan of West Usk Lighthouse, Jessica Bridgeman of Peterstone Court, Brecon, and staff at tourist offices and national park offices across South Wales. Thanks also to co-author David Atkinson, and the Lonely Planet team of editors and cartographers.

OUR READERS
Many thanks to the travellers who used the last edition and wrote to us with helpful hints, useful advice and interesting anecdotes:

Ken Ashton, Michael Bidinger, Robert Braiden, Geoff Bridgman, Jerome Brown, Virginia Buehler, JM Cimelli, Jeremy Cook, Carys Dafydd, George Dupe, Emmanuel Fankhauser, MJ Feaver, Emily Garner, Christian Glockner, Marcia Hershkovitz, Charlotte Hindle, Lawrence Hourahane, Stacey Jenks, MD Jones, Funda Kemal, Ton Kersten, Stefan Lammel, Soong Lee, Sharon Lim, Charlie Martel, Andrew Maynard, Neil McDermott, Colleen McLaughlin, Nards and Chona Novicio, Jojo O'Neill, Abigaile Phole, William Ponissi, Melissa Powell, Linda Press, Marie-Louise Sahraoui, Emma Stewardson, Anna and Bernard Swift, Karen Taylor, Linnett Turner, Benjamin Vogler, Chris Walford, Jeffrey Walter, Cris Walus-Ffordd, Rosemary Wilding, Stephen Williams, Andrew Young

---

THE LONELY PLANET STORY

The story begins with a classic travel adventure: Tony and Maureen Wheeler's 1972 journey across Europe and Asia to Australia. There was no useful information about the overland trail then, so Tony and Maureen published the first Lonely Planet guidebook to meet a growing need.

From a kitchen table, Lonely Planet has grown to become the largest independent travel publisher in the world, with offices in Melbourne (Australia), Oakland (USA) and London (UK). Today Lonely Planet guidebooks cover the globe. There is an ever-growing list of books and information in a variety of media. Some things haven't changed. The main aim is still to make it possible for adventurous travellers to get out there – to explore and better understand the world.

At Lonely Planet we believe travellers can make a positive contribution to the countries they visit – if they respect their host communities and spend their money wisely. Every year 5% of company profit is donated to charities around the world.

ACKNOWLEDGMENTS

Many thanks to the following for the use of their content:

Paul Allen, Jessica Bridgeman, Arwel Hughes, Dan James, Brian John, Iwan Llywd, Andrew Logan, Colin Pressdee, Nona Rees, Dr Greg Stevenson, Eleri Williams.

SEND US YOUR FEEDBACK

We love to hear from travellers – your comments keep us on our toes and help make our books better. Our well-travelled team reads every word on what you loved or loathed about this book. Although we cannot reply individually to postal submissions, we always guarantee that your feedback goes straight to the appropriate authors, in time for the next edition. Each person who sends us information is thanked in the next edition – and the most useful submissions are rewarded with a free book.

To send us your updates – and find out about Lonely Planet events, newsletters and travel news – visit our award-winning website: **www.lonelyplanet.com/contact**.

Note: we may edit, reproduce and incorporate your comments in Lonely Planet products such as guidebooks, websites and digital products, so let us know if you don't want your comments reproduced or your name acknowledged. For a copy of our privacy policy visit www.lonelyplanet.com/privacy.

Index

INDEX

INDEX

000 Map pages
000 Photograph pages